TRANSFORMATIONAL GROWTH AND EFFECTIVE DEMAND

Transformational Growth and Effective Demand

Economics after the Capital Critique

Edward J. Nell

Professor of Economics
New School for Social Research

NEW YORK UNIVERSITY PRESS
Washington Square, New York

Manufactured in Hong Kong

First published in the U.S.A. in 1992 by
NEW YORK UNIVERSITY PRESS
Washington Square
New York, N.Y. 10003

Library of Congress Cataloging-in-Publication Data
Nell, Edward J.
Transformational growth and effective demand: economics after the capital critique / Edward J. Nell
p. cm.
Includes bibliographical references and index.
ISBN 0-8147-5769-3
1. Capital–History. 2. Profit–History. 3. Economic development–History. I. Title.
HB501.N37 1992
339.5–dc20 91-6928
CIP

For my mother, **Marcella**, who always supported me
And for my father, **Edward**, who would have

Contents

Introduction

This collection of essays is not intended primarily to contribute to the critique of neo-Classical theory, even though individually many of these papers first appeared in the course of debates over the validity of certain neo-Classical propositions. Rather, the reason for bringing them together at this time is that, when they are read in conjunction with one another, it can be seen that the critique presents the basis for an alternative approach to understanding the economy, building on the Classics and Marx. For more than a century the real foundations of this alternative have been submerged: the message of the Classics – Smith and Ricardo especially – has been systematically distorted and misinterpreted by the determined neo-Classical attempt to read them only as precursors of the marginalists. The publication of *Production of Commodities by Means of Commodities*, the great work of Sraffa, and the subsequent Capital Theory Controversy, together with the work of Joan Robinson, Nicholas Kaldor, Luigi Pasinetti, Pierangelo Garegnani, Michio Morishima, John Hicks, Richard Goodwin and many others, should have made it clear by now that whatever incipient marginalist elements may have lurked in the Classics, another vision altogether dominated their writings – and is relevant today. That way of thinking about economic analysis has been called 'the surplus approach', since it takes its start from the fact that production, using labor and produced means of production, normally results in a surplus. More is produced than is needed to support the workers and replace the used-up means of production; and this surplus is distributed through market processes as wages to labor, rents to land and profits on the value of capital. Prices indicate the exchanges that must be made to replace used-up means of production so that another round of production can take place again, in the same way, consistently with the distribution of the surplus between the various claimants through the market mechanism. Notice that this implies a difference in logical form and function between prices of commodities and 'factor prices,' the rate of profit and the wage rate. When the price equation is set up in matrix form, commodity prices are derived from the characteristic vector in the solution, whereas the rate of profit and the wage rate follow from the characteristic root.

The price equations have as their mirror image, so to speak, a set of quantity equations, relating the rate of balanced growth and *per capita* consumption. Just as the profit and wage rates are inversely related, so are the growth and consumption rates; and just as the rate of profit is associated with a set of relative prices, the growth rate is similarly associated with a set of relative industry sizes. When the wage rate (or the rate of profit) is determined, the other distributional variable and the set of relative prices follows; when either consumption or growth is determined, the other variable and relative sector sizes follow. Prices and quantities are thus capable of being separately determined; savings behavior, and the influence of distribution on investment, will link the two through the working of effective demand, at least under some conditions, but the straightforward *simultaneous* determination, central to the neo-Classical vision, is not present here.

1 TEMPORARY EQUILIBRIUM AND THE RATE OF PROFIT

The conventional picture holds that prices are indicators of relative scarcities, and that prices adjust so as to bring about the most efficient allocation of the resources available at any given time. The Capital Theory Debate showed that neither capital nor labor were governed by a scarcity pricing process; neither the rate of profits nor the wage rate behave in the required fashion. Moreover, there is no escape through an appeal to 'general equilibrium' theory, for if provision is made for the formation of a general rate of profit, a model based on the normal neo-Classical assumptions, namely given specific resources (produced means of production), a given technology (set of methods of production), and given preferences will – accidental cases aside – be overdetermined. If the rate of profit is neglected then, of course, an analysis can be made of the relation between supply based on given equipment, labor and natural resources, and demand based on preferences constrained by the income generated by ownership of the resources (including labor). But such a 'temporary equilibrium' is really no equilibrium at all, whether considered *ex post* or *ex ante*. For example, taking the *ex post* perspective, firms employing means of production in ways that earn lower than normal profits will try to discard them and acquire other more profitable equipment, or shift such resources into uses that earn the greatest possible profit. Taking the *ex ante* viewpoint, suppose that some firms expect that their equipment, put to normal use at market-clearing prices, will earn profit at a lower rate on the value invested in it either than other equipment which they could acquire, or than they could earn by putting it to other uses. If expectations are formed rationally, and firms make use of all information available to them at reasonable cost, they will anticipate the market-clearing prices and realize that they will not make as high a return on their invested capital as they could get elsewhere. Surely such firms would be foolish to try to supply the available demand at market-clearing prices; they should at once get out of low profit-rate activities and into those that provide the best obtainable rate of earnings on the value of their holdings. Hence, if earnings below the general rate of profit are foreseen, as they must be if expectations are rational, the 'temporary equilibrium' will never happen; if they are not foreseen, then it is not a genuine equilibrium, but a temporary position resulting from imperfect knowledge, which will be corrected as soon as firms learn from their experience, at which point they will rearrange their holdings of means of production.

The relation between capital, exchange value and profit, then, has to be approached differently. Prices are not indicators of relative scarcities, and they are not determined by market-clearing processes. Rather they reflect technological interdependence and the requirements of distribution, and they interact with demand in a very different manner than that indicated by conventional theory. Some of these differences can be captured pictorially. (See pp. 10, 12 and 18, *et passim*.)

2 CONTRASTING PICTURES

The neo-Classical way of thinking is often summed up in a simple and familiar diagram, with boxes indicating Households and Firms, and circles the Factor and Product Markets. Money flows in one direction, goods and services in the other. Households maximize utility, Firms profit (*NOT* the rate of profit); Households demand goods and supply factor, Firms demand factors and supply goods. The diagram is simple – and telling, especially in its combination of symmetry and abstraction. There is neither production nor distribution in the Classical sense; production is subsumed under supplying goods, and distribution becomes demanding factors. Households and Firms behave in symmetrical ways; both react passively to signals and essentially choose from among pre-determined options, constrained by similarly pre-determined givens.

By contrast the Classical scheme, of Smith and Ricardo as much as Marx, can be presented in an alternative diagram, based on a Social Pyramid and an Industrial Park, as well as markets and flows of funds. The Social Pyramid signifies the class structure, in particular that the upper class receives profits as a result of ownership, while the lower class must work for wages, and the unemployed constitute a reserve labor force. The Industrial Park displays the exchanges between industries which maintain the viability of the system of production. The surplus is distributed as profit, which is channeled through the financial system. Government performs two functions, regulating the flow of traffic – the stoplights – and adding to or subtracting from it, to maintain an appropriate level of traffic.

The orthodox diagram is deliberately abstract and stylized; Households and Firms are both contained in boxes of the same size, set opposite to one another, implying or suggesting that Firms and Households play the same kind of role in the economy, are of equal importance, but act in symmetrically opposite ways – Firms supplying final goods and demanding factors, Households supplying factors and demanding final goods. Factor markets and final goods markets are both contained in circles, also set diametically opposite each other. By implication both are markets in the same sense – that is, work on the same principles of supply and demand – and both mediate exchanges between households and firms.

The Classical diagram is deliberately concrete. The factory buildings have doors and windows, and the smokestacks are polluting the air. The bank building has columns, and the Social Pyramid has steps – for social climbing. The implication is that such details matter; the outcome of market processes depends on them for they provide sources of power and points for bargaining. Prices depend on the transactions within the Industrial Park, given the level of wages that must be paid. Overall demand depends on wages and salaries and the government, which together determine Consumption, and on Investment and finally on Government Spending.

The alternative vision thus centers on the exchanges needed to bring about reproduction and distribution, and the pattern of expenditure that results from distribution and from the incentives to accumulation. Production generates a surplus, the claims to which are determined through the processes of the market – but the size of the surplus, which depends on the volume of production, is itself partly determined by the market. The marketplace is seen as an arena in which social conflicts are fought out according to certain rules, but the struggle has direct economic consequences. Nor can economics be understood apart from these conflicts.

3 OVERVIEW OF THE BOOK

Part I presents the essential ideas underpinning these contrasting visions, and lays down the challenge that the Classical picture is significantly superior in its treatment of essential features of production and distribution. The general features of the Classical and Marxian systems are explored, and in particular it is shown that the rate of exploitation, when interpreted as a measure of the intensity of work, determines and explains the rate of profit and prices.

In Part II this claim is developed further. Important flaws in the neo-Classical treatment of produced means of production, the choice of technique and the formation of a general rate of profit are examined. These problems undermine a number of important claims normally taken for granted in mainstream writings – that prices reflect relative scarcities, that income is a payment for, and made in proportion to, a productive contribution, for example or, more generally, that distribution is a species of exchange. But if distribution is the assignment of claims over shares of a surplus, then it is not a species of exchange. The prices that bring about such a distribution may have nothing to do with relative scarcities. Further, if the distribution tends to be stable, the prices will also tend to be stable.

Capital, then, is not a 'factor of production;' it is a way of organizing production, giving rise to a certain pattern of claims against the surplus, inversely relating those of wage and profit receivers.

It is natural, therefore, to ask whether there are other, similarly well-established ways of organizing production and distribution, and whether any such preceded the emergence of capitalism. In Part III this question is taken up, and the working of earlier systems is described, particular care being paid to the way in which the incentives built into these systems leads to a systematic undermining of their foundations. When such undermining itself gives rise to technological innovation, this is the process of transformational growth. After an initial discussion of primitive agriculture, traditional agrarian societies are examined, with a special emphasis on European feudalism (but also taking a look at the American West). It is shown that in the early systems the production and distribution of the surplus through exchange is properly analyzed by means of the labor theory of value, but that the transformation of traditional agrarian society into modern capitalism involves the development of a modern pricing system, based on the rate of profit. Chapter 16 shows that key changes in technology have a major impact on the way markets work.

This leads on to Part IV, in which the implications of this picture for macroeconomics are explored. The surplus approach raises the question of stability in distributive shares; when shares are stable, long-run or benchmark prices will also be stable, even if there are fluctuations in demand. This in turn suggests a reconsideration of industrial technology; mass production methods are designed to make it possible to vary output in response to short-term fluctuations in demand, while keeping productivity, and therefore running costs, constant. Hence prices will tend to be stable, while output and employment vary with changes in demand, which provides a foundation for the macroeconomic theory of aggregate demand. Chapter 17 develops the crucial arguments.

But the conventional formulation of macroeconomics will have to be reconsidered. According to the textbooks, equilibrium is reached when household saving equals business' planned investments spending. But household savings are problematical; in the US they tend to be offset by households' debt payments for home mortgages and consumer durable finance. By contrast business profits, and business retained earnings, are unquestionably withdrawals. The basic principle can be reformulated to state that employment – which in the short run generates the surplus – adjusts to provide the profits which offset investment. Framed in this way the principle allows us to see the connections between the payment of money income, as wages and profits, and production in response to expenditure pressure. Three separate concepts can be clearly distinguished: income, output, and expenditure; these are commonly conflated in mainstream models, which seldom introduce an explicit equation for income as wages plus profits – with the consequence that they misspecify the income determination process. When corrected this provides a better approach to employment and the labor market, for it shows that employment is likely to vary directly, rather than inversely, with the real wage in the short run. It also enables us to distinguish clearly between investment plans and investment spending; the former depends on long-run considerations, including technological innovation, expected market growth and other factors that may be difficult to model with any precision – summed up by Keynes as 'animal spirits'. But the current level of spending in carrying out previously detemined plans depends on current sales revenues in relation to capacity, the current level of interest rates, dividends and stock prices, the expected levels of these in the immediate future, the current real wage, and similar variables. Investment spending can thus be readily modeled, and reveals a pattern of cyclical instability grounded in the working of the financial system. A new and significantly different view of inflation emerges, as the process by which the market determines who shall bear the burden of an adjustment to a change in costs or distribution. This takes on added dimensions when corporations are able to exercise some degree of control over the direction of market growth. Prices and investment will become even more closely related in these conditions. Finally, the section closes with critiques of the macroeconomics of the right, the center and the left – Friedman, Patinkin and Marglin – in each case for failing to spell out the process by which income – wages plus profits – is generated in conditions of mass production.

Part V concludes the book by drawing out some of the implications of the surplus approach for understanding questions of justice. The first two studies (*Chapters 26 and 27*) draw out the implications of the capital critique for the 'Chicago' perspective on the economy, while the third (Chapter 28) examines the ideal of pure socialism. Quite apart from the issue of taking literally what is at best an analogy, the Chicago account of the marriage market and the family rests heavily on invalid marginalist relationships. The same applies to their account of the entrepreneur and his just rewards. By contrast, Chapter 28 suggests that the surplus approach is well-adapted to an examination of principles of fairness and just distribution.

4 FINAL REMARKS

The surplus approach requires a careful account of the way claims to the surplus are translated into money; for the Classics, this was the problem of the circulation of money. It was treated extensively, and unsatisfactorily, by Marx in Volume II of *CAPITAL*. But it has largely disappeared from the modern scene. These studies are addressed to current issues dividing economists, and for this reason the discussion of monetary circulation does not appear in the present work. Since it is important, I have tried to deal with it elsewhere; the interested reader is referred to Part III of *Keynes After Sraffa*. Policy issues related to the surplus approach were examined in *Prosperity and Public Spending*.

No attempt will be made in these papers to develop the *n*-sectoral analysis of prices and the rate of profit, or growth and consumption. Well-known results will simply be assumed here; even wholly new points (as in Chapter 4) will be explained in the simpler two-sectoral format. Joint production problems will be ruled out on the grounds that for the most part in manufacturing principal products and by-products are clearly identifiable (so that single-product results carry over), and genuine joint production occurs chiefly in primary industries, in which profits are governed by different forces, and consist largely of capitalised rents. The notation follows standard practice and, as far as possible, has been kept consistent from chapter to chapter. But there are some differences, and each paper defines the symbols used in it.

Acknowledgements are indicated separately in each Chapter, but a special debt is owed to Keith Povey and his staff for a fine job with a difficult typescript.

Finally, there will be found some overlap and repetition; it has been kept to a minimum, but in their present form the studies can each be read independently, and this seemed desirable.

Preface: Joan Robinson – a Memoir*

When I first met her in the fifties, I liked to think of Joan playing opposite Humphrey Bogart in a John Huston film about the Resistance. She'd have been perfect – black clothes and red stockings, a commanding presence, cool, tough, single-mindedly loyal, fiercely partisan. Strong progressive opinions, but no nonsense about accepting dogmas, Marxist or otherwise. Critical of bourgeois society and its hypocrisy. A fighter, fearless and tough as they come.

Perhaps not a film, though. Joan was always part of real life, not of art. Later I thought, more like the Sandinistas – an English Nora Astorga! But again, perhaps not. Nora Astorga seems comfortable as a woman; I don't think Joan was. Which may partly account for what many found disproportionately harsh in her criticism.

Yet it was really not the harshness which was the problem; her opponents complained, but perhaps they deserved what they got. There was a lack of balance in her work between the positive or constructive and the negative and critical. Her emphasis, and the conclusions she highlighted, in her principal contributions have mostly been critical: in capital theory, of course. But consider her essay on Marx; it was her criticism of the labor theory of value that caught attention. As for Keynes, it is her critique of 'bastard Keynesianism' that is remembered. Even ingenious theorems like the 'Golden Rule' were developed during the course of a critique of marginal productivity theory. *The Accumulation of Capital* ends up in a set of disconnected scenarios designed to show what was wrong with Harrod's approach, on the one hand, and neo-Classical thinking on the other. Even *The Economics of Imperfect Competition* had a primarily critical objective – to undermine the marginal productivity theory of wages, and the associated ideas of perfect competition. (Of course, it also had the positive aim of explaining the existence of excess capacity in conditions that were clearly in some sense competitive.) And finally, after initially welcoming Sraffa's great contribution, she turned critical of the efforts of some of her closest friends and associates to develop a constructive account of capitalism on the foundations Sraffa laid. It was an equilibrium theory, she argued, and equilibrium can tell us nothing about history. At a stage in her life where she might have been expected to sum up her life's work in a way that might have provided guidance for her students and followers, she

* G.R. Feiwel (ed.) *Joan Robinson and Economic Theory* (London: Macmillan, 1989).

offered a critique of the whole project: instead of answers, she gave us *What Are the Questions?*

Well, why not? The profession certainly needs critics, and harsh ones. Look at virtually any mainstream journal these days and you will find pre-Keynesian thinking, standard and marginal productivity theory, perfect competition, and all the rest, parading through the pages as if there were nothing wrong.

But this is exactly the point. You can't beat something with nothing. No matter how fierce the criticism, not matter how well delivered the blows, neo-Classical theory never dies. Like a vampire it rises from the grave the next night, to prey on the unwary. Only those protected by the amulet of another theory will be safe from its ravages. And that is the protection that many of Joan's students and followers sought, but which she never provided.

Yet she might have. The materials were certainly there, particularly in *The Accumulation of Capital*, and the later *Essays*. The presentation may be deficient, but the conception is clear: here, for the first time in academic economics is a two-sector 'classical' growth model, turning on an inverse relationship between wages (=consumption) and growth (financed by saving out of profits). Neither prices nor choice of technique are governed by scarcity relationships; by contrast, investment, depending chiefly on 'animal spirits', governs both output and profits, (given the saving rate) and thus, indirectly, the choice of technique. Prices depend on technical coefficients and on profits, and so, ultimately on investment. Her objective was to extend Keynes's vision to the long run, showing that investment governs savings, the active dominates the passive, there also, exactly reversing the neo-Classical growth models developed by Solow, Swan, Meade, Uzawa *et al.* She tried to provide both the vision and some of the technical foundations.

My favorite among her later works has always been *Exercises in Economic Analysis*, a relatively good-tempered and constructive work, full of common sense and shrewd insight. (Also excellent diagrams that students have to draw for themselves.) But it was rudimentary, from a technical point of view. It contained the basis for a theory of accumulation, of the rate of profit and the rate of interest. It set forth a theory of the mark-up, and, by way of contrast, an account of scarcity prices. It contrasted socialism and capitalism, with many perceptive insights; and it dealt with effective demand, and provided important hints about the working of the monetary system. It contained criticism, of course, but the positive side was much more in evidence. These were the topics that provided a basis for an alternative account of the working of the economy. The material was there, but it needed more work, not only by Joan, but by a school of supporters. It could have been developed, but so far it has been neglected. (A later attempt, jointly with John Eatwell, fell between two stools; it did not dig deep enough to build new theory, but it was too abstract for a textbook.) Her later work became overwhelmingly critical. In her last years, she was acutely aware of what she called the failure to found an alternative school, and she lamented the drift back to neo-Classicism, occurring even at Cambridge.

Yet the simplest explanation for the failure of the alternative vision is that it has never been fully developed. Where is the constructive non-Neo-Classical work to compare with James Meade's multi-volume magnum opus? Where is the alternative to Samuelson's *Foundations*, Hicks's *Value and Capital*? To the constructions of Arrow and Debreu, or Arrow and Hahn? An alternative vision is one thing, an alternative construction quite another. *The General Theory* makes too many concessions, *Production of Commodities* is a prelude, a foundation, but the edifice is still to be built. *The Accumulation of Capital*, or the later *Exercises*, reworked and developed fully, as a positive theory, could and should have been part of such a construction, but it has yet to be erected.

These essays are offered as a contribution to this project.

Part I
Method and Approach

In the approach to economics advocated here the object is to understand the way a social system provisions itself – in particular, how it produces, distributes and uses its surplus, through the working of markets. So we must start with the elements of a social system, rather than with abstractly conceived, rational individual agents. Of course, we will abstract, but we cannot abstract too freely, lest we lose something essential to the working of the system. Chapter 1 sets up a simplified picture of the social system and its relation to the problems of exchange, distribution and expenditure; it sketches the way the system is to be analyzed, and contrasts the conventional picture with the surplus approach. Chapter 2 develops the importance of the theory of value, contrasting choice theories and theories basing prices on the conditions for reproduction, and showing how this contrast underlies conflicts in the analysis of equilibrium prices, distribution and growth. Chapter 3 develops the Marxian contribution, and in particular distinguishes the general and the special labor theories of value, arguing for the superiority of the general labor theory to the mainstream approach, while relegating the special labor theory to a secondary position, as a reasonable approximation, on the one hand, and an important particular case, on the other. Chapter 4 develops the labor theory further, drawing on Marx's treatment of exploitation as intensity of work, in order to provide a general solution to the problem of the relationship between the rate of exploitation, prices and the rate of profit, showing, in a simple model, that understanding the causes and consequences of changes in the intensity of work in production makes it possible to handle relationships that create trouble for virtually all other schools of thought.

1 The Revival of Political Economy*

I

Since the latter decades of the 19th century, orthodox economic theory has made its main business the demonstration that a well-oiled market mechanism will produce the most efficient allocation of scarce resources among competing ends. This preoccupation has in turn dictated a characteristic mode of analysis, in which the economy is conceived in terms of 'agencies,' or institutions, which, whatever their other differences, find their common denominators in terms of their market functions. Thus Rockefellers and sharecroppers are both 'households,' GM and the corner grocery are both 'firms.' Households, rich and poor, all demand 'final goods' and supply labor and other 'services' (meaning the use of capital and land); firms, big and small, demand labor and other factor services, and in turn supply final goods.

This way of subdividing the economy fits neatly into the framework of 'rational choice.' Factors supply services and demand goods in the amounts and proportions that will maximize their 'utilities,' given their 'initial endowments,' a polite way of referring to property holdings. It can be shown that the amounts finally chosen, the so-called equilibrium supplies and demands, will be simultaneously compatible solutions to all these different individual maximizing problems.

The task of high theory, then, is twofold: first, since the models are complex, *to show that there are, indeed, such simultaneous, mutually compatible solutions*. This is not obvious, and, in fact, not always true. Secondly, of equal mathematical and of greater ideological importance, are what might be called the Invisible Hand Theorems, which *show that the system of market incentives will direct the economy toward these equilibrium prices, supplies, and demands*. In other words, the Invisible Hand Theorems demonstrate that the system is automatically self-adjusting and self-regulating.

This architecture of thought has many strengths. Market incentives often *do* direct the system in various predictable ways. Maximizing is, under some conditions, an indispensible part of rational behavior, and so must be spelled out. That it is all done at an exceptionally high level of abstraction

* *Social Research*, 39(1) (Spring 1972). Also *Australian Economic Papers*, Summer, 1972.

is not only not an objection, but – it is claimed – may be a positive merit. The analysis is not cluttered with irrelevancies.

But when all is said, the theory of the efficiency of competitive markets has never provided much practical insight into historical reality. Since it presupposes effective market incentives and institutions devoted to maximizing behavior, it cannot easily be applied to the study either of pre-market economics or of post-market ones – i.e., ideal communist (or anarchist) societies. More important, traditional theory fails to provide a good model for studying the working and misworking of present-day capitalism.

There is a simple reason for this very important failure. Basically, orthodox theory is a theory of markets and market interdependence. It is a theory of general equilibrium as applied to *exchange*, extended almost as an afterthought to cover production and distribution. But exchange is a limited aspect of economic, much less social, reality. Therefore, orthodox theory is not a theory of economic power and social class, much less of a social system in its entirety. As we have noted, the initial 'endowments,' wealth, skills, and property of the populations are taken as *given*. Moreover, since the object of the theory is to demonstrate the tendency toward equilibrium, class and sectoral conflict tend to be ruled out almost by assumption.

As a result, the orthodox approach has comparatively little interesting to say about such important socioeconomic questions as the distribution of wealth and income. It cannot say how these came about originally; nor how different they might be under another kind of economic system. It does, however, have one major claim to social and historical relevance. It offers a definite though limited theory of the division of the value of net output between land, labor, and capital in a market system. This is known as 'marginal productivity' theory. Briefly, it states that each agent in the system will tend to be rewarded in proportion to – and as a limiting case, in direct equivalence with – the contribution he makes to output. Thus a man earns what he (literally) makes; a landlord reaps what he (metaphorically) sows.

But with the revival of interest in recent years in the great problems of Political Economy, this central claim has come under increasingly heavy attack. This attack, which began as particular and limited objections to specific orthodox doctrines, has in the past few years developed into an alternative conception of the economic system as a whole. It is no longer simply a rival theory of market dispensations – a 'non-neo-Classical' theory; nor can it be regarded merely as a return to the approach of the Classical greats – Smith, Ricardo, and Marx. It is both of these, but it is also considerably more. In currently fashionable terminology, it is the emergence of a new paradigm.

II

To see this, let us contrast the view of income distribution given by the new paradigm with that of orthodox marginal productivity theory. At first glance, marginal productivity theory appears eminently sensible. Essentially, it states that factors – land, labor, and capital – will be hired as long as they produce more than they cost to hire. Expanding the employment of any one factor, the others held constant, will (the theory assumes) cause the returns on the extra units of that factor to decline, since it has proportionately less of the others to work with. Thus employment will cease when the declining returns to the factor in question just equal the cost of hiring more of the factor. Competition will cause each factor to be used up to the point where the gain from employing it equals that obtainable from the other factors. The total earnings of any factor will then be equal to the amount of it that is employed, times its marginal product, summed up over all the industries in which it is used. Clearly the relative shares of factors – land, labor, and capital – will then depend on their respective marginal products.

So far, so good. To be sure, this story depends on the existence of markets, specifically on markets for land, labor, and capital, so that the theory won't be much use in examining the emergence or evolution of the market system. But note that, in a sleight of hand so deft as to have passed virtually unnoticed for an intellectual generation, the theory attributes responsibility for the distribution of income (under market competition) wholly and solely to the impersonal agency of *technology*. It is technology, not man, nor God, least of all politics, that has decreed what the shares of labor and capital are to be in the total product. *For it is technology that determines how rapidly returns diminish*. Thus only through technological changes, inventions that alter the engineering possibilities, can relative shares be changed. For if income shares are to change, marginal products must change faster or slower than they will change simply by the slow changes in the relative supplies of factors – e.g., population growth. Thus everything depends on how rapidly marginal returns to the different factors diminish, relative to one another, and this is a matter that depends only on technology.[1]

From this perspective the class struggle is an illusion, and unions are valuable only as mother substitutes – providers of security and a sense of identification. Minimum-wage legislation may or may not raise wages, but in all cases the effect will depend entirely on what the technology permits. Only moves that change the relative marginal products of labor and capital can affect income distribution (though even they might not change if, for example, the movement in the relative amounts of labor and capital employed just offsets the changes in their marginal products). The influence of factor supplies is felt only through marginal productivity. Hence technology is what finally determines income distribution. Aggregate demand, monetary policy, inflation, unions, politics, even revolutions, are, in the end, all alike, irrelevant insofar as Who Gets What.

Socialist and left-wing economists, indeed social critics generally, have always gagged on this.[2] Property and power, they maintain, are the essential elements in class struggles and sectional conflicts; it is ridiculous to say they don't matter – that the outcome, given the competitive market, is predetermined by the accidents of technological inventiveness. From their vantage point, income distribution – the division of society's annual product among the members of society – is *the* central question. For if we put income distribution at the center of the stage, the concern of the orthodox theorists with how factors spend their incomes seems relatively minor. The framework of rational choice looks flimsier and more makeshift; essentially a consumer-oriented theory, it has come to resemble so many consumer products: ingenious, brilliant, but unsuited to human needs.

This is not to say that the Political Economist rejects the theory of rational choice outright: he rejects it merely as an appropriate framework for the analysis of production and distribution *in the aggregate*. The framework he erects in its place is one that reveals the *links* between sectors and classes; shows how the products of one industry or set of industries are used as inputs by other industries (whose products, in turn, are used by still others); and makes clear how the earnings of one class are spent supporting production in some sector or industry. These interindustry and intersectoral relations are crucial to understanding how changes in demand or in technology transmute themselves into prosperity for some, disaster for others. Links between revenue from sales, social classes, and spending are crucial for understanding how the distribution of income is established and maintained in the face of considerable changes in the composition of output and in government policy.

The difference may seem one more of emphasis than of substance, but putting income distribution at the center and relating it to different patterns of linkages, of payment streams, and of technological dependencies between industries, sectors, and classes, leads to an altogether different vision of how the economy works.

III

The new vision can be called a 'general equilibrium' approach, if one likes. But it immediately departs from the orthodox meaning of that phrase by emphasizing the interdependence of *production*, rather than of markets; technical and institutional '*interlocks*' – or their absence – rather than purely market relationships.

A second difference between the new approach and the old lies in the treatment of 'substitution.' In the old picture, substitution is the law of life on both the supply and demand sides. In response to price changes, different patterns of goods and/or factors will be chosen; when prices change, cheaper things will be substituted for more expensive ones in household budgets and industrial processes. The problem is that this conventional picture assumes that households and firms have *given* ends – the maximization of 'utility' or output respectively. Hence, it does not deal with the more important questions of introducing altogether new products and processes, changes that often alter the parameters of the system or perhaps even the consciousness of society. Even within the narrow focus of the neo-Classical lens, however, many alleged cases of 'substitution' involve something quite different – technological progress, changes in the nature of the product, external effects on parameters of the system, and so on. Indeed, in this wider sense, neo-Classical substitution is only a *special* case, and that is how the matter is treated in the new vision.

Thirdly, the old vision treats the consumer as sovereign, and the effects of his choices enter into the determination of all major variables. This, of course, does not render the old vision incapable of discussing market power, producer sovereignty, or the 'new industrial state.' But, inevitably, such phenomena appear as special cases, limitations on the *general* principle of consumer sovereignty. In the new vision the consumer is cut down to size from the start. Her preferences have little or no effect on prices or income distribution.

As a consequence, markets and the 'price mechanism' are not seen in the new vision as a stable method of bringing about social optimality. On the contrary, prices are seen as determined largely from the supply side, and so depend on income distribution, which in turn may be influenced by many nonmarket and even noneconomic considerations. Ideologically, this means that the 'market' should not be seen as some sort of alternative to bureaucracy, or as a method of allocating resources. Allocation depends on distribution, which depends at least in part on property and class.[3]

A further fundamental difference can be seen when we consider the *purposes* of the two visions. The basic constituents of the old vision are consumers and firms, agents whose optimizing behavior, individually or in the aggregate, the equations of the models describe. In particular, maximizing behavior is what the theory is all about, and the *object of the theory, by and large, is to predict the consequences of such behavior*. But the circumstances in which this behavior takes place are taken for granted.

By contrast – and oversimplifying – the new vision is primarily interested in structure, in the patterns of dependency between established institutions, in how the system hangs together, and how it works or fails to work. The job of economic theory is to delineate the *blueprint* of the economic system, of the environment in which economic behavior takes place. The basic constituents of theory are industries, sectors, processes, or activities, defined in technological terms; so defined, the new vision's basic constituents normally will not coincide with decision-making 'agencies.' Neither the word 'household' nor the word 'firm,' nor any synonym for either, appears in Sraffa's *Production of Commodities by Means of Commodities*, the basic work laying the foundation of the new paradigm. For decision-making, the prediction of behavior or of what *will* happen, is not the goal. The new vision is concerned with seeing how an economy keeps going, what is *supposed* to happen; from that to discover what makes it break down and what makes it develop into an economy of a different kind. These are seen as questions addressed primarily to the analysis of the system of production, and of the social relations surrounding production.

The central distinction between the two visions, then, lies in the treatment of production and distribution. For the traditional neo-Classical economist, production is a one-way street, running from primary 'factors' to 'final products.' Among the primary factors are land, labor, and, above all, *capital*, each receiving in competition a reward proportional, in some sense (depending on market circumstances), to its 'contribution.'

But not so in the new paradigm. The notion that the three traditional factors are on the same footing is discarded altogether. The great achievement of the Marginalist Revolution, as seen by its 19th century proponents – namely, the development of a unified theory applying to all three factors – is dismissed. This can be seen nowhere so clearly as in the new conception of 'capital,' in reality a revival of a point well understood before the Marginalists confused things. 'Capital' has two meanings. On the one hand, it is property in the means of production, enabling owners of equal amounts of claim in these means to receive equal returns (given competitive conditions). In this sense it is a homogeneous fund of value, capable of being embodied in different forms. On the other hand, 'capital' also means produced means of production – that is, specific materials, tools, instruments, machines, plant, and equipment, on which, with which, and by means of which labor works. In this sense it is a set of heterogeneous, disparate products. *Capital goods are not the same thing as capital.* 'Capital' is relevant to the analysis of the division of income among the members of society, but a nonspecific fund has no bearing on production. 'Capital goods' are relevant to the study of production, but have no bearing on the distribution of income, since profit is earned and interest is paid on the *fund* (value) of capital invested, regardless of its specific form. 'Capital goods,' specific instruments, can only be converted into a fund of 'capital' on the basis of a given set of prices for those instruments; but to know these prices we must already know the general rate of profit (in a reasonably competitive capitalist economy).[4] Hence the amount of 'capital' cannot be among the factors that set the level of the rate of profit. But in the orthodox, or neo-Classical, theory the 'contribution' of 'capital' to *production* supposedly determines the demand for capital, which together with the supply determines the rate of profit. This must be rejected. No sense can be given to the 'contribution' to production of a *fund* of capital (Ch. 7).

This is not to say that *saving and investment*, and their long-run consequences, are irrelevant to determining the rate of profits and relative shares. Quite the reverse; by eliminating the alleged 'contribution of capital' in production as an influence or determinant of distribution, we open the way for a theory of distribution based on the relation between the growth of spending, of capacity, and of the labor force, on the one hand; and on the market power available to the various parties, on the other. Unequal rates of inflation of money wages and prices necessarily imply changes in the relative shares going to capital and labor, as Keynes pointed out in the *Treatise on Money*, his earlier major and now neglected work. Inflation is partly a consequence of the ratio of demand to supply, but it also reflects relative market power. And here is where the rules of the game – the rules of property – come in. For property confers advantages, though not absolute ones, in the setting of prices and in bargaining for money wages. Exactly what these advantages are, how they work, and by what kinds of forces, are among the questions that a theory of distribution should be able to answer. (See Chs 9 and 10.)

In short, the new vision adopts a picture of the relation between production and distribution altogether distinct from that which has ruled the economist's roost since the Marginalist Revolution. This, in turn, entails rejecting some widely used techniques of empirical analysis, in favor with both radical and orthodox economists. In particular, 'production function' studies – e.g., of technical progress, the contribution of education, the effects of discrimination, and of shares during growth – all involve a fatal flaw. For insofar as they proceed by assuming that a factor's *income share* indicates in any way its *productive power* at the margin, they are based on precisely the relationship that the new vision rejects.[5]

It thus seems that conventional theory, although it contains much of value and importance, contains serious deficiencies.[6] The neo-Classical theory of the general equilibrium of production, distribution, and exchange holds that the payments in the *factor markets are exchanges* in the same sense as payments in the *product markets*. 'Distribution is the species of exchange,' wrote Edgeworth, 'by which produce is divided between the parties who have contributed to its production.' Distribution, say the proponents of the new vision, is *not* a species of exchange; and capital *goods*, rather than capital, contribute to production. The ideological teeth begin to bite; an exchange, in equilibrium, means that *value equivalent is traded for value equivalent*. No exploitation there. But if distribution is *not* a form of exchange, then we must ask Who Whom?

This catalogue of differences, and especially the last point, can be nicely illustrated by comparing two simple diagrams that visually summarize the two paradigms. The first, Figure 1.1, adapted from Samuelson

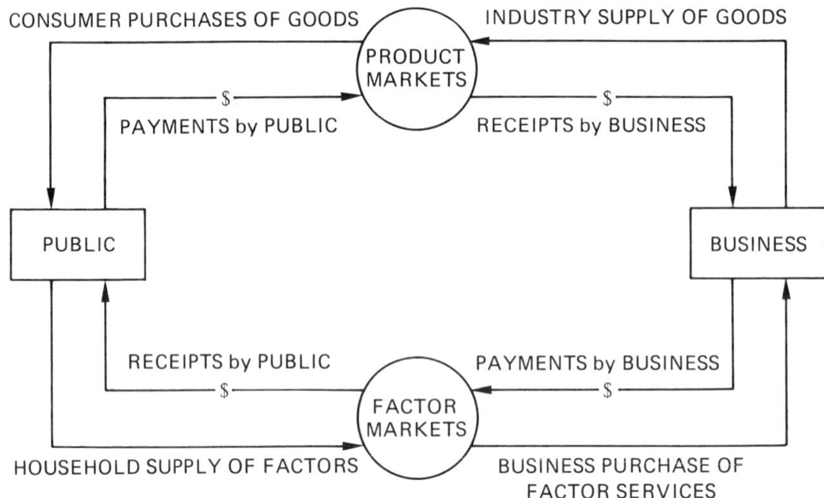

Figure 1.1

(1948–present) and echoed in all major textbooks, presents what might be called a same-level division of society: business and the public (producers and consumers) confront each other more or less as equals in the markets for both products and factors. (The equality is an overall one; there are some large or allied firms, some collective consumers.) Households demand final goods and services and supply the services of productive factors, in both cases in accord with what economists rather pompously call 'their given relative preference schedules,' meaning, what they like best. Businesses supply final goods and services according to their cost schedules in relation to the prices that consumers are prepared to pay, and demand the services of productive factors according to their technical opportunities and needs in relation to consumer demand for products.

So goods and services flow counterclockwise, while money flows clockwise. In each set of markets, *equivalents are traded for equivalents*, the value of goods and services flowing in one direction being just matched by the stream of revenue in the other. No exploitation is possible in competitive equilibrium. The value of household factor supplies just matches aggregate household demand, and the output of goods and services matches business demands. This may seem to ignore the fact that households save and businesses invest, meaning that some final demand flows not from the Public but from Business. But that is easily allowed for. To finance this demand, Business must borrow Household savings, by supplying bonds that the public demands. Bonds are treated as a kind of good, flowing counterclockwise. These points enable the microflow picture to be summed up as a macroflow picture, illustrating in the simplest way how macro rests on microfoundations.

Obvious objections to this economic schema can easily be raised. For instance, not all 'households' are on a par, since some *own* all the firms between them, while the rest merely *work* for the firms. Also the distribution of profit and similar income is not an exchange, since the only 'service' that the owner of a business (in his capacity as owner) need supply in return for its profits is that of permitting it to be owned by him. He does bear risks, of course, but so do the employees who will be out of their jobs in the event of failure. Other objections were mentioned earlier in the charge that orthodox neo-Classicism ignores technological interdependences and institutional relationships, as the circular flow picture makes evident. Nowhere in it can one find social classes or any specific information about patterns of technical interdependence.

All these objections look at first like strong empirical problems that neo-Classicists should meet head on. In fact, however, the customary orthodox defense is oblique and of dubious validity. To the charge that their model rests on unrealistic assumptions, they reply that the *only* test of a model is the success of its predictions. So there is no *a priori* error in making unrealistic assumptions. Moreover, 'simplifying assumptions' and 'theoretical constructs' are bound to be, in some sense, 'unrealistic,' and there is no predicting without them. Unrealistic assumptions may therefore be warranted and the warrant is philosophical, positivism itself.

We will return to these defenses. But first consider quite a different picture of capitalist society. Figure 1.2 epitomizes the new approach, which, if the old is 'neo-Classical,' could be dubbed 'Classical–Marxian.' It cannot be claimed that this is the only, or necessarily the best, distillation of an alternative picture from that tradition, but it will serve to illustrate the contrasts.

To keep Figure 1.2 comparable to Figure 1.1, we retain the circle for the final goods market and the box standing for industry, though we shall interpret both quite differently. 'Households' and the 'factor market' disappear altogether. Instead we have a pyramid, representing the social hierarchy, divided into two parts: a small upper class of owners and a large lower class of workers. Owners own industry and receive profits; workers work for industry and receive wages. Workers consume, but do not, in this simplified model, save; owners both consume and save, in order to invest.

Now consider the flows of services and money payments. Labor is the only 'factor input;' other inputs are produced by industry itself, which is assumed to have access to land, mines, etc. (We are lumping landlords and capitalists together.) Hence we might expect to be able to value the total product in terms of labor, and though the mathematics is complicated, this can indeed be done, though not in all cases. The arrows running back and forth between factories represent interindustry transactions, the exchanges between industries necessary to replace used-up means of production. The Net Social Product is sold for Total Receipts, and consists of all goods over and above those needed for replacement. These can be divided (for

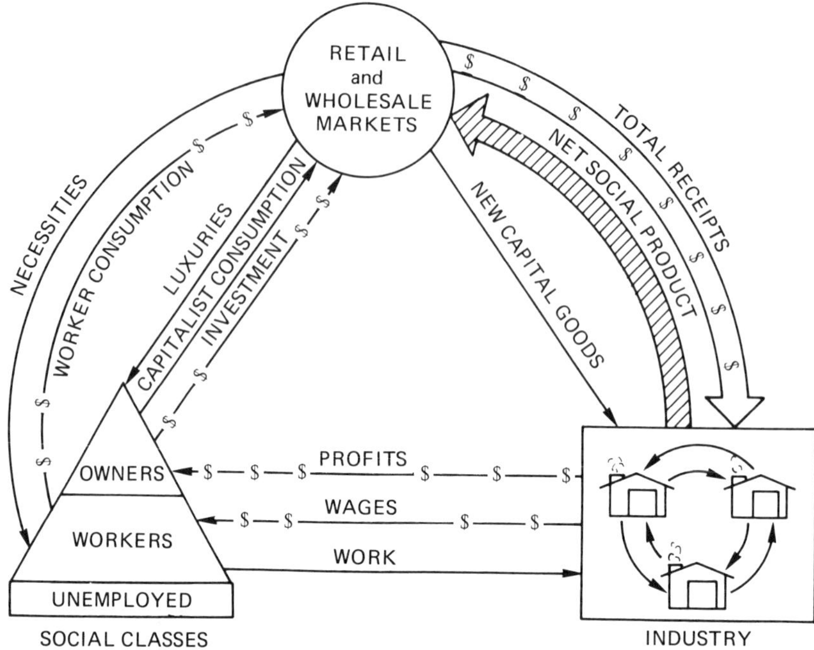

Figure 1.2

convenience) into Necessities, Luxuries, and New Capital Goods.[7] Necessities go for Worker Consumption, Luxuries for Capitalist Consumption, and New Capital Goods are installed in the factories in return for Investment payments. Hence, the national accounts work out:

> Total Receipts = Net Social Product = Wages + Profits = Wage Consumption + Capitalist Consumption + Investment Demand = Necessities + Luxuries + New Capital Goods.

From the point of view of Political Economy, however, the most important fact is that while wages are paid for work, and one can (and in some circumstances should) think of the wage bill, equal here to Worker Consumption, as reproducing the power to work, *profits are not paid for anything at all.* The flow of profit income is not an exchange in any sense. The Samuelson diagram in Figure 1.1 is fundamentally misleading; there is no 'flow' from 'household supply' to the factor market for capital. The *only* flow is the flow of profit income in the other direction. And this, of course, leads straight to that hoary but substantial claim that the payment of wages is not an exchange either, or at any rate, not a fair one. For Wages plus Profits adds up to the Net Income Product; yet Profits are not paid for anything, while wages are paid for work. Hence the work of labor (using the tools, equipment, etc., replacement and depreciation of which is already counted in) has produced the entire product. Is labor not therefore exploited? Does it not deserve the whole product?

IV

The latter question opens Pandora's box; as for the former, it all depends on what you mean. What does certainly follow, however, is that distribution is *not* an exchange, profits are not paid *for* anything and serve no function which cannot be met in other ways. This may not be exploitation but it shows clearly that the traditional economic justification – the 'reward' for services – cannot be applied to profits, interest, dividends, and the like. Moreover, since the payment of profit is no exchange, there can be no equilibrium in the usual sense. A century-old school of thought, holding that our troubles come from the *excessive* profits sucked in by giant monopolies, and idolizing small competitive enterprise earning 'normal profits,' is thereby undercut. There is no merit in 'normal profit;' indeed there is no such thing. The issue for Political Economy is the profit system itself, not its alleged abuse.

But surely, under both capitalism and market socialism, do not profits serve the essential function of indicating where investment can most advantageously be directed? Does not the *rate* of profit, similarly, serve to allocate productive resources between producing for current consumption and expansion for the future?

There are two things wrong with this common claim. First (as sophisticated neo-Classical economists will quickly admit), the function of profits and the rate of profit as indicators require merely that they be *calculated, not that they be actually paid out.* Calculated profit indicators are compatible with many different incentive schemes (e.g., salary bonuses to managers of state-owned enterprises, moral incentives, etc.). Second, profit-based indicators are only one set among several. In a stationary economy, for example, the correct indicators to achieve maximum output would be based not on profits but on *labor values*![8] Indeed, profit indicators alone are likely to be misleading; the rate and pattern of growth must also be considered in trying to identify the best investment plans. Thus, from the strict economic point of view, forgetting social complications, the best choices for maximizing consumption may differ from the best choices for maximizing growth. Once we allow for quality, the effect on the environment, and so on, the variety of possible indicators becomes considerable.

To return to the diagram in Figure 1.2: the new model helps us to understand how the division of income comes about. Remember that the orthodox doctrines held that the distribution of income was determined in the factor market, by the marginal 'contribution' of factors in conjunction with their relative scarcity. The diagram makes it clear that income distribution interacts with all aspects of the economy, not just with the 'factor market.' This point can be made quite simply, though its consequences are far-reaching. Labor's share is given by the real wage times the amount of work. But the *real* wage is the *money* wage divided by an index of consumer goods prices. The money wage is set in the labor market, but prices are set in the final goods market. Labor's share, then, depends on *both* markets. Thus the system is interdependent in ways no hint of which can be found in orthodox teaching.[9] (See Ch. 24.)

This puts inflation in a new and clearer light. The standard approach is to distinguish 'demand-pull' inflation (originating in the final goods market) from 'cost-push' inflation (originating in the factor market). Very few actual cases seem to fit either category. On the new approach this should come as no surprise, for the question has been wrongly posed. This issue is not where inflation originates, but how fast it proceeds in different markets. In the orthodox diagram it is natural to suppose that a price increase in the product market will be transmitted directly to the factor market, and vice versa. Unless costs and prices rise together the circular flow cannot continue unimpeded. In the new diagram it is evident that this is not so – costs and prices rising in the same proportion will be the special, limiting case. In all other cases the effect will be to raise or lower Profits. When wages rise faster than prices, there will be Profit Deflation; when prices rise faster than wages, Profit Inflation, to use the terminology suggested by Keynes in the *Treatise on Money*. In all cases except the limiting one, then, inflation will affect income distribution and so aggregate demand and employment.[10] (See Ch. 23.)

What determines the relative rate of price and wage increases? The first answer, of course, must be 'supply and demand,' and this is surely right. For example, large numbers of unemployed will tend to act as a drag on money wages. But the same balance of supply and demand may have a very different total impact on price in different circumstances, depending on market power; on the financial position of companies and unions; on the ability to make use of the law, or state agencies, to manipulate the press and the media; and so on. These considerations are preeminently ones of Political Economy, but they play an essential role in theory, for they determine the relative responsiveness of markets, and hence the relative speed of wage and price inflation.

V

We have now presented and contrasted the two paradigms. The neo-Classical one is far better known, and most contemporary work is conceived in its terms. But if the preceding argument is sound, it is significantly misleading. The new paradigm, by contrast, is clearly more realistic sociologically, and is capable of handling questions, such as those concerning property income and social class, that the other tends to submerge.

These two claims, that the old paradigm is misleading and the new more realistic, suggest that there is a strong *prima facie* case for adopting the new. This conclusion, however, is widely resisted, and the reasons, already mentioned, are interesting. Those who defend the old approach often contend that a paradigm cannot be 'misleading' in its representation of institutions *if it leads to models that predict well*. 'Realism' is not important; abstraction must take place, and a model can abstract from anything, so long as it performs well.

Such a defense must be seen for what it is. It is a methodological claim, and one based on a particular, and today rather questionable, philosophy of science. One straightforward retort might be that neo-Classical models have not done very well on their chosen ground.[11] Prediction has not been the greatest success of modern economics. But a more fundamental response would be to challenge the methodology itself. There is no time to argue the case now, but there is an intuitive appeal to the idea that a model of social institutions must be a good representation of things as they are at a given moment of time, regardless of how they work out over time. To demand of economics that it predict what *will* happen may be asking too much.[12] In modern industrial societies the economic system is too closely interlocked with other aspects of society; it cannot be isolated enough for effective tests to be run. But to add a long string of *ceteri paribus* clauses simply tends to reduce predictions to vacuity. Instead, we must examine the definitions and assumptions of our models for their realism, and for the extent to which they incorporate the essentials. If they are realistic, then the working of the model should mirror the working of the economic system in relatively simple and abstract form. To argue this further would take us far afield.[13] It should be clear, though, that the case we have presented can be defended from the methodological objections of the Positivists.

In short, the new approach presents a coherent picture of the economy, perfectly adapted to modern empirical methods and capable of providing technical analysis of a sophisticated nature.[14] But it has not been developed for its own sake, or simply because it presents a better, more accurate picture of capitalism. The new picture is intended precisely as *Political* Economics, as a guide to the criticism of the capitalist socioeconomic system. Its basic challenge to orthodox thinking is that, in treating the distribution of income as a form of exchange, it misrepresents the way the system works. But if it is not an exchange then someone is getting something for which he is not giving a value-equivalent. The step to social criticism is then short.

Orthodox economics tries to show that the markets allocate scarce resources according to relative efficiency; Political Economics tries to show that markets distribute income according to relative power. It is good to know about efficiency, but in the world we live in, it tends to be subservient to power.[15] By failing to appreciate this, and consequently failing also to accord the distribution of income between labor and capital a properly central role, orthodox economics has become cut off from the central economic issues of our time, drifting further into ever more abstract and mathematically sophisticated reformulations of essentially the same propositions. The heart of the matter is the concept of 'capital' and its relation to social class and economic power. When this is put right, as in the new paradigm, economic theory can once again speak to the critical issues of the day.

Appendix: Post-Keynesian Flow Diagrams

The reader should first refer back to the discussion of the 'neo-Classical picture' on pp. 10–11, and Figures 1.1 and 1.2. Figure 1.2 suggests relationships not evident in the circular flow model. Owners consume without working; workers consume without owning.[16] Production and intermediate transactions (which largely set relative prices, i.e., 'real' exchange ratios) occur in the manufacturing sector, which supplies the Social Product and pays out Wages and Profits to Workers and to Banks and Boards of Directors respectively. However, the model shows that the Financial Management then decides how much will be distributed to owners and how much will be retained for investment and liquidity purposes.

Consumer demand is subdivided here, showing separate propensities to consume and save out of earned and property income. (The flow of property income *to* households will be determined in the money, bond and stock markets.) Investment demand is presumed to depend on competition in growth, constrained by the need for funds. An important point is that money *wages* and the volume of employment are determined in the labor market, where they are obviously influenced by the level of capacity utilization, desired investment, and other factors influencing the demand for labor. Money *prices*, however, will be set in the market for final goods. However, given the rate of profit, or the rate of growth, *relative* prices will be determined by the production equations, and will be set in intermediate transactions. That is, money prices are set in a market of business vs households; relative or real, prices in business vs business transactions.

The net social product will be a kind of 'surplus,' including, however, wage goods. The notion of surplus can be defined as the net output over and above whatever goes to replace the total means of production and sources of energy used up in the course of producing. Strictly speaking, of course, wages should not be counted in a surplus; so the net social product here is really surplus *plus* wages. The idea is important, however, for it anchors the concept of national income firmly in the sea of technology, in contrast to the neo-Classicals who leave it floating in the ethereal skies of 'utility.' The final total of Aggregate Demand and Supply, then, will depend on the interaction of all of these parts, and so will be determined together with the distribution of income.

A number of differences should be evident between this and the neo-Classical diagram in Figure 1.2. Wage-earners' Consumption primarily reproduces their ability to work. In any case the total Consumer demand depends on the distribution of income. Only work in the production sector is productive. Distribution of income and exchange of goods are completely different; owners and workers have separate economic roles, and the financial sector mediates between owners and the firms they own, which are run by managers. Money prices and relative prices are determined in different markets, and thus only the money wage, not the real wage, is set in the labor market. (The real wage will therefore only emerge from interaction of the entire system.)

Thus, the relationships suggested in this simple model are different and rely on different methodological strategies from those of the neo-Classicists. The latter predicate behavioral functions of *individual* decision-makers, paying little attention to institutional detail, except where it can be expressed in behavioral functions (as

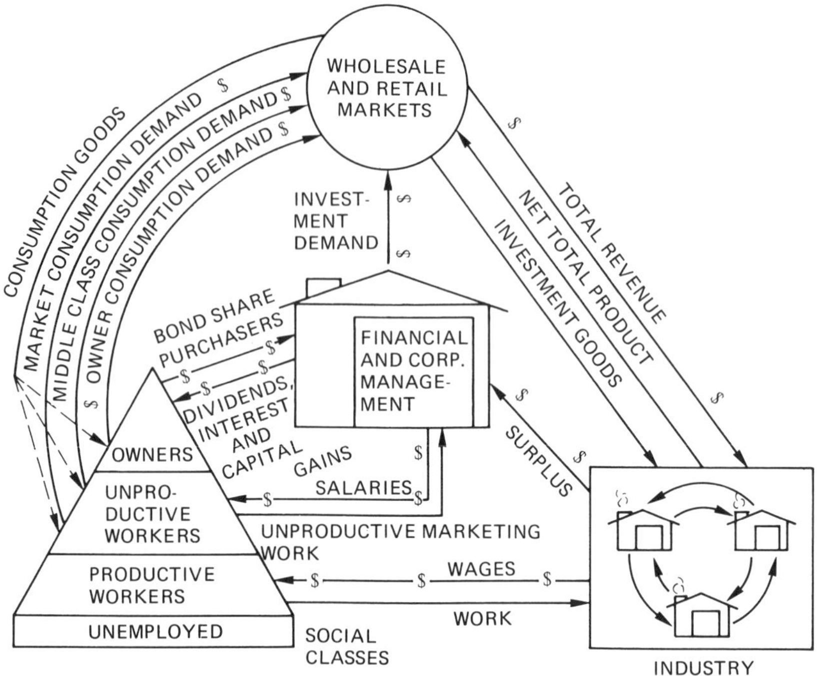

Figure 1A.1

in the imperfect competitor's downward-sloping demand curve or the kinked oligopoly demand curve). By way of contrast, 'Classical-Marxian' theorists base their equations on institutional structures and tend to use fewer behavioral equations. This reflects a difference in political theory. Neo-Classicists see behavior characteristically as the outcome of maximizing decisions; Classical-Marxian theorists find behavior expressed (as with the classical savings function) in sociological and institutional data. They do not discard maximizing; on the contrary, it is seen both as an instrument for deciding the best means to an end and sometimes, but by no means always or necessarily, as a description of what men do. This reflects a difference in philosophies of mind and theories of action. Neo-Classicists treat 'sound' theory as the upshot of testing predictions with success; Classical-Marxian theorists insist that the 'specification' of a model, that is, the relationships we postulate, and the 'identification' of the results of testing (to use the technical term for interpretation) be determined by reflecting on what *must* be the case for our capitalist industrial institutions to maintain themselves and work the way they do. All models must be grounded in the basic blueprint. Two further comments:

1. Figure 1A.1 can be simplified by leaving out the Financial Management sector. The resulting picture brings out more sharply the contrast between Wages, which are paid for Work, and Profits, which are paid because of ownership rights, and not in exchange for anything at all. Profits are important, *given the system*, because, as Figures 1A.1 and 1.2 make clear, they provide the funds which finance investment. But they are not paid in exchange for anything and workers have no say in their disposition. Investment decisions, which, of course,

affect workers, too, are the exclusive prerogative of the capitalist class. Nothing of this is indicated by the conventional diagram.

2. Figure 1A.1 can also be made to reveal another aspect of the modern economy, at a relatively small cost in additional complexity. Some work obviously contributes to the output of goods and services; some work equally obviously does not. This is the ancient distinction between 'productive' and 'unproductive' labor. Baran and Sweezy (1900) have given this a rather different twist, by distinguishing the costs of *producing* goods and services from costs of *marketing* (realizing) them, including in these latter not merely advertising, promotion, and selling costs, but also, along with finance and lobbying, all those costs which are related to supporting the capitalist system as such. (Of course, any system will engender some supportive costs; so the foregone opportunity is really the difference between the cost of supporting the current system and that of supporting an alternative.) According to Baran and Sweezy these non-productive costs come out of the 'surplus' generated by productive labor, using the instruments, plant and equipment available. This is defined as the excess of total output over and above the goods and services required to support productive labor, to replace the used-up means of production and to make up for depreciation of equipment. This surplus, then, will be divided by the Financial and Corporate Managements between Ownership Income (Dividends, Interest, and Realized Capital Gains), Investment, and Marketing Costs, with Owners returning a portion in the form of Bond and Share Purchases and spending the remainder of their income on Capitalist Consumption. Among other things this makes it clear that Marketing Costs, the costs of running the capitalist system, compete with Investment for funds. (See Ch. 17, sections 4 and 5.)

   The distinction between productive and unproductive labor has often been criticized, and some of this criticism is valid. Certainly there are many cases which it would be difficult to classify. But it is hard to deny that there is a clear distinction in principle between work in production and work in marketing. It is one thing to argue over where to draw the line, quite another to hold that there is no line to be drawn. The purpose here is simply to exhibit this distinction, indicating its relation to the Profit System.

The Social Accounts are now: Wages + Salaries + Dividends, Interest and Realized Capital Gains − Bond and Share Purchases = Wages + Surplus = (Worker + Middle Class + Owner) Consumption Demand + Investment Demand = Value of Consumption Goods + Value of Investment Goods = Net Total Revenue = Net Total Product.

Government can be added in two ways. First, traffic lights can be drawn, showing government regulation, and secondly, at the lights, government can add to or siphon off the flow of traffic.

Notes

1. The point can be put more accurately in technical language: relative shares will change with factor supplies according to the elasticity of substitution, which, in turn, depends only on technology. If the elasticity of substitution is unity, then proportional changes in factor ratios will just be offset by proportional changes in marginal products, so that relative shares will be unaltered. In other cases, changes in the relative amounts of factors employed will alter relative shares,

but both by how much and in what direction will depend solely on the technology.

2. Of course, the available technical possibilities do influence income distribution. Clearly, if it is known that a machine can do a certain job now being performed manually, the laborer doing the job would be most unwise to ask more than the annual cost of installing and running the machine. But this point can be made without accepting the strait jacket of marginal productivity theory. This is important because the technical possibilities of substitution are only one of several sets of influences that bear upon the division of the national income. Differential rates of inflation, both between wages and prices and between sectors, the aggregate level of employment and monopoly power, are at least equally important, for example. Marginal productivity theory tends to blind us to these influences, or to treat them as 'market imperfections,' exceptions rather than the normal working of the system.
3. There is also an interesting technical point. In the neo-Classical vision macroeconomic relationships are supposed to be based on markets and the price mechanism, which are seen as fundamental. But in the new vision, prices depend on income distribution, and that, insofar as it is determined by economic forces, depends largely on macroeconomic factors. The direction of causal influence is reversed.
4. This is perhaps the central issue in the recent dispute over capital theory between the 'two Cambridges,' Cambridge, England, maintaining the view presented here, against Cambridge, Massachusetts, which argued that the essential neo-Classical story could be developed in a 'heterogeneous-capital' model. Unfortunately, to do this, Cambridge, Mass. found it had to assume conditions in which a simple Labor Theory of Value held! It is now widely agreed that neo-Classical capital theory is defective. For a thorough discussion see G.C. Harcourt, *Cambridge Controversies in the Theory of Capital* (Cambridge: Cambridge University Press, 1972), and Part II of the book.
5. Put this baldly, of course, it seems an extraordinary assumption for anyone to make seriously. Given what we know about how our society works, if we read the newspapers (or the Valachi papers), we would never in our ordinary thinking expect to explain a change in the income of a group primarily by reference to a change in its marginal productivity. We would certainly think of demand and supply, and of income elasticity; these would provide the framework within which bargaining, power plays, and politics would settle the final (or temporary) outcome. Marginal productivity might or might not come into it; just as it might or might not be measurable, but it would hardly be decisive. Is the shift in the income going to the top few per cent since 1960 to be taken seriously as reflecting an increase in their marginal productivity? Is the relative rise in professional income from 1900–1970 evidence of a long-term upward drift in their productivity at the margin? Yet, in spite of common sense and advanced theory, the production-function studies, aggregate and individual, continue.
6. This should be distinguished from the commonplace (though correct) criticisms that opportunities for substitution are not legion, that changes in techniques of production and consumption are time consuming and costly, that information is hard to come by (and perhaps should be treated as itself a product!), that mobility is sluggish, foresight myopic, and expectations an irregular compound of habit and hope. These points will be readily admitted, for they merely indicate how far the actual world falls short of its own ideal type. The point of the present criticism is that the neo-Classical ideal market economy is *not* a

picture of how the economic system would work under ideal conditions, for it fundamentally misrepresents the relationship of distribution to exchange, whether conditions are 'ideal' or not.

7. The traditional interest in classifying goods along lines such as these, largely abandoned in the face of positivist criticism – these are just value judgements – has been revived in the light of Sraffa's important and far-reaching distinction between basics (goods that enter directly or indirectly into the means of production of all goods) and nonbasics.
8. See R. Goodwin, *Elementary Economics from the Higher Standpoint* (Cambridge: Cambridge University Press). The point follows directly from the Golden Rule of Accumulation, which states that consumption per head is maximized when the rate of growth equals the rate of profit. When the rate of growth is zero, then in the stationary state, for optimality – maximum consumption per head, or in this case, maximum national income per head – the rate of profit must be zero. But the prices which obtain when the rate of profit is zero can easily be shown to be equal to the amounts of direct and indirect labor embodied – i.e., the labor theory of value holds.
9. This diagram also illustrates a proposition first discovered in the 1930s by the great Polish Marxist economist, Michel Kalecki, who independently and at the same time set forth the main propositions of the *General Theory*.

   Investment, I, is the change in the capital stock, written $\triangle K$, where '$\triangle$' means 'change in,' and comes entirely from savings out of profits. Let 's_p' stand for the fraction of profits saved. So $\triangle K = s_p P$, where P is profits. Divide both sides by 'K,' the capital stock. We have

   $$\frac{\triangle K}{K} = s_p \frac{P}{K}$$

   But

   $$\frac{\triangle K}{K} = g, \text{ the rate of growth}$$

   and

   $$\frac{P}{K} = r, \text{ the rate of profits.}$$

   Hence $g = s_p r$, a simple formula connecting the growth rate and the profit rate. Remembering that $\triangle K = I$, we also have

   $$\frac{I}{s_p} = P = rK.$$

   So, for a given technology, *profits are higher and the growth rate lower the greater is the average propensity of the capitalist class to consume out of profits*. The extreme simplicity and great generality of this proposition, even now not widely known in the profession, are typical of the results obtained by the new approach.
10. A parallel point should be made about the relative prosperity of different sectors during inflation. The relative rates of price and wage inflation will determine the relative changes in profits, which (on the assumption that most

investment is financed by retained earnings) will set the relative growth rates. Thus inflation, except in the limiting case, will over the course of time bring about changes in the composition of the aggregate economy.

11. See Sidney Schoeffler, *The Failures of Economics: A Diagnostic Study* (Cambridge, Mass.: Harvard University Press, 1957). The record has not improved much since this book was published.
12. See Adolph Lowe, *On Economic Knowledge* (New York: Harper Torch Book, 1959), pp. 55ff., passim.
13. For an examination of these points, see Martin Hollis and Edward Nell, *Rational Economic Man* (Cambridge: Cambridge University Press, 1975).
14. The picture can be very much improved as a representation of the modern economy by channeling Profits, not directly to owners but to 'Wall Street,' where Banks, Boards of Directors, and Financial Institutions decide how much to retain, how much to invest, and how much to pay out in dividends. Then Capitalist Consumption will come out of Distributed Profits and Realized Capital Gains, and Savings will flow back to Wall Street in the form of bond and share purchases. This properly separates ownership and control, and shows the separation of financial and production decisions, the former dominating the latter. The model can also be modified to take account of worker savings, which, however, are empirically inconsequential.
15. Power, of course, is usually enhanced by efficiency, but the two are nevertheless quite distinct. Economic power ultimately rests on the ability to inflict a loss – the stick. A subsidiary form is the ability to bribe – the carrot. If economists paid as much attention to bribery and extortion as they do to marginal utility, we would be able to develop rough quantitative indices, by means of which one could sensibly discuss (and plan strategy to alter) the distribution of economic power in society.
16. The model can be adapted to account for worker savings.

References

Baran, P. and Sweezy, P.M. (1966) *Monopoly Capital*, (New York: Monthly Review Press).

Samuelson, P.A. (1948–present) *Economics*, 1st–13th edn. (New York: McGraw-Hill).

2 Theories of Growth and Theories of Value*

1 INTRODUCTION

A number of recent treatments of growth, otherwise widely divergent in approach, have found themselves confronted by certain common problems.[1] For example, a series of questions has arisen with respect to the concept of capital: how should it be measured? Does it consist of one 'capital good' or of many goods? Should materials and depreciation be included as part of the capital upon which returns are calculated? Should the wage bill likewise be included? Secondly, some closely related questions concerning distribution have emerged, for the concept of capital adopted in a model determines to a considerable extent both what the model will say about the relation of the return to capital to the wages of labor and how this relation will be affected by growth. Consideration of relative shares leads naturally to a third question concerned with the relation between the amounts of the various factors advanced and the output produced. If this relationship, the 'production function,' is to be of any use in the study of technical changes during growth, it must be disaggregated to exhibit the structure of production as a set of relationships between technologically specific inputs and outputs. But in this case 'capital' will be composed of different specific goods in different industries, with the result that the notion of a 'marginal physical product of capital' must be discarded as meaningless. This requires the development of some alternative theory of distribution.

These problems are commonly believed to be inseparable from the consideration of growth, that is, to result from the fact that the models are designed to deal with an expanding economy. Yet this is not actually the case, as Walras, for example, knew. Even in a stationary economy, if there is net production, all the above difficulties about capital and the formation of a general rate of return arise.[2] If inputs and outputs are broken down into their specific components, then capital in different industries will consist of different sets of goods, with the result that a marginal productivity theory cannot be employed. But if specific inputs are not shown, then the supply and demand equations for intermediate goods will not be stated explicitly.[3] Moreover, when inputs are shown specifically a compli-

* *Economic Development and Cultural Change*, 16(1) (1967) pp. 15–26, reprinted in G.C. Harcourt and N. Laing (eds,) *Capital and Growth* (Harmondsworth: Penguin).

cation is introduced into the determination of prices. For it is customary to assume that prices are set so as to return at least a normal level of profit on the capital advanced. Yet when capital consists of a multiplicity of separate items, its quantity must be expressed in value terms, which can only be done when the prices of the individual items are known.

This suggests that some at least, of these questions arise not so much from the fact that it is growth which is being examined as from the type of value theory which is assumed to underlie the growth model. Most models of growth are implicitly or explicitly set in the context of a Walrasian general equilibrium theory, which, as Wicksell long ago pointed out,[4] cannot easily accommodate a concept of capital – a fatal shortcoming in a theory which is expected to provide the foundations for growth theory. Fortunately, it is no longer necessary to rely on Walrasian theory; enough is known about the mathematical properties of linear production systems to place growth models in a Ricardian setting. The purpose of this study will be to contrast Walrasian and Ricardian general equilibrium theories, taking each in simplest form, and to suggest that providing a Ricardian value theory as the context for growth models eliminates the difficulties outlined above.

1. By a 'Walrasian theory of value' we mean a model[5] in which there are a large number of consumers, variously endowed with property, and a large number of producers of each kind of good or service. Each consumer's preferences are described by a utility function, with positive first and negative second derivatives. Each producer's technical possibilities are described by a production function, also normally assumed to have positive first and (after a point) negative second derivatives. Consumers purchase final goods, maximizing their utility subject to the constraints of their incomes: they sell the services of factors, balancing disutility against expected return. Firms purchase factors, balancing expected productivity against cost, and sell final goods, setting quantities and prices so as to maximize their profits. Goods and services thus move in a circular flow: producers sell final goods to consumers, and with the proceeds from such sales they purchase factor services from consumers, which they combine into final products. With the proceeds from the sale of factor services consumers buy final products in accordance with their utilities. Competition ensures that demands and supplies will be equated in every market and that excessive profits will be eliminated. Briefly, marginal utility and marginal cost determine equilibrium in the final goods market; marginal disutility and marginal productivity do so in the factor market.

   By contrast, in a 'Ricardian theory of value'[6] firms and consumers are not mentioned; only industries are shown – or rather, only the techniques of production appear, each industry being defined by the technique it employs. These are taken as given and are assumed to be costly to change.[7] Given a set of techniques, including the amounts of labor needed for production at the unit level, the system will be termed 'productive' if and only if more of at least one good can be produced per period than is consumed in the aggregate in production, while at least as much is produced of every other good as is consumed. With given techniques productivity can be increased, for example, by cutting down on the labor-time required per unit output. Prices are set so as to cover the technical costs of production, which are shown explicitly, and to return a uniform rate of profit in all industries.[8] Final demand will determine the allocation of labor among the industries, but operating an industry at a higher or lower level of intensity will not affect prices, given the usual assumptions. Since the technical composition of each industry's input is shown explicitly, each industry's capital will be made up of different combinations of goods; hence, to set the level of normal or uniform profits, the prices of the inputs will have to be known. But since the outputs of some industries are the inputs of others, all prices and the rate of profit will have to be determined together. Yet the rate of profit cannot be determined until the share of profits is given. Once relative shares are fixed, however, prices, the wage rate, and the profit rate can all be determined. Relative shares can be fixed, say, by collective bargaining. Given a wage rate, prices will be determined by the competitive condition that the rate of profit must be the same in every industry. To see the effect of changes in relative shares on prices, suppose the wage rate rises. At the given initial prices, labor-intensive industries will have to devote a greater than average share of their sales proceeds to paying their wage-bill, leaving a less than average return on capital, while capital-intensive industries will find themselves in just the opposite position, with a greater than average return. To equalize the rate of profit, therefore, when the wage rises the prices of labor-intensive goods must rise, while those of capital-intensive goods must fall.

The contrast between Walrasian and Ricardian theories of value could hardly be sharper. The most obvious difference, and the one most frequently discussed, concerns substitution. In a Ricardian system the coefficients of production are fixed; whereas in a Walrasian system continuous neo-Classical production functions are assumed.[9] But this difference is both overworked and ultimately less important than others. For switches in technique are possible in Ricardian systems, and Walras in fact assumed fixed technical coefficients. More fundamental differences emerge when we look at the way the flow of transactions is presented. In Walrasian theory economic transactions are pictured as a circular flow of goods and services; in each market, whether for goods or for factors, the stream of goods moving in one direction is matched by a corresponding traffic traveling the opposite way. By contrast, modern Ricardian theory puts a good deal of emphasis on the fact that the payments to capital are dispositions of a surplus and do not involve any kind of exchange. There simply is no corresponding stream moving in the opposite direction. In Walrasian theory both prices and quantities are determined by supply and demand acting in conjunction; in simple Ricardian theory prices are determined wholly by the conditions of supply: demand is relevant only to the determination of quantities. In Walrasian theory intermediate products are eliminated as far as possible; in Ricardian theory such products are given pride of place. In a Walrasian system both supplies and demands are closely tied to individual decision-making units; in a Ricardian system no such units are assumed. A Ricardian system shows the interlocking of possibilities and necessities, rather than motives, plans, and information.

2. The significance of these contrasts for growth theory must now be shown explicitly. Since much of this significance arises from the Ricardian distinction between matters of technology and matters of appropriation – between features of the system which depend on techniques of production and features which depend on division of the product – it is important to begin by examining the Ricardian concept of what is to be divided – i.e., the net product, or 'surplus.'

In a Ricardian model the net output is a physical surplus of output over and above the amounts needed for replacement, to make good depreciation, and (in some models) for the maintenance and support of the working population in the customary style.[10] We can represent net output more formally by means of a set of interdependent single-product industries, using only 'circulating' means of production:[11]

$$\begin{array}{l} C_{11}\ C_{12}\ \ldots\ C_{1k} \rightarrow C_1 \\ C_{21}\ C_{22}\ \ldots\ C_{2k} \rightarrow C_2 \\ \hline C_{k1}\ C_{k2}\ \ldots\ C_{kk} \rightarrow C_k \end{array}$$

Each process will require the products of others, and at least one good must be used directly or indirectly by all processes. A composite consumption good supports labor, assumed fixed in amount. Normally some processes will produce goods that do not return to the system as inputs; these processes can be thought of as luxury industries. The surplus will be the vector. $(C_t - \Sigma_i C_{i1}, C_2 - \Sigma_i C_{i2}, \ldots C_k - \Sigma_i C_{ik})$. The physical composition of the surplus can be varied (e.g., in response to demand) by reallocating labor (the 'fixed factor') among the industries. Such reallocation leaves prices, and value relationships generally, unaffected.

When the rate of profit and prices are added, the system generally becomes:[12]

$$\begin{aligned}
(1 + R)(C_{11}P_1 + C_{12}P_2 + \ldots + C_{1k}P_k) &= C_1P_1 \\
(1 + R)(C_{21}P_1 + C_{22}P_2 + \ldots + C_{2k}P_k) &= C_2P_2 \\
\hline
(1 + R)(C_{k1}P_1 + C_{k2}P_2 + \ldots + C_{kk}P_k) &= C_kP_k
\end{aligned}$$

Here the whole surplus goes to profit. When part of the surplus goes to labor, the wage can be shown as a uniform return paid on the basic subsistence wage, and the rate of profit will fall in proportion to rises in the wage.

One reallocation can be defined in which the ratios of the net amounts of each good produced to the total amount of that good consumed in production will all be the same. This common ratio will be the maximum rate of profit, and also, of course, the maximum possible rate of growth. So this ratio can be interpreted as the ratio of the value of the surplus to the value of the total current or circulating input.[13]

A surplus can be put to many uses. It can be used for the public benefit in the form of common goods, for privately consumed luxuries, to fight wars, or to support a lavish government. Or it can be reinvested productively, leading to growth. But in a private enterprise system, before one can say anything about the *allocation* of the surplus among these competing ends (or even about the influence of consumer preferences upon its composition), one must consider the logically prior question of its *distribution*. For in an economic system based on private property, everything produced belongs to someone, but the activity of production is carried out cooperatively by a number of different parties who, therefore, have competing claims. More specifically, the (value of the) net product must be divided among workers, managers, owners of capital, and owners of land, though it is convenient for many purposes to lump the first two and last two together and treat the product as being divided between wages and profits. This division is accomplished through the competitive market at the same time that the exchanges necessary for reproduction take place. The market mechanism, therefore, is obliged to do two things at once. It must allocate goods to make reproduction possible, and it must distribute the full value of product as wages and profits, which means, among the other things, deciding how much shall go to each.

In general, this decision cannot be analyzed in a static framework, for it both depends upon and affects growth. For example, when population growth equals or exceeds the rate of growth of capital, competition among laborers may force the wage down toward the cost-of-living level, raising profits toward their maximum. When population growth is less than the rate of growth of capital, competition between employers will bid wages up, lowering profits. Such changes in distribution can be expected to affect savings, since workers and profit-takers will normally have different saving propensities. And changes in the rate of profit can be expected to affect decisions to invest.

This suggests a view of competitive price determination somewhat different from that which has become customary, for it means putting the conflict between labor and capital in the foreground, making relative prices depend on the outcome of this conflict.

3. In the system described above, the outputs of some industries served as the inputs of others. This makes it possible to trace chains of direct and indirect mutual dependence, which presents a further contrast with neo-Classical thinking. For economic thought in the Walrasian tradition emphasizes the interdependence of markets, while neglecting the more fundamental technological interdependence of production. At first glance this may seem strange, since surely the analysis of one leads to the study of the other. But in a strictly neo-Classical world this connection cannot be made so easily, for the factors influencing supply and those determining demand are assumed to be separate. In the neo-Classical view of the economy, markets are connected not because the various products are consumed in the production of one another, but because, for example, an increase in the amount of any good purchased draws demand away from other markets; and similarly, an increase in the amount of any good produced draws factors away from the production of other goods. Production is regarded as a sort of one-way street, in which ultimate 'factors' are converted into 'final products' and all intermediate steps are ignored, as attention is concentrated, on the one hand, upon the conditions influencing the sale of final products and, on the other, upon the payments to the 'factors.' In a system of this kind production might be technologically interdependent,[14] but it is not necessary that it be so, for the scarcity of factors is a sufficient condition for the interdependence of markets.

It makes a good deal of difference in a growth model whether the interdependence emphasized is that of markets or of production. For if it is the former, the arguments of the production function will be factors which are specific not to technology but to the payment of income. Further, both supplies and demands will be tied to the decision-making units, the firm and the household. But the technological knowledge and the social conventions underlying production and consumption respectively are part of the common environment of all firms and households, and while for some purposes it may be important to emphasize the individual character of decisions to produce and consume, in the long term it may well be that this is less important than the influence of the common background. The introduction of irrelevant particulars concerning decision-making is made possible only by sacrificing the consideration of relevant technological facts.

4. In Classical (as in Marxian) economics, the focus of attention is the

cf. K. Arrow and F. Hahn, *General Competitive Analysis* (San Francisco: Holden-Day, 1980).

6. The best example of a modern Ricardian model is P. Sraffa, *Production of Commodities by Means of Commodities* (Cambridge, 1960). Also cf. L. Pasinetti, *Lectures* in *The Theory of Production* (New York: Columbia, 1975).
7. Alternatively, it could be assumed that the time required to change to a new technique is greater than one period of production.
8. The modern Ricardian approach outlined here, while in important ways akin to a Leontief system, nevertheless must be sharply distinguished from the latter. A Leontief system represents production in the same way and is similarly concerned with technological interdependence and the role of intermediate goods. But a Ricardian system is principally concerned with the relation between prices, wages, and profits under competitive conditions. Leontief systems never deal with a uniform rate of profit on capital nor with the effects of changes in distribution upon prices. Further, insofar as Leontief systems take account of fixed capital, they treat it as a necessary element in production and neglect its effects upon profits and prices. Cf. W. Leontief, *Structure of American Economy* (New York, 1952).
9. It is worth remarking that part of the process of development has been the reduction in the cost and difficulty of switching techniques; the difficulties in the way of this accomplishment (as well as the complexities involved in practice in switching techniques) should not simply be assumed away.
10. Cf. Ricardo, *Principles of Political Economy and Taxation*, Ch. 1 [P. Sraffa (ed.), *Works and Correspondence of David Ricardo*, Vol. I] (Cambridge, 1951). Also P.A. Samuelson, 'Wages and Interest: A Modern Dissection of Marxian Economic Models,' *American Economic Review*, 47 (December 1957).
11. There are several ways of relaxing this assumption. If goods used in different industries are written off in the same number of periods, the columns showing the depreciation each period – which figures in circulating capital – can be multiplied by the write-off time. Alternatively, partly depreciated durable equipment can be treated as a joint product, produced along with the regular output.
12. When there is no surplus, call the matrix of inputs C and the matrix of outputs P. Then for the price equation we have $Cp = Pp$ or $(C - P)p = 0$, a unique and positive solution of which is guaranteed by the fact that $C - P = 0$, given certain other restrictions on the matrices. For a full discussion, cf. David Gale. *Theory of Linear Economic Models* (New York, 1960) Ch. 8.
13. For a proof that a maximum rate of profit always exists, is unique, and is associated with a unique set of positive prices, cf. Sraffa, *Production of Commodities*, Chs IV and V. Also cf. F. Seton, 'The Transformation Problem,' *Review of Economic Studies* (June 1957), and Pasinetti, *op. cit*, 1975.
14. Walras, however, maintained that references to intermediate goods could be eliminated by 'reducing' them to equivalent expressions containing only primary factors. Cf. Walras, *Elements*. Lesson 20.
15. It is sometimes thought that a measure of the quantity of capital currently being invested can be got by considering the amount of consumption sacrificed. But this simply transfers the difficulties of measurement to consumption. An economy with a single consumption good is no more plausible than an economy with a single capital good. Also, the attempt to estimate the rate of return on investment by the ratio of later consumption to sacrificed current consumption runs into two difficulties. First, the growth rate need not equal the profit rate

(i.e., the productivity of capital is a different matter from its profitability), and second, the concern is for the return on capital in general, and not just on investment. (Cf. Ch. 8).

16. The owners of capital (the recipients of property income) are frequently said to sell the capital's 'service' to a firm, the factor price of the capital being the interest or dividend they receive in return. But this is just a play on words, for the 'owners of capital' are also, *ipso facto*, the owners of the firm. They are therefore 'selling' this service to themselves. The 'firm' only appears to be different from the owners of its capital because of their limited liability; but important as this is, in this context it means merely that they can lose no more on a given project than they choose to put into it. Yet the project is still theirs.

3 Value and Capital in Marxian Economics*

Neo-Classical theory roots value in the act of exchange, which is undertaken by the parties in order to gain. The theory shows that under the postulated conditions all parties will gain from exchange in terms of their subjective preferences. This then generalizes into the theory of optimal allocation of scarce rewards by means of the price mechanism, which makes it possible to incorporate production into the theory as a special case of indirect exchange. Value arises from the interactions of isolated, rootless 'individuals' acting in terms of their abstract 'preferences,' expressed as a consistent ranking of the bundles of commodities assumed to be 'available' on the one hand and 'scarce' on the other. Where these individuals come from, how they are supported, what their preferences are based on, how and by whom the commodities have been produced, and by whose authority the 'initial endowments' were conferred – all are assumed to be irrelevant to the foundation of value-in-exchange. Whatever the answers to such questions, value arises because the parties to exchange stand to gain in terms of their preferences, so long as these are consistent and 'convex,' and goods are scarce. Value arises from convex preferences coupled with scarcity.

One feature of this approach is worth mentioning. Value, which appears to be a relationship between commodities – the value of this chair in apples or in gold or paper money – is shown to be a relationship between, on the one hand, economic agents (their preferences), and between these agents and nature (scarcity) on the other. At this very general level, the neo-Classical approach meets Marx's definition of the task of the theory of value, explaining how 'exchange of commodities [which] is a definite social relation between men . . . has assumed in their eyes the fantastic form of a relation between things.' Beneath this appearance lie the real relationships which hold between people. On this, neo-Classicals and Marxists can agree. But then the paths diverge. Neo-Classicals ground value in the act of exchange, which in turn is governed by preference and scarcity. For Marx, value arises from the relationships governing the process of production and reproduction – the process which maintains the social order. The key to the working of that process lies in the relation of wages to labor, which is therefore the foundation upon which the theory of value must be built.

* *Public Interest*, Fifteenth Anniversary Issue: 'The Crisis in Economic Theory' (1980). Reprinted in D. Bell, and L. Kristel (eds) *The Crisis in Economic Theory* (New York: Basic Books, 1982).

1 MAINSTREAM OR MUD PUDDLE?

Swimmers in the mainstream of economics have noted how cloudy the waters have become, even at the source. The neo-Classical theory of value is no fountain of inspiration, bubbling and sparkling with new ideas. To an increasing number of economists it is a source of intellectual pollution. It doesn't explain demand; its concept of production is naive. Thus it doesn't help with the theory of prices. It is difficult, arcane, and finally rests on assumptions that are not only 'unrealistic,' but quite simply false. Four sets of complaints are commonly articulated.

First, it bases value on exchange, treating production (in rather an afterthought) as a special kind of exchange. But reproduction commodities used to produce commodities used to produce commodities (counting support of labor as an input) – makes exchange a moment in the circuit of production and reproduction. Such an input–output account is arguably essential to any analysis of a social system's continued ability to support itself or expand. It therefore seems more fundamental than any account which takes the agents and the supplies of goods to be traded as *given*. But in that case the mainstream theory has its starting point wrong.

Secondly, the agents involved in exchange are typically described with extreme abstraction, although the environment in which they operate is one in which quite definite and historically-specific rules of property apply. Surely it would be more appropriate to develop the theory based not on abstract agents but on the institutional forms, abstracting only from inessential details. This, however, would require a close study of the history and sociology of labor, of the different social classes of households, of the business corporation, and so on, to determine at different periods what were and were not inessential details. It would mean trading generality for content. (Cf. Part III)

Thirdly, the central notion of preference itself is so abstract as to be virtually inexplicable. Interpersonal comparisons of 'utility' generally are forbidden; preference scales are usually considered 'ordinal,' although in certain game theory situations cardinal utility is held to be permissible. But what are these preferences based on? This we are told is a question the economist cannot ask. The grounds of choice are a matter of the agents' ultimate decisions, and the descriptive sciences can do no more than record what their subjects choose. This is a position, central to positivism, which modern moral philosophy has largely thrown over, and economics would do well to follow suit. The observing economist can – and must – question the choices he observes being made, not in terms of his own values and social philosophy, but in terms of the agents'. An agent has not revealed a preference if he has made a mistake, or miscalculated, or forgotten. The point of (theoretically) constructing preference scales from 'market data' is to show that the law of demand (that the sign of the substitution effect is negative) can be derived. But this is a 'lawlike proposition;' it supports counter-factual conditionals – statements, that is, of the form 'what would happen if . . .' So the *actual* behavior must reveal the agents' *typical* disposition or commitment to behave in a certain way. And how can we tell whether the behavior we are observing is typical? (Cf. Hollis and Nell, 1975.)

The course we normally take in everyday life is to discover whether the agent has *good reason* to behave that way typically. If so, then we can count the behavior as 'projectible;' in similar circumstances, he will normally choose such a course of action; it will be a means to an end, or will fulfill his obligations, or is expected and socially approved behavior. In the case of the theory of the firm, this can be done. Selling for a certain price, or buying a quantity of input at a certain price, will contribute to maximizing profit (or growth, or sales, or the value of invested capital – although there is little agreement about which of these is the appropriate target and when). But in the case of consumers, or in the pure theory of exchange, there is nothing to go on. There are no reasons for preferences; they are simply postulated to be there. More of any good is always better, but increasing abundance provides diminishing improvement. No other explanation is given – and within the framework none is possible – of why a consumer prefers one bundle of commodities to another, or is indifferent to the choice. But this is obviously wildly at variance with everyday life and with the informal logic of the process of making comparisons and choices. When we choose a bundle of goods we can always explain why, and we frequently have to, to our wives, children, employers, and tax collectors. More is not always better, not even somewhat better. Goods are chosen because they have characteristics that serve needs or functions. These needs, in turn, depend on what kind of household it is; that is to say, on status, family, and employment. The characteristics of a commodity and the fact that these will serve or help serve certain clearly defined functions provide the reasons for choosing the good. Choices must be made subject to a budget, and this sets up a very typical economic problem. But the details of this problem are not abstract at all. They depend on what kind of household it is, the social as well as economic constraints it faces, the ordering of priorities among the needs that have to be met, and so on. Since the kind of household depends, in part at least, on the job of the breadwinner, household demand will be influenced by the structure of production. Causality runs from the supply side to the demand side, just the reverse of 'consumer sovereignty.' (Cf. Ch. 17, section 2)

Finally, there is the notion of scarcity itself. Scarcity in neo-Classical theory is, as is choice, essentially *timeless*. Moreover, it is a relationship between output or 'endowments' and wants, which is assumed to be insatiable. But an economy exists through time only by continually replacing the material basis for production. What is left over after such replacement – the *net* output – is what is available for purposes other than the support of continued existence. And an obviously central question is, who will control that surplus and decide how it is to be used? Scarcity for some way be the result of plenty for others. Moreover, over time the relationships may change, or *be* changed, by conscious political action.

The traditional alternative to the mainstream theory of value is the Labor Theory of Value (LTV). Both can be said to agree that the problem is to show how what appear to be relations among things are really social relations among persons. But neo-Classical theory treats these as timeless relations between the abstract preferences of socially unspecific individuals, in conjunction with given endowments and postulated scarcity, whereas the Marxian tradition grounds value in the class positions of agents in a specifically capitalist system engaged in a continual process of reproducing itself over time.

But, notoriously, the Marxian theory of value is a mare's nest of tangled issues and unresolved problems. Even among serious scholars there are disputes over exactly what is being claimed, and whether certain propositions are or are not true; that is, provable within the accepted framework of the theory. One could agree, as argued above, that the Marxian approach is superior, yet still shy away from the intense and sometimes rancorous dispute. How can concepts that will reveal the interconnections of the system we live under come out of such often graceless polemics? Yet the fierceness of the debates stands in reasonable ratio to the magnitude of the issues involved. *For what is at stake is our understanding of the central concepts of the system: value and capital.*

2 THE GENERAL LABOR THEORY OF VALUE

Broadly speaking, all recent work on the LTV written in the Marxian tradition agrees that the starting point must be a conception of the economic system as capitalist; that is, as characterized by ownership of capital, institutionalized in business firms, employing workers who live on their wages, and engaging in production which uses up commodities in producing them. But from the common starting point very different roads are taken. One group led by Ian Steedman strenuously rejects all consideration of labor values, arguing that the representation of the system in terms of physical inputs used up or consumed and produced is completely adequate for all serious analysis, and that further consideration of 'labour value' is a metaphysical exercise and a waste of time. Worse, the labor theory stinks of dogmatism and is haunted by the ghost of Stalin. A second group argues that the so-called 'detour through labor values' is necessary or useful in revealing the underlying relations of exploitation. A large set of authors, however, reject much of this discussion as 'economistic,' and regard the LTV as a set of philosophical propositions about the nature of capitalist commodity exchange with no particular implications for the specific values of variables in economic models, though defining the meaning of such variables. A related group also holds that the LTV is basically philosophical, but argues that its world-historical meaning implies that at bottom relative prices are 'governed by values' in some ill-defined sense. Some of these writings are distinctly fundamentalist; Marx is the Word, and the Word, like butter, is there to be spread, not analyzed. 'Obscurantist' is Steedman's Word, and it fits.

First, what exactly does the Labor Theory of Value say? This, of course, is part of what the argument is about. But certain points can be made. At a general level it says that the fact that commodities 'have value' is to be explained by the fact and only by the fact that they are products of wage labor, which is to say exploited labor. To 'have value' is to be exchangeable in a regular way for a universal equivalent. For a universal equivalent to exist, exchange ratios between any two commodities must be consistent with the exchange ratios of either with any third. The ultimate insight of the LTV in its most general form is that value as a society-wide phenomenon, expressed in universal equivalence with money ('everything has its price'), can only arise in social circumstances of class conflict. If commodities exist, if things have exchange-value, then there must be exploited labor, and so at least potential class conflict. No 'harmony' is possible through the market, since value and commodity exchange, and so class conflict, are preconditions for markets.

Let's call this general doctrine the GLTV and take a closer look at the claim that value is the reflection of class conflict in the mirror of economics. All activities which can be privately organized are commodities, and so have value – and the key condition for this arrangement is that labor be exploited. This is a large claim, and it is not the way everyone has read Marx. For instance, it has become commonplace to remark, and to lament, that Marx simply took over Ricardo's position on the LTV, in the process, of course, both developing it and placing it in a social and historical perspective. But on this view, Marx's theory is still substantially that of Ricardo; embodied labor is what explains exchange-value and so prices, whereas the level of wages in relation to total output is what explains profits. As Ricardo recognized, however, these two propositions cannot coexist under free competitive conditions, except in the special case, assumed by Marx in *Capital*, Volume I, of all industries or departments having equal organic compositions of capital. For capital will flow to where rates of return are highest, thus establishing a uniform rate of profits, and the resulting prices will not reflect embodied labor.

But in fact the first nine chapters of *Capital*, Volume I are devoted to a completely different set of issues in which prices and the rate of profits figure neither as the targets of the inquiry, nor among the explanatory concepts. When Marx finally does set about to determine a quantitative concept, it is not the rate of profit but the rate of surplus-value (rate of exploitation), and this comes only in Chapter IX. Are the first eight chapters just a prelude, presenting the social and historical background? *That certainly is not what Marx thought!*

Capital begins with a discussion of commodities and money, moves on to the transformation of money into capital, and then shows that the production of surplus-value in the labor process is the foundation of the earning power of capital. The entire discussion, although illuminated by examples drawn from history, moves on the plane of theory. It is *not* a presentation of socio-historical background; it is the central core of Marx's theory, leading up to the determination of the rate of surplus-value.

Commodities, the form in which the wealth of capitalist societies presents itself, have two aspects, use-value and exchange-value. These in turn correspond to two aspects of the labor which produces them: concrete, specific labor which produces use-value, and abstract labor which generates exchange-value. Concrete labor is easy to understand, but exactly what abstract labor is and how it produces value is not yet explained, partly no doubt because the Ricardian LTV was the most common currency of political economy at the time he wrote and could be taken for granted. Instead, Marx enters on a long and detailed examination of the forms of exchange-value, culminating in the General Form of Value which 'results from the joint action of the whole world of commodities. . . . A commodity can acquire a general expression of its value only by all other commodities, simultaneously with it, expressing their values in the same equivalent . . .' The general form of value requires some commodity to act as universal equivalent. But insofar as a commodity does so, it cannot be used as a means of production or of subsistence or of luxury consumption. It no longer is the use-value it once was; it is money. 'The difficulty lies, not in comprehending that money is a commodity, but in discovering how, why and by what means a commodity becomes money.'

The commodity which becomes money already has value. 'When it steps into circulation as money, its value is already given. . . . This value is determined by the labor-time required for its production . . .' Exchange requires not only a universal equivalent, but a fit and proper one. 'The truth of the proposition that, "although gold and silver are not by nature money, money is by nature gold and silver," is shown by the fitness of the physical properties of these metals for the functions of money.' For there to be general commodity production, there must be fully developed exchange, and for Marx that *requires* that exchange-values be expressed (and compared) in universal equivalent form, and carried out by means of circulating money.

But if money is the universal medium by which commodities are exchanged, then capital will have to circulate in money form. The capitalist advances money for commodities, then sells commodities for money.

But this makes no real sense. Selling commodities for money and then buying commodities again is practical enough. The exchange-value of the two sets of commodities may be the same; but the use-value of the second set to the owner will be higher.[1] By contrast, buying commodities for a sum of money and selling them again for that same sum is a complete waste of time. (Marx is assuming all commodities sell for their cost of production, and that all exchanges are fair and equal; no agents in the market have any special privileges.) To assume that on resale commodities can fetch more than they cost, *in general*, is contradictory. 'Suppose, then, that by some inexplicable privilege' a seller is able to sell at some percentage above what he previously paid. He seems to pocket a gain. Then he goes to buy, and finds all other sellers now offering only at the higher price. Or suppose one capitalist is clever enough to take advantage of another; what the one gains the other loses. The total amount of value in circulation is unaltered. 'If equivalents are exchanged, no surplus-value results, and if non-equivalents are exchanged, still no surplus-value. Circulation, or the exchange of commodities, begets no value.'

At this point Marx states exactly what he is up to: 'The conversion of money into capital has to be explained on the basis of the laws that regulate the exchange of commodities, in such a way that the starting-point is the exchange of equivalents. Our friend, Moneybags, who as yet is only an embryo capitalist, must buy his commodities at their value, must sell them at their value, and yet at the end of the process must withdraw more value from circulation than he threw into it at starting. His development into a full-grown capitalist must take place, both within the sphere of circulation and without it. These are the conditions of the problem. *Hic Rhodus, hic salta!*'[2]

We began from universal commodity production; all activities are commodities, so human work will be also. And the solution lies in the buying and selling of labor power. The buyer pays its cost of production, the (socially determined) subsistence wage, but obtains its use-value, namely the worker's capacity to work for a period of time. What the worker does in this time depends on what the buying of labor power can get out of him. Workers work; work means changing the form of materials – cutting, shaping, processing, and so on. The faster, harder, or longer a worker works for subsistence pay, the more material input he converts to output.

Marx analyzes the labor process with great care, and his chapter on 'The Working Day' has never been surpassed for controlled outrage in exposing injustice. Material input, wear and tear of machinery, and so on, summed up, form the 'constant' capital that must be advanced. Such capital is simply converted into output, adding its own value, but no more. The wage bill, however, is 'variable' capital; it is spent on the purchase of labor power which, if coerced or cajoled suitably, can produce in a day more than the value needed to pay its subsistence. The ratio between the time worked 'for the capitalist' and the time worked 'for himself' (producing what it would take to buy his subsistence) is the rate of exploitation.[3] Thus by buying materials, equipment, and labor-power at cost or true value, and selling goods produced by labor for cost or true value, a capitalist is still able to turn a profit.

In short, the first nine chapters of *Capital* are devoted to relating commodities, values, and free exchange to capital and the exploitation of labor. And the latter explains the earning power of capital, which in turn explains the driving force of its circulation – the motivation which runs the whole system.

3 THE SPECIAL LABOR THEORY OF VALUE

A more specific level of theory holds that the value of a unit amount of a commodity is the sum of the abstract, socially necessary labor directly and indirectly embodied in it. Let us call this SLTV. This is not a simple claim and is widely misunderstood. For one thing, the terms are complex. 'Abstract labor' means labor conceived simply in terms of its status as wage-labor, and measured in time, regardless of the specifics of job or skill.[4] 'Socially necessary labor time' means the time needed according to the best methods known and in use at the historical moment in question. Labor indirectly required, of course, is the labor required by the non-worker inputs. So the formula for value gives the amount of time – put in by those with the status of wage earners – that *would be required*, directly and indirectly, to produce the commodity. What results is a set of simultaneous linear equations, easily handled by matrix methods. Value in exchange, then, is the ratio of the labor value of any good with any other good taken as a standard.

Now a very important implication of this definition of value is that the exchange ratios implied are such that the excess of the value of every department's output, over the value required to replace its means of production and subsistence, will stand in the same ratio to the cost of supporting direct labor. That is, the ratio of 'value of output minus value of means of production and subsistence' to 'direct labor time employed' is the same in every department or industry. This has important implications.

First, since the surplus is measured in labor time, we have a pure ratio expressing the productivity of the direct labor employed. If the surplus is appropriated by the owners of the means of production, then the ratio can be interpreted as showing the time workers worked to produce what they needed to replace their own means of subsistence in relation to the time they worked to produce surplus-value for their employer – the rate of exploitation. Moreover, the existence of the mathematical dual to the set of equations implies that means of production and labor could be reallocated among the departments so that the physical net output consisted only of means of subsistence.[5] Thus the rate of exploitation can be expressed as a ratio of quantities of surplus consumer goods to required consumer goods.[6] If these consumer goods were used to support servants, entertainers, police, and the like, this would then be interpreted as the ratio of unproductive or surplus labor to necessary or productive labor. Note also that since the rate is expressed in labor-time, its reciprocal is the proportional 'slowdown' or work-to-rule which, if carried out in every department, would totally eliminate the surplus. That is, a proportional slowdown in every department, equal to the reciprocal of the rate of surplus-value, would result in an output the value of which would just cover replacement of means of production and subsistence.

This leads directly to a fundamental point. For Marx, in *Capital*, the labor process is one in which workers *work*, that is, convert material inputs into output by means of their labor power. So there are two different kinds of 'technical coefficients,' those which tell us the material inputs required per unit output (regardless of how long production takes), and those which tell us the labor *time* needed for unit production (regardless of the amount of input required). Of course, there may be interactions, but the first depends on engineering, while the second depends on incentives and morale, the willingness of workers to work, or the ability of capital to coerce them. Marx runs the first kind of coefficients under the heading 'constant capital,' and the second under 'variable capital.' It is variable capital, then, which produces surplus-value; labor works faster or harder, so converting more input into output. A general slowdown can eliminate surplus-value (and, in the dual, the surplus product). Only as much would be produced in a given length of time as is needed, directly and indirectly, to replace the means of subsistence needed to support labor for that time. A faster rate of production, more intensive work or longer hours per day, applied across the board, would increase surplus-value.[7]

But suppose workers performed no work. Suppose machines, carefully programmed robots, carried out actual production, drawing energy from sunlight, the tides, geothermal sources, etc. Computers might devise most of the programs. The human being would then relate to the production process 'more as watchman and regulator,' stepping 'to the side . . . instead of being its chief actor' (*Grundrisse*, p. 705). Of course, there will be paperwork concerned with the bureaucracy, or with the struggle for markets and against taxes.[8] But no matter how fast or slow, well or badly, such work is done, within wide limits the output produced would be unaffected. How, in such a situation, could we speak of 'variable capital' or define a rate of exploitation?

Marx himself seems to conclude that the SLTV must be set aside: 'As soon as labor in the direct form has ceased to be the great well-spring of wealth labor time ceases and must cease to be its measure, and exchange-value [must cease to be the measure] of use-value. The *surplus labor of the mass* has ceased to be the condition for the development of general wealth, just as the *nonlabor of the few*, for the development of the general powers of the human head.' If labor's direct work is not the source of the surplus, labor time is not the measure of value.

But does this means throwing over the GLTV as well? Quite the contrary. Whereas manual labor can only be appropriated once, while it is being expended, some kinds of mental labor can be appropriated, as it were, once and for all. For the result of such mental labor is 'the business of invention,' 'when . . . all the sciences have been pressed into the service of capital.' This dramatically heightens the contradiction between the essentially social nature of production and the private mode of organizing it and appropriating its fruits. The processes of scientific discovery and engineering development depend on the accumulated knowledge of the human race. But they are tied down to the making of profit for the benefit of particular capitalists. What is exploited here is not the power to perform material work, but humanity's potential to think creatively. The difference, and it is a crucial one, is that the return to capital is not immediate, but is spread out over an indefinite and unpredictably long period of time. But the scientist is paid his wages, and the use-value of his product – of his ideas – is appropriated by capital.

4 SCRAPPING THE SLTV

It is time for a close and more critical look at the Special Labor Theory of Value. If, in fact, commodities exchanged at ratios of labor-values, employers would then obtain surplus-value in relation to the labor they employed, not in relation to the total value of the means of production advanced. That total value is the value of their capital, and under capitalist production capital will be moved about until all capital tends to earn the same return on its value. The implication of this is that exchange-ratios must be such that the 'exchange-value of output' minus 'exchange-value of means of production and subsistence' stands in the same ratio for every department to the 'exchange-value of means of production and subsistence,' not to the 'direct labor time employed.' So in capitalism relative prices will not be equal to ratios of labor-values, except in the case where the ratio of the value of means of production to the value of subsistence is the same in all departments.

But Marx defines the rate of profit as $S/(C + V)$, where 'S' is surplus-value, 'C' is constant capital, and 'V' variable capital, all expressed in labor-values. So if prices are governed by the rate of profit, his definition of the rate of profit will not, except by a fluke, be correct. Nor, in fact, will his definition of the overall organic composition of capital. What should we conclude?

The most controversial position (Steedman, 1977; Hodgson, 1976) may be the easiest to start with. If exchange-values are governed by the rate of profit, and will therefore not usually equal labor-values, why bother with the Labor Theory of Value at all? It was an interesting insight, and of importance in the history of the subject, but as a proposition about relative prices, it is wrong. So forget it. Moreover, the Sraffa system is perfectly capable of dealing with cases like the robot economy above, where even Marx acknowledges that labor-values are inapplicable. This does not necessarily mean throwing over the general insight – the GLTV.[9] (Still less does it offer any consolation to partisans of supply and demand or choice theory.) All it means is scrapping the specific labor-value formulae. But it has sometimes been taken to mean that, given the quantities of inputs and outputs, exchange-values can be calculated on various assumptions about the disposition of the surplus, quite regardless of class positions or class conflict. Some have argued that the same equations could be used to describe systems in which supposedly there was 'no class conflict,' leading critics to charge that 'neo-Ricardians' think of socialism simply as 'capitalism without capitalists.'

On the face of it, such a use of the equations is inconsistent with the GLTV, which holds that the existence of commodity exchange, a precondition for generalized value-in-exchange, implies that there is exploited labor. If it is argued that the prices are calculated simply for 'accounting purposes,' the question becomes, why are the accounts kept? What costs are being minimized, at whose expense and for whose benefit? If labor is a cost, what does cost minimization imply for workers? These 'accounting calculations' are not neutral in their implications. Not to see this is to miss – or reject – the point of the GLTV.

Abandoning the SLTV while retaining the GLTV, however, leads to some striking positions, which may prove of considerable importance to the future development of Marxism. First, labor-values have nothing and the rate of profit has everything to do with prices. So traditional supply and demand are out the window, and we have a new general equilibrium theory in which prices are a function of the rate of profit, and so of distribution. Secondly, distribution in its turn reflects the balance of class forces; distribution is not determined by purely economic relationships, contrary to neo-Classical thinking. The model shows precisely how and when class struggle affects economic variables, so it helps to locate 'economic laws' in the wider field of historical materialism generally. Thirdly, the approach is capable of great mathematical sophistication – in effect, Sraffa and von Neumann are conjoined to Marx, producing a Marxian dynamic general equilibrium–disequilibrium approach (Morishima, 1974; Abraham-Frois and Berrebi, 1976). Many normal topics of mainstream concern can be dealt with (e.g., the effects of taxes, subsidies, welfare) while many traditional Marxian subjects, such as the reserve army, mechanization, and the falling rate of profit, can be dealt with in a far more elaborate and sophisticated way.

Apparently, then, there are great advantages to developing Marxian economics by dropping the SLTV while retaining the GLTV. Yet this trend has met strong resistance. One line of argument holds, in effect, that the distinction between the GLTV and SLTV is artificial. They are inseparable: They stand or fall together. Marxism is an organic unity, the parts of which are mutually supportive and cannot be questioned. Like an oyster, but less digestible, it must be swallowed whole.

A better argument, but still defective (Amin, 1978), is that the use of physical quantities permits no comparison of changes in the economic base. When new products or processes are introduced the physical system changes, and the new exchange-values cannot, in general, be compared with the old. But labor-values can be compared. Hence it is argued the SLTV is superior to an approach based on physical quantities and exchange ratios. However, both rates of profit and rates of exploitation, being pure ratios, can be compared. This is the point of the 'switching' arguments. And under capitalism it will be the rate of profit that will govern the movement of capital. All that is necessary is to calculate which processes or products, if introduced, will generate the highest rate of profit. These will be the ones eventually adopted unless, of course, there are institutional or political barriers. There is no need to detour through labor-values.

The fundamentalist arguments are wrong, though the last point can be restated in a more acceptable form, as we shall see. So long as the GLTV is taken as the basis for the interpretation of the variables of the model, the case for dropping the SLTV as (part of) the account of exchange-values looks sound enough, so far. But the matter cannot be left there. There is the not altogether irrelevant question of what is, in fact, the case.

It has been customary for decades among economists of all stripes to dismiss the SLTV as 'unrealistic.' Yet this dismissal has been based on theoretical grounds, not on empirical investigation. The argument has already been presented. Capital-to-labor ratios differ in different industries, and capitalism tends to establish a uniform rate of profit. Therefore prices cannot equal ratios of embodied labor. Good, but what do the *facts* say?

Unfortunately, the facts are a little shy of speaking right up, but with a bit of coaxing they can be heard to murmur something like, 'perhaps Ricardo was right after all.' To study the problem one has to make use of input–output tables, and the data collected there are not presented in 'physical' terms. So the coefficients have to be adjusted, and this (along with many other things) may introduce bias. Nevertheless, allowing for such problems, labor-values can be calculated from input–output data, and so can the theoretically correct (uniform rate of profit) prices. Then the labor-values and the 'correct' prices of production can be compared to the 'actual' prices (which of course are highly aggregated). Preliminary calculations, surprisingly enough, suggest that labor-values are much closer to actual prices than the theoretically superior prices of production (Shaikh, 1982). Moreover, it appears, and is well known from other studies, that changes in labor productivity account for by far the greatest part of price changes. If this is so, then it would seem that labor-values and changes in labor-values provide a simple and reasonably accurate working hypothesis for predicting both the prices ruling at a given time, and changes in prices over time. This ought to be of interest to practical economists. Indeed, it is something of a comment on the ideological state of mind in the profession that this suggestion provoked such vicious attacks that the effects can only be described as chilling; some of those working on the idea came to feel they might be endangering their careers. The idea that the SLTV might be a reasonable empirical approximation, though theoretically inadequate – for Marxist reasons – was too much. Economists don't appreciate irony.

5 THE SLTV REINTERPRETED: THE FUNDAMENTAL THEOREM

Nevertheless, this is a sideshow. So far the partisans of Marx after Sraffa seem to have a good case theoretically. The second group of writings, however, whittles this down. Understandably, in view of ambiguities in the tradition, Steedman, et al., have misconceived the role of the SLTV by treating it, in Ricardian fashion, as a theory of price. But it is not; like the GLTV it is a theory of the origin (or grounds) of the surplus – that is, of the basis of profits and other forms of net income (and also, in the dual, of net output).[10] GLTV shows that commodities having value is the consequence of the exploitation of labor, where labor is itself a commodity. SLTV, then, determines the rate of exploitation and the associated commodity values. What is needed to complete this is the demonstration that to any given rate of exploitation there corresponds a definite and unique positive rate of profit. And that is given by the solution to the transformation problem.

In other words, the relation between labor-values and prices of production is a red herring. The correct transformation is not of values into prices, it is the proof that to every rate of exploitation there corresponds a unique rate of profit – that is, exploitation and the rate of profit are functionally connected. This Morishima terms the Fundamental Theorem of Marxian economics.

But Steedman still has a point. Values and the rate of exploitation are determined *along with* prices and the rate of profit, by the same fundamental data. So why are they any more or any less important? They are simply the solutions to the same system of equations when the rate of profit is zero, and the entire surplus is appropriated in proportion to direct labor. However, this argument misses the point that when labor works, the speed, intensity, and the like, of that work is what determines the rate of exploitation.

So there is no 'detour' through labor-values. The issue is not to explain prices; it is to explain *profits*. The point of the SLTV is to determine the rate of exploitation, to uncover the underlying grounds for the existence of profits, and to demonstrate a formal connection between these grounds and the rate of profit.

6 CHANGES OF TECHNIQUE

Now we come to an apparently devastating objection, which is, perhaps, the centerpiece of Steedman's position. Suppose there are several 'techniques' of production for some or all of the commodities. The choice of technique which maximizes the rate of exploitation (notoriously) need not be the same as that which maximizes the rate of profits. So the rate of exploitation is not only irrelevant; it would also be misleading. Or, put another way, a given rate of exploitation implies different profit rates in different techniques. But the techniques will be adopted on the grounds that they maximize the rate of profit. So we have to know the rate of profit to know the technique in order to calculate the corresponding rate of exploitation. The Fundamental Theorem has it just the wrong way around. Again the rate of exploitation *et hic omnia genus* seem to have led us to red but indigestible herrings.

This conclusion is strongly bolstered by two further arguments which are not easy to explain intuitively. One concerns joint production. The other, fixed capital, in the Sraffa–von Neumann tradition is a *special* case of joint production. [Each year the industry both ('jointly') produces its product(s) and depreciates its machinery.] In both cases some labor-values can turn out to be negative, even though prices and the rate of profit are positive. So a paradox can be constructed: positive profits and negative surplus value. 'Marxists should therefore concentrate on developing the materialist account of why production conditions and real wages are what they are, leaving the discussion of "value magnitudes" to those concerned only with the development of a new Gnosticism.'

Admirers of the caves of Nag Hammadi may wish to rephrase this, but the message is clear and strong. The mechanics of these arguments are mathematically formidable. But the framework in which they move has drawn fire. Critics, especially Morishima, have charged that the joint-production arguments depended on an arbitrary and unjustified assumption that the number of products just equalled the number of processes. Instead, all the possible processes should be considered, and the choice of the best made in accordance with cost-minimization. In other words, the 'choice of technique' problematic should be extended to cover joint production. Steedman accepts this, and agrees with Morishima's revised analysis of the joint-production case. So there is no need to go over the paradoxes of "negative value"; we can concentrate on choice of technique, taking single-product industries as the illustrative case.

There are serious problems here. First, (unlike the 'method of physical quantities' generally) the choice of techniques problematic, borrowed from neo-Classical production-function theory, is genuinely asocial and ahistorical, as Joan Robinson never tired of stressing. Secondly, the choice of techniques argument moves on a different level of abstraction than the claim that the rate of exploitation explains the rate of profit. And, thirdly, the argument, once it is set in historical time, *does* require a specification of the rate of exploitation. These three points are closely related.

A set of techniques – one for each commodity – makes up a technology according to modern theory. At any moment there will normally be known a number of different ways of producing at least some commodities. So the different techniques can be grouped together in different technologies. In a technology, then, a given level of the real wage will imply a set of prices and the rate of profit. But the technology *chosen* will be that one which maximizes the rate of profit. For simplicity, assume *either* with Marx, that all the techniques in each technology have the same organic composition of capital, *or* with Sraffa, that all technologies are in standard proportions. Then the real wage, rate of profit trade-off is a downward sloping straight line. The vertical axis represents output of consumer goods, so the real wage can be marked out on it. The horizontal axis represents the rate of profits. The slope of each line, then, is the capital–labor ratio for that technology.

At any given time there will be an actual technology in place. Social systems do not rise full-blown, like Venus from the waves. For this actual system the rate of exploitation will be determinate. In each sector an actual labor force is employed under established working conditions, and between them and their employers there will be a *modus vivendi*. Both sides will be constantly pushing to change this, employers to increase productivity and reduce costs, employees to raise wages and improve working conditions, but Steedman is surely right that for many purposes it is legitimate to 'freeze' the balance of forces in the workplace and analyze the working of the system for a given level of productivity and real wages.

Now let us say that we are examining a prospective change in a currently existing technology. We know the present rate of exploitation (output per worker divided by the wage); we know its output over capital, profits over capital, and its capital–labor ratio (output per worker divided by the output over capital).

The new technology does not yet exist. (Of course, this new technology may include many of the same industries now in place, but at least some must be new.) The present real wage may carry over in the new situation. That presumably depends on the labor market. But new technology creates a new workplace situation; new jobs will have to be defined, and new factories built. Relations in these new work situations cannot be 'frozen' – no one knows what they will be. Of course, assumptions about work intensity can – and must – be made, but until they are it will be impossible to determine how much the new technology's capital–labor ratio varies from that of the currently existing technology. (For simplicity, I am basing the discussion on the non-Marxian assumption that profit is not figured on advanced wages.) Productivity will vary considerably depending on how long, how hard, and with what care and attention workers will work; and if workers do not like the new set-up and are careless and wasteful, unit costs will rise and profits decline. But leaving this aside, suppose that engineers can predict with reasonable accuracy what the material inputs per unit output should be, and that the number of workers needed to operate the technology, and the wage required to sustain a worker for a given period of time are also known. This is enough to tell us the horizontal intercept of the wage–profit frontier. For whatever the speed with which workers work, the input per unit of output remains the same. But it does not give us the frontier's vertical intercept, nor consequently its slope – which is to say, we cannot yet know whether the new technology is superior to the existing one at all levels of the existing wage, or at only some levels, or not at all. For that we have to know also how much work – processing input into output – workers will do in a given amount of time. *And that is simply asking, in Marx's sense, what is the rate of exploitation?* (Cf. Ch. 4, esp. Fig. 4.6.)

If we turn back to the paradoxes of 'negative value' we find the same thing. Steedman does not distinguish coefficients falling under constant capital from those under variable capital. The effects of changes in the speed or intensity of work are therefore not examined. So he has not really confronted Marx's problem, though his examples do call attention to the importance of the patterns of technological interdependence. Where these are complex, conclusions from simpler cases may not carry over. However, not much work has been done analyzing what kinds of industries engage in what kinds of joint production; indeed, not much has been done defining categories of joint production. (Definitions have been developed for 'by-products' in which most of the conclusions from the single-product case carry over, see Nell, 1964; Schefold, 1971.) But the question is too technical to go into further. As for fixed capital, there are two serious problems with the Sraffa–von Neumann approach that have not yet received the attention they deserve. First, if fixed capital is to be treated as a joint product, how much should appear as output when capacity is under or over-utilized, that is, when we adapt the analysis to the consideration of questions of effective demand? (Nell, in Lowe, 1976, p. 292.) Presumably if the normal output is down when capacity is under-utilized, the equipment appearing as joint product will be *up*, since it has been depreciated less. But it may all have been used at less than normal intensity, or some of it left idle, while the rest ran as usual. Are these equivalent? Do managers have a choice? Secondly, for Marx capital must be continually turned over from commodities into money form. Thus, when the part of constant capital corresponding to the depreciation of fixed equipment is realized in the sale of the product for money, it will then be invested in a sinking fund, which will earn interest. Hence the total capital will be unchanged in amount, and in earning power, if the rate of interest equals the rate of profit. Only the form will be changed, progressively, with more of it in funds and less in the value of equipment, until the time for replacement comes when the sinking fund matures (Nell, 1964). These questions, capacity utilization and turnover, need answers before the Sraffa–von Neumann approach can claim to be an adequate concept of fixed capital for Marxian analysis.

So the 'choice of technique' and related arguments fail. The analysis moved at too abstract a plane; it was developed without regard to the fact that any change of technology involves moving from one concrete, actual situation, in which the balance of forces in the workplace can (often) reasonably be taken as known and 'frozen,' to a new, as yet untried, situation in which it can only be estimated. More importantly, the 'balance of class forces' – and therefore the position of the wage–profit frontier – depends on different kinds of factors from those determining material input into output. Social and political questions predominate in the former, engineering in the latter. Marx sought precisely to separate, and then relate, these two categories of influences on the rate of profits.

7 HOW DO WE GET THERE FROM HERE?

So what does it all amount to? The Sraffa-based critique of Marx is surely correct that, theoretically, labor-values are of no relevance in explaining prices (though, ironically, they may yet prove a useful empirical approximation). Marx's account of the rate of profit as $S/(C + V)$ is wrong, and his attempts to solve the transformation problem failed. Attempts to defend Marx on these specific points are a waste of time and effort. But the LTV played a larger and a different role for Marx. In its general form it relates capitalist commodity production and the existence of exchange-value to the exploitation of wage-labor, and more specifically, it determines the rate of exploitation in a sense which shows it to be a causal determinant of the rate of profit. So Steedman's claim that socio-technical conditions and the real wage are all that count is misleading, and his claim that 'the rate of profit is . . . *logically prior* to any determination of value magnitudes' must be rejected. On the contrary, it seems the rate of exploitation must be known in order to determine the rate of profit.

Where does this get us, though? We undoubtedly understand Marx much better, and a powerful array of mathematical techniques has been developed for Marxist and other non-standard economics. A coherent and sophisticated alternative to conventional value theory seems to be taking shape, though no doubt still containing many unresolved issues. *But how is a better understanding of Marx, or for that matter of value and capital, going to help us understand the economic crisis of our times?* What does all this argumentation, ingenious and abstruse as it is, promise in the way of insight into the malignant follies of our age? Marx, after all, wrote about a very much earlier stage of capitalism.

Consider some of the economic issues of today: inflation and unemployment, formerly thought to be opposites, moving together; stagnant productivity in the West; runaway energy pricing by cartels and powerful multinationals; massive dependency on armaments spending; ubiquitous waste and social misallocation; ill-designed and unmanageable cities; dwindling supplies of essential resources and a world population explosion; widespread destruction of ecological balance; the pillage of the Third World and the resulting reactions; and on and on. All this in the context of a period of historically unparalleled scientific and technological creativity. What have value and capital, or Marx's theories, to do with this?

It is surely impossible to answer this here. The best I can do is sketch the outline of an answer. To begin with, a flexible approach, based on Marx and the Classics generally, will be rooted . . in the actual situation of the system, at a moment of historical time. It has become what it is as the result of a particular path of historical development. The pure logic of the system can and must be considered, *but it is the logic of a system on a path of historical development.* Moreover, that development is powered by internal tensions and conflicts – 'contradictions' – which are tending to undermine the very processes by which it works. Conflict, latent or open, is absolutely endemic to the system – buyer vs. seller, employer vs. employee, borrower vs. lender, as well as firm vs. firm and worker vs. worker. Some conflicts are more fundamental than others, and the GLTV holds that the most fundamental of all is capital versus labor, taken in all its dimensions.

Secondly, no clear line can be drawn between economic and social or political conflicts, or even between economic and political processes. Politics, very often, is simply economics pursued by other means. This applies to capital as well as to labor. Not surprisingly the scope of state activities, and the cost of them, expands to encompass these demands, and to try to keep the conflicts within bounds, (Of course, there are political and social issues that are not, at least in any immediate way, related to economic concerns. In this connection there is an extensive Marxist literature about the influence of material factors 'in the last instance.') Neo-Classical theory, however, defines a sharp boundary between what can be analyzed by its methods, and what falls outside its purview. Since it is a theory of choice under constraints, it can be applied widely, if unsuccessfully, in explaining many political choices, marriage and divorce, job discrimination, and other issues. 'Widely,' because being abstract, it is quite general; 'unsuccessfully,' because it starts from the individual with given preferences operating in a given environment, where both 'preferences' and environment are conceived in limited and misleading ways. Neither the development of the individual's consciousness, nor the development of the institutions in and through which individuals function are possible subjects of inquiry. 'What are the effects of mechanization upon worker alienation' is not a question that can be raised in orthodox labor market analysis; it is inescapable in the Classical-Marxian framework.

Thirdly, capital is not a 'factor of production' earning a return in virtue of its 'productive contribution' at the margin. It is a social relationship; it is the way production is organized and the product appropriated. The existence of capital as self-expanding value depends upon the exploitation of wage-labor. This again is the point of the GLTV. So when multinational capital moves into new areas, formerly organized non-capitalistically, new institutional arrangements must be created. A proper 'climate for investment' must be established. This means a labor force, labor discipline, protection for property in the means of production, suitable finance, and so on. These can involve major social upheavals and political changes, all too evident throughout the Third World, from South Korea through South America to South Africa.

Some of these changes are the results of conscious political decisions. (One should never underestimate the conspiracy theory of history. Even paranoids have *real* enemies.) But many, and perhaps the largest, are not. They are the outcomes of the process of capital accumulation. This is not steady-state growth. It is the creation and management of a force of wage-laborers by capital in pursuit of its only legitimate goal, high and steady profit. The massive shift of people to the cities in search of work, for example, is an indirect and largely unintended result of technical progress and reorganization resulting from the invasion of agriculture by corporate capital.

Fourthly, the Marxian approach forces us to recognize that productivity and technical change have social and political dimensions. We have already seen that productivity depends on the clash of interests – and wills – in the workplace. It also depends on common interests; the more successful the business, the higher the wage it can afford. Productivity is the outcome of a complex symbiotic process, an important aspect of which is the development of technology. For technology is not merely control over Nature, it also provides control over Man. The division of labor and the factory system provided ways of *controlling* the pace and quality of work, as do modern assembly-line methods. Technology provides for social control and discipline in the workplace. So the development of technology is not socially neutral; it will reflect class interests and sociopolitical pressures. 'Economies of scale,' for example, may refer to lower unit material costs, or to greater effectiveness in controlling markets or disciplining labor. The appropriation of science and engineering for private interests, setting up walls of secrecy, distorts and even comes to block scientific development.

Fifthly, we get a very different perspective on markets. For one thing the 'labor market' and the 'capital market' are quite different in nature and working from the markets for goods. To understand a market requires having a clear picture of the respective positions of the parties on either side of it. The GLTV provides this for the labor market, and moreover, in doing so, explains the origin of the net returns which are the subject of the bargaining among the different types of capitalists in the capital markets. The SLTV explains the size of such returns and the 'transformation' relates exploitation and productivity to profits. But besides the relationship of the labor market to capital, the LTV also provides insight into employment and effective demand. Returns must be realized in money form; if sales are not made, exploitation merely means piling up inventory. The rate of exploitation will not be reduced, however; instead, workers will be laid off. Lay-offs, in turn, reduce consumer spending, so lead to lower sales revenue and hence lay-offs. The SLTV, in fact, can be developed as an employment multiplier, showing the repercussions of a change in sales of final goods on employment throughout the system. This offers a practical alternative to marginal productivity theory, and has been extensively developed, first by Kalecki, and now by the contemporary 'post Keynesians.'

Prices, in turn, must be explained in terms of the mark-up required to obtain a target rate of return. Here Steedman's themes are paramount. Long-term prices are determined by the rate of profits, which depends on real wages, productivity, and technical coefficients. Exploitation depends on real wages as well as intensity of work, and real wages depend on money wages in relation to prices. Effective short-run pricing policies can, therefore, contribute to a favorable rate of exploitation. Such policies are the results of collusion, power plays, politics and governmental regulation, marketing, mergers and takeovers, and many other strategies designed to bring about stable and profitable markets. Price competition is one route to this end, but only one. Competition is a short-lived state of affairs; it is the race to get the monopoly – but it ends like the race between whales and minnows, with the winners swallowing the losers. The neo-Classical picture of 'the price mechanism efficiently allocating scarce resources' should be hung next to the round square in the Gallery of the Theatre of the Absurd. The Invisible Hand, if it is to be found anywhere, is likely to be found picking the pockets of the poor.

I could go on. Our approach to the theory of value and capital provides a framework for re-thinking population questions, for re-examining the historical growth of capitalism in the Age of European Expansion, for re-thinking the role of the State and the causes of its growth. It provides the basis for a new approach to the development of technology. But most of all, it provides the conceptual linkages showing how all these different aspects of human society are bound together in a central unity: the organization of production by capital. The problems outlined earlier are all, in some part, attributable to the consequences, and normal working, of this form of organization. '[T]hey belong to a state of society, in which the process of production has the mastery over man, instead of being controlled by him . . .'

Notes

1. 'So far as regards use-value, it is clear that both parties may gain some advantage. Both part with goods that, as use-values, are of no service to them, and receive others that they can make use of . . . With reference, then, to use-value, there is good ground for saying that exchange is a transaction by which both sides gain. It is otherwise with exchange-value.' Marx, *Capital*, Volume I, Chapter 1.
2. Marx attached an important footnote to this passage which explains why he insisted on assuming the SLTV throughout Volume I: '[T]he formation of capital must be possible even though the price and value of a commodity be the same; for its formation cannot be attributed to any deviation of the one from the other.' He knew perfectly well that, in general, prices deviate from value – Volume III was drafted before Volume I was written – but he wanted to forestall the notion that the existence of profit could be explained by a systematic discrepancy between price and value. Hence 'to explain profit at all, it must first be explained on the assumption that prices equal values.' Dobb made this point in 1939.
3. It should be evident that this argument does not depend on whether the true values of goods are measured by ratios of embodied labor times or by prices. The subsistence goods support labor for a given time; whatever their prices are, the real wage is thus the equivalent of a certain amount of labor time. Hence the rate of exploitation can be expressed in terms of the division of the working day. Steedman is surely right on this point.
4. The distinction between abstract and concrete labor must not be confused with the distinction between simple and skilled labor, both of which are concrete. The reduction of skilled labor to simple is, for Marx, largely a matter of history and custom, including the ability (or lack of it) of groups to entrench themselves and enhance their status. It 'rests in part on pure illusion, or to say the least, on distinctions that have long since ceased to be real, and that survive

only by virtue of a traditional convention, in part on the helpless condition of some groups of the working class' (Marx, Volume I, p. 192, No. 1). Concrete labor is the practical work of producing use-values; abstract labor is the condition of being exploited, measured as the amount of time in simple labor equivalents spent working in that status. A good deal of academic labor has been expended on the question of determining the reduction of skilled to simple labor. It is not clear that such labor is socially necessary; Marx regarded the reduction as exogenous to value theory. (For a related view, cf. Bowles and Gintis, 1978.)

5. It is now widely recognized that Marx had unusually acute insight into the mathematical structure of economic problems (Morishima, 1974). His attempts to formulate his system were often cumbersome and inept, but he was developing arguments for which there were as yet no adequate mathematical tools. Matrix algebra was 40 years in the future. The Perron–Frobenius theorem was first proved in 1907.
6. 'In the "transparent" modes of exploitation, the rate of exploitation is immediately obvious: the serf works for three days on his or her own land and for three days on the master's. Neither the serf nor the lord is blind to this fact. But the capitalist mode of exploitation is opaque. On the one hand, the proletarian sells labor power, but seems to be selling labor, and is paid for the eight hours of work put in, not just for the four that would be necessary for maintenance; on the other hand, the bourgeois realizes a profit which is calculated in relation to the capital owned, not to the labour exploited, so that this capital seems to the capitalist to be productive' (from Amin, 1977, p. 13).
7. But wouldn't industries or departments all produce at different speeds, depending on the particular working conditions in each? Industries, however, are interdependent. One which produced faster than the rest will find, on the one hand, its supplies used up before its suppliers have completed production, and on the other, its product finished before its customers are ready to buy. Inventory policy smooths this out, of course, but *given* an inventory policy, a speed-up out of line with its customers and suppliers will lead an industry to where it has to lay off workers and wait. The basic industry, therefore, with the slowest rate of production regulates all the rest, a result familiar from critical path analysis.
8. It is important to realize that faster or better work in circulation (sales, finance, etc.) does produce a faster turnover, and therefore *does* contribute to surplus-value in Marx's sense. The robot economy suggested is very far removed from any advanced capitalist economy today.
9. Abandoning values and relying on physical quantities has sometimes been taken as equivalent to rejecting Marx's insights into exploitation (Roosevelt, 1975). Steedman specifically denies this.
10. This is brought out very clearly in a note circulated by Steedman concerning a long-standing problem in the interpretation of 'socially necessary labor-time.' Steedman holds that this *must* mean the labor time required in the best-practice technique; otherwise the exchange ratios will not be the correct equilibrium ones. Marx, however, several time asserts that required labor is that with 'the *average* degree of skill and intensity prevalent at a given time' (*Capital* I, p. 39, my italics). Steedman is correct for his purposes, but his method would *overestimate* both the actual surplus-value produced and the rate of exploitation. Marx is right, if his purpose is the theory of exploitation.

Bibliographical Notes

An excellent introduction to Marx's thought is R. Heilbroner, *Marxism: For and Against* (New York: Norton, 1980). A more advanced discussion is M. Dobb, *Political Economy and Capitalism* (London: Routledge, 1940). In the end, however, the only way to understand Marx is to read him. *Capital* consists of three volumes: Volume I presents the Labor Theory of Value and the associated doctrine of exploitation, culminating in the General Law of Capitalist Accumulation; Volume II examines the turnover of capital-monetary accumulation – analyzing the conditions for balance between the sectors in the process of (expanding) reproduction; Volume III moves from 'values' and the 'underlying' categories of Marxian analysis to the practical categories of the business world – prices, profits, interest, credit, and rent. In Volume III we are given Marx's version of the 'transformation,' the movement from value analysis to the categories of the real world. Heilbroner's *Nature and Logic of Capitalism* (New York: Norton, 1985) will help.

Reading *Capital* is notoriously difficult. But a great deal of help is provided by comparing the argument of *Capital* with corresponding points in *Theories of Surplus Value* (New York: Progress Publishers, 1971), where Marx contrasts his work with that of others, or in the *Grundrisse* (New York: Vintage Books, 1973) where Marx sketches the overall plan of his life's work.

The four complaints raised against neo-Classical economics are developed in the following works, among others:

M. Hollis and E. Nell, *Rational Economic Man* (Cambridge: Cambridge University Press, 1975).
M. Lutz and K. Lux, *Humanistic Economics: Fundamentals and Applications* (Boston: Benjamin-Cummins, 1979).
J. Robinson, *Economic Heresies: Some Old-Fashioned Questions in Economic Theory* (New York: Basic Books, 1971).
V.C. Walsh and H.N. Gram, *Classical and Neo-Classical Theories of General Equilibrium: Historical Origins and Mathematical Structure* (Oxford: Oxford University Press, 1980).

The most fundamental work providing the basis for a critique of modern economics is P. Sraffa, *Production of Commodities by Means of Commodities* (Cambridge: Cambridge University Press, 1960). That this work lays the groundwork for powerful – some would say decisive – criticism of marginalist theory is well known. An apparent paradox, however, is that these same foundations provide the basis for the critique of the Labor Theory of Value.

•

The text distinguished four positions on the Labor Theory of Value. The following representative works present the basic ideas of the different positions:

I. I. Steedman, *Marx After Sraffa*, New Left Books, 1977. G. Hodgson, 'Exploitation and Embodied Labor Time,' *Bulletin of the Conference of Socialist Economists* (March 1976).
M. Morishima, *Marx's Economics: A Dual Theory of Value and Growth* (Cambridge: Cambridge University Press, 1973); and, with qualification, 'Marx in the Light of Modern Economic Theory,' *Econometrica* (1974).

II. J. Roemer, 'Marxian Models of Reproduction and Accumulation,' *Cambridge Journal of Economics* (March 1978).
E. Wolfstetter, 'Positive Profits with Negative Surplus Value: A Comment,' *Economic Journal* (1976).
G. Abraham-Frois and E. Berrebi, *Theory of Value, Prices and Accumulation: A Mathematical Integration of Marx, von Neumann and Sraffa* (Cambridge: Cambridge University Press, 1976).
W.J. Baumol, 'The Transformation of Values: What Marx "Really" Meant (an Interpretation),' *Journal of Economic Literature* (March 1974).
D. Laibman, 'Values and Prices of Production: The Political Economy of the Transformation Problem,' *Science and Society* (Winter 1973–4).

III. F. Roosevelt, 'Cambridge Economics as Commodity Fetishism,' *Review of Radical Political Economics* (Winter 1975). Reprinted in E. Nell (ed.), *Growth, Profits and Property* (Cambridge: Cambridge University Press, 1980).
H. Ganssmann, *The Use Value of Marx's Theory of Value*, unpublished manuscript.
P. Armstrong, A. Glyn, and J. Harrison, 'In Defense of Value – A Reply to Ian Steedman,' *Capital and Class* (Summer 1978).
A. Shaikh, 'Political Economy and Capitalism: Notes on Dobb's Theory of Crisis,' *Cambridge Journal of Economics* (March 1978). Reprinted in *Political Economy in the New School* (New School for Social Research, 1980).

IV. D. Yaffe, 'Value and Price in Marx's Capital,' *Revolutionary Communist* (January 1975).

•

Other references mentioned in the text:

S. Amin, *The Law of Value and Historical Materialism* (New York: Monthly Review Press, 1978).
S. Bowles and H. Gintis, 'The Marxian Theory of Value and Heterogeneous Labor: A Critique and Reformulation,' *Cambridge Journal of Economics* (June 1977).
D.G. Champernowne, 'A Note on John von Neumann's Article on "A Model of General Economic Equilibrium,"' *Review of Economic Studies* (1945–6).
A. Lowe, *The Path to Economic Growth* (Cambridge: Cambridge University Press, 1976), with Appendix by E.J. Nell.
E.J. Nell, 'Models of Behaviour with Special Reference to Certain Economic Theories,' thesis (1964).
J. von Neumann, 'A Model of General Economic Equilibrium,' *Review of Economic Studies* (1945–6).
B. Schefold, *Theorie der Kuppelproduction* (private print, 1971).
A. Shaikh, 'The Transformation from Marx to Sraffa (Prelude to a Critique of the Neo-Ricardians),' (1982), in A. Corchuelo, ed., *Nuevos Desarrollos de la Teoria Economica* (Cali-Columbia: CIDSE Universidad del Valle).

4 Understanding the Marxian Notion of Exploitation: the 'Number One Issue'

According to Samuelson, 'The Number One Issue in Appraising Karl Marx's Theoretical Innovations' is 'what Marx claimed as most originally his . . . namely [his] way of handling "surplus value"' (1977, p. 250).[1] 'It is precisely Marx's models in Volumes I and II of equalized-rates-of-positive-surplus-value-markups-on-direct-wages-alone that have seemed bizarre to most non-Marxian economists,' who have therefore joined in a 'near-universal rejection . . . of these . . . paradigms as (a) gratuitously unrealistic, (b) an unnecessary *detour* from which Marx in Volume III had to beat a return, even though . . . he was too stubborn or too unperceptive or too unscientific to admit [it]' (ibid.).

This, he repeats, 'has been the Number One issue in the debates about Marxian economics throughout the years of [his] professional life.' He gives his own opinion:

> Save as only an admitted first approximation, justifiable for dramatic emphasis and hortatory persuasiveness or defended because of its obvious greater simplicity of algebraic structure, the paradigm of equalized-rates-of-surplus-values is an unnecessary detour from the alternative paradigm of equalized-rate-of-profit that Marx and mainstream economists inherited from Ricardo and earlier writers. The digressing Marxian alternative paradigm not only lacks empirical realism as applied to competitive arbitrage governing capital flows among industries and competitive price relations of different goods and services, but also is a detour and a digression to the would-be student of monopolistic and imperfect competition, to the would-be student of socialism, to the would-be student of the modern mixed economy and its laws of motion, to the would-be student of the historic laws of motion of historic capitalism. (Samuelson 1977, p. 251).

* Reprinted from G. Feiwel (ed.), *Samuelson and Neo-Classical Economics* (Boston: Kluwer–Nijoff, 1982). I am grateful to Ulrich Krause, Heinz Kurz, and Anwar Shaikh for detailed comments and criticism. This paper develops themes raised in Chapter 3, and in doing so repeats some material.

Lest there be any doubt, he later states 'for dogmatic clarity' the position he thinks serious economists, Marxian and non-Marxian, will ultimately agree on:

> 1. *No* new analytical insight is given, statically or dynamically, by Marx's own novelties of theoretical analysis that involve – *macro*economically or *micro*economically – the concept of the 'rate of surplus-value,' either in the form of s_j/v_j or of S_j/V_j, $\Sigma s_j/\Sigma v_j$ or $\Sigma S_j/\Sigma V_j$
>
> (a) into the explanation of the distribution of income between labor wages and property capital return, or
>
> (b) into the determination of society's general profit rate (or total of profit return), or
>
> (c) into the microeconomic empirical configuration of goods and prices in a system of perfect or imperfect competition (or of imperfect knowledge, or of stochastic exogenous disturbance) or
>
> (d) into the realities of the class struggle or the understanding of power relations between groups and governments, internationally or nationally, or
>
> (e) into the ethical nature of 'exploitation' and inequality of income (Samuelson 1977, pp. 295–6).

(To this he adds three qualifications: The algebra of the surplus value regime is easier to handle, so it might have expository uses; if labor intensities in different sectors are similar, labor values might be useful approximations to prices; and blind alleys may be interesting or suggestive, even though blind.)

Samuelson, in effect, poses two questions:

1. What insight do we get from the study of the rate of surplus value that we do not get from a study of the rate of profit?
2. Why and how does the rate of surplus value 'explain' the rate of profit in a way that the rate of profit does not equally 'explain' the rate of surplus value?

His answer to the first is that there is no such insight and to the second that there is no such explanatory power.

1 EXPLAINING EXCHANGE VALUE

Samuelson's argument has concentrated almost exclusively on the comparison, for given (single-product) physical input and labor coefficient matrices, of the different accounting regimes of labor values, with a uniform rate of surplus value, and prices of production, with a uniform rate of profit. As is well known now (since Sraffa and known to mathematically inclined students of the subject before), the labor-value accounting regime corresponds to the intercept of the wage rate – rate of profit frontier at which the rate of profit is zero. (All that is necessary is to convert labor values into ratios.) Hence the two regimes are connected by a one-to-one mapping. (Samuelson's 'eraser theorem' amounts to saying that if an economy is at one point on the wage-profit frontier it is not at some other point.) The analysis of the 'transformation problem' is simply an examination of the properties of this mapping and can tell one no more, or less, than what these are, given the various possible properties of the matrix, whether wages are advanced or not, the durability of capital and nature of depreciation, and so forth.

The question of what are the economically relevant mathematical characteristics of the price system can best be answered by examining the price system itself. However, these characteristics will all have a mapping into the value system, so one could look for them there (though they might not be so readily recognizable). But neither system provides any 'explanation' for the other; they are simply connected by a one-to-one mapping.

If this were the only issue, it would be hard to see what all the fuss has been about. But it is certainly not the issue that chiefly interested Marx. Indeed, the properties of the price system, of paramount concern to neo-Classical economists, were located by Marx at a different level of theory altogether. (Chaps. 6–12, and 42, 43 and 45 of Vol. III analyze the working of the price system; Chap. 50, 'Illusions Created by Competition,' concerns its interpretation. The price system is a surface phenomenon; the theory of value concerns the deep structure.) The main question for Marx, one not usually raised by modern mainstream economists (in spite of its obvious importance in Third World countries today and in economic history generally), is why there is such a thing as value-in-exchange at all. This question has two parts. There is, first of all, the logical question of what social conditions must exist for there to be, and to continue to be, value-in-exchange and second, the historical question of how and when these social conditions came into existence (and, of course, how they are developing over time).

This question may be neglected by modern economists, but it was not always so. Walras, for example, devotes a good deal of attention to the logical question (1954, Lessons, 3, 5, and 10; see especially p. 101, 'Rareté, the cause of value-in-exchange'), and so does Wicksell. Samuelson himself discusses the 'law of scarcity' in the early pages of his famous textbook and uses it to explain why there are few, if any, 'free goods' (i.e., why everything has a price), the modern equivalent of explaining the existence of value-in-exchange.

The neo-Classical or mainstream answer is cast in terms of scarcity and individual preferences, the necessity of 'economizing' or 'making choices' in a world with not enough to go around. The Marxian tradition has always rejected this answer as inadequate to the question. The issue is not, 'Why do we have to make choices?' (to which a correct, though unilluminating, answer is surely, 'Because there isn't enough, given all that we want'), but 'Why are the choices we face of this kind, given what we have?' And this leads to a wholly different perspective.

The reason we face the kinds of choices we do is that we live under the kind of social arrangements that we have. 'Choices' are not made in the abstract; choices are necessarily between these commodities and those, this job and that, one investment or another, and they are made by persons occupying specific social roles with definite obligations and responsibilities – housewives or heads of households, managers or directors of firms. The array of choices that people face depends on the system of production and the distribution of claims to the product. These social arrangements, in turn, must be supported and reproduced. It is in this context in which value arises and must be defined.

To put it with dogmatic clarity, value arises not because choices have to be made, but because a surplus has to be brought into existence and appropriated. Moreover, this surplus is produced by workers working with means of production that they use up; the workers must be supported and the means of production replaced at the same time that the surplus is appropriated. This leads to a special and important peculiarity of capitalism: Replacement and appropriation are both accomplished at the same time, through the market – that is, by means of exchange. Yet an exchange, in equilibrium, is always an exchange of equivalents. How, then, can a *surplus* be appropriated, in value terms, through exchange?

In Marx's analysis this is the key question, and the answer lies in the nature of the commodity, labor. The buying and selling of labor power is the fulcrum on which the entire theory of value turns. It explains the origin of the surplus, the nature of exploitation, and the inherent connection between exploitation and value. Let's review section 2 of the previous chapter.

The General Labor Theory of Value

This connection between exploitation and value simply does not exist in neo-Classical economics, so it will be useful to examine it more closely. At a general level Marx argued that the fact that commodities 'have value' is to be explained by the fact and only by the fact that they are products of wage labor, which is to say, exploited labor. To 'have value' is to be exchangeable in a regular way for a universal equivalent. For a universal equivalent to exist, exchange ratios between any two commodities must be consistent with the exchange ratios of either with any third. The ultimate insight of the LTV in its most general form is that value as a societywide phenomenon, expressed in universal equivalence with money ('everything has its price'), can arise only in social circumstances of class conflict. If commodities exist, if things have exchange value, then there must be exploited labor. No 'harmony' is possible through the market, for value and commodity exchange, and so class conflict, are preconditions for markets.

We have called this doctrine the GLTV; let us now look at the claim that value is the reflection of class conflict in the mirror of economics. All activities that can be privately organized are, or produce, commodities and so have value; the key condition for this arrangement is that labor be exploited, which in turn implies a division of society into owners of means of production and workers who 'own' only their capacity to work. This is not the way everyone has read Marx. For instance, it has been claimed that Marx simply took over Ricardo's position[2] on the LTV in the process, of course, both developing it and placing it in a social and historical perspective. In that case Marx's theory would still be substantially that of Ricardo; embodied labor would explain exchange value and so prices, while the level of wages in relation to total output would explain profits. The central questions would be those Samuelson tackles on the working of the price system.

But in fact the first nine chapters of *Capital*, Volume I, are devoted to a set of issues completely different from those that interest Samuelson. Prices and the rate of profits figure neither as the targets of the inquiry, nor among the explanatory concepts. When Marx finally does set about to determine a quantitative concept, it is not the rate of profit, but the rate of surplus value (rate of exploitation), and this comes only in Chapter 9. Are the first eight chapters just a prelude, presenting the social and historical background? *That certainly is not what Marx thought.*

Capital begins with a discussion of commodities and money, moves on to the transformation of money into capital, and then shows that the production of surplus value in the labor process is the foundation of the earning power of capital. The entire discussion, although illuminated by examples drawn from history, moves on the plane of theory. It is *not* a presentation of socio-historical background; it is the central core of Marx's theory, leading up to the determination of the rate of surplus value.

Commodities, the form in which the wealth of capitalist societies presents itself, have two aspects, use value and exchange value. These in turn correspond to two aspects of the labor that produces them: concrete specific labor, which produces use value, and abstract labor, which generates exchange value.[3] Concrete labor is the practical work of producing use values; abstract labor is the condition of being exploited, measured as the amount of time in simple labor equivalents spent working in that status.

Marx next enters on a long and detailed examination of the forms of exchange value, culminating in the general form of value that '. . . results from the joint action of the whole world of commodities . . . A commodity can acquire a general expression of its value only by all other commodities, simultaneously with it, expressing their values in the same equivalent . . .' (1967, p. 66). The general form of value requires some commodity to act as universal equivalent. But insofar as the commodity does so, it cannot be used as means of production or of subsistence or of luxury consumption. It is no longer the use value it once was; it is money. 'The difficulty lies, not in comprehending that money is a commodity, but in discovering how, why, and by what means a commodity becomes money' (ibid., p. 92).

The commodity that becomes money already has value.[4] For general commodity production to exist, there must be fully developed exchange, and for Marx that *requires* that exchange values be expressed (and compared) in universal equivalent form and carried out by means of circulating money.

If money is the universal medium by which commodities are exchanged, then capital will have to circulate in money form. The capitalist advances money for commodities, then sells commodities for money. But this makes no sense. Selling commodities for money, and then buying commodities again, is practical enough. The exchange value of the two sets of commodities may be the same, but the use value of the second set to the owner will be higher.[5] In contrast, buying commodities for a sum of money and selling them again for that same sum is a complete waste of time. (Marx is assuming that all commodities sell for their cost of production and that all exchanges are fair and equal; no agents in the market have any special privileges.) To assume that on resale, commodities can fetch more than they cost, *in general*, is contradictory.[6] 'Circulation, or the exchange of commodities, begets no value' (ibid., p. 163).

At this point Marx states exactly what he is up to:

> The conversion of money into capital has to be explained on the basis of the laws that regulate the exchange of commodities, in such a way that the starting-point is the exchange of equivalents. Our friend, Moneybags, who as yet is only an embryo capitalist, must buy his commodities at their value, must sell them at their value, and yet at the end of the process must withdraw more value from circulation than he threw into it at starting. His development into a full-grown capitalist must take place, both within the sphere of circulation and without it. These are the conditions of the problem. *Hic Rhodus, hic salta*![7]
>
> (Marx 1967, p. 166).

We began from universal commodity production; all activities are commodities, so human work will be also. The solution lies in the buying and selling of labor power. The seller pays its cost of production, the (socially determined) subsistence wage, but obtains its use value – namely, the workers' capacity to work for a period of time. What the worker *does* in this time depends on what the buyer of labor power can get out of him.

Workers work; work means changing the form of materials, cutting, shaping, processing, and so on. The faster, or harder, or longer hours a worker works for a day's subsistence pay, the more material input he will convert into output. Marx examines the labor process with great care, and his chapter on 'The Working Day' eloquently expresses outrage over injustice, but also offers analysis. Material input, wear and tear of machinery, and so on, summed up, form the 'constant' capital that must be advanced. Such capital is simply converted into output, adding its own value, but no more. The wage bill, however, is 'variable' capital; it is spent on the purchase of labor power, which, if coerced or cajoled suitably, *can produce in a day more than the value needed to pay its subsistence*. The ratio between the time worked 'for the capitalist' and the time worked 'for himself' (producing what it would take to buy his subsistence) is the rate of exploitation.[8] Thus, while buying materials, equipment, and labor power at cost or true value and selling the goods produced by labor for their cost or true value, the capitalist is still able to turn a profit.

In short, the first nine chapters of *Capital* are devoted to relating commodities, values, and free exchange to capital and the exploitation of labor; the latter explains the earning power of capital, which, in turn, explains the driving force of its circulation, the motivation that runs the whole system. This, then, is the general answer to the question why we face the kinds of choices we do. It is the *general* form of the labor theory of value.

Samuelson's Interpretation

Given that Marx devoted the first nine chapters of *Capital*, Volume I, to the discussion of the issues just summarized, why does Samuelson ignore this and assume that Marx's object in proposing a 'labor theory of value' was to explain prices? If that had been his purpose, he was not only incorrect, but *he himself knew it*, since Volume III was drafted before Volume I was written in final form! Why does Samuelson think he would put forth an incorrect theory of prices when he had already worked out (albeit imperfectly) many of the aspects of a correct theory? Samuelson's answer appears to be that Marx was committed, for ideological reasons, to the LTV and was reluctant to admit that he had to give it up. But this does not account for the discussion just examined, which has nothing to do with explaining prices or profits and focuses wholly on connecting universal value-in-exchange with the exploitation of labor in a class society.

Marx's argument can be separated into three stages. The first and most fundamental is that the exchange accomplishes two things simultaneously – exchanging the replacement goods to permit reproduction and appropriating the surplus. It must be shown how this can be done consistently with exchange as the exchange of value equivalents. The key to this is the unique nature of labor power, which in turn sets the stage for the examination of the labor process as the source of surplus value. Labor is hired and paid a wage for a given time. But the work it does in that time depends on what the capitalist can cajole or coerce out of it. This is the conflict at the point of production. If labor works sufficiently slowly, there will be no surplus. If it works faster or harder, there will be. But capital directs the work and can replace lazy or rebellious workers with other who are more energetic or more compliant. Finally, the competition of capitalists establishes a uniform rate of profits and thereby sets the prices of production for the commodities so produced.[9]

Samuelson, wedded to the theory that value derives from utility in conditions of scarcity, simply ignores the first two stages of Marx's argument. Not surprisingly, he then finds that the third stage doesn't seem to make sense. Let's look at his discussion more closely.

He starts with a no-surplus model. Exchange value is determinate, but there is nothing left over for profits or for taxes. Then, '. . . perhaps because of an invention that makes venison more digestible, the minimum needed wage drops . . .' (1971, p. 406). The appeal to an unexplained invention to account for the surplus is no accident; it crops up again a few pages later. For Marx, of course, the surplus arises because it is *produced*; workers produce it because capitalists make them *work* long enough hours, or hard enough in given hours, in order to generate it. Exploitation is a matter of structural coercion. Circumstances are so arranged that a large mass of people must agree to do as they are told by others in order to support themselves and their families. Samuelson completely ignores this.

Moreover, he also misses the fact that once a surplus exists, exchange accomplishes two objects at once – replacement and appropriation. He not only has no answer to how this can be done consistently with exchange as the trade of value equivalents – he is apparently not even aware of the question.

Having 'invented' a surplus, Samuelson's next move is to discuss how Malthusian population pressure combined with growth resulting from savings out of profits would determine the real wage and therefore the rate of profit. He himself, evidently, does not feel that this is an adequate approach to long-run questions, but he argues that Marx was mistaken, in terms of his own model, to dismiss bourgeois economics. Insofar as the model is valid, it could be as legitimately claimed by neo-Classicists as by Marxists. Marx, of course, discusses accumulation, wages, and the growth of the labor force in Chapter 25 of Volume I, 'The General Law of Capitalist Accumulation,' to which Samuelson does not refer. The analysis of accumulation, absolutely basic in Marx, takes place at a *different level of abstraction* than does the analysis of value and exploitation. The GLTV exhibits the central relationship of the capitalist mode of production. The GLCA states the basic 'law of motion' of the capitalist system; the latter, therefore, presupposes and builds on the former.

Thus, Samuelson's discussion should have remained at the same level of abstraction as Marx's and should have directed itself to the same question – the explanation of value-in-exchange in conditions in which a surplus is produced under capitalist relations of production. By shifting levels – and ignoring Marx's and later Marxist discussions of GLCA – he makes it seem that modern growth analysis can answer questions in Marxian value theory. By ignoring the first two stages – and the real purpose – of Marx's inquiry, he makes it seem that Marx simply had two theories of prices, a bad one to which he was ideologically committed and a good one, which was insufficiently worked out.

So, to understand the Marxian notion of exploitation, the best course is to do what Samuelson should have done – that is, set up a simple model of production and exchange and analyze it, according to the various prevailing theories. I will consider three treatments of the question of exchange value: the standard Marxian, the neo-Classical, and what has been termed the neo-Ricardian system. Since value is perhaps the most fundamental concept of economics, a theory of value should be able to handle all plausible and simple cases. The model we will now examine, however, though simple and plausible, presents serious problems for each of the three approaches just mentioned. However, a Marxian analysis, based on the first nine chapters of Volume I, handles the matter easily and shows exactly how the rate of exploitation determines both the rate of profit and prices.

2 A SIMPLIFIED MODEL

Consider the following simplified economy. There are two producing institutions. Each uses the other's product as means of production, but *workers in each consume only their own product*. We begin with 'simple commodity production,' assuming that workers in each sector own their own means of production.

Let the two goods be n and m. The producer or producers of m work l_m days using n_m means of production to produce 1 unit of m output. The producer or producers of n work l_n days using m_n for this unit of output. The two (sets of) workers both do different kinds of work, since they work up different means of production, and have completely different consumption patterns. Taking the price of n as unity, we have for exchange equations:

$$n_m + w_m p_m l_m = p_m \tag{4.1}$$

$$m_n p_m + w_n l_n = 1 \tag{4.2}$$

where w_m is the 'wage' of the m-producers and w_n the 'wage' of the n-producers. (Even though both sets of workers are paid in 'real' terms, in the form of the respective producer's consumption good, both must be expressed in *value* since that good must be traded for means of production.)

Eliminating p_m yields w_m in terms of w_n:

$$w_m = \frac{n_m m_n + w_n l_n - 1}{l_m(w_n l_n - 1)} = \frac{1}{l_m}\left(1 + \frac{n_m m_n}{w_n l_n - 1}\right) \tag{4.3}$$

and, clearly,

$$\frac{dw_m}{dw_n} = \frac{-n_m m_n l_n l_m}{[l_m(w_n l_n - 1)]^2} < 0. \tag{4.4}$$

By substituting (4.3) into (4.1), we obtain p_m in terms of w_n:

$$p_m = \frac{1 - w_n l_n}{m_n}, \text{ and } \frac{dp_m}{dw_n} = -\frac{l_n}{m_n}. \tag{4.5}$$

So we see that p_m varies continuously and monotonically with the division of the gains between the parties. The real wage will be uniform for the two producers (even though paid in different commodities) when $w_n = w_m p_m$. In this case the original system reduces to two equations in two unknowns, the price and the uniform real wage. But in *general* the exchange ratio of the products, the price system, is indeterminate until the *division of gain*, or *the relative worth of the two different lines of work*, has been settled.

No analogous problem arises in the pure exchange economy. It is not just a matter of relative pay scales; it is an issue of direct confrontation, for what one gains the other loses. The difficulty of reducing all labor to simple, abstract labor receiving a common wage is now in plain view; different lines of work are not only wholly different, they are also interdependent, as a consequence of which the gain of one is the other's loss.

Continuing with the model, we write the quantity equations for the two parties:

$$q_m = m_n + c_m q_m l_m \tag{4.6}$$

$$1 = n_m q_m + c_n l_n \tag{4.7}$$

Here q_m stands for the *relative* quantity of m to n – the number of wheelbarrows per hundredweight of apples needed in equilibrium. The scale of the system will not be fixed until we know the amount of labor.

Solving (4.6) and (4.7) we can obtain the same relation between c_m and c_n that we found before between w_m and w_n:

$$c_m = \frac{n_m m_n + c_n l_n - 1}{l_m(c_n l_n - 1)} . \tag{4.8}$$

Using this and solving for q_m, we obtain:

$$q_m = \frac{1 - c_n l_n}{n_m} \text{, and } \frac{dq_m}{dc_n} = - \frac{l_n}{n_m} . \tag{4.9}$$

Equations (4.5) and (4.9) together imply:

$$p_m = \frac{n_m}{m_n} q_m, \tag{4.10}$$

provided that $w_m = c_m$ and $w_n = c_n$.

This result can be obtained another way, by multiplying, first, equations (4.1) and (4.2) by the quantities, q_m and 1, and then equations (4.6) and (4.7) by the prices, p_m and 1. The resulting equations are respectively equal to each other; comparing them, we see that either (4.1) and (4.6) or (4.2) and (4.7) yield $p_m m_n = q_m n_m$, provided that $w_m = c_m$ (which from (4.8) and (4.3) implies $w_n = c_n$). (Notice that this is the same relationship between prices and quantities that would follow from a *uniform* ratio of net earnings to direct labor (absorbing the whole surplus), which equaled the *uniform* rate of consumption per head, with the entire surplus consisting of the consumer goods in the proportions in which they are consumed in the aggregate. We will come to the surplus shortly.)

The provision in (4.10) amounts to assuming that conditions are stationary and that each producer consumes only one of the goods. These assumptions, though at the cost of some complexity, can easily be relaxed. Equation (4.10) clearly yields a straight line when graphed (Figure 4.1). For later, we will want the relationship between w_m and q_m.

From (4.3) we have:

$$w_n = \frac{1 - m_n p_m}{l_n}$$

Hence:

$$w_m = \frac{1}{l_m}\left(1 - \frac{n_m}{p_m}\right). \tag{4.11}$$

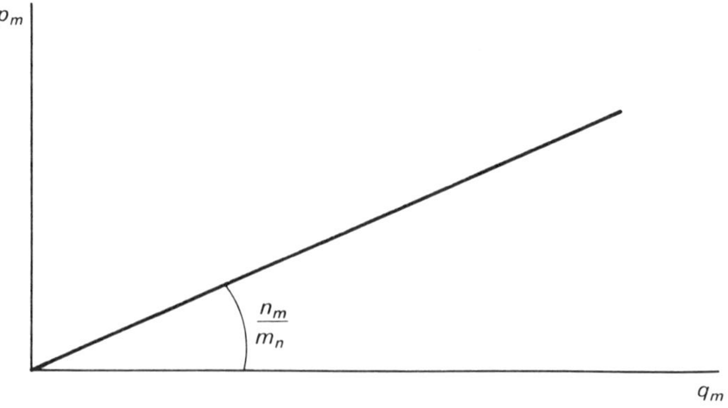

Figure 4.1

Clearly,

$$\frac{dw_m}{dp_m} = \frac{n_m}{l_m} \; p_m^{-2} > 0, \text{ and } \frac{d^2w_m}{dp_m^2} = -\,2\,\frac{n_m}{l_m} \; p_m^{-3} < 0.$$

Substituting from (4.10):

$$w_m = \frac{1}{l_m}\left(1 - \frac{m_n}{q_m}\right), \tag{4.12}$$

which obviously has the same shape – namely, that of a hyperbola that approaches – infinity when $w_m = 0$, and $1/l_m$ when p_m approaches infinity. When $w_m = 0$ the curve cuts the horizontal axis at $p_m = n_m$ (Figure 4.2).

Standard Marxism and Neo-Ricardian Theory

The difficulties this simple model poses for the three approaches to the theory of value are readily seen. Standard treatments of Marxism, for example, face a serious problem interpreting the concept of labor time. Workers in the two sectors perform different tasks, presumably using different skills and facing different problems and dangers. An hour of labor time, therefore, does not mean the same thing in the two production processes. A common way of circumventing the issue is to interpret labor as the product of the consumption that supports it. Two different lines of work are comparable even though the jobs performed and skills employed are different because the labor time is supported by the same consumption. But this avenue is closed here, since the two sets of workers consume

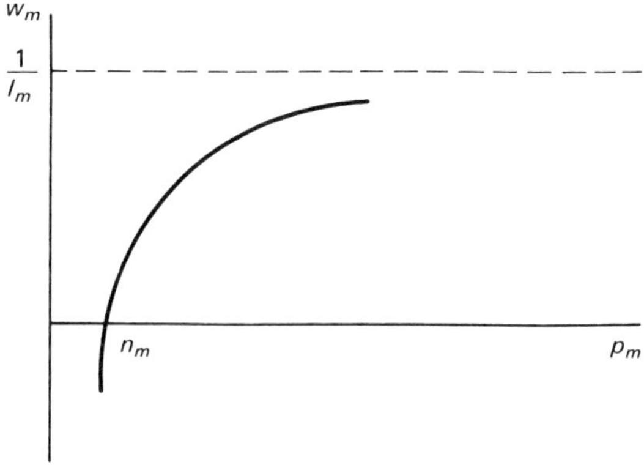

Figure 4.2

different commodities. If labor time has no meaning, however, standard Marxism is in serious trouble. Since c, v, and s are all expressed in labor time, no analysis is possible without a well-defined basic labor unit.

The concept of simple commodity production also comes to grief. Interpret each sector as a guild, owned by its workers and operating at a stationary level (no growth). Each guild consumes its own product and trades with the other for means of production. According to the traditional doctrine, each set of workers should obtain the same net earning per unit of direct labor. This would suggest equilibrium at the point, $w_n = w_m p_m$. But there is absolutely no reason for this. There is no unit of direct labor; there are *two* kinds of direct labor with no connection between them until their relative value is established. Simple commodity production is indeterminate in this case.

Neo-Ricardian models customarily write a vector of labor times in the different sectors. This is invalid in the present model for the same reasons. Hence these models, too, cannot handle this case. Of course, this need not bother proponents of such an approach, since once a rate of profit is introduced, prices can be determined. Since neo-Ricardians are opposed to the labor theory of value as an account of prices, this would appear simply as a special case supporting their general position.

However, the flaw in neo-Ricardian models lies in the fact that they have no explanation of the surplus. It is simply there – by postulate. The matrix of 'input coefficients' is assumed to be 'productive.' Like Samuelson they rely on exogenous 'inventions' that have somehow taken place in the past. However it happened, it has already taken place and has nothing to do with the analysis of exchange value and reproduction. We shall return to this point in a moment; first, there is the question of how a neo-Classical approach would handle this model.

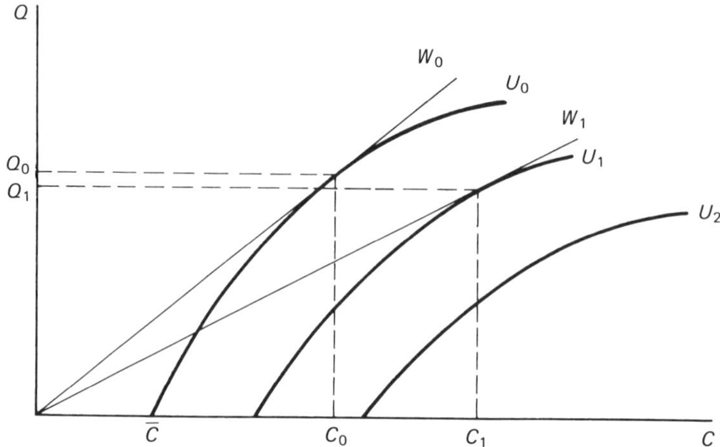

Note: A rise in the wage, from W_0 to W_1, leads to a higher level of consumption, C_1, and a higher level of utility, U_1, but to a lower output, Q_1.

Figure 4.3

Neo-Classical Theory

There are two possibilities, a short-run or stationary-state analysis in terms of the disutility of labor, and a long-run approach, which adds consideration of the rate of profit and time preference. According to conventional theory, the amount of labor performed will depend on the disutility of additional labor as compared with the utility yielded by the reward in consumption. This can be illustrated by a simple diagram (Figure 4.3) in which we measure the quantity of output on one axis and the amount of consumption on the other. Iso-utility curves then show the amount of consumption that would be required to compensate for the disutility of the labor involved in producing given amounts of output[10] (remembering that production coefficients are fixed).

If Q is measured on the vertical axis, then a definite amount of consumption, $C = \bar{C}$, will be required to compensate for the disutility of producing any Q at all, and as Q increases more and more C will be needed to compensate additional Q. Next, add a line from the origin, representing the 'wage' obtained by producing the output. Since there are constant returns, this will be a straight line rising from left to right. The point where this line is tangent to an iso-utility curve gives the absolute quantity the producer will produce and the corresponding total consumption he will obtain at that wage.

We can draw the diagrams for different assumptions about the shape of the utility functions. For example, assume that for C_m, a rise in the real wage (a downward swing of the line) will call forth more labor – that is, Q_m

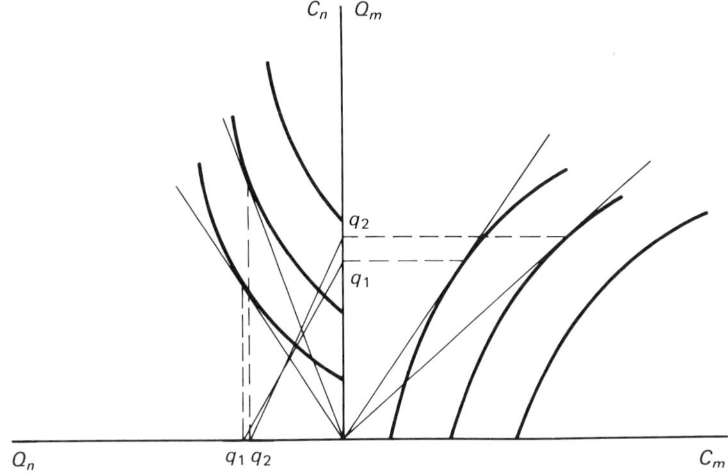

Figure 4.4

increases. But in the case of Q_n, let a rise in the real wage result in a diminished willingness to work, so Q_n decreases. Put two diagrams together by flipping the second one over on its side and plotting C_n along the Q_m axis (Figure 4.4). Then join up the points on the respective Q axes that correspond to a given wage pair. Thus to (w_{m1}, w_{n1}) there corresponds the line q_1q_1, the slope of which gives the *relative* quantities produced. When w_m falls and w_n rises, there will be a new relative quantity line, q_2q_2. We can thus read off the relationships between w_m and q_m; they will depend on the assumed shapes of the indifference curves. Starting from $w_m = 0$, no m will be offered; w_n will be at its maximum, so $Q_n > 0$, but will be low. Then as w_m rises and w_n falls, *after a point* Q_m will rise, while Q_n will also increase. If

$$\left| \frac{dQ_m}{dw_m} \right| > \left| \frac{dQ_n}{dw_n} \right| ,$$

the curve will have a steep positive slope; otherwise it will be shallow. If the two are equal, then relative quantities will be constant.

Suppose, however, that both producers have regular labor-consumption indifference maps. Then as w_m rises, after a point Q_m rises, and as w_n falls, Q_n falls; hence both effects will cause Q_m to rise with w_m. Suppose both producers have perverse indifference maps. Then as w_m rises, Q_m, initially positive, falls, and as w_n falls, Q_n rises up to a point. Hence the relative quantities will fall as w_m rises.

Since these cases are all expressed as functional relationships between w_m and q_m, we can graph them on the diagram of equation (4.12), which

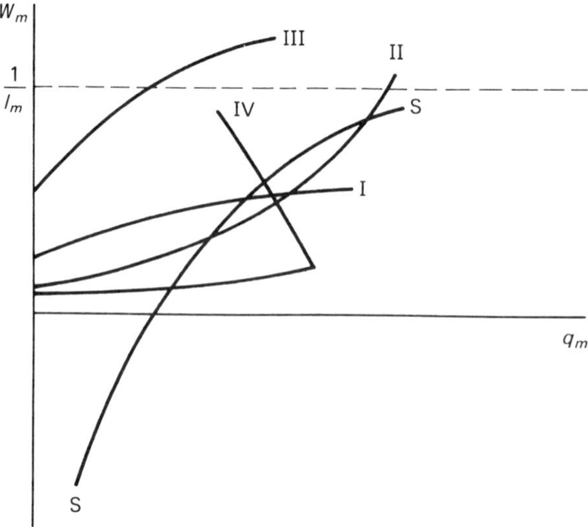

Figure 4.5

expresses the structural relationship between w_m and q_m. (We are assuming that initial supplies are suitable.) However, the resulting graph is not a conventional supply and demand diagram. The structural equation is not analogous to either a supply or demand curve; it shows the pairs, w_m and q_m that *can and must occur together* if the structural assumptions of our simple context are fulfilled. The behavioral relationships, on the other hand, show the w_m necessary to call forth or, more precisely, to compensate for the disutility of producing a certain q_m. An intersection of the two curves, then, is a point at which the chosen (or acceptable) balance between work and consumption is compatible with the structural possibilities and constraints.

Figure 4.5 illustrates four plausible cases; many others can easily be imagined. *SS* is the structural curve, and the others represent different possible behavioral curves corresponding to different assumptions about the indifference curves. Curve *I* represents the case in which both are regular and the minimal wage for the *m*-producer is feasible. A small rise in w_m will cause a large increase in q_m, and we can expect a single intersection. Curve *II* represents the case in which the indifference curves of the *m*-producer are perverse and those of the *n*-producer regular, with the minimal wage feasible. Initially the rise in w_m will, after a point, call forth more *m*-production, while the fall in w_n will reduce *n*-production. But then the perverse effect takes over, and the curve turns sharply up. Two intersections are therefore likely (though there would be none or a tangency point, if the perverse effect took over very early). Curve *III* is the reverse case, in which the *m*-producer has regular, and the *n*-producer perverse, indifference curves. In this case the curve first rises steeply and then flattens when the perverse effect takes over. Unless this is quite early there will be no intersection; otherwise, one. Finally, curve *IV* represents the case in which both producers have perverse indifference maps. The curve begins from a positive w_m intercept and at first rises with a shallow slope, exactly like curve I. But when the perverse effects take over, the curve bends sharply back, now rising from right to left (i.e., the slope becomes *negative*), so that there will be two intersections, unless the perverse effects occur very early.

Stability questions have not been defined for this simple context, so it would be inappropriate to analyze such matters here, beyond remarking that just below the upper of the two intersections of curve *II*, more w_m is available than is required to call forth that q_m, while the reverse is true just below the lower of these two intersections. However the parties react to out-of-equilibrium situations, this kind of consideration will eventually play a determining role.

The Initial Endowments

The initial endowments clearly pose a problem. Assuming an equilibrium exists, the structural equations determine the *relative* outputs, and the behavioral equations determine the *absolute* levels. Hence if the initial endowments of means of production are to be fully and exactly utilized and are to be reproduced regularly, then one and only one set will be compatible with any given equilibrium, since only one set of initial inputs could yield the equilibrium outputs while being fully utilized.

If either or both of the endowments are too small; the equilibrium outputs cannot be produced. But if either or both were too big, equilibrium could be established simply by not using a portion of the endowment. The part not used, however, would then be kept for means of production next period, thus reducing replacement demand, or would be traded for the consumption good, thus reducing current consumer demand. Or, finally, it could be used for some combination of both.

Assume first that one endowment is too big and the other just right, for equilibrium. In terms of Figure 4.5 it is easy to see how the excess endowment could be used to permit the system to end up with the equilibrium output, so that when the excess endowment is used up, the system would be able regularly to reproduce the correct endowments. Suppose that there is excess endowment of m. It might seem, then, that a portion of the excess m should be kept by the n-producers as means of production for next period. This would effectively reduce the coefficient, m_n, to a lower value, m'_n, shifting the structural curve inward and making the curvature more pronounced. If the remainder of the excess m went to consumption, then more m could be produced for any given utility map.

This would shift the behavioral curve outward. If the excess endowment were divided so that these two shifts exactly offset one another, this would leave the intersection of the behavioral and structural curves at the same point on the relative quantity axis. The resulting behavior would use up the excess endowment but reproduce the proper relative quantities for the following period, when the curves would return to the positions corresponding to the actual coefficients.

In cases like *IV*, where the curves have opposite slopes, these two movements are clearly offsetting, and the division that will preserve the equilibrium quantities can easily be calculated. But a difficulty arises in cases like *I* and *II*, where the curves have the same slopes, for then both movements tend in the same direction.

The above is necessary to reach the correct relative quantities for reproduction, but it is inconsistent with the price system. The endowment of m is given to the producer of n; hence the producer of n will retain part of his excess endowment, or additional means of production, and will trade the rest to the producer of m, who is also the consumer of m. But the producer of m has to trade m for n at the correct price, $p_m = (n_m/m'_n)(q_m)$; to increase the consumption of m, the producer of n would have to take that much less m in exchange for the n required as means of production for m. The correct price follows from the (revised) coefficients and the quantities alone; to reduce the amount of m exchanged any further would raise its price above the proper level, in effect making a gift of the excess m. In other words, with an excess endowment of only one good, transactions leading to the equilibrium cannot take place consistently with the postulates of scarcity and value, in conjunction with the price equations.[11]

Completing the Model

So far we have treated only part of the neo-Classical analysis. To develop a complete model we should have to include an examination of time preference and the rate of profit. But it will not actually be necessary to enter into a detailed discussion of such a model, for two striking facts immediately confront us. The first is that the theory of time preference and the rate of return is an *additional* consideration; it does not supplant the theory of the disutility of labor. Hence the difficulties uncovered above still stand. For instance, once we introduce the rate of profit, the equations read:

$$(1 + r)n_m + w_m p_m l_m = p_m. \tag{4.13}$$

$$(1 + r)m_n p_m + w_n l_n = 1. \tag{4.14}$$

These must now be interpreted as representing specifically capitalist institutional arrangements. We have left simple commodity production behind. Assuming that all profits are invested and all wages consumed:

$$(1 + g)m_n + c_m q_m l_m = q_m. \tag{4.15}$$

$$(1 + g)n_m q_m + c_n l_n = 1. \tag{4.16}$$

Eliminating p_m yields,

$$w_m = \frac{1}{l_m}\left[1 + \frac{(1 + r)^2 n_m m_n}{(w_n l_n - 1)}\right]; \tag{4.17}$$

so that, given r, w_n is determined as a hyperbolic function of w_m. Thus, if capitalists' time preference determines a level of the rate of profit, an analysis similar to that just examined will be needed to determine w_m and q_m and thus w_n. As we have just seen, there is no reason to suppose that any solution exists or, if it does, that it will be unique. Hence, a long-run neo-Classical approach is beset with the same difficulties that afflict the short-run stationary version.

Worse is to come. The model has no concept of labor-in-general. It can be argued that even though existing workers are specialized both as to skills and consumption, so that they will not shift employment, new entrants or potential new entrants to the labor force are not so restricted. Hence, once we are considering the long-run position of the economy, we must introduce some concept of a real wage made uniform by competitive pressures.[12]

Perhaps surprisingly, this is not at all difficult. We define ω in analogy with the rate of profit, as the percent of extra consumption – or real wages – over the level socially necessary and normal for subsistence. Thus we must introduce a socio-historical subsistence norm; but once we take this as defined, the competitive pressures generated by potential new entrants to the labor force will see that the percentage by which the actual wage exceeds this is kept the same in the two sectors. The equations are now:

$$(1 + r)n_m + \omega w_m p_m l_m = p_m. \tag{4.18}$$

$$(1 + r)m_n p_m + \omega w_n l_n = 1, \tag{4.19}$$

where w_m and w_n are now taken as fixed. Eliminating p_m gives r in terms of w:

$$1 + r = [1 - \omega(w_n l_n + w_m l_m) + \omega^2(w_n l_n w_m l_m)]^{1/2}. \tag{4.20}$$

3 THE MARXIAN SOLUTION

The surplus emerges because employers make workers do more work in a given time than is needed to reproduce the goods they consume during that time. This must now be shown in the equations. We introduce a variable, t, to indicate the speed of production, the number of times input is converted into output during the period for which wages are paid. Since each sector uses the other's output as means of production, the two sectors must coordinate the timing of production. If one sector finished before the other, it would not be able to sell its product since the other would not yet be in a position to buy. If the faster-producing sector nevertheless kept its workers on, at make-work jobs, it would lose the advantages of speeding up. But if it laid its workers off while waiting for the other sector to finish, it would confirm workers in the belief that working harder or faster just leads to unemployment.[13] With a uniform t, then we have

$$(1 + r)tn_m + \omega w_m p_m l_m = tp_m. \tag{4.21}$$

$$(1 + r)tm_n p_m + \omega w_n l_n = t. \tag{4.22}$$

We define these variables so that when

$$t = \omega = 1, r = 0; \tag{4.23}$$

(i.e., the economy can just support and reproduce itself). A positive rate of profit will emerge when $t > \omega \gtreqless 1$. For $\omega = 1$, the subsistence wage, t therefore represents the rate of exploitation. When $t > 1$, $\omega = 1$, a surplus will be produced. Aggregate gross production will be in the same proportions as in the simple reproduction case ($t = 1$). Hence aggregate *net* production will be in the same ratio as the subsistence wage bills. The surplus, in other words, will consist of quantities of the two consumer goods, in the same ratio they are required for subsistence. The ratio of this composite surplus product to the aggregate means of subsistence does not depend on prices; it is a pure quantity ratio, which reflects the intensity of work.[14] Since the quantities in the numerator and denominator consist of the composite subsistence good, the ratio measures 'unpaid labor' to 'paid labor;' it is precisely Marx's rate of exploitation. It in no way implies that relative prices equal ratios of direct plus indirect embodied labor times. On the contrary, we can see from the equations that prices will depend on the rate of profits. The rate of profit, however, depends on t, the measure of the rate of exploitation. Hence *exploitation explains both prices and the rate of profit, even when labor is fully heterogeneous*.

This can be seen by solving the equations for r in terms of t:

$$r = [(t - \omega w_n l_n)(t - \omega w_m l_m)]^{1/2}[t^2 m_n n_m]^{-1/2} - 1; \tag{4.24}$$

and for p_m in terms of t:

$$p_m = [(t - \omega w_n l_n)tn_m]^{1/2} [(t - \omega w_m l_m)tm_n]^{-1/2}. \tag{4.25}$$

Thus the choice-of-technique arguments fail. The analysis moved at too abstract a plane; it was developed without regard for the fact that any change of technology involves moving from one concrete actual situation, in which the balance of forces in the workplace can (often) reasonably be taken as known and 'frozen,' to a new, as yet untried situation, in which it can only be estimated. More important, the 'balance of class forces' – and therefore the position of the wage-profit frontier – depends on factors different in kind from those determining material input into output. Social and political questions predominate in the former, engineering in the latter. Marx sought precisely to separate, and then relate, these two categories of influences on the rate of profits.

4 SUMMARY

Samuelson claims that the labor theory of value is totally without use value. No new insights are provided by any of its concepts. The rate of surplus value does not explain the rate of profits, and labor values provide an incorrect account of prices. Marx simply followed a blind alley when he developed the argument of Volume I.

But Samuelson failed to look at the structure of Marx's argument. Marx provided an account of value-in-exchange and showed this to depend on the conditions in which labor is exploited and compelled to produce a surplus, which capital appropriates through the exchange mechanism. Marx's approach proved able to handle a simple but significant model in which Marx*ist*, neo-Classical, and neo-Ricardian analyses all came to grief. Exchange accomplishes both replacement and distribution, exploitation explains the production of the surplus, and the rate of exploitation explains both prices and the rate of profit. Far from following a detour, Marx's route lay right along the turnpike. Neo-Classical theory pictures value-in-exchange as arising from the interaction of relative preferences and relative scarcity, given some postulate of insatiable wants. In contrast, Marx sees value as the expression of the exploitation of labor; exchange accomplishes at one and the same time both the allocation necessary for reproduction and the appropriation of the surplus, while understanding the buying and selling of labor power provides the key to grasping the origin of the surplus. The neo-Classical picture leads one to analyze markets in terms of harmony and optimization. Marx's approach takes one beneath the surface to class conflict at the point of production and relates this to the circulation of capital (the turnover between money-form and commodity-form), the interdependence of sectors, and the appropriation of the surplus in the form of profits. This provides the foundation for a *political* analysis of economic relationships.

Appendix: A Generalization

The 2×2 model developed so far can easily be generalized. Let A be a productive, irreducible input–output matrix with circulating capital. Then let L be a matrix of different kinds of labor inputs, and B be a matrix of the consumption goods consumed by the different kinds of labor. (In relation to the earlier notation, these would be:

$$A = \begin{bmatrix} O & m_n \\ n_m & O \end{bmatrix}, \quad L = \begin{bmatrix} l_m & O \\ O & l_n \end{bmatrix}, \quad B = \begin{bmatrix} W_m/t & O \\ O & w_n/t \end{bmatrix}$$

So we can write the price equation:

$$p = (1 + r)\, pA = wL,$$

where $w = pB$ is fixed.

So

$$p = (1 + r)\, p[A + BL]$$

Then if $B = 1/t\ \hat{B}$

where $\hat{B} > 0$ and is such that

$$\hat{p} = \hat{p}\ (A + \hat{B}L) \text{ with } \hat{p} > 0,$$

we can show that r and p are functions of t alone, and that r increases with t.

This can be seen by rewriting the price equation as

$$p = p\ [(1 + r)\ A + 1/t\ \hat{B}L].$$

Then, from the irreducibility of A, we know

$$e[(1 + r)\ A + 1/t\ \hat{B}L] = 1$$

and so the relative prices will be determined by $(1 + r)/a + 1/t\hat{B}L$.

Clearly, given the irreducibility of A, r is a function of t alone and since A, $\hat{B}$ and L are given, so is the price vector. Moreover, $t < t'$ implies $r < r'$. For if $t < t'$ and $r < r'$, then $1 = e[(1 + r')A + 1/t'\hat{B}L)] < e[(1 + r)A + 1/t\hat{B}L] = 1$, a contradiction. Thus r varies directly with t; speeding up raises profit.

Notes

1. Though this study is critical of Samuelson, it should be said at the outset that his work on Marx is admirable both for its vigor and its clarity. It marks a milestone in the serious reevaluation of Marx.
2. As Ricardo recognized, however, embodied labor won't do under free competitive conditions, except in the special case, assumed by Marx in Volume I, in which all industries or departments have equal organic compositions of capital. Capital will flow to where rates of return are highest, thus establishing a uniform rate of profits, and the resulting prices will not reflect direct embodied labor, although, as we shall see, they will vary with changes in the productivity of labor.
3. Concrete labor is easy to understand, abstract labor more difficult. The distinction between them must not be confused with the distinction between simple and skilled labor, both of which are concrete. The reduction of skilled labor to simple is, for Marx, largely a matter of history and custom, including the ability (or lack of it) of groups to entrench themselves and enhance their status. It 'rests in part on pure illusion, or to say the least, on distinctions that have long since ceased to be real, and that survive only by virtue of a traditional convention, in part on the helpless condition of some groups of the working class,' (Marx 1967, Vol. I, p. 192, no. 1).
4. 'When it steps into circulation as money, its value is already given . . . This value is determined by the labor-time required for its production' (Marx 1967, p. 92). [Exchange requires not only a universal equivalent, but a fit and proper one. 'The truth of the proposition that, "although gold and silver are not by nature money, money is by nature gold and silver," is shown by the fitness of the physical properties of these metals for the functions of money' (ibid., p. 89)]. When Marx's theory determines the money wage, it also fixes the real wage. Hence, though Marx's insistence that money is an essential moment in the turnover of capital, so that exchange value *must* be expressed in money terms, is fundamental to understanding both effective demand and accumulation in Marxian terms, the theory of exploitation can make use of the neo-Ricardian equation system.
5. 'So far as regards use-value, it is clear that both parties may gain some advantage. Both part with goods that, as use-values, are of no service to them, and receive others that they can make use of. . . . With reference, then, to use-value, there is good ground for saying that exchange is a transaction by which both sides gain. It is otherwise with exchange-value' (Marx 1967, p. 157).
6. 'Suppose, then, that by some inexplicable privilege' a seller is able to sell at some percentage above what he previously paid. He seems to pocket a gain. Then he goes to buy and finds all other sellers now offering only at the higher prices. Or suppose one capitalist is clever enough to take advantage of another; what the one gains, the other loses. The total amount of value in circulation is unaltered. 'If equivalents are exchanged, no surplus-value results, and if non-equivalents are exchanged, still no surplus-value' (Marx 1967, p. 160).
7. Marx attached an important footnote to this passage, which explains why he insisted on assuming the SLTV throughout Volume I '. . . the formation of capital must be possible even though the price and value of a commodity be the same; for its formation cannot be attributed to any deviation of the one from the other' (1967, p. 166). He knew perfectly well that, in general, prices deviate from value – Volume III was drafted before Volume I was written – but he wanted to forestall the notion that the existence of profit could be explained by a systematic discrepancy between price and value. Hence 'to explain' profit at

all, it must first be explained on the assumption that prices equal values.' Dobb made this point long ago (1972, Chapter I).

8. It should be evident that this argument does not depend on whether the true values of goods are measured by ratios of embodied labor times or by prices. The subsistence goods support labor for a given time; whatever their prices are, the real wage is thus the equivalent of a certain amount of labor time. Hence the rate of exploitation can be expressed in terms of the division of the working day. Samuelson and other critics are surely right on this point.
9. These are, of course, not separate stages in reality; they are separated *methodologically* for the purposes of analysis. The first part of Volume I examines the first stage; later parts of Volume I take up the second stage. (The section on 'Primitive [*original* – a mistranslation) Accumulation' indicates some of the ways by which society became divided into a class of owners and a mass of propertyless workers). Volume III then (not altogether adequately) shows how a rate of profit and prices of production will be formed on the basis of the surplus value so produced.
10. Recall our strong assumption that each group of workers consumes only its own product. Here 'tastes' are pronounced and uncompromising; no doubt if the two groups of workers were willing to consume each other's goods baskets, at suitable tradeoffs, neo-Classical theory would fare better. But that is admitting that orthodox theory cannot handle strong differences in tastes, even while it celebrates individual variety. The argument is designed to show that none of the three usual approaches can handle 'heterogeneous labor,' while Marx's theory can. To assume that both set of workers have the same or similar utility functions violates the terms of the problem.
11. Suppose there were excess endowments of both goods. An intuitive argument suggests that, in general, there can be no presumption that equilibrium can be reached, using all of both endowments. Start with the division of *m* between consumption and means of production (assuming the best case, that the curves are shaped so that the shifts are offsetting) on the hypothesis that all excess *n* is used for means of production. The formula $p_m = (n'_m / lm'_n)q_m$ then gives the price at which *m* and *n* must exchange, and the problem will be that the portion of *m* consumed causes the actual exchange ratio to diverge from this. By allocating a suitable part of the excess *n* to consumption, however, this would be remedied; the *m*-producer could trade excess *n* to the *n*-producer for his excess *m*, and all will be well if this consumption trade takes place at the same exchange ratio, p_m that prevails in the trade for means of production. But any allocation of *n* to consumption will shift the function expressing the willingness to produce *n* for a given wage w_n. Hence an allocation of excess *n* to consumption must be matched by a corresponding allocation of *m*, to keep the relative amounts in the equilibrium ratio, q_m. It is clear that these changes need not lead to the desired pattern of exchange, for as the allocation of excess *n* to consumption is increased, the allocation of excess *m* to consumption will also increase, and for exactly the same reason both 'effective coefficients' will move in the same direction. Hence, while cases may well exist in which the trade of excess endowment for consumption purposes will take place at the price that prevails in the exchange of means of production, there can be no general presumption that such an all-around exchange ratio exists.
12. Notice that this is not a way open to simple commodity production. According to that scheme, workers own their own means of production. Hence new entrants would inherit a position from retiring workers, so would enter *already specialized*. No competitive pressures would be generated.

13. Of course, inventories could be carried, but at a cost that would have to be compared to the costs of finishing up and waiting. *Given* an inventory policy, however, the slowest producer sets the pace; no one can produce at a faster clip than that, apart from the inventory leeway.
14. The dual of this, however, will be found at the point on the wage-profit frontier where $r = 0$ and $\omega = \omega$. The prices associated with this point will equal ratios of embodied labor time; and ω_{max} will equal the rate of exploitation just defined. (For further analysis, see Nell, 1964, pp. 155–221.)
15. Ulrich Krause has pointed out in private correspondence that these results neatly generalize. For an earlier treatment of exploitation and work intensity, extended to heterogeneous labor, see Nell (1964).
16. Accepting neo-Classical theory's proposed determination of t or t/ω would just get it out of the frying pan into the fire. By the same token we should have to accept a time preference determination of the rate of profit. As we noted earlier, that means adding two equations, one for t/ω and one for r, to a system that has only one degree of freedom. (Since t/ω is a ratio of intensity of effort to pay, it is the appropriate variable for utility theory to determine.)
17. If we relax the either/or assumption above – equal capital–labor ratios in all sectors, or being in the standard proportions – then the wage rate–profit rate frontiers will no longer be straight lines, and they may intersect several times. This is significant for the critique of neo-Classical theory, but has no bearing on the present argument.
18. The argument and the diagram are presented, for simplicity, on the un-Marxian assumption that profit is not figured on advanced wages. If wages were advanced as part of capital, then changes in the intensity of work would change not only the vertical intercept but also the horizontal one of the wage–profit frontier. A speedup, for example, would increase output for a given wage bill, raising the rate of exploitation and profits in the same proportion, but only part of capital, constant capital, would be raised in that proportion. Hence the maximum rate of profit would be raised.

References

Dobb, M. (1972) *The Political Economy and Capitalism: Some Essays in Economic Tradition* (Westport, Conn.: Greenwood Press).

Krause, U. (1981) 'Heterogeneous Labour and the Fundamental Marxian Theorem,' *Review of Economic Studies*, 48, pp. 173–8.

Marx, K. (1967) *Capital*, 3 Vols (New York: International Publishers).

Nell, E.J. (1964) 'Models of Behavior with Special Reference to Certain Economic Theories,' B. Litt. (Oxford).

Nell, E.J. (1980) 'Value and Capital in Marxian Economics,' *Public Interest*, Fifteenth Anniversary Issue: 'The Crisis in Economic Theory.'

Samuelson, P.A. (1971) 'Understanding the Marxian Notion of Exploitation: A Summary of the So-Called Transformation Problem between Marxian Values and Competitive Prices,' *Journal of Economic Literature*, 9(2), pp. 399–431.

Samuelson, P.A. (1977) *The Collected Scientific Papers of Paul A. Samuelson*, Vol. 4, H. Nagatani and K. Crowley (eds) (Cambridge, Mass.: MIT Press).

Walras, L. (1954) *Elements of Pure Economics*, W. Jaffe (ed.) London: Allen & Unwin).

Part II
Capital Theory in a Growing Economy

The accumulation of capital is the starting point for the surplus approach and, accordingly, Chapter 5 surveys the neo-Classical attempt to give marginal productivity answers to Keynesian questions in a growth model and summarizes the resulting controversy over the nature of capital, concluding with a critique of 'steady growth' and a brief introduction to transformational growth. The next three studies (Chapters 6–8) take up particular points in the capital critique. Chapter 6 explores the implications for the theory of the firm, contending that neo-Classical theories of distribution and of the the firm are inconsistent with one another. Chapter 7 provides a thorough treatment of reswitching, demonstrating its generality and the strength and implausibility of the assumptions needed to rule it out, even in relatively simple models. It also covers a number of closely related issues involving marginal productivity concepts, concluding that, in general, the relationship between 'capital goods' and 'capital funds' required by neo-Classical theory does not exist. Chapter 8 examines the suggestion that, even if the inverse relation between capital–intensity and the rate of profit does not exist, the efficiency properties of the price system can be demonstrated, since the rate of return will always correctly measure the ratio of benefits in future consumption to sacrifices of present consumption. This theorem is shown to hold only in special conditions, and to rely on very special definitions of terms and to require particular institutional assumptions. The fifth study (Chapter 9) turns to a consideration of alternative theories of distribution, arguing that the role of institutions and institutional and technological change in determining distribution has not been adequately examined. Finally, the last study of Part II (Chapter 10) argues on purely analytical grounds that no steady-state growth path can exist for a class society. In class societies, growth must be transformational; it cannot be steady. This leads us therefore to Part III, on Transformational Growth.

5 Accumulation and Capital Theory*

As Joan Robinson's views matured, the study of expansion through the accumulation of capital moved more and more to central stage, and she increasingly sought to group other questions around it. Yet it proved a difficult nut to crack. Accumulation has been analyzed by economists in two very different ways, between which she moved uneasily. The most common has been to see it as the expansion of the productive potential of an economy with a given technology, which may be improved in the process – this was her basic stance. But it has also been understood as the outright transformation of the technical and productive organization of the economy, an outlook of which she thoroughly approved, but which played almost no role in her analytics.

The first approach bases its thinking on the idea of steady growth, subsuming the concerns of the second under the heading of 'technical progress'. The resulting analysis rests on a conception of capital as productive goods, or, in more sophisticated versions, as a fund providing command over productive goods. This is not wrong; it is merely inadequate. Capital must also be understood, and this is the second approach, as a way of organizing production and economic activity, so that the accumulation of capital is the extension of this form of organization into areas in which production, exchange and distribution were governed by other rules. This conception of capital, in contrast to the first, more limited notion, emphasizes the importance of organization; so understood, technology and engineering are not abstract science, existing apart from capital; they are ways of organizing production, and so have an institutional dimension. Accumulation then implies the transformation of institutions as well as production, and steady growth is not applicable (except perhaps as a benchmark).

Besides the distinction between steady state and transformational growth, there is another principal division in the way that economists have thought about accumulation, and here Joan Robinson chose sides quite unambiguously. One view sees it as 'ploughing back' part of the surplus arising from production; the other as the process of adjusting a scarce resource to its optimal uses, as determined by the market. According to the first, the classical 'surplus' approach, accumulation consists of the productive

* G.R. Feiwel (ed.), *Joan Robinson and Modern Economic Theory* (London: Macmillan, 1989).

investment of part of society's net product – the surplus of output over necessary consumption and the requirements for maintaining capital intact – in order to expand productive capacity to take advantage of new or developing markets. The study of accumulation, therefore, needs to explain both the availability of the surplus and the motivation for ploughing it back – and, referring to the previous distinction, this can be examined either as steady-state expansion or as part of a process of transformation.

The originators of the classical tradition saw accumulation primarily as a transformation of the economy. Smith stressed institutional changes, in particular the development of markets and the removal of state barriers, but his analytics were incomplete and partially incorrect. Ricardo offered only a rudimentary explanation of the surplus, in the 'iron law of wages'; accumulation, however, he saw as the natural activity of capitalists, although it would be limited by the rise of food prices caused by the extension of cultivation to marginal lands, shifting distribution in favor of rent. Marx located the origin of the surplus in the exploitation of labor, and found the cause of the tendency of the rate of profit to fall in the interaction of competition and technological advance, rather than in pressure on marginal land. Rosa Luxemburg accepted Marx's framework, but located the limits to accumulation in a systematic failure of domestic demand to keep pace with the expansion of capacity, requiring the conquest of overseas markets. Each offered a picture with a grand sweep, painted in large strokes. Modern 'surplus' theory, even Joan Robinson's, is more circumspect and less interesting.

The other approach, which Joan Robinson totally rejected, sees accumulation or decumulation of capital simply as the adjustment of a particular factor of production to its equilibrium level, as determined by supply and demand. In this conception (exemplified, e.g. by Hayek, 1941, Ch.xx), factor equilibrium is defined in terms of the optimal allocation of scarce resources to competing tasks (in turn defined by the equilibrium final bill of goods, again determined by supply and demand). The supply of capital may either be taken as given, along with that of land and labor, or it may be seen as governed by saving behavior, and so responsive, through time preference, to the rate of interest. Demand for capital will be governed by its productivity at the margin, as with the other factors. Equilibrium in a particular sector comes when supply to that sector equals the demand for capital arising in it; equilibrium in general comes when the overall supply of capital equals the overall demand for it. So, according to this conception, accumulation occurs only when the economy is in disequilibrium – it is the movement along the path to equilibrium, or to a new equilibrium, occasioned perhaps by a shift in preferences or the effects of a technical innovation. The central economic problem is the optimal allocation of scarce resources, and accumulation of capital is simply an adjustment towards this objective – a perspective which Joan not only rejected, but held to be incoherent, since 'capital' was not a factor of production in the required sense. Nor could such an approach account for technical progress.

This last judgement may have been misguided. Allocation is a matter of given resources and given competing ends; it is clearly not suited, therefore, to the analysis of transformation. But neo-Classical ingenuity should not be underestimated. Technical knowledge itself can be treated as a scarce resource, and the incentives to produce it and allocate it optimally can be studied by neo-Classical methods. Thus the allocation approach can give rise to an account, albeit a little far-fetched, of the long-term transformation of the economy. And it does address the issue of the incentives to innovate, which Joan never did.

But a reallocation process has a natural ending at the equilibrium point, whereas capital accumulation appears to be limitless. A stationary equilibrium must be a point of 'bliss', in which no further capital can be usefully employed. Hence net saving must be zero, and all net income consumed. Locked into such an allocation/disequilibrium framework, the supply and demand approach would be unable even to examine adequately the (Keynesian) contention that a capitalist system must either expand or collapse into recession, the starting point for Robinson's approach. It was saved from this fate by the development of the neo-Classical growth model, based on the aggregate production function, and thus combining aspects of the traditional 'surplus' approach with supply and demand, a mix to which Joan Robinson fiercely objected. The neo-Classical model provides an account of 'steady growth' over the long run, that is, uniform expansion of all outputs and all inputs, taking place together with regular technical progress. Its working, in turn, is based on the traditional theory of competitive factor markets, with substitution between labor and capital in the process of production, where both factors are expressed in aggregate terms, and where 'factor prices' function analogously to commodity prices in the usual theory of markets.

1 THE KEYNESIAN PROBLEMATIC

The question of substitution initially arose because a simple Keynesian growth model with a given capital–output ratio led Harrod to the disturbing conclusion that neither steady growth nor optimal allocation could be achieved. Aggregate demand equals investment times the multiplier, or I/s, in the simplest case, where s is the average and marginal propensity to save. Aggregate supply, then, is the capital stock times its productivity, or K/v, where v is the capital–output ratio. So the growth rate, $G = I/K = s/v$. This is the rate which equates supply and demand; hence it is the one that business will find satisfactory. But nothing has been said about the labor force or employment; so the equilibrium growth rate need not be consistent with the growth of the labor force (adjusted for neutral technical progress), a condition which cannot be optimal. Nor is that the only problem. When I is too low, so that $I/K <$ full employment s/v, $I/s < K/v$, and there will be excess capacity; so businesses will be inclined to reduce I still further. Similarly when I is too large, there will appear to be capacity shortage, and businesses will be inclined to increase I still more. The system gives the wrong signals, and a deviation from steady growth will tend to worsen, rather than correct itself. (Cf. Ch. 23, Section 3)

Joan Robinson's reaction was to question the use of the capital–output ratio as an accelerator in the account of deviations from the steady path. Investment decisions were more complex and the possibilities more numerous and less disastrous than this suggested. But the neo-Classicals got in first.

2 THE NEO-CLASSICAL RESPONSE

Substitution in response to price signals appears to 'correct' these Keynesian problems. The neo-Classical model determines a path of steady and stable full employment growth. For instance, when the rate of growth of labor, in efficiency units (the 'natural' rate of growth), persistently exceeds the rate, s/v, determined by the propensity to save and the capital–output ratio (the rate that will just balance aggregate demand and aggregate supply), the real-wage will tend to fall, leading firms to substitute labor for capital. As a result, v, the capital–output ratio will decline, raising the rate of growth, s/v. So long as the production function is 'well behaved' (linear and homogeneous, positive first and negative second derivatives, marginal product of capital tends to infinity as K/L tends to zero, and tends to zero as K/L to infinity), there will exist a value of v that will equate s/v to any natural rate of growth. Technical progress which leaves the K/Y ratio unchanged (Harrod-neutral) will not affect the steady-growth path; technical progress which leaves the ratio of the marginal products of capital and labor unchanged (Hicks-neutral) will change the path, but the economy should adjust smoothly to the new equilibrium. In the Keynesian case, investment determined savings; here that causality is reversed (and so the instability disappears – by fiat): in the long run, all saving will be invested; persistent excess capacity (resulting from planned saving > planned investment at full employment) would drive down the rate of interest by lowering the return (or raising the risk) on existing securities; the lower rate of interest will then raise investment up to the full employment level.

Of course, Joan Robinson would have none of this. It was pre-Keynesian in its approach to saving and investment, and it treated capital as a scarce factor, whose price – the rate of interest – fell as its amount relative to other factors rose. But capital is not a simple factor; it consists of miscellaneous produced means of production added together in value terms. Nor is this 'adding-up' arbitrary or insignificant; capital is shifted about from one line of industry to another precisely in response to the return obtained on the *amount* of it, as measured in value. This led to the famous controversy. But Joan Robinson objected to the neo-Classical model even on its own terms.

3 OPTIMALITY AND THE GOLDEN RULE

In neo-Classical theory, equilibria tend also to be optimal, but very early in the game she showed that in general the steady-growth path will not be. An optimal path ought to be one along which *per capita* consumption is at a maximum. Consumption is output minus investment, and investment must grow at a fixed rate in order to fully employ the growing labor force. Now consider different capital–output ratios: if the marginal product of capital at a certain v adds more to output than is required to equip the labor force, consumption rises; if it adds less, consumption falls. Since the marginal product falls as v rises when the marginal product of capital just equals the additional investment required for the growing labor force, consumption will be a maximum. But there is no reason to expect this level of the marginal product to be associated with the capital–output ratio that makes s/v just equal to the rate of growth of the labor force.

The proposition that consumption per head is maximized when the rate of profit equals the rate of growth is sometimes called the 'Golden Rule of Growth.' Under constant returns, it has another disconcerting implication for neo-Classical theory. In the stationary state, a positive rate of profit implies that the choice of technique (of the capital–output ratio) is suboptimal. In the stationary state (the normal assumption underlying textbook price theory), only a zero rate of profit is consistent with optimal technique. But a zero rate of profit implies that the labor theory of value governs long-run prices! Either long-run prices are determined by growth theory, or they reflect labor values, or the techniques in use are suboptimal. (Non-constant returns make this more complicated, but the heart of the problem remains: allocation theory cannot determine long-run prices and optimal techniques independently of growth theory, and therefore of the 'surplus approach.') Joan Robinson opted for the last of these, arguing that a 'benevolent authority' would choose the optimal technique because it would set prices so that the rate of profit equalled the planned growth rate, whereas the market system, in general (and in practice), would not. But the choice of technique was only part of the conventional story; there was also the matter of the impact of a new technique, and how to analyze this.

4 TECHNICAL PROGRESS

Treating technical progress as a shift of one kind or another in the production function limits the field of study to changes in method, overlooking the introduction of new products, and indeed, whole new sectors. Treating it as autonomous or as a function of time, even, as in 'learning-by-doing,' time on the job, ignores the important influence of demand pressures. Neo-Keynesians, by contrast, treat technical progress as primarily occurring in manufacturing as a response to the growth of demand, so that the rate of technical progress depends on the relative size of manufacturing and on the rate of growth of demand, a relationship known as 'Verdoorn's Law,' which has been widely confirmed. But Joan herself was inconsistent on the subject. In her programmatic remarks she stressed the transformational effects of technical changes, but her analytic work was largely confined to attempts to classify innovations according to their impact on distribution, considered primarily from the supply side, but taking into account the impact of changes in distribution on effective demand. The obvious fact that new products transformed household technology, and so altered living patterns and the structure of family life, radically changing demand, nowhere figured in her analytical work. The distributional effects, however, can also lead to changes in the valuation of capital, a favorite topic of hers. For such changes in valuation invalidated the modelling of capital and distribution in terms of supply and demand.

5 CAPITAL THEORY

The standard version of neo-Classical theory treats capital as a factor of production, on a par with labor and land, where factors are understood in broad terms, and are supplied by households and demanded by firms. The scarcity principle rules: prices are high when a factor is relatively scarce, low when it is plentiful. (The activity analysis version likewise rests on relative scarcity, but it treats each capital good and each form of land or labor separately, determining its marginal product as a shadow price, thereby avoiding difficulties over capital-in-general. But for that very reason activity analysis cannot easily analyze the forces that bear on capital as a whole – for instance, saving and investment and their relation to the rate of interest.) The 'surplus' approach of the classics, especially as developed by Marx, conceives capital as an institution: it is a way of organizing production by means of control over produced means of production, which permits processes of production to be valued so they can be bought and sold. These two approaches are obviously different, but are they necessarily incompatible? Joan Robinson thought so; the high priests of Cambridge, Massachusetts, did not. The capital theory controversy developed over the neo-Classical attempt to show that the aggregate production function's implied ordering of techniques, according to an inverse relationship between profitability and capital intensity, could be constructed in a disaggregated classical or 'surplus' model.

Each point on a neo-Classical production function (whether aggregate or not) represents the adoption of a method of production: the firm or the economy as a whole has fully adjusted its plant and equipment. Moving from one point on a production function to another thus means scrapping old plant and replacing it with new, which implies a burst of exceptionally high activity in the capital goods sector. This will normally be compatible with continuous full employment in the neo-Classical framework only if the consumption goods sector is the more capital intensive, a condition for which there is no economic rationale (Uzawa, 1961), or if certain other special conditions are met (Solow, 1962; weakened by Drandakis, 1963). Moreover, even neo-Classical theorists have shown that very special and strong assumptions, excluding a wide range of plausible technologies and initial conditions, are needed to bring about equilibrium growth (Hahn, 1966). And once we step outside the neo-Classical framework the problem of 'traverse' (moving from one growth path to another), even with a *given* technique, can be shown to imply capacity surplus or shortages in one or more sectors, normally accompanied by temporary overall unemployment (Hicks, 1965; Lowe, 1976). All these points at least indirectly serve to validate Joan Robinson's long-standing contention that mainstream theory construes equilibrium as the end-point of a dynamic process, but has never produced a satisfactory, general account of how or why an economy out of equilibrium would ever get into it. But while Joan finally came to feel that this was her deepest line of criticism, the capital controversy revolved around the application of the scarcity principle to capital and its 'price', the rate of return.

In marginal productivity theory a technique is uniquely designated by (K/Y, K/L); moreover, each K/Y is uniquely paired to its corresponding K/L, and as a direct consequence, each K/L is uniquely associated with a marginal product of capital. But suppose a technique were most profitable at one rate of profit (marginal product of capital), and then also proved the most profitable at another level of the profit rate. If this could happen, the neo-Classical production function would not uniquely determine the choice of method of production. Yet the general possibility of this phenomenon ('reswitching') is easily demonstrated (see Appendix). Moreover, the inverse 'demand' relationship between capital intensity and the rate of profit need not hold; hence the principle of scarcity cannot be invoked to explain the 'use' of capital in production (see Appendix).

Not only the neo-Classical approach is at risk here. If the technique of production which is chosen is the most profitable, and if, in general, there are no grounds for presuming that increasing capital intensity is associated with a lower rate of profit, the Marxian doctrine of the falling rate of profit is likewise rendered suspect (Okishio, 1961) (see Appendix). Profit-maximizing business, operating in competitive conditions, will never choose a technique with a lower rate of profit. Joan Robinson always insisted that Marx's analytics be subjected to the same harsh criticism she inflicted on the orthodox.

6 CONCEPTUALIZING PRODUCTION

Orthodox economists underestimating the importance of dynamics, have argued that the capital controversy revealed nothing more than some anomalous cases which create trouble for the theory of adjustment to equilibrium. But the problem Joan Robinson initially posed concerned the *meaning* of capital as a produced element in the process of production.

Neo-Classical production theory, whether aggregate or not, postulates diminishing marginal output as the amount used of a factor is varied in relation to other factors. If factors are paid the value of their marginal products, as the theory of competitive behavior asserts, then factor reward, e.g. the rate of profit, should fall as the amount of the factor, capital, increases in relation to labor. (If reswitching occurs, it can be demonstrated that at least one of the switches will show a positive relation between capital per worker and the rate of profit.) Once we step outside the conventional approach this inverse relationship is not intuitively plausible: increasing the amount of capital employed in a production process is a more complex matter than employing more labor. Capital consists of all the various means of production; it is a *set* of inputs. In fact, it is more (and more complicated) than that: at the beginning of production the capital of an enterprise consists of its plant and equipment, its inventory of materials and its wage fund (minus various obligations). A little later it consists of somewhat depreciated plant and equipment, together with the worked-up inventory of marketable goods, while the materials and wage fund have disappeared. But (allowing for changes in indebtedness during production, etc.), although the actual goods in which its capital is embodied are different in the two situations, the business will sell for the same price – it has the same capital value. To vary the amount of capital is to change the size or the nature of the entire process, and it is not at all obvious what effect this will have on the rate of profit.

A second problem concerns influences running in the other direction, from the rate of profit to the amount of capital. When the rate of profit changes, competition requires prices to change. (Suppose, *ceteris paribus*, that the real-wage rose, requiring the general rate of profit to fall; to keep the rate uniform, so capital will not tend to migrate to the relatively high-profit industries, the prices of labor-intensive products will have to rise relative to capital-intensive ones.) But if the prices of produced means of production change, then the 'amount of capital' embodied in *unchanged* plant and equipment can vary, and this can come about because of variation in the rate of profit. Moreover, the amount of capital embodied in unchanged equipment can vary in either direction when the rate of profit changes, since the direction of relative price changes depends only on relative capital intensity, about which no general rules can be given. The neo-Classical ranking of techniques according to capital intensity and the rate of return has to be considered an inadequate representation of the real complexities involved in choosing techniques and using capital in production. So the neo-Classical answer to the Keynesian problem is not adequate, nor can the neo-Classical theory of scarcity and substitution be applied to the problem of understanding the forces behind accumulation. Neo-Classical theory *misconceives* capital.

7 NEO-KEYNESIAN THEORY

But, paradoxically, the alternative to the neo-Classical theory of steady growth, developed in Cambridge by Joan Robinson and others, provides an answer that also appears to imply a stable full employment equilibrium, guaranteed by market price flexibility, although based on a different conception of the market, but still retaining the conception of accumulation as the expansion, rather than the transformation, of a given system. The overall saving ratio is considered the weighted average of saving out of wages and profits, the weights being the respective income shares. Here the propensity to save out of profits is assumed to be relatively high, and that out of wages to be low. Then, if the natural rate of growth $> s/v$, eventually the money-wage rate would tend to fall, and this, *ceteris paribus*, would raise the profitability of investment. As a result the overall saving ratio would rise, bringing s/v up to the full employment level. If s/v is greater than the natural rate, on the other hand, the resulting excess capacity would lower profitability, and tend to bring s/v down. Thus it is not necessary to assume easy and unrealistic substitution; the capital–output ratio can remain fixed, and yet market adjustments will direct the system towards the full employment growth path. (Moreover, such a 'classical' saving function could replace the proportional saving function in the neo-Classical growth model, with the result that shifts in the production function would affect the K/Y ratio, but leave the rate of profit unchanged, rather than the reverse.)

Like the neo-Classical, this scenario sees the natural rate of growth as the center of gravitation, towards which the system adjusts. But it has sometimes been given another, more Keynesian interpretation. If, at the level of normal capacity utilization, investment demand were to exceed savings, multiplier pressure would drive up prices – since output could not be (easily) increased. Money wages, on the other hand, would not be driven up, since employment could not be (easily) increased, either, for when plant and equipment is operating at full capacity there are no more places on the assembly lines – the full complement of workers has already been hired. Thus the excess demand for goods will *not* translate into excess demand for labor, and prices will be driven up relative to money-wages: a profit inflation. Thus the overall saving ratio will rise, until the pressure of excess demand is eased. So, in the long run as well as in the short, savings adjusts to investment. Understood in this way, as Joan Robinson and Luigi Pasinetti insisted, the second scenario contradicts the neo-Classical one, rather than complementing it. (Cf. Ch. 24.)

8 INVESTMENT AND THE ACCELERATOR

But this is still not fully Keynesian, or at least not Harrodian, for the emergence of excess or shortage of capacity must be allowed to influence investment plans – the 'accelerator', or capital stock adjustment principle. Joan Robinson objected to this, on the reasonable grounds that Harrod's (and especially Samuelson's) use of the idea was too mechanical, and less plausibly, that it was not obvious to business that a change in demand would be permanent. But business success depends on being able to make that kind of judgment correctly; that is what marketing is all about. Once long-run demand has changed, either capacity or utilization has to be adjusted. But if capacity utilization is flexible, then there is no reason for prices, or, therefore, distribution, to change. Since Joan Robinson argues that prices and distribution do adjust, she must accept that capacity constrains upward movements and is expensive to carry when demand falls. Hence she must accept some form of modified 'accelerator'.

Starting from full capacity, when $s/v >$ actual or current I/K, there will be a slump; when $s/v < I/K$ prices will be bid up relative to money-wages. Money wages, in turn, will tend to rise or fall according to whether the actual rate of growth lies above or below the natural. If the actual rate lies above the natural, this will tend to rise the natural and lower the actual. There are thus three rates of growth: the actual, I/K, the warranted, s/v, and the natural, and six possible permutations of these. It can be shown (See Ch. 24) that in only two cases is there an unambiguous tendency for all three rates to converge; in these cases the actual rate lies between the warranted and the natural rates, so that money-wage inflation and price inflation move in opposite directions, causing the real wage to change. A rise in the real wage will lower the warranted rate and (less certainly) raise the natural rate; a fall will do the opposite. Hence in the two cases where the change lies in the right direction, the rates will tend to converge. In two others, the rates of inflation lie in the same direction, but plausible additional assumptions imply that they will not be equally rapid, so that the real wage will change, bringing a tendency to converge. But in two cases the real wage will tend to move in the wrong direction, and there seems to be no possibility of convergence at all; quite the opposite (Nell, 1982). So the Keynesian approach suggests that the full employment (or, indeed, any) steady-growth path should not be treated as a center of gravitation; it may or may not be what the market tends to bring about.

9 CAPACITY CONSTRAINTS?

It has been objected (Vianello, 1985, following a suggestion of Garegnani) that business routinely carries excess capacity, so that there are no binding constraints. But this is a misconception; 'normal capacity' will be a point or range of optimal usage. It can be exceeded, but at a cost, which means lowering profits below their normal range. Hence if the additional demand is permanent it will require additional capacity, either through new construction or by incurring once-for-all expenses for reorganizing present plant. In either case, we have investment expenditure, but the first means additional output from the capital goods industries, and must be underwritten by a reduction in consumption. The second, however, is a form of technical progress; no additional capital goods are required and no changes in consumption are necessary. What is required are changes in the methods and allocation of labor and in the organization of work. It may be costly to bring these about, but the costs will largely be labor and forgone output. Incurring these costs is an investment, but not one which has to be underwritten by a change in the real wage; it will normally come about through a cutback in production, while labor and managerial costs continue to run (though for different purposes). Thus the investment will be financed by the once-for-all *reduction in profits*, to be repaid by higher output and profits later. This is the mechanism which accounts for the fact that increases in the growth rate, as in the US during World war II, can be accompanied by an unchanged or even substantially increased real-wage. Contrary to the Vianello-Garegnani argument, there is no need to discard the insight that the full or normal capacity rate of growth is connected to the normal rate of profit through the propensity to save/retain earnings. But there are other difficulties.

10 CAPITAL VALUE AND PROFIT

Ironically, this neo-Keynesian approach falls foul of the same problems that plague the neo-Classical standard version. For once we leave the one-sector framework, the neo-Keynesian theory implies that excess aggregate demand will bid up, not the price level in general, but the relative price of capital goods – for the excess demand is entirely concentrated in the investment goods sector, and there is no discussion of how this could be transmitted to the consumer goods sector. Moreover, if both prices did rise relative to money wages, consumer goods demand would fall. But this would not indicate a possible equilibrium, for such price increases would leave the profit rate unequal in the two sectors. Thus the neo-Keynesian claim must be that a bidding up of the relative price of capital goods will raise the rate of profit, leading to higher savings, etc., but in a two-sector model it is easily seen that this will only be the case when the capital goods sector is the more capital intensive (see Appendix). So the validity of the approach depends on an arbitrary condition (which becomes even more arbitrary as the number of sectors increases).

Even worse, suppose that the capital goods sector is the more capital intensive, and consider a small rise in the growth rate to a new equilibrium level, requiring an increased production of capital goods (alternatively, a fall in the actual rate below the equilibrium). The corresponding new overall capital–labor ratio will be higher than the initial one; but to maintain full employment there will have to be a diversion of resources to the industry with the lower capital–labor ratio. To preserve full employment the capital goods sector would have to be contracted; but to increase the growth rate it has to expand. (A similar argument holds for a decline in the equilibrium growth rate.) In the case where a rise in the price of capital goods would increase the rate of profit, permitting the neo-Keynesian mechanism to work, the system could not adjust to the new steady-growth path, since the two conditions for adjustment contradict one another (see Appendix).

In fact, adjustment from one steady-growth path to another turns out to be difficult in general, even without changes in technique. A change in the growth rate requires changes in the relative sizes of sectors, which means shifting labor and resources, but these are normally used in different proportions, or in different combinations. And some can only be used in certain sectors and not in others. The 'traverse' from one steady path to another will normally involve both unemployment and shortages, and it may be difficult to actually reach a new path before the conditions determining it change. The 'steady-growth' approach to accumulation may face insurmountable problems, if it is supposed that equilibrium paths trace out stylized history. But that profit and growth incentives may contradict one another, or that traverses be difficult in no way undermines the theory. Indeed, these may be crucial insights, even if still oversimplified, into real problems of accumulation (Halevi, Laibman and Nell, 1992).

11 THE SIGNIFICANCE OF STEADY GROWTH

But, then, what is the importance of the steady-growth path? For the neo-Classical approach it is an extension of the concept of equilibrium to the case of expansion over time; for some neo-Keynesians it represents a center of gravitation, a point towards which the system would move, or around which it would oscillate. For others it may simply be a point of reference – how the system would work *if* certain contrary-to-fact assumptions held. Real processes will normally be different, and can be classified by their distance from such a point of reference.

Following Joan Robinson, steady growth with continuous full employment been termed a 'golden age'; desired capital accumulation equals the natural rate of growth. But a low desired rate, well below the initial natural rate, might create a large reserve army of unemployed, forcing down real wages and lowering the birth rate, so that the natural rate would fall to the depressed desired rate – a 'leaden age.' A desired rate above the natural rate may bid up real wages enough to lower the rate of profit until the desired rate falls to the natural – a 'restrained golden age.' A 'bastard golden age' occurs when the desired rate cannot be achieved because the real wage cannot be driven down sufficiently, the attempt resulting in inflation. Other possibilities can be envisioned, depending on the adjustment mechanisms postulated. For example, when the initial stock of capital is not appropriate to the desired rate of accumulation, it will have first to be adjusted but the part of the capital goods sector that produces capital goods for its own use may be too large or too small for easy adjustment to the desired rate, giving rise to 'platinum age' patterns of accumulation. The catalogue is endless, but its value is limited, as Joan Robinson herself came to see.

But her disillusionment with growth theory arose from an increasing concern for the texture of history, coupled with a growing disdain for the smooth and polished surfaces of equilibrium. These latter are crystalline and timeless, collapsing the unknowable future and the unalterable past into an artificially determinate present. History, by contrast, is rough edged and open ended, filled with conficts, accidents and mistakes. The models show us smooth sailing; the real world is awash in rough seas.

This contrast is surely overdrawn. Equilibrium cannot model history, but equilibrium models may, nevertheless, have a point. Not all concepts of equilibrium are neo-Classical. Consider 'reproduction' models: what conditions must be met for the present system to reproduce itself with its present (or some other) distribution of income? Or: what conditions must be met for the present system to expand at the maximum rate permitted by its present (or some other) distribution of income and propensities to save? Or: what conditions must be met for the present system to move from its present growth path to one implied by a new distribution of income? Such questions are not only not meaningless; they must be answered if we are to analyze the actual movement of an economy – or try to plan and control such movement. Steady-growth models have a point, but they are not the whole story.

Steady growth, in fact, appears to be best analyzed as a supply-side concept. Its most elaborate development, in fact, is strictly supply side – as the von Neumann ray, or, in Sraffa's terms, the standard commodity, where the industry sizes of the system have been so adjusted that the net product of the economy as a whole consists of the same commodities in the same ratios as its aggregate means of production. The warranted rate of growth, by contrast, balances supply and demand. But it is an imperfect growth concept, for it balances aggregate supply and aggregate demand *at a moment of time*; it does not balance the growth of supply with the growth of demand. The von Neumann ray is an analysis of the growth of supply– but so far there does not exist a comparably detailed analysis of the growth of demand. (But see Ch. 17.)

12 ACCUMULATION AND TECHNICAL CHANGE

This not only brings to light a defect in the theory of steady growth; it also raises the question of the relation of steady growth to the accumulation of capital. For the best established empirical proposition in the study of consumer behavior states that as income increases consumer demand will increase non-proportionally – it will shift in a characteristic manner. Hence there is little point in trying to complete the theory of steady growth with an account of steady growth in demand; it doesn't happen.

In actual fact, steady growth has never taken place. The history of capitalism is a history of successive booms and slumps, but perhaps even more striking, of slow but persistent long-term shifts in crucial relationships. (Joan Robinson seems to have largely overlooked this regularity in her concentration on the disorderliness of history.) For two centuries labor shifted out of agriculture and migrated to the cities to work in manufacturing industry. For over half a century now labor has shifted into services, first from agriculture and then, later, from manufacturing as well. For almost a century the relative size of the government sector has been rising, whether measured by share of GNP or by share of employment.

These points lead to a major criticism of the treatment of technical progress in accumulation: whether it is presented as shifting the production function, as learning by doing, or in a 'technical progress' function, and whether conceived as embodied or disembodied, it has been treated as leading to the extraction of greater output from given resources, in the context of steady growth. But technical progress introduces new products as well as new processes, and together these change the forms of social life.

This is reflected in the changing importance of the major sectors of the economy, in the changing class structure, and in the changing patterns and nature of work. None of these points seem to have been captured by Joan Robinson's work, nor do they figure in most current analyses, in part because of the preoccupation with steady growth, based on an overly simplified concept of capital as productive goods. When capital is understood as also being a form of organization, then the link between accumulation and the transformation of institutions can be forged. Another reason, perhaps, may be that technical progress has been approached too timidly, and without understanding its dual relation to the growth of demand. For technical progress both stimulates the growth of demand and responds to it.

13 STEADY GROWTH vs TRANSFORMATIONAL GROWTH

In practice, steady growth is an impossibility, for at least three reasons. First, land and natural resources are limited, and high-grade ores and high-fertility lands are the first to be used. As they are used up over time, productivity falls unless and until technical progress offsets the decline – but such technical progress will have to involve new products. Second, as mentioned, Engel curves imply that consumption patterns will be changing. And finally, if propensities to save differ in the different social classes (and if workers receive interest on their savings, and capitalists salaries for managing capital) then the relative wealth of the classes will be changing over time, leading to changes in the composition of demand (see Ch. 10 in this volume). The first point implies that costs will tend to rise, the second two that demand for consumer goods will tend to rise more slowly, as time passes. All three, therefore, point to long-term stagnation in the absence of major technological changes.

This does not simply mean increasing the productivity of currently employed processes; it means the development of new processes and new products – both for consumers and for industry. It means electrification, or the internal combustion engine, the airplane, or perhaps, the computer. The changes must be of sufficient importance to lead to an investment boom resulting from widespread scrapping of present plant and equipment, as well as the development, concurrently, of large-scale new markets, as consumers introduce the new products into their living patterns. And as new plants are built economies of scale can be realized, making it possible to lower prices, so as to reach new markets in lower levels of the income distribution. Capital organizes markets and marketing as well as production.

New household products have emerged because a way has been found to perform some normal daily activity better or more cheaply, by, in effect, shifting it from the household to industry, capitalizing it. New industrial processes, usually involving new products as well, have emerged as the result of mechanizing activities formerly performed by workers, enabling them to be done better, or more cheaply, or more reliably. Mass production goods have replaced home crafts; the mechanization of agriculture, in conjunction with Engel's Law, has displaced farm labor; the rise of manufacturing, to build the factories and then to supply the new goods, has provided employment for the displaced labor – but at greatly reduced hours of work per week, providing more hours to spend on consuming.

The rise of mass production and the consequent urbanization have created new problems, among others periodic mass unemployment, which in turn had to be dealt with by an expanded government. And today, traditional mass production is being transformed by the computer and the chip, with consequences we cannot yet fully forsee.

The interlocking emergence of new products and new processes, creating new markets and new industries, can be termed 'transformational growth,' in contrast to steady growth. This is what is missing in Joan Robinson's work. But it is here that the true story of the accumulation of capital, and the causes of the wealth of nations, will be found, although to date this study has been left to the province of economic historians.

Appendix

The main points of the capital controversy can be illustrated in a simple two-sector model, of consumer goods and capital goods, sometimes interpreted as agriculture and industry.

1 THE MODEL

$$\begin{aligned} &\text{Price:} && 1 = r\alpha p + b\beta && \\ & && p = rap + wb && (5.A1) \\ &\text{Quantity:} && 1 = gbT + c\beta && \\ & && T = gaT + c\alpha && (5.A2) \end{aligned}$$

Greek letters stand for consumer goods. Roman for capital, *as* and *αs* for capital inputs, *bs* and *βs* for labor inputs. The price and quantity of the consumer goods are taken as unity, r is the rate of profit, g the rate of accumulation; w is the wage rate and c the rate of consumption per worker. p is the price of capital goods and T the output of capital goods, both in relation to consumption goods. The unit volume of consumption goods can be taken as the basic basket of goods required to support a unit amount of labor, and the quantity equations can then be interpreted so that T is capital goods per head and c consumption per head.

This model will now be elaborated in various contexts to present significant results that were demonstrated in fuller and more sophisticated ways during the course of the controversy.

2 THE RATE OF PROFIT AND GENERAL EQUILIBRIUM

First, convert this model to a simple activity analysis model; instead of the ratio T of capital goods (iron) to consumption goods (corn), we have the absolute outputs of each, x_c and x_I, and instead of the price ratio, p, we have p_c and p_I.

The standard version of neo-Classical theory deals with factors in competitive conditions: laborers compete with one another for jobs, and capital funds flow towards the highest rate of return. The activity analysis model determines the earnings, for example, of particular machines or workers. But these earnings are rents and are subject to the requirement that

> [the] permanent fund of capital . . . is put into such forms that the rent secured by one concrete form or capital-good, is as large a fraction of its value as is that received by another . . . This equalizing force determines the number of capital-goods of each kind; and this, again, governs the rents they severally earn (Clark, 1956, p. 125).

The question confronting us is whether the modern activity analysis model is compatible with the capital theory of the standard version of neo-classical theory.

The implications of admitting that some of the goods in the initial endowments may be produced means of production are dramatic. Consider a simple model, containing two such goods:

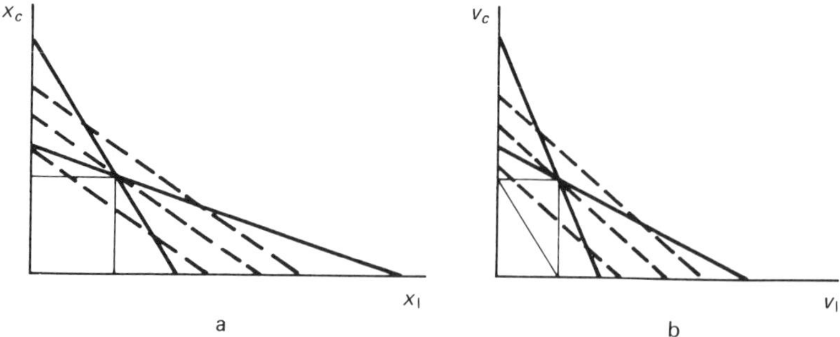

Figure 5A.1

Max:	$x_c p_c + x_I p_I$	Min:	$Cv_c + Iv_I$	(1)
Subject to:	$\beta x_c + \beta x_I \leqslant C$	Subject to:	$\beta v_c + \alpha v_I \geqslant p_c$	
	$\alpha x_c + \alpha x_I \leqslant I$		$\beta v_c + \alpha v_I \geqslant p_I$	
	$x_c, x_I > 0$		$v_c, v_I > 0$	

Let the demand function $F(p, v)$ be such that prices satisfying it result in the production of both corn and iron, and further suppose that these quantities permit the necessary replacement to take place. No loss of generality is involved; this merely guarantees a solution compatible with replacement. Now let us follow the Walras–Cassel procedure. Consider the diagram first of the maximizing (Figure 5A.1a), then of the minimizing (Figure 15.A2b) problem.

In Figure 15.A1a, as long as the slope of the price ratio lies between the slopes of the two constraints, both goods will be produced.

In Figure 15.A1b, if both goods are produced, both resources will be assigned positive values. The minimizing problem yields these shadow values, which represent the rentals that can be obtained from the commodities. The slope of the line joining the optimal value of v_1 to the optimal value of v_c gives the ratio of the rental values.

The slope of v_I/v_c need not equal p_I/p_c. If it did, p_I/p_c could not be changed without changing v_I/p_c as long as the change stays within limits prescribed by the slopes of the constraints.

Shift the intersection of the constraints in the max problem to the origin. The construct perpendiculars to the constraint lines at the origin. These normal lines span a cone, and any line in this cone will be perpendicular to a line through the origin, *between* the constraints. The cone therefore defines the set of price vectors for which the optimal point v_I/v_c remains unchanged. This set may be quite large.

But if $(v_I/v_c) \lesseqgtr (p_I/p_c)$, then $(v_I/p_I) \lesseqgtr (v_c/p_c)$; that is, the ratio of rental earnings to supply price for the two goods will be different. But capitalists will invest their capital in (pay the supply price of) equipment whose earning power is the highest. Hence in the Walras–Cassel equilibrium model, all capital funds will flow into the purchase of only *one* of the goods, the one whose rental value in relation to supply price is the greatest. (Even more simply, output prices and input prices for the same good can only differ by a small markup for handling – which would imply $v_I/v_c = p_I/p_c$ contrary to the Walras–Cassel results.)

Clearly, this is inconsistent. But a failure to reproduce of the initial supplies of the model, is incompatible with the notion of capital as a freely moving fund, self-maintaining and responsive to competitive pressures and opportunities. It follows that the standard version and the activity analysis approaches are *not* mutually compatible. The standard version rests on a *broad* conception of factor, allowing for a wide substitution among particular capital goods and workers in its account of the equilibrium of the firm. But this leads straight to the internal difficulties discussed earlier and, fundamentally, to the Cambridge (UK) critique (Ch. 7).

Activity analysis, since it has no theory of the firm, has no such internal difficulties, and on its narrow conception of factors, it is not subject to the Cambridge critique of factor pricing.

But for precisely these reasons, it stands directly opposed to the standard version and to the important idea that the cost and return on capital will both be uniform in different areas and will tend to equality with each other.

Without a theory of the firm, it is difficult to examine market structure and adjustments. But a theory of the firm cannot be grafted onto the activity analysis model without providing an account of the firm's *cost and capital structure*. The model cannot accommodate this, however, for it would require consideration of factor markets broadly defined. Hence these are mutually exclusive approaches rather than alternative tools in the economist's famous kit, and both stumble over the capital concept.

The Cambridge critics think they know what has gone amiss: net income is not, in general, a payment for productive contribution; rather, it is the distribution of a surplus in accordance with property rights that reflect mostly class position. 'Capital' is not a factor of production, nor is it to be identified with a set of material means of production: raw materials, intruments and means of subsistence:

> What is a Negro slave? A man of the black race. The one explanation is as good as the other. A Negro is a Negro. He only becomes a slave in certain relations. A cotton spinning jenny is a machine for spinning cotton. It becomes *capital* only in certain relations. Torn from these relationships it is no more capital than gold in itself is money . . . Capital . . . is a social relation of production (Marx, 1976).

These points are developed further in Ch. 6.

3 THE UNIFORM RATE OF PROFIT AND THE BALANCED GROWTH RATE

Steady growth means expansion along a balanced path, investment in which is underwritten largely by saving out of profits, which must be earned at a uniform rate. Both the balanced growth rate and the uniform profit rate are conventionally supposed to be established by movements of capital in response to competitive incentives – yet these movements are inconsistent.

Assume that 'agriculture' – consumer goods – is the relatively labor-intensive sector. Then let us suppose that initially, the wage – equal in both sectors – stood at its maximum level, with profit sufficient only for replacement. Assume, further, that all wages are consumed and all profits invested. Now let the wage fall from its maximum level to subsistence. Since agriculture is the relatively labor-intensive sector, it will now have the highest profit in relation to the value of its means of production. Thus, according to the implicit theory, capital should flow into agriculture, expanding supply while reducing it in industry – the capital goods sector – thus bidding down grain prices relatively to the prices of industry's products.

But a capitalist economy is an expanding one; the point of profits is that they underwrite accumulation. As the rate of profit is formed profits are invested and the capital stock expands. In order to expand in a balanced way, however, the sectors must stand in the correct proportions to one another. Moving from zero expansion – simple replacement – to expansion at the maximum rate when the capital goods sector is capital-intensive, requires an increase in the relative size of industry, which is to say a shrinkage in agriculture, just the *opposite* of the movement required to equalize the rate of profit!

Writing out the system in full, assuming circulating capital and that profit is figured in advanced wages:

Price equations	*Quantity equations*
(1a) $(1 + r)(a + wb\pi) = 1$	(3a) $(1 + g)(a + c\alpha\theta) = 1$
(2a) $(1 + r)(\alpha + w\beta\pi) = \pi$	(4a) $(1 + g)(b + c\beta\theta) = \theta$

Here (a, α) are the machinery inputs in industry and agriculture, respectively, and (b, β) the consumer good requirements at subsistence level; w and c are the wage rate and the rate of consumption per head (both are *percentages* of subsistence levels); π and θ are relative prices and relative quantities, respectively (taking capital goods as the unit this time).

Eliminating w and c we obtain,

$$\pi = \frac{\beta}{b}[1 - (1 + r)a] + (1 + r)\alpha$$

$$\theta = \frac{\beta}{\alpha}[1 - (1 + g)a] + (1 + g)b \qquad (5A.3)$$

$$\frac{\delta\pi}{\delta r} = a - \left(\frac{a\beta}{b}\right) < 0 \qquad \frac{\delta\theta}{\delta g} = b - \left(\frac{a\beta}{\alpha}\right) < 0 \qquad (5A.4)$$

So the movement of capital into agriculture which will reduce π, so as to raise r, will raise θ and so reduce g, which contradicts the assumption that $r = g$, since all and only all profits are invested. More generally, when $r = g$,

$$\theta = \frac{b}{\alpha}\pi \qquad (5A.5)$$

Equilibrium θ and π must always move together. But to effect a change in π by means of supply and demand, capital must move so that the ratio of industry sizes moves inversely with π. So a movement of capital which brings prices nearer to prices of production moves outputs away from those required for balanced growth. This cannot be. The whole picture is mistaken. Capital almost never moves in response to current price differentials. Investment depends on expected market growth; and prices are set to provide the profits to finance investment. So they have little or nothing to do with current supply and demand (see 9 below; also Chs 16 and 17; see also Nikaido, 1980).

4 THE MARGINAL PRODUCTIVITY THEORY OF WAGES

Neo-Classical economists have held that distribution was determined in the factor market in the same way that prices and quantities were determined in the product market. The theory of marginal productivity, which has always been the foundation of this view, holds that: (1) in competition each unit of a factor will receive the

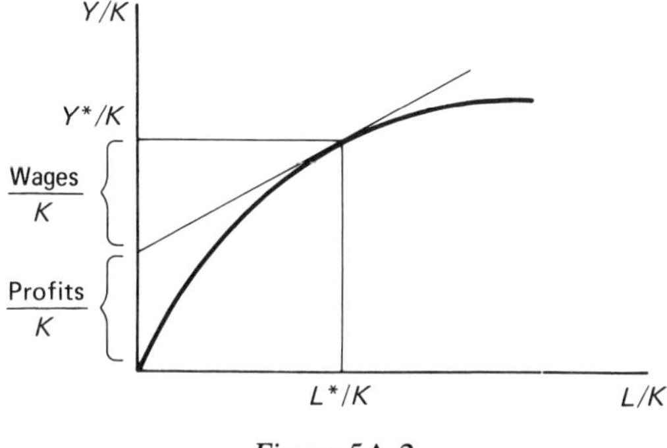

Figure 5A.2

value of the extra product the employment of an extra unit of the factor brings as reward, and (2) that as employment of a factor increases, with other factors constant, the amount of extra product from further employment declines. This can be shown easily in a diagram. Plot output per employed plant, Y/K, on one axis, and amounts of labor per plant, L/K, on the other. As we apply more men to the factory, output goes up, but by a smaller amount each time. For a certain ratio of labor to capital, L^*/K, there will be a corresponding Y^*/K. The tangent to the curve at that point will measure the marginal product, and the point where the tangent intersects the vertical axis will divide the output of the factory between wages and profits. The slope of the tangent is $(\text{wages}/K)/(L^*/K) = w$ (see Figure 5A.2), the wage rate, and by definition:

$$\frac{Y^*}{K} = \frac{\text{wages} + \text{profits}}{K}$$

These basic ideas can be developed in a number of ways. For instance: the relationship may be conceived as one between aggregate output – the whole capital and entire labor force of the society; total wages; profits and output can be determined together with investment, savings and growth. Whatever method is used, the ultimate thought remains that factor rewards represent productive contributions at the margin and that these contributions diminish as factor employment increases.

The claim that distribution is really a form of exchange and that factor incomes are proportional to contributions has always encountered opposition. In the past, this centered on the difficulties in separating the contributions made by the various contributing factors. Cassel has commented that 'If a pit has to be dug, the addition of one more man will make little difference . . . unless you give the man a spade.' A homely illustration; yet, one can translate the example to the modern factory and consider adding a man to a well-designed, properly running assembly line, where his marginal product will be zero. Subtracting a man – if the plant is well designed, without redundant workers or featherbedding – will bring the process to a halt: the marginal product will equal the total. Sir Dennis Robertson (1951), commenting on Cassel's observation, provided the neo-Classical answer.

> If ten men are set to dig a hole instead of nine, they will be furnished with ten cheaper spades instead of nine more expensive ones; or, perhaps, if there is no room for him to dig comfortably, the tenth man will be furnished with a bucket and sent to fetch beer for the other nine. Once we allow ourselves this liberty, we can exhibit in the sharpest form the principle of variation – the principle

> that you can combine varying amounts of one factor with a fixed amount of all the others; and we can draw, for labor or any other factor, a perfectly definite descending curve of marginal productivity.

Robertson admits that where the technique of production is rigidly fixed, marginal productivity theory is inapplicable; he claims that it applies where technique is variable and that under such conditions, a unique inverse relation exists between the wage and the labor to capital ratio.

In fact, Robertson qualifies the claim considerably, admitting 'that there seems to be a certain unreality about the assumption' [that the forms of capital and organization can change without the amounts changing].

5 EXAMINATION OF ROBERTSON'S CLAIMS

One can adopt some well-known theorems from current literature and analyze these claims. With a little mathematics – but not much – the results will prove to be of striking simplicity, yet great generality. Start with the income identity in real terms:

$$Y = wN + rK \tag{5A.6}$$

where Y is output; w, the wage; N, the number of workers; r, the rate of profit; and K, the total capital stock.

Then, dividing by K:

$$\varphi = wn + r \tag{5A.7}$$

where φ equals Y/K and n equals N/K. Differentiating:

$$d\varphi = ndw + wdn + dr \tag{5A.8}$$

from which it follows that

$$w = \frac{d\varphi}{dn} \tag{5A.9}$$

if and only if $-n$ equals dr/dw. This is to say that the wage will equal the marginal product of labor if, but only if, a certain special condition is met. This condition is that all sectors in the economy must have the same capital to labor ratios – a most unlikely circumstance. In general, therefore, with a given technique – or, for that matter, if techniques vary – the wage will not equal the marginal product of labor.

Consider the second claim and suppose there are two techniques, competitive in the sense that for a given wage both return the same rate of profit:

$$\varphi_1 = wn_1 + r$$

and

$$\varphi_2 = wn_2 + r \tag{5A.10}$$

This means that below the given wage technique 1 would yield a slightly higher r, than would technique 2. Combine the two equations and regroup:

$$w = \frac{\varphi_1 - \varphi_2}{n_1 - n_2} \tag{5A.11}$$

At the so-called switching point, the wage identically, even trivially, equals the marginal product of labor. Lest anyone think this somehow profound, observe that equation (5A.11) states no more than that when two techniques, operating at a given rate of profit and paying everything out as wages or profits, also pay the same wage, then the technique using more labor per unit of capital must produce proportionately more output per unit of capital.

Modern analysis confirms the first two of Robertson's propositions. What about the third? When methods of productions can be varied – that is, when nine expensive spades can be turned into nine cheaper ones, a bucket and beer – is the result a 'perfectly definite descending curve of marginal productivity'?

The answer is devastating, unambiguous and by now well known. The law of scarcity requires that as labor becomes more plentiful with respect to capital, the real wage should decline and the marginal product diminish. However, the distribution variables (w and r), the real-wage rate and the profit rate – defined as identical with marginal products at switching points – move in a capricious and haphazard way as the relative scarcity of labor to capital varies. In fact, the marginal product might rise, jump about discontinuously or move in any imaginable manner, without apparent rhyme or reason. There appears to be no way that a monotonic, inverse relation between the real-wage or profit rates and relative scarcity can be derived; therefore, most neoclassical writers introduce it simply as a postulate, a method which, in the words of Bertrand Russell, 'has many advantages; the same as theft over honest toil' (1919, p. 71).

These are strong words, but the demonstration is simple. The two sectors – agriculture and industry – set out above and some high school algebra will suffice. The equations showed revenues equal to cost-plus in each sector.

$$p = rap + wb$$

$$1 = r\alpha p + w\beta$$

Solving each for p, equating the results and rearranging:

$$\frac{(1/\beta - w)(1/a - r)}{rw} = \frac{\alpha/\beta}{a/b} \tag{5A.12}$$

This can be illustrated by a simple, very instructive diagram (Figure 5A.3) which shows the relatedness of prices, profits and wages. Plot w against r, marking off $1/\beta$ and $1/a$ on the w and r axes, respectively: $1/\beta$ is the maximum wage rate; $1/a$, the maximum rate of profit consistent with positive prices; α/β is the machine to man ratio in agriculture; a/b, the machine to man ratio in industry. Consider the shaded portions of the diagram in Figure 5A.3; they represent the left side of equation (5A.12). When $\alpha/\beta < a/b$, that is, whenever industry uses more machines relative to manpower than agriculture, the curve bulges outwards; when $\alpha/\beta > a/b$, that is, when agriculture uses more machinery per man than industry, the curve bends

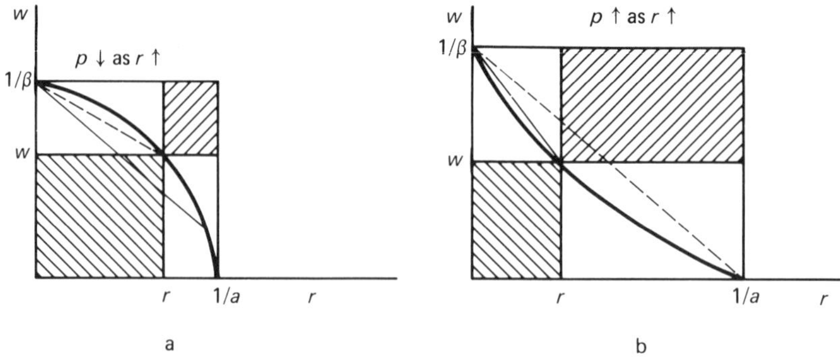

Figure 5A.3

inwards. This means that, for a given real-wage, the rate of profit will be higher for both sectors whenever industry is more heavily mechanized than agriculture.

6 PRICES

Now for prices. Income, by definition, equals wages and profits – ignoring land and rents. In equilibrium, income also equals consumption and investment. Dividing all these magnitudes by the total labor force:

$$y = rk + w \tag{5A.13}$$

$$y = gk + c \tag{5A.14}$$

where y is output per man; k is capital per man; g is growth rate; gk = investment/ labor force; and c is consumption per head.

In general, it follows that:

$$k = \frac{c - w}{r - g} \tag{5A.15}$$

In particular, however, ratios of capital value to labor for techniques producing the same good are to be compared. Let this be the consumption good, grain. Then g equals 0; so, $c = 1/\beta$ is the maximum value, the same as the maximum wage. Hence:

$$k = \frac{1/B - w}{r} = \frac{1}{n} \tag{5A.16}$$

and k, the capital to labor ratio, will be indicated by the solid lines from 1/ß to the curve in the diagrams in Figure 5A.3.

Clearly, when the curve bulges out – when industry is more mechanized – as w increases, the slope measuring k gets flatter. That is, as w increases the ratio of labor to value of capital also increases. Thus, contrary to accepted opinion, the wage varies directly, rather than inversely, with the ratio of labor to capital.

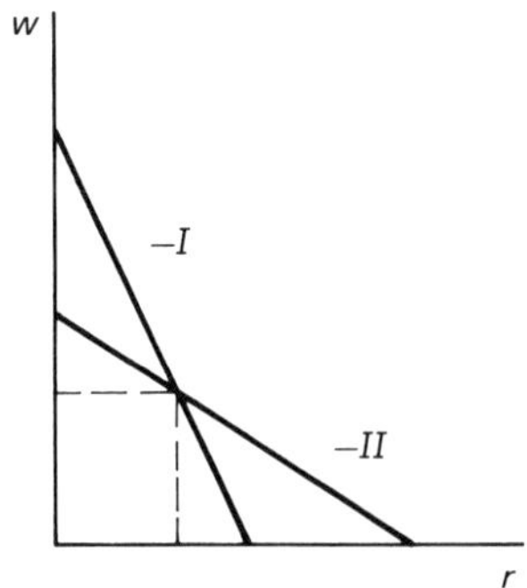

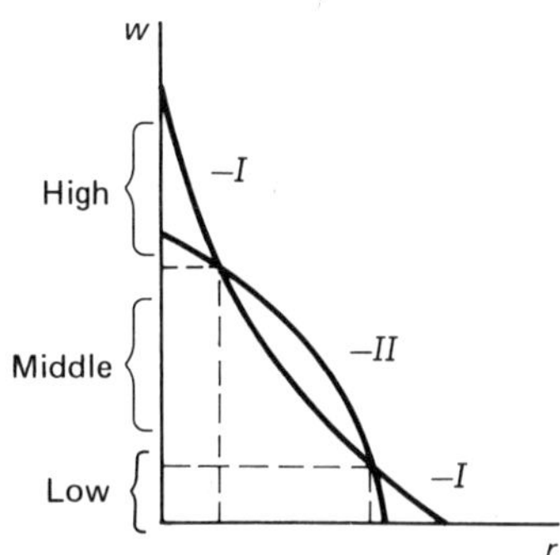

Figure 5A.4

Before the dunce cap is placed on the head of modern economics, we had better look again at those switch points. We saw earlier that if $dr/dw = -n$, the wage would equal the marginal product of labor. A close look at equation (5A.12) gives a clue: when $\alpha/\beta = a/b$, equation (5A.12) will be a straight line:

$$w = \frac{1}{\beta} - \frac{ar}{\beta} \tag{5A.17}$$

or rearranging:

$$\frac{-a}{\beta} = \frac{1/\beta - w}{r} \tag{5A.18}$$

and

$$\frac{dw}{dr} = \frac{1}{n} = \frac{-a}{\beta} \tag{5A.19}$$

The straight line case is a good candidate for the neo-Classical conditions. Consider two such techniques which cross. As the wage falls, it becomes profitable to switch from technique *I* to *II* – that is, from a technique with less labor to capital to one with more plentiful labor in relation to capital This confirms the neo-Classical picture, although only in a very special case.

Suppose that technique *I* bends inwards and *II* outwards; for low levels of the wage, technique *I* will be most profitable. For middle-level wages, technique *II* will be best; finally, for high wages technique *I* will be best again (see Figure 5A.4).

At the high-wage switching point, the system moves from a more labor-using technique to a less labor-using one as the wage rises. At the low-wage switching point, the movement is reversed. As the wage rises, the highest profit is obtained as more labor-intensive techniques are used. As the wage rises, it becomes profitable to adopt a method of production which uses more labor in relation to capital. This result simply cannot be reconciled with neo-Classical doctrine, and there is no way to avoid a plentiful supply of such cases. (Cf. Ch. 7.)

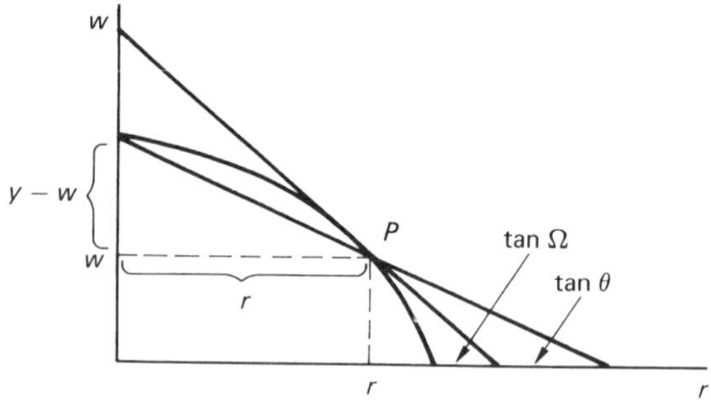

Figure 5A.5

7 THE RATE OF PROFIT AND THE MARGINAL PRODUCT OF CAPITAL

It is easy to show that in *general* the rate of profit will not equal the marginal product of capital. Write the income distribution equation in *per capita* terms.

$$y = rk + w \tag{5A.13}$$

Then

$$dy = kdr + rdk + dw \tag{5A.20}$$

and $dy/dk = r$ if and only if $dw/dr = -k = K^*/L$, i.e. $\tan \Omega = \tan \theta$ (Figure 5A.5).

There is no reason to suppose that this condition will normally, or indeed, ever, be met.

Consider a conventional returns-to-scale neo-Classical production function, $Y = Y(K, L)$. This can be written $Y/L = Y(K/L, 1)$ or $y = y(k)$. From Euler's theorem

$$w = \delta Y/\delta L = y(k) - ky'(k) \tag{5A.21}$$

and

$$r = \delta Y/\delta K = y'(k), \; (y'(k) = dy/dk) \tag{5A.22}$$

Then, $dw = y'dk - ky''dk - y'dk = -ky''dk$; $dr = y''dk$.
Hence,

$$\frac{dw}{dr} = \frac{-ky''dk}{y''dk} = -k = \frac{-K}{L} \tag{5A.23}$$

This, we saw above, is the condition which must be met for the rate of profits to equal the marginal product of capital, and is met in the labor theory of value case. Hence, when the latter holds, the wage–profit trade-off frontier can be represented by a neo-Classical production function.

However, in one special and implausible case, suppose all industries, whatever they produce, use capital goods and labor in the *same proportions*. Then when the

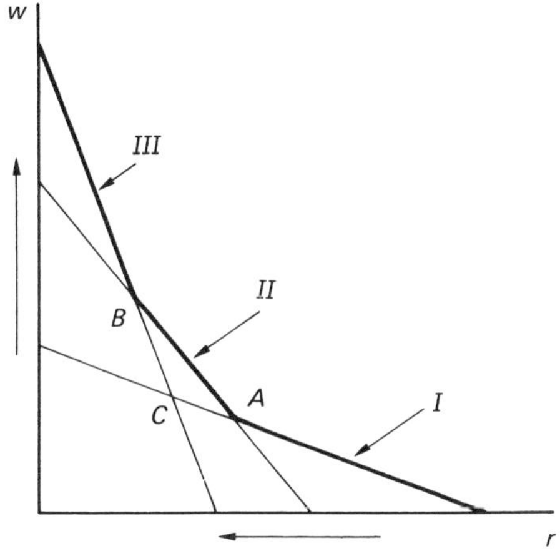

Figure 5A.6

wages rise and the rate of profit falls, no revaluation of capital goods will be necessary.

Hence, $w/r = dw/dr = K/L$ (ignoring signs). In this special case, then, marginal productivity theory will hold. Such a wage–profit rate of trade-off can be drawn as a straight line, and three such lines will cross at switch points A, B and C (Figure 5A.6). C, of course, will never appear, since the economy will move along the 'frontier' indicated by the heavy shading. Switch points A and B are 'neo-Classical' – as w rises and r falls the system moves to more capital-intensive techniques. (Consider the switch from *I* to *II* at A: *II* has the higher output per man – maximum wage – so to have equal profit rates at A, *II* must have a higher value of capital per man.)

8 CAPITAL THEORY AND THE GOLDEN RULE

Solving for p and T, as in Nell (1970):

$$p = \frac{b}{\beta + r(\alpha b - a\beta)} \tag{5A.24}$$

$$T = \frac{\alpha}{\beta + g(\alpha b - a\beta)} \tag{5A.25}$$

and then the value of capital per man will be:

$$pT = \frac{\alpha b}{[\beta + r(\alpha b - a\beta)][\beta + g(\alpha b - a\beta)]} \tag{5A.26}$$

The wage–profit trade-off can be written:

$$w = \frac{1 - ar}{\beta + r(\alpha b - a\beta)} \tag{5A.27}$$

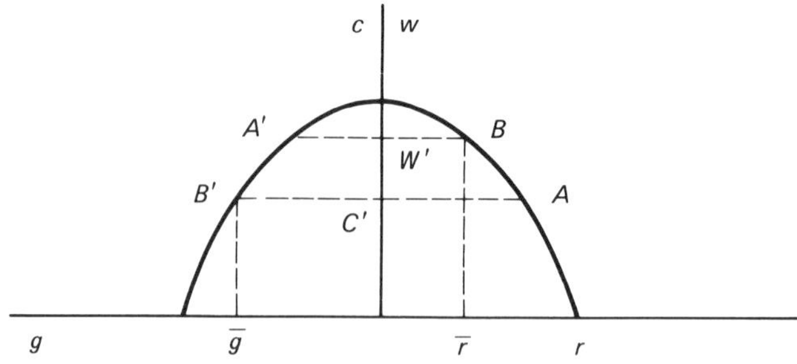

Figure 5A.7

so that

$$\frac{dw}{dr} = - \frac{\alpha b}{[\beta + r(\alpha b - a\beta)]^2} \tag{5A.28}$$

Hence, when $r = g$, when the golden rule holds,

$$pT = \frac{-\,dw}{dr} \tag{5A.29}$$

and

$$\frac{r}{w}\ pT = - \frac{r}{w}\frac{dw}{dr} = \frac{r}{w}\ k \tag{5A.30}$$

When $r = g$, price and real Wicksell effects exactly offset one another. So even though the $w - r$ relationship is not a straight line, the value of capital per man is given by its slope, and its elasticity measures the distribution of income.

Neo-Classical distribution theory will not find much comfort from this. Adopting a diagram and notation by Spaventa (4, 1970), we can first show the above case and then the more general one. Let $v = pT$, or the value of capital per man, $H = w + rv = c + gv$, or the value of net output per man. Then, from the ratio theorem, $v = c - w/r - g$ which can be seen in Figure 5A.7 as the slope either of the line AB or the line $A'B'$. Clearly as $r - g \rightarrow 0$ this line will tend to approach the tangent.

When $g = 0$, on the other hand, the value of capital will equal tan θ. Suppose, then, that $r = g$, so the tangent measures the value of capital per man, and the elasticity at a point relative shares. Then in Figure 5A.7 which illustrates the case in which the capital sector is the more capital intensive, as the rate of profit falls with a given technique the value of capital per man will also fall, just the reverse of the neo-Classical postulate. Now consider a second technique which double-switches with the first. If $g = r$ then *both* switches will be forward, but the value of capital per man will still vary directly rather than inversely with the rate of profit on the section of the frontier between the two switches. For discrete techniques this can only be eliminated by postulating, implausibly enough, that the consumer goods sector is the more capital intensive of all techniques appearing on the frontier. *Two* special conditions must hold before the neo-Classical relation between r and v can be justified.

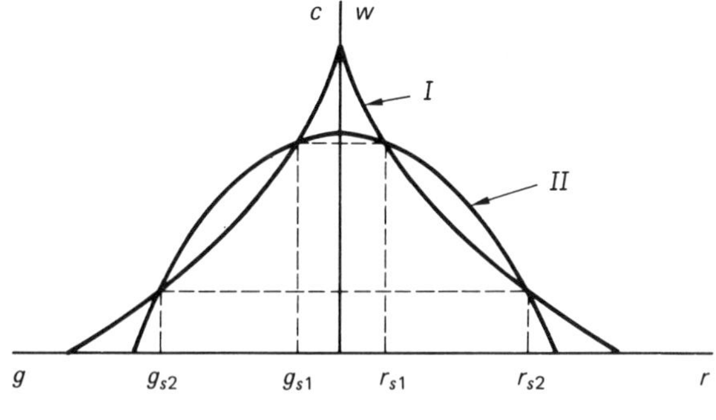

Figure 5A.8

As I just indicated, the second switch will not necessarily be backward, if the rate of growth is not zero. The general condition is easily seen from Figure 5A.8. If $g = g_{s1}$, then when $r = r_{s2}$ and the techniques switch, both techniques have the same value of capital per man. So, if $g > g_{s1}$, when $r = r_{s2}$, and the switch goes from *II* to *I*, the movement will be from a higher to a lower value of capital per man, a forward switch. Similarly, when $g < g_{s1}$ and $r = r_{s2}$ the switch will be backward, from a lower to a higher value of capital per man.

Exactly parallel remarks hold for the first switch. If $g = g_{s2}$ and $r = r_{s1}$ then the value of capital per man in the two techniques will be the same. If $g < g_{s2}$ the switch will be forward, but if $g < g_{s2}$, then technique *I* will have the lower value of capital per man, so with a small rise in the rate of profit at r_{s1} the system will go from a less to a more capital-intensive technique.

9 TWO CONCEPTS OF PRICE

Scarcity prices are flexible, rising in times of shortage and falling when supplies are plentiful. Scarcity prices are therefore indicators of the relative availability of goods. Production prices, by contrast, do not vary with shortages and surpluses, or with changes in output – special circumstances aside – because they are set to provide the profits needed to finance the capital required for production. Production prices are not wholly independent of demand, but what is considered in setting them is not the current market, but the possibilities of market growth (Ch. 17).

Joan Robinson repeatedly contrasted these two, stressing that each was appropriate to certain economic conditions, and/or to certain aspects of economic problems.

The significance of the capital theory controversy in this regard is that it has shown that production prices cannot be treated as a special kind of scarcity price, with capital as the scare factor, whose marginal productivity is reflected in the rate of profit. The two conceptions of price are totally distinct: scarcity prices make sense in certain kinds of planning, and in non-industrial, pre-capitalist markets, whereas production prices are those which rule under industrial capitalism.

Since production prices do not vary with changes in output, they provide, as Hicks (1965) noted, an appropriate setting for the Keynesian theory of effective demand. So, contrary to much modern literature, it is not necessary to assume 'sticky' money-wages or prices to establish the Keynesian picture (cf. Ch. 17).

10 THE FALLING RATE OF PROFIT AND THE CHOICE OF TECHNIQUE

Some Marxists have argued that if we discard the neo-Classical conception of competition, we can see pressures at work which will explain the tendency of the rate of profit to fall as the outcome of competitive choices of methods of production. Firms will seek to increase their profit margins by reducing their variable costs through an expansion of their fixed plant and equipment. They will, in short, substitute equipment for workers. With higher margins, they can afford to cut price and intensify the competitive struggle for markets. Since anyone can gain by doing this – attracting customers from the rest – all will adopt this course, and the prevailing method of production will more or less rapidly change to one with a higher margin but lower profit rate.

Formally, this argument is the same as that advanced by Gallaway and Shukla in the capital theory controversy – that firms will maximize profits rather than the rate of profits, so from any set of possible techniques, they will always choose the method of production with the highest profits per head (Gallaway and Shukla, 1974; Laibman and Nell, 1977). This is an argument about which method of production will be chosen under the influence of competitive pressures, not about the path of movement of the economy over time. To convert this point into a story of movement, Marxists must explain why firms find themselves, in the first place, operating techniques with lower profits per head but higher rates of profit than the one entailed by the profit margin maximization criterion. Presumably, the more capital-intensive, lower profit rate techniques are invented later, under the pressure of competition. But this is an *ad hoc* explanation, not a theory.

A further problem arises in trying to use this choice of technique argument to explain the tendency of the *rate* of profit to fall. But the *rate* of profit in general – uniform across all industries – only exists because of the pressures of competition: according both to Marx and the classical tradition, capital flows from low *rate* of profit areas to high profit rate areas, leading to rising prices in the former and falling ones in the latter, until actual prices have come to approximate prices of production, and the rate of profit has reached an appropriate degree of uniformity. Marx was explicit: 'capital withdraws from a sphere with *a low rate* of profit and invades others, which yield a higher' (italics mine) (Marx, vol. III, Ch. 10).

But this means that capitalists are motivated to disinvest in one sphere of industry and invest in another by consideration of the rate of profit. Marx describes this as a process of competition between capitals. Why, then, would capitalists come, at another point, to *ignore* the rate of profit and invest on the basis of profit margins, rather than profit rates? Moreover, by so shifting capital, they would (as we have shown) create a 'disproportionality crisis,' bringing about a collapse in growth. (This point is independent of objections to the 'implicit theory' of the movement of capital, for such objections argue for an even more fully specified theory of investment, which would rule out simple profit maximization.)

But the most serious problem with this argument is that it misconceives the theoretical position of the capitalist firm in two important respects. It fails to understand or analyze the firm as a unit of capital, and therefore as *constantly expanding, i.e. accumulating*. And it fails to appreciate the fact that firms undertaking large investments in fixed capital must normally raise funds to do so. Competition faces two ways – towards the market for products, but also towards the markets for labor and finance capital. Neglect of accumulation, on the one hand, and of competition in the market for funds, on the other, have allowed the story to seem plausible. Once these are properly fitted into the picture it will be clear that competitive firms must consider their profit rates, and cannot ever choose techniques on the basis of profit margins.

What follows is a study of the *logic* of choosing methods of production under capitalist institutions, on the assumption that a uniform rate of profit exists, and outputs are priced accordingly.

As a preliminary, it is useful to see that once accumulation is taken into account, the argument can run into trouble even on its own grounds. For simplicity and to avoid a long discussion over depreciation, assume a circulating capital model, with profit calculated on advanced wages (variable capital). Then in an obvious notation, in per capita terms:

$$w(1 + r) + rk = c + g(w + k) \tag{5A.31}$$

On the left we have net national income as wages plus profits, on the right, net national product as consumption plus investment. Manipulating, we find

$$w + k = \frac{c - w}{r - g}, \tag{5A.32}$$

that is, the value of capital per worker is given by the slope of a chord connecting the wage–profit rate point and the consumption growth rate point on the contours representing the respective trade-offs. As is well known, these contours will normally be duals and will be identical in shape (Nell, 1970; Spaventa, 1970; Laibman and Nell, 1977). They can both therefore be represented by a single curve. Let the vertical axis measure c and w, the horizontal, r and g. When $g = 0$, then c equals the maximum level of w, and the intercept of the curve measures the value of net output *per capita*. But when $g > 0$, and $g = r$ the vertical intercept of the chord measures net output *per capita* (point H). So the profit margin will be $H - w$, so the mark-up will be $(H - w)/w$, and clearly the size of this margin depend not only on w, but also on g.

Now consider two of these curves, A and B, which cross at one switch point. Initially the economy uses method A. Let us take the wage rate as given, at w. Assume little or no capitalist consumption and substantial savings out of wages. The growth rate will then be g, the maximum attainable with method A, and the rate of profit will be r_{0A}. Method B then becomes known and available. For simplicity, assume it is a straight line. The profit maximization criterion indicates a shift to method B, since $J - W_0 > H - W_0$. However, as is evident from the diagram (Figure 5A.9), this shift also results in a *higher* rate of profit! Far from an explanation of the tendency of the rate of profit to fall, we now have a tendency of the rate of profit to rise. Moreover, if we have chosen W_0 appropriately, the chord giving the value of capital per head in method A will be parallel to the straight line representing method B; i.e. the organic (value) composition of capital will be the same in both techniques! By choosing W_0 a little higher, then, we could arrange it so that the value composition of capital was *higher* in method A. In that event, going from method A to method B would mean a falling organic composition and a rising rate of profit. Many other combinations can be worked out, as a little experimentation will show. There can be no *general* presumption here any more than in neo-Classical theory, that the 'profit maximizing' criterion will uniformly lead to a succession of techniques in which the organic (value) composition of capital is higher and the rate of profit lower. (For an example of 'reswitching' according to this criterion, see Chapter 7.) On the contrary, it could lead to a succession of techniques with progressively lower organic compositions and higher

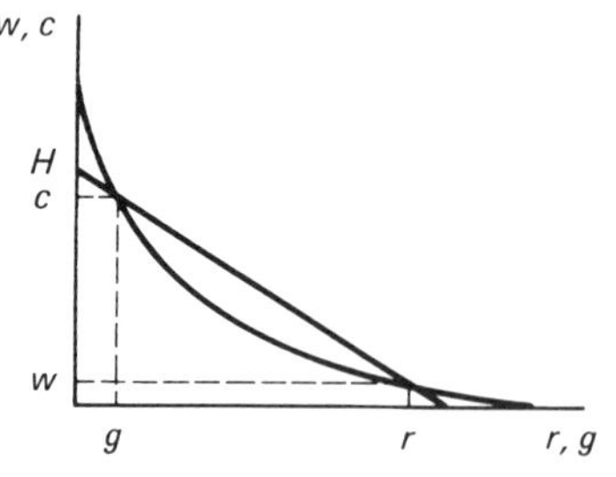

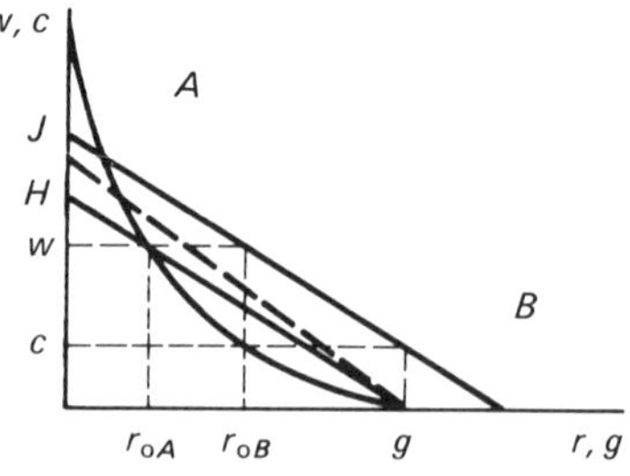

Figure 5A.9

rates of profit, or for that matter, to almost any other combination of changes. No definite rules can be laid down. (Note that this has nothing to do with the question of mechanization. There are many reasons for believing that technical progress in capitalism will take the form of displacing labor by machinery, but this is no guarantee that *value* of capital per man will rise in any regular way.)

Now let us return to the analysis of the actual process by which competitors move from the use of one method of production to another. This is supposedly the result of competitive pressure. Let us assume that the techniques, the growth rate and the wage rate are such that the preceding story will hold: the new technique will have a higher organic composition, a lower profit but a higher profit margin.

At the conclusion of the write-off period, or upon the emergence of a purchaser for the existing plant, the firm will have on hand the money value of its 'method *A*' plant. This will consist of its equity plus its borrowed capital. The latter it will presumably have to repay or roll-over. Hence it will have available for investment only *its equity in the initial plant* (assuming that it received a satisfactory purchase price or that it successfully recovered its initial investment before scrapping). The new plant, by assumption to have the same capacity, will employ fewer workers, but more fixed capital. Hence long-term borrowing requirements will rise, though short-term working capital needs will be less. Thus the firm contemplating a switch to 'method *B*' will have to increase its long-term debt–equity ratios. However, at the same time it faces a serious difficulty: method *B* generates a lower *rate* of profit. Hence, while it has a larger long-term debt it also has a reduced ability to pay. The competitive market interest rate will either equal the rate of profit or differ from it by a fixed margin, representing the premium for risk, etc. In any case, its movements will be governed by the rate of profit (or the rate of growth). Let us assume that the rate of interest equals the initial rate of profit. To pay the interest on the debt required to finance the method *B* plant, the firm will either have to *reduce its retained earnings* or cut *its dividend payments*. Either way it reduces the value of its equity. If it cuts dividends, its shares will no longer be so welcome in portfolios; if it reduces its retention ratio, s_0, it will not be able to expand as fast as its competitors, for *two* reasons: a lower rate of profit and a lower retention ratio. Thus the original growth rate of the firm was $g_0 = s_{c0}r_A$, whereas the later one will be $g_1 = s_{c1}r_B$, where $s_{c0} > s_{c1}$ and $r_A > r_B$. Other firms which do not make the shift to method *B* will be able to maintain their retention ratios intact, so they will continue to grow at the rate g_0; hence the firm or firms that switch to method *B* will grow more slowly and their market shares will fall.

Of course, it is more likely that, foreseeing competitive disaster, banks would refuse to finance a plant constructed to operate method *B*. The argument was that firms would be *forced* to adopt method *B*, because anyone who does can cut price, having a larger margin. But the margin over variable costs has to cover fixed costs and investments, and before a firm can shift into method B, it must enter into fixed-cost contracts for the financing of its new plant. Even if a firm did use its higher margin to cut price temporarily (postponing its debt servicing?; postponing further investment?) it could not *supply* the new business it attracted, without expanding still further, which its reduced profit rate makes it impossible to do so.

This Appendix has presented enough of the capital theory controversy, in simplified form, to make it clear that production prices – prices which distribute the surplus while effecting the exchanges required for re-supplying producers – cannot be treated as a special kind of scarcity prices. We have not considered joint production and we have remained within the confines of very simple models, but the results do generalize, and the next few chapters will take the argument further.

References

Arrow, K.J. (1962) 'The Economic Implications of Learning by Doing,' *Review of Economic Studies*, 29, pp. 155–73.

Cassel, G. (1932) *The Theory of Social Economy* (London: E. Benn).

Clark, J.B. (1956) *The Distribution of Wealth* (New York: Kelley).

Domar, E. (1957) *Essays in the Theory of Economic Growth* (New York: Oxford University Press).

Drandakis, E. (1963) 'Factor Substitution in the Two Sector Growth Model,' *Review of Economic Studies*, 84, pp. 217–28.

Gallaway, L. and V. Shukla (1974) 'The Neo-Classical Production Function,' *American Economic Review*, 64, pp. 348–58.

Garegnani, P. (1970) 'Heterogeneous Capital, the Production Function and the Theory of Distribution,' *Review of Economic Studies*, 37, pp. 407–36.

Goodwin, R. (1970) *Elementary Economics from the Higher Standpoint* (Cambridge: Cambridge University Press).

Hahn, F. (1966) 'Equilibrium Dynamics with Heterogeneous Capital Goods,' *Quarterly Journal of Economics*, 80, pp. 633–46.

Halevi, J., D. Laibman and E.J. Nell (eds) (1992) *Beyond the Steady State* (London: Macmillan).

Harrod, R. (1939) 'An Essay in Dynamic Theory,' *Economic Journal*, 49, pp. 14–33.

Hayek, F. (1941) *The Pure Theory of Capital* (London: Routledge).

Hicks, J.R. (1965) *Capital and Growth* (Oxford: Clarendon Press).

Jorgensen, D. (1960) 'A Dual Stability Theorem', *Econometrica*, 28 (4).

Kaldor, N. (1955) 'Alternative Theories of Distribution,' *Review of Economic Studies*, 23, pp. 83–100.

Laibman, D. and E.J. Nell (1977) 'Reswitching, Wicksell Effects, and the Neo-Classical Production Function,' *American Economic Review*, 67, pp. 878–88.

Lowe, A. (1976) *The Path of Economic Growth*, (Cambridge: Cambridge University Press).

Marx, K. (1976) *Wage Labor and Capital* (New York: International Publishers).

Marx, K. (no date) *Capital*, Vols. I, II, III (New York: International Publishers).

Nell, E.J. (1967) 'Theories of Growth and Theories of Value,' *Economic Development and Cultural Change*, 16, pp. 15–26, reprinted in G. Harcourt and N. Lang (eds), *Capital and Growth* (Harmondsworth: Penguin).

Nell, E.J. (1970) 'A Note on Cambridge Controversies in Capital Theory,' *Journal of Economic Literature*, 8, pp. 41–44.

Nell, E.J. (1982) 'Growth Distribution and Inflation,' *Journal of Post-Keynesian Economics*, 5, pp. 104–13.
Nell, E.J. (1988a) *Prosperity and Public Spending* (Boston and London: Allen & Unwin).
Nell, E.J. (1988b) 'Transformational Growth and Stagnation,' in C. Kurdas *et al*, *The Imperilled Economy* (New York: Monthly Review Press).
Nikaido, H. (1983) 'Marx on Competition'. *Zeitschrift Fuer Nationaloekonomie*, 43 (4), pp. 337–362.
Okishio, N. (1961) 'Technical Change and the Rate of Profit,' *Kobe University Economic Review*, 7, pp. 85–90.
Pasinetti, L. (1977) *Lectures on the Theory of Production* (New York: Columbia University Press).
Robertson, D. (1951) 'Wage Grumbles,' *Readings in the Theory of Income Distribution*, W. Fellner and B. Haley (eds) (Chicago: Richard Irwin) pp. 221–36.
Robinson, J. (1953) 'The Production Function and the Theory of Capital,' *Review of Economic Studies*, 21, pp. 81–106.
Robinson, J. (1956) *The Accumulation of Capital* (London: Macmillan).
Robinson, J. (1962) *Essays in the Theory of Economic Growth* (London: Macmillan).
Robinson, J. (1963) *Exercises in Economic Analysis* (London: Macmillan).
Russell, B. (1919) *Introduction to Mathematical Philosophy* (London: Allen & Unwin).
Solow, R. (1956) 'A Contribution to the Theory of Economic Growth,' *Quarterly Journal of Economics*, 70, pp. 65–94.
Solow, R. (1962) 'Substitution and Fixed Proportions in the Theory of Capital,' *Review of Economic Studies*, 29, pp. 207–18.
Spaventa, L. (1970) 'Rate of Profit, Rate of Growth and Capital Intensity in a Simple Production Model,' *Oxford Economic Paper*, 22, 129–47.
Sraffa, P. (1960) *Production of Commodities by Means of Commodities* (Cambridge: Cambridge University Press).
Uzawa, H. (1961) 'On a Two Sector Model of Economic Growth,' *Review of Economic Studies*, 29, pp. 40–8.
Vianello, F. (1985) 'The Pace of Accumulation,' *Political Economy: Studies in the Surplus Approach*, 1, pp. 33–51.

6 Capital and the Firm in Neo-Classical Theory*

How does a social system maintain and reproduce itself? How are capitalist social relationships maintained and reproduced? Many neo-Classical models are inconsistent at various points with the requirements for the maintenance and reproduction of capitalist relationships.

1 TWO VERSIONS OF NEO-CLASSICAL THEORY

All forms of neo-Classicism postulate household utility functions as the basis for demand. The standard version (SV) treats supply symmetrically – postulating the existence of a definite number of firms whose technical production possibilities are each described by a production function relating inputs and outputs. However, neo-Classicism can also be developed by the methods of activity analysis (AA), in which no firms are represented at all.[1] Production functions in activity analysis show the inputs required for a *product*, rather than the inputs required by a *firm*. Only firms can make market decisions; the cost of a product, in the abstract, may be interesting, but it is the cost *to the firm*, not in the abstract, that will be relevant to the firm's strategy in the marketplace and in the competitive environments that firms face and create for one another.

It is because the standard version deals with the concrete activities of firms, rather than with the abstract technology of products, that it must employ what is misleadingly referred to as an 'aggregative' concept of capital. The point is not so much that the various inputs under the firm's control are valued and aggregated. As participants on all sides of the capital controversy have observed, this in itself is of little interest. *Given* the prices, it is easy to 'aggregate' capital goods; *without* prices, no proxy measure will do. Everyone agrees. The question is, why bother aggregating capital?

The answer is as basic as it is obvious. A firm's capital is what makes it what it is. 'The firm' is the institutional form a particular capital takes. Its permanent existence is not as a set of capital goods, but as a *fund* of capital, embodied from time to time in capital goods, such as plant, equipment, and inventories. But capital remains while capital goods are used up, and inventories are converted to output and sold off. All of which is another

* *Journal of Post Keynesian Economics*, II (4) (Summer 1980).

way of saying that the activity of a firm is making a profit in the *turnover* of its capital. Marx captured the essence of the process in a simple formulation encompassing what he called the circuits of productive, commodity, and money capital.

$$M - C\begin{matrix} \nearrow L \\ \searrow MP \end{matrix} \ldots P \ldots C' \left\{\begin{matrix} C \; - \\ - M' \\ C \; - \end{matrix}\right. \left\{\begin{matrix} M - C\begin{matrix} \nearrow L \\ \searrow MP \end{matrix} \ldots P \ldots C' \\ m - \bar{c} \end{matrix}\right.$$

Money capital is used to buy means of production and labor, which then produce an expanded set of commodities, C', sold again for money, M', which then exchanges for productive commodities, C, and for luxury consumption, $\bar{c}$ (Marx, 1967, Vol. II, Ch. 4).

Marx's way of representing the circuits of capital highlights the fact that capital is regularly transformed from capital goods into inventories, into sales revenue, and into capital goods again. At the point when it is in money form, the managers of capital must decide on the most advantageous selection of capital goods. The inherent – and sequential – connection between capital as a fund and capital as plant and equipment is made plain. Of course, in any realistic account, there are restrictions on the extent to which changes in the form of invested capital can be made at any given time. But this is no comfort to those who assume 'malleable capital.' J.B. Clark, who understood very well the dual modes of existence of capital as a fund and as instruments of production,[2] gives the example of New England capital leaving whaling for textiles. No ships were converted to mills. 'As the vessels were worn out, the part of their earnings that might have been used to build more vessels was actually used to build mills. The nautical form of the capital perished; but the capital survived and, as it were, migrated from the one set of material bodies to the other' (1956, p. 118). Such mobility has traditionally been taken to establish a tendency to form a uniform rate of profit. At the very least, nonuniformity of the rate of profit on capital funds is inconsistent with equilibrium in competitive conditions. And, of course, the rate of profit must clear the capital market.

An exactly analogous point holds for labor. Competitive workers are on short-term contracts – 'daily wages' – that either side can abrogate costlessly. Hence workers will always seek employment at the highest wages, while employers will try to hire only those willing to work for the lowest wages. The only position consistent with equilibrium is one in which the wage is uniform, at a level that clears the labor market of each of the noncompeting labor groups.

Such points are elementary and are widely acknowledged in the neo-Classical SV theory. Surprisingly, these elementary features of competition are not consistent with the AA version of Neo-Classicism as generally presented.

2 FEATURES OF NEO-CLASSICISM

Activity analysis is analytically powerful and permits a far more detailed representation of the economy. To understand the relations between activity analysis and the earlier thinking, let us try to sum up the main features of neo-Classicism in a few basic propositions. This will not be easy. Neo-Classical writers had different interests, and frequently advanced different and competing theories. But there are certain common threads, and these can be woven into a fabric of ideas. Not all Neo-Classical writers would be content to wear the resulting garment, at least without alterations, and some might claim it was made of whole cloth. Nevertheless, here it is.

Neo-Classical economic theory explains the market system by establishing the forces determining prices and quantities exchanged, showing how and to what extent the resources are allocated efficiently and welfare achieved. The method is to determine a behavioral equilibrium. Prices, rates of return, and (less often) quantities are treated as signals to which behavior responds. Supply and demand functions thus have a stimulus-response form. Agents who demand final products and supply factor service are 'households;' agents who supply final products and demand factor services are 'firms.' Nothing essential depends on who or how many are capitalists and workers. Whether one is a capitalist or a worker is a matter of preference – 'labor can hire capital just as readily as capital can hire labor,' in the absence of inflexibilities and imperfections in markets. Agents' behavior is described by carefully specified functions, showing how far the agent should carry a desired course of action and stating exactly the constraints binding him. Objective factors such as initial endowments are clearly separated from subjective ones like expectations and uncertainty. Market analysis proceeds by building on the behavior of the individual firm and household units, determining first their individual equilibria, then by aggregation the equilibrium of the market as a whole and, by extension, the general equilibrium of the whole system. The product and factor markets are linked, since the demand for factors is derived from the demand for products, while the demand for products depends on the earnings from the sale of factor services. Intermediate products, however, are neglected. Markets for factors and for final products are analyzed in similar ways. In each case the supply and demand functions represent agents' solutions to constrained maximizing problems as price variables are assumed to change parametrically. Equilibrium exists for sets of values of the variables at which all agents are satisfied. This can be interpreted to mean either that all markets clear, or that no agent can be made better off without some other agent becoming worse off. These two interpretations overlap but are not equivalent. Equilibrium is interesting because it is assumed that there must be some 'tendency to equilibrium' in real markets.

The preceding is intended as a general account of the neo-Classical approach broad enough to encompass both the standard version and the general equilibrium model of Walras and Cassel. The standard version incorporates the effect of competition in equalizing the wage on all substitutable grades and skills of labor and in equalizing the rate of return across the entire field of capital goods within which capital funds can be invested. The Walras–Cassel or activity analysis model treats each capital good and each type of labor separately, determining their efficient use and particular rental values.

3 INITIAL ENDOWMENTS OF CAPITAL: GOODS OR FUNDS?

This difference leads to a difficulty when we come to consider how neo-Classical theory presents the social context within which economic activity is to take place. A universal property system is assumed, sometimes explicitly, more often implicitly; all means of production are owned, generally by private institutions, normally households or firms, where ownership implies alienability. Hence all products are owned by the owner of the means of production, or by the contractual operator of those means, according to the terms of the contract. So far, so good; though sparse in detail. The trouble comes in specifying the 'initial endowments,' for neo-Classical theory is not about to try to explain how property of various kinds came to be concentrated in certain hands. Given the initial distribution of ownership of factors, the theory determines equilibrium in product and factor markets, and examines the conditions under which these equilibria define efficient allocations of resources and welfare-maximizing patterns of consumption. How the initial distribution of ownership came about, however, is none of its concern.

In assuming an initial distribution, a problem arises. Households' endowments of land and labor are easily specified. It would also be appropriate to endow them with capital. But, capital funds or capital goods? If households are given specific machines, we are no longer operating with the broad concept of the factor. Households will trade their endowments of machines, each trying to obtain the most profitable selection. More of this later; the point is that initial endowments of specific goods will be traded. So we have left the framework of the standard version. But if households are endowed with *funds*, we have to ask how a *value* concept can be given meaning in advance of the determination of prices.

Even endowing households with funds, however, does not free the standard version from factor market problems. There is a general difficulty concerned with the relationship between the concept of capital, as a 'factor' supplied by households and demanded by firms, and the concept of the firm itself, the owner of the means of production and therefore of the product and the liabilities incurred in production.

4 CAPITAL AS PROPERTY, AND THE PROBLEM OF RESIDUAL INCOME

The expenditure of households is constrained by their incomes, which are obtained by selling the services of factors of production. But there is a curious difficulty here. Under competitive profit maximizing, firms equate value of the marginal product to the competitive factor price. An important constraint enters, however: the income paid out consists of claims in real terms, and these claims must exactly 'add up' to the real product produced. Suppose that the claims issued were less than the product; then the firm would necessarily be the owner of the residual and could not be in equilibrium. Part of the product would then be distributed in accordance with a principle other than marginal productivity.[3] Suppose that the claims added up to more than the product. At least one factor must then end up with less than its marginal product. But which one, and why?

So for neo-Classical competitive equilibrium, two conditions must be met: factors must receive their real marginal products, and these payments must exactly add up to the total product. These are *necessary* but not *sufficient* conditions. Both could be met, while factor supplies were out of equilibrium. But if they are *not* met, the system is not merely in 'disequilibrium:' rather, it is a case where the model itself is an *improper representation* of neo-Classical ideas.

The distinction is subtle but important. A disequilibrium position is one from which agents *could* conceivably move toward the equilibrium. By contrast, an unstable position is one in which incentives are so structured that agents' choices will tend to move them away from equilibrium. A system may possess no equilibrium, meaning that no set of choices can simultaneously satisfy all agents. These are all to be distinguished from the case in which the model *improperly* represents the underlying ideas,[4] as in an inconsistency between the *functional relations* postulated, and the *meanings assigned* to the variables of the model. Thus, when the income paid out according to marginal products does not add up to the output produced, the residual income is not the same as a 'disequilibrium factor reward'; a different *kind* of income appears – positive or negative incomes that are *not* the result (either implicitly or explicitly) of a sale of factor services. Where could such incomes come from? Income in excess of costs will be a net surplus; are there surplus goods as well?

Such questions are clearly disruptive; they portend a shift to a different framework of ideas, one that views production, organized along class lines, as resulting characteristically in a surplus appropriated by the dominant class, through the exchange and property system. The magic of neo-Classicism lies precisely in its ability to make the surplus disappear as all income results from a sale and payment for productive services.

So the problem stems from the need to reconcile two ideas basic to neo-Classicism: the concept of the firm as one of the basic agents in the market, and the doctrine that income payments represent a market sale of factor services. The idea of the firm as an agent supplying products in the market requires that the firm be the residual claimant – the owner of the total product, including all liabilities incurred in production. But the conception of income as the sale of factor services requires that any residual net claims to product, positive or negative, incurred by the firm be represented as the proceeds of a sale of a factor service, as the service of 'entrepreneurship' – which, however, has never been specified in any concrete way. It is seen only as the service of incurring the residual claims, assumed to involve risk, so the service has been called 'risk bearing.' But this is simply the service of being the residual claimant, that is, of being the firm.[6]

Even the risk is peculiar. For, in competition, in stationary conditions, the earnings of entrepreneurship depend wholly on the returns to scale. With constant returns entrepreneurship earns nothing; if returns diminish, then total product is greater than factor payments and entrepreneurs residually claim the difference, while if returns are increasing, total product is less than factor payments and entrepreneurs absorb the loss. So either there is residual income or at least one factor does not receive its marginal product. Either way, outside of constant returns, the neo-Classical theory fails to account for distribution. But if returns are constant, the firm's long-run marginal cost curve is horizontal, and so its size is indeterminate under competition.

5 RETURNS TO SCALE AND THE EQUILIBRIUM OF THE FIRM

The problem lies in reconciling the concept of the firm with the notion of income as a reward for the productive contributions of factors.[7] The simplest way around the problem has been to adopt Wicksteed's solution: to assume that production functions are linear and homogeneous. This solves the problem of distribution without determining the size and equilibrium of both the firm and the market independently of demand, which is the unfortunate consequence of following the route suggested by Walras and Wicksell.[8] Moreover, only a linear and homogeneous production function makes sense in the aggregate case, where there cannot be a residual claimant, since aggregate capital includes the equity, and so the ownership, of all firms.

There is nevertheless a heavy price to pay for this solution. Three points spring to mind. First, the assumption of constant returns requires that technical progress be treated as a *shift* in the production function. But for long-run problems this seems artificial. On what grounds could one distinguish between a shift and a movement along a function? Second, the scissors no longer cut with both blades. The long-run marginal cost curve is horizontal, so prices are fixed independently of demand. Third, the size of the firm and the distribution of output between firms is altogether indeterminate. All three of these, and particularly the third, cut deeply into the standard version's ability to deal with the analysis of particular markets.

Perhaps this discussion could be summed up by looking at it formally. The neo-Classical approach requires that factor markets be analogous to product markets. Looking at the aggregate picture, we have five variables to determine: the real wage, the rate of interest, the amount of labor employed, the amount of capital used, and the total output. But there are six equations to determine them: demand for labor, demand for capital, supply of labor, supply of capital, the production function, and the distributional identity. It is the overdetermination which gives rise to the overpayment or underpayment of income, the positive or negative residual incomes. To eliminate this awkwardness, neo-Classical theory makes the distributional identity depend on the production function, reducing the number of independent equations to five. But this creates problems for the theory of the firm, since the cost curves of producers reflect the same data that determine distribution.

If making sense of marginal productivity theory requires one to assume that production functions are linear and homogeneous, one might as well go all the way and adopt the Walras–Cassel approach, leaving the position of the firm indeterminate, but gaining the advantages of mathematical power, coupled with a detailed representation of production.

6 CONSISTENCY OF THE TREATMENT OF CAPITAL IN THE TWO APPROACHES

Some economists view the two approaches as complementary, drawing for some purposes on the standard version, for others on the Walras–Cassel model. This is unobjectionable when the problem concerns a particular event in a particular market, but the standard version cannot hold for the economic system as a whole. If they are both to be taken as true, with each revealing a different aspect of the truth, then they must be mutually compatible. We consider their capital theory aspects by examining a simple Walras–Cassel general equilibrium model (amplifying the argument of the Appendix to Ch. 5).

Let there be a vector of resources, $r = r_1, \ldots, r_m$ representing nonproduced means of production. Let $x = x_1, \ldots, x_n$ represent the outputs of the n various goods. A, the input matrix, is $m \times n$, showing the amounts of resources per unit output of the goods. p is the price vector and v the vector of rental values of the resources. The model can be formulated in programming fashion as follows:

$$\begin{array}{llll} \max & p'x & \min & r'v \\ \text{Subject to} & Ax \leqslant r & \text{Subject to} & A'v \geqslant p \\ & x \geqslant 0 & & v \geqslant 0 \\ & x = F(p, v) & & \end{array}$$

The function F gives the demands for the goods, x, as a function of prices and the incomes of households received from the rental of their resources.

A principal concern of those who have worked with this equilibrium model has been to show that it possesses a plausible solution.[9] A crucial question concerns the resources vector, r: the resources enter into production but are not themselves produced,[10] and evidently need no renewal. For if they were used up or worn out, the 'equilibrium' determined would be at most a one-shot affair; an equilibrium configuration must not only be capable of persisting, it must also account for all the market-related costs and benefits. If using the resources wears them down, a 'user cost' must be represented.

Are there any productive resources capable of being appropriated which are not used up? Ricardo spoke of 'the original and indestructible powers of the soil'; but after the Dust Bowl we know better. Space or location might be an example, but such things 'enter production' more in a metaphorical than in an engineering sense. In general, in ignoring depreciating resources, the model lacks application because it *misrepresents the nature of production* – an error of commission, not merely an 'unrealistic' omission.

Yet this is easily remedied. Let some of the commodities produced be the same goods as the resources. The stock of resources can then represent the initial endowments, and the coefficients denote the user cost, to be made good by replacement.

The implications of admitting that some of the goods in the initial endowments may be *produced means of production* are dramatic. Consider a simple model, containing only corn and iron:

$$\begin{array}{llll} \max & x_c p_c + x_I p_I & \min & C v_c + I v_I \\ \text{Subject to} & a_{cc} x_c + a_{cI} x_I \leqslant C & \text{Subject to} & a_{cc} v_c + a_{Ic} v_I \geqslant p_c \\ & a_{Ic} x_c + a_{II} x_I \leqslant I & & a_{cI} v_c + a_{II} v_I \geqslant p_I \\ & x_c, x_I > 0 & & v_c, v_I > 0 \end{array}$$

Let the demand function $F(p, v)$ be such that prices satisfying it result in the production of both corn and iron, and further suppose that these quantities permit the necessary replacement to take place. No loss of generality is involved; this merely guarantees a solution compatible with replacement. Of course the fact that the goods appear both as output and as input raises the question of whether the ps will be compatible with the

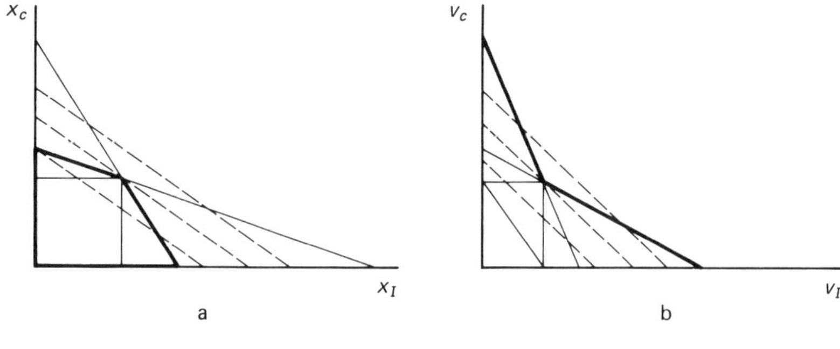

Figure 6.1

vs. Let us closely observe the Walras-Cassel procedure. Consider the diagram first of the maximizing (Figure 6.1a), then of the minimizing (Figure 6.1b) problem.

In Figure 6.1a, as long as the slope of the price ratio lies between the slopes of the two constraints, both goods will be produced.

In Figure 6.1b, if both goods are produced, both resources will be assigned positive values. The minimizing problem yields these shadow values, which represent the rentals that can be obtained from the commodities. The slope of the line joining the optimal value of v_I to the optimal value of v_c gives the ratio of the rental values.

The slope of v_I/v_c need not equal p_I/p_c. If it did, p_I/p_c could not be changed without changing v_I/v_c as long as the change stays within the limits prescribed by the slopes of the contraints.[11] But if

$$\frac{v_I}{v_c} \lesseqgtr \frac{p_I}{p_c},$$

then

$$\frac{v_I}{p_I} \lesseqgtr \frac{v_c}{p_c};$$

that is, the ratio of rental earnings to supply price for the two goods will be different. But capitalists will invest their capital in (pay the supply price of) equipment whose earning power is the highest.[12] Hence in the Walras–Cassel equilibrium model, all capital funds will flow into the purchase of only *one* of the goods, the one whose rental value in relation to supply price is the greatest.

This result could be reached more simply. It follows directly from the fact that a good's price as output cannot in general differ from its price when used as input, except for a markup due to handling, shipping, etc.

Hence, if μ is such a markup, $p_c = \mu v_c$ and $p_I = \mu v_I$, which implies $p_c/v_c = p_I/v_I$. But as we have just seen this result does not in general follow from the imputation procedure. Indeed if we imposed a requirement relating p_c/p_I and v_c/v_I the demand function would be redundant. Prices would be determined by production and distribution, independently of demand.

Clearly, a divergence of p_c/p_I and v_c/v_I is inconsistent with the reproduction of the initial supplies of the model, which means that reproduction, in turn, is incompatible with the notion of capital as a freely moving fund, responsive to competitive pressures and opportunities. It follows that the standard version and the activity analysis approaches are *not* mutually compatible. The standard version rests on a *broad* conception of a factor, allowing for a wide substitution among particular capital goods and workers in its account of the equilibrium of the firm. But this leads straight to the internal difficulties discussed earlier and, fundamentally, to the Cambridge (UK) critique as explained in the next chapter.

Activity analysis, since it has no theory of the firm, has no such internal difficulties, and on its narrow conception of factors, it is not subject to the Cambridge critique of factor pricing. But for precisely these reasons it stands directly opposed both to the standard version and to important strands of neo-Classical tradition. Without a theory of the firm, it is difficult to examine market structure and adjustments. But a theory of the firm cannot be grafted onto the AA model without providing an account of the firm's *cost and capital structure*. The model cannot accommodate this, however, for it would require consideration of factor markets broadly defined. Hence these are mutually exclusive approaches rather than alternative tools in the economist's famous kit, and both stumble over the capital concept.

The Cambridge critics think they know what has gone amiss: net income is not, in general, a payment for a productive contribution; rather, it is the distribution of a surplus in accordance with property rights that reflect mostly class position. 'Capital' is not a factor of production, nor is it to be identified with a set of material means of production: raw materials, instruments, and means of subsistence:

> What is a Negro slave? A man of the black race. The one explanation is as good as the other.
>
> A Negro is a Negro. He only becomes a slave in certain relations. A cotton spinning jenny is a machine for spinning cotton. It becomes *capital* only in certain relations. Torn from these relationships it is no more capital than gold in itself is money. . . .
>
> Capital . . . is a social relation of production (Marx, 1976).

Once this is cleared up, the way is open for an account of incomes that allows for the characteristic differences between profits and wages, in particular, and for the differences between the positions of the classes that predominantly receive each form of income.

In summary, each of the two principal versions of neo-Classicism has its characteristic defect, namely the absence from it of the concept of capital that defines the other. Each is therefore fatally one-sided, and represents a failure to live up to Clark's original vision. But the two versions share a further flaw: neither can offer an adequate theory of the firm, for neither is able to integrate the theory of the firm – in which supply price is based on costs – with the theory of distribution, in which costs reappear in the guise of factor incomes. But the doctrine of prices as signals of efficient allocation requires that costs represent relative scarcities, which means that no factor incomes can be pure residuals – all must be determined by supply and demand. This causes the theory of the firm to break down, since rising supply prices cannot be explained. Nor can an adequate account be given of the relation between capital funds and capital goods. The result is a complex, three-way incompatibility: neo-Classical theory cannot simultaneously encompass a full-bodied concept of capital (funds *and* goods successively), a concept of the firm in which its position defines the nature of the market, and a theory of distribution determined by supply and demand in factor markets.

The central doctrine of Neo-Classicism – that competitive markets tend to bring about an 'efficient allocation of scarce resources' – is therefore fundamentally suspect, and the way is open to treat capital, not as a 'scarce factor' but as a social relationship whose institutional form in the modern world is the corporation, which is maintaned and reproduced by economic activity. For many contemporary economists, this marks a welcome scientific advance, a triumph of reason over ideology.

Notes

1. Activity analysis is a method that is perfectly valid in what we term 'programming' models in *Rational Economic Man* (Hollis and Nell, 1975), or what Lowe calls 'instrumental' analysis. But activity analysis has been used to develop the Walras–Cassel theory of general economic equilibrium, an approach that differs significantly from the standard version of Neo-Classicism. The problems we shall be discussing do not arise in activity analysis, as such, but in its application to the Walras–Cassel scheme.
2. [Capital itself is] . . . a fund, a sum of active and productive wealth that continues in industry, as successive instruments of production live, as it were, their productive lives and die' (Clark, 1956, p. 121). Or again: 'We may think of capital as a sum of productive wealth, invested in material things which are perpetually shifting – which come and go continually – although the fund abides' (pp. 119–20). Clark is less detailed than Marx. He does not represent

the circuits explicitly, nor does he distinguish commodity from productive capital, although the distinction is latent in his work. But the idea that capital must be understood as a process by which a fund of value expands through undergoing a succession of changes in form is clearly central to Clark's theory.

3. An additional fictitious 'factor' could be defined to receive the residual, created expressly for the purpose of receiving the residual product. (How does one define the supply function for this factor?)
4. Cf. Hollis and Nell (1975) where we argue that the ideas *cannot* be adequately represented because the conditions for the continued existence – which we contend, necessarily means regular *reproduction* – of the agents, not only are not shown, but cannot be shown, consistently with the image of production as a 'one-way street' from factors to final products.
5. The output produced in a system of private property always and necessarily belongs to someone, so the assignment of the rights to it and claims over it must be *exact* at all times, whether or not that assignment is compatible with the agents' plans, incentives, and motivations. But if the system is supposed to determine earnings on market principles – that is, by supply and demand – then there can be no portion of output falling to a residual claimant, nor can real claims be distributed in excess of output, for that would imply a net liability on the part of the residual claimant, the firm. Income as a residual contradicts the basic idea that income results from the sale of factor services, that is, that it is a reward for a productive contribution.
6. There is thus implicit in the view we are adopting the notion that each individual can, as a formal matter, be regarded as owning two types of resources: 1) his resources . . . 2) A resource that reflects the difference between the productivity of his resources viewed solely as hired resources and their productivity when owned by his firm – we may call this "Mr. X's entrepreneurial capacity" . . . It should be emphasized that this distinction between two types of resources is purely formal. Giving names to our ignorance may be useful; it does not dispel the ignorance. A really satisfactory theory would do more than say there must be something other than hired resources; it would say what the essential characteristics of the "something other" are' (Friedman, 1960, p. 95). The trouble is that the 'essential characteristics of the something other' contradict the notion that all incomes are rewards for productive services. Hence these characteristics, which are perfectly obvious, must be concealed behind opaque names.
7. One of the strengths of the 'partial equilibrium' approach was that it helped to conceal these internal difficulties. To analyze the behavior of the firm, one assumed the income and behavior of factors as given and derived the cost curves from the production function. The implications for the income received by factors need not be taken into account. Later, when considering distribution, the behavior of the firm and the product market would be taken as given, without considering the implications of distribution for the cost curve of the firm.
8. Assume the following. The notation should be obvious:

(1) $P = P(L, K)$	The well-behaved production function.
(2) $\pi_L = \dfrac{\partial P\pi}{\partial L}$	Factors will each be employed up to the point where the value of their marginal product equals their price.

(3) $\pi_K = \dfrac{\partial P\pi}{\partial K}$

(4) $P = \dfrac{\partial P}{\partial L} L + \dfrac{\partial P}{\partial K} K$ The value of the total output must be distributed as wages to labor and interest to capital.

(5) $C = \pi_L L + \pi_K K$ Total cost of production equals total income paid out.

From the form assumed for the production function we know that $\lambda NP = P(\lambda L, \lambda K)$ where λ is an arbitrary proportionality factor. N varies from greater than unity to less than unity as P increases; hence $N = N(P)$ and $dN/dP < 0$. When L and K are increased by the factor λ, C increases by λ also: $\lambda C = \pi_L \lambda L + \pi_K \lambda K$. Since P is increased by λN, $\Delta P = P_2 - P_1$, and since $P_1 = P(L, K)$, $\lambda N\, P_1 = P_2 = P(\lambda L, \lambda K)$, $\Delta P = P(\lambda N - 1)$, or $\Delta P/P = \lambda N - 1$. By a similar argument, it is clear that $\Delta C/C = \lambda - 1$. Consequently, the ratio of the proportionate change in P to the proportionate change in C will be:

$$\frac{\Delta P/P}{\Delta C/C} = \frac{\lambda N - 1}{\lambda - 1}.$$

Taking limits and rearranging:

$$\frac{dP}{P} = \frac{dC}{C}\,\frac{\lambda N - 1}{\lambda - 1}$$

Suppose $N = 1$. Then, for that value of P, $dC/C = dP/P$ or $dC/dP = C/P$, which says that marginal cost equals average cost. When $N > 1$, $\dfrac{\lambda N - 1}{\lambda - 1} > 1$, and consequently $dC/dP > C/P$; marginal cost less than average cost.

Equations (1) and (4) will be satisfied together only when $N = 1$. Under the above assumptions there is one and only one such point, where $dC/dP = C/P$. Both price and quantity are determined independently of demand.

9. Unfortunately, the equilibrium does not guarantee the survival of consumers (cf. Koopmans, 1958, p. 41). Moreover, rather strong assumptions are required to ensure survival. This is therefore 'equilibrium' in a rather weak sense – markets clear, but the system may not be able to survive.

The assumptions on preferences and substitution required for existence and uniqueness are not our concern here.

10. Such resources are 'nonbasics' in Sraffa's classification. 'Being employed in production, but not themselves produced, they are the converse of commodities which, although produced, are not used in production' (Sraffa, 1960, p. 74). In arguing that 'reproduction' is the fundamental economic concept. Hollis and Nell argued, in *Rational Economic Man* (1975), that any economic system had at least two basic products. Basics and nonbasics differ fundamentally in their relationships to other economic variables, but the distinction is unknown in neo-Classical thinking.

11. Shift the intersection of the constraints in the max problem to the origin. Then construct perpendiculars to the constraint lines at the origin. These normal lines span a cone, and any line in this cone will be perpendicular to a line

through the origin lying *between* the two constraints. The cone therefore defines the set of price vectors for which the optimal point remains unchanged.

12. The standard version deals with factors in competitive conditions; laborers compete with one another for jobs, and capital funds flow toward the highest rate of return. The activity analysis model determines the earnings, for example, of particular machines or workers. But these earnings are rents and are subject to the requirement that

> [the] permanent fund of capital . . . is put into such forms that the rent secured by one concrete form or capital-good, is as large a fraction of its value as is that received by another . . . This equalizing force determines the number of capital-goods of each kind; and this, again, governs the rents they severally earn (Clark, 1956, p. 125).

The question confronting us is whether the modern activity analysis model is compatible with the capital theory of the standard version.

References

Clark, John B. (1956) *The Distribution of Wealth* (New York: Macmillan).

Dorfman, R., Samuelson, P., and Solow, R. (1956) *Linear Programming and Economic Theory* (New York: McGraw-Hill).

Friedman, M. (1960) *Price Theory: A Provisional Text* (Chicago: Aldine).

Hollis, M., and Nell, E.J. (1975) *Rational Economic Man: A Philosophical Critique of Neo-Classical Economics* (New York: Cambridge University Press).

Koopmans, T.C. (1958) *Three Essays on the State of Economic Science* (New York: McGraw-Hill).

Laibman, D., and Nell, E.J. (1977) 'Reswitching, Witchell Effects, and the Neo-Classical Production Function', *American Economic Review*, 67 (5).

Marx, K. (1967) *Capital*, Vol. 2 (New York: International Publishers).

Marx, K. (1976) *Wage Labor and Capital* (1848) (New York: International Publishers).

Sraffa, Piero (1960) *Production of Commodities by Means of Commodities* (Cambridge: Cambridge University Press).

7 Reswitching, Wicksell Effects, and the Neo-Classical Production Function*

David Laibman and Edward J. Nell

The Cambridge debate over capital theory has raised doubts about the validity of the neo-Classical theory of distribution (see G.C. Harcourt). As this theory is widely assumed in empirical work, and often drawn upon in the analysis of policy, a demonstration that it is seriously flawed would require extensive rethinking of many areas of mainstream economics. Accordingly, two principal lines of defense have been advanced. The first, an oblique defense, accepts the critique, but asserts that only a simplifying 'parable' has been damaged. The main corpus of neo-Classicism, general equilibrium theory, remains unscatched. The second is a counterattack, and contends that a well-ordered neo-Classical production function can be constructed after all (see Gallaway and Shukla, 1974, and refutations by Garegnani and by Sato, 1976).

In this study we explore further dimensions of the problem by returning to the classical work of John Bates Clark to inquire into the issues of reswitching of techniques and negative price Wicksell effects (rises in the value of capital per man as the profit rate rises within a given technique) in a variety of settings. In the first section, following Clark, we set forth the problem of establishing the relation between the fund of capital as held in portfolios, and the heterogeneous capital goods used in production. The second section presents a two-sector indecomposable model with only circulating capital and profit formed on the wage as well as on capital-good inputs in primal (price) and dual (quantity) form. It is the model best adapted to the task of verifying the Clarkian story weaving behavior concerning capital funds and constraints concerning capital goods into an operational demand curve for 'capital.' In the third section, the reswitching possibilities are examined, and a special case identified for which a 'nonreswitching theorem' does in fact hold. The fourth section examines the problem of negative price Wicksell effects and their impact on the attempt

* *American Economic Review*, 67(5) (1977).

to construct a 'surrogate' production function. The concluding section states results; the core of the matter, however, is that the capital controversies, against the rigorous Clarkian background, demonstrate the ill-founded character of both the aggregate production function and the general equilibrium defenses, and open the way for new approaches to distribution drawing on the post-Keynesian and Marxian heritage.

1 CAPITAL FUNDS AND CAPITAL GOODS

Reswitching of techniques and perverse changes in the value of capital arise in the connection between two equally significant and practical concepts of capital – the portfolio concept, a homogeneous fund of value, shifted about in pursuit of the highest rate of return, and the productive concept, heterogeneous goods and equipment designed for specific uses. This is how the problem of capital theory was first posed by Clark.[1]

The fund of capital moves in response to profit, and its effect is to produce a uniform rate of profit: 'Given a certain permanent fund of capital . . . it is put into such forms that the rent secured by one concrete form or capital-good, is as large a fraction of its value as is that secured by another' (Clark, p. 125). But Clark did not think that capital goods themselves would be shifted around. Capital proper is mobile, capital goods are fixed. He wrote: 'Capital is . . . the subject of competition; but capital-goods are not. The capital that is competed for does not consist in instruments – concrete, visible, moveable and ready for any one of a dozen different uses; there is no stock of capital-goods that has such adaptability' pp. 256–7).

In short, for Clark the problem of capital theory is that new capital is supplied and existing capital held in response to the rate of return on *funds*, while entrepreneurs, also necessarily motivated by the rate of return on the value of their investments, always demand capital for the purpose of embodying it in particular capital *goods*. What is required is a systematic connection between capital funds and capital goods, consistent with the relationship of each to the rate of profit. Clark's answer was that the more capital intensive a project, in terms of funds, the less an additional increment of funds could contribute to increasing the returns obtainable from it, by improving or altering the capital goods. Better technical ideas will be used first; it becomes progressively more difficult, hence more costly, to make technical improvements. Thus additional infusions of funds to improve capital goods will yield progressively smaller increments of profit. But the rate of return on the whole capital will be set, because of competition, by that on the final increment. Hence, with a given labor force, increasing capital funds can be embodied in alternative sets of quite different capital goods, which can be clearly ranked according to the associated rate of profit; the more expensive, more capital intensive the capital goods, the lower the rate of profit.

Clark thus does *not* put forth a simplistic 'aggregate capital' theory of marginal productivity, or 'parable.' The fund of capital is a reality, significant in determining business behavior. On the other hand, the demand for capital can only be understood in terms of concrete heterogeneous capital goods. Economists who confine their analysis to heterogeneous capital goods are unable to deal with the supply side or with financial matters, while those who deal only in aggregate capital are incapable of analyzing the specifics of production and technical choice, and the corresponding rental values of particular capital goods. For Clark, neo-Classical capital theory must encompass both funds and goods, and the connection between them must be consistent with the supply and demand framework. This is the point of constructing the aggregate production function, exactly as Paul Samuelson did, and it is this which the Cambridge critics contend they have shown to be impossible, in general.

2 THE TWO-SECTOR MODEL

In reconsidering the condition for successful coordination of capital funds and capital goods within a supply and demand framework, the appropriate model is a genuinely circulating capital model, in which the rapid turnover of capital goods releases funds that can migrate within a time frame consistent with a given set of conditions in financial markets. Thus, capital funds can 'travel' from one set of capital goods to another in response to profit incentives, as in Clark's example of New England capital leaving whaling for textiles.[2] If capital goods turn over in the same time span as wage capital – the given production-payment period – profit must be formed on the capital advanced as wages as well as that advanced on materials.[3]

The price equations for an indecomposable two-sector model, incorporating the above assumption, are

$$1 = (1 + r)(a_{01}w + m_1 + n_1p_2) \tag{7.1}$$

$$p_2 = (1 + r)(a_{02}w + m_2 + n_2p_2) \tag{7.2}$$

where r is the rate of profit, w the wage rate, p_2 the price of commodity two, m_1 and m_2 the input coefficients of commodity one into commodities one and two, respectively, and n_1 and n_2 the input coefficients of commodity two into commodities one and two, respectively. (Commodity one is the numeraire.)

The price equations yield a wage–profit contour:[4]

$$w = \{1 - (m_1 + n_2)(1 + r) + (m_1 n_2 - m_2 n_1)(1 + r)^2\} + \{a_{01}(1 + r) + (a_{02} n_1 - a_{01} n_2)(1 + r)^2\} \quad (7.3)$$

and an expression for the price of commodity two:

$$p_2 = \frac{a_{02} + (a_{01} m_2 - a_{02} m_1)(1 + r)}{a_{01} + (a_{02} n_1 - a_{01} n_2)(1 + r)} \quad (7.4)$$

We now write down the quantity equations, dual to the price equations (7.1) and (7.2). These show the composition of output per head and the disposition of the labor force. Letting T_1 be output per head of commodity one, T_2 be output per head of commodity two, c can be consumption per head, where consumption is limited to commodity one (the numeraire),[5] and g is the uniform (steady-state) rate of growth, we have:

$$T_1 = (1 + g)(m_1 T_1 + m_2 T_2 + c) \quad (7.5)$$

$$T_2 = (1 + g)(n_1 T_1 + n_2 T_2) \quad (7.6)$$

$$1 = a_{01} T_1 + a_{02} T_2) \quad (7.7)$$

Eliminating T_1 and T_2, we find the consumption-growth curve:

$$c = \{1 - (m_1 + n_2)(1 + g) + (m_1 n_2 - m_2 n_1)(1 + g)^2\} + \{a_{01}(1 + g) + (a_{02} n_1 - a_{01} n_2)(1 + g)^2\} \quad (7.8)$$

which is parametrically identical to the wage-profit contour (7.3).

The most common approach to choice of technique assumes that the techniques compared have one process in common; goods are defined independently of the uses to which they are put, so that a sector's choice of technique is not affected by, nor does it affect, the choice of technique by any other sector. Further assuming that the numeraire sector (sector one) is the one with the technique held in common, use the following compact notation for the case of two techniques:

$$s = s_1 = a_{01}$$

$$t = (a_{02}n_1 - a_{01}n_2)$$

$$t_1 = (a_{02}n_1 - a_{01}n_2)_1$$

$$j = (m_1 + n_2)$$

$$j_1 = (m_1 + n_2)_1$$

$$k = (n_1m_2 - m_1n_2)$$

$$k_1 = (n_1m_2 - m_1n_2)_1$$

The subscript 1 applied to the t, j, and k refers to the second technique. Equating the expression for the wage in the two techniques ($w = w_1$), we get the switching equation:[6]

$$(1 + r)^2 + \frac{s(k_1 - k) + tj_1 - t_1j}{tk_1 - t_1k} \cdot \qquad (7.10)$$

$$(1 + r) + \frac{s(j_1 - j) + (t_1 - t)}{tk_1 - t_1k} = 0$$

For reswitching of techniques to occur, (7.10) must have two positive roots for which $0 \leqslant r \leqslant r_0$, where r_0 is the maximum rate of profit at which either w or w_1 becomes zero. Sato neatly derives the range of values for the technical coefficients within which this condition is fulfilled.[7]

3 VARIETIES OF RESWITCHING

Reswitching of techniques – in which a single technique is the most profitable at both high and low rates of profit – is the impasse that brings the Clark expedition to a halt. We examine it under a variety of assumptions.

The Gallaway and Shukla Assumption

We add to the record our counterexample to the 'general nonreswitching theorem' proposed for the case in which all k_i, $t_i > 0$:

Parameter	*Technique A*	*Technique B*
a_{01}	1.0	1.0
m_1	0.1	0.1

Parameter	*Technique A*	*Technique B*
n_1	1.0	1.0
a_{02}	0.55872	0.56712
m_2	0.135872	0.261712
n_2	0.35872	0.11712

Using (7.9), we have $s = s_1 = 1$, $t = 0.20$, $t_1 = 0.45$, $j = 0.45872$, $j_1 = 0.21712$, $k = 0.10$, $k_1 = 0.25$.

Substituting these values into (7.10) and simplifying yields:

$$(1 + r)^2 - 2.6(1 + r) + 1.68 = 0$$

which factors neatly into

$$[(1 + r) - 1.2][(1 + r) - 1.4] = 0$$

Thus there are two positive roots, $r_1 = .2$ and $r_2 = .4$. The maximum rate of profit for the first technique is $r_{0_1} = 0.6129$, for the second $r_{0_2} = 0.61176$; hence, both roots fall within the required range.[8] The Gallaway and Shukla examples join the ranks of the standard reswitching examples which violate the unjustified assumption k_i, $t_i > 0$ (see n. 7).

Principal Diagonal = 0

It is possible to find an economically meaningful condition strong enough to yield the conclusion that the Clark story requires – but it is a very special case, indeed. The condition that

$$j = j_1 = 0 \qquad (7.11)$$

gives the required result. For then the switching equation becomes

$$(1 + r)^2 + \frac{s(k_1 - k)}{k_1 t - k t_1}(1 + r) + \frac{t_1 - t}{k_1 t - k t_1} = 0 \qquad (7.10')$$

By definition, now, k_i, $t_i > 0$. For there to be two positive real roots the term associated with $(1 + r)$ must be negative and the constant term positive. First, suppose $k_1 t > k t_1$. Then $k_1 < k$ implies $t > t_1$, so the constant term will be negative. But if $k_1 > k$, the $(1 + r)$ term will be positive. Next suppose $k_1t < kt_1$. If $k_1 < k$, the $(1 + r)$ term will be positive. But if $k_1 > k$, then $t_1 > t$, which will make the constant term negative. Hence, there cannot be two positive roots, and reswitching is ruled out.

This tells us at best that neo-Classical theory can only deal with highly specialized and unusual cases of changes in technique. An adequate theory will have to range further afield, into regions where the marginal productivity principle can give no guidance. Reswitching is not a peculiar or 'perverse' phenomenon; on the contrary, it is generally possible, and it is the neo-Classical case that is special.

Intersectoral Switching of Techniques

Comparison of techniques with one process in common considerably limits the generality of the results, for in a multisector world, it means comparing economies which differ in one process only.

Consider the problem of choice of techniques as Joan Robinson originally posed it: there are a number of identical islands in a sunny archipelago, the engineers of which all read the same book of blueprints. For historical or extraeconomic reasons different wage rates prevail on different islands. Arrange the islands in order, according to their wage rates. The question of 'reswitching' now carries no implication that there is any change from one technique to another and then back; rather we wish to know if an island with a low wage and one with a high wage might find the same technique most profitable, while an island with a middling wage chose a different one.

The assumption that the techniques differ in only one process carries the implication that producing the second good in a different way would nevertheless yield a product capable of entering just as it did before into the first process. While this may often be the case, it is also commonly true that the specifications laid down by industrial consumers of a product limit or determine product design, materials, machine tooling, and the method or production in general. The modern neo-Classical assumption that many different methods exist for producing exactly the same product simply ignores the inherent connection between the potential uses of a thing and the way it is made.[9] If a change in the method of production changes the qualities of the product, this may in turn require a change or adaptation in the method of production of the second good.[10]

The mathematical argument[11] that the total number of processes cannot exceed the total number of unknowns – the $n - 1$ prices, plus the wage and the rate of profits – is perfectly correct, but begs the question. For this argument assumes that the systems are in contact, and that the equations are to be solved simultaneously. Then only at switch points will prices be identical across techniques; hence, the price system will tell us which method is cheaper.[12] But in comparing island economies or more generally in choosing methods of production, we are interested not in prices but in profit rates and capital values, so the fact that the techniques are associated with different price structures will not affect the decision.

Reswitching examples in this case are readily available; see the one below with k_i, $t_i > 0$, as in Section 3.

Parameter	*Technique A*	*Technique B*
a_{01}	10.000	10.730
m_1	0.200	0.100
n_1	1.000	1.000
a_{02}	3.000	3.219
m_2	0.220	0.275
n_2	0.100	0.100

Here, technique A is used at low profit rates; there are switch points at $r = 0.09$ and $r = 0.32$, approximately, and technique A returns for r between 0.32 and $r_0(B) = 0.6085$.

Profit Maximization

If the world were coming to an end tomorrow, firms would maximize profits instead of the profit *rate*.[13] The rate of return becomes irrelevant, since growth is moot, and in the immediate future everything will be bygones. In the Clarkian world, and indeed the real world, however, there is a capital market; rental values of capital goods are ultimately governed by the rate of interest on capital funds. Efficiency shadow pricing of given endowments of resources, as in much contemporary general equilibrium theory, could not be acceptable to Clark. So long as the ratio of rental earnings to endowment (replacement) value remains nonuniform, capital funds will move, until the ratio of rents to value of holdings is equalized. Marginal product shadow prices are not, in general, equilibrium prices.

Suppose an entrepreneur invested in a method of production that maximized profits per head but yielded a lower rate of profit. He must borrow capital and pay the going rate of interest, while facing the same prices and wage rates as all other producers. Profit rate maximizers will be able to pay a higher rate of interest, thus attracting the entire supply of capital to themselves; profit maximizers would prove unable to meet competitive costs.

Still, since profit maximization is closely related to the general equilibrium defense against Cambridge criticism, we consider the possibility of reswitching in the circulating capital model, in which the technique is chosen which maximizes profits per head (π). For the aggregate economy, we have the quasi identity.

$$w(1 + r) + rk = c + g(w + k) \tag{7.12}$$

This gives net national product seen as wages plus profits on the left, consumption plus net investment on the right (remembering that in a model where wages are advanced, so must consumption be accumulated and advanced). Solving for the value of the total capital flow,[14]

$$w + k = (c - w)/(r - g) \qquad (7.13)$$

The value of capital per head is then given by the slope of the chord connecting the wage-profit point and the consumption-growth point on the single curve representing both the wage-profit and the consumption-growth contours (equations (7.3) and (7.8)). The w or c intercept of this chord, then, gives the value of net output per head, and the r or g intercept, the ratio of the value of net output to the value of capital.

If g goes to zero, the w-intercept of the chord comes to coincide with the w-intercept of the contour itself. In this zero-growth case, the value of net output per head is invariant to the rate of profit, and the technique with the highest w-intercept will always produce the maximum profits per head, whatever the level of the wage.[15]

While the growth rate is irrelevant to the reswitching issue as conventionally defined, it is important in this case, because the value of profits per head unlike the profit rate is not invariant to the composition of output. To give our argument some rope, we assume a high growth rate, implying substantial savings out of wages (we are concerned with the possibility, not the empirical likelihood, of reswitching; examples using weaker assumptions can undoubtedly be found).

In Figure 7.1, two techniques are drawn with no conventional reswitching, and no negative price Wicksell effects (see the next section). The growth rate is g_0, the maximum rate for technique A. Consider three levels of the wage: at w_1, $\pi_A = h - w_1 > \pi_B = 0$; at w_2, $\pi_B = j - w_2 > \pi_A = k - w_2$; finally, at w_3, $\pi_A = m - w_3 > \pi_B = n - w_3$. Clearly, on the profit-maximization criterion, technique A is most profitable at the high- and low-wage levels, and technique B is most profitable at the intermediate level. The inescapable curse of reswitching reappears.

4 NEGATIVE PRICE WICKSELL EFFECTS AND THE SURROGATE PRODUCTION FUNCTION

The neo-Classical story, whether in rigorous-Clarkian or jelly-parable form, requires an inverse monotonic relationship between the rate of profit and fund- or real-capital, respectively. In the absence of reswitching and perverse shifts in the value of real capital at switchpoints (capital reversing), validation of the inverse relation would depend on the premise of infinite substitutability, unless it were shown that the value of capital varies

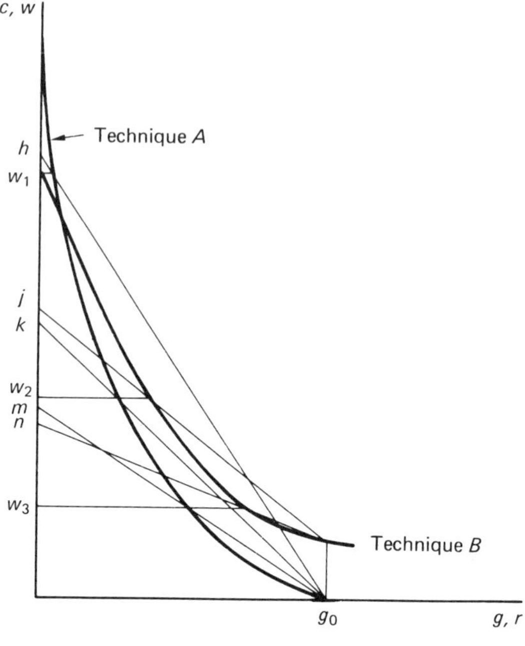

Figure 7.1

inversely with the profit rate within a single technique. In view of the attention devoted to this condition and its relation to efforts to construct a surrogate production function, we will examine, within the circulating-capital two-sector model, the conditions necessary for absence of negative price Wicksell effects (increases in the value of capital per unit of labor as the profit rate rises).[16] In Figure 7.1, as noted above, the value of capital per man is the slope of the chord connecting the $c - g$ point and the $w - r$ point; if this slope is to rise with a rise in the profit rate, the contour must be concave from below, and the condition for negative price Wicksell effects is thereby identified: the wage–profit (or consumption-growth) contour must have a negative second derivative.

Gallaway and Shukla attribute the absence of negative price Wicksell effects to their assumption $k_i, t_i > 0$, which we have already shown to be without economic justification. We will now show that it is also necessary that profit be calculated on the wage. The two conditions are jointly sufficient, as Gallaway and Shukla demonstrate in their original article, but neither alone will suffice.[17]

Consider the following examples: First, suppose that the condition $k_i, t_i > 0$ holds, in the strongest possible form – $m_1 = n_2 = 0$ – but that profit is not calculated on the wage. Let $a_{01} = 1$, $a_{02} = 0.2$, $n_1 = 0.1$, $m_2 = 0.8$. The wage–profit contour is

$$w = \frac{1 - 0.08\,(1 + r)^2}{1 - 0.02\,(1 + r)^2}$$

and $r_0 = 2.5355$, $w_0 = 0.902$. Let $R = (1 + r)$. Then

$$dw/dR = (-\,0.2R)\ /$$

$$(1 + 0.04R^2 + 0.0004R^4) < 0$$

$$d^2w/dR^2 = (-\,0.2 + 0.008R^2 + 0.00024R^4)\ /$$

$$(1 + 0.04R^2 + 0.0004R^4)^2$$

which is < 0 for $R \leqslant 3.5355$.

Now consider a case where profit is calculated on the wage, but where $t < 0$, $k = 0$. Let $a_{01} = 1$, $a_{02}, = 0.2$, $m_1 = 0.1$, $m_2 = 0.7$, $n_1 = 0.1$, $n_2 = 0.7$. Then $k = 0$, $j = 0.8$, $t = -\,0.68$, and $s = 1$. The maximum rate of profit is 0.25. Differentiating (7.3), we obtain

$$dw/dR = (-\,0.544R^2 + 1.36R - 1)$$

$$+ (R^2 - 1.36R^3 + 0.4624R^4)$$

which is negative between $R = 1$ and $R = 1.25$;

$$\frac{d^2w}{dR^2} = \{0.5032R^4 - 2.627R^3$$

$$+ 5.5488R^2 - 5.44R + 2\} + \{0.2138R^7$$

$$-\,1.258R^6 + 2.774R^5 - 2.72R^4 + R^3\}$$

which is also negative in the range $1 \leqslant R \leqslant 1.25$.

Only when both the capital-intensity condition k_i, $t_i > 0$ holds, *and* profit is figured on the wage, will negative price Wicksell effects be eliminated.

This double condition suggests that the attempt to rule out valuation perversity ends up on the horns of a dilemma. First, we observe that the model in which profit is not formed on the wage is most appropriate as an analog to the real world of real capital stocks, fixed in form for long periods of time, compared to which the stocks of financial capital tied up in payrolls ar negligible. With the value of capital dominated by stocks of physical capital, the possibility of 'perverse' swings in value relative to profit rates is all the greater.

However, as explained above, we seek to give full play to the Clark story in which financial capital 'migrates' from one physical body to another; we therefore return to the model with profit calculated on the wage, in which negative price Wicksell effects are less likely. But we now observe that the 'well-ordered' neo-Classical production function requires more than the nonreswitching of techniques. Marginal products must equal rates of factor payment. More generally, Samuelson's surrogate production function is constructed on the basis of a central and defining property of linear homogeneous production functions – that the elasticity of the wage–profit frontier measures relative shares.[18] But when the rate of profit is calculated on the wage these properties cannot hold consistently with marginal productivity theory. Starting with the net income equation, in obvious notation:

$$Y = wN + rwN + rK \tag{7.14}$$

Rewrite in per capita terms:

$$y = w + r(w + k) \tag{7.15}$$

Differentiating, and manipulating,

$$dy = dw + rdw + wdr + kdr + rdk \tag{7.16}$$

$$\frac{dy}{dk + dw} = r + \frac{dw}{dk + dw} + \frac{dr}{dk + dw}(k + w) \tag{7.17}$$

This implies that

$$\frac{dy}{dk + dw} = r \text{ if and only if} \tag{7.18}$$

$$\frac{dw}{dr} = -(k + w)$$

The marginal net product of total capital equals the rate of profit if and only if the slope of the wage–profit curve equals the value of total capital (ignoring sign). There is, of course, no reason to suppose this condition will be met; but if it is, then the elasticity of the wage-profit curve measures relative shares:

$$-\frac{rdw}{wdr}=\frac{r(k+w)}{w} \tag{7.19}$$

But the reciprocal condition that the marginal product of labor equal the wage must also hold.[19] Rewriting the net income equation and using $\phi = Y/K$, $n = N/K$ in per unit of capital terms:

$$\phi = (1+r)wn + r \tag{7.20}$$

we find, using the same method as before,

$$d\phi = (1+r)ndw + (wn+1)dr + (1+r)wdn \tag{7.21}$$

$$\frac{d\phi}{dn} = (1+r)w, \text{ if and only if} \tag{7.22}$$

$$\frac{dw}{dr} = -\frac{wn+1}{(1+r)n}$$

which, rearranged, is equal to

$$\frac{dw}{dr} = -\frac{k+w}{1+r}$$

Thus the marginal net product of labor will equal not the wage, but the wage *marked up by the gross profit rate*, if and only if the slope of the wage–profit curve equals the value of capital *discounted by the gross profit rate*. In the model with profit calculated on the wage, then, the two marginal productivity conditions cannot be simultaneously met. The model does not generate a surrogate for use in the neo-Classical parable.

And thus the dilemma: With profit formed on advanced wages, negative price Wicksell effects *can* be ruled out, but the marginal productivity conditions fail; in the opposite case, the latter conditions and their surrogate properties are preserved – here the reswitching and capital-reversing problems are not even considered – but only by incurring the necessary possibility of negative price Wicksell effects.

A final remark: Calculating profit on the wage appears to abandon a crucial neo-Classical position, one stated very forcefully by Clark, namely the labor and capital are separate, independent, and symmetrical factors, cooperating in production and receiving rewards commensurate with their contributions. To figure profit on the wage bill amounts to a return to one of the oldest conceptions of capital as, in part, a wage fund. This conception is alien to the structure of capital as it has evolved in modern industrial conditions, but it does undermine the 'factors of production' approach; we therefore wonder whether it is consistent with the defense of neo-Classical theory.

5 CONCLUSION

We have shown that the continuing attempts to rule out perverse phenomena in the neo-Classical theory of production and distribution have validated the contention of the Cambridge critics: that the crucial connections between Clark's capital funds and capital goods cannot be made in the way required, except in special and implausible conditions.

But the central point is not whether reswitching, capital reversing, and counter-indicated valuation shifts are empirically likely or unlikely.[20] The critics' deeper contention is rather that the supply and demand framework within which the problem of distribution is posed must be reassessed. One approach, mentioned earlier, is to abandon the fund concept of capital; this is the path taken by the general equilibrium theorists. This would have been just as unacceptable to Clark as the opposite reduction of capital to 'aggregate' jelly, now largely seen to be inadequate. Equilibrium prices which assign rental values to capital goods but fail to provide a uniform rate of profit[21] on capital funds will not do, for they simply make impossible any theory of the central institution of the capital market.

It is not our purpose to argue the case against general equilibrium theory here. We do wish to assert what will seem to many a great irony: that the Cambridge critics of neo-Classical theory are closer to Clark than either the general equilibrium enthusiasts or the would-be defenders of the parable, such as Gallaway and Shukla. The controversy has shown that, despite the vigor of Clark's original vision, it is not possible to consistently relate capital goods (in the theory of production) and capital funds (in the distribution of income to property ownership) within a comprehensive supply and demand framework that rules out social relations other than market relations grounded only in exogenously given technology and preferences. If anything is to be learned from this, it is to retain Clark's appreciation of the complexities of the capital concept in developing the institutionally richer post-Keynesian and Marxist theories of distribution.

Notes

1. Clark states: 'It is inevitable that both capital and capital goods should be subjects of economic study. There are problems concerning each of them that have to be solved; and this fact appears in an unfortunate way, in all those treatises on political economy in which the single term, capital, is used to designate productive wealth. Invariably does the application of this term shift from capital, as we define it, to capital-goods, and vice versa. This two-fold meaning of one important word has made endless trouble and confusion. . . .

   'The early economists all defined capital as consisting in instruments of production, such as tools, buildings, raw materials, etc. . . . Yet, having defined capital in this way, they were forced – as anyone must be – to revert to the common conception of it as a fund describable in terms of money, when they entered on the consideration of interest (p. 122).'

   See Hicks (1963), 'Commentary,' pp. 342–4 for a similar distinction.
2. Clark states: 'As the vessels were worn out, the part of their earnings that might have been used to build more vessels was actually used to build mills. The nautical form of the capital perished; but the capital survived and, as it were, migrated from the one set of material bodies to the other' (p. 118).
3. The assumption that profit is formed on materials alone dominates the circulating capital models in the literature; see Piero Sraffa, Hicks (1965), Samuelson, and Michael Bruno *et al*. While this procedure is most congenial to other aspects of the neo-Classical vision (see 4 below), its justification is that circulating capital is conceived as a simple surrogate for fixed capital stocks. The immobility of fixed capital, however, makes the capital market adjustment story appear extremely dubious, as movements of capital can only be in response to uncertainly held expectations of future rates of return.
4. Suppose commodity two were taken as numeraire; then the price equations would be

$$p_1 = (1 + r)(a_{01}\, w + m_1 p_1 + n_1)$$

$$1 = (1 + r)(a_{02} + m_2 p_1 + n_2)$$

   with the wage-profit contour

$$w = \{1 - (m_1 + n_2)(1 + r) + (m_1 n_2 - m_2 n_1)\,(1 + r)^2\} \\ + \{a_{02}(1 + r) + (a_{01} m_2 - a_{02} m_1)(1 + r)^2\}$$

5. This single departure from full generality makes consumption per head, in physical units, dimensionally homogeneous with the wage rate. If both commodities were consumed, consumption per head would have to be evaluated using the price ratio, and the consumption-growth tradeoff would not be independent of, let alone dual to, the wage–profit tradeoff.
6. When profit is not calculated on the wage, the wage-profit curve will be

$$w = \{1 - (m_1 + n_2)(1 + r) + (m_1 n_2 - m_2 n_1)(1 + r)^2\} \\ + \{a_{01} + (a_{02} n_1 - a_{01} n_2)(1 + r)\}$$

   Comparing this with (7.3), we see that the only difference consists in a factor of $(1 + r)$ in the denominator. When, solving for switch points, we set $w = w_1$, the factor $(1 + r)$ will cancel out. Hence, given the technologies, switch points are the same whether or not profit is figured on the wage.

7. Gallaway and Shukla (1974) propose a restriction on the coefficients sufficient to render commodity prices 'positive and finite for all positive values of r.' This seemingly reasonable restriction is in fact excessive; all that is necessary for an economically reasonable model is that prices (and the wage) be positive for $0 \leqslant r \leqslant r_0$ (where r_0 is the maximum rate of profit), which is guaranteed by the well-known Perron–Frobenius Theorem – the maximal eigenvalue of a non-singular matrix, and it alone, has an all-positive eigenvector associated with it. A rigorous but nontechnical presentation will be found in Ch. 5 of Sraffa. A simple demonstration for nonmathematicians: rewrite the numerator of (7.4) as

$$a_{02}\{1 - m_1(1 + r)] + a_{01}m_2(1 + r) \qquad (7.4')$$

Now consider a *comparison system* with $n_1 = n_2 = 0$. This system will have a maximum rate of profit $\hat{r}_0$ greater than r_0 of the system given by (7.1) and (7.2). For the comparison system, setting $w = 0$ in (7.3), we find $1 + \hat{r}_0 = 1/m_1$. For this value of r, (7.4′) reduces to $a_{01}m_2/m_1 > 0$, demonstrating that the numerator must be positive for $\hat{r}_0$, hence for r_0 and for all r such that $0 \leqslant r \leqslant r_0$. A symmetrical demonstration, this time with $m_1 = m_2 = 0$ in the comparison system, applies to the denominator of (7.4), which must therefore be positive for all relevant r in any productive technology. The 'counterexamples' tabulated by Gallaway and Shukla are therefore all perfectly valid examples of reswitching, as prices are positive for profit rates lower than the maximum rate; see Garegnani (1976). The Gallaway and Shukla restriction applies to (7.4); it is $a_{01}m_2 - a_{02}m_1 > 0$, $a_{02}n_1 - a_{01}n_2 > 0$. This implies a very special and arbitrary ordering of the coefficients. Let $A = n_1/n_2$, $B = a_{01}/a_{02}$, $C = m_1/m_2$. The Gallaway and Shukla restriction implies $A > B > C$. Call this ordering ABC. The possible orderings then are: ABC, CAB, BCA, ACB, BAC, CBA. In short, Gallaway and Shukla focussed on one out of six possible configurations of the coefficients. For our purposes we note here that their ordering implies all k_i, $t_i > 0$.

8. The Gallaway and Shukla proof of their nonreswitching theorem relies on comparison of the ratio of the numerators of the wage-profit curves of the two techniques (N) with the ratio of the denominators (D). Their account of the denominator ratio curve is correct; it has a negative first and a positive second derivative, falling but flattening out and remaining positive throughout the range $0 \leqslant r \leqslant r_0$. But in their account of the N curve (p. 355, Figure 5, and p. 356, Figure 7), they fail to realize that it may cut the D curve from above, and then flatten out more rapidly (or begin to rise) and cut it again, within the relevant range. This is what happens in our reswitching example in the text, as shown by these computations, for selected values of r:

$r = 0$	$N = 0.8281$	$D = 0.8275$	$N > D$
$r = 0.2$	$N = 0.8051$	$D = 0.8051$	$N = D$
$r = 0.3$	$N = 0.79481$	$D = 0.79485$	$N < D$
$r = 0.4$	$N = 0.785276$	$D = 0.785276$	$N = D$
$r = 0.5$	$N = 0.7773207$	$D = 0.776119$	$N > D$

9. For a critique of this assumption, see Martin Hollis and Edward Nell (1975) Ch. 9, especially pp. 234–40, 245–8. As regards the assumption, see Clark:

'This complementarity of producers' goods must always be considered; since a poor machine introduced into an equipment of good ones has the effect of taking something from the productive power of the other parts of the equipment' (p. 248). For Clark, altering methods and improving products go hand in hand, and a method cannot be altered without its suppliers of inputs appropriately improving their products (pp. 246–52).

10. Perhaps the best-known case of switching where both sectors always change methods together is Samuelson's construction of the surrogate production function. Since the two sectors always have the same capital-labor ratio, they will both cease to be most profitable at the same time. The techniques always have different price structures, even at switch point, with prices equal to labor values in each case.
11. See Sraffa (1960) pp. 81–2; Bharadwaj (1970) p. 415.
12. Moreover, this is necessary for the rate of profit to equal the real marginal product of capital at a switch point. Consider two techniques in aggregative terms: $y_1 = rk_1 + w$, $y_2 = rk_2 + w$. Clearly, $r = (y_2 - y_1)/(k_2 - k_1)$. This can be interpreted as a 'marginal product' *only* if the two systems have identical price structures at the switch point. Moreover, it is an accounting marginal product, and cannot be used to determine the rate of profit.
13. In their reply to Garegnani and Sato, Gallaway and Shukla revert to a profit-maximization assumption as a second line of defense.
14. See Spaventa (1970) and Nell (1970) for the derivation of this relationship for models in which profit is formed on physical capital only.
15. This is the Gallaway–Shukla case, which thus rests on the arbitrary restriction $g = 0$. Note that to rule out reswitching, these authors are ready to rule out *any* switching of techniques – and this in the name of a defense of neo-Classicism!
16. Gallaway and Shukla, in attempting to rule out this phenomenon by showing that $d^2w/dr^2 > 0$ for a single wage-profit curve (7.3), mistakenly argue that this is a necessary condition for a 'factor price contour [which is] monotonically decreasing and decreasing at a decreasing rate throughout the positive quadrant' (p. 357). They seem to have forgotten that Samuelson's surrogate production function is made up of *linear* wage–profit tradeoffs.
17. It is easy to see why figuring profit on the wage helps to rule out negative price Wicksell effects. There is a massive 'composition effect' working against them. Since the rate of profit is formed on the wage, the wage is part of capital, and a rise in profits involves a fall in the capital flow equal to the fall in the wage. The rise in the price of physical capital inputs must be huge to offset this fall and ensure an overall rise in the value of capital.
18. Write a linear homogeneous 'well-behaved' production function in per capita form: $y = y(k)$. Then $r = y'(k)$ and from Euler's Theorem, $w = y(k) - ky'(k)$; $dr/dk = y''(k)$; $dw/dk = y'(k) - y'(k).\ (dk/dk) - ky''(k)$. Hence $dw/dr = (dw/dk)/(dr/dk) = -k$, $rdw/wdr = -rk/w = -rk/wL$. The wage–profit frontier is derived from the cost-minimizing problem which is dual to the output maximizing usually associated with the production function; see Samuelson (1962) p. 202, n. 2.
19. This is not explicitly recognized by Amit Bhaduri. Nevertheless it can be shown that the condition does indeed hold in his model which calculates profit on physical capital only.
20. But see Peter Albin (1975), who examines the case of a major lumber company switching from horses and men to mechanized methods of hauling logs with a rise in wages, and then back to horses and men with a further rise.
21. Except with linear Engel curves, constant returns, and a very special set of initial conditions.

References

Albin, P. (1975) 'Reswitching: An Empirical Observation,' *Kyklos*, 1 (28) pp. 149–54.

Bhaduri, A. (1969) 'On the Significance of Recent Controversies on Capital Theory: A Marxian View,' *Economic Journal*, 79, pp. 532–9.

Bharadwaj, K. (1970) 'On the Maximum Number of Switches Between Two Production Systems,' *Schweizerische Zeitschrift für Volkswirtschaft und Statistik*, 106, pp. 409–29.

Bruno, M. *et al.* (1966) 'Nature and Implications of the Reswitching of Techniques', *Quarterly Journal of Economics*, 80, pp. 526–53.

Champernowne, D.G. (1954) 'The Production Function and the Theory of Capital: A Comment,' *Review of Economic Studies*, 2 (21) pp. 112–35.

Clark, John B. (1956) *The Distribution of Wealth: A Theory of Wages, Interest and Profits* (New York: Macmillan).

Gallaway, L. and V. Shukla (1974) 'The Neoclassical Production Function,' *American Economic Review*, 64, pp. 348–58.

Gallaway, L. and V. Shukla (1976) 'Reply,' *American Economic Review*, 66, pp. 433–6.

Garegnani, P. (1966) 'Switching of Techniques,' *Quarterly Journal of Economics*, 80, pp. 554–67.

Garegnani, P. (1970) 'Heterogeneous Capital, the Production Function and the Theory of Distribution,' *Review of Economic Studies*, 37, pp. 407–36.

Garegnani, P. (1976) 'The Neoclassical Production Function: Comment,' *American Economic Review*, 66, pp. 424–7.

Harcourt, G.C. (1972) *Some Cambridge Controversies in the Theory of Capital* (London, New York).

Hicks, John (1963) *Theory of Wages* (London) 2nd edn.

Hicks, John (1965) *Capital and Growth* (New York).

Hollis, Martin and Nell, Edward J. (1975) *Rational Economic Man: A Philosophical Critique of Neo-Classical Economics* (London, New York).

Nell, E.J. (1970) 'A Note on Cambridge Controversies in Capital Theory,' *Journal of Economic Literature*, 8, pp. 41–4.

Robinson, J. (1954) 'The Production Function and the Theory of Capital,' *Review of Economic Studies*, 2 (21) pp. 81–106.

Robinson, J. (1970) 'Capital Theory Up to Date,' *Canadian Journal of Economics*, 3, pp. 309–17.

Samuelson, P.A. (1962) 'Parable and Realism in Capital Theory: The Surrogate Production Function,' *Review of Economic Studies*, 29, pp. 193–206.

Sato, K. (1976) 'The Neoclassical Production Function: Comment,' *American Economic Review*, 66, pp. 428–33.

Spaventa, L. (1970) 'The Rate of Profit, Rate of Growth and Capital Intensity in a Simple Production Model,' *Oxford Economic Papers*, 22, pp. 129–47.

Sraffa, Piero (1960) *Production of Commodities By Means of Commodities* (London, New York).

8 The Black Box Rate of Return*

'(. . .) What is the proper scope of capital theory, and on what real problems can it throw light?

(. . .) The highbrow answer is that the theory of capital is (. . .) a part of the fundamentally microeconomic theory of the allocation of resources, necessary to allow for the fact that commodities can be transformed into other commodities over time. Just as the theory of resource allocation has as its "dual" a theory of competitive pricing, so the theory of capital has as its "dual" a theory of intertemporal pricing involving rentals, interest rates, present values and the like. In both cases, a complete price theory is also a theory of distribution among factors of production (. . .)' (R.M. Solow, *Capital Theory and the Rate of Return*, 1963, p. 14).

1 INTRODUCTION

In his de Vries lectures (1963) Solow developed 'middle-brow' capital theory, using the social rate of return on investment as the organizing concept. Later, in his famous contribution to the Dobb *Festschrift*, he took steps towards the elaboration of a highbrow theory. Now Mario Nuti (1974) has provided a masterly summary of neo-Classical highbrow capital theory, together with a brief and brilliant commentary on current controversies as seen by strollers along the banks of the Charles – all the more remarkable for being written while punting on the Cam.

These controversies are intricate and difficult, but by now a few main lines of agreement stand out among neo-Classical economists. The Clark parable has been abandoned, if with regret in some quarters, though none in Mario Nuti's. But general equilibrium theory, and particularly intertemporal allocation theory, is held to be wholly immune to 'Cambridge Criticism'. In a general equilibrium framework, 'capital theory is an extension of ordinary resource allocation and price theory' (Solow, 1963, p. 15), and the fact that no monotonic inverse relation exists between the

* *Kyklos*, 28(4)(1975). This study circulated for a long time in draft form, and I owe an unusually large number of debts for helpful comments and criticism. Thanks are especially due to E. Burmeister, G.C. Harcourt, Luigi L. Pasinetti, C.R. Ross, R.M. Solow, and, above all, Luigi Spaventa, who independently arrived at many of the same results.

total stock of capital and the rate of return has no bearing on general price theory. The crucial point is to demonstrate the *efficiency* properties of the price system – that prices provide accurate guides to efficient resource allocation. Thus the rate of return must equal the contribution of savings at the margin, just as all other prices, and the wage, must measure marginal contributions. For the proportionality of revenues and productive contributions at the margin is the centerpiece of the neo-Classical vision of the price mechanism – it is the rock on which the temple is built wherein we worship the efficiency of Mammon (Nell, 1973).

The implication is that the distribution of net income, as Edgeworth saw long ago, is a special case of efficiency pricing. It would be hard to find a proposition more at variance with the whole of Classical, let alone Marxian, economics.[1] To be sure Nuti does not think neo-Classical theory *does describe* the actual working of capitalist economies. On the contrary, he holds that neo-Walrasian theory cannot accurately describe it, because full equilibrium requires forward markets for labor, which would invest workers with contractual claims to income, in conflict with the priorities established by capitalist institutions. But a system which *could* establish such markets, centrally planned socialism, for example, would then fit the general equilibrium picture, and competitive pricing in such a system would provide a realistic paradigm of efficiency. This is in many ways an ironic elaboration of Solow's view that '(. . .) the best way of understanding the economics of capitalism may be to think about a socialist economy (. . .)' (1963, p. 11) for, after all, 'the theory of perfectly-competitive capitalism is in many respects the theory of a planned or socialist economy' (p. 15).

2 DISTRIBUTION, EFFICIENT PRICING AND INTERTEMPORAL SUBSTITUTION

But is distribution in a market system in any reasonable sense a special case of efficiency pricing? Certainly in a Sraffa type of system neither the wage nor the rate of profits are *formally* the same as prices. Mathematically the rate of profits is derived from the characteristic root of the input-output matrix, while prices follow from the associated vector. These mathematical notions express different formal properties of the system, and are susceptible of quite different economic interpretations. Prices can be seen as expressing the exchanges necessary to carry out reproduction consistently with some pre-assigned division of the surplus, while the rate of profit expresses the ratio of the part of that surplus going to capital to the capital advanced. The corresponding dual variables would then express the growth rate which that profit could support if it were invested, and the proportions in which the physical commodities would have to stand to one another in the investment. There is no justification here for treating the rate of profits as a 'price' of any sort, whether of capital or of investment. Nor is there any ground for supposing that it measures either the 'scarcity' or the 'productive contribution' of any factor, real or imagined. Yet Nuti states that, '(. . .) The equality between the interest rate and the rate of return on investment (when both are constant over time) is a condition for equilibrium and efficiency (. . .) for Sraffa as well as Solow (. . .)' (1963, p. 361).[2]

He goes even further later, when he argues that Sraffa's approach '(. . .) based on wage-profit relations has no overwhelming advantage over the general equilibrium approach. It is a general equilibrium approach with the preference side chopped off (. . .)' In some respects, this may confuse formal and substantial identity. Certainly some neo-Classical writers, e.g. Solow, have used sets of equations formally the same as Sraffa's. But their substantive interpretation of these equations – what makes the mathematics economics – has generally not been the same. Neo-Classical writers have never made use of the distinction between basic and non-basic goods; nor have they been concerned with the relations between 'labor embodied' and 'labor-commanded' standards of value; nor have they been concerned with distinguishing '(. . .) such properties of an economic system as do not depend on changes in the scale of production or in the proportions of "factors"' (Sraffa, p.v.) from properties that do.[3]

Still, Nuti has a point, but it might better be put this way: a Sraffa-type wage-profit model could be substituted for the production-distribution side of a neo-Classical general equilibrium model. The resulting model would be closed, given the usual structure of preferences, and would be able to analyze the relation between basic and non-basic sectors, and also the returns to the ownership of goods like land which though themselves not produced, enter into production. (Morishima has worked extensively with such models.)

But these matters do not, and cannot, bear on the central features of Nuti's argument, for the latter is based on a different form of modern economic theory in which production is not represented explicitly at all. In place of current inputs and outputs Nuti provides a model of *intertemporal substitution possibilities*. Within this framework he analyzes intertemporal production *choices* in the light of intertemporal wealth and utility maximization. Since this point is of great significance in what follows, his analysis deserves a close look:

He begins by defining a price, $p\,(1, 0)$ representing the present value of the consumption good at time 1, at which a unit of consumption at time 1 exchanges for consumption at time 0, which defines a one-period interest rate, r

$$r \equiv \frac{1}{p(1, 0)} - 1$$

at which the consumption good can be lent or borrowed over the period. Then

> 'If consumption at time 1, c_1 can be transformed into consumption at time 0 (or vice-versa) at a rate of dc_1/dc_0 in production or consumption activities, we can express this rate of transformation in terms of a rate ϱ, defines as
>
> $$\varrho \equiv -\frac{dc_1}{dc_0} - 1$$
>
> where ϱ is the marginal rate of return on one-period investment if dc_1/dc_0 denotes productive transformation, or the marginal rate of time preference if dc_1/dc_0 denotes substitution in the highest attainable utility level.
>
> The equality between transformation rates and relative prices,
>
> $$-\frac{dc_1}{dc_0} = \frac{1}{p(1, 0)}$$
>
> implies
>
> $$\varrho = r$$
>
> i.e. the equality between the interest rate, the marginal rate of 'time preference,' and the marginal rate of return on investment.
>
> This equality is not, *in itself*, a theory of the determination of the interest rate. (It) indicates *either* a partial equilibrium situation of an individual consumer or producer for a *given* interest rate; *or* the property of the solution of an intertemporal general equilibrium system, where initial endowments, tastes and technology are fully specified for each individual, and the interest rate is *simultaneously determined* by the intertemporal choices of wealth-maximizing and utility-maximizing agents operating in perfect markets.'

3 THE MEANING OF SOLOW'S THEOREM

The clue may lie in the first word quoted – 'If . . .'. So long as Mario Nuti *postulates* that consumption at one time can be transformed at a certain rate into consumption at another time, and *defines* the one-period rate of interest by the price at which a unit of consumption at one time exchanges for a unit at another, his analysis, like a pardoned

President, is unimpeachable. The equality between transformation rates and relative prices, the standard neo-Classical equilibrium condition, implies that the interest rate, so defined, equals the marginal transformation rate, so postulated. This is no different in principle from the method of many other neo-Classical writers, who have postulated the existence of an aggregate production function, together with competitive conditions, and proceeded with the help of equilibrium conditions to derive the usual theorems on the efficiency of the price mechanism.

There is much to be said for this approach; indeed it has the support of Bertrand Russell, who writes, 'Postulating what we want has many advantages; they are the same as the advantages of theft over honest toil.' What has been stolen here, rather than earned, is the right to claim that intertemporal transformations of consumption can take place at a rate capable of being brought into equality with the rate of profit earned on the production of the consumption goods. For the intertemporal transformations are not specified; we are shown consumption at one time and the changed consumption at other times. In between, whatever happens is concealed in the Black Box.

The starting point of the Cambridge Controversy over the aggregate production function was the challenge to the original sin. Joan Robinson's complaint was not that the aggregate relationships could not be postulated, but that they could not be *demonstrated*, when methods of production were explicitly specified in input-output terms. Mario Nuti, it seems has missed the analogous point in the present discussion. For his model cannot possibly help to clear up the argument between Solow and Pasinetti; he begins by postulating what is at issue.

By contrast, Solow's paper in the Dobb *Festschrift*, like Samuelson's paper on the surrogate production function, sets out to meet the challenge. Solow's theorem is designed to *show* that when methods of production and relations of distribution are fully specified,[4] intertemporal efficiency properties hold for the rate of interest. In particular the rate of interest will measure the ratio of benefits in future consumption to the sacrifices of present consumption involved in making a switch between methods of production. Even more ambitiously, he argues that because of this equality, private and social rates of return will coincide.

The theorem needs only simple algebra. For reasons which will become plain in section 6, I shall write everything in *per capita* terms. Let y be output per head, w the wage rate, r the rate of profit, g the growth rate, c consumption per head, and k capital per man. All are aggregate variables; the implications of this aggregation will be taken up later, in section 5. We then consider a switch point between two techniques using circulating capital and operating in stationary conditions:

$$y_1 = w + (1 + r)\,k_1 = c_1 + k_1 \qquad (8.1)$$

$$y_2 = w + (1 + r)\, k_2 = c_2 + k_2 \tag{8.2}$$

Suppose the economy actually proceeds from Technique 1 to Technique 2. There will have to be a 'transition' step, where capital per head, k_2, is provided out of income per head, y_1. The consequence will be reduced consumption per head, $\bar{c}$:

$$y_1 = \bar{c} + k_2 \tag{8.3}$$

Solow then defines the Social Rate of Return, ϱ, as:

$$\varrho = \frac{c_2 - c_1}{c_1 - \bar{c}}$$

and substituting from (8.1) and (8.2) we get:

$$\varrho = \frac{y_2 - y_1}{k_2 - k_1} - 1 = \frac{w + (1 + r)\, k_2 - w - (1 + r)k_1}{k_2 - k_1} - 1 \tag{8.4}$$

$$\varrho = r$$

At *any* switch point, and quite apart from any definition of the social rate of return:

$$r = \frac{y_2 - y_1}{k_2 - k_1} - 1 \tag{8.5}$$

This is a tautology pure and simple, and cannot explain prices or profits. If any part of marginal productivity theory rests on (8.5), it is in trouble, for, except in a one-commodity world, prices and so the rate of profits, must be known *before* the RHS can be computed. Hence nothing which rests on this equation can explain prices or profits.

But Solow is quite justified in pointing to the fact that his social rate of return is defined in terms not simply of (8.1) and (8.2), but also of (8.3), the 'transition step'. He is concerned, not simply with the fact that a switch point exists, but with the sacrifice of consumption, and subsequent gain, involved in *making* the switch.[5]

Solow's theorem, then, is not so much an equilibrium condition as a *validation* of a proposed equilibrium condition. He shows that it is indeed possible for a rate of return to be computed on the social benefits in consumption resulting from a sacrifice of consumption, consistently with a rate of profits being earned in the production of the consumption good and its inputs, i.e. these two rates will be mutually compatible. To see the point, suppose the contrary: Suppose that the rate of return resulting from discounting the stream of benefits arising from a sacrifice of consumption systematically *differed* from the rate of profits earned in the production of the consumer goods. Then saving and investment could not be brought into equilibrium with the holding of present capital; neo-Classical capital theory could not possess a complete equilibrium. If the rate of return lay above the rate of profit, businesses would try to scrap their equipment and get into new investment, while if the rate of return lay below the rate of profit, new savings would be channeled into bidding for presently existing properties. In either case the market value of currently operating plant would be affected, thereby creating disequilibrium in current production and distribution.[6] Hence Solow's theorem should be interpreted as a demonstration that a Fisherian theory of saving and investment can be grafted on to the wage–profit model. It is not an equilibrium condition itself; rather it demonstrates the possibility of a Fisherian equilibrium.

4 SOLOW'S THEOREM IN A GROWING ECONOMY

Yet it is surprising that Solow, who is principally concerned with investment and growth, should have presented and examined his theorem principally for stationary conditions. Surely in the stationary state no one is willing to forego present for future consumption, at least at the rates available? For if they were willing to make the sacrifice necessary to switch techniques; then they would also be willing to make the sacrifice necessary to invest in expansion in a given technique in which the same return will be realized.[7]

Let us consider what happens when growth is taking place at a positive rate, g:

$$y_1 = w + (1 + r)\, k_1 = c_1 + (1 + g)k_1 \tag{8.6}$$

$$y_2 = w + (1 + r)\, k_2 = c_2 + (1 + g)k_2 \tag{8.7}$$

And suppose that a transition from Technique 1 to Technique 2 takes place without disturbing the growth rate:

$$y_1 = \bar{c} + (1 + g)\, k_2 \tag{8.8}$$

Then,

$$\varrho - \frac{c_2 - c_1}{c_1 - \bar{c}} = \frac{y_2 - y_1}{(1 + g)(k_2 - k_1)} - 1 \tag{8.9}$$

Hence, substituting again,

$$\varrho = \frac{w + (1 + r)k_1 - w - (1 + r)k_2}{(1 + g)(k_1 - k_2)} - 1 = \frac{r - g}{1 + g} \tag{8.10}$$

So when $g = 0$, $\varrho = r$; when $g = r$, $\varrho = 0$; when $g > r$ (e.g. all profits *and* some wages saved), $\varrho < 0$.

This is the correct analogue to Solow's argument, for in effect, he assumes an unchanged growth rate of zero. But suppose the transition *does* disturb the growth rate. Before the transition, Technique 1 is operated in stationary conditions, $g = 0$, while afterwards, Technique 2 is operated in a growing economy, $g > 0$. Then we have:

$$y_1 = w + (1 + r)k_1 = c_1 + k_1 \tag{8.1a}$$

$$y_2 = w + (1 + r)k_2 = c_2 + (1 + g)\, k_2 \tag{8.2a}$$

$$y_1 = \bar{c} + (1 + g)k_2 \tag{8.3a}$$

so that

$$\varrho = \frac{c_2 - c_1}{c_1 - \bar{c}} = \frac{y_2 - y_1 + k_1 - (1 + g)k_2}{(1 + g)k_2 - k}$$

$$= \frac{r(k_2 - k_1) - gk_2}{k_2 - k_1 + gk_2} \tag{8.4b}$$

More generally, suppose there is an initial growth rate g_1 and a later rate g_2:

$$y_1 = w + (1 + r)k_1 = c_1 + (1 + g_1)k_1 \tag{8.1b}$$

$$y_2 = w + (1 + r)k_2 = c_1 + (1 + g_2)k_2 \tag{8.2b}$$

$$y_1 = \bar{c} + (1 + g_2)k_2 \tag{8.3b}$$

and

$$\varrho = \frac{c_2 - c_1}{c_1 - \bar{c}} = \frac{r(k_2 - k_1) + g_1k_1 - g_2k_2}{(k_2 - k_1) + g_2k_2 - g_1k_1} \tag{8.4b}$$

Clearly when $g_1 = g_2 = r$:

$$\varrho = \frac{r(k_2 - k_1) - g(k_2 - k_1)}{(k_2 - k_1) + g(k_2 - k_1)} = \frac{r - g}{1 + g} = 0$$

as before, and when $g_1 = g_2 = 0$, $\varrho = r$, Solow's special case. But, *in general*, the social rate of return will not equal the switching rate of profit. If $g_1 \neq g_2$, Solow's Theorem will hold if and only if $g_1k_1 = g_2k_2$, that is, if the ratio of the growth rates equals the ratio of the capitals, certainly a very special case.

Now consider the simple case where $g = s_\pi r$, s_π being the propensity to save out of profits, $0 < s_\pi \leqslant 1$. Then,

$$\varrho = \frac{r(1 - s_\pi)}{1 + s_\pi r} \tag{8.11}$$

and,

$$\frac{\partial \varrho}{\partial r} = \frac{(1 - s_\pi)(1 - r)}{s_\pi r} > 0, \quad \text{if } s_\pi < 1 \tag{8.12}$$

For given r, varying s_π gives:

$$\frac{\partial \varrho}{\partial s_\pi} = - \frac{-2r^2(1 - s_\pi)}{(1 + s_\pi r)^2} < 0$$

So when $s_\pi = 0$, $g = 0$ and $\varrho = \varrho\text{max} = r$; but when $s_\pi = 1$, $g = r$, and $\varrho = 0$. There is, however, a curious case involving reswitching, where (8.10) and (8.11) do not hold. This can be illustrated for a two-sector case with a diagram (Figure 8.1) showing the primal and dual sides, the tradeoffs, that is, between w and r, and c and g, together with the saving function, which relates g and r. The w, r curves are plotted in the upper right quadrant and the c, g curves in the upper left. Let us suppose that $0 < g < r$, and, further, that s_π is such that when r is at switch point S_2, g falls at the level corresponding to S_1. According to (8.11) $\varrho > 0$, since $0 < s_\pi$ 1. But in these circumstances,

$$k_1 = \frac{c - w}{r - g} = k_2 \tag{8.13}$$

Hence $y_1 = y_2$, which implies $c_1 = c_2 = \bar{c}$, from which it follows that $\varrho = \%$. The social rate of return is undefined in this case. Notice that an exactly parallel case could be constructed if all profits and some wages were saved, at such a rate that when r stood at the level corresponding to S_1, g would be

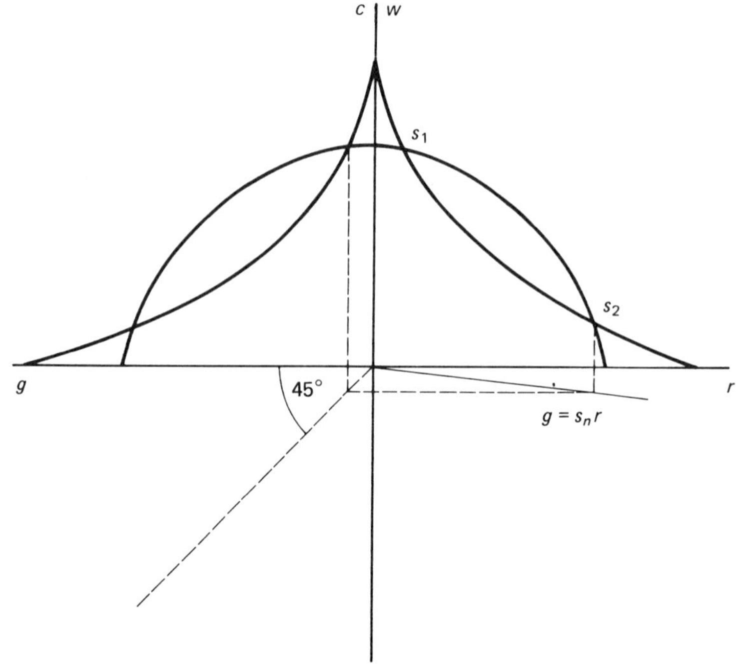

Figure 8.1

found at the level corresponding to S_2. According to (8.11), under these circumstances $\varrho < 0$, but in fact ϱ will be undefined.

Now consider the relation between the social rate of return and the switching rate of profit when r is at S_2, but g varies over its entire range. First, suppose $g < r_{S_1}$. In this case there will be a rise in the value of capital per head when the system moves from Technique 1 to Technique 2, so there will be a sacrifice in consumption per head in making the transition, followed by a gain in consumption. This is the sort of case Solow has in mind, but even if $\varrho = r_{S_2}$ for some value of $g < r_{S_1}$, it will not for any of the others. If $r_{S_1} < g < r_{S_2}$ there will be a fall in both the value of capital per man and in the amount of consumption per head. If $g > r_{S_2}$ there will be a fall in the value of capital per man coupled with a rise in consumption per man, so the social rate of return would be negative. Finally if the Golden Rule holds, if $g = r_{S_2}$, then $c_2 = c_1 = w$; consumption will be the same in both techniques, so there will be no gain at all, and $\varrho = 0$.[8]

5 CONSUMER GOODS AND CAPITAL GOODS

So far everything has been simple. Too simple, in fact, for something essential has been concealed. The analysis has implicitly assumed that all goods figure both as consumption goods and as means of production. To see this assume there are two goods A and B. Then in balanced growth:

$$
\begin{aligned}
y_{A_1} &= c_{A_1} + (1 + g)k_{A_1} \\
y_{B_1} &= c_{B_1} + (1 + g)k_{B_1}
\end{aligned}
\tag{8.14}
$$

Now consider a transition from one method of production to another (or as Spaventa shows, from one pattern of consumption to another with an unchanged method of production). This requires altering the capital:

$$
\begin{aligned}
\bar{c}_A &= c_{A_1} - (1 + g)(k_{A_2} - k_{A_1}) \\
\bar{c}_B &= c_{B_1} - (1 + g)(k_{B_2} - k_{B_1})
\end{aligned}
\tag{8.15}
$$

So, where p is the price of the capital good:

$$
\begin{aligned}
\bar{c} &= \bar{c}_A + p\bar{c}_B = c_{A_1} + p\bar{c}_{B_I} - (1 + g)(k_{A_2} + pk_{B_2} - (k_{A_1} + pk_{B_1}) \\
&= c_1 - (1 + g)(k_2 - k_1)
\end{aligned}
$$

Hence

$$
k_2 - k_1 = \frac{c_1 - \bar{c}}{1 + g} \tag{8.16}
$$

and since, from (8.1) and (8.2), $r - g = (c_2 - c_1) / (k_2 - k_1)$

$$
\frac{r - g}{1 + g} = \frac{c_2 - c_1}{c_1 - \bar{c}} \tag{8.17}
$$

Now suppose only one good, say A, is consumed, while both figure as means of production. Then

$$
c_1 - \bar{c} = (1 + g)(k_{A_2} - k_{A_1}) = (1 + g)\ k_2 - k_1 - p\ (k_{B_2} - k_{B_1}) \tag{8.18}
$$

From (8.17) and (8.18) we obtain:

$$
\varrho = \frac{c_{A_2} - c_{A_1}}{(1 + g)\ (k_{A_2} - k_{A_1})} \tag{8.19}
$$

Since good A is both consumption and means of production, numerator and denominator are comparable. The denominator coefficients are fixed, and the numerator simply depends on the consumption differences between the techniques. Hence given a rate of growth, ϱ will be fixed. Suppose $\varrho = r$ for some level of g, and consider a change in saving habits which would raise g and lower c; both of these will lower ϱ. In general if $\varrho = r$ for some level of g, it will not for any other.

Now look at (8.18) again. Only if $k_{B_2} = k_{B_1}$ would (8.17) hold. But under those conditions capital and consumer goods are effectively homogeneous; we are back to an analogue of the one-sector model. If $k_{B_2} > k_{B_1}$ the transition cannot take place without a one-period (or longer) drop in g, or a divergence in growth rates between sectors, and/or unemployment of some resources. Such transitions are both realistic and important (Lowe, 1955), but they are not consistent with intertemporal equilibrium analysis, and they cannot be part of this analysis. The only possible case, therefore, is where $k_{B_2} < k_{B_1}$ – and the transition is irreversible. But even so Solow's Theorem will not generally hold.

6 A NEW DEFINITION OF THE SOCIAL RATE OF RETURN

Solow briefly considers the case of a 'growing labor force' in section 7 of his article. In this discussion he introduces a *different* conception of the social rate of return, though he does not seem to realize this. He argues, '(. . .) the one-period transition amounts to a sacrifice of $c_1 - \bar{c}$ in consumption in the current period in return for a stream of consumption gains equal to $(1 + g)(c_2 - c_1)$ next period, $(1 + g)^2(c_2 - c_1)$ in the period after that, and so on. The social rate of return is the discount rate, ϱ, which discounts the value of this stream to the value of the current consumption foregone' (Solow, 1967, p. 37, changed to my notation). So we have

$$c_1 - \bar{c} = \frac{(1 + g)}{1 + \varrho}(c_2 - c_1) + (1 + g)^2 \frac{(c_2 - c_1)}{1 + \varrho^2} + \ldots \tag{8.20}$$

or

$$\begin{aligned} 1 + \varrho &= (1 - g)\left(\frac{c_2 - c_1}{c_1 - \bar{c}}\right)\left(1 + \frac{1 + g}{1 + \varrho} + \frac{(1 + g)^2}{(1 + \varrho)^2} + \ldots\right) \\ &= (1 + g)\left(\frac{c_2 - c_1}{c_2 - \bar{c}}\right)\left(\frac{1 + \varrho}{1 + \varrho - (1 + g)}\right) \\ &= (1 + g) + (1 + g)\left(\frac{c_2 - c_1}{c_1 - \bar{c}}\right) = (1 + g) + (1 + g)\frac{r - g}{1 + g} \end{aligned} \tag{8.21}$$

Hence, $\varrho = r$, as before.

This is worth looking at more closely. First there are questions arising from the algebra; then there is a problem of interpretation. The algebra works only if the sequence converges, and that will be true only if $\varrho > g$. But for $\varrho > g$, it must be the case that

$$\frac{c_2 - c_1}{c_1 - \bar{c}} > 0 \text{ i.e. } \frac{r - g}{1 - g} > 0$$

This rules out, for example, a growth rate financed by all of profits together with some worker savings, and more generally, all cases where worker savings exceed capitalist consumption. It also means that Solow's Theorem, in this form, is incompatible with Golden Rule growth; ϱ, by this formula, will be *undefined* if $r = g$. Hence the discounting formula gives results that differ from those derived from the earlier definition of the social rate of return. The conclusion must be that there are two different notions of the social rate of return here.

Next the matter of interpretation. As a matter of logic the sacrifice is necessarily a *per capita* sacrifice, while the gain, *as Solow portrays it*, is an absolute, *but not a per capita*, gain. Labour grows at whatever long-term rate is postulated: 0 in the stationary state, $g > 0$ in any other case. The one-period sacrifice is defined for a *given* labour force; hence it is necessarily a per capita sacrifice. But the later stream of benefits comes with a growing labor force, and hence, with a given distribution, a growing consuming population. Solow (p. 37) writes the stream of gains as '(. . .) $(1 + g)(c^* - c)$ next period, $(1 + g)^2(c^* - c)$ in the period after that (. . .)' neglecting to point out that the consuming population 'next period' is $(1 + g)$ times its size this period and $(1 + g)^2$ times its present size in the period after that. To derive an expression for ϱ, the sacrifice and benefits must be homogeneous, and since the sacrifice *must* be *per capita*, so must be the benefits. Hence the correct discounting expression is

$$c_1 - \bar{c} = \frac{c_2 - c_1}{1 + \varrho} + \frac{c_2 - c_1}{(1 + \varrho)^2} + \ldots \qquad (8.22)$$

that is,

$$1 + \varrho = \frac{c_2 - c_1}{c_1 - \bar{c}}\left(1 + \frac{1}{1 + \varrho} + \frac{1}{(1 + \varrho)^2} + \ldots\right)$$

from which it follows that,

$$\varrho = \frac{c_2 - c_1}{c_1 - \bar{c}} = \frac{r - g}{1 + g} \tag{8.23}$$

It may be objected[9] that if a single person puts $1.00 in his family bank account and earns 10 c. during a year in which he gives birth to 1/10 of a child, that it will still be true that the rate of interest on the initial saving is 10%, even though the per capita return is zero. Though presented as an objection this illustrates the point perfectly. The interest at the bank is analogous to the rate of profit in production; the family's $1.00 sacrifice and $1.10 return provides the basis for Solow's concept of the rate of return, and if figured *per capita* this will *not* be equal to the rate of interest. If we ignore the fact that the benefits must accrue in part to persons who performed no sacrifices (babies in the analogy, but new workers in the model) we could save the theorem. But only at the price of making the talk of 'sacrifice' and 'benefits' meaningless, since the benefits no longer go exclusively to those who make the sacrifices. Individuals responsive to market forces, which is what the Fisherman's Tale is all about, will be induced to sacrifice present consumption by the prospect of *their own* stream of future gains in consumption. The discounting formula for the society must be the aggregate of individuals' discounting calculations, and if there are more individuals (receiving the uniform wage and consuming/saving at the common rate) they will have to be added in. Only a rate of return derived from the aggregation of individuals' discounting calculations could be the basis for a Fisherian time-preference theory for determining the rate of profit. It should be added, however, that the ambiguity uncovered here shows that in general, in intertemporal calculations, private and social rates of return *do not* coincide.

7 AN ANALOGUE OF THE SOCIAL RATE OF RETURN IN A SOCIALIST SETTING

If Solow's theorem is not generally correct – if the Black Box does not contain what Nuti and Solow think it contains – then Fisherian theory cannot be grafted onto the wage-profit model in the general case of a growing economy (the only case where investment makes sense when there is no 'unobtrusive postulate') quite apart from any other deficiencies in the Fisherian approach, such as those adduced by Pasinetti. For as Nuti correctly points out, the wage-profit model '(. . .) investigates the necessary properties of a solution without sponsoring any particular theory of how that (. . .) solution has come about'. Yet we must not jump to conclusions too rashly. So far we have only investigated the case for a capitalist economy; it is possible that the Fisherian approach may work better (or, perhaps, differently) in the context of socialist institutions. Solow, it is true, tells us that the social rate of return is a '(. . .) technocratic notion (. . .) entirely independent of the institutional arrangements of the economy (. . .),' but perhaps we had better see for ourselves.

So let us imagine a different economy. To avoid arguments about 'state capitalism' let us choose a market socialist 'labor-managed' economic system. Workers manage factories, and pay interest to the State Treasury on their capital. They also save by buying Treasury bills and receive interest on their savings. The State Treasury, in turn, receives an interest on the capital of the enterprises, out of which it meets the expenses of the state administration, making the remainder available at the going rate to enterprises wishing to expand. Under this system interest payments on capital replace taxes, thereby ensuring that there will be no distortion of the market by government. The long-run equilibrium conditions are that the same wage and the same rate of interest should prevail everywhere; hence given the desired overall rate of growth, set by the government, the rate of interest will be given by $r = g/(1 - a)$ where a is the fraction of every dollar coming in to the Treasury which goes to administration costs.[10] Consider such a system on the margin of doubt between two methods of production, I already being used, and II which will yield higher growth rates at lower *per capita* consumption levels. To switch from I to II, paying the same rate of interest and growing at the same rate after the transition as before, it will be necessary to curtail income payments to workers, but they will benefit from higher income in the future. Following Solow, we can identify their sacrifice as their original wages, $L(w_1 - \bar{w})$; and we can readily see that their permanent gain will be $L(w_2 - w_1)$, the difference between the final wage and the original. Hence the dual to Solow's social rate of return can be defined as the ratio of the discounted value of the perpetual stream of returns to the initial one period sacrifice of wage income. This initial sacrifice will be $(w_1 - \bar{w})L$ and the gain in each period will be $(w_2 - w_1)L$ multiplied by the growth rate appropriately compounded. Clearly the amounts of labor cancel out, and we have

$$w_1 - \bar{w} = \frac{(1+g)}{1+\varrho}(w_2 - w_1) + \left(\frac{1+g}{1+\varrho}\right)^2 (w_2 - w_1) + \ldots \quad (8.24)$$

or,

$$1 - \varrho = (1+g)\left(\frac{w_2 - w_1}{w_1 - \bar{w}}\right) + \frac{(1+g)^2}{(1+\varrho)}\left(\frac{w_2 - w_1}{w_1 - \bar{w}}\right) + \ldots$$

$$1 - \varrho = (1+g)\left(\frac{w_2 - w_1}{w_1 - \bar{w}}\right)\left[1 + \frac{1+g}{1+\varrho} + \left(\frac{1+g}{1+\varrho}\right)^2 + \ldots\right] \quad (8.25)$$

$$1 - \varrho = (1 + g)\left(\frac{w_2 - w_1}{w_1 - \bar{w}}\right)\left(\frac{1 + \varrho}{(1 + \varrho) - (1 + g)}\right)$$

$$\varrho = g + (1 + g)\left(\frac{g - r}{1 + r}\right)$$

Observe that $\varrho > g$ is necessary for convergence, which requires

$$\frac{w_2 - w_1}{w_2 - \bar{w}} > 0, \quad \text{i.e. } g > r$$

The second term of this expression gives the *one-period rate of return* in this model. The one period sacrifice is $w_1L - \bar{w}L$, and the gain in the immediately following period will be the difference between the old and new wage rates multiplied by the *expanded* labor supply, $(1 + g)(w_2 - w_1)L$. So the one-period rate of return is

$$\varrho = (1 - g)\frac{(w_2 - w_1)L}{(w_1 - \bar{w})L} = \tag{8.26}$$

$$\frac{(1 + g)[c - (1 - g)k_2 - (1 + r)k_2] - [c + (1 + g)k_1 - (1 + r)k_1] -}{(c + (1 + g)k_1 - (1 + r)k_1] - [c + (1 + g)k_1 - (1 + r)k_2]}$$

$$\frac{[c + (1 + g)k_1 - (1 + r)k_1]}{(c + (1 + g)k_1 - (1 + r)k_1] - [c + (1 + g)k_1 - (1 + r)k_2]}$$

$$= \frac{(1 + g)[(1 + g)(k_2 - k_1) - (1 + r)(k_2 - k_1)]}{(1 + r)(k_2 - k_1)} = (1 + g)\frac{(g - r)}{(1 + r)} \tag{8.27}$$

Note that here again we have two distinct concepts of the social rate of return, one derived from substitutions in the formula for benefits over sacrifices, the other from discounting the stream of income-differences to zero. Again the discounting formula will not be valid for the Golden Rule, or for any case where $r > g$.

In the short run – looking ahead one-period only – when the rate of profit is zero, the market socialist social rate of return is $g + g^2$, but in the long run it will be $2g + g^2$. In the short run when the Golden Rule holds, when $r = g$, the market socialist social rate of return will be zero, but in the long run it will equal g, for the first notion, but be undefined for the discounting formula. This is the true, and *only*, market socialist analogue to Solow's case. When the profit rate is zero, the dual of the stationary state, the market socialist social rate is not equal to g, because of the growth of the labor force. The conclusion has to be that only in the very special case of the Golden Rule, and only for one of the two notions of the rate of return, will a sacrifice of wages under market socialism be rewarded at a rate consistent with marginal productivity principles. In general this 'social rate of return' does *not* 'behave like a marginal product'. Moreover it is usual to think that r will normally be larger than g; but if r is sufficiently larger, then the first notion of the dual social rate of return will be *negative*.

Yet it may seem we have reached these conclusions too hastily. A *given* work force makes the sacrifice at a given time. Surely the *return* should be figured only for those workers who make the sacrifice. The fact that the wage bill expands because more workers are brought in must be irrelevant; the rewards must go to those who made the sacrifice. In such a case the one period and the perpetual rates of return will be identical, and both will be given by:

$$\varrho = \frac{w_2 - w_1}{w_1 - \bar{w}} = \frac{g - r}{1 + r} \tag{8.28}$$

In this event, if $r = 0$, then $\varrho = g$, and we have the exact analogue of Solow's original case. Unfortunately, however, r may very well lie above g, which suggests that the dual social rate will normally be negative by one formula, but undefined by the discounting formula. A carefully managed market socialist economy, of course, might try to balance r and g exactly, but this does not seem very plausible.

But if we accept the argument here that a *given* work force makes the sacrifice, and therefore should obtain the reward, we are entitled to make the same argument in Solow's original case. He defined the sacrifice as giving up consumption now, in order to make the shift between techniques, in return for higher consumption later, rather than lower wages now for higher wages later. But he computed the reward in *total* consumption, in a growing economy, regardless of the fact that much of the additional consumption would be done by those who had made no initial sacrifice. If we follow Solow's lead then the only case where anything resembling his result holds for the dual social rate occurs when $r = g$, and then only for one of the two notions of the rate of return.

In any case the question whether those who make a sacrifice (whether of consumption or of wages) obtain all or only a part of the benefits (the rest going to society) is *precisely* the question whether 'private and social rates of return will coincide' (Solow, 1963, p. 65). It was to answer this question, indeed to show that when private and social marginal products coincided then so would private and social rates of return, that Solow first defined his concept of the social rate of return. The ambiguity we have just uncovered confirms further our earlier contention that even when the social rate of return equals r, or its dual equals g, we cannot conclude that private and social rates of return are equal.

8 CONCLUSIONS

Nuti begins by postulating intertemporal productive transformations capable of being set equal to the rate of profit on capital in current production, and this begs the central question. By contrast, Solow's argument is directed to the real issue: is a Fisherian equilibrium generally possible in a world of fully specified (single-product, circulating capital) technologies? His answer is that it is. Pasinetti's attack was directed at what he took to be the implicit theory of the determination of the rate of profit. Solow objected that his theorem in no way depended on how the rate of profit was determined; he was interested in showing that the interest rate accurately measured the social rate of return to saving-investment. The latter can be thought of, in Fisherian style, as an index of savers' willingness to shift consumption to the future, and can therefore be used in allocation theory. Solow's argument is ultimately designed to justify the extension of price and allocation theory to profits and distribution, to maintain the central neo-Classical thesis that distribution is a special case of efficiency pricing, exactly as in Mario Nuti's model.

This is the heart of the issue. *Outside* the neo-Classical tradition market prices even in 'competitive' conditions may be seen as indicators of power, not efficiency, while distribution reflects the class structure, not 'rational intertemporal substitution'. The economy will normally function, and function quite well, in disequilibrium, and there may be no special reason to suppose that there exists any tendency to move to equilibrium, that is, for markets to clear. Moreover, markets may set up pressures for the system to move in directions that are not technically feasible, leading to crises and difficulties of various sorts (Lowe, 1955 and 1976). These realistic questions, often having political implications, tend to be excluded from the domain of pure theory under the auspices of the neo-Classical vision, and, as a consequence are often unduly neglected, in favor of meaningless discussion of 'rational choice.'

If the argument of this paper is correct the Fisherian intertemporal approach cannot be grafted onto the wage-profit model, at least in the way so far proposed. The intertemporal general equilibrium model used by Nuti thus contains a fatal defect: The rate of return determined by discounting future streams of consumption will not in general equal the current rate of profit. Just as reswitching and capital-reversing showed the Clark parable invalid, so this shows that the Fisherman's Tale, amplified by the modern followers of Arrow and Debreu, must end as fishermen's stories always do, with a lament for the big one that got away.

Notes

1. Mario Nuti suggests at several points that his views are consistent with Marxian economics. Marx certainly never mentions the efficiency properties of prices, but it might be held that he wrote before these had been generally recognized – or that he was implicitly aware of them, but lacked the proper analytical concepts developed by later writers in the scientific analysis of exchange. In one of the later sections of Volume III he repeatedly returns to the fact that '(. . .) average profit figures practically, in the mind and calculation of the capitalist himself, as a regulating element, not merely in so far as it determines the transfer of capitals from one sphere of investment into another, but also in all sales and contracts which embrace a process of reproduction extending over long periods (. . .).' And further, 'A part of the average profit in the form of interest confronts the functioning capitalist independently as an assumed element in the production of commodities and their value. No matter how much the magnitude of the interest fluctuates, at each moment and for every capitalist it is a given magnitude entering into the cost price of the commodities produced by him (. . .).' Certainly this shows that Marx was aware of market incentives and their influence in the allocation of resources. But the title of the section also shows what he thought of the resulting doctrines of efficiency resulting from responses to market incentives – 'Illusions Created By Competition.'
2. Part of Nuti's point is that for Solow the equality between the rate of return on investment and the rate of profit is an *equilibrium condition* and not, as some have charged, a tautology. This point, as we shall see, is well-taken, in part, but it certainly does not follow that the equilibrium is also efficient.
3. Perhaps most important, they have not been concerned with developing a theory of exploitation – that is, a theory of the division of a surplus produced by productive labor working with reproducible equipment between the competing claims of the various social classes. Nuti admits this, but apparently feel that a 'focus on the relations between the incomes of classes rather than classless individuals' does not constitute an overwhelming advantage.
4. In single-product, circulating capital terms. It needs to be emphasized that this is only a *first step* towards a full specification. Joint production and fixed capital remain to be considered, and very little is known about such models.
5. Harcourt citing Pasinetti (1969), for example, remarks that Solow is '(. . .) open to the charge that he had shown that at the rate of profits at which two economic systems (techniques) are equi-profitable, that is the rate of profits at which they *are so* (. . .)' (Harcourt, 1972, p. 168). This comment applies to equation (8.5), but not to equation (8.4).
6. Equilibrium might be restored by further developments, of course, but that is no part of the present discussion. Solow explicitly disavows any interest in *determining* the rate of profit.
7. Much traditional theory discusses temporary sacrifices to move from one stationary state to another, as when Robinson Crusoe stops fishing to make a net. Yet these discussions generally depend on the 'unobtrusive postulate' – diminishing returns – to explain why Robinson stops making nets, i.e. why no further capital-deepening takes place. In the absence of this postulate, when neo-Classical theory is revealed 'in its full generality' (Solow, 1970), it is not clear why the incentives to one-shot investment would not also encourage regular expansion.
8. Cf. Nell (1970) sections 4 and 5.
9. R.M. Solow, in correspondence (24 January 1974).

10. This, of course, is the familiar Pasinetti result, transferred to 'market socialist' conditions.

References

Bruno, M., Burmeister, E., and Sheshinski, E. (1966) 'Nature and Implications of the Reswitching of Techniques', *Quarterly Journal of Economics* (November).
Harcourt, G.C. (1972) *Some Cambridge Controversies in the Theory of Capital* (Cambridge: Cambridge University Press).
Lowe, A. (1955) 'Structural Analysis of Real Capital Formation,' in M. Abramovitz (ed.), *Capital Formation and Economic Growth* (Princeton: NBER) pp. 581–634.
Lowe, A. (1976) *The Path of Economic Growth* (Cambridge University Press).
Marx, Karl (1969) *Capital*, 3 Vols (New York, International Publishers).
Morishima, M. (1967) *Theory of Economic Growth* (Oxford: Oxford University Press.)
Nell, E.J.: (1970) 'A Note on Cambridge Controversies in Capital Theory,' *Journal of Economic Literature* (March).
Nell, E.J. (1973) 'The Fall of the House of Efficiency,' in S. Weintraub (ed.), *Income Inequality*, The Annals of the American Academy of Political and Social Science (September).
Nuti, Mario (1974) 'On the Rates of Return on Investment,' *Kyklos*, 27 (2).
Pasinetti, Luigi (1969) 'Switches of Technique and the "Rate of Return" in Capital Theory,' *Economic Journal* (September).
Pasinetti, Luigi (1970) 'Again on Capital Theory and Solow's "Rate of Return",' *Economic Journal* (June).
Pasinetti, Luigi (1974) 'A Reply to Dr. Nuti on the Rate of Return,' *Kyklos*, 27 (2).
Solow, R.M. (1963) *Capital Theory and the Rate of Return*, F.M. De Vries Lectures, (Amsterdam).
Solow, R.M. (1967) 'The Interest Rate and The Transition Between Techniques,' in C.H. Feinstein (ed.), *Socialism, Capitalism and Economic Growth, Essays Presented to Maurice Dobb* (Cambridge University Press).
Solow, R.M. (1970) 'On the Rate of Return: Reply to Pasinetti,' *Economic Journal* (June).
Spaventa, Luigi (1973) 'Notes on Problems of Transition Between Techniques,' in J. Mirrlees and N. Stern (eds), *Models of Economic Growth* (London: Macmillan).

9 The Theory of Income Distribution*

Neo-Classical theory *is* a Story for the Faithful. Those of us outside the Flock, in our unguarded moments, tend to regard it in much the same way Betrand Russell saw theology, and with about the same respect. Of course, as professionals with sober expressions, we will solemnly discuss competitive equilibrium and the elasticity of the marginal product curve, as of old we might have disputed whether or not God, being omnipotent, could make a stone too heavy for Himself to lift. Neither in economic nor in natural theology are the questions easily resolved; disputes are intricate, intellectually fascinating, and, as formal logic, often aesthetically delightful. But quite meaningless. Time and effort spent on the fine points of neo-Classical theory appear to Heretics a shocking waste of scarce intellectual resources.

These are strong words. Surely a theory so widely believed cannot be so lightly dismissed? Quite so; but as both the history of religion and the Pen and Bronfenbrenner books show, the Faithful do not listen to heresy. They do not seem to know what the critics object to, or why. In what follows I shall sketch the position(s) taken by Pen and Bronfenbrenner in their rather different but really excellent books, and then try to indicate some of the major shortcomings of the Faith. Finally, I shall try to pull some of the major shortcomings together by contrasting the alternative *viewpoints*, or in more fashionable terminology 'paradigms' for distribution theory, and in doing so I shall argue that neo-Classical theory is fundamentally pre-Keynesian.

1 PEN AND BRONFENBRENNER

These are both very good books indeed. Pen, especially, is a master of exposition at all levels; he presents the basic data of personal income distribution in the most dramatic and striking way imaginable. He organizes a parade of income recipients, lowest incomes first, with each recipient stretched or squashed to a height corresponding to his or her income.[1] Both books give exceptionally clear accounts of basic neo-Classical theory. Pen literally begins with the elements of supply and demand and works his way through to the CES production function and beyond, something of a

* *Journal of Economic Literature*, X (2) (1972).

tour de force. But the discussion always remains elementary and uncritical, as far as theory is concerned, though he is very much aware of the limited applicability of marginal productivity. By contrast, Bronfenbrenner is alive to the many difficulties and theoretical complexities of the neo-Classical position. In this respect his book deserves high praise. It is a pleasure to follow him through the myriad cross-currents of argument on some recondite subject to a definite and defensible, if frequently unorthodox, conclusion. He also presents a good account of the statistical and interpretive problems in testing neo-Classical theory, though, in my opinion, he underestimates the charge that the production function has been mis-identified, and he is too ready to defend Solow and Douglas.[2] But he is perhaps less sensitive than Pen to the limited usefulness of the theory, even in the best of conditions.

Though he doesn't quite say it openly, Pen raises a serious question in this connection. Like Bronfenbrenner, he vigorously supports conventional theory, and gives heavy lumps both to critics and to proponents of alternative theories, mainly Kaldor and Kalecki.[3] Yet he sharply qualifies its range of application: where we find

> . . . inputs into production in which the connexion with the outputs is . . . indirect, and the qualitative differences . . . great and at the same time . . . uncertain, . . . marginal productivity no longer forms a guideline. This applies in the first place to executive and staff work . . . Consequently, these renumerations are fixed in another way: social conventions, the power structure, considerations of prestige and status play a much larger part than marginal productivity. And that also holds good for the renumeration of people not working in industry: of teachers, for instance . . . and of doctors . . .

If we take this literally – and Pen means us to – later on he discusses the role of status and the power structure in executive compensation – marginal productivity applies only where labor inputs of uniform quality are directly connected with a physical product, in conditions of full technical knowledge and no uncertainty.

But in developed countries white collar workers now comprise more than half the labor forces; call it half. From the remaining half substract service workers (12 to 15 per cent), farm proprietors and managers (3 per cent), industrial foremen and supervisors (12 per cent), and we are left with 20 to 25 per cent of the labor force. But even for many ostensibly manual production line jobs, the connection with output is indirect, uncertain and hard to estimate physically. Suppose this group is a minority, say no more than a quarter of such jobs. Then, at best, the marginal productivity theory would apply to about 15 per cent of the labor force. But things never are at their best. Firms do not have full knowledge either of their technical possibilities or of their market circumstances – or perhaps what economic theorists think firms should know is not actually there to be known. (For example, there may be fixed coefficients and no other technical possibilities.) Bronfenbrenner mentions a remark made to him by E.E. Witte, the labor arbitrator, that 'no form of marginal analysis had ever been raised by either employer or employee representatives in any proceeding in which he has participated.' So even when the theory could be applied it might still not be a correct description of what is done. Finally, as Bronfenbrenner points out, even if true, it might be true only some of the time: firms, particularly large corporations, may have multiple and conflicting goals, and so might behave on some occasions as profit maximizers, on others as revenue or market share maximizers, on still others they might react defensively, e.g., by labor-hoarding.

What is left? As a theory of wages, we can say that marginal productivity applies part of the time and not always well to a tiny minority of the labor force, perhaps allowing for lack of knowledge and multiple goals no more than 3 or 4 per cent.

Clearly such a theory should be thought of as a *special* case. Yet both Bronfenbrenner and Pen treat it as a general rule. The reason is not hard to find. To reject neo-Classical distribution theory would entail reconstructing large parts of the theory of the firm, and of long-run supply generally. It would signal the break-up of the neo-Classical paradigm.[4] That is what the critics want, but neither author is ready to hear such impertinence.

These remarks are suggestive, but no more. I should now like to turn to some specific problem areas, where, it seems to me, certain shortcomings of the Faith can be seen.

2 THE PERSONAL AND THE FUNCTIONAL DISTRIBUTION

Both authors (especially Pen), unlike Ferguson, attach considerable importance to the personal distribution. Both rather critically canvass a number of attempts, largely built on 'chance,' to explain the shape of the personal distribution. Both reject the claim that there has been an 'Income Revolution;' both see the need to explain the persistence of inequality not only among the population but also as between regions and nations. Finally, both raise questions about the relation between the personal and the functional distribution. Curiously, neither exploit one of the strengths of marginal productivity theory, namely that it can rather easily be used to analyze both functional and personal distribution. The 'human capital' approach is precisely an application of neo-Classical thinking to personal distribution. Yet Pen does not even mention it, and Bronfenbrenner gives it only a paragraph.

My own feeling is that they are right, but it makes their defense of the

Good Old Theory all the more curious. Surely, most of us would agree that marginal productivity theory is on stronger ground in a microeconomic context? Bronfenbrenner gives no reasons for his neglect; Pen, though he does not discuss 'human capital' explicitly, does give reasons and they are instructive if hardly novel. Put very broadly, Pen argues that to understand the forces shaping the personal distribution, economists must incorporate a good deal of sociology into their thinking. It simply will not do to examine the abstract choices of assumed 'individuals' and 'firms.' Given the power structure of corporations, executives at the top largely set their own pay; from these levels down the pay structure reflects relative position in the hierarchy. The return on education depends on the pay of the jobs the education fits one for, i.e., the pay as determined by level in the hierarchy, not by *marginal productivity* (there are no measurable outputs). How, then, is pay set? According to Pen (this is what Ferguson doesn't like), largely by considerations of status and prestige, in accordance with society's value judgements. To explain it we need to know how social value judgements are formed; to change it (pre-tax), we must know how social values are changed.

Pen devotes the last 120 pages of his book to a discussion, without parallel in recent literature, of norms for judging and policies for improving the personal distribution, not only of income, but of the quality of life. If nothing else does, these pages make this book indispensible reading for any course on income distribution and social policy. Progressive taxation, profit sharing, transfers, strengthening competition, improving education – *pre* and *post* school – democratizing the corporation, nationalization, redistribution of property and wealth, full employment, changing the architecture and class structure of cities – are all discussed with wit and perception. Yet something is missing. A scheme that improves the personal distribution, by any norm Pen accepts, will tread on some influential and well-manicured toes. These toes may be persuaded, in the light of the general social well-being, to accept a modicum of discomfort, and most of Pen's discussion assumes that possibility. Surely this is right; social groups *can* be persuaded to accept even very painful sacrifices in the interests of the whole. Witness the progressive income tax. And this example also illustrates what is missing in Pen. For though he discusses the power structure *within* a corporation, he offers no systematic analysis of the (economic) power structure in society *as a whole*. Yet that is what the *functional* distribution, which he wishes to leave intact (p. 290) is all about. The flow of profits to business reflects market power in relation to consumers on the one hand and labor on the other, and it *provides business with both means and motives for resisting egalitarian changes in the personal distribution*. Means, because the flow of profits, together with the resources of the companies, provides the wherewithal for political lobbying. Motives, because profits are realized through sales and the pattern of consumption depends on the distribution of income. This is illustrated, in a highly aggregative way, by Marx's 'schemes of reproduction,' as developed by Kalecki and Joan Robinson. There is a 'duality,' expressed in the 'classical savings function,' between Marx's departments – producing wage goods, luxury goods and capital goods respectively – and the division of income between wages and profits (the latter dividing between investment and luxury consumption.) If capital goods are non-malleable a fall in capitalist consumption, e.g., through progressive taxation or profit sharing, means a drop in sales, and so in profits, for the luxury goods sector. Even if capitalists as a whole, voting as private citizens, agreed to such a measure, the capitalists of the luxury sector, in their capacities as business executives, would resist it. The gain will be spread thinly; the loss, not to capitalist households, who have agreed to the measure, but to business, will be concentrated. Even if the measure is enacted the luxury industries can resist its implementation.

Surely the wage goods industries gain an exactly offsetting amount and so should lobby for the measure? This overlooks an important asymmetry, familiar from discussions of the 'compensation criteria.' The marginal utility of a given addition to income is less than the loss in marginal utility of the same amount subtracted, when both parties start from the same position, and have comparable utility measures. The interpretation here is obvious. A gain in sales is always welcome, but when normal profits are being earned, it is not necessary, to solvency. A loss in profits, however, brings the risk of bankruptcy. The asymmetry arises from the fact that a fall in sales raises the risk of bankruptcies, whereas a rise above normal operations does not further reduce it. Hence a decline will be resisted more strongly than a gain will be encouraged.

Pen's failure to appreciate the relations between the functional and personal distributions stems partly, I would suggest, from his acceptance of the neo-Classical approach to the former.

3 THE CONSTANCY OF RELATIVE SHARES

Both authors express a cautious skepticism here. They note that on the whole the share of 'pay,' wages plus salaries in GNP, has risen. Nevertheless, as they admit, this is largely explained by the decline in agriculture and other forms of self-employment. If one takes out government employment the increase is further reduced. Even without these adjustments both US and UK data show that the greatest increases happened during the two World Wars. The trend before 1960 largely reduces to two discontinuous jumps.

But the issue may not be best posed as one of 'pay vs profits.' Kalecki thought of it as 'net business income vs variable costs,' which latter are largely composed of non-supervisory labor charges. And this, as both C.H. Feinstein and B. Haley show, remains fairly stable in both the US and the UK even through the wars.

The theoretical differences between these two ways of analyzing the movement of shares are considerable. The first is the more traditional. 'Pay' is what labor gets for its services; 'profit' is the pound of flesh that the owners of capital can extract for making the services of capital goods available to potential producers. Pay and profits, then, are rewards for the services that the factors respectively contribute to production, which gives rise to the natural and plausible doctrine that these rewards will be proportionate to their contributions, which, in turn, depend on technology.

By contrast, the other view sees the question of shares as one of the mark-up business can impose in bargaining with labor over money wages and in setting prices to consumers. From this perspective the question is largely one of market power, and one is immediately led to consider both institutional arrangements (collective bargaining, and monopoly) and the impact of changes in aggregate demand, respectively, on the goods market and on the labor market.

From the first point of view we might expect shares to shift gradually, but decidedly, in favor of labor, as both capital and labor become more specialized, so that the ability to substitute one for the other declines. From the second viewpoint, however, we might expect shares to move in favor of capital as concentration increases, unless offsetting influences could be found. Kalecki thought the cheapening of raw materials, through exploitation of the poorer nations, provided such a factor. More recently, Sutcliffe and Glyn (1972) have sketched quite a different picture. They argue that the union movement, the commitment to full employment, and the increased specialization of labor (raising training costs) have strengthened the power of labor to push up money wages, at a time when international competition and the world liquidity crises have weakened business' ability to pass such increases on in the form of price inflation. The result is a profit squeeze, which they document from 1960 for a number of countries, though their primary focus is on the UK.

Their argument seems both interesting and plausible, but it is not compatible with marginal productivity theory. One can always say that because markets are imperfect, in the short run price inflation and wage inflation can diverge. But this is not what Sutcliffe and Glyn, any more than Kalecki, are saying. They claim that there has been a *historical* change in the disposition of market power, and that this is showing itself in the trend in shares. Such a claim cannot easily be meshed into the Good Old Theory, to which we must now turn.

4 THE DEMAND FOR PRODUCTIVE SERVICES

Both authors present neo-Classical theory as essentially a theory of the supply and demand for productive services. Minor quibbles aside, the two presentations, at their respective levels, are admirable. They are so clear, in fact, that they call up a strong feeling of skepticism in the heretic. Suppose one were explaining the law of gravity to an intelligent nine-year old. If you drop an object it will strike the ground with a *force* which depends on the mass of the object and the acceleration due to gravity, but with a *velocity* which depends on the height from which it was dropped and the acceleration due to gravity. Thus the force is independent of the height, and the velocity of the mass. Naturally, he will have to be shown. This will not be difficult to arrange. A step-ladder, a stop-watch, scales, some solid objects, pencil and paper for calculation, and some ingenuity in explaining 'force' – and both parties should end up the wiser, one way or another.

Now let us set the scene for the Law of Variable Proportions. We cannot baffle a nine-year old with index numbers. The 'output' made from the many different proportions of inputs must be the *same*. So must be the jobs performed in the course of making it. It will not do to say we can make a table of wood or of metal; they are not the same. Nor can we say we can make the table by hand or by machine; the skills required of workers are different. Where shall we find our simple example? Not, so far as I know, in any of the common text-books. In the three-quarters of a century that this theory has ruled the classrooms, no one has produced a simple but detailed and convincing real-life example drawn from industry.[5]

Nor is this a mere quibble. A paradigm should have paradigmatic cases. But if we take seriously the twin requirements of homogeneity in output and in labor input, the scope for smooth substitution *as understood in the neo-Classical vision* seems drastically reduced. This is not to deny the importance of substitution in production. Both Sraffa and Joan Robinson give it a central place in their work (as did Marx). But it is to claim that neo-Classical thinking seriously misrepresents the process. The characteristics of a product depend on what goes into it and the skills required of workers depend on how the inputs are put together.

Once we insist that whatever substitution 'parable' we tell must accurately represent technology, at least with respect to economically relevant matters,[6] we rapidly move into the world of fixed coefficient models with vintage capital goods. The reason is not so much that rigidity is 'more realistic' than flexibility, for there frequently are one or more roughly alternative methods of producing roughly the 'same' good. Rather, it is that choice between methods is discrete, often costly, and usually made between a small number of techniques.

But theories are discarded in favor of other theories, not because of awkward facts. The fixed-coefficient, discrete technology approach does offer new theoretical insights. For example, in a *given* 'productive'[7] technology we can derive a 'wage-profit trade-off,' showing the inverse relationship between the wage rate and the profit rate. This function has a number of important properties, which shed new light on the labor theory of value, on the movement of prices with costs, on the nature of rents and quasi-rents, and, of course, on the valuation of capital. 'Switches' between techniques take place at points where two trade-off functions intersect; the envelope of the intersecting trade-off functions defines the 'surrogate production function,' and the essence of the Cambridge Criticism is the proof that this will not normally be 'well-behaved' in the neo-Classical sense.

5 THE RATE OF PROFITS

The central theoretical issue, at least for the critics of orthodoxy, is the determination of the rate of profits. The neo-Classicals put forward two candidates, both designed to bring 'capital' and its 'price,' the rate of profits, under the umbrella of neo-Classical allocation theory. The first is a relatively simple 'parable,' useful in empirical work; the other is a full-dress, general equilibrium theory, which supposedly provides rigorous under-pinning for the first. These two models, as seen by the critics, both depend on a single idea: that a simple monotonic relationship can be found, which holds *independently of prices*, between the value of a set of capital goods and the general rate of return. In the 'parable' the set of goods consists of the entire capital stock, which is supposed to stand in a monotonic inverse relationship to the rate of return, reflecting its relative scarcity, as, for example, in an aggregate production function. In the full-dress, heterogeneous capital models[8] the rate of profits is set by the rate of return, obtained *à la* Irving Fisher, by sacrificing present consumption for future consumption. It is supply and demand again, this time for investment, measured in terms of sacrificed consumption. The stream of future benefits obtained by saving and investing gives rise to what Solow calls the 'social rate of return,' by which investment projects can be ranked, as in the Keynesian 'marginal efficiency' schedule. This gives demand. On the supply side, the greater the rate of return, the greater will be the amount of present consumption sacrificed, in accordance with utility theory. This should provide the basis for an investment theory, capable of determining both the rate of growth and the rate of profits. Of course it ignores questions of both effective demand and liquidity preference. In an important sense, it is pre-Keynesian.

Unfortunately, both the simple J.B. Clark parable and the more complex MIT–Irving Fisher model fail to work for essentially the same reason, now known as the 'Cambridge Criticism.' That is, reswitching and capital reversing not only show that the value of capital need not be uniquely and monotonically related to the rate of return. They also show that low rates of return do not necessarily go with high consumption per head.[9] Furthermore, if there is *more than one consumption good*, changes in the pattern of consumption with unchanged prices and rate of profits may raise or lower the value of consumption per head.[10] Finally, the connection between the Irving Fisher rate of return and the general rate of profits has been challenged. Pasinetti (and, separately, myself) have criticized Solow's demonstration that the rate of return characterizing the difference in the consumption streams associated with two techniques must equal the rate of profits at which an economy would switch between them. If Solow's demonstration is unsound, the determination of the 'social rate of return,' in his sense, will not help to provide a theory of the rate of profit – the latter need not necessarily measure the 'social return to saving.'

These matters are at the center of the fighting on the disputed frontiers of knowledge. Nevertheless, by now certain articles of the eventual peace treaty are clear. Most important, it is now generally conceded that the J.B. Clark parable is theoretically invalid. (The truly faithful, however, do not let this intrude upon their worship. Aggregate production function studies continue, justified by their excellent empirical 'results' in spite of the fact that most methods of estimating technical progress *presuppose* marginal productivity theory.) It is also widely agreed that reswitching and capital-reversing cause trouble for the general-equilibrium Walras–Fisher approach.[11] But some adherents maintain that the criticisms are not decisive, or perhaps even very important. Demand theory can accommodate Giffen goods, and we have known for years that general equilibrium systems may have multiple equilibria. Now we have discovered a few more cases of 'perverse' behavior.

But the Cambridge Criticism cuts deeper. Neo-Classical theory brings capital and its 'price' – the rate of profits – under the aegis of the principle of scarcity. That is its great achievement – the extension of the principles of allocation to the field of distribution. It is for this that the 'unobtrusive postulate' is necessary. But the claim that capital-intensity moves inversely to the rate of return is supposedly descriptive of *technological possibilities*. Hence there follows the striking and ideologically significant implication: distribution depends solely on technology and factor proportions. (In the Cobb–Douglas case even factor proportions do not matter.) This is what the critics cannot stomach. Other matters – aggregate demand, the monetary system, the corporate power structure, unions, the structure of industry – perhaps even the state of politics, all do seem relevant. The MIT version blames the distribution of income not so much on technology alone as upon its interaction with our preference for present as opposed to future consumption. The market – bless its heart – does no more than provide us with an income distribution which *efficiently* allocates current resources between investment and consumption. Again the digestive tracts of the critics rumble. Fortunately the Criticism also weakens this model. To re-strengthen neo-Classicism in either version, to preserve the Faith, it has seemed necessary to bring some, at least, of the excluded variables into the fold, and set them moving in epicycles.

6 ALTERNATIVE APPROACHES TO THE THEORY OF DISTRIBUTION

For this the faithful, reasonably enough, expect applause from their critics. After all they have liberalized the dogma. Too much, say their own conservatives. But the heretics are stubborn and ungrateful. It is still all wrong. The argument is over strategy not tactics, and the heretics want an alternative approach. We had better see what these are.

The easiest way to do this compactly is to set 'stylized' versions of the main rivals side-by-side in a table. Let us distinguish four theories: Neo-Classical (Aggregate PF), Neo-Classical (Social Rate of Return), Neo-Keynesian (Kaldor) and Neo-Marxian (Kalecki). For each we will indicate the Target Variables to be determined, the Variables Determined Outside the *purely distributional* system, the Mechanism by which the target variables are determined, the assumed Nature of Production, and finally the Variables Determined Residually, together with any Additional Constraints. This is quite a lot but it fits neatly enough into a small table.

We take as given: (1) A Distribution Identity, $\pi Y = wN + rK\pi$, where π is the price level, w the money wage rate, and r the general rate of profits. This is common to all theories. (2) $\phi(Y, K, N) = 0$, a Production Function, where Y is real output, K the stock of capital, and N the volume of labor employed. No form is specified, as the theories disagree as to the correct form.

Determined variables	*Variables determined outside*	*Mechanism*	*Residually determined variables*	*Nature of production function*	*Additional constraint*
NC(APF): w/π, N, r K	None	Supply & Demand	Y	Well-Behaved NC Form	'Adding up'
NC(SRR): r, ΔK	K, N	Supply & Demand	Y, w/π?	Fixed Coefficients or Surrogate	None
$N - K$: r, ΔK	K, N, ΔK?	Saving & Investment	Y, w/π	Fixed Coefficients	None
$N - M$: w/π	K, N	Bargaining & Monopoly Power	Y, r	Fixed Coefficients	None

Neo-Classical theory relies on Supply and Demand in factor markets. In the mainstream version this effectively overdetermines the system, requiring additional constraints on the production function, ensuring 'adding-up.' In the alternative version (as in Walras), the rate of return is set in the investment market, and the general equilibrium equations then adjust prices so that a uniform rate of net return is established for all capital goods. Such a model need not define an aggregate production function. Marginal productivity conditions will therefore remain strictly microeconomic; there is neither a 'marginal product of capital' nor a 'marginal product of labor' in this model. Hence there can be no demand curve for labor in general, in the usual sense. Still, none is needed if full employment is assumed, and the work–leisure choice suppressed. Not surprisingly this approach is structurally similar to the Neo-Keynesian, particularly later versions of that theory which treat investment as (at least partly) a function of profits. Then ΔK as well as r will be determined by the Saving–Investment Mechanism. The Neo-Marxian approach stands out in marked contrast to all the rest. The real wage is determined through power relations in two quite separate markets. Prices are set in accordance with a mark-up that depends on monopoly power; money wages depend on the respective bargaining power of the two sides. But unlike the other, this approach cannot easily be combined with a full employment assumption, for the realization of profits depends on savings propensities of capitalists.[12]

Contemporary thinking among the critics of orthodoxy is unquestionably much more interested in developing, and blending, the insights of the last two approaches, than in modifying or rearranging the neo-Classical ideas. But before we can explore why this is so, or what is being done, we must fend off the neo-Classical backlash.

7 PRE-KEYNESIAN THINKING ONCE AGAIN

Pen and Bronfenbrenner are good representatives of their side, and they do battle honorably. Both present Kalecki concisely and fairly; both criticize him on essentially the same grounds, and, as they think definitively. The grounds are interesting: Kalecki's basic equation for the wage share is:

$$\frac{W}{A} = 1 - \bar{\mu}\left(1 + \frac{R}{A}\right)$$

where W is the wage bill, A real national income, R total raw material costs, and $\bar{\mu}$ a weighted average of the degree of monopoly for the entire economy.

According to this equation the share of wages will fall as the degree of monopoly rises, but this can be offset by exploitation of the Third World, shifting the terms of trade so as to reduce raw material costs. Neat, but not acceptable, both authors argue. For if the degree of monopoly is zero – perfect competition – labor will get the entire national income; yet under perfect competition capital remains both scarce and productive. Presumably it should therefore command a price reflecting this.

This argument rests on what has to be proved, that 'capital' is a scarce good with a price. If the rate of return is not a price, but a reflection of power, then the claim that in the absence of power it will be zero makes perfectly good sense. Moreover, given Kalecki's saving hypothesis, perfect competition is the only case where the choice of technique will be optimal.[13] For $W/A = 1$ implies that the growth rate will be zero, in which case it equals the profit rate, fulfilling the Golden Rule. In all other cases capitalist consumption entails a suboptimal choice of technique. For the realization of profits depends on Investment and Capitalist Consumption, according to the equation $I/s_p = rK$, which also implies that the growth rate $= s_p r$.

Pen and Bronfenbrenner have failed to see that Kalecki's theory consists of two complementary parts: the degree of monopoly and the costs of materials determine costs and markup, on the one hand, and the pattern of consumption and investment spending determine output and employment, on the other. Only by taking these together do we get the complete theory.

The inability to see that saving and investment determine profits, and not the other way around, comes out even more clearly in their respective discussions of Kaldor's work.[14] Pen goes out on a limb here, which is a pity, since he falls off it. He presents a simplified version of Kaldor in terms of a given I and Y, and a shifting propensity to save of workers, and shows that 'by saving slightly more' (200 percent!) the workers could reduce profits to nil (provided I remains unchanged!). Figures apart – neither numbers nor interpretation are in line with Kaldor's intent – this is simply not Keynesian in spirit. Investment is the volatile element; saving propensities are relatively stable. Worse is to come. He goes on '. . . [Kaldor has] distorted all causalities. [He] assume[s] that the workers can save more, or less, *without the average propensity to save changing*! The only influence of an increasing s_w is on labor's share; s remains as it is. That is entirely unnatural.' (Italics in original.)

Was the Keynesian Revolution unnatural? The case had better be argued in full. The average propensity to save remains unchanged, because we have assumed both full employment and a level of investment demand. In Keynesian thinking, saving adjusts to investment, and where the saving ratio is a weighted average, the weights must adjust. Of course, Pen takes the case where a savings propensity rises; neither Kaldor nor anyone else would deny that the normal response would be a decline in Y. But if

Government policy prevented Y from falling there would have to be an increase in labor incomes to absorb the excess consumer goods. To repeat, savings and investment determine profits through the adjustment of savings to investment. That is why the approach is called Keynesian.

Bronfenbrenner likewise advances the pre-Keynesian cause 'With full employment maintained exogenously, a higher non-wage share (plus a wider differential between "class" saving ratios) produces a higher growth rate and/or a higher capital coefficient. There is no reason to suppose a reverse pattern leading to the income distribution as dependent variable.'

No reason? If we *assume* that technology and factor proportions can explain shares, then it might seem plausible to hold that causality runs in the pre-Keynesian direction from profits through savings to investment. Or we may collapse savings and investment into one, and determine savings–investment and the rate of return together from time preference and the schedule of investment opportunities. But if we accept the Cambridge Criticisms these courses are not open to us. Income distribution cannot be blamed on the engineers and the birth rate; the rate of profits does not arise from our misguided passion to consume the fruits of our labor at once. The share which falls to the capitalists emerges from the interaction of aggregate demand, the growth rates of capital and labor, the monetary system, and monopoly power. True, many neo-Classicals, Fergusnn among them, would readily admit this – for the *short run*, calling attention to the deeper forces of technology and time-preference at work in the long run. These forces operate in a comfortable full employment world (disturbed only by occasional unruly demands for wage increases), in which savings govern investment, and the rate of return, in equating them, also ensures that investment will assume its optimal technical form. Keynes warned that no such world exists; the message from Cambridge today is that no such forces exist.

Notes

1. The effect is very dramatic, as two examples indicate. It begins with marchers of negative height, walking upside down; it lasts one hour, and not until 48 minutes have passed do the marchers reach average height!
2. H. Simon and F. Levy (1963) have shown that comparing the coefficients derived from a (cross-sectionally) fitted Cobb–Douglas with actual shares does not provide a valid test, since the same results would follow from simple cost functions. More recently Franklin Fisher has shown that Cobb–Douglas aggregate functions are a consequence of constant shares, given our estimation procedures (Fisher, 1971). In an unpublished paper (1971) Anwar Shaikh of Columbia has shown that the equation Solow (1957) fits can be derived from the identity (in self-evident notation)

$$Y = \frac{w}{\pi} N + rK \tag{9N.1}$$

and that it will always integrate into a Cobb–Douglas if shares are constant. Lydall (1971) points out, first that if technical progress is introduced since it cannot be measured independently, the Cobb–Douglas no longer provides empirical support for neo-Classical theory, and second, that marginal productivity theory incorrectly predicts the size distribution of firms.

I have argued in (1972) along somewhat different lines. Assume fixed coefficients and a single technique, Harrod-neutral technical progress, and initially balanced growth. Then let the actual rate of growth rise temporarily above the natural. A rate of construction of plant and equipment in excess of newly available labor will, under competition, lead to a scramble for labor in which money wages will be bid up. Let us assume that prices cannot be forced up as rapidly. Then, differentiating 1) (and ignoring technical change),

$$dr = \frac{wN}{K\pi} \left(\frac{d\pi}{\pi} - \frac{dw}{w} \right). \tag{9N.2}$$

A little manipulation, however, shows that this is simply

$$\frac{dr}{d(w/\pi)} = \frac{N}{K}, \tag{9N.3}$$

which is the condition that characterizes the 'factor price frontier' of a well-behaved production function. If and only if 3) holds

$$\frac{dY}{dK} = r \tag{9.4}$$

Hence, data generated by 2) will 'confirm' (9.4), even though no marginal changes have taken place.

3. Pen leaves out Kennedy altogether, and dismisses Weintraub as a 'caricature of Kalecki.' Bronfenbrenner does much better, but wrong-headedly tries to assimilate Kennedy to the neo-Classicals and looks for price theory in Weintraub.
4. *Of course*, large parts of present theory would be salvaged. Many important neo-Classical ideas are better seen as *instrumental*, in Adolph Lowe's sense, than as descriptive. These particularly will take their place among the methods of operations research, though, given their high level of abstraction, they may not prove very useful.
5. Textbook examples usually involve applying labor to land, i.e., farming, not the best illustration of industrial production. If the Law of Variable Proportions is supposed to describe *industrial* processes, it would be nice to have an example. Coefficients that vary with *output* (which are plentiful) will not do either. Moreover, even the farming examples are questionable except as special cases. E. Boserup has argued (1965) that more intensive agriculture involves a dramatic change in the quality of work, entailing very considerable social changes. Robert Heilbroner, however, has pointed out to me that there is a textbook case meeting all neo-Classical specifications: Widgets.
6. The two we have mentioned are certainly relevant. Kelvin Lancaster has argued (1966) that utility functions take *characteristics* of products, rather than

the products themselves as arguments. (The famous 'diet problem' in linear programming is an example.) Even a relatively minor change in a product's characteristics resulting from substitution among inputs could lead to a noticeable change in demand. No comment is needed on the importance of the skill mix, or of job ratings, on the labor market.

7. Let C be a square non-negative matrix of inputs, each row showing the current inputs, including user cost, of each commodity or factor required to produce a unit output of a given commodity. Then, assuming single-product industries, the unit diagonal matrix, I, will represent outputs. It is customary to define the system as *productive* if there exists a non-negative vector $\bar{x}$ (representing a set of production intensities) such that $\bar{x} > \bar{x}C$.
8. It is difficult to spell out this second neo-Classical model, since it is not written out in full anywhere, showing how it can answer the questions the critics are asking. Instead it leads a shadowy existence in footnotes and unpublished papers, and in the sometimes cross, but always tantalizing, remarks of Robert Solow, when he speaks of 'neo-Classical theory in its full generality.' Does the rate of return follow from 'time-preference?' Or from the 'demand for wealth,' *à la* Modigliani? Does the real wage, then, follow as a residual? If there is no aggregate production function, there cannot be a marginal product of labor. But if time preference enters into the determination of the rate of return, we would expect, on grounds of symmetry, that work-leisure preference would figure in the labor market. Such an equation could prove awkward, however. For if fixed coefficient techniques and given initial capital determine the (full employment) amount of labor, while the real wage follows as a residual, there will be no room for it.
9. Thus the Cambridge Criticism undermines the demand schedule of the 'parable' and the supply schedule of the MIT–Fisher model. But the demand schedule of the latter is also suspect once we move away from Solow's simple one-consumption-good model. As is now well-known, there are many investment criteria which under plausible circumstances give different rankings. Moreover, under economically-plausible circumstances the internal rate of return is not unique (Harcourt, 1962): In any case, Solow's rate of return is the return to society from investment, not to capitalists from capital. It is a long step from this to a theory of the rate of profit.
10. This could be true even though the *propensity* to consume or to save out of income were fixed!
11. A Walras–Fisher model cannot explain the rate of profit in the stationary state. Does capital receive no return in the stationary state? Does the whole national income go in wages to labor, when the rate of growth is zero? Wicksell criticized Walras on this very point (1954, pp. 167–8).
12. Assume that all savings comes out of profits. Then $\Delta Y/Y = \Delta K/K = S/Y \cdot Y/K = s_p P/Y \cdot Y/K = s_p r$. Hence $\Delta K/K = s_p r$, so Capitalist Total Spending: I/s_p = Total Profit on Capital: rK.
13. According to Joan Robinson, if there were perfect competition, price would be driven down to prime cost whenever there is under-capacity utilization of plant. The theory of imperfect competition was developed precisely to show why this does not happen.
14. 'Now, it is clear that capitalists may decide to consume and invest more in a given period than in the preceding one, but they cannot decide to earn more. It is, therefore, their investment and consumption decisions which determine profits, and not vice versa' (Kalecki, 1954, p. 46).

References

Boserup, E. (1965) *The Conditions of Agricultural Growth: The Economics of Agrarian Change Under Population Pressure* (London: Aldine).
Bronfenbrenner, M. (1971) *Income Distribution Theory* (London: Aldine-Atherton).
Dorfman, R., Samuelson, P. and Solow, R. (1958) *Linear Programming and Economic Analysis* (London: John Wiley).
Douglas, P. (1934) *The Theory of Wages* (London: Macmillan).
Feinstein, C.H. (1968) 'Changes in the Distribution of the National Income in the U.K. Since 1960,' in J. Marchal and B. Ducross (eds), *The Distribution of the National Income* (London: Macmillan).
Ferguson, C. (1969) *The Neo-Classical Theory of Production and Distribution* (Cambridge: Cambridge University Press).
Ferguson, C. (1971) 'Capital Theory Up to Date: A Comment on Mrs Robinson's Article,' *Canadian Journal of Economics* (May).
Fisher, F. (1971) 'Aggregate Production Functions and the Explanation of Wages: A Simulation Experiment,' *Review of Economics and Statistics*, 53, pp. 305–25.
Haley, B. (1968) 'Changes in the Distribution of Income in the US,' in J. Marchal and B. Ducross, *The Distribution of National Income* (London: Macmillan).
Harcourt, G.C. (1962) 'Investment-Decision Criteria, Capital Intensity and the Choice of Techniques,' *Czechoslovak Economic Papers*, 9.
Harcourt, G.C. (1969). 'Some Cambridge Controversies in the Theory of Capital,' *Journal of Economic Literature* (June).
Kalecki, M. (1954) *Theory of Economic Dynamics* (London: George Allen & Unwin).
Kennedy, C. (1964) 'Induced Bias in Innovation and the Theory of Distribution,' *Economic Journal*, (October).
Keynes, J.M. (1930) *Treatise on Money*, 2 Vols (London: Macmillan).
Lancaster, K. 'A New Approach to Consumer Theory,' *Journal of Political Economy*, 74.
Lowe, A. (1964) *On Economic Knowledge* (New York: Harper Torch Books).
Lydall, H. (1971) 'A Theory of Distribution and Growth with Economies of Scale,' *Economic Journal*, 181 (March) pp. 91–112.
Marx, K. (1867–94) *Capital*, Vol. I 1867; Vol. II 1885; Vol. III 1894 (Chicago: W.H. Kerr).
Nell, E. (1968) 'The Social Rate of Return and the Switching Rate of Profit,' University of East Anglia, unpublished paper.
Nell, E. (1971) 'Capital Theory: Profit Inflation, Exploitation and Maximizing,' New School for Social Research (New York) unpublished paper.
Nell, E. (1972) 'Population Pressure and Intensity of Cultivation,' *Peasant Studies* (February) (Chapter 11 in this volume).
Nell, E. (1972) 'The Wage-Profit Trade-off,' New School, unpublished.
Pasinetti, L.L. (1969) 'Switches of Technique and "the Rate of Return" in Capital Theory,' *Economic Journal* (September).
Pen, J. (1971) *Income Distribution* (London: Allen Lane).
Robinson, J. (1955) 'The Theory of Distribution,' *Collected Economic Papers*, II (Oxford: Basil Blackwell).
Robinson, J. (1971) 'Capital Theory Up to Date: A Reply,' *Canadian Journal of Economics* (May).
Samuelson, P. (1967) 'Parable and Realism in Capital Theory: The Surrogate Production Function,' *Review of Economic Studies*, xxix, pp. 193–206.

Samuelson, P. and Solow, R. (1956) 'A Complete Capital Model Involving Heterogeneous Capital Goods,' *Quarterly Journal of Economics*, LXX (November) pp. 537–62.

Shaikh, A. (1971) 'Laws of Production and Laws of Algebra: A Note on Cobb–Douglas Aggregate Production Functions,' Columbia University, unpublished paper.

Simon, H. and Levy, F. (1953) 'A Note on the Cobb–Douglas Function,' *Review of Economic Studies* (June).

Solow, R.M. (1957) 'Technological Change and the Aggregate Production Function,' *Review of Economics and Statistics*,

Solow, R.M. (1963) *Capital Theory and the Rate of Return* (Amsterdam: North-Holland).

Solow, R.M. (1970) 'In the Rate of Return: A Reply to Pasinetti,' *Economic Journal* (June).

Sutcliffe, R. and Glyn, A. (1972) *The Crisis of British Capitalism* (London: Pelican).

Weintraub, S. (1958) *Approach to the Theory of Income Distribution* (London: Chilton Books).

Wicksell, K. (1954) *Value, Capital and Rent* (London: George Allen & Unwin).

10 On Long-run Equilibrium in Class Society*

The notion of equilibrium and the distinction between two kinds, long run and short, has been fundamental to almost all economic analysis of the past century. By contrast, the classics and Marx sought for the 'laws of motion' of capitalism. These latter do not define a long-run equilibrium, and it will be the claim here that a full-fledged, long-run equilibrium is not possible in a class society. This is not exactly Joan Robinson's position, but it is close, and it builds on some of her favorite themes.

We shall take it that the predominant sense of 'equilibrium' describes a position of the economy in which no agent has any incentive to change behavior; it is therefore a behavioral concept. The classics, by contrast, analyzed structure, and turned to behavioral notions only when dealing with market fluctuations around the economy's 'natural' position. (By 'behavior' we mean stimulus-response patterns, as in supply or demand functions; 'structure', on the other hand, refers to roles and institutions, which have to be maintained or reproduced. Of course, structure implies propensities to kinds of behavior, and behavior occurs in a structural setting, but the two are nevertheless significantly different.) Such 'natural' positions are inherent in the economy's structure; attempts to interpret them as positions of long-run (behavioral) equilibrium must be rejected, if the contentions of this paper are correct. To see what is involved, let's examine the notion of equilibrium.

Arrow, in concert first with Debreu (1954) and later with Hahn (1971), has greatly deepened our understanding of Hicks' (1939) notion of 'temporary equilibrium', itself a development of the older notion of short-run equilibrium, elaborated most fully by Marshall (1895). Marshall's 'short period' was defined by the fact that some or most factors of production could be varied, so that output could be adjusted, but at least one factor remained fixed. In simple models, labor was treated as variable while land and/or capital were held fixed. So, ignoring noncompeting groups and other barriers to entry, the wage rate would be made uniform across different lines of work by competition. But if capital is fixed (and in modern 'temporary equilibrium' all factors are fixed in amount), then in

* G.R. Feiwel (ed.), *Joan Robinson and Modern Economic Theory* (London: Macmillan, 1989). Thanks for comments and discussions on earlier versions of this paper go to G.C. Harcourt, Cigdem Kurdas, Heinz Kurz and Anwar Shaikh.

the short period returns to capital invested in different lines of activity might vary, for the forces of competition would not have time to take effect. In the long run, however, capital, too, could be shifted between lines of activity, and this ebb and flow in search of the most profitable opportunities would only cease when returns to capital invested stood in the same proportion in all spheres. For if returns were non-uniform, there would exist an incentive to disinvest in low return areas and reinvest where returns are high. The analogy with the 'law of one price' is exact.

Ricardo and Marx both recognized this, and made the establishment of uniformity in the rate of profit central to their analysis of the formation of prices, though not in an equilibrium context. Likewise, the early neo-Classical thinkers, Marshall, Walras, Wicksell, Clark, and others, all held both that uniformity in the rate of profit was essential to the establishment of long-run equilibrium, and that the analysis of the economy's long-period positions was a central task of economic theory, perhaps even its most important one.

But starting in the 1930s both these tenets were abandoned, as main-stream thinkers came to adopt the approach of 'temporary equilibrium.' The chief difference between this and the older notion of short-run equilibrium is that it no longer relies on the broad concept of a factor of production, such as labor in general, or capital, considered as a fund capable of adopting different forms – that is, of being invested in different sets of productive equipment. Instead, it takes each type of labor and each particular capital good as given, and it determines the appropriate shadow price or rental value. The ratio of this rental value to supply price is not considered; only the supply and demand conditions are examined, and the equilibrium prices are those that clear the markets. But such equilibria are temporary, and therefore it may be appropriate to investigate sequences of them. One of the properties of such sequences could be that rental value–supply price ratios for the various capital goods would tend to converge as the sequence lengthens to infinity. But this has not been much investigated; it is likely, however, that along the way the relations between capital values and the rates of return may be highly irregular or 'perverse.'

1 THE QUESTION OF THE RATE OF PROFIT

Serious questions can be raised about this approach, particularly when we require our models to exhibit fully the production of means of production, i.e. of capital goods. Why would owners of any capital goods accept a lower rate of return on the value of their productive equipment than was available to others, even in the short run? The short-period equilibrium is either reached by a process of *tâtonnement*, or through recontracting, either of which would provide plenty of opportunity for owners to search out and compete for the best returns. Information, foresight and mobility are all assumed to be perfect, so all owners of capital goods (and, *mutatis mutandis*, labor) not only know where the best returns will be, but could threaten to shift their activity there. Moreover, some aspects of methods of production are normally assumed to be variable, so that the temporary equilibrium will reflect a cost-minimizing choice of techniques. That makes it even harder to see why owners of factors would not insist on the best rate of return on their investment.

The crucial missing element in this approach is what Marshall called 'free capital', and Hicks (1965) has referred to as the 'fund' concept of capital. Capital, as J.B. Clark knew very well, alternately takes the form of a fund of value and a set of productive goods. As the goods are used up in production, output results and is sold, returning the capital in the form of investible funds, which will at all times seek the highest returns. Thus even in the short period, there will be some capital in the form of funds – last period's depreciation, plus this period's new saving – which will potentially be shifting about in search of the highest rate of return. Even if this process is not modelled explicitly, its implication – the tendency to seek the highest rate of return – must be incorporated.

So long as the returns from using equipment in relation to its supply price are unequal, the pressure for such shifting will continue to exist. Once the rate of return is uniform, capital will no longer tend to move about, disrupting prices. But this brings us face to face with a surprising and in some quarters unwelcome implication, namely that, given a set of methods of production with certain commonly assumed characteristics (single product, 'productive', constant returns, no technical change, at least one basic good, and one primary factor – labor), the establishment of a uniform rate of profit is sufficient to determine both the choice of the method of production and the set of equilibrium prices, including the real-wage, independently of demand, and therefore of market clearing. Such prices have nothing to do with scarcity; they reflect embodied labor (Arrow and Hahn, 1971, p. 45; Pasinetti, 1975, Ch. 5). Or, to put the point perhaps more revealingly, in a manner favored by Joan Robinson, they reflect a different conception of the function of the price system. Instead of indicating the most preferred choice among constrained alternatives, thus measuring scarcity as it affects behavior, prices show the exchanges that would be required to bring about the reproduction of the system with a particular distribution. This is a structural notion; it doesn't picture behavior occurring in response to stimuli, so it doesn't depend on assumptions about knowledge, rationality, veridical perceptions, mobility of factors, or the like, all of which are crucial to behavioral theories (Nell, 1967, 1984). This view of the price system, therefore, does not involve the concept of equilibrium in the sense we are using the term, although as we shall see, Hicks has given it an equilibrium interpretation, treating it as simply an alternative approach, on the same level as the method of temporary equilibrium.

2 THE 'METHOD OF GROWTH ECONOMICS'

The different way that prices work seems to be the chief reason that Hicks came to consider what he called 'Growth Economics,' in which prices are determined by the rate of profit (itself inversely related to the real wage), as a separate 'method' of dynamic economics, on the same level of generality as the 'Temporary Equilibrium' method, but more useful because more suited to combination with 'Fixprice' thinking, i.e. the microeconomics of Keynes, Robinson, Harrod and the cycle theorists (Hicks, 1965, Part I). The 'Temporary Equilibrium' method is defective, in Hicks's view, because of its inadequate treatment of uncertainty, its assumption of perfect competition, but, above all, because it assumes, it *has* to assume (for otherwise prices would not be determinate), that markets clear each period. Because in 'Growth Economics' prices are determined by distribution, rather than by supply and demand, it is not necessary to assume unrealistic market clearing; hence the model is capable of providing the price-theoretic foundations for macroeconomics. But this introduces a new dimension, the growth of the economy, as a result of investment. The relationship of this to profits and distribution in long-run equilibrium must now be considered.

3 THE UNIFORM GROWTH RATE

The essential idea of a growth equilibrium is that all variables expand at the same positive rate, which must also be determined. This replaces the earlier, static idea of long-run equilibrium, in which all variables are fully adjusted, but essentially fixed, i.e. growing at the rate of zero. This requires closer examination.[1]

Growth in long-run equilibrium must be uniform; that is, all industries and sectors must be expanding at the same rate. If some industry were growing faster than its suppliers, for example, once inventories of suppliers were exhausted (and the running down of inventories itself would represent a change in capital holdings) the suppliers would have to try to change their output allocation in order to sustain the fast-growing industry. But they would not be able to do so, because (in an interdependent system with at least one basic) *their* suppliers would not be able to keep up. So the faster-growing industry would have to slow down. Similarly, if an industry were growing more slowly than its suppliers – or customers – then it would both have the incentive and the means to expand more rapidly. Of course, non-uniform growth is easily possible, at least for short periods, even when the economy is operating at or near normal full capacity. But it is not sustainable without changes in inventories and/or in average costs, so it is not a possible position of equilibrium. Only a uniform rate could be that.

A rate of growth is the ratio of output at the end of one period to output at the end of the previous period. But when the good in question is a produced means of production – a capital good, a 'basic' – then the growth rate (the potential, or full capacity growth rate) is the ratio of the output of the good to the amount of it used directly and indirectly as input. Such a ratio can be defined for every capital good. Assume either that capital goods last one period only, or that they all have the same lifetime and depreciate linearly. Then consider the set of all capital goods used directly or indirectly in each other's production – Sraffa's basics. The growth rate of this set will be constrained by the lowest ratio of output to the vertically integrated means of production; and the highest growth rate sustainable from period to period will be achieved when all such output to use-as-input ratios are uniform (Pasinetti, 1975; Brody, 1970; Mathur, 1965). But in that case the ratios of the various outputs to one another will be the same as the ratios of the various inputs to one another; the economy's output will be a 'composite commodity' consisting of the same goods in the same proportions as the aggregate of its capital goods inputs. (This conception can be extended to the case of capital goods with different lifetimes and different patterns of depreciation (Sraffa, 1960).)

4 THE RATE OF PROFIT AND THE RATE OF GROWTH

Finally, let's examine the relation between the rate of profit and the rate of growth in equilibrium. First, consider the question of uniformity. Movements of capital from low to high profit industries generate the uniform rate of profit; but it is also movements of capital, from slack to 'bottleneck' industries, which bring uniformity in growth rates. Hence, if either the growth or the profit rate is upset, causing capital to shift about, the uniformity of the other will be threatened. Since the same cause (movements of capital between sectors) establishes both uniformities, anything which incites such movements threatens both. The uniformities must therefore be considered interdependent.

Next, taking the two rates as uniform, consider the relations between them. We will begin with some quite specialized institutional assumptions, but these have been chosen to bring out certain connections, which hold more generally. Consider a set of capitalists who deal in machinery and capital goods. They themselves do not operate the equipment; they merely lease it out to entrepreneurs. Each period they buy the entire output of the capital goods industries, which they then make available to producers in both the consumer goods industries and in the capital goods sector itself. Let us suppose that all production is organized in this way; producers are entrepreneurs who earn only salaries and 'pure profits,' which are zero in long-run equilibrium. Hence the equilibrium leasing fees, or rentals, must enable the capitalists to cover their own consumption and to purchase this period's output of capital goods. Part of current output will simply replace the capital goods used up or depreciated in the course of current production; if the leasing fees cover no more than this there will be no net profit. But if the current output of the capital goods sector is greater than replacement and depreciation, the ratio of such current output to the capital goods used to produce it will be the rate of growth of the capital stock, and the leasing fees will have to be sufficient to permit the capitalists to purchase this current output. The surplus of the leasing fees over the amount required for depreciation will be the capitalists' net profit, which will have to exactly equal their consumption plus what they need to buy the additional output which represents the growth of this period's production over last period's. If we neglect capitalist consumption for the moment, this period's net leasing fees go to purchase the capital goods which will serve as next period's net investment. The rate of profit is given by the ratio of the leasing fees to last period's output (this period's invested capital), while the rate of growth is the ratio of next period's invested capital to this period's, and in equilibrium these will clearly have to be equal, since there could be arbitrage between owning the leasing industry and owning producing industries.

This argument made some very special institutional assumptions, but it brought to light the general relationship between accumulation in value terms, based on profits minus planned capitalist consumption, and real investment, which is the acquisition and installation of the equipment produced by the capital goods producers. In long-term equilibrium, growth must be balanced and growth in value and in real terms must proceed at the same rate.[2]

To put it another way: if either the rate of profit or the rate of accumulation is nonuniform, we *know* that prices and outputs must change from period to period, and, moreover, we will often have enough information to say which prices and/or which outputs will change and in which directions they will move. So if we are to define a long-period equilibrium, by contrast to temporary equilibrium, as a position in which agents are not only satisfied, but which will be maintained from period to period so long as the fundamental data remain unchanged, we must require uniformity of these two rates (automatically achieved in a zero-profit stationary state, for both rates are then uniform at zero), and the appropriate relationship between them.

5 A CLAIM OF THE CRITICS

But critics of orthodox economics have claimed that the notion of equilibrium itself was inconsistent with capitalism. (Lenin's notion of uneven development surely implies this.) To put it in contemporary terms, can capitalism proceed along a path of steady growth? Alternatively, can capitalism be studied using the 'method' of Growth Economics, that is, by comparing (hypothetical) situations of economies, similar in various respects, but growing at different rates, and/or with different rates of profit? We have now developed the concept of long-run equilibrium in a capitalist economy; let's examine the challenge of the critics.

We began from the dual nature of capital, as freely movable funds, and as produced means of production, which led to the notions of the uniform rate of profit and of accumulation, and the critique of the Temporary Equilibrium approach. But we have not yet considered the implications of the most basic fact about the capitalist system: that it is a class society.

6 CAPITALISM AND SOCIAL CLASSES

The concept of class, as it is used in sociology, is ambiguous and multi-dimensional, but for the purposes of developing an abstract economic theory we can adopt a simple and consistent notion, such as figured in the work of Smith and Ricardo (and to some extent, Marx, although his use of the concept goes beyond economics and raises new problems). For our purposes, class is based on the kinship system: classes are classes of families, that is, of working household units, which function both as consumers, supporting the workers and decision makers of this generation, and as producers of the next generation. Working-class families own very little wealth, not enough to provide a living income, and so must be supported by working for wages. Working-class offspring will generally marry within the working class, just as children of capitalist families will marry within their class. Capitalist families are defined by the ownership of wealth on a substantial scale, which yields profit income, and entails rights to make decisions about the uses to which means of production will be put. But working-class families will normally save, for precautionary reasons, if for no other, and so will accumulate wealth, which will yield them profit income, in addition to their wages. And capitalists will have to manage their wealth, making decisions about how and where to invest it. By normal definitions this is work, entitling them to a salary, particularly in view of the fact that managing investments requires skill and information. (Moreover, because of such specialization, capitalist managers will also handle the savings of workers.) Hence, in addition to profit income, capitalist households will normally also draw salaries. The *per capita* level of salaries, however, will be much higher than the working class wage rate, reflecting both the ability of the status and prestige conferred by wealth to command income, and returns to the investment in the acquisition of skills.

7 A SIMPLE MODEL OF GROWTH EQUILIBRIUM

If we were to write it out in full there would be at least three sectors, one producing capital goods (of various kinds), another consumer goods for workers, and one producing a higher grade of consumer goods for capitalist households. However, for simplicity we can aggregate the sectors. It is necessary to assume that all household income-expenditure functions are linear; otherwise, and realistically, as the system expands the proportions of spending on different goods would change. For simplicity we shall assume that all households in each class are identical. For the system to be in Growth Equilibrium, the various sectors must all expand at the same rate, and industries must earn the same rate of profit on their invested capital. Under these circumstances prices will remain constant, making it easy to aggregate output, income and capital. Hence, using an obvious notation, we can write, using '*w*' and '*c*' to indicate workers and capitalists,

$$Y = C_w + C_c + I = W + P = xK \tag{10.1}$$

where $W = W_c + W_w$, $P = P_c + P_w$, $K = K_c + K_w$, and

$$L_w = nK, \text{ and } L_c = mK \tag{10.2}$$

where x, n and m are the ratios of output, factory labor and management, respectively, to capital.

Now consider the implication of long-run equilibrium for the class structure: the relative wealth and income of the two classes must remain constant (if either changed, the ratio C_w/C_c would have to change), so both classes must find their wealth expanding at the same rate, and must receive income from wealth in the same proportion, which is to say that their wealth holdings yield the same rate of profit. So we can write,

$$\frac{P_c}{K_c} = \frac{P_w}{K_w} = r \tag{10.3}$$

and

$$\frac{S_c}{K_c} = \frac{S_w}{K_w} = g \tag{10.4}$$

showing that the wealth holdings of the two classes both earn returns at the same rate and grow at the same rate. However, the wealth of the two classes is very different *per capita*, capitalists being substantially wealthier, though how much is not at issue here. So,

$$\frac{K_c}{L_c} = \frac{aK_w}{L_w} \qquad (10.5)$$

where $a > 1$ is the coefficient indicating the extent to which capitalists are wealthier.

Next we must consider wages and salaries. The possession of wealth not only provides direct returns in the form of profits, but (notoriously) confers advantages in the earning of income, partly through the influence of position, and partly through the development of skills – so-called 'human capital'. In long-run equilibrium the effect of wealth on earning power must be the same for all forms and holdings of wealth and all types of work. Hence the ratio of salaries *per capita* to the wage-rate must be the same as the ratio of capitalist wealth to working-class wealth. So,

$$\frac{W_c}{L_c} = \frac{aW_w}{L_w} \qquad (10.6)$$

Dividing (10.5) into (10.6) and then into (10.4) gives us,

$$\frac{S_c}{W_c} = \frac{S_w}{W_w} \qquad (10.7)$$

so that, writing 's_c' and 's_w' for the respective saving propensities, which reflect the different circumstances of the classes,

$$\frac{s_c(P_c + W_c)}{W_c} = \frac{s_w(P_w + W_w)}{W_w}. \qquad (10.8)$$

Dividing (10.6) into (10.5) and then into (10.3) yields,

$$\frac{P_w}{W_w} = \frac{P_c}{W_c} = \frac{P}{W} \qquad (10.9)$$

so we can rewrite (10.8)

$$s_c \frac{P}{W} + s_c = s_w \frac{P}{W} + s_w \qquad (10.10)$$

from which it follows that,

$$\frac{P}{W} = \frac{s_w - s_c}{s_c - s_w} = -1, s_w \neq s_c \tag{10.11}$$

(When $s_w = s_c$ the result will be indeterminate.)[3]

8 CLASS WEALTH AND THE SALARY/WAGE DIFFERENTIAL

Should we assume that the salary/wage differential echoes the wealth ratio of the two classes? The argument is that in long-run equilibrium the power of capital to increase wages, or more generally earned incomes, must be the same everywhere. Otherwise, there would be attempts to create institutions to take advantage of the ability of capital to produce higher earnings in some areas. Suppose capital could augment worker earnings in some particular line; workers could then pool savings, and then boost the earnings of some select few, who would then divide the additional earnings among those who had contributed to the pool (very much as the extended family chips in to send a promising son to college). Note that the argument is not that this will tend to equalize returns; it is rather that if returns are not equalized, then these disequilibrium movements will occur.

Still, let's consider the case where, instead of (10.6) we have

$$W_c/L_c = bW_w/L_w \tag{10.6'}$$

from which we get

$$S_c/W_c = a/b(S_w/W_w) \tag{10.7'}$$

Manipulating further

$$P/W = [(a/b)s_w - s_c]/[a/b(s_c - s_w)] \tag{10.11'}$$

which will be > 0 if and only if $(a/b)s_w > s_c$, i.e. $as_w > bs_c$, or $a/b > s_c/s_w$. This is both arbitrary and implausible. For the profit–wage ratio to be positive, wealth must augment capitalist salaries very little if it affects their saving very much; the higher s_c in relation to s_w, the lower b has to be in relation to a. But if wealth promotes class differences in saving, will it not also bring about class differences in earned income?

9 GROWTH EQUILIBRIUM vs CLASS BEHAVIOR

A negative profit–wage ratio does not make sense; the system is inconsistent. Let us see what has gone wrong. From (10.5) and (10.6) we obtain,

$$\frac{W_c}{K_c} = \frac{W_w}{K_w} \tag{10.12}$$

hence adding to (10.3),

$$\frac{P_c + W_c}{K_c} = \frac{P_w + W_w}{K_w} \tag{10.13}$$

Income per unit of wealth is the same in the two classes, although, of course, income *per capita* is higher for the capitalists, so the growth rates of wealth cannot be the same unless the saving ratios are identical. But the respective saving ratios reflect the different positions of the classes; higher *per capita* wealth and income should produce a higher saving ratio. Working-class households will spend most of their income on essentials; saving will therefore be expensive in terms of forgone necessities. By contrast capitalists will only have to give up luxuries in order to save.[4]

Looking at it another way, since their current consumer needs are well provided for, capitalist households can afford to set funds aside for the future, whereas working-class households must give prime consideration to filling current needs. So it is inherent in the concept of a class society that the saving-consumption behavior of the two classes should be different, but the conditions of long-run equilibrium require their behavior to be the same.

10 DIFFERENT PROPENSITIES TO SAVE OUT OF WAGES AND PROFITS

This last point is more complicated than it might seem. Clearly if both classes have the same proportional saving function both will accumulate at the same rate. But this is not necessary; from (10.3) and (10.12), we find

$$\frac{P_c}{W_c} = \frac{P_w}{W_w} \tag{10.14}$$

So if the saving propensities out of profits and out of wages are the same for both classes, even though different for the different kinds of income, then each class will have the same average propensity to save, overall, and hence will accumulate at the same rate.

Granted that there can be good reasons for saving to take place at different rates out of different kinds of income, e.g. that the payments of wages and profits were timed differently, but there is equally good reason to suppose that the respective patterns of saving behavior will be different in the two classes.[5] Suppose we add further subscripts to distinguish each class's propensity to save out of each kind of income. Then we have four distinct saving propensities, two for each class, and we write:

$$S_c = s_{cp} P_c + s_{cw} W_c \text{ and } S_w = s_{wp} P_w + s_{ww} W_w \tag{10.15}$$

so, following the same procedure, we find

$$s_{cp} \frac{P_c}{W_c} + s_{cw} = s_{wp} \frac{P_w}{W_w} + s_{ww}, \text{ yielding}$$

$$\frac{P}{W} = \frac{s_{ww} - s_{cw}}{s_{cp} - s_{wp}} \tag{10.16}$$

The most plausible case will be $s_{cp} > s_{cw} > s_{wp} > s_{ww}$, which implies that P/W will be negative. Since $s_{cp} > s_{wp}$ is very reasonable, a positive ratio would require that workers save more from wages than capitalists from salaries, which does not make economic sense, given our assumptions on the nature of the class system.

11 MANY SOCIAL CLASSES

These results can easily be generalized. Suppose there are m classes, $i = 1, \ldots, m$, each receiving both kinds of income. Then we rewrite (10.3) and (10.4),

$$P_i = rK_i \tag{10.3'}$$

$$S_i = gK_i \tag{10.4'}$$

Next we suppose that earned income for any class consists of two parts, a basic socially determined subsistence wage – the same for all – and an additional portion which reflects the command of wealth. This last may be thought of as due to investment in the acquisition of skills in proportion to wealth, with the skills also being rewarded proportionally. This amounts to contending that 'human capital' must be held in proportion to non-human, as a requirement of long-run equilibrium. But this then poses the problem that the two kinds of capital, human and non-human, must either earn the same rate of return, or we must explain the differential. Alternatively, the fraction of earned income proportional to wealth could be considered as a command over income provided by privilege and social prestige, a kind of monopoly rent available to those with the inside information and contacts which follow the ownership of property. In any case, let w_{oi} stand for the conventionally determined subsistence component of the wage; then,

$$w_i = w_{oi} + b_i K_i \qquad (10.17)$$

where w_i is the total wage received by each class, basic plus wealth-determined, and b_i is the coefficient for each of the i social classes indicating the influence of its wealth in procuring earned income.

In the 'human capital' interpretation, however, b would have to be uniform for all groups, since everyone's capital must earn the same return in equilibrium. Taking the more general case where b can vary between different classes.

$$S_i = s_i(w_i - w_{oi} + P_i) \qquad (10.18)$$

which states that saving by the ith class will take place out of profits and wealth-related earned income. Alternatively,

$$S_i = s_{wi}(w_i - w_{oi}) + s_{pi} P_i \qquad (10.18')$$

Then using (10.17) we have

$$S_i = s_i(b_i + r)K_i, \text{ or from (10.18')}: S_i = (s_{wi} b_i + s_{pi} r)K_i \qquad (10.19)$$

It follows that,

$$s_i(b_i + r) = g = s_j(b_j + r) \qquad (10.20)$$

or:

$$s_{wi} b_i + s_{pi} r = g = s_{wj} b_j + s_{pj} r$$

And this in turn implies

$$r = [s_j b_j - s_i b_i]/[s_i - s_j) \qquad (10.21)$$

which will be > 0 if and only if $b_j/b_i > s_i/s_j$. Alternatively,

$$r = [s_{wj}b_j - s_{wi}b_i]/[s_{pi} - s_{pj}) > 0 \text{ iff } b_j/b_i > s_{wi}/s_{wj}$$

In both cases the condition is wholly arbitrary; even worse, it implies that the class whose wealth generates more income must save less out of it, as a condition for the rate of profit to be positive in long-run equilibrium, i.e. for the system to make minimal economic sense. (This is a generalization of 10.11′.) Now consider

$$[s_k b_k - s_i b_i]/(s_i - s_k),\ k \neq j$$

If either s_k or b_k differ from s_j or b_j, then the calculated value of r will differ also. If there are more than two classes whose saving behavior, or the earning power of whose wealth differ, then the rate of profit cannot be uniform, even if the conditions for its being positive are met.

Finally, from (10.21), in the human capital case, where $b = b_j = b_i$, it follows that $r = -b$. If wealth invested in human skills contributes to earning power at a positive rate, uniform in all social classes, and if saving takes place at different rates in these classes, then non-human wealth will suffer loss at the same rate that human wealth earns returns, in order for the classes to accumulate at the same rate, i.e. for their wealth holdings to maintain a constant ratio.

12 MORE ON HUMAN CAPITAL

Suppose the return on human capital were treated as another form of the return to capital as such, so that the part of the earnings from work which are due to the holding of wealth were added to ordinary profits to determine the (augmented) rate of profit. Then we would have,

$$P_i + b_i K_i = rK_i, \text{ or } r = P_i/K_i + b_i \qquad (10.3'')$$

Clearly for r to be uniform all classes must have the same wealth-salary coefficient, b. Since wages are now w_{oi}, the socially determined subsistence wages, all saving will come out of wealth-related income, i.e. augmented profits. Hence,

$$S_i = gK_i = s_i(b_i + P_i/K_i)K_i = s_i r K_i \qquad (10.4'')$$

Hence for g to be uniform,

$$s_i\, r = s_j\, r = g;$$

all classes must have identical saving behavior.

13 CORPORATE RETAINED EARNINGS

So far we have worked with a highly simplified picture of capitalism, in which its most characteristic institution, the modern corporation, has not even been mentioned. To rectify this, while keeping the argument manageable, we continue to assume that there are two classes of households, workers and capitalists, both receiving both profit and wage income, in proportion to their wealth. But now their (non-human) wealth is held explicitly in the form of shares in corporations, the number and distribution of which we take to be fixed. Income from such wealth comes in the form of dividends distributed by the corporations. Hence, in addition to distributed earnings, there will or may be undistributed earnings retained by the companies. These when invested will increase the value of the corporations' operating systems. So in anticipation of such successful investments, the shares of the companies will appreciate, and this appreciation along with savings will determine the expansion of wealth holdings.

Each class, therefore, saves and spends out of its income, which it receives as wage and dividend payments, but passively accepts the capital gains which result from the rise in the value of the shares it holds. As before, the classes can be presumed to have different consumption patterns, so that long-run equilibrium will require their wealth holdings to grow at the same rate:

$$[s_w(W_w + D_w) + N_w\Delta\$]/N_w\$ = [s_c(W_c + D_c) + N_c\Delta\$]/N_c\$ \quad (10.22)$$

where D_w and D_c are the dividends received by the two classes, N_w and N_c are the numbers of shares held respectively by the classes, while '\$' is the price of a share, and Δ is the operator 'delta'. Then, since corporations borrow and invest the savings of households, company growth will be:

$$g = [RP + s_w(W_w + D_w) + s_c(W_c + D_c)]/N\$ \quad (10.23)$$

where P is total profits, so that RP is retained earnings and $(1 - R)P = D_w + D_c = D$, distributed profit. In long-run equilibrium company growth must equal the expansion in household wealth; hence adding the numerators and denominators of (10.22) and comparing to (10.23), we see that the rate of increase in share values must equal the ratio of retained earning to the value of corporate invested capital.

Just as accumulation rates must be equal, so must profit rates; hence

$$[D_w + N_w\Delta\$]/N_w\$ = [D_c + N_c\Delta\$]/N_c\$ = P/N\$ = r \quad (10.24)$$

which implies,

$$D_w/N_w\$ = D_c/N_c\$ = D/N\$ = (1 - R)P/N\$ \quad (10.25)$$

As before we have,

$$W_c/L_c = aW_w/L_w, \text{ and } N_c\$/L_c = aN_w\$/L_w \qquad (10.26)$$

from which

$$W_c/N_c\$ = W_w/N_w\$ = W/N\$ \qquad (10.27)$$

Hence, using (10.24)

$$W_c/W_w = N_c\$/N_w\$ = [D_c + N_c\Delta\$] / [D_w + N_w\Delta\$]$$

$$= \{W_c + D_c + N_c\Delta\$\}/\{W_w + D_w + N_w\Delta\$\} = Y_c/Y_w \qquad (10.28)$$

where Y stands for the total income of a class.

Similarly, we can derive

$$[D_c + N_c\Delta\$] / W_c = [D_w + N_w\Delta\$] / W_w = P/W \qquad (10.29)$$

Thus in long-run equilibrium both class incomes and functional shares are determined in a fixed ratio.

Now divide (10.22) by (10.27) and rearrange, obtaining

$$s_w(1 + D_w/W_w) + N_w\Delta\$/W_w = s_c(1 + D_c/W_c) + N_c\Delta\$/W_c. \qquad (10.30)$$

But from (10.27) and (10.29) we know that $N_w/W_w = N_c/W_c$ and that $D_w/W_w = D_c/W_c = P/W$, so rewriting, we get

$$s_w + s_wP/W = s_c + s_cP/W \qquad (10.31)$$

which yields

$$P/W = [s_c - s_w] / (s_w - s_c) = -1 \qquad (10.32)$$

as before.

Introducing corporations does make a difference; under the assumptions here, the higher the retention rate, the higher will be the equilibrium growth rate (since there is no consumption out of capital gains). The corporation is the institutional form designed to promote capital accumulation in modern conditions (see Marglin, 1974). But it does nothing to resolve the conflict between the conditions required for long-run equilibrium and the differential behavior patterns inherent in class society, which results in the economically impossible equation (10.32).

14 ACCUMULATION, RELATIVE SHARES AND CLASS SIZES

The problem, of course, arises from imposing the condition of equal rates of accumulation on an economy in which saving and consuming behavior will be conditioned by social class. Let us now see what happens when we drop that requirement.

From (10.2) we see that the ratio of the sizes of the two classes in m/n, and we can now relate this to relative rates of growth and relative shares. From (10.5), then, we have,

$$K_c/K_w = aL_c/L_w = am/n \tag{10.33}$$

But we know that

$$K_c/K_w = P_c/P_w = W_c/W_w \tag{10.34}$$

so that $P/W = am/n$.

From (10.1) and the definitions we can derive

$$\frac{dK}{K} = \left(\frac{K_c}{K}\right)\frac{dK_c}{K_c} + \left(\frac{K_w}{K}\right)\frac{dK_w}{K_w} \quad \text{or}$$

$$g = \theta g_c + (1 - \theta)g_w, \text{ where } \theta = K_c/K \tag{10.35}$$

Hence from (10.33)

$$\theta = (am/n) \,/\, [am/n + 1], \text{ and } 1 > \theta > 0 \tag{10.36}$$

Next suppose that the saving behavior of the classes is such that their saving propensities are directly proportional to their *per capita* wealth. If the constants of proportionality are the same,

$$s_c = as_w, \text{ and since } Y_c/K_c = Y_w/K_w,\ g_c = ag_w \tag{10.37}$$

Hence,

$$g = [(1 + \theta)(a - 1)]g_w, \text{ and } g_c > g > g_w \tag{10.38}$$

Next from (10.1) and (10.2) we find

$$dY/Y = dK/K = g = dL_w/L_w = dL_c/L_c \tag{10.39}$$

Now consider (10.5): $K_c/L_c = aK_w/L_w$. We know that

K_c grows at rate g_c

L_c and L_w grow at rate g

K_w grows at rate g_w

so K_c/L_c tends to rise over time while K_w/L_w tends to fall. But it is an important feature of the class system, on the assumptions here, that wealth makes it possible to command additional earned income, and just as the rate of profit must be uniform in equilibrium, so must be this power to command earned income, as in (10.12). But this brings us to (10.6): $W_c/L_c = aW_w/L_w$. The salaries per head of capitalists will tend to rise, while the wage per worker will fall. In quite a literal sense, the rich get richer and the poor get poorer.

To maintain the consistency of the equations, the parameter a must rise over time, at the rate $g_c - g_w = g_w(a - 1)$. This ensures the consistency of equations (10.5), (10.6) and (10.12). But it also means that θ rises over time: capitalists' share of total wealth increases, and, accordingly, P/W also rises. It is common in models of growth equilibrium to assume that g is given by the requirement that capital should accumulate at the same rate that the labor force (in efficiency units) is growing. In this case, (10.38) implies that g_w must be falling over time. In any event, if a is rising, g_c/g_w will also rise at the same rate. Hence, in the very long run, in the limit, all wealth must tend to concentrate in the hands of capitalists. Working-class wealth must shrink to an insignificant proportion of total wealth, and working-class earnings must tend to the socially determined subsistence level.

15 METHODS OF ECONOMIC ANALYSIS

The message is not that, under capitalism, wealth will tend to concentrate: that may or may not be true, but an argument as abstract as this cannot decide the issue. What has been shown is rather that the idea of long-run equilibrium sits uncomfortably in a model of class society. Yet this conclusion raises a considerable methodological problem. For we have previously seen that the method of Temporary Equilibrium is defective. To correct these defects it was necessary to allow for the formation of a rate of profit, which made it possible to determine prices on the basis of distribution and technology, independently of supply and demand, thereby creating a theory of value capable of providing a basis for macroeconomics. Yet the rate of profit is necessarily connected to the rate of growth; one cannot be in equilibrium without the other. But once we consider the equilibrium rate of growth, we are in trouble with the relative wealth of the classes. However, if long-run equilibrium is impossible in a class society, then the method of Growth Economics must similarly be considered defective. But can we do without the notion of equilibrium? Joan Robinson certainly thought so. But then how can the position of the economy at a moment of time, or its movement through time, be determined?[6]

The problem lies in the notion of equilibrium as a position in which no agent has an incentive to change his pattern of behavior. This is always problematical, because in a competitive, class society various groups are always struggling with one another, and so will always be on the lookout for new means or methods to improve their positions. This is one basic reason why such systems are technologically and organizationally innovative. And it means that any approach which defines equilibrium in terms of the absence of incentives to change behavior is thereby precluded from studying the incentives to innovation. But even when questions of innovation are ruled out, as in the context of the preceding discussion, the equilibrium approach demands that the social order be modelled as reaching a *settled* state. Yet it may be one of the deepest truths about capitalism that it is never settled, that it is always changing, and that this is built into the fabric of the class structure itself.

To abandon equilibrium is not to abandon economic theory. Smith, Ricardo and Marx looked for 'laws of motion' rather than positions of short-term or long-term equilibrium. To be sure, Marx's 'prices of production' and his condition for sectoral balance can be interpreted as equilibrium conditions in the modern sense. But that is not how they have to be understood. Instead, they could be seen as conditions for *reproduction*, structural conditions which have to be met if the system is to reproduce itself, that is, maintain itself in its present state (which may be a state of proportional or non-proportional expansion). Given these structural conditions, we can then ask whether the system is likely to produce behavior which will satisfy them. In other words, the problem is broken into two parts: on the one hand, there is the calculation of the conditions for the system to continue to operate successfully – and, on the other hand, the analysis of what happens when these are not met. These comprise the structural analysis. Such structural conditions need not be thought of as 'centers of gravitation'; they may function simply as regulating ideals – benchmarks to which actual behavior can be compared, not only by the observing economists, but more importantly by the agents of the system themselves. Then there follows the study of behavior, to see what behavior is required to fulfill the structural conditions, and whether the system will tend to generate it. This method, which Adolph Lowe has long advocated (Lowe, 1965, 1976; Hollis and Nell, 1975; Nell, 1984), derives from classical thinking and because it partitions the question of the economy's position into structural and behavioral components, it avoids determining variables by relying on a notion of harmonious reconcilation, in which no one will have any incentive to change their course of action.

Notes

1. The built-in static bias of neo-Classical theory has tended to obscure the fact that for a capitalist economy the normal condition must be a state of growth. The problem of optimal allocation under scarcity is essentially static; it is an important subject, but it is not a good point from which to start the study of industrial capitalism. Capitalists compete, and in general size will provide advantages in competition; faster growing firms will tend to displace more slowly growing ones in the long run. Hence, even if most firms were willing to opt for the easy life, the few ambitious ones would force the rest to follow suit. So long as even one capitalist or firm proposes to improve its competitive position by investing, the rest must follow suit, or lose out in the long run – unless it can be assumed that size confers no competitive advantages whatsoever. Since this is unrealistic, in general competition will tend to lead a capitalist system to expand.
2. Garegnani (1976) and others have argued recently that the proper approach to economic theory is to determine the 'long-period position' of the economy, and then compare alternative positions for different values of key parameters. The long-period position is chiefly defined by the existence of a uniform rate of profit, and it is suggested that the development of the Temporary Equilibrium method came about because neo-Classical theory had difficulty working out a 'supply and demand' treatment of capital and the rate of profit. For Garegnani the normal rate of profit and the associated prices are 'centers of gravitation,' towards which the economy tends to move. Hence the idea of Temporary Equilibrium cannot be accepted, but by the same token, the rate of profit cannot be formed without Growth Equilibrium. A theory of 'gravitation' must also be a theory of investment. And if the 'long period' is sufficient to establish the uniformity of the rate profit, it must also establish the uniform rate of growth, for the reasons given in the text.
3. This discussion has some affinity to a celebrated argument of Pasinetti's (1962). But in Pasinetti's system workers receive both forms of income, but capitalists only get profits. Hence, dividing (10.4) into (10.3), we get an expression for r/g, which is

   $P_c/s_cP_c = P_w/s_w(W + P_w)$, and simplifies to

   $s_cP_w = s_w(W + P_w)$.

   Substitute this into the investment-savings equation:

   $I = s_w(W + P_w) + s_c P_c$

   $= s_c(P_w + P_c) = s_cP$, and dividing by K

   $g = s_cr$

   Worker's saving can be ignored because, in equilibrium, what they save out of all forms of income must equal what the capitalists would have saved, had they received the profits which go to the workers. But the entire argument turns on the assumption that capitalists receive only profits, although they both save and consume. A similar argument can be advanced on the assumption that workers receive only wages, although they both save and consume. The justification is that their wealth – accumulated savings – must be managed by capitalists, whose (monopoly) charges for their services eat up the entire earnings. Alternatively, we can think of the bulk of workers savings as being institutional, pension funds, managed by capitalists for their own benefit. It can be objected that workers would not save if they received no profit returns, but this is wrong, for their accumulated wealth raises their wages above subsistence. ('Subsistence' here means a conventional level; if it were biological they would not be able to save.) So (10.3) is irrelevant, and the system consists of (10.4), (10.5) and (10.6), from which we derive (10.7), and then

$$s_c(P + W_c)/W_c = s_w W/W_w, \text{ so that}$$

$$s_c(P + W_c) = s_w W_c$$

which states that the savings of capitalists are equal in long-run equilibrium to what the working class would have saved had they received the wages which went to capitalist managers. Substituting in the investment-saving conditions;

$$I = s_w W_w + s_c(P + W_c) = s_w W_w + s_w W_c = s_w W. \text{ So we can write,}$$

$$g = s_w(1/v - r)$$

where v is the capital–output ratio and r the rate of profit. The growth rate is independent of the capitalist saving propensity.

4. Saving propensities must be constant because of the assumption that income expenditure functions are linear. Without such an assumption long-run equilibrium would not be possible, for rising incomes would then lead to changes in the composition of output.
5. Moreover there are good reasons to avoid such an assumption. Consider,

$$S_w = s_w W + s_p P_w = gK_w$$

$$S_p = s_p P_c = g_{kc}$$

$$P_c/K_c = P_w/K_w = r$$

Following the procedure above to obtain r/g and simplifying, we find,

$$s_p P_w = s_w W + s_p P_w, \text{ which implies}$$

$$s_w W = 0, \text{ which is absurd.}$$

6. Disequilibrium methods are now widely used to provide microfoundations for macroeconomics (Harcourt, 1977). But such methods simply explain one mystery by another: macro quantity adjustments are explained by the assumed rigidity of some wage rate or price, but this rigidity is itself left unexamined, apart from casual references to unions and oligopoly. The purpose of the exercise is to retain the supply and demand framework, which determines prices and quantities together, yet still make room for macroecnomics. From the perspective taken here, the *ad hoc* assumptions of rigidity simply show up the defects of the Temporary Equilibrium method.

References

Arrow, K.J. and F. Hahn (1971) *General Competitive Analysis* (San Francisco: Holden-Day).

Brody, A. (1970) *Proportions, Prices and Planning* (New York: American Elsevier).

Debreu, G. (1954) *Theory of Value* (New York: John Wiley).

Eatwell, J. and M. Milgate (eds) (1983) *Keynes' Economics and The Theory of Value and Distribution* (New York: Oxford University Press).

Garegnani, P. (1976) 'On a Change in the Notion of Equilibrium in Recent Work on Value and Distribution,' reprinted in Eatwell and Milgate (1983).

Harcourt, G.C. (ed.) (1977) *The Microeconomic Foundations of Macroeconomics* (London: Macmillan).

Hicks, J.R. (1939) *Value and Capital* (Oxford: Clarendon Press).

Hicks, J.R. (1965) *Capital and Growth* (Oxford: Clarendon Press).

Hollis, M. and E. Nell (1975) *Rational Economic Man* (Cambridge: Cambridge Univerity Press).

Laibman, D. and E. Nell (1977) 'Reswitching, Wicksell Effects and the Neo-Classical Production Function,' *American Economic Review*, 67 (5) (December).

Lowe, A. (1965) *On Economic Knowledge* (New York: Harper & Row).

Lowe, A. (1976) *The Path of Economic Growth* (Cambridge: Cambridge University Press).

Marglin, S.A. (1974) 'What Do Bosses Do? The Origin and Functions of Hierarchy in Capitalist Production,' *Review of Radical Political Economy*, 6 (2) (Summer).

Marshall, A. (1895) *Principles of Economics* (London: Macmillan).

Mathur, G. (1965) *Planning For Steady Growth* (Oxford: Blackwell).

Nell, E. (1967) 'Theories of Growth and Theories of Value', *Economic Development and Cultural Change*, 16 (1), reprinted in G. Harcourt and N. Laing (eds), *Capital and Growth* (Harmondsworth: Penguin).

Nell, E. (1984) 'Structure and Behavior in Classical and Neo-Classical Theory,' *Eastern Economic Journal*, 11 2 (April).

Pasinetti, L. (1962) 'Rate of Profit and Income Distribution in Relation to the Rate of Economic Growth,' *Review of Economic Studies*, 29.

Pasinetti, L. (1974) *Growth and Income Distribution* (Cambridge: Cambridge University Press).

Pasinetti, L. (1975) *Lectures on the Theory of Production* (New York: Columbia University Press).

Robinson, J. *Collected Economic Papers*, 5 Vols (Oxford: Blackwell).

Sraffa, P. (1960) *Production of Commodities by Means of Commodities* (Cambridge: Cambridge University Press).

Part III
Transformational Growth

Transformational growth is the central idea with which we propose to develop the surplus approach. The normal working of the system of production and exchange sets up incentives to innovate in various ways. The introduction of innovations, in turn, leads to new patterns of dependence and independence, which change the way the system works, setting up new patterns of incentives. This is the way technology develops; technologies are not 'chosen' from among a set of blueprints – they evolve under the pressure of economic incentives, and they affect the way economic institutions work. This perspective is introduced in the first essay in the guise of the pressures that lead to the replacement of slash-and-burn agriculture by settled cultivation. The simple and popular 'population pressure' models turn out to be neo-Classical theory in disguise; besides the errors, what is neglected is the role of coercion. The second essay takes up the correlative role of technical change, showing that the pressure created by the rise of towns to carry out trade led to technical changes that altered the patterns of interdependence, and therefore the power relationships that determined the distribution of the surplus. This analysis is carried further in the third study (Chapter 13) in which the transformation of static agrarian society to growing capitalism is shown to be explained by the same pressures that transform surplus value into capitalist profit and labor values into profit-based prices. The labor theory of value is shown to have considerable explanatory power in feudal conditions, even though markets are largely undeveloped. Other institutions, particularly courts, generate pressures that perform functions later handled by competition. Some of these pressures, particularly in the guilds, are further examined in the fourth study (Chapter 14), while the fifth study (Chapter 15) shows that the cyclical fluctuations between agriculture and industry generate a pattern of systematic expulsion, forcing labor out of agriculture into industrial employment or into an industrial reserve army. The final study of Part III examines the price mechanism of early capitalism, and concludes that it tends to stabilize output and employment through the price mechanism – imperfectly, to be sure – but nevertheless in the manner suggested by the supporters of Say's Law. However, this creates incentives for individual firms to innovate in certain specific ways. The result is a change in the nature of the system; Craft technology is replaced by Mass Production, and Say's Law by the multiplier. The era of effective demand begins.

11 Population Pressure and Methods of Cultivation: a Critique of Classless Theory*

Population pressure has recently emerged as a fashionable explanation both for the shift from semi-nomadic slash and burn agriculture to settled cultivation and for the intensification of already settled cultivation. Thus Boserup (1965) and her followers account for an entire sequence of agricultural transformations through population changes. Others explain the fifteenth-century decline of rents and agricultural prices coupled with the prosperity of laborers and artisans by the decline in population following the Black Death. Or again, a seemingly new orthodoxy, which replaces the Hamilton-Keynes thesis, holds that the Elizabethan inflation resulted not so much from an influx of New World treasure, as from the rapid growth of population in the sixteenth century.

Yet these arguments frequently conflate very different economic doctrines. Textbook marginal productivity theory explains change by the movement in costs, given changes in factor supplies, but assumes those factors are of uniform quality. Ricardian theory also addresses the supply side of the question, but assumes that land is of variable quality, and so treats the labor and land markets quite differently. (Both simple marginal productivity theory and the Ricardian model can be found in the works of E.H. Phelps-Brown and M.M. Postan.) Finally appeal is sometimes made to 'supply and demand,' pure and simple, with no attempt to go behind the supply curve to the original conditions of production. A population increase raises the demand for food and land and increases the supply of labor; hence, food prices and rents rise, while wages fall. (The outstanding example of this type of thinking is B.H. Slicher van Bath.)

Not only are all of these very different doctrines, even the arguments are not mutually compatible. In particular, Bosreup's thinking, more closely attuned to anthropology than the others, compels critical reconsideration of the rest. For her, description of intensification is incompatible with the smooth adjustments pictured by conventional theory, and her criticisms of the Ricardian movement to marginal land are well taken, though not

* Reprinted from S. Diamond (ed.), *Towards a Marxist Anthropology* (The Hague: Mouton, 1974).

necessarily decisive. But, most importantly, she requires us to think about the effects of population pressure in an altogether new way. All three of the conventional models postulate a direct connection between population changes and changes in factor supplies and/or final demands. But the 'factor of production' is not population, it is work. An increase in population does not lead directly to an increase in work; instead, the effects proceed indirectly, through pressure on food supplies, to changes in work habits as the pattern of cultivation is intensified. Any given method of agriculture must be described according to the work habits it imposes, and any changes in cultivation imply changes in the nature, amount, timing, and conditions of work. These will not come about easily for the process involves major social change.

But once this is understood, population pressure is no longer decisive. It may be important, but then again it may not. The issue is the changing pattern and intensity of work, to which class relationships and coercion are at least as relevant as population pressure.

Marx certainly rejected all theories which sought to ground economic or social change in autonomous population changes; he particularly attacked Malthus. Many current population theories are explicitly anti-Malthusian – Boserup for instance. But from the Marxian perspective the arguments tend to be trivial. For neo-Malthusians, the methods of agricultural production set limits on the possible size of populations; for the more modern population theorists, it is the pressure of population that determines which of the possible methods of agricultural production will be adopted. That is, population pressure will cause intensification of land use, rather than, as the neo-Malthusians believe, the intensity of land use being a consequence of climate and the natural fertility of the soil, a consequence which places an upper limit on population.

The obvious comment is that both could be right – the causal influences could be reciprocal. Population growth caused by expanded agricultural output presses at a certain point upon the available land, given the method of cultivation. To support the expanded population requires a shift to more intensive methods. Once the shift is made, output per man-year, though not per man-hour, is increased and population growth can continue. Indeed, this seems to be precisely what the moderns are saying; they differ from the Malthusians not in denying the connection between abundance or scarcity in the food supply and a growing or stagnant population, but rather in emphasizing the importance of population pressure in bringing about greater intensity of cultivation.

The quarrel over Malthusianism, then, is a sham. There are two variables: population size relative to arable land and intensity of cultivation. Further, there are two equations: the population that a given land area can support increases with the intensity of cultivation, and the larger the population, the greater the pressure will be to intensify cultivation. A

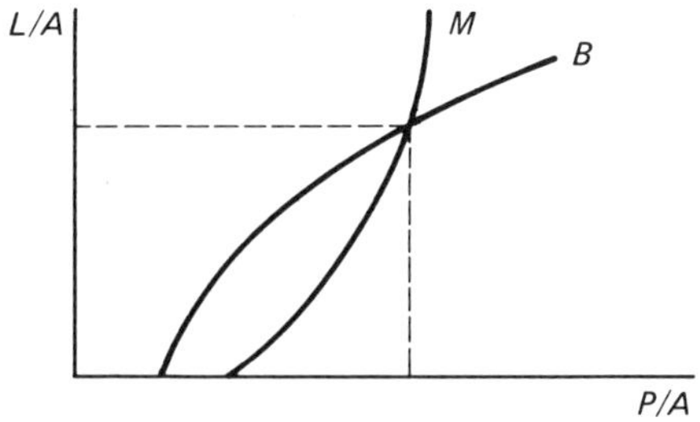

Figure 11.1

number of *technical* questions arise here – do the equations have a solution? Is there more than one possible solution? What are the properties of the solutions? However, there is surely no quarrel of principle. The two propositions together determine the two variables.

An illustration will show both how mechanical the argument is and how strongly it depends on its own assumptions. Both relationships show the variables moving in the same direction. It would be natural to assume that the Malthusian would exhibit diminishing returns, while the Boserupian would show increasing resistance to intensifying cultivation as population per arable land area increased. We could express this in a diagram (Figure 11.1), plotting population per arable acre (*P*/*A*) on the horizontal axis and labor-time per acre (*L*/*A*) on the vertical. *P*/*A* has to reach a certain level before the *M* curve begins to rise, but it rises with increasing steepness, reflecting diminishing returns. The *B* curve also begins only after a certain level of *P*/*A* is reached. If the initial *P*/*A* for the *B* curve lies above the initial point for the M curve, then the population will be governed exclusively by Malthusian considerations – pressures to intensify are too weak or make their appearance too late. Otherwise the two forces will interact. Where the curves cross, population pressures and methods of cultivation will be in balance. Should population rise above this equilibrium point it could not be supported because the pressures to intensify (as exhibited in the *B* curve) would not be strong enough to push the society to the method of cultivation required.

So far so good, though it is all a bit like engineering. (We can easily imagine a society moving out along these curves, but can we imagine it moving *back and forth*?) Are there really diminishing returns to intensification? Many economists think there may be increasing returns. And will there necessarily be increasing resistance to intensification? Suppose with increasing organization the ability to resist progressively weakens. Then we have the situation illustrated in Figure 11.2, in which intensity of cultivation is exclusively determined by Boserup. This sort of analysis is neat, but it may also be misleading. Neither of the 'variables' are quite what they seem, nor are they always capable of varying in the ways postulated.

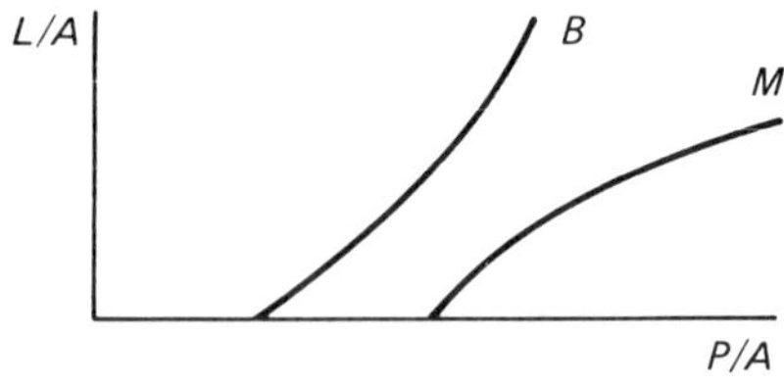

Figure 11.2

Population size depends upon family life and upon the work habits of the society. It is interwoven with the most basic strands of social life and cannot possible be considered autonomous. The rise of the population depends among other things upon the marriage age, the desire and pressure for large or small families, the normal work expected of women, the knowledge and skill in means of birth control, and the effectiveness of traditional medicine and its consequences both for survival in childbirth and for life expectancy. A population too large or growing too rapidly for the society's land and resources can be controlled in a variety of traditional ways – through exposure of babies and emigration, through a rise in the marriage age, through limitations on family size in certain sections of society, and so on. Similarly, a population too small for resources can be expanded. The important point is that the size and rate of growth of population should not be considered *exogenous*; population pressure does not *impinge on* society, it is *created by* the society.

Let us take as an example the situation often offered as a counter-instance, namely the rapidly growing population all over the Third World. There can be no reasonable doubt that this phenomenon is pointing toward a catastrophe of almost unimaginable proportions. But it should also be clear that these population increases are anything but autonomous (and, to make the ideological point, *therefore* no one's responsibility). They are the direct consequence of imperialism. They result from the impact of the advanced technology and market systems of the West on largely peasant agriculture. The impact of modern medicine is widely acknowledged, yet at least some of these societies *could have* adapted to this impact, but have not done so. Generalizing in this area is dangerous, but it is generally true in peasant societies that large families are a good thing. The children can do enough work, after a time, to more than pay their way. Moreover, they are the parent's old age insurance, and it is important that enough children survive to support the aged parents, especially so as the market comes to dominate the countryside. Better too many children than too few. The high rates of population growth in the Third World can thus be seen, in part, as rural society taking out insurance against the vicissitudes resulting from the impact of the West.

Now consider the other variable in population pressure explanations of social change, the intensity of cultivation. This is not to be confused with output per man-year, and it had little to do with output per acre. It refers to the input of effort per man per year. Cultivation is said to become more intense when a new method is substituted for an old, and output per man-hour in the old is higher than in the new, but output per man-year is greater in the new. In other words 'intensifying agricultural production' means working less productively but harder or longer and so producing more, perhaps substantially more.

In Marxian terms the point seems very simple. Let s_1 be the old, higher rate of surplus-value, and s_2 the new; let L_1 be the old amount of labor time worked, and L_2 the new. Then, for $s_1L_1 < s_2L_2$ while $s_1 > s_2$ – that is, for the *mass* of surplus-value to increase while the *rate* falls – the proportional increase in labor time worked must exceed the proportional fall in the rate of surplus value:

$$\left|\frac{dL}{L}\right| > \left|\frac{ds}{s}\right|$$

In primitive societies, the rate of surplus value is defined by the proportion of time that cultivators and direct laborers must work to produce their own support, divided into total output. But much time which *could* be spent working is actually spent in other activities. This time could be called 'potential surplus-value' and could be taken as evidence of the affluence of the system. In a sense, it is. But, in actual fact, that time can rarely be harnessed without a major change in social structure. It may be potential, but it remains only potential; production is not the name of the game.

As a consequence, the new method of production, say settled cultivation as opposed to slash and burn, will be characterized by a rate of surplus value composed of less *relative* and more *absolute* surplus value. The labor time needed to produce necessities will be higher, but the length of the average working day will be longer.

Putting the matter in Marxian terms is useful because it leads to the heart of the matter. The assumption implicit among population theorists is that enlarged net output goes to support an enlarged population. Yet, it may or it may not. What happens to it surely depends on the method of production. This is the subject of the theory of surplus-value. To develop these ideas further in general terms would be inappropriate here. Instead, I shall argue that population pressure need not in general, though it may on occasion, be part of the explanation of intensification of cultivation, while, by contrast, the organization of production, especially coercion and competition, must always be considered. To make this argument I shall critically examine what is widely regarded as one of the best and most imaginative statements of the modern population pressure thesis, Boserup's *The Conditions of Agricultural Growth* (1965).

Just where she is most original, Boserup's argument is most questionable. She contends that population pressure will cause or bring about a shift to more intensive methods, which are less productive per man-hour, though because of the longer and harder work entailed, more productive per hectare and per year. These methods will normally have been known to the society before, and may even have been used on occasion, as in the case of intensive market gardening on the fringes of early medieval towns. She rightly points to the considerable evidence that both primitive and peasant societies are capable, when it suits them, of very rapidly assimilating new products and new techniques. The refusal to adopt the new methods should not, then, be ascribed to ignorance, nor to the inertia of tradition, but rather to an economic judgement that the extra output is not worth the extra work.

This raises two sets of questions. The first concerns her claim that, initially, the more intensive methods are not adopted, though known and understood, because the extra output is not worth the extra work; the second, her claim that when adopted, they are introduced in response to population pressure.

In connection with the first, there seems (to an economist) to be an implied assumption that work will not be done beyond the point where its marginal disutility is just compensated by the extra output. But this kind of thinking is not consonant with the evidence she cites. For example, under long fallow cultivation there are often periods of hunger, because not enough land has been cleared Arguably, on a rational calculation, the extra output would have been worth more than the disutility of the additional labor. But 'Anthroplogists stress the lack of foresight and the general inclination to shun hard agricultural work' (Boserup 1965, p. 54). If so, might not such lack of foresight and disinclination to work account for the unwillingness to adopt more intensive methods, even if they were substantially more productive per man-hour, provided they required substantially more labor per year? There are other reasons for not working more than the judgment that the extra reward is not worth it, and by her own account these apparently were operative on occasion. Boserup's argument is that more productive methods will not be adopted until population pressure causes a sufficient increase in the utility of extra output to offset the disutility of extra work.

But the failure to adopt more intensive and more productive methods can be explained as quite a different sort of economic calculation. It can be seen as the consequence of switching from less to more intensive cultivation in piecemeal fashion, in a setting where production is organised on an individualistic basis modified by certain communal rights. The argument is relatively simple, and depends on the fact that a process only partially

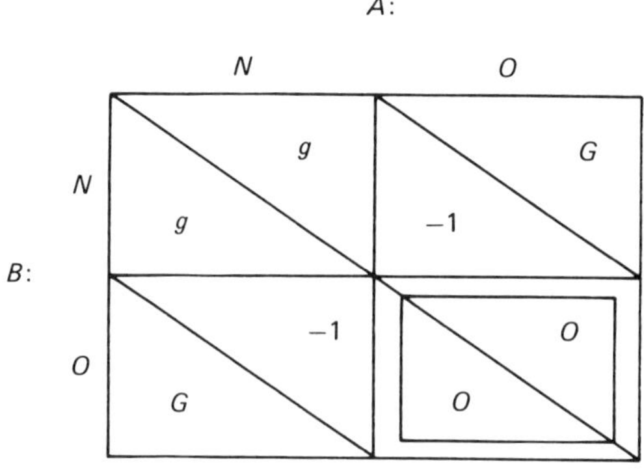

Figure 11.3

adopted may set up a peculiar pattern of payoffs. Consider an example discussed by Boserup. According to her

> . . . grazing rights may delay . . . the change-over to feeding with cultivated fodder plants, because an individual cultivator who desires to introduce this innovation would have to carry the full burden of producing the fodder and feeding it to the animals while [the] benefit of reduced pressure on communal grazing land accrues to other cultivators. (1965, pp. 85–6).

This is an acute observation, but it has nothing particularly to do with grazing rights, and it provides an alternative explanation for the resistance to intensive methods. Wherever this pattern of costs and payoffs obtains, the introduction of a more productive method can be blocked. What counts is that the 'full burden' on the innovator must reduce his earnings below what he could make on the old system, while the 'benefits of reduced pressure' going to non-innovators should raise their earnings above what they could make under the new more productive method. This can be represented in a "game theory" table (Figure 11.3). We simply divide the society into two groups, *A* and *B*. For these purposes we need not specify which represents the innovators, or even how large they are relative to one another. Let the new method be *N* and the old *O*. The initial position, where both groups use *O*, we shall take as the zero point. If both groups shifted to *N*, both would make a gain, *g*. But if either *A* or *B* shifted to *N* and the other did not, the one who shifted would make a loss, − 1 (from bearing the full burden), while the one who stuck with *O* would make a larger gain, *G* (reaping the 'benefits of reduced pressure' on resources.)

As we can see at a glance, whichever course *A* chooses, *B*'s best choice is *O*, since *G* is greater than *g* and 0 is greater than − 1. Whichever course *B* chooses, *A*'s best choice is *O*, since *G* is greater than *g* and *O* is greater than − 1. By not making the shift when the other does, one party gains more. By making the shift when the other does not, the other party loses more than if he stood pat. Strategy *O*, *O* will therefore tend to be adopted, even though *N*, *N* is better for both groups.

This pattern of benefits and burdens during the process of switching methods is not implausible for many of the cases Boserup discusses; it relieves her of the necessity of arguing that, in general, relatively extensive, long fallow methods of cultivation are more productive per manhour. More importantly, it makes it clear that lack of sufficient population pressure is not the reason for not adopting the more productive methods.

The same kind of argument can be applied to another topic. Boserup explains the coexistence of different methods of cultivation by introducing the additional assumption, which does not follow from her main argument, that the rate of technological change depends on the rate of population growth. Thus, the higher the rate of population growth, the faster the spread of the plow, or perhaps, for it is not quite clear, the faster we pass from stick to hoe to plow to tractor. So long as the population growth is slow, so also will be technological change, and we can expect to find methods of cultivation coexisting. 'Thus, the slowly penetrating new systems . . . would . . . coexist for long periods with older systems within the same village or . . . region' (1965, p. 56).

Now consider the argument we have just examined, but take, this time, the shift from long fallow to short. We shall have to be rather hypothetical, but will try to follow Boserup (1965, pp. 30–3, 80–1). Those who shift to short fallow cultivation have to expend more labor in hoeing, weeding, and manuring during the growing season, but their greatest effort must come in clearing the fields of roots and stones. This is a task in which teamwork pays off well. The larger the group making the shift the greater the manpower available for clearing, and the more easily and rapidly fields can be cleared. But those who do not shift to settled cultivation will find themselves better off as more make the shift, for there will be fewer claimants to the better plots of forest or bush land. Thus, if only a small group shifts to settled cultivation, they will find clearing and also harvesting (in which a large labor force is valuable) difficult. If a larger group shifts, providing sufficient labor, there may well be a significant reduction of pressure on forest or bush plots.

The circumstances we have described can be expressed in diagrammatic form (Figure 11.4).

If a small group shifts, forest cultivators benefit from reduced pressure, while the small group is actually worse off. If a large group shifts, forest cultivators benefit considerably, and the newly settled cultivators also gain. Now the question is, how considerable are these gains and losses? Suppose population is pushing against a forest area in which there are two grades of

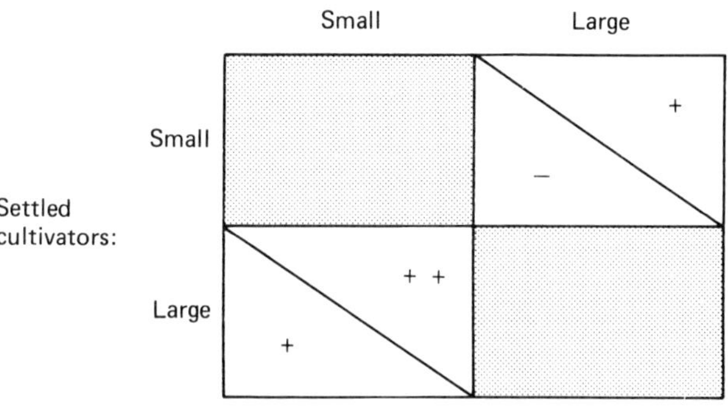

Figure 11.4

land, one considerably worse than the other. The gain to practitioners of the old method from a switch of even a small number may then be more than the gain from the new method if everyone pursued it. As before, a small group shifting might lead to burdens sufficient to overbalance any gain from the new method. In such circumstances the case we have just mentioned would hold; even though short fallow methods were superior in productivity per man-hour to long fallow ones, they would not be adopted.

But the pattern of gains and losses might be rather different. Suppose that a small movement from the old method to the new resulted in little or no benefit to practitioners of the old. Only a fairly large shift would reduce the pressure on resources enough to yield perceptible gains. The situation is illustrated in Figure 11.5.

We now identify one group as Large, the other as Small and rewrite Figure 11.3 on the basis of Figure 11.4. For Large, *N* is the best choice

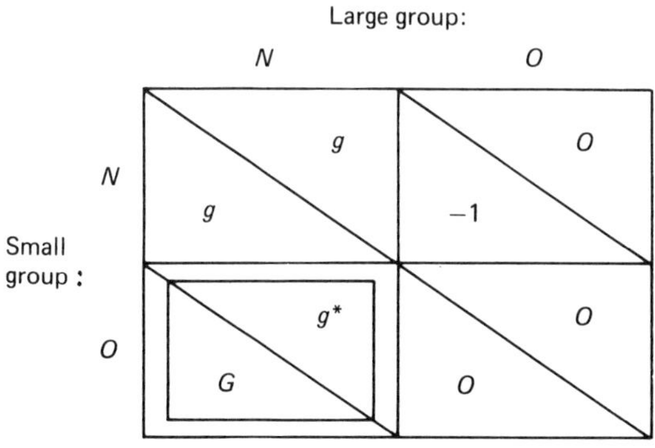

Figure 11.5

whatever Small does, since g is greater than O, and g^* is greater than O. (It is immaterial whether g^* is less than g or greater than g, though presumably g^* is less than g.) For Small, O, is the best choice whatever Large does, since G is greater than g and O is greater than -1. Hence, the 'equilibrium outcome' will be, as indicated, (G, g^*), even though the total benefits may be less than in (g,g) if $(g - g^*)$ is greater than $(G - g)$. Thus an inferior method may continue to be employed by a minority, even though everyone would be better off if it were wholly phased out. We do not have to assume, as Boserup does, that the rate of innovation closely depends on the rate of population growth to explain the coexistence of different methods of cultivation.

The second set of questions I raised concern Boserup's claim that intensification of land use results from population pressure. The main difficulty here is that her claim is vague. The exact pattern of incentives is not explained, nor are the institutions or mechanisms through which the pressure exerts itself identified. It has to be so, for a more precise specification would raise unanswerable questions. For example, why should population pressures not be resisted? Many primitive and not-so-primitive peoples have practiced crude forms of population control, such as exposure. Alternatively, population pressure, leading to land shortage, might lead to a rise in the marriage age of women, and a consequent reduction in the natural reproduction rate. There are many other possible effects of population pressure which could in a similar way lead back to a reduction of that pressure. Why are these ruled out and the typical response taken as a rise in the intensity of cultivation?

Secondly, why should population pressure lead a society to value additional output more highly in terms of labor? Boserup's implicit argument seems to be that increased population with a given method of cultivation will, after a point, result in reduced consumption per head, thus raising the marginal utility of output. According to conventional theory, work will be performed up to the point where its marginal disutility will just be compensated by the utility of the additional output. Hence, population pressure, in this view, would naturally lead to increased willingness to work harder.

But it should be obvious that the argument above simply does not answer the question.[1] Instead of working harder, a society might expand the area of land under its control, by conquest if necessary. Alternatively, it might encourage emigration or colonization. At times, it might simply accept reduced consumption or enforce such reductions on powerless and ill-fated groups within it. If a population increase is supposed to lead to reduced consumption per head, the exact mechanism and incentive pattern which leads to this must be explained.

One piece of traditional Ricardian analysis, his discussion of differential rent, does suggest a very precise way in which population pressures would affect consumption per head in a primitive society, such as one practicing forest or bush cultivation. According to Boserup (1965, pp. 79–81) all members of a tribe have a general right to practice cultivation in a certain area, but families develop specific rights to particular plots. Then '. . . with increasing population, as good plots become somewhat scarce . . . a family is likely to become more attached to the plots they have been cultivating . . . because it is becoming difficult to find better plots elsewhere . . .' (1965, p. 80). Boserup sees this as a reason for shortening the period of fallow; families hurry back to the better plots. Perhaps. A better alternative would be to develop a system for adjudicating and enforcing specific rights; then, when population increased, progressively more plots of land would be cultivated, and a systematic and enforceable difference in prosperity would emerge between those families with specific rights to the better plots of land and the rest. This is in addition to the distinction discussed by Boserup between those who possess general rights to cultivate and 'strangers' who do not.

This leads to perhaps the most important criticism of her argument. Once a class society emerges, another explanation for intensification of land use (in her sense) is available, one that responsible scholars tend cautiously to avoid, coercion. A certain increase in output needed to support an increased population can be got only by a more than proportional increase in hard work. Even if we question Boserup's argument in general, this must surely have been the case sometimes. The desiccated, anemic, neo-Classical conclusion is that the implied fall in average consumption per head provides an incentive to work harder. Why not an incentive to make others to work harder? Population pressure is surely one of the oldest and most obvious factors behind military expansion. But it is not the only, nor perhaps even the main, factor.

For if it becomes possible for one class or group to make others work harder for its benefit, then they may be motivated to do so whether there is population pressure or not. Once we admit that coercion is a factor, population pressure as an explanatory variable recedes into the background. We should not think of coercion as physical force primarily. Undoubtedly, it does rest on force, but the technology of intimidation is multifaceted and reached a state of high development early in civilized history.

Settled cultivators are easier to tax and control. A ruling class may compel intensive cultivation not only for the additional output, but also for greater convenience and certainty in obtaining the surplus. Recognition of this may be one reason behind the refusal of contemporary peasants still practising forest cultivation to take advantage of apparently generous offers of government advice and technical assistance to adopt more modern methods (Boserup 1965, pp. 33, 65). To develop this further would be to go beyond a critique of Boserup. Once we allow that coercion and exploitation are possible, and, indeed, the normal case, we do not need to rely on population pressure for explanation (though it may still, of course, be correct in some cases). On the contrary, changes in the relative strengths of classes and competing factions, and the causes of these changes (among which population pressure might figure, along with many other factors) become the basic explanatory variables. Boserup's most important contribution is to show that changes in the pattern of cultivation are social changes. Such changes come about through the exercise of power and influence, political as well as economic. Such power cannot be reduced to mere numbers; the system, not the size, is what counts.

Note

1. Traditional, or neo-Classical theory, if interpreted strictly, takes far too simple-minded a view of the incentives which will lead people to work, as the Hawthorne experiments and the writings of A.H. Maslow and others have shown. If we interpret neo-Classical theory broadly, so as to include as remuneration such factors as status and prestige, the views of others, control over own working conditions, the attention and interest of superiors, and so on, we effectively make the theory vacuous – the point at which the marginal disutility of work equals the extra remuneration offered becomes whatever point at which work stops. For a nice parody, see Robinson (1952); for a discussion of incentives see Brown (1960).

References

Boserup, E. (1965) *The Conditions of Agricultural Growth* (Chicago: Aldine).
Brown, J.A.C. (1960) *Social Psychology of Industry* (New York: Penguin).
Robinson, Joan (1952) 'Beauty and the beast,' in *Collected Economic Papers*, vol. 1 (Oxford: Oxford University Press).

12 Economic Relationships in the Decline of Feudalism: an Examination of Economic Interdependence and Social Change*

The object of this study is theoretical rather than historical or narrative; it proposes an analysis of arguments, not a reconstruction of events. But to appraise the logic of historical arguments we must know something of the relationships between events. Hence we shall first examine an outline of what happened, and then schematize that outline in a way which will set in relief the temporal development of the principal relationships we shall need to examine. We will then consider three arguments which purport to account for these developments, and from the rejection of these arguments we shall advance a new theory, developed further in the next two chapters.

1 THE CHANGES IN FEUDAL SOCIETY, 1000–1500

The year 1000 is usually held to mark the end of the period of the 'feudal disintegration of the state' and the beginning of a sometimes slow and halting trend towards the re-establishment of central authority. But in the 11th century governing power still rested largely in the hands of the local nobility, whose allegiance to their overlords was tempered by the impregnability of their own castles and strongholds. The arts of war, and the elaborate accoutrements they required, were the monopoly of the landed nobility and their retainers, for only the landed class could afford the equipage and the time required to master the skills of using it. The great bulk of the population lived in the countryside in a state of servitude, bound to the soil by tradition as well as law, owing services and payments in kind to their lord. The only universally acknowledged authority was the Church, but its temporal power could be defied with impunity as easily as that of any other superior.

* *History and Theory*, 6 (1967). In revising this study I have been much helped, in very various ways, by comments from W.J. Barber, R.L. Benson, M. Dobb, J. Herbst, P. Kilby, S. Lebergott, W. Mudd, O. Nell, N. Rudich, P.M. Sweezy, and R. Vann. I am grateful to all of them.

During the 12th century significant changes were occurring in feudal society. Towns had grown and trade expanded; new towns were being founded, and were proving a profitable source of revenue for lords. Changes in agriculture were taking place, rendering it more productive, but in the process changing the traditional patterns of country life. Two developments were particularly important: the new methods of cultivation required a different lay-out of fields and allowed families to live in larger villages, and the increased productivity made possible the production of goods for sale in a relatively distant market.

By the end of the 15th century a very different kind of society had emerged all over Western Europe. Speaking rather generally, it was one in which local autonomy was circumscribed, either in favor of a strong central government, as in France and England, or in favor of powerful princes, as in Germany and Italy. The political organization was far more complex, in that the influential interests were of different kinds, rather than, as before, all drawn from a single class possessed of land and military power. No longer could one speak of a single homogeneous elite; the old hierarchy had been shattered, though remnants of it remained in possession of significant power. A general characterization of the change can be given in the following terms: in the 11th century the political and economic position of the single dominant elite was secured and advanced by its command of the means of coercion; by the end of the 15th century the economic positions of the various competing elites rested either upon their control of one form or another of production or upon their dominant position in trading, and the ability to wield military power had come to rest to a very considerable degree upon the possession of a form of economic power not dependent on control of the land. The nobility remains a significant class, but it no longer draws its strength entirely from its military position; it has been transformed into an economic class, based primarily on land, but sometimes involved in trading ventures, sharing the domination of society with merchants and the urban artisan gilds.

Many historians, following Pirenne, have tended to group the principal social and economic changes in society during this period into two categories. First, there are those changes in the countryside which are associated with the commutation of feudal dues and labor services to money payments, and then there are those developments associated with the rise of towns and the emergence of urban laws and freedoms. The connecting link between these two sets of developments is frequently taken to be the growth of trade and production for sale in a distant market. This fairly conventional picture must now be examined.

Commutation could proceed in a variety of ways; dues and services were sometimes commuted only partially or temporarily, occasionally leaving a choice to the peasant. The leasing for various terms of the demesne lands for money rents normally accompanied commutation. But whatever the form it took, it is generally agreed that the long-run effect of commutation and leasing was to shift the burden of feudal obligation from the person of the peasant to the position he occupied; rents are owed not because of station at birth; but in virtue of holding a tenancy. Commutation, in effect, turned the peasantry into freemen, which frequently implied the right to sue in higher courts, and so implicitly curtailed the judicial powers (and so 'profits from justice') of the local nobility.

The rise of towns brought parallel developments, since trade required a quite different legal environment from that prevailing under feudal disintegration. Buyers and sellers must be able to contract on equal terms and have equal access to legal enforcement of their contracts. This implicit equality of status came to be reflected in the structure of government, which, at times, was distinctly democratic. Again the development of trade led to the emergence of freedoms.

The difficulty with this not uncommon picture, from our point of view, is that it fails to stress certain important relationships. For example, we are interested not merely in the amount of trade but also in its terms; not merely in whether rents are paid in kind or in money but also in which economic forces determine their amount.

We shall now present an alternative sketch of the major changes in feudal society from the 11th to the 15th century, illuminating these changes with lights of a somewhat different color. In examining a broad sketch of this sort a number of qualifications must be borne in mind. First, it must not be supposed that the changes indicated took place uniformly everywhere in Western Europe. Different societies obviously developed at different rates; what we are suggesting is that the same trend was observable everywhere. (In general the dates at which events took place are less important for the thesis we shall advance than the serial order of their occurrence.) Secondly, the changes we are examining are not qualitatively the same everywhere, nor are the relationships constant; the same antecedents may sometimes produce different consequences, and vice versa. (For example, the development of trade sometimes leads to commutation and the lightening of the feudal burden, sometimes to an intensification of labor services and feudal dues.) Some such differences we shall want to explain as due to deeper causes, but others we shall ascribe to differences in the situations in which the same basic pattern of development took place. In particular, while the process to be described began earlier in the South, its full course can be seen best in Northern Europe. Finally, some such cases may simply be 'accidents,' from the point of view of the argument that will be presented here; that is, such cases, while not inconsistent with our argument, cannot be explained by any of the processes or modifications of the processes considered here. Thirdly, especially during the period 1300–1500, Western European society suffered from a series of natural disasters, some of which had profound social consequences, e.g. the Black Death, poor harvests, invasions from the East. The effects of such factors depends partly upon the nature of the factor and partly upon the ability of the social structure to respond to it, but since these external events both affected different areas to varying degrees and struck different areas at different stages of development, they contribute further to the uneven and variegated unfolding of the process we shall seek to describe. Fourthly, the frequent occurrence of pillaging and banditry at certain periods poses a special difficulty, for some such activities must be considered endemic in the feudal system at any time since it is an essential feature of feudal society that military force is decentralized. But these activities are a direct application of military power to economic ends, and on occasion may well be the expression of an inability on the part of the possessors of military force to resist economic pressures. We might thus have an index of economic conflict in the extent to which the nobility engages in banditry at the expense of trade. But in the first place not all warlike activity is of this sort; and secondly, such activity is not merely redistributive, it tends to break the system apart, so delaying or altering the economic relationships that were developing. Finally, no society can be adequately described without an account of its religion, ideology and letters, and of the state of its arts. Even an economic description requires reference to these in a limited way, for such activities must be supported, and developments in science and the arts make possible technological progress. But these matters must be left to one side; we shall find that changes in applied technology are of central importance, but we shall not ask why these discoveries occurred when they did.

With these qualifications in mind we shall now present a schematic account of the development of certain key features of the structure of Western European society from 1100–1500. This account does not pretend to be exhaustive even of essentials; it is intended only to isolate and highlight features relevant to the later argument. Nor is it intended to be strictly accurate; on the contrary the facts here are 'stylized.'[1] Minor trends are ignored to emphasize the major ones. Discrepancies in statistical or documentary evidence are deliberately smoothed over to exhibit the general pattern, and accidental or special features are dropped, along with divergences that depend on local circumstances. What emerges is a general picture somewhat different from most textbook accounts, but containing, I think, no surprises.

1100–1300

By the year 1100 an agricultural revolution was well underway. The heavy iron plow had made its appearance, and improved harness had been developed, permitting the substitution of the horse for the ox in ploughing and farm labor, and the three-field system of crop rotation, introducing large-scale production of legumes, was supplanting the older, less productive two-field system as fast as the barriers of manorial customs and rights could be broken.[2] This revolution continued throughout the greater part of the period, as new lands were opened and swamps were drained. Population increased steadily, and the prices of farm products rose.[3] Since village size was limited by the availability of fields near enough to be reached by a team of oxen within a reasonable time (later horses which move faster and allowed villages to increase in size), population growth either meant subdivision of existing fields or the founding of 'villes neuves.' The new methods were most easily introduced in new lands, since no conflicts arose there over changing traditional procedures or rights. To induce peasants to move to the new lands and/or to adopt the new methods, feudal dues were often lightened, or in some cases abolished outright, and the peasantry of the new lands were often given (or later obtained) free status.[4]

Rising agricultural prices generally meant rising land values, and rising seigneurial incomes.[5] (But it should not be assumed that the high prices paid in the towns were automatically reflected in the prices received in the countryside.[6]) The principal sources of income for the nobility were feudal dues, revenue from the sale of demesne products, tolls levied upon trade passing over roads, bridges, etc., and dues paid for the (required) use of buildings, milling equipment, etc.[7] At the beginning of the period the nobility had judicial rights over all those under their jurisdiction, and they generally constituted the strongest military force in their immediate area.[8] By 1300 their position was declining in both these spheres.[9] In 1100 the feudal countryside was still predominantly self-subsistent, meeting a great part of its needs for non-agricultural products through the demesne workshops, the 'gynaceas.'[10] But by 1300 the countryside had come to purchase a great part of its cloth, many of its farm implements, and much of the arms and armor for the feudal military establishment from the towns.[11]

By 1100 the growth of towns was already well underway, and commerce had become extensive, consisting in Southern Europe mainly of trade in luxuries, in the North mainly of trade in necessities.[12] The prices of town products on the whole stayed steady or rose at a lower rate than agricultural prices throughout the years 1100–1300.[13] The towns progressively became free of feudal restrictions and developed a system of government of their own. Trade remained relatively free of mercantile restrictions, and entry into the guilds relatively easy,[14] though merchants in the cloth trade frequently attempted to exclude weavers, dyers and fullers from guild membership. Merchants found themselves able to make great fortunes buying cheap and selling dear, or lending at high interest rates. By the year 1300 the wealth and influence of a distinct class of merchants had become evident in all major towns.[15] But this date marks the apogee of this class; with the development of artisan guilds town government ceased to be the exclusive prerogative of the merchant class, and the new restrictions tended to benefit artisans more than merchants.[16]

1300–1500

During these years agricultural productivity remained roughly constant whether measured by land, labor or seed.[17] But agricultural prices fell steadily, as did seigneurial revenues.[18] Population increased to 1348, when the Black Death struck. Plague epidemics and war had reduced the population by almost 25% by 1400, but in the 15th century growth began again.[19] Wages rose both in towns and in the countryside. Town wealth grew relatively to that of the countryside. Falling prices and rising wages put great pressure on landlords; labor services were commuted for fixed money payments in many areas, and attempts were made to shift industry to the countryside. Brigandage, extortion and exactions upon trade by the nobility increased, sometimes leading to open warfare between nobles and towns.[20] Legislation regulating wages and prices led to strife between nobles and peasants. In such warfare the nobility generally, though not universally, proved successful.[21]

In the towns the position of the great merchant families steadily declined, while that of artisans, craftsmen and industrial workers improved.[22] By the end of the 15th century real wages reached a point which they were not again to attain for 400 years.[23] Town laws became more complex, partly in order to benefit the towns at the expense of the countryside, partly in order to benefit artisans at the expense of merchants (or vice versa, at times). Civil strife between *maiores* and *minores* broke out intermittently in the towns. Merchants, finding that the simultaneous decline of farm and rise of product prices tended to close off the opportunities for profitable arbitrage, began both to buy land and become renters and to engage in industry directly through the 'putting-out' system.[24]

During the 15th century two curious stalemates were reached, in which political and military power successfully checked but could not wholly prevent the exercise of superior economic power. In the first, industry and commerce were able to turn the terms of trade dramatically to the advantage of the towns, but the towns were powerless to protect trade from the ravages of noble extortion and brigandage. The feudal nobility could maintain itself so long as its military supremacy remained; but technology worked steadily against it, for the new armaments were manufactured in the towns. The second stalemate occurred in the towns, where the traditional merchant families, who had tended to dominate town government, found themselves unable to keep down the prices charged by the producers, the artisans and craftsmen of the *minores*. By striking more or less temporary alliances with the nobility the merchants were able to draw on force to keep order – the old order. But given their divergent interests in other areas such alliances tended to be short-lived. Again greater economic power lay on one side, force on the other, and the result was stalemate. In France and England the modern centralized state was born in the course of the protracted struggles ensuing from these stalemates.

2 THEORIES OF THE DECLINE OF FEUDALISM

Three principal explanations have been advanced to account for the transformation of the feudal order. These are respectively the trade theory, the population theory, and the class struggle theory. We shall argue that while each of these directs attention to significant aspects of this historical period, yet each has certain specific defects. Though specific to each case, these defects will be seen to follow from a shared misconception of the kind of explanation required for these events.

The classic exposition of the trade theory of the decline of feudalism is given by Pirenne, where it begins simply as the obverse of his theory of the decline of the post-Roman Western world.[25] He sees the break-up of trade and the decay of towns following from the Moslem domination of the Mediterranean, achieved in the 8th century. When Christian hegemony in the Mediterranean was re-established trade redeveloped, and the towns, which had withered, began once again to grow.[26] New towns developed from forts as merchants, drawn from the ranks of vagabonds and the dispossessed, settled in faubourgs outside the walls of the fortresses.[27] To deal with the settling of accounts a new system of law was required, and merchant law arose, based on certain specific freedoms.[28] At first the nobility tended to favor and encourage the towns. As they grew trade spread and landlords began to produce for the market. The growing prosperity of the towns attracted the more enterprising peasantry. But the prosperity of the towns provided an incentive for the lords to increase production for the market; hence demand for labor increased just as supply tended to diminish.[29] To attract and keep serfs the lords had to relieve them of their burdens and pay them in money.[30] Freedom and the money economy thus tended to spread together.[31]

Pirenne's argument can be given two different interpretations, for it is not entirely clear whether trade or money broke up the feudal economy. The two are of course, related but the economic significance of the argument is different. The first interpretation stresses the dependencies created by production for sale in a distant market, and these would be the same even if that exchange were conducted through barter. The second interpretation stresses the significance of setting forth obligations in terms of a universal unit of account and medium of exchange, whose value can be presumed fixed; this development need not coincide with the changeover to production for the market.[32]

But however one wishes to amend the trade theory it suffers from irremediable defects. First, to trade one must have something to trade. But the opening of trade does not increase the ability to produce.[33] More specifically, the growth of towns requires the existence of a surplus of agricultural output over the needs of the countryside, since the towns must be fed. But the opening of trade does not increase agricultural productivity.[34] Secondly, this approach tells us nothing about the terms of trade, or about their determinants. Among a certain class of economists it tends to be an article of faith that all parties gain from trade, in some sense or other; in practice this is not necessarily true, still less does it follow that all parties gain equally. But if we are to understand why one economic class rose relatively to another, we must surely know something about the terms of the trade between them. Thirdly, towns are supposed not merely to grow relative to the rural economy, but to grow absolutely. But to explain growth which is not simply the result of resources shifted from one sector to another, it is necessary to analyze the determinants of investment. Yet Pirenne's discussion of trade tells us nothing about investment. Finally, it is not clear why trade is supposed to benefit the towns more than the countryside. Why should it not enrich the feudal nobility, and strengthen rather than dissolve the feudal order? The increase in trade and the development of production for the market can be regarded equally plausibly as opportunity for intensifying feudal exactions or as a reason for reducing them or commuting them to money payments. The incompatibility of commerce and feudal order is asserted but not demonstrated.

There can be no doubt that the revival of trade played a significant role in the process we are investigating, and the population theory, to which we now turn, is not so much an alternative as a complementary theory, designed to remedy some of the shortcomings just noted. Perhaps the best-known exposition is given by Postan,[35] who divides the period 1100–1500 into two phases, the first being a period of expanding trade, the second of contracting trade, with the dividing point falling somewhere in the early fourteenth century. He argues that the waxing and waning of commerce followed primarily from changes in population.[36]

During the first phase population rose steadily and trade rose with it. The development of trade required the development of trading centers, and the law governing these centers necessarily differed from that prevailing throughout the rest of society: the towns were islands of freedom in a feudal sea.[37] The rising population had to be fed, and the pressure of demand on supply led to the opening of new lands, to marginal lands being brought into cultivation, with the result that agricultural costs at the margin, and so prices, rose.[38] This process slowed down in the early 14th century, and reversed itself after the Black Death of 1348.

The second phase began in earnest with the terrible social dislocation brought by the plague. Trade was disrupted; demand and supply were both substantially reduced. But different groups were affected in different ways. In the towns the merchants found themselves faced with declining markets and with guilds and guild restrictions designed to protect the artisan's share. Merchants gradually found themselves forced out of business, and many began to invest in land or in urban real estate.[39] The decline in the scale of the market meant that the advantages of large scale production could not be so readily realized, hence costs increased in urban industries, with the result that prices tended to remain high. But just the reverse occurred in agriculture, for the decline in population meant releasing marginal, low-return (high-cost) lands from production, and this fall in marginal costs was reflected in falling agricultural prices. This meant that prices tended to move in favor of towns and town wages reflected this. The result was a drift of agricultural labor to the towns, which reduced the labor supply in the countryside. This led in turn to upward pressure on wages in rural areas at the very time that agricultural prices were declining.[40] The feudal lord was thus caught in a wage–price squeeze with no apparent means of escape. Faced with steadily falling revenues, and finding attempts at legal regulation ultimately ineffectual, the nobility turned increasingly to outright extortion and banditry.[41]

Undoubtedly population and trade in the second period fell together in some rough way, and equally surely the causes of this are to be found in pestilence and war; it is also clear that they rose together in the earlier period.[42] But these observations are in fact not to the point, for there would be nothing very surprising if population and commerce merely rose and fell together in the same proportion. It is the remarkable conjunction of certain further facts which requires explanation. First, both the population and the wealth of towns grew in the first period at a more rapid rate than did population as a whole; but in the second period, though trade declined at least as much as population, the wealth of towns did not. Within towns, however, the prosperity of merchants fell relatively to that of other groups. Secondly, paradoxically enough, the period during which the towns were growing and when the merchants became wealthy was the period during which the terms of trade tended to move against the towns, while during the period in which the towns were stagnant and the merchants declining the terms of trade moved markedly in favor of the towns. Postan's explanation accounts for the changes in the terms of trade, but fails to deal with the question of *growth*. Why do merchants invest, and why do they become wealthy when the terms of trade are disadvantageous? By contrast, when the terms of trade turn against the nobility, their revenues fall, and they remove land from cultivation, i.e. disinvest. In the first period, of course, population is rising rather than declining, but parity of reasoning would suggest that during this period the size and prosperity of towns and the merchant class should have grown proportionally less than population, and the numbers and prosperity of the countryside and nobility more. But this was not the case.

The argument that population changes affect different sectors unequally, thus changing the price-ratio of their products, depends upon the assumption that diminishing returns prevail in agriculture and constant or increasing returns in industry. Quite apart from theoretical considerations, to which we shall come in a moment, these assumptions are very dubious historically. The period during which agricultural prices tended generally to rise coincides with the period during which major agricultural improvements were being introduced; moreover, the productivity of the new 'marginal' lands was, if anything, higher than average, since the new methods could be introduced on these lands with least resistance. Moreover, there is evidence to suggest that during the period in which agricultural prices fell productivity remained constant.[43] Thus the movement of prices cannot be explained by the movement of costs.

But the most serious objections are theoretical. First, if the Black Death hit the cities hardest, as is usually believed, then if agricultural production were cut back in proportion to the fall in urban demand, there would be a surplus of rural labor; in this case supply and demand considerations suggest that wages would tend to *fall* in the countryside until a sufficient number of peasants had migrated to the towns. Secondly, ignoring this short-run question, explaining the rise in wages and craft-earnings by the fall in population is difficult to reconcile with the explanation of the price-scissors by the different movement of costs with output in the towns and in the countryside. For the former depends on there being an inflexible relation between capital or land and labor, whereas the latter, if interpreted as meaning the variation of costs with capacity utilization, depends on a flexible relation between capital or land and labor. This difficulty could be avoided by interpreting the variation of costs with output as an exclusively long-run phenomenon only at the cost of giving up the explanation of rising wages. If the cost variation were long-run, the effects on prices would show up only when the scale of capital installations was changed, adjusting supply to demand and eliminating the pressure on wages. Further, the rise in town prices would have to wait until plant and equipment was used up and replaced by smaller units. Since the fall in population meant a fall in demand, capital equipment would be used less intensively and so depreciate more slowly, so the effects on urban prices would emerge only after a considerable lag.

Thirdly, it is simply not correct to argue from the fall in agricultural marginal costs to the conclusion that, given constant urban unit costs, seigneurial real incomes are falling relative to real incomes earned in towns, unless seigneurial incomes are regarded as 'differential rents'. For if agricultural prices remained constant the fall in costs produced by the cut-back in production would mean a rise in profits on marginal units; the fall in price in such circumstances is usually attributed to competitive pressures which equalize profit rates in all sectors. (It is this equalization of profit rates which gives rise to differential rents on the 'intra-marginal' units.) But in that case the fall in prices precisely implies unchanged returns per unit outlay. The total *amount* of profit earned, of course, falls, because the total amount exchanged declines; but agriculture and industry are equally affected in this respect, and the fall in agricultural prices implies that the same rate of return is being earned in both sectors. But this implies no change in the relative positions of town and countryside as regards the return on *capital* and in any case provides no explanation for changes in wages. Moreover, as the references to 'profit' and 'capital' indicate, this line of argument assumes institutions which did not develop until much later (and the emergence of which we wish to explain.) There is simply no justification for regarding the 'rents' which formed the basis of seigneurial incomes during this period as differential rents. On the contrary, the various feudal dues incorporated a major portion of what is now thought of as profit, and many of the later changes in the institutional arrangements in the countryside were concerned precisely with freeing profits and capital from feudal exactions and restrictions. This leads to a more general point.

Postan's argument rests to a considerable extent on the proposition that prices will change as costs change. The usual justification for this presupposes competitive markets for land, labor and capital ('free entry'); but this institutional context was not available in this period. Neither land nor labor could be freely bought and sold, and while capital could be raised, 'usury' was prohibited, and the methods of circumventing this prohibition were awkward and sometimes costly. Even more important, the object of Postan's argument is to explain from population changes those changes in the state of trade which, by affecting the political and social activities of merchants and nobles, led to the transformation of feudal institutions into modern capitalist institutions. But this means that his argument presupposes the very institutional context, free competitive factor markets, whose emergence it is ultimately supposed to explain.

Neither the trade nor the population theory is acceptable in its present form, though both embody significant insights. Dobb and Nabholz have tried to draw on these insights by putting them in a somewhat different theoretical setting, where the principal engine of social change is the class struggle. Dobb regards the inefficiency of the feudal system of production as a fundamental factor, for, with the development of trade and luxury expenditure and growing need for military retainers, the requirements of the nobility for revenue increased, leading them to increase their exactions upon the peasantry.[44] But this did not lead to an increase in output; instead it provoked massive and illegal emigration to the towns or to new lands, which were being opened in the attempt to increase revenues. The expansion of towns, at first the result of the opening of new opportunities for commerce, accelerated with the population of the countryside, and urban industry benefited from the large pool of available labor. The Black Death exacerbated the rural labor shortage, but did not cause it.[45] After the emergence of the disproportion of demand and supply wages rose steadily, and demesne cultivation declined, while the tendency to lease the demesne lands grew. Lords were obliged to reduce the obligations of their serfs and tenants in order to keep them at all. But the feudal system, though weakened, survived, for with the growth of population and the rise of towns a new supply of labor and the possibility of increased revenue through production for the market emerged in many areas. Thus the feudal bonds were maintained, though often in different forms.[46] In England the final abolition of feudalism did not come until the English civil war; in France it came only with the Revolution.

Dobb sees the initial pressures in the class struggle as coming from the nobles; Nabholz regards the pressures initiated from below as the more significant.[47] With the progress of commerce and the development in the countryside of production for the market there comes a blurring of the line between free and unfree peasants. The financial burdens of the free are increased while the personal obligations of the unfree are reduced or commuted. Thus the two classes of peasants tend to coalesce at the time when the ties of personal dependence between lords and serfs are decaying. The position of the lords is weakened politically by the loss of judicial rights implied in the dissolution of these feudal ties, and economically by the fall in the value of money, since this erodes the purchasing power of fixed rents. Among the peasantry there emerges a class of well-to-do free peasants, prosperous but socially disadvantaged, and subject to continual economic harassment by the nobility.[48] This class provides the leadership for a sustained struggle for complete economic and legal independence, which in France, England and Germany breaks into open civil war.

The most obvious difficulty with these versions of the class struggle theory is that each must rely on a *deus ex machina*, in Dobb's case the increased desire of the nobility for revenue,[49] in Nabholz the rise of the 'kulaks.' Not only are these explaining factors themselves left unexplained; they also invoke the kind of social change which should itself be part of what is to be explained. For example, insofar as Dobb explains the increased demand for revenue he does so by pointing to the increased cost of maintaining the feudal establishment. But to say that the feudal order decayed because it became too costly to maintain is in some ways simply to redescribe the question, not to answer it.

While it may often be illuminating to call attention to a class struggle, the existence of such a struggle is not sufficient to explain the rise or decline of a social order, for that depends upon the outcome of the struggle. The determinants of this outcome are by no means always the same as the causes of the conflict, and calling attention to the one may distract it from the other. Dobb and Nabholz have pointed to a number of factors which led to the struggle between the nobility and the peasantry – the desire for revenue on the one side and for independent status on the other – but they have not adequately explained why the peasantry after 1300 were in a better position to enforce their demands.

This leads to a final point. In trying to explain the improved condition of the peasant and the weakened position of the noble, both point to the effects on the countryside of the increasing prosperity of the towns, first in offering attractive alternative employment to the peasant, and secondly in stimulating the lords' desire for revenue. But the effect of the towns is even more profound (as Dobb himself later points out[50]), for the countryside and town trade with one another, and the changes in terms of this trade reflect the relative economic power and prosperity of these two sectors. But these terms do not depend on the class struggle between lords and peasant, though they will certainly be relevant to the outcome of that struggle. There *is* a class struggle involved in the explanation of the terms of trade, but it is between the bourgeoisie of the towns and the nobles, not between peasants and nobles; and it is concerned with prices not wages.

3 EXPLANATION BY FACTOR AND BY NETWORK

The explanandum under consideration is the change in the nature and composition of the elite in Western European society between 1100 and 1500. None of the three authors posed the problem in exactly this way, nor did they all consider the same aspects of the change, or even exactly the same periods of time. But from their work we were able to extract explanations directed to this phenomenon, conceived in much the same way. We must now consider what can be learned from the defects found in these explanations.

All three have the same form; they are what we shall call 'factor explanations.' This does not mean that a *single* factor is identified as the explanans; none of these authors does that, though each does attribute primary responsibility to one factor. Rather a group of factors is set apart, and these features of society are treated as independent variables causing changes in dependent variables. For example, it is argued that, 'The expansion of trade leads to an increase in the size and wealth of towns,' and 'a decline in population leads to a relatively greater decline in seigneurial than in artisan incomes.' Each of the three explanations is made up of chains of such individual factor-explanation statements.

But such chains of factor-explanations run into two difficulties. First, there is the danger of treating redescription as explanation, together with the related problem of explaining *obscurus per obscuriorem*. If the first step is open to such objections the rest of the chain is irrelevant. Secondly, the chain may turn back upon itself, becoming circular, if effects coming further along in the chain react upon the initial factors. In other words, it may not be possible to isolate genuinely independent variables. Thus, for example, trade stimulates production, production at a high level encourages specialization and the division of labor, which in turn requires trade; or, again, a rise in population leads to an increase in output by making possible the realization of returns to scale, the higher output leads to higher wages, which in turn lowers the death rate and the marriage age, bringing a further increase in population. If anything, such folding back is more likely in multi- than in single-factor explanation chains.

If no independent variables, which are not themselves part of what is to be explained, can be isolated, then the factor-chain approach is useless. The appropriate procedure at this point is to consider the relations between the variables, rather than the variables themselves, as the explanans, so that any explanation will be found in the relationship of these relations. In this approach we picture society as an interdependent whole, concentrating our attention on the relations between the parts, rather than on the parts themselves. Instead of a causal chain we have a network of mutually dependent relationships; and these relationships are such that a change in any one of them will have clearly determinable effects upon the others. This approach, we shall argue, is the appropriate one for explaining changes in the social order.

It is important to be clear what is meant by 'factor' and by 'network.' For example, if some relation in a network changed, say because of technical improvements and/or a new division of labor, that change might itself be called a 'factor,' and the whole argument dubbed a 'factor explanation' in consequence. This would be a mistake. By a 'factor' we mean a variable which itself describes a part of the fabric of society. The volume of trade, the population, and the typical attitudes and motives of the members of a social class are good examples of factors, changes in which will normally lead to changes in other variables. Now suppose that formerly a rise in trade led to increased productivity, due to economies of scale, but that now a rise in trade leads to a rise in unit costs and diminished productivity, due to the strain on transport facilities and pressure on land and natural resources. In the sense intended the changes in the volume of trade and in productivity are 'factor changes,' but the change in the relation between them (from varying directly to varying inversely) is not. But to examine the changed relation by itself is not very illuminating; to understand this change the relation itself has to be seen in context, and its dependence on other variables, as well as the further relations between those variables, must all be set forth. When this has been done a sector of the network of social dependencies will have been revealed.

It might still be argued that a change in some relation should be treated as the basic element in any explanation, since it brings about the various other changes. Though it is true that the initial change sets off a train of consequences, what has to be explained is not merely why a series of interacting changes happened, but why this series took on a particular form. The original change merely set off the chain of events; it had no power to shape or direct them. To understand why the subsequent series of events took the form it did we must understand the network of relations and dependencies between the features of society which the initial event disturbed.

Factors are included in the network if they stand in ascertainable relationships of mutual dependence. The average size of peasant holdings, for example, might depend on the price of grain, which in turn might depend in part upon peasant productivity, and productivity upon the size of holdings. But other relationships will depend on factors not included in the social network. The output of grain in relation to seed input on land of a certain quality will depend in part upon the weather, a factor which does not depend on the social network, though modern technology may be bringing some aspects of it under control. Whether a factor is included in the network of a particular society will depend principally on the degree of control that society can exercise over it. A factor should be considered endogenous if and only if changes in it are brought about (not necessarily consciously or intentionally) by some identifiable social process. The network consists of the set of all relationships between endogenous factors.

A change in one of the relations in this network can properly be called exogenous, if the change is not attributable to the influence of any factor included in the network. A 'network explanation,' then, traces the consequences of an exogenous change in some relation or set of relations through the network constituting the productive basis of society. Such an explanation is not concerned with why events happened at a certain time; it rather seeks to account for the form they took on and the order in which they took place.

Of course, not all relationships between economic, social and political variables should be included in the network. Society is too varied and complex to be shown in full; nor need one do so for the purposes of examining social change, for we are interested (here) only in those changes fundamental to the social order, and so we eliminate from consideration accidental or inessential features. By this last phrase we mean features that could be drastically altered or abolished altogether, while the society remains able to function much as before in all other respects. In other words, we shall eliminate from consideration all institutions which, while themselves economically dependent on the rest of society, do not in turn support dependent activities. For example, painting and religious worship are excluded by this stipulation. The activities which are essential – but not the workings of the ecclesiastical courts – are those without which society cannot continue, and these activities are primarily concerned first with providing a living, tools, and socially necessary training to the population, and secondly with the maintenance of order and the enforcement of rules of conduct. The two classes of relationships with which we shall be concerned are thus economic and political, in the older and richer sense of that term. (We shall not draw the customary sharp distinction between the political system of feudal society and its underlying economic basis. On the contrary, the changing relation between control over the means of coercion and over the means of production will be a central theme in this analysis; nor can this changing relation be understood apart from the interdependence of the activities of maintaining order and producing.)

The normal working of the system – of the network of relationships – will, over time, set up stresses, leading to innovations. For example, the specialization of the guilds produces finer goods; these displace the products of the gynaceas – thereby improving the trading position of the towns *vis-à-vis* the countryside. The peasants on better lands become more prosperous and the lords seek for ways to exact higher dues from them. Each of these, and other, changes arise from the normal pattern of activities, but once the change occurs, the effects spread through the entire network, and the consequences, magnified by the interactions, are often of far greater significance than the change itself would lead one to expect. But this is the nature of transformational growth. It is not the change itself, e.g. a change in technology, but the amplification of the change through its impact on the network of relationships that matters for understanding economic history.

The economic relationships to be examined arise primarily on the supply side, and are not generally connected with what is often considered to be the fundamental problem of economic science, the allocation of scarce resources among competing ends. In general, the kinds of economic decisions modern theory describes are not relevant to these problems, and in particular the opportunities for substitution of any kind are limited or non-existent. What much modern theory treats as 'imperfections of the market' must here be taken as the basic conditions of economic activity; complementarity and market rigidity must be treated as methodologically fundamental.

The model of these economic relationships must show how the society produces enough to feed itself and keep itself going, and so must show the exchanges necessary for this, i.e., the trade in necessities. But any model which can do this will also show which sectors and activities depend how much on which others. Since the model will exhibit the working of the whole society, all economic dependencies will be revealed; but power is simply the inverse of dependency. To the extent that dependency exists on one side of the market, economic power exists on the other.

Economic power concerns the ability to obtain economic advantages through market bargaining. This can be done in two ways – respectively the positive and negative sides of economic power. Very roughly, these can be termed 'bribing' and 'extorting.' Positive economic power, 'bribing,' is the ability to act in the market so as to influence some outcome favorably, e.g. by bidding up prices, spoiling the market for competitors, cornering the market, etc. Negative economic power, 'extorting,' is the ability to wait, to hold out, and by so doing compel the market to meet certain terms. Negative economic power consists in being to some degree self-sufficient relative to the others in the market. Of the two, negative power is the more important, for it arises from the economic needs for others, whereas positive power only plays upon their wants.

In any reasonably well developed market two kinds of competition are to be found. Each seller competes with his fellows for the available trade, and each buyer competes with the others for the available merchandise. However, in addition to such competition along each side of the market, there is competition across the market between buyers and sellers; the more buyers must pay the more sellers gain, and vice versa. The first kind of competition is concerned with the allocation of custom, the second with the distribution of gain. But the two interact; the fiercer the competition on one side, compared to that on the other, the worse that side will do across the market. Conversely, the weaker the position on one side the more its members will tend to compete against each other for what profits there are to be had. When there is economic mobility, when trade can shift channels freely, competition along the market will tend to smooth out differentials, establishing a uniform price for each kind of commodity; but it is competition across the market that establishes the levels of prices and sets the terms of trade. It is in this latter competition that economic power is exercised and that the effects of economic dependence are felt, and such competition, of course, exists in any kind of market transaction, regardless of the mobility of trade.

In across the market competition negative economic power, which is the inverse of dependency, plays the more important role. Hence when dependencies change, the distribution of this power will change, and with it the ability to affect the terms of exchange. We must now examine how this is relevant to the explanation of the changes in feudal society.

4 THE INTERDEPENDENCE OF THE URBAN AND RURAL ECONOMIES (A PREVIEW OF CHAPTER 13)

By 1500 the feudal nobility no longer possessed an unchallenged position in society; they not only had now to share power with the great merchant princes of the towns, but even the craft guilds were able to wield influence. The transition had been from a society with a ruling class of uniform character, based on military force, to a society in which the ruling elite had become complex and divided, composed of elements depending on different and competing sources of revenue, and living different styles of life, but all based on economic power, while military power was tending to concentrate in the hands of the central authority.

The explanation of this change which we shall now present finds the basic causes in a series of technological developments, which first change the relations of dependence between different economic sectors, and ultimately affect the relation between economic power and military power, thus altering the relations between the classes resting respectively on the possession of the means of coercion, the various types of means of production, and the control of commerce. On the basis of these technological changes we distinguish three successive stages or phases in this development, which we shall examine in order. In the first stage agricultural productivity rises enabling towns to be supported. The countryside is self-sufficient, whereas towns depend on the countryside for their food supply, and the military power of the nobility rests on the productive abilities of the countryside. (Mercenaries may be used, but they are supplied by the countryside.) In the second stage a merchant class emerges possessing a monopoly of information about trading conditions, and able to create and take advantage of price differentials. Nobility and to some extent peasantry come to depend on towns for the superior cloth produced there, and towns become able in part to supply and defend themselves. In the third stage the countryside becomes heavily dependent on towns for a variety of goods, and the nobility come to depend on urban craftsmen for the new kinds of armor and weapons. Highly skilled craft work develops, requiring customers and producers to come together, which tends to squeeze out the merchants. The change in the character of warfare erodes the nobility's monopoly of military power.

It should be remembered that the argument which follows is abstract; the phases described here as successive often blended in reality. Nor will any attempt be made to determine the exact scope of this abstract argument; it may well be that the development of certain parts of Western Europe, particularly in the South, cannot be fitted to this pattern. We shall also here abstract from the fact that men will frequently occupy more than one position in the social structure. Thus merchants may invest in land or in manufacturing; and nobles will sometimes put up the capital for trading ventures. Such diversification of interest has two consequences. First, it means that, e.g. the decline of seigneurial incomes does not necessarily coincide with a decline in the incomes of seigneurial families. Secondly, it means that those in a position to exercise economic power at the expense of certain other groups will not always be motivated to do so. History will seldom perfectly recapitulate theory.

In the first phase the prevailing economic relationships were those of feudal society proper; they represent the initial position from which the process of development began. We shall now consider an idealized model of those relationships. For this purpose we shall suppose that we are analyzing a country district having no contact with the outside world, composed of a limited number of large manors, each presided over by a noble and his military retinue, and worked by a large number of peasants. We shall first explain the sense in which the countryside is self-sufficient, then examine the economic relationships involved in the manorial economy, and finally consider the trade between the countryside and town.

It is oversimplified to suppose that each manor or villa is itself self-sufficient should not be accepted; what is essential is rather that the countryside as a whole be self-sufficient. But individual manors can specialize to a greater or less degree. The importance of this lies in the fact that specialization both increases productivity and requires trade; but the trade required here all takes place within the 'natural economy.' The consumption goods required by towns can be produced in the required proportions if specialization is carried out appropriately. Thus we can treat the countryside, the agricultural sector, as a unit producing a single composite consumption good (consumed by peasants, retainers and towns folk), made up of the various individual items in the appropriate proportions.[51] This good represents the surplus produced by the countryside above its own needs, including seed and the replacement of tools, materials, etc.

Now let us consider the economic relationships on the manor. In the manorial system land is divided between peasant holdings and the demesne. The peasant supports himself and his family out of the earnings from the sale of the produce of his holding. He owes his lord a certain amount of time working the demesne land, and this time will be set so that the surplus accrues to the lord.[52] Thus only as much land will be distributed to peasants, and only as much time will be left them, as is needed for them to produce their own subsistence. Hence, assuming all land to be of equal quality, both the ratio of demesne land to peasant holdings and the ratio of time owed in labor services to time working peasant holdings will equal the ratio of the total surplus composite consumption good to the amount required to support the peasantry of the district. It is easy to see this when every manor is fully self-sufficient and produces the composite consumption good on its own demesne. But specialization changes nothing essential; it merely regroups the various processes in a way permitting them to operate more effectively. Hence every manor will demand labor services in the same ratio, the ratio of total non-peasant consumption of the district to total peasant consumption, which we shall therefore call the 'feudal rent ratio.' Even when the various manors of a district are fully specialized this ratio can be determined independently of prices, since it is a ratio of quantities of the composite consumption good, and so depends only on the technology.

Given the feudal rent ratio the remaining economic relationships, prices and quantities, can be determined. Since the methods of production are given, quantities follow from the assumption that the net output is to consist of the composite consumption good, for this determines the allocation of resources to the various branches of the natural economy. Prices also follow, though their determination is somewhat more complicated.[53] We have already seen that prices remain unchanged by the shifting of resources from one line of production to another; this holds true of the feudal rent ratio as well. Even when the surplus does not consist of the composite consumption good the ratio of the *value* of the surplus to the *value* of the consumption goods required by the natural economy will be the feudal rent ratio. Hence whatever the composition of the surplus produced for the support of the feudal establishment and for trade with towns all economic relations in the natural economy are determinate.

The meaning of the feudal rent ratio is simply this: on land of equal quality exchange between specialized or partly specialized manors will take place at prices such that the value of the demesne produce accruing to every lord stands in the same proportion to the amount of labor producing it,[54] in other words, the productivity of labor is the same on every manor, as would necessarily be the case if each manor produced the composite consumption good.

Of course, land is *not* all of the same quality, and this benefits the peasant. Typically the best land will be taken for the demesne. But the peasantry cannot be pushed below subsistence. Consider now the peasant on the poorest land; he will have to work the longest to maintain himself and his family, so he will have the least time available to work for his lord. (Either he will have to farm a similar acreage more intensively than others, or, the land being poorer he will require more of it, in which case the larger area to be covered means more time will be needed for plowing, seeding, harvesting, etc.) But common justice and the requirements of administration require that all peasants should be treated alike, for they owe services in virtue of their condition as serfs, not because they have a particular holding.[55] Hence, when the quality of land varies the feudal rent ratio will be determined on the land of poorest quality, and the peasants on 'intra-marginal' land will earn 'differential rents.' (A rise in population will therefore lead to the emergence of a class of rich peasants and a decline will tend to reduce their incomes, not those of landlords. But a decline in population might also lead to a rise in the average size of holdings and a lowering of the intensity of cultivation. This is likely to result in a decline of productivity per acre and a rise in productivity per man, so that rent per acre will fall, while peasant incomes rise.)

Now let us examine first the towns and then the trade between town and countryside. From our point of view it does not matter how or why towns began; but one cause of their origin is easy to see. In a district in which manors specialize and trade with one another, it is cheaper in terms of transport costs for everyone to take their goods to a central market, returning with their purchases, than for them to travel to one another to engage directly in trade.[56] District market towns will therefore develop to economize on the transport costs required by the trade resulting from the specialization of manors. The land for such towns and the 'capital' (fund) needed to support the initial population during the construction and founding stage will be provided by a nobleman, who, in return will receive dues from the market and from the administration of justice.

Such towns will do more than provide a market; the surplus accruing to the nobility can be transformed into something more useful and more attractive. Trade with distant parts can turn it into silks and spices; local manufacture can turn it into finely woven cloth. The towns will therefore produce luxuries for the nobility (and for those peasants whose better land yields them a differential earning), the countryside supplying it with the composite consumption good and any other materials, etc. required for manufacture or trade.[57] Some goods will be produced wholly for use within towns; their quantities and prices will be determined exactly as the quantities and prices of their counterparts in the countryside were.

Since the towns receive their consumption goods and raw materials from the countryside, they are in a dependent position; but what they produce is a luxury, which the countryside can do without. The towns cannot compel the countryside to sell to them; if the countryside chooses to hold out the towns will starve. Nor is any alternative to buying from the countryside available; towns cannot acquire land, for land is not alienable in a feudal system, nor can they look elsewhere for sources of supply, for wherever they look they will find a feudal countryside not dependent upon urban products. The countryside, for its part, can store its products, use them to support larger military establishments, or ship them to another town not disposed to hold out for higher prices. In extreme cases of conflict, the nobility might be tempted to found a competing trading center.

The outcome of this across-the-market bargaining is determined in part by the situation on each side of the market. Speaking schematically, when the towns are producing the amount of, say, cloth the nobles want, then the best strategy of any townsman *vis-à-vis* his fellows is to lower his price and try to sell first. For if he lowers and the rest try to hold out for better terms, he will sell his goods first, saving on storage costs and making it possible to begin the next round of production sooner than the rest. Since supply and demand are, ex hypothesi, in balance, and the countryside in a better position to hold out, the other town merchants will eventually have to meet the lower price. If a given merchant lowers and the rest also lower, all will sell at roughly the same time and no one will gain any advantage. If he holds out and they accept the lower price, he sells last, incurring storage costs and a delay in beginning the next round of production. If all hold out together no one gains any relative advantages, but if the nobles look to their interests, given their strong position the townsmen will have to meet their terms in the end.

For the nobles (or rather, their stewards) the best strategy is clearly to hold out for a high price. If one estate accepts a lower price for its products, it will sell first, saving perhaps on storage costs (though since the manor's winter supplies must be stored in any case the greater part of such costs will be fixed and marginal storage costs very low) but losing on the price. If all lower all lose. If one estate or group of estates holds out for a high price and others do not, those who hold out sell last, but since the town needs all the supplies available, the townsmen will eventually have to meet their price. Finally, if all estates or groups of estates hold out together all will gain. Thus, when all available supplies are in demand the best strategy for any estate, regardless of what the rest do, is to hold out for a high price. For a townsman the best strategy, regardless of what his fellows do, is to accept a lower price and sell first.

When supply and demand are not in balance the outcome will be rather different. If supply is greater than demand some cloth will not readily find a market, and will tend to push down the price of the rest. But a producing establishment cannot be maintained if its costs cannot be covered. A fall of price below cost means a loss in operating funds, and this reduction in the amount of funds invested will continue until the output corresponding to the reduced capital just meets the demand. Conversely, when demand exceeds supply, estates will compete with one another for the available merchandise, bidding up the price. To be certain of getting any cloth at all an estate will have to be among the first buyers, and under these circumstances the townsmen can afford to hold out until prices rise to the point where the investment of the gains would produce an output just meeting the demand. When demand and supply balance again the price will readjust to the level reflecting the dominant position of the countryside.

In the long run, therefore, the terms of trade will strongly tend to favor the nobility. Agricultural prices in terms of town products will tend to be high, and will tend to rise as the productivity of towns increases. However, increases in agricultural productivity, instead of lowering agricultural prices (raising the prices of town goods), will lead to an increase in the town population, and a corresponding expansion of urban production. (Assuming town goods to be in demand this would be preceded by a temporary rise in urban prices, attracting the marginal or surplus peasantry.)

Within the town there will normally be a number of different establishments producing fine cloth and luxuries, some of which will be more

Under these conditions a general surplus of unskilled labor provides no bargaining advantage to employers. If any group of workers chooses to hold out, they can prevent the project from going forward; hence they are in a position to demand a share in the earnings of the enterprise in proportion to their numbers, the time they put in, and the degree of skill they possess. Very often they will be paid on a piece-rate basis, so that in effect they sell a product rather than their labor.

This means a decline in the price of the composite consumption good produces earnings for craft work, in whatever line, in proportion to the number of workers employed.[60] Initially this means that the value productivity of craft labor rises uniformly in all crafts, while the value-productivity of agricultural labor (the feudal rent ratio) declines. A large part of the power to command the surplus has thus been transferred from the nobility in the countryside, through the merchants to the artisans in the towns.

Hence a decline in the price of the composite consumption good (in terms of town goods) produces earnings for craft work, in whatever line, in proportion to the number of workers employed.[61] Initially, value productivity of craft labor rises uniformly in all crafts, while the value productivity of agricultural labor (the feudal rent ratio) declines. A large part of the power to command the surplus has thus been transferred from the nobility in the countryside, through the merchants to the artisans in the towns.

In the beginning the major share of the surplus went in feudal rents and dues to the nobility, in virtue of their dominant bargaining position *vis-à-vis* both towns and peasants. A relatively small share went as differential earnings to peasants on intra-marginal lands and to craftsmen of superior skill or in advantageous locations. Expansion through the investment of these earnings and through population growth made possible further specialization and division of labor, reducing the cost and improving the quality of town goods, until it became advantageous for the nobility to abolish the gynaceas and purchase all manufactured goods from towns. With this development towns and countryside became interdependent, with the advantage in bargaining gradually shifting to the towns, as they consolidated their control over the markets. Initially merchants, the only group with access to market information, were in the best position to gain from interdependence, since they could establish and maintain a differential between purchase and sale prices. But the specialization and individuality of craft work militated against the merchant, since it called for direct contact between craftsman and customer. As specialization increased, craft earnings, and with them journeymen's wages, tended to rise at the expense of merchants and nobles, just as previously merchants had gained at the expense of the feudal nobility. Merchants, however, retained an advantageous position in lending, and nobles could maintain their income by commuting labor services to money rents, and improve it by attaching obligations to specific holdings rather than to personal status. In the long run this changed the nature of the social bond between peasant and lord; in the short run it eased the way for peasant migration to the towns and helped to transmit the pressures from rising craft earnings and wages to the countryside.

Each transition represents changes in the network of social relations due to population growth and technical change. The initial increase in agricultural productivity that made the establishment of towns possible must have been exogenous, and a good part of the subsequent development may also have been so. But once the system had begun developing, both population growth and technical change were at least partly endogenous. Population increase came about at least partly in response to intra-marginal peasant prosperity, which in turn it enhanced. Technical development, especially specialization and the division of labor, was partly a response to an expanded market – 'the division of labor is limited by the extent of the market' – and partly a consequence of the investment of the intra-marginal earnings in improved equipment and superior establishments.

These developments must now be explored more carefully, for they resulted in a kind of stalemate, lasting for a full century, and finally broken by the emergence of early forms of capitalistic relationships in production. The next two chapters will take up these issues.

Appendix: Wage and Price Trends in the Middle Ages

Statistical evidence from the Middle Ages is at best fragmentary, and no analysis of it can be much more than suggestive. But a few important trends stand out. Some of the evidence for these is presented below.

It is worth noting that the same trends are observable in many different parts of Europe and under very different social and political conditions; for example, agricultural prices fell in England and in Eastern Prussia during the 15th century, and in England these prices fell and real wages rose both during the relative domestic stability of the early years of Henry VI and during the civil strife of the Wars of the Roses (see Tables 12A.1–12A.5).

Table 12A.1 English wheat prices

Period	*Wheat price in shillings (per qr)*	*Wheat price in grains of silver (per qr)*
1160–79	1.89	534
1180–99	2.60	744
1200–19	4.33	1082
1220–39	4.19	1047
1240–59	4.58	1144
1260–79	5.62	1404
1280–99	5.97	1491
1300–19	7.01	1734
1320–39	6.27	1547
1340–59	6.31	1372
1360	7.55	1508
1380–99	5.57	1113
1400–19	6.37	1188
1420–39	6.65	1107
1440–59	5.56	926
1460–79	6.02	812
1480–99	6.40	852
1500–19	6.91	920

Source: Postan (CEHE, 1952, pp. 166, 205).

Table 12A.2 Prices of rye in Koenigsberg

Years	*Prices (silver)*
1399	100.00
1405	89.29
1432	85.32
1448	79.81
1494	49.84
1508	36.48

Source: Postan (CEHE, 1952, p. 207).

Table 12A.3 English prices of wheat and animal products

Years	*Wheat*	*Animal products and cattle*
1351–75	100	100
1376–1400	71	88
1401–25	70	99
1426–50	70	89
1451–75	55	76
1476–1500	53	68

Source: Postan (CEHE, 1952, p. 209).

Table 12A.4 English prices of iron expressed in wheat

1300–50	100
1351–60	159
1389–1400	352

Source: Postan (CEHE, 1952, p. 208).

Table 12A.5 The make-up of the composite consumption good

	1453–60 %	*1790s* %	*1904–13* $	*Weights* %
1. Farinaceous	20.0	53.0	16.0	20.0
2. Meat, fish	35.0	12.0	21.5	25.0
3. Butter, cheese	2.0	7.0	16.0	12.5
4. Drink (malt, hops, sugar, tea)	23.0	9.0	24.0	22.5
Subtotal, Food	80.0	81.0	77.5	80.0

Table 12A.5 *continued*

	1453–60 %	*1790s* %	*1904–13* $	*Weights* %
5. Fuel and light	7.5	7.5	9.0	7.5
6. Textiles	n.a.	11.5	13.5	12.5
Total	87.5	100.0	100.0	100.0

Note: Table 12A.5 shows the main classes of items in consumption at three different times during the five centuries studied by Phelps-Brown and Hopkins. The fourth column shows the weights they used.

Source: Phelps-Brown and Hopkins (EEH, 1962, p. 180).

The price of the composite consumption good is graphed in Figure 12A.1, from 1300 to 1900. Figure 12A.2 shows the money wages of an average laborer, and the real wage for seven centuries is shown in Figure 12A.3. We will refer to these again in Chapter 14, when we discuss the centuries' long fall in real wages.

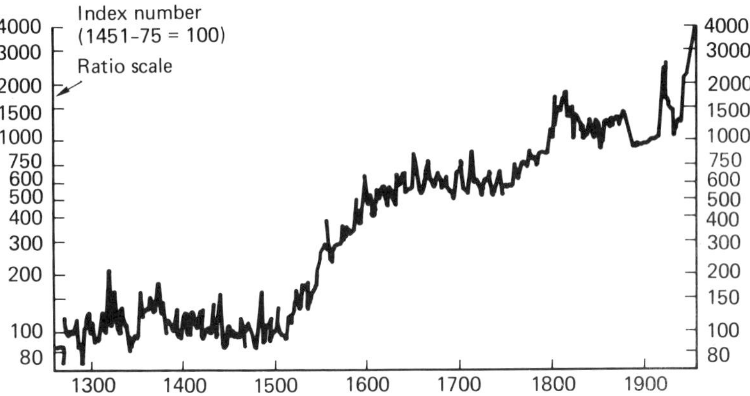

Figure 12A.1 Price of composite unit of consumables in Southern England, 1264–1954.

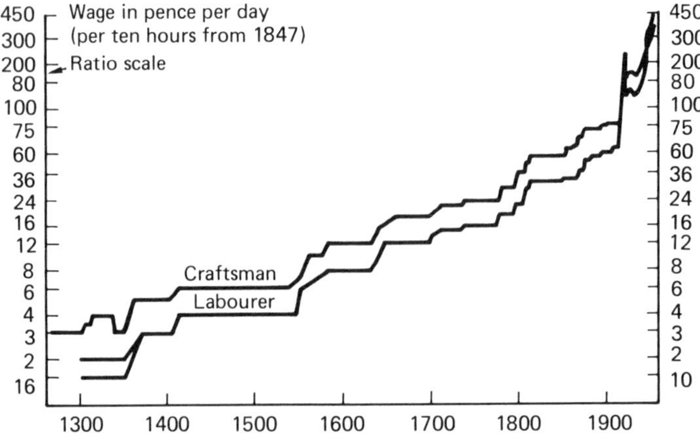

Figure 12A.2 Wages of building craftsman and labourer in Southern England, 1264–1954

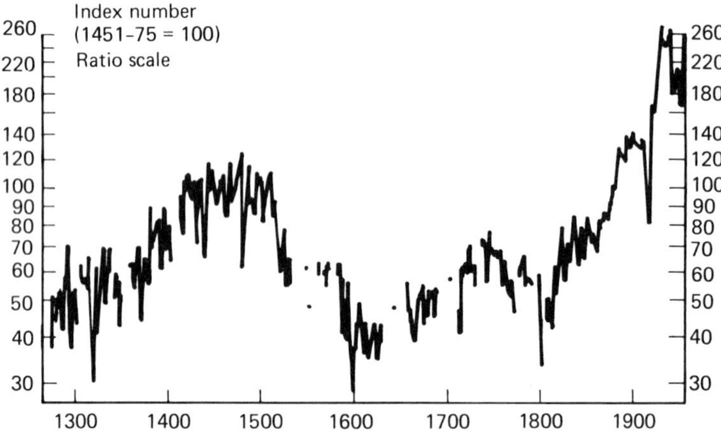

Figure 12A.3 Changes in the equivalent of the wage rate of a building craftsman expressed in a composite physical unit of consumables in Southern England, 1264–1954

Notes

1. Economists interested in growth often make use of this approach, cf. N. Kaldor, 'Capital Accumulation and Economic Growth,' in F.A. Lutz and D.C. Hague (eds), *The Theory of Capital* (London: Macmillan, 1961).
2. White (1962) Ch. II, esp. pp. 72–6.
3. Postan (CEHE, 1952) pp. 159–68.
4. Ganshof (CEHE, 1941) pp. 279–81, 317–20.
5. Postan (CEHE, 1952) pp. 165–8.
6. Dobb (1963) pp. 89–91.
7. Ganshof (CEHE, 1941) p. 316.
8. Previté-Orton (1960) pp. 24–7.
9. Ganshof (CEHE, 1941) p. 322.
10. Pirenne (1937) p. 81.
11. Postan (CEHE, 1952) pp. 171–4.
12. Postan (CEHE, 1952) pp. 119–29; Lopez.
13. Postan (CEHE, 1952) pp. 155–68.
14. Hibbert (CEHE, 1963) pp. 181–98.
15. Pirenne (1963, 1937, 1946).
16. Pirenne (1963) Chs 6, 8.
17. Beveridge (EEH, 1954).
18. Postan (CEHE, 1952) pp. 191–216; (esp, 198).
19. Pirenne (1937) p. 192; Postan (CEHE, 1952) pp. 213–16.
20. Postan (EHR, 1939) pp. 166–7; Dobb (CEHE, 1939) (1963) p. 49.
21. Nabholz (CEHE, 1941) pp. 412–21, pp. 558–9. Bridbury (1962) pp. 77–82 & Appendix II.
22. Pirenne (1963, 1937, 1946); Postan (CEHE, 1952) pp. 216–219; Cipolla (CEHE, 1963) pp. 411–15.
23. Phelps-Brown and Hopkins (EEH, 1962; 1986).
24. Postan (CEHE, 1952) p. 217; Carus-Wilson (EEH, 1954).
25. Pirenne (1937) pp. 25–35, 66–85.
26. Pirenne (1937) pp. 1–20.
27. Pirenne (1963) pp. 1–26.
28. Pirenne (1963) pp. 34–54; (1937) pp. 49–57.
29. Pirenne (1937) pp. 66–86.
30. Pirenne (1937) pp. 66–86.
31. Pirenne's argument, as given here, applies primarily to the earlier of our two periods. During the 14th and 15th centuries, he argues that the earlier progress was halted first by 'natural and political calamities' (Pirenne, 1937, pp. 192–3), and then by the development of rigid guild restrictions, 'urban protectionism,' which stifled trade (Pirenne, 1937, p. 206, *et passim.*)
32. Sweezy suggests a third interpretation of Pirenne, namely that the real significance of the re-opening of Mediterranean commerce lay in the backwardness of Western Europe compared to the Arab world; hence the transformation of feudalism should be seen as the result not so much of trade as of the impact of an advanced economy upon a backward one. Cf. Sweezy *et al.* (n.d.) pp. 62–3.
33. No appeal can be made to the principle of comparative advantage unless both parties initially produced all the goods traded, and specialized after the opening of trade. Specialization, not trade, is responsible for the increased production; but Pirenne neither discusses the opportunities for nor the advantages of specialization nor why it would benefit towns more than countryside.
34. It might be objected that the productivity, the ability to produce, was already present, but not being used, for lack of an outlet for the products. This is the

'disguised unemployment' argument, familiar in modern development economics. As in the modern case, there is no evidence of this; on the contrary, it seems probable that the nobility extracted as much as they could from the peasantry to support their large, semi-military establishments. Nor was the standard of living of the peasantry so high that additional output would have been regarded as superfluous. In any case, even if trade did provide a stimulus to take up slack in production, the stimulus is only half the story.

35. Postan (CEHE, 1952) pp. 191–216; (1939).
36. Postan (CEHE, 1952) pp. 191–216; (1939).
37. Postan (CEHE, 1952) pp. 172–4.
38. Postan (CEHE, 1952) pp. 214–16.
39. Postan (CEHE, 1952) p. 217.
40. Postan (CEHE, 1952) p. 207.
41. Postan (CEHE, 1952) p. 166.
42. That the plague was a disaster beyond comparison cannot be doubted, but its long term effects on population and economic potential can easily be exaggerated. First, plague carries off the old, the infirm, the already sick and the very young – all of whom require support but add nothing to society's productive powers. Secondly, it accelerates inheritance, putting the young and energetic in command of society's resources at the very time that charges on these are reduced, which, in turn, leads to a tendency for the marriage age to fall and the birth rate to rise. Cf. Glass and Eversley (1965) p. 31, *et passim*.
43. Beveridge (EEH, 1954).
44. Dobb (1963) p. 42.
45. Dobb (1963) p. 49.
46. Lords adapted and reinterpreted feudal obligations in order to levy taxes on the revenues from growing markets and trade. (Bridbury, 1962 Chs III, IV, V.)
47. Nabholz (CEHE, 1941) pp. 498–500.
48. Nabholz (CEHE, 1941) pp. 504–5.
49. Dobb provides an interesting explanation for the rise of a rich upper stratum in the peasantry (1963, pp. 60–2).
50. Dobb (1963) pp. 82, 88–91.
51. The surplus need not consist of this set of goods. The agricultural system (including the workshops) is based on a set of given techniques, which specify the inputs during the year to produce the various outputs. These inputs are (more or less) fixed per unit output, which implies that on land of any given quality, constant returns to scale obtain. That is, changing all inputs, including land, by some factor changes output by the same factor. This means that resources, labor, land, tools and materials can be shifted between the different activities so that the surplus will consist of more of one kind of good and less of another, if desired. Since costs are constant, and since, in a system of this kind, costs determine prices (as we shall explain below), such shifts of resources do not change prices.
52. It may be objected that this assumes a 'profit-maximizing' nobility, and that the Middle Ages was a time when records show a great pre-occupation with other-worldly matters. But perhaps there has been less a change of outlook than a change in the sections of society keeping records. In any case we do not have to assume universal economic motivation, but only that those so motivated will prosper at the expense of those not so motivated, e.g. that the nobility who fail to keep up their estates and revenues will find their ability to wage war diminished, and will find themselves prey to their neighbors (or seneschals) or sinking into debt. Nor is it necessary to assume 'economic rationality,' as that is

usually understood; nobles may spend a good part of their incomes quite irrationally, so long as they extract it efficiently from their peasants.

53. Specialization requires exchange; each manor has used up goods during the year (seed, tools, raw materials) and must stock up the composite consumption good for the next year. Revenue must cover such costs, but prices cannot be determined by such considerations alone. If we wrote down a set of equations for prices with such costs on the left hand side and revenues from the sale of output on the right, they could not balance for any values of the unknown prices since the quantities produced (appearing on the right) exceed the quantities used up (appearing on the left) by the amount of the surplus. To determine prices, therefore, we must show the distribution of the surplus as rent by introducing the feudal rent ratio; when we multiply every appearance of the composite consumption good on the left-hand or cost side by the feudal rent ratio, the equations will balance. Interpreted, this means that revenues must be such that replacements can be made and a food supply laid in, leaving a surplus for the lord in proportion to the amount of peasant labor he commands.
54. When specialization takes place the manors are mutually dependent; no one has any advantage in bargaining. In particular cases, of course, this would not be true.
55. Cf. Stephenson (1954) pp. 45, 52, 55, 59, 68, 81, 82, 83, 88, 90, for citations from medieval documents in which dues of various kinds are levied upon all peasants alike, in virtue of their condition.
56. This point can be illustrated by the example of a merchant carrying 6 tons of goods one ton of which he will sell to each of 6 manors, each located one mile from each other. If each manor purchases from the merchant in the village and returns, the total cost is that of 6 ton-miles, plus 6 miles unburdened travel. But if the merchant has to deliver to each manor his costs will be those of (6 + 5 + 5 + 4 + 4 + 3 + 3 + 2 + 2 + 1 + 1) = 36 ton-miles, plus 1 mile unburdened travel. If there are direct roads between manors (on the outside of the hexagon) his travel costs will be (6 + 5 + 4 + 3 + 2 + 1) = 21 ton-miles, plus 1 mile unburdened travel. Given medieval transport charges the difference between these figures could amount to a significant proportion of the value of the goods.
57. As we have seen this can be done without disturbing the set of prices or the feudal rent ratio, since neither are affected by the shifts in resource allocation involved in changing the composition of the net output of the countryside.
58. How do merchants make a profit? The cloth merchants sell part of the cloth to the nobles for all of the silver; then pay all of the silver to the craftsmen for all of the cloth. The craftsmen pay all the silver to the grain merchants for part of the grain; the grain merchants pay all the silver to the nobles for all the grain. Grain merchants thus have 'earned' an amount of grain, cloth merchants of cloth. The former will sell grain to the latter and buy cloth; these transactions can easily be carried out since both have idle money available; or they can be done by straight barter.
59. As feudal society moved into this stage, the silver mines of Europe, which had hitherto produced at an annual rate higher than the rate of growth of output, began to give out, while the rise of petty industry and craft production required increasing amounts of circulating capital. The ratio of the annual production of silver to the total amount of silver appears to have fallen below the ratio of the annual increase in output to total output, leading to a downward drift of the general level of money prices. Cf. Postan (CEHE, 1952, pp. 211–12). Such a

fall might lead to some dishoarding or to a melting down of plate, but for other reasons the demand for ornamental silver probably rose in this period. These movements of the general level of prices must be kept distinct from the changes in the terms of trade, the ratio of agricultural money prices to urban money prices.

60. Differential changes in productivity in the various crafts will tend to disrupt this, but it seems likely that market pressures would tend to keep it uniform. Suppose the ratio of earnings to labor rose especially high in one craft. This would attract apprentices and provide an incentive to expand output. Supply will be contracted in other crafts (or fail to grow at the appropriate rate) and over-expanded in the high earning one, with the result that the latter price will tend to fall, while others tend to rise, until the earnings ratios are equalized.
61. The sketch presented does not deal with the changed position of the Church in the two periods, nor have we taken account of the Church as an independent political and juridical authority. There are good reasons for this omission. The influence of the Church was undisputed only in the spiritual realm; in the secular and temporal world, moral suasion often served the Church's ambitions well, but its ends were more readily achieved and better secured when it commanded military force or wielded economic power. Thus we should expect the history of the Church to reflect the transition from a primarily land-based society where political dominance rests largely on control of the means of coercion, to a more complex society where political eminence is based at least as much on economic power, the possession of which is not confined to a single group. This change in the structure of the elite can be seen reflected in the different social composition of the higher clergy and princes of the Church in the two periods.

References

Becker, John (1965) 'The Composition of Anglo-Norman Armies,' *Speculum*, Vol. 40.

Becker, M.B. and Brucker, G.A. (1956) 'The Arti Minori in Florentine Politics, 1342–1378,' *Medieval Studies*, 18.

Beveridge, W. (EEH, 1954) 'The Yield and Price of Corn in the Middle Ages.'

Bishop, T.A.M. (EEH, 1954) 'Assarting and the Growth of the Open Fields.'

Bloch, Marc (CEHE, 1941) 'Rise of Dependent Cultivation and Seigneurial Institutions.'

Bloch, Marc (1961) *Feudal Society* (2 vols), L.A. Manyen (trans.) (London).

Boissonnade, P. (1964) *Life and Work in Medieval Europe*, E. Power (trans.) (New York).

Bowsky, W.M. (1954) 'The impact of the Black Death upon Science, Government and Society,' *Speculum*, Vol. 39.

Bridbury, A. (1962) *Economic Growth: England in the Later Middle Ages* (London).

Carus-Wilson, E.M. (EEH, 1954) 'An Industrial Revolution of the Thirteenth Century.'

Carus-Wilson, E.M. (EEH, 1954) 'Evidences of industrial growth on Some Fifteenth Century Manors.'

Carus-Wilson, E.M. (CEHE, 1952) 'The Woollen Industry.'
CEHE – *Cambridge Economic History of Europe*, 3 vols:
I (1941) *The Agrarian Life of the Middle Ages*, J.H. Clapham and E. Power (eds) (Cambridge).
II (1982) *Trade and Industry in the Middle Ages*, M. Postan and E.E. Rich (eds) (Cambridge).
III (1963) *Economic Organization and Policies in the Middle Ages*, M. Postan, E.E. Rich, and E. Miller (eds) (Cambridge).
Cipolla, C.M. (CEHE, 1963) 'The Economic Policies of Governments: The Italian and Iberian Peninsulas.'
Commons, J.R. (1959) *Legal Foundations of Capitalism* (Madison, Wisc.).
Dobb, M. (1963) *Studies in the Development of Capitalism* (London).
Douglas, David (1939) 'The Norman Conquest and English Feudalism,' *Economic History Review*, 9, (2) (May).
EEH – *Essays in Economic History*, 3 vols (1954, 1962, 1966), E.M. Carus-Wilson (ed.) (London).
Fryde, E.B. and M.M. (CEHE, 1963) 'Public Credit, with Special Reference to North-Western Europe.'
Ganshof, F.L. (CEHE, 1941) 'Medieval Agrarian Society in its Prime: France, the Low Countries, and Western Germany.'
Glass, D.V. and Eversley, D.E.C. (eds) (1965) *Population in History* (London).
Herlihy, David (1958) 'The Agrarian Revolution in Southern France and Italy, 801–1150,' *Speculum*, 33.
Hibbert, A.B. (CEHE, 1963) 'The Economic Policies of Towns.'
Hilton, R.H. (EEH, 1954) 'Peasant Movements in England Before 1381.'
Kerridge, Eric (EEH, 1962) 'The Movement of Rent, 1540–1640.'
Kosminsky, E.A. (EEH, 1962) 'Services and Money Rents in the Thirteenth Century.'
Lopez, R.S. (CEHE, 1952) 'The Trade of Medieval Europe: The South.'
Lutz, F.A. and Hague, D.C. (eds) (1961) *The Theory of Capital* (London: Macmillan).
Miller, E. (CEHE, 1963) 'The Economic Policies of Governments: I, II.'
Nabholz, Hans (CEHE, 1941) 'Medieval Agrarian Society in Transition.'
Neilsen, Nellie (CEHE, 1941) 'Medieval Agrarian Society in its Prime: England.'
Nef, John U. (1964) *The Conquest of the Material World* (Chicago).
Phelps-Brown, E.H., and Hopkins, Sheila V. (EEH, 1962) 'Seven Centuries of Building Wages.'
Phelps-Brown, E.H., and Hopkins, Sheila V. (EEH, 1962) 'Seven Centuries of the Prices of Consumables, Compared with Builders' Wage-Rates.'
Pirenne, Henri (1946) *Medieval Cities* (Princeton).
Pirenne, Henri (1937) *Economic and Social History of Medieval Europe* (New York).
Pirenne, Henri (1963) *Early Democracies in the Low Countries* (New York).
Postan, M.M. (EEH, 1954) 'Credit in Medieval Trade.'
Postan, M.M. (1939) 'The Fifteenth Century,' *Economic History Review*, 9 (2) (May).
Postan, M.M. (EEH, 1954) 'The Rise of a Money Economy.'
Postan, M.M. (CEHE, 1952) 'The Trade of Medieval Europe: The North.'
Previté-Orton, C.W. (1960) *A History of Europe, 1198–1378* (London).
Rogers, J.E. Thorold (1866–1902) *A History of Agriculture and Prices in England* (Oxford).
Roover, R. (CEHE, 1963) 'The Organization of Trade.'
Russell, J.C. (1965) 'Recent Advances in Medieval Demography,' *Speculum*, 40.

Shelby, L.R. (1964) 'The Role of the Master Mason in Medieval English Building,' *Speculum*, 39.
Stephenson, C. (1954) *Mediaeval Institutions: Selected Essays*, Bryce D. Lyons (ed.) (Ithaca, NY).
Sweezy, P.M. *et al.* (n.d.) *The Transition from Feudalism to Capitalism* (New York).
Thrupp, Sylvia (CEHE, 1963) 'The Gilds.'
Weber, Max (1961) *General Economic History*, F. Knight (trans.) (New York).
Werverke, H. van (CEHE, 1963) 'The Rise of the Towns.'
White, Lynn (1962) *Medieval Technology and Social Change* (Oxford).

13 The Transformation of Agrarian Society*

The familiar differences between Greenwich Village in 1974 and, say, Warren, Illinois (pop. 3000), where my grandparents farmed, in 1874, are not only those between rural and urban societies, nor are they summarized by the distinction between the 20th and the 19th century or between one level and distribution of prosperity and another. Warren in 1874, more like Greenwich Village in 1774 than itself today, represents one kind of economy; Greenwich Village today and Warren today, represent another. This difference in kind is not explained by technological changes, nor by levels of prosperity, nor even by distinctive property systems, though all are relevant. Warren in 1874 was (embryonically) capitalist but still bore the trappings and in many ways behaved like earlier forms of society. Property relations, we shall see, are fundamental – but not by themselves capable of defining the difference between a settled, traditional and largely static society, and an expanding, technologically dynamic, business-oriented one.

The problems addressed in this study concern the transformation of traditional society into capitalist society. This is a huge topic, and no study can hope to touch on more than a few of its many complexities. The principal feature of this changeover in Marx's analysis is the formation of the landless and propertyless proletariat, concurrently with the concentration of ownership and control of the means of production in a relatively few hands. Important as this is, it is a different development than those considered here, where the central theme will be the formation of a uniform rate of surplus value in conditions where the labor market is not yet highly developed, and the labor force only imperfectly mobile. Competition in the market is not the only form of pressure that can determine the pattern of exchange and distribution. But with the growth of the market, market relationships erode and displace older arrangements governing work and distribution, thereby providing a basis for the formation of a rudimentary rate of profit, establishing the process of accumulation.

At first, however, the emergence of the market in the stationary conditions of traditional society reinforces, rather than undermines, the dominant pattern of exchange and distribution, based on labor values. In these conditions, produced means of production play the same role as natural endowments, and the market's reflection of scarcity will mirror the assign-

* Written for this volume.

ment of the surplus in proportion to the direct labor expended. But as the institutions of traditional society break down under economic pressures, markets for means of production will form, generating incentives to accumulation. This ushers in a new phase, in which the system begins to work differently, but the pattern of exchange will continue to reflect labor values during a long transition period.

To keep the argument manageable, society will be assumed to be divided into two spheres: Industry and Agriculture, the former located for the most part in towns and cities. Further, only a very simple class structure will be considered. Classes will be defined by their positions in the process of production; there will be lords and serfs (bound to the land) in the countryside, and petty craftsmen or guildsmen in the towns; but I shall also discuss free farmers and capitalist farmers, and the main part of the discussion will concentrate on the familiar simplified society of propertyless wage-laborers, capitalists (both in Agriculture and in Industry) and landlords. The argument will examine and justify the implicit claim of Marx and Engels that the (logical) transformation of values into prices of production, of surplus value into profit, interest and rent, provides an appropriate framework for examining the historical transformation of a largely agrarian static society into an expanding capitalist system. It will come down firmly on the side of those who interpret the labor theory of value 'historically', rather than merely 'analytically'. But it should be clear that there need be no conflict between the two interpretations: the historical transformation implies the logical. The most contentious question has always been the historical validity of the labor theory of value in any period. (Morishima and Catephores, 1978, especially Ch. 7). The challenge has been to show how labor values could be established and maintained through economic pressures. In what follows, we will try to explain this and, as well, issue a challenge of our own – if exchanges in traditional society did not gravitate around labor values, then what did they reflect?

1 THE TRADITIONAL SYSTEM

Traditional society, covering the better part of human history, was not only predominantly agricultural, it was also economically static. Neither profits (as known in capitalism, and in some contemporary versions of socialism) nor investment and growth could be found. Nor was there regular technological innovation. The change therefore has been threefold: from a largely agricultural to a largely industrial, from a non-profit-calculating to a profit-oriented, and from a stationary to a developing economy. But we should not infer, as some have done, that traditional society lacked markets and market incentives, and instead functioned as a 'natural economy.' Some precapitalist societies may have; others definitely did not.

There were many versions of traditional society. Static, agricultural, non-profit-calculating societies have been based on river valleys, on the manorial system, on a frontier with free land (the 19th century Western lands in the USA), on slavery, on a caste system, and on many other foundations. Not all of these were wholly agrarian; Northern Europe in the 15th century had an industrial sector run by a powerful guild system. It also operated in monetary terms. And traditional society need not be literally static: the Western frontier was rapidly expanding and innovative and Medieval Europe underwent dramatic economic and social changes. The point, however, is that these changes were not – or at least not chiefly – endogenous. The frontier did not grow through the savings and investment it generated; both population and funds came from outside. Medieval Europe changed from within, but the changes were not compatible with the system: they brought about the destruction of one form of society and replaced it with another!

Most important, an economic system not based on profit may still have markets, even well developed ones, in which exchanges may be made with an eye to private, monetary gain. Any interdependent production system implies that exchanges must take place between the activities; and such exchanges have often taken place in highly elaborate and fiercely competitive markets. The great fairs and markets of the Middle Ages spring to mind, as do the famous activities of the Phoenicians in the Ancient world. Even where production was primarily locally self-sufficient, there were local markets and, judging from the voluminous accounts of litigation in the manorial records of the Middle Ages, gains and losses in these transactions were calculated pretty finely. But the basis for calculation was not profit on capital – i.e., on total means of production. Gain is not synonymous with profit *on capital*. To put it another way, profit calculations are a special case of calculating gain, a case that depends on a particular institutional structure.[1]

Any productive economic system generates a surplus. When the system is stable and embodied in organized institutions, this surplus will be regular and, God willing and weather permitting, will appear year in and year out. If the system is interdependent, then the process of exchange will also have to be consistent with the assignment of the surplus to certain persons or classes. If the entire product is brought to market (or assigned according to imputed market values) then the struggle for gain will be a struggle for a share of the surplus. Competition in the market will involve moving into areas and channels of trade where gains are the greatest or the easiest to obtain, leaving those where gains are low or difficult or uncertain, making use of political devices and regulation to assure that one's own line of trade gets at least a fair slice of the cake, and so on. But such competition does not depend on figuring gain on the basis of capital – that is, the value of the total means of production advanced. Exchange can be, and for centuries was, carried on for gain, and work and production were performed for the market, without the desired gain being profit on capital. The gain was not profit, and what it was earned in proportion to was not capital.

To understand this, consider that in traditional societies, where the land, buildings and most production facilities are not alienable, which is to say that they cannot be bought and sold by the producers (indeed, the uses to which land and facilities are put often cannot be easily changed at all), gain is rightly and rationally proportioned to the length and intensity of effort, the direct labor time, rather than to the value of the entire means of production. For gain to be figured on the value of the entire means of production, and for such computation to provide a motive to market behavior, the means of production must be alienable property, with the organization of production concentrated in a single institution. Where peasants farm individually, but market collectively, sharing the proceeds as in the German Mark Associations, the value of the entire means of production has no practical significance. Nor does it in the guilds of the towns in the Middle Ages. Instead the competitive market, in conjunction with courts and other institutions, will set up pressures that will tend to equalize the return on the length of labor time (adjusted for intensity of work) required under normal conditions to produce the article and bring it to market.

2 THE LABOR THEORY OF VALUE

We had better examine this more closely, first looking at the labor theory of value, then at the way institutions channel competitive pressures. I shall use a variant of a familiar notation in which lower-case letters stand for inputs and variables associated with urban industry, and capitals stand for those concerned with agriculture. Urban industry is not highly advanced. Capitalists, when they enter the model, will earn and reinvest profits, which they compute on the entire sum of their advances, including their wage bill. Products of urban industry – 'manufacture properly so-called' in Marx's term – include cloth, tools, equipment, weapons, clocks, early machinery and so on. I shall assume that urban industry produces a composite input good, 'machines,' whose components are always used in the same proportions, and similarly that agriculture produces a composite consumption good, 'corn,' again always consumed in the same proportions. We can thus write the input–output matrix

$$\begin{matrix} a & b \\ A & B \end{matrix}$$

where the top row shows 'machine' and 'corn' (labor support) inputs into machine production, and the bottom row machine and corn inputs into corn.

b and B represent corn needed to support the requisite number of laborers at the established subsistence level for one year. a and A, however, represent the required machinery which presumably lasts for more than one year. Hence we should figure annual depreciation. For simplicity, however, I shall use a circulating capital model, which can easily be adjusted for a common depreciation rate in both industry and agriculture; r and g, when we come to them, will be the net rates of profit and growth, and w will be the gross (subsistence plus net) wage rate (a pure number – e.g., 120%). W_m, the maximum wage, will be the rate of surplus value, and $\hat{w}$ the net wage. The corresponding dual variables, standing for consumption, are c_m and C, with p for the price ratio of machines in terms of corn, and v the corresponding ratio of the labor values of machines to corn. The output ratio of machines to corn will be X. Finally, ϱ is the level of absolute rent per unit of land.[2]

To carry on the argument we must first look at the labor theory of value. The simplest statement of it is perhaps also the most generally applicable: the labor value of a unit of a commodity is the sum of the labor directly and indirectly embodied in it. This formulation has the advantage that it can be derived immediately from the matrix of coefficients, without our even knowing how productive the matrix is. Using the notation above, and adding that L_i will stand for the direct and indirect labor embodied in i = Industry or Agriculture respectively:

$$L_I = aL_I + b \tag{13.1}$$

$$L_A = AL_I + B \text{ and} \tag{13.2}$$

$$L_I/L_A = v = b \,/\, [Ab + B(1 - a)] \tag{13.3}$$

It is easy to see that this is the same exchange ratio that will prevail under an equal rate of surplus value in the two sectors:

$$v = av + W_mB \tag{13.4}$$

$$1 = Av + W_mB \tag{13.5}$$

Solving, we have:

$$v = b \,/\, [Ab + B(1 - a)] \text{ and } W_m = (1 - a) \,/\, [Ab + B(1 - a)] \tag{13.6}$$

The dual showing consumption and replacement, is:

$$X = aX + Ac_m$$

$$1 = bX + Bc_m$$

Clearly,

$$c_m = Wm$$

and

$$X = A / [Ab + B(1 - a)]; \text{ hence}$$

$$v = (b/A)X \tag{13.10}$$

Under relatively primitive conditions labor values are readily calculated and widely understood. According to Engels, 'the peasant of the Middle Ages knew fairly accurately the labour-time required for the manufacture of the articles obtained by him . . . The smith and the cart-wright of the village worked under his eyes; likewise the tailor and shoemaker . . . The peasants, as well as the people from whom they bought, were themselves workers . . . The same holds good for exchange between peasant products and those of the urban artisans . . . At the beginning . . . not only does the peasant know the artisan's working conditions, but the latter knows those of the peasant as well . . . People in the Middle Ages were thus able to check up with considerable accuracy on each other's production costs for raw material, auxiliary material, and labour-time.' In the same passage Engels concludes: 'Not only was the labour-time spent on these products the suitable measure for the quantitative determination of the values to be exchanged; no other was at all possible. Or is it believed that the peasant and the artisan were so stupid as to give up the product of ten hours' labour of one person for that of a single hour's labour of another?' The argument is cogent. Under primitive conditions the production of many items in daily use is vertically integrated to a high degree – division of labor having not yet taken place to a high degree – and the total labor time required is widely known. Direct and indirect labor requirements could be readily understood and[3] easily calculated to good approximations. To effect exchange on any other basis would imply someone's giving up more labor-time that he received in return, a manifestly unfair bargain. And what alternative rule could have governed exchanges? (Markets were not developed enough for supply and demand to work through market-clearing – and labor markets did not exist at all, in the modern sense.) Or is it argued that there was no general rule, so that exchanges were by nature irregular and chaotic? But manorial records show a high degree of regularity, and writings of the time indicate that people had a strong sense of normal and fair values: indeed, the latter received a good deal of attention from the Church.

But rude and primitive conditions are not really to the point: capitalism developed out of a much more sophisticated society, in which there existed a well-oiled monetary system, widespread trading, and an elaborate division of labor. It is here that the implications of the equivalence established above can be seen. For if there are market mechanisms and/or other pressures tending to establish a uniform rate of surplus value in this more elaborate system, exchanges will continue to take place at rates representing ratios of labor value. This conclusion does not depend in any way upon who gets the surplus value; it may go as earnings to master craftsmen, or as wages to apprentices, or it may be appropriated by the nobility, the State and the Church in the form of *per capita* labor services or rents, taxes, and tithes. But so long as distribution takes place through a *per capita* rate of surplus value, the same in all sectors, exchange rates – relative prices – will be ratios of labor values.

This conclusion will not be disturbed by the development of new methods of farming or of production of goods. For the best technique will be the one yielding the highest rate of surplus value, and so long as the choice is made upon this basis, the labor theory of value will continue to hold.

To repeat an earlier point, in traditional society there is no reason for profit calculation. There are no capital markets in the precapitalist world; indeed there is no alienable property, as we know it. One guild or nobleman cannot buy out another, or enter a take-over bid. Journeymen, day-laborers, can move from one place to another, which would tend to keep the earnings within a trade or craft uniform within a region. But means of production – capital – cannot be shifted from one line of activity to another. Hence there is no pressure to form a uniform rate of profit. Nor does a rate of profit make sense in a social system without property in the means of production. If there is neither a single agency controlling the entire process for its own benefit, nor the means of shifting the resources so controlled into other activities, what point would there be to computing rates of profit?[4] What would there be for competition to act on?

3 A DIFFERENT TRADITIONAL SYSTEM

Now consider (in an idealized version) virtually the opposite of the European land tenure system – the Western frontier. In Europe, '*nulle terre sans seigneur*'; on the frontier rich prairie land is almost free (a one-time lump sum payment equal to a few weeks' wages in the Eastern cities buys enough land to raise a family comfortably). Laborers migrate and take land; carpenters, craftsmen, blacksmiths, shopkeepers follow. A minimum standard of income is set by the surplus that can be earned by the least skilled effort and time in farming, on the poorest land; for if the prices commanded by farm products do not support the least competent, worst placed farmers, they will disappear, and farm output will decline accordingly. This level of income will also set a standard for wages in the East, since workers paid less will have an incentive to uproot and move West. Farmers settle where the return on their effort and time is highest; craftsmen ply their trade rather than farm only if the return on time and effort is comparable. A shopkeeper or craftsman will not be motivated by profit on capital; the question is whether they could obtain a better return on their labor-time in farming than by plying their crafts; if so, it would make sense to switch to farming. Self-employed businessmen are not capitalists; capitalism requires the employment of others. It is also important that the self-employed artisan (like the farmer) owns tools and means of production that are specific to his trade, but non-specific within it. To move to a new area or new line within a trade is easy; but to move outside the craft is much more difficult – unless it is to farming, where there are no trade secrets and the skills are widely disseminated. Thus only the return to direct labor matters when it comes to practical decisions about what lines to concentrate in.

In farming (and other seasonal work) much the same is true, but for an additional, perhaps deeper reason. The self-employed farmer must raise enough to support himself and his family the year round, but he will work full-time at farming only part of the year. In the off season, in his fallow time, he will do his farm maintenance, construction, tool making, fencing and ditching, and the like. For the most part this work again is overhead; it is non-specific, draws on generally available skills, and does not, and should not, enter into his decisions about the mix of crops, time to slaughter and so on, which will be determined by earnings to direct labor.

Fallow time has another implication. If the fallow time is sufficient for the manufacture of implements and construction of buildings, as in a fairly primitive economy, then the rate of surplus value also shows the maximum rate of expansion (through immigration, or over a longer period through population growth) of both the labor employed and net output. Non-capitalist expansion is certainly possible, though only under special conditions.

A negligible overhead payment, and a good deal of overhead work, will put a healthy worker in a position to support himself and his family by farming; a skilled craftsman would have to do better in terms of direct earnings to justify plying his trade (to say nothing of the time spent learning it!). The earnings to direct labor thus govern choices, and the return to farming sets the standard other trades must match. The goods produced by each trade will then exchange in terms that reflect the value of the labor that is required to produce them directly, added on to the value of the other goods used up in production – which, of course, is indirect labor. But in a frontier economy, where land is free, neither prices nor the earnings that motivate production and allocation decisions will be based on the calculation of profit on investment capital. For if new land is (virtually) free the value of existing land will reflect only clearing and improvements. We have an example of what Marx called 'simple commodity production.'

4 CONFLICT WITH THE CONVENTIONAL WISDOM

Simple and sensible as these essentially institutional observations are, they contrast sharply with the conventional wisdom of both supporters and critics of Marx. The standard view holds simply that the labor theory of value is wrong; it is irrational in a competitive market and could not except by accident provide an accurate description of actual prices. It is argued that Marx was well aware of its shortcomings, and never intended its assumption that commodities exchanged at labor values to be taken as 'realistic;' on the contrary, it was adopted for heuristic purposes only. In precapitalist societies the labor market would be insufficiently developed to permit the reduction of skilled labor to simple labor, or to form a uniform rate of surplus value. In the absence of a labor market, goods markets cannot be fully formed, and without developed markets there will be no pressures to form uniform, normal prices. But as markets develop with the emergence of capitalism a rate of profit will be formed, and prices will reflect this. Hence labor values can never appear in practice. Both critics and many defenders of Marx agree that the labor theory of value is useless as an instrument for analyzing actual exchange relationships.

Such agreement is surprising both in the light of what Marx and Engels actually said, and in view of the fact that many of the institutional arrangements just discussed are still widely prevalent today. Inadequate markets clearly do not prevent the formation of 'normal' prices. Moreover, even contemporary input–output studies show that labor values are a good approximation to actual prices (Ochoa, 1984; Val'tukh, 1987). Yet the conventional wisdom should not be lightly dismissed, and it focusses its critique on the rate of surplus value, which is held to be inconsistent with competitive pressures. The case for the historical validity of the labor theory of value must therefore show in detail that it does make sense to suppose that a uniform rate of surplus value could be established in a precapitalist economy that lacks a fully developed labor market. The argument will draw on the example of 14th century Northern Europe (Cf. Ch. 12).

5 A MANORIAL ECONOMY

Suppose that we are analyzing a country district which has no contact with the outside world, composed of a limited number of large manors, each presided over by a noble and his military retinue, and worked by a large number of peasants. Each noble in turn owes military services in the form of armed horsemen for a period of time and dues in grain or money to a higher lord, up to the highest noble of the region, who owes similar services and dues to the crown. Obligations are set on a capitation basis at every level; a tithe – a ten% *per capita* tax – likewise supports the Church. The military forces provide the region's protection from invaders and bandits; the payments of grain and/or money support the local judiciary and administration, including the manorial households and workshops, which performed domestic crafts – sewing, making butter and preserves, butchering and curing meats, milling and baking, tanning and leather work, etc. We shall first explain the sense in which the countryside is self-sufficient, then examine the economic relationships involved in the manorial economy, and finally consider the trade between the countryside and town.

It is oversimplified to say that each manor or villa is itself self-sufficient, but true that the countryside as a whole is self-sufficient: individual manors can specialize to a greater or less degree. This is important because specialization both increases productivity and requires trade; but such trade all takes place within the 'natural economy.' The consumption goods required by towns can be produced in the required proportions if specialization is carried out appropriately. We can thus treat the agricultural sector as a unit producing a single composite consumption good (consumed by peasants, retainers and towns folk), made up of the various individual items in the appropriate proportions. This good represents the surplus produced by the countryside above its own needs, including seed and the replacement of tools, materials, etc.

Now consider how the manor produces its surplus. In the manorial system land is divided between peasant holdings and the demesne. The peasant supports himself and his family out of the earnings from the sale of the produce of his holding. From his status at birth – which is to say, independently of his particular holding – he owes his lord a certain amount of time working the demesne land. This time will be set so that the lord's lands can be worked effectively. The rest of the time the peasant will spend working his holding to support himself and his family. Only as much land will be distributed to peasants, and only as much time will be left them, as is needed for them to produce their own subsistence. Hence, for the moment assuming all land to be of equal quality, both the ratio of demesne land to peasant holdings and the ratio of time owed in labor services to time working peasant holdings will equal the ratio of the total surplus composite consumption good to the amount required to support the peasantry of the district. It is easy to see this when every manor is fully self-sufficient and produces the composite consumption good on its own demesne. But specialization changes nothing essential; it merely regroups the various processes so they can be operated more efficiently. Hence every manor will demand labor services in the same ratio – the ratio of non-peasant consumption of the district to total peasant consumption – which I shall therefore call the 'feudal rent ratio.' Even when the various manors of a district are fully specialized this ratio can be determined independently of prices, since it is a ratio of quantities of the composite consumption good, and so depends only on the various coefficients.

Given the feudal rent ratio the relationships of prices and quantities can be determined. Since the methods of production are given, quantities follow from the assumption that the net output is to consist of the composite consumption good, for this determines the allocation of resources to the various branches of the natural economy. Prices also follow, and since the technology is relatively primitive, there will be no economies of scale, and coefficients will be fixed.[5] So prices will remain unchanged by the shifting of resources from one line of production to another; this holds true of the feudal rent ratio as well. Even when the surplus does not consist of the composite consumption good the ratio of the value of the surplus to the value of the consumption goods required by the natural economy will be the feudal rent ratio. Hence whatever the composition of the surplus produced for the support of the feudal establishment and for trade with towns, all economic relations in the natural economy will be determinate.

The meaning of the feudal rent ratio is simply this: on land of equal quality exchange between specialized or partly specialized manors will take place at prices such that the value of the demesne produce accruing to every lord stands in the same proportion to the amount of labor producing it: in other words, the productivity of labor is the same on every manor, as would necessarily be the case if each manor produced the composite consumption good. This implies, of course, that exchanges take place, records are kept, and tithes and taxes paid, in terms of prices which equal ratios of direct and indirect embodied labor. The labor theory of value holds.

6 THE QUESTION OF MARKETS

To the modern mind, this may seem impossible. Markets of all kinds were poorly developed, and with the great majority of the population bound to the land, there were no labor markets at all in the modern sense. How, then, could prices be established and maintained? How could equal rent ratios on different manors be enforced? If the peasantry had been free to move, manors would have had to bid for workers, offering packages of land parcels and rights to retain crops (real wages) in return for obligations – labor services and dues – so that the resulting bidding and shifting of workers would have tended to establish a uniform ratio of real wages to obligations to perform labor services, (i.e., a uniform rate of surplus value). Moreover, competition between lords would require them to put downward pressure on real wages, tending to force them to a common level – that which will support the socially defined norm of household life for the rural worker. Markets and competition could thus provide pressures that would have defined equilibrium levels and kept prices, wages and earnings close to those levels. But how could this be done in the absence of adequately developed markets? For markets were not adequately developed, and when they did develop, markets for land and means of production emerged at the same time – which led to the formation of a rate of profit, rather than a rate of surplus value.

Markets are not the only institutional forms able to generate economic pressures, however – even if they are, so far, the most systematic and effective. The Medieval world depended on another system, the courts of law, ecclesiastical and civil, which functioned to enforce, and keep within proper bounds, the obligations and duties required by the system's hierarchical relationships. The Church thought in terms of the good of the system as a whole – the Just Price was that 'price which enables the seller just to keep up that household which his state of life, whatever it may be, does on the average require' (Coulton, 1945, 332). The civil courts varied in different countries and different eras, but always had to moderate the demands of the powerful in the light of the need to retain the allegiance of the weak. Serfs resisting additional demands of their lord appealed to a court presided over by the lord's bailiff – but were represented in this court by the reeve, elected by the village. Some issues could be appealed to higher courts; freemen could take their cases to the king's Court, and cases were settled in the light of tradition and custom. The courts had a double interest: they had to ensure that the vassals of the higher nobility were able to meet their obligations, which meant that the serfs had to provide enough services and dues to support the vassals. But at the same time the serfs could not be so overloaded that they became rebellious or engaged in systematic shirking or sabotage. The higher nobility had a double interest also: they wanted their vassals to be prosperous enough to meet their obligations, but not so prosperous as to become powerful enough to mount a challenge to their overlords. Nor should any single vassal become so prosperous as to outshine the rest. The Crown, like the Church, had a long-term interest in protecting the weakest, the serfs and free laborers, both because it was their labor on which the system ultimately rested, and because an alliance of King and commoner weakened the base of any nobles powerful enough to present a potential challenge to the Throne.

Church doctrine, tradition and social pressure, and the decisions of the courts thus tended to establish prices such as to just permit the earnings that would provide a household with a standard of living appropriate to the average of its station. Feudal obligations, both in towns and in the countryside, were *per capita* payments, and these were set according to station at birth, and adjudicated and enforced in the courts. Everyone had to pay equally according to his or her station. Wages and incomes were thus set according to custom at a socially defined subsistence, graded by social rank, higher ranks being 'worth' more than lower, and the surplus was paid to the higher ranks at a uniform *per capita* rate by the lower. Hence a uniform rate of surplus value tended to prevail (insofar as actual conditions approached the ideal), enforced by the court system, which, assisted by custom and tradition, also evaluated the relative worth of different occupations and stations in life. Finally, insofar as labor mobility did exist, it would also work to even out differences in rates of exploitation; and even rudimentary markets would tend to establish prices that gravitated around the long-term costs of production, which in these circumstances would be direct and indirect labor costs.

7 SOCIAL DIFFERENTIATION WITHIN CLASSES

Earlier we assumed that land was all of the same quality. Of course, it is not, and this benefits the peasant. Typically the best land will be taken for the demesne. But the peasantry cannot be pushed below subsistence. Consider now the peasant on the poorest land; he will have to work the longest to maintain himself and his family, so he will have the least time available to work for his lord. (Either he will have to farm a similar acreage more intensively than others or, the land being poorer, he will require more of it, in which case the larger area to be covered means more time will be needed for plowing, seeding, harvesting, etc.) But common justice and the requirements of administration imply that all peasants should be treated alike, for they owe services in virtue of their condition as serfs, not because they have a particular holding. Hence, when the quality of land varies the feudal rent ratio will be determined on the land of poorest quality that still remains in cultivation, and the peasants on 'intramarginal' land will earn 'differential rents.' Over time, as particular plots become attached by tradition to certain families, social differentiation develops within the peasantry.

8 A SIMPLE MODEL

The argument will be clearer if put formally. Suppose there are n commodities produced on the manor, each by a single process involving labor and some, at least, of the other goods (as seed or tools, etc.). Further, suppose that as much or more of every good is produced than is consumed during one year, and that more is produced of at least one. Some subset of these n goods, in certain given proportions, constitutes the 'composite consumption good,' denoted by C. The system of production can then be written:

$$\frac{\begin{array}{l} c_{11} \mathbin{\&} c_{12} \mathbin{\&} \ldots \mathbin{\&} c_{1n} \mathbin{\&} C_1 \rightarrow c_1 \\ c_{21} \mathbin{\&} c_{22} \mathbin{\&} \ldots \mathbin{\&} c_{2n} \mathbin{\&} C_2 \rightarrow c_2 \end{array}}{c_{n1} \mathbin{\&} c_{n2} \mathbin{\&} \ldots \mathbin{\&} c_{nn} \mathbin{\&} C_n \rightarrow c_n} \tag{13.11}$$

where c_{ij} stands for the amount of the jth good used as input in the ith process, and C_i stands for the amount of the composite consumption good needed to support the labor used by the ith process.

Since the population is taken initially as given we can compute the total amount of the composite consumption good required to support the manorial economy for one year. Let us express this by the expression, $\Sigma C_i = 1$. To find the productivity of labor in this economy we subtract from the amount of each good produced the total amount of it consumed or used up in production during the year – that is, from the quantity produced we subtract the quantity used either as input or as subsistence to make that production possible. In the formulas above, the cs are the coefficients; to find the net product we need, in addition, the quantities, q_i. Then,

$$q_1c_1 - \Sigma\, q_ic_{i1},\ q_2c_2 - \Sigma\, q_ic_{i2},\ \ldots,\ q_nc_n - \Sigma\, q_ic_{in} \tag{13.12}$$

(where the amount of the jth good in C_i, the composite subsistence good, is understood to be included in the amount of the jth good used as input).

This set of goods will include many or all of the same goods that figure in C, but they generally will not appear in the same proportions. However, it is possible to find a particular set of quantity multipliers, q_i which, applied to the original table, will so readjust it that, while using the same amount of labor [$\text{sum}_i\ C_i = 1$], the system will produce a net product consisting of the composite consumption good.

$$\frac{\begin{array}{l} [q_1c_{11} + q_2c_{21} + \ldots + q_nc_{n1}] + (1 + F)q_1C_1 = q_1c_1 \\ [q_1c_{12} + q_2c_{22} + \ldots + q_nc_{n2}] + (1 + F)q_2C_2 = q_2c_2 \end{array}}{[q_1c_{1n} + q_2c_{2n} + \ldots + q_nc_{nn}] + (1 + F)q_nC_n = q_nc_n} \tag{13.13A}$$

The productivity of labor in this economy, or the 'feudal rent ratio,' will then be a ratio of quantities, and can be determined independently of prices.[6] Writing 'Σ' for 'sum,' the formula for the ratio will be,

$$F = [q_1c_1 - \Sigma q_ic_{i1},\ q_2c_2 - \Sigma q_ic_{i2},\ \ldots,\ q_nc_n - \Sigma q_ic_{in}] \,/\, \Sigma q_iC_i$$

Given this ratio prices can be determined:

$$c_{11}p_i + c_{12}p_2 + \ldots + c_{1n}p_n + (1 + F)C_1p_c = c_1p_1$$

$$\begin{array}{c} c_{21}p_1 + c_{22}p_2 + \ldots + c_{2n}p_n + (1 + F)C_2p_2 = c_2p_2 \\ \hline c_{n1}p_1 + c_{n2}p_2 + \ldots + c_{nn}p_n + (1 + F)C_np_c = c_np_n \end{array} \qquad (13.13B)$$

(There are n prices of the n goods, and since C is a composite good its price, p_c, is simply the set of the prices of the individual components of C.) When the equations are in the q proportions both sides contain the same quantities in the aggregate. Hence one of the equations can be inferred from the rest, and a solution can be found in which the various prices can be expressed in terms of one of their number. But whatever the proportions the solutions are the same. F may appear as a ratio of quantities in the q-proportions, but in all other proportions the ratio of the value of the net output to the value of the total composite consumption will be F, and prices likewise will be the same. The prices are designated by the symbol 'p', but it can easily be seen that they are ratios of labor values, since they establish a uniform ratio of the value of the surplus to the direct labor (measured by the subsistence supporting it) in each process, thus making them equivalent to the ratio 'v' examined earlier.[7]

9 TOWNS AND TRADE

Now let us examine first the towns and then the trade between town and countryside. From our point of view it does not matter how or why towns began, but one cause of their origin is easy to see. In a district in which manors specialize and trade with one another, it is cheaper in terms of transport costs for everyone to take their goods to a central market, returning with their purchases, than for them to travel to one another to engage directly in trade. District market towns will therefore develop to economize on the transport costs required by the trade resulting from the specialization of manors. The land for such towns and the initial support for the founding population during the construction and early stages will be provided by a nobleman who, in return, will receive dues from the market and from the administration of justice.

Such towns will do more than provide a market; the surplus accruing to the nobility can be transformed into something more useful and more attractive. Trade with distant parts can turn it into silks and spices; local manufacture can turn it into finely woven cloth. The towns will therefore produce luxuries for the nobility (and for those peasants whose better land yields them a differential earning), the countryside supplying it with the composite consumption good and any other materials, etc. required for manufacture or trade. Some goods will be produced wholly for use within towns; their quantities and prices will be determined exactly as the quantities and prices of their counterparts in the countryside were.

Suppose there are *m* town goods, some used only in the production of town goods, others exported to the countryside. The demand pattern of the countryside is known, so the system will be adjusted to produce the appropriate surplus for export. Assume the t's are so defined. The equations are:

$$\begin{aligned} t_{11}p_1 + t_{12}p_2 + \ldots + t_{1m}p_m + C_1e &= t_1p_1 \\ t_{21}p_1 + t_{22}p_2 + \ldots + t_{2m}p_m + C_2e &= t_2p_2 \\ \hline t_{m1}p_1 + t_{m2}p_2 + \ldots + t_{mm}p_m + C_me &= t_mp_m \end{aligned} \tag{13.14}$$

Here *e* stands for the exchange ratio of urban and rural goods, the price of *C* in terms of town goods, or the terms of trade between town and countryside. Once *e* is determined, the rest of the system follows as above.

Since the towns receive their consumption goods and raw materials from the countryside, they are in a dependent position; but what they produce is a luxury, which the countryside can do without. The towns cannot compel the countryside to sell to them; if the countryside chooses to hold out, the towns will starve. Nor have they any alternative to buying from the countryside; towns cannot acquire land, for land is not alienable in a feudal system, nor can they look elsewhere for sources of supply, for wherever they look they will find a feudal countryside which does not depend upon urban products. The countryside, for its part, can (at some cost) store its products, use them to support larger military establishments, or ship them to another town not disposed to hold out for higher prices. In extreme cases of conflict, the nobility might be tempted to found a competing trading center.

In the long run, therefore, the terms of trade will strongly tend to favor the nobility. Agricultural prices will tend to be high in terms of town products, and will tend to rise as the productivity of towns increases. However, increases in agricultural productivity, instead of lowering agricultural prices (raising the prices of town goods), will lead to an increase in the town population, and a corresponding expansion of urban production. (Assuming town goods to be in demand, this would be preceded by a temporary rise in urban prices, attracting the marginal or surplus peasantry.)

Within the town, there will normally be a number of different establishments producing fine cloth and luxuries, some of which will be more productive than others. But competition will tend to establish a uniform price of urban goods in terms of the composite consumption good, and this price will have to be high enough to permit the least productive establishment to survive. When trade between towns develops, so that arbitrage between different markets becomes possible, the price must settle at the level where the least productive establishment in the most backward town can just survive. All 'intra-marginal' establishments thus will earn quasi-rents from their superior productivity. In this way a well-to-do class can emerge in the towns.

Initially the size of towns will be determined by the size of the rural food surplus (given the lords' demand for urban luxury goods), and the entire urban surplus will go to the feudal lords. Define 'e' as the fraction, y, of the urban surplus that trades for the rural surplus. When $y = 1$, towns will be in a purely dependent position. But as they develop, towns will become able to retain a portion of their surplus, pushing $y < 1$

$$e = y[\text{urban surplus}]/\text{rural surplus} \tag{13.15}$$

Under these circumstances the set of equations for the urban sector will in the aggregate contain the same quantities on both sides, so that one price can be taken as the standard and the rest expressed in terms of it. Again it can be shown that these equations always have one and only one all-positive solution.[8]

10 DEPENDENCY AND DIFFERENTIAL EARNINGS

When urban and rural industry become interdependent rurally produced goods not entering into C will gradually be dropped in favor of more sophisticated, better-made town goods. Suppose that c_1 is such a good, and that t_1 is the corresponding (perhaps composite) town good replacing it. The equations for the rural sector then become:

$$\begin{array}{l} t_{21}(1/e) + c_{22}p_2 + \ldots + c_{2n}p_n + (1 + F')\, c_2 p_c = c_2 p_2 \\ \hline t_{n1}(1/e) + c_{n2}p_2 + \ldots + c_{nn}p_n + (1 + F')\, c_n p_c = c_n p_n \end{array} \tag{13.16}$$

Note the important implication here that town goods vary as a block against 'corn' – i.e., against the composite output of the rural sector – even though only a few town goods enter directly into production in the countryside. Suppose one product used in the countryside came to command more corn in relation to its labor value than other urban goods; since town goods are used directly and indirectly in each other's production, other producers would attempt to raise their prices to the producers of the favored good, refusing to provide supply unless allowed to share in the gain. To avoid such struggles, dividing the town against itself, the aldermen who control access to the marketplace will try to set prices to the advantage of the town as a whole. Once the countryside becomes seriously dependent on even a single major urban product, this will gradually be translated into a general improvement in the ability of urban goods to command corn.

In equation (13.6) F' is the new potential feudal rent ratio, made possible by the higher productivity of agriculture once town-made tools have replaced rural inputs. But the actual ratio will be the same as before, since urban goods will rise in price, so that the benefit of the increased productivity will accrue to the towns, in the form of a rate of surplus value, s, earned by the guilds. This will come through the adjustment of e, the exchange rate between town and country goods, as a result of pressure exerted by the towns, pushing y below unity. The new equations will be,

$$\begin{aligned} t_{11}p_1 + t_{12}p_2 + \ldots + t_{1m}p_m + (1 + s)C_1e' &= t_1p_1 \\ t_{21}p_1 + t_{22}p_2 + \ldots + t_{2m}p_m + (1 + s)C_2e' &= t_2p_2 \\ \hline t_{m1}p_1 + t_{m2}p_2 + \ldots + t_{mm}p_m + (1 + s)C_me' &= t_mp_m \end{aligned} \tag{13.17}$$

Here $e' < e$, and s is the ratio of net earnings to labor, the rate of surplus value in the towns. Producers in the countryside introduced town-made goods in the expectation that their superior productivity would raise the feudal rent ratio, so that $F' > F$; the increased bargaining power of townsmen will lower e, but it cannot fall below the level at which $F' = F$. If this were to happen, the countryside would shift back to the old methods. Hence the earning rate of the towns, s, will be limited by the ability of town goods to enhance productivity in the manorial economy:

$$s = (F' - F)[\Sigma\, C_r]/[\Sigma\, C_u] \tag{13.18}$$

That is, s equals the difference between the productivity of labor using town goods and its productivity without them, multiplied by the ratio of total rural subsistence to total urban subsistence. Assuming townsmen to push their bargaining advantages[9] s will rise to this level. When the quality of urban goods has improved and the cost of a change back to the older methods has become prohibitive, e can fall to a point where F', the actual feudal income, lies below F. In such a case F' must be substituted for F in the equation for s (13.18).

This adjustment will go one step further when the prolonged use of town-made goods has resulted in the loss of the corresponding skills in rural areas. Then it will no longer be possible to return to the old ways; at this point town goods will rise still further in price, until $s = F'$ (i.e., until a common rate of surplus value is established throughout the system).

The incentives to develop technology in ways that undermined the feudal nobility arose in the first place from the position of towns under the conditions that Bloch termed 'the feudal disintegration of the state'. In the Ancient World the state could guarantee the supply of grain and foodstuffs to the towns. But in the Middle Ages the towns had to depend on the market for their supplies; they had to earn their subsistence through trade. Hence to ensure a steady supply, in good times and bad, they needed to have the countryside as dependent on them as they were on it.

Differential earnings become possible when competition establishes uniform prices and a uniform ratio of net earnings to labor, and there is some element or factor entering into production which varies in quality but is not itself produced. In the rural economy land is such a factor. Let L_1 stand for the different qualities of land, and @ for the corresponding differential earnings, which as we have seen, will go to the peasantry. Then

$$\begin{aligned} \varrho_1 L_1 + c_{11}p_1 + \ldots + c_{1n}p_n + (1 + F)C_1 p_c &= c_1 p_1 \\ \varrho_2 L_2 + c_{21}p_1 + \ldots + c_{2n}p_n + (1 + F)C_2 p_c &= c_2 p_2 \\ \hline \varrho_n L_n + c_{n1}p_1 + \ldots + c_{nn}p_n + (1 + F)C_n p_c &= c_n p_n \end{aligned} \tag{13.19}$$

Prices and the feudal rent ratio are determined on marginal or 'no rent' land; this is expressed by the condition that one of the differential rents be 0, i.e.:

$$\varrho_1 \, \varrho_2 \ldots \varrho_n = 0 \tag{13.20}$$

The same formal mechanism can be applied to towns, where the nonproduced factor might be location in relation to the market, access to water power of varying strength and reliability, or some other positional factor. (There is no reason to suppose that only one such factor exists.)

Initially these differential earnings will accrue to the peasantry and the artisans respectively. But with the development of interdependence between the sectors an important shift in the pattern of distribution takes place. As *e* falls, the nobility will attempt to maintain their position by commuting services for rents, and attaching the rents to particular holdings rather than requiring them on the basis of status. This makes it possible for the lords to pick up the differentials, but it also frees the serfs from attachment to the land by birth, making their relation to their lords contractual. They are therefore able to migrate to the towns where artisan earnings are available. To retain their peasants, lords will therefore be obliged to pay wages or permit earnings comparable to artisan wages and earnings. In general, lords will need labor in proportion to the land they control, and however high labor's earnings may be, some rent is better than none. Lords will therefore bid against each other and against towns to have their holdings worked, up to the point where the only land available cannot provide rent. Thus when labor is free and mobile, the peasantry will tend to (or threaten to) migrate to the towns, leading to a bidding up of wages and earnings in the countryside until these are equal to those of artisans in the towns, which in time will leave the former feudal lords reduced to the status of landlords, able to obtain only differential rents. But the result will be gradually to establish a uniform rate of surplus value throughout the entire economic system – now paid in money rather than in kind; as this happens, wages in the countryside will come to reflect artisan earnings in the towns, and the terms received by lords will be squeezed to the minimum, as the prices of agricultural products fall relative to urban goods.

11 THE FORMATION OF A RATE OF PROFIT

Under the conditions of traditional society, then, feudal institutions, particularly courts, and a rudimentary market system will tend to enforce a uniform rate of surplus value. But over time the growth and integration of the market will have an unsettling effect on these institutional arrangements: for the wider the market the more complex and varied the information required, and therefore the more significant the position of those who have ready access to it. Merchants and guilds standing at the end of a chain of production (e.g., dyers, as opposed to fullers, spinners and weavers) are granted what amounts almost to a natural monopoly of market information. They are therefore in a position to establish a differential between the price they charge the customer and the price they pay to earlier stages of the production chain. More important, they are in a position to make the earlier stages dependent on them, perhaps even sufficiently dependent to have to borrow materials and even tools from the merchants and masters of the final stages. At this point, it makes sense for merchants and masters to calculate the return they receive from such advances (as shown in the next chapter).

So the monopoly of information by merchants and guilds in final stages leads naturally to calculation of return on advances at the same time that it provides opportunity and means for establishing control over the means of production. Profit calculation emerges, as the old institutional forms break down. No longer is control democratic; instead, workmen receive material to work up, and are paid for their time and effort. Even though craftsmen still own their tools and often their place of business, we can see the beginnings of the wage-labor system.

The next step is to establish full control by collecting the workmen together under one roof, the factory system, where the capitalist owns the place and the tools of production. Such a system enables the master to standardize the product and control its quality, while directly supervising the pace and quality of work. The advantages are by no means confined to scale of operation as that notion is customarily understood. Economies of scale may have existed, although for the most part they are associated with a later stage, in which division of labor is practised, but even without them the factory system is advantageous to the masters because of the control it offers over work.

In the towns, masters fought for control over the guilds, and competed for apprentices and journeymen. An important element in this competition was control over the means and places of production. But obtaining such control was costly, and the costs had to be considered among the advances for production, hence one of the expenses on which returns had to be figured.

The development of profit calculation and the consolidation of control over the means of production in a few hands, for whatever reason it comes about, changes the institutional nature of competition. The competition of workers for earnings gives way to the competition of capitals for profits. Competition for earnings does not set up a tendency to expand, but competition among capitals does.

A similar process took place in the countryside. The struggle of the lords to appropriate the differentials alters the nature of the payment: from an obligation of status it becomes a payment for the right to use a particular plot of land. The land, in turn, becomes the property of the lord, an economic asset, whose value depends on its earning power.

12 COMPETITION, CAPITAL MOBILITY AND THE RATE OF PROFIT

Assume, then, that competition for profit emerges in the towns among the merchants and well-placed guild masters. Economists of all schools argue that with the breakdown of institutional barriers to the mobility of capital – that is, with the development of markets for property and shares in businesses – movement of capital out of low into high profit spheres adjusts prices to form a more or less uniform rate of profit on capital.

Marx (1965) is explicit on this:

> capital withdraws from a sphere with a low rate of profit and invades others, which yield a higher profit. Through this incessant outflow and influx . . . it creates such a ratio of supply to demand that the average profit in the various spheres of production becomes the same, and values are, therefore, converted into prices of production.

The language differs from that of the ordinary neo-Classical textbook describing the 'entry' and 'exit' of firms, but the idea is fundamentally the same. Indeed, modern growth theory can put it much better, for prices of production are the dual variables to the outputs required for balanced growth. The profit motive and the supply and demand price mechanisms will thus transform traditional static markets into capitalist ones, where equilibrium prices reflect the valuations appropriate to an expanding economy.

This simple and traditional picture is flawed. It could not have happened that way, for the good reason that supply and demand will lead to the expansion of the wrong sector. If Agriculture is the relatively labor-intensive sector, as most economists agree it was, and so has the highest surplus value in relation to the value of its means of production, the development of property markets and capital mobility should lead capital to flow from Industry into Agriculture. This will expand the supply of corn and reduce the output of machinery, thus bidding down grain prices relatively to the prices of industrial products. If Agriculture is the relatively labor-intensive sector, then the labor-value of corn will be higher than its price of production, so the movement of capital will tend to adjust the exchange-ratio in the right direction. But the point of profit is accumulation: a capitalist society is an expanding one. Will this movement of capital be compatible with the changeover from a static to an expanding economy? The equations for growth and consumption are:[10]

$$(1 + g)(a + cAQ) = 1 \tag{13.21}$$

$$(1 + g)(b + cBQ) = Q \tag{13.22}$$

from which, eliminating c, we obtain

$$Q = (B/A)[1 - (1 + g)\,a] + (1 + g)b, \text{ and} \tag{13.23}$$

$$dQ/dg = (b - aB/A) < 0 \tag{13.24}$$

That is, the movement of capital into Agriculture, which is supposed to reduce the exchange ratio from value to price of production, raises Q, which tends to reduce g! A move from a static economy to an expanding one requires a reduction in the output of Agriculture and an increase in that of Industry. This disjunction between the requirements of theory and of history does not depend, in fact, on the assumption that Agriculture is the relatively labor-intensive sector. If we assume for simplicity that all profits are invested, then $r = g$, and

$$Q = (b/A)P \tag{13.25}$$

Where P is the price ratio.

When profits are uniform and growth is balanced. Equilibrium Qs and Ps must therefore always vary together. But to alter P by means of supply and demand, capital must move so that the ratio of actual outputs varies *inversely* with Q. A movement of capital which brings the actual price ratio nearer to prices of production will therefore move the actual outputs further from the balanced growth path. In short, it seems that the profit motive and the price mechanism cannot establish a uniform rate of profits, consistently with the investment of profits for the purpose of expansion.

Perhaps we are being too hasty, though. The development of capitalism will bring high productivity growth to Industry. Even with prices remaining fixed at the level of labor values, if its productivity expands enough, Industry could become the high profit sector, even though Agriculture apparently remains the relatively labor-intensive sector. Under these conditions surely capital would be attracted into Industry. This is true, but it will not dispose of the problem; for we now have two grades of labor, more productive Industrial labor and less productive Agricultural labor, with the implication that workers moving from farms to towns will, with training, become more productive. Accordingly we must express Industrial labor in terms of equivalent units of untrained Agricultural labor. With this adjustment, however, Industry will now appear as the labor-intensive sector, consistently with its being the more profitable when prices are fixed at the level of labor values. But according to equations (13.23) and (13.24), when Industry is labor-intensive, a change from a static to an expanding economy requires increasing the relative size of Agriculture: capital should leave Industry and flow into farming! (Cf. Ch. 5, Appendix.)

In short, it seems that the profit motive and the mechanisms of supply and demand cannot establish a uniform rate of profits, consistently with the emergence of an expanding economy. Competition alone cannot form prices of production out of values; the market cannot perform the historical mission economists have assigned it.

13 THE TRANSFORMATION OF SURPLUS VALUE INTO PROFITS

Marx thought that capital movements certainly could transform values into prices of production, but he did not think that they would, for a very important reason: a barrier existed in the form of landed property. The former feudal nobility had turned into proprietors of land, and would not permit capitalist farming without charging a fee for the privilege of making profits on their premises. Marx termed this fee 'Absolute Rent,' and held that its amount depended on the difference between values and prices of production. Capital, in short, could not move freely into Agriculture, and the formation of a rate of profit would be inhibited there by the necessity of paying Absolute Rent.

A reconstruction of this view permits a very simple solution to the transformation problem, which avoids the difficulties just discussed, is compatible with the historical facts, and also leads to an interesting proposition on technical change. A comment of Baumol's provides a good beginning:

> any explanation of pricing as an end in itself was of very little consequence to Marx, for the primary transformation was not from values into prices, but as Marx and Engels repeatedly emphasize, from surplus values into the non-labor income categories that are recognized by the 'vulgar economists', i.e. profits, interest, and rent (1974, p. 52).

Engels in the Preface to Vol. II of *Capital* (1967) (p. 10) refers to moving from 'an understanding of surplus-value in general' to 'an understanding of its transformation into *profit and ground-rent*' (my italics). Baumol claims that the real point is the transformation of the surplus value produced by exploitation into the familiar categories of unearned income. If this is correct there is no reason why surplus value should all be transformed into profit. A transformation into profit *and ground-rent* is also possible.

The exchange ratio between the sectors remains at the traditional level, reflecting labor values. But instead of the surplus value going to workers, or being treated as a *per capita* levy, it is treated as a rate of profit. Wages are paid at the socially determined subsistence level; hence $w = 1$. We have

$$(1 + r)(av + b) = v \tag{13.26}$$

$$(1 + r)(Av + B) = 1 - \varrho, \text{ so that,} \tag{13.27}$$

$$\varrho = (1 - v)(Av + B)/(av + b) \tag{13.28}$$

and for the growth path (assuming all profit invested):

$$(1 + g)(ax + A) = x \tag{13.29}$$

$$(1 + g)(bx + B) = 1 - \varrho, \text{ so that,} \tag{13.30}$$

$$\varrho = (1 - x)(bx + B)/(ax + A)$$

the same as above, since $v = (b/A)x$. Further,

$$r = g = \{1/[a + B(1 - a) + Ab]\} - 1 \tag{13.32}$$

The profit rate and the growth rate are determined wholly in Industry, given the technology and labor values. A rate of profit is formed in Industry,[11] and the same rate will be established by capitalist tenant farmers in Agriculture, with landlords collecting Absolute Rent. ϱ follows from the Agriculture equation (13.28) as a residual. The profit consists of what formerly appeared as the 'net earnings' of workers in industry, $bP(W_m - 1)$, and the investment for growth consists of the machinery, $AQ(c_m - 1)$, formerly required as input for Agriculture, when Agriculture was producing the maximum level of consumption goods. Here, because there is no price change, there is no problem of resources shifting in the wrong direction. The profit rate and the growth rate are formed together, by the shift of earnings from workers (who consume) to capitalists (who invest), and the equivalence of the reduction in consumption and the increase of investment is guaranteed by the duality properties of the labor theory of value. For the actual exchange ratio between Agriculture and Industry remains equal to the ratio of the labor values; hence, even though surplus value is transformed into profit and ground-rent, values are not transformed into prices of production. The market remains in a stable position. This vindicates Marx's assumption, in Vol. I of *Capital* (1967), that actual exchanges and payments under profit-motivated capitalism are consistent with the labor theory of value. Certainly it suggests that we should not so readily concede Samuelson's claim that,

> By now the crucial issue is no longer whether Vol. III's prices are more realistic under competition than Vol. I's values: critics and Marxians are agreed that these prices certainly are (1971, pp. 418–9).

The effects of technical change, particularly in Agriculture, are now clearer. The rate of profit and labor values are connected by the Industry equation; hence

$$dr/dv = b/[av + b]^2 \tag{13.33}$$

On the other hand it is clear from inspection of the labor value system, that L_A varies directly with B/A; and consequently that v varies inversely with the labor-intensity of Agriculture. A fall in B/A will thus increase r and, since r and ϱ are inversely related, it will reduce ϱ. Rent will decline and profits increase in both sectors, when Agriculture is mechanized.

14 RAILROADING SURPLUS VALUE

This result seems to hold only for countries in which an established precapitalist dominant class controls the land. Turning, however, to our example of simple commodity production, something analogous might be found in the relations between the Western frontier and the established metropolitan areas of the Eastern seabord. There is no space to develop the argument here, but the point can be made in a simplified example. We remember that we assumed a frontier with free land. The effect of free land, it was argued, would be to establish a uniform rate of surplus value in the frontier economy. Moreover, it would also destroy Eastern farming, as farmers migrated to the free lands and, by so doing, established a wage rate in the industries of the East equal to the rate of surplus value in Western agriculture, minus the amortized costs of moving. This in turn will tend to establish an exchange ratio between Western farm products and Eastern industrial products based on labor values, leaving profits, apart from differentials, dependent on moving costs, and on supplies of new labor preventing the wage from rising.

Eastern capital has had time to become established, and immigrant labor will have to take what it can get. Surplus value will therefore be appropriated as profit; in the West, as the frontier closes, the earlier settlers will employ the later, paying wages no higher than they need, likewise seeking to appropriate the surplus as profit. But the Western grain has to travel East, and Eastern products West, and this provides the railroad with an opportunity to establish a marketing monopoly, permitting a differential between the price paid to the farmer, and the value at which it is sold in the East. Assume that railroads employ fixed capital T, embodied in tracks and rolling stock; they also require variable capital t, man-hours or working time per unit of output. The higher t, the faster goods will be shipped, and the lower the losses due to spoilage, hence the more competitive the railroad, but against this must be set the higher expense in wage costs.

Let us take the employment per unit shipment, t, as a variable, with the wage set at a socially defined normal level. In both East and West the more successful operators among the self-employed have developed into employers of others. Then, taking the wage as unity, with P_e, the price ratio of agricultural products to industrial in the East, equal to labor values, and given at the outset, the equations are:

$$(d + r)(A) + (1 + r)BP_w = P_w \qquad \text{Western Agric.} \qquad (13.34)$$

$$(d + r)(T) + (1 + r)tP_e = P_e - P_w \qquad \text{Transport} \qquad (13.35)$$

$$(d + r)(a) + (1 + r)bP_e = 1 \qquad \text{Eastern Industry} \qquad (13.36)$$

(Here d is the rate of depreciation of capital equipment, assumed given.) P_e is the labor value ratio; hence the rate of profit is determined by the (Eastern) Industry equation; P_w then follows from the (Western) Agriculture equation, and the amount of worktime per unit shipment in railroads, t, follows from the Transport equation. Here the railroad plays the role of the feudal class, and its earnings are the equivalent of absolute rent.

But P_e will be only a starting point, and t may become determined partly by technology and partly by work-norms. When P_e is variable and t fixed, we still have three equations to determine three unknowns: P_e, P_w, and r; but the solution will not be so straightforward, since it requires a cubic equation in r. Nor will either of the prices necessarily reflect labor values.

15 INNOVATION AND GROWTH

So, under appropriate circumstances, the labor theory of value can correctly describe capitalist market relationships and must be considered indispensible in the analysis of the emergence of capitalism. We have, in fact, met a general challenge issued by Marx:

> To explain, therefore, the general nature of profits, you must start from the theorem that, on an average, commodities are sold at their real values, and that profits are derived from selling them at their values, that is, in proportion to the quantity of labour realized in them. If you cannot explain profit on this supposition, you cannot explain it at all (1965, p. 42).

Yet so far we have discussed only a primitive stage of capitalism, in which the feudal rentier class still retains its strength. This cannot last, for capitalists (both industrial and agricultural) are investing and accumulating, while the landed classes consume. But the investments of the former will raise the rental incomes of the latter, eventually creating a barrier to further accumulation. This Ricardian problem can be solved by innovation, creating new products and new processes. Innovation will make it possible to grow more profitable crops, using less land, thereby reducing the pressure of rents on profit – a point well understood at least since the time of J.S. Mill.

But the issue here is a different one. The introduction of new products will also tend over time to create prices of production, as the older products are phased out. New products will be produced by means of existing products, which will enter the production equations of the new industries at labor value prices. Thus a new industry producing a good, '*n*', will require inputs, including labor, in certain proportions; we can suppose either that existing industries lend a certain fraction of their capital (industries contributing in such a way that the aggregate will result in goods in the correct proportions), or that a similar fraction is contributed from the industries' net investment. The price of the new product will have to be set to earn a rate of profit at least equal to the rate of interest on the loan of the new capital, the components of which, however, will still be valued in terms of embodied labor. Hence this will be a kind of intermediate price of production, a way-station between labor-values and full-fledged prices of production. But as new products replace old, the system will gradually shift towards a competitive capitalist price system, with a uniform rate of profit. (Land will be priced at the capitalized value of its rents, thus becoming simply another form of capital.) But it is innovation more than competition which brings about these changes.

The fact that rates of profit and growth can emerge consistently with relative prices remaining fixed at labor-value ratios has important consequences for technical change. For it creates a significant price incentive to innovate by substituting relatively cheap industrial products for relatively expensive agricultural ones, in short to substitute durable goods and machinery for labor.

The value of a machine is its indirect plus direct labor cost, which can readily be compared to the amount of direct labor the machine can displace in the process of producing a given output. Since the ratio of indirect to direct labor costs is higher in industry than in agriculture, industry's prices of production will be higher than their labor values; a machine capable of doing the job of a certain amount of labor and whose value is equal to that amount of labor will be on the margin of substitution when prices equal values, but will not be introduced under prices of production. Prices being frozen at the level of labor-values encourages mechanization.

It is also possible to sketch a simple and plausible mechanization cycle. When prices are fixed at labor-values, the tradeoff between the wage rate and the profit rate is a straight line, the slope of which measures the ratio of capital to labor. Shifting to more mechanized processes of production can thus be expressed as moving from a shallower to a steeper wage–profit tradeoff line. When prices are not equal to ratios of labor values, wage–profit tradeoffs are not straight lines, and no simple relationships, such as described below, will hold between mechanization, capital-intensity and the rate of profit.

Now suppose that, as a result of growing urbanization, the rate of population increase falls off, so that capital accumulation begins to outpace the growth of the labor force. At this stage in history, the real wage will tend to track movements of the money wage – Keynesian problems are still waiting in the wings. So the labor shortage will tend to raise wages above the normal level, providing a spur to greater mechanization since, as can be seen in Figure 13.1, at a higher than normal wage, the more mechanized technique yields a higher rate of profit. The displaced labor, however, will put a drag on the labor market, pushing down the wage towards the normal level again. The rate of profit will rise, but since the economy is now operating more capital-intensive processes, it will not rise all the way back to its previous level. Eventually, the displaced workers will be absorbed, and growth will accumulate sufficient capital (urbanization will reduce

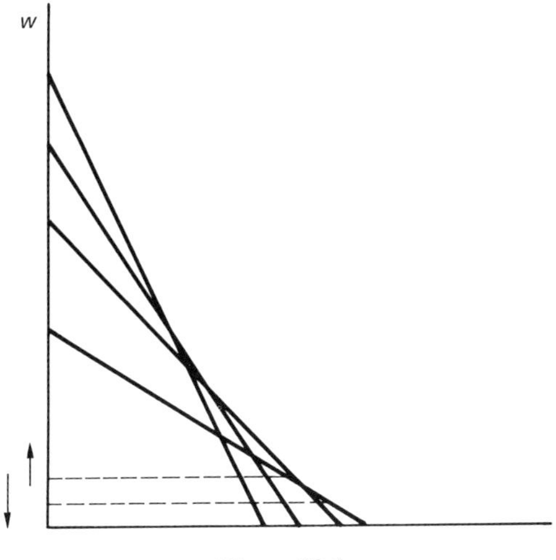

Figure 13.1

family size) to recreate the shortage of workers, and the wage will be bid up again. A new round of mechanization will ensue; the displaced workers will push wages down, the rate of profit will rise, but once again the rise will be less than it would have been with the previous technique. As this cycle repeats itself over time, the profit peaks should exhibit an unmistakeable downward drift. Capital-intensity rises over time, and the rate of profit drifts downward.

16 FINAL REMARKS

The emergence of modern capitalism required the transformation of a static agrarian economy, dependent on traditional rules, and working as much through courts as markets, into a growing, market-oriented industrial system. The traditional economy exhibited a definite pattern of exchange and distribution – it regularly produced a surplus that was distributed, in the ideal case, as a uniform rate of surplus value, and the normal exchange ratios were therefore proportional to the direct and indirect labor embodied in the goods being traded. But the working of this system tended to generate pressures that tore it apart. With the breakdown of traditional society came the development of the market, but at first, so long as land was held in fief and crafts were organized into guilds, the labor market supported exchange at labor values. Nor did the initial emergence of a rate of profit, as land and businesses became marketable, lead prices to move away from labor values. Absolute rent absorbed the potential difference between labor values and prices of production. Competition and the market could not, and did not, play the role assigned to them by the conventional wisdom. Labor values will remain in place until innovation has replaced the traditional products and methods of production. During this long transition, there will exist very strong incentives to mechanization, and the conventional relationship between capital-intensity and the rate of profit will hold.

Notes

1. Profit-earning production, arguably, is necessarily monetary, because it involves contracts for deferred payments. But non-profit-calculating surplus production, such as in the feudal system, may also be fully monetized, meaning that all transactions are recorded in money of account, and are carried out through a medium of circulation. This was substantially the case in the late Middle Ages, and the growing monetization facilitated the development of markets for land and for production facilities. But the question of monetary circulation raises additional issues, while not being central to those posed here. See Nell (1967; 1968; 1988) and especially (1991, Part III).
2. I shall use the preceding notation for much of this study. However, at one point it will be necessary to examine the sectors more closely, and at that time we will have to switch techniques, and make use of a more disaggregated model.
3. Engels' Appendix to *Capital*, Vol. III (1965, pp. 897–8).
4. Samuelson (1971) argues that the interest cost of time must be taken into account: 'In the real world, of 1776, 1817, or 1970, time was money and interest (or profit, they are the same thing when uncertainty is ignorable) rates were not zero. Interest will compound as a cost . . . So . . . bourgeois economics . . . did expect competitive price ratios to differ from embodied labor contents.' This is assertion, not argument. Of course, if profit is calculated, and paid or received, it will compound, and prices will differ from values. But if it is not calculated, and neither paid nor received, it won't compound either. The question still remains: what kinds of institutions require the calculation of profits, and the establishing of a uniform profit rate, and what kinds do not? Alienable property under unitary control does entail profit calculation and, combined with expansionist competition for markets, will lead to the formation of a common rate of profits. But when land is held under feudal tenure, and tilled with labor services owed as dues, it does not make sense to calculate profits on capital. There isn't any capital – for the means of production are not alienable, and the labor is supported not by wages but by farming an assigned tenancy. Nor does it matter for this question if feudal tenants pay in money rather than in labor services or in kind. It is the nature of the relationship, not the nature of the payment, that is at issue.
5. 'Supply and demand' will be reflected in the fluctuations of market prices – in so far as there are developed markets – but they should be thought of as forming a ratio, not as functions. When supply exceeds demand prices will be driven down, when there is a shortage prices will be bid up. But the idea that supply is an increasing, demand a decreasing, *function* of the (parametrically given) market price is wholly inappropriate here. Such functions depend on substitution of final goods in consumption patterns and of factors in methods of

production, respectively. The Medieval economy provided few, if any, opportunities for either – normal production and consumption can both be most reasonably treated as represented by fixed coefficients which, of course, may change from time to time under various kinds of pressure. But these changes will be exceptions; the rule will be the unchanging norms of tradition. So long-term normal prices will depend on the conditions for reproducing and distributing the surplus, while normal outputs will reflect the needs established in the normal conditions of life. Given the few opportunities for substitution, or even choice, in medieval circumstances, supply and demand functions have no place in the story.

6. Two complexities are left out of this account. First, not all goods take exactly one year to produce; but any process that is repeated (say) three times during a year can be entered in the table with a multiplier of three. Secondly not all goods are used up in a year, but similarly, the column showing the consumption of a good that lasts (say) two years can be reduced by one-half. More difficult cases can be dealt with by elaborations of these techniques.
7. To understand the role of the feudal rent ratio in the equations, conduct a simple thought experiment: Suppose all laborers, on manors and in craft shops in the towns, began to work more slowly and less effectively – all in the same proportion. Less would be produced, and the rent ratio would fall, until at a certain point the slowdown would eliminate the surplus entirely. Such a system can be written

$$c_{11}p_1 + c_{12}p_2 + \ldots + c_{1n}p_n = c_1p_1$$

$$c_{21}p_1 + c_{22}p_2 + \ldots + c_{2n}p_n = c_2p_2$$

$$\overline{\phantom{c_{n1}p_1 + c_{n2}p_2 + \ldots + c_{nn}p_n = c_np_n}}$$

$$c_{n1}p_1 + c_{n2}p_2 + \ldots + c_{nn}p_n = c_np_n$$

Each row represents an industry, which can be thought of as composed of a (large or small) number of firms using the same technique and responding to market forces in the same way and at the same time. (This makes it possible to take the industry as the unit of analysis.) The $p_1, \ldots, p_n$, represent barter exchange ratios; the left side of each equation is cost of production, the right revenue. Since total output equals total input, cost equals revenue; if output exceeded input the difference would have to be distributed on the cost side as profits or wages. Given the equality of cost (plus earning) and revenue, when the industries are connected (i.e., when at least one good figures directly or indirectly in the production of all, there will always be one and only one all positive set of barter prices).
8. Following the thought experiment of n. 7 above consider a level of e such that the town surplus earnings ratios is unity (i.e., zero surplus). Then, an intuitive proof can be given, (which also holds for the countryside equations, and *a fortiori* for any trade pattern between the two), running as follows:

> Let I stand for the matrix of outputs (each taken as a unit amount) and C for the matrix of inputs. The assumption that exactly as much is produced as is consumed in producion can be stated $s'(I - C) = 0$. The assumption that every good enters directly or indirectly into the production of every good means that no smaller group of industries is self-sufficient. Because of this connectedness, we can rearrange the rows and columns of C so that each entry along the diagonal shows the use of the previous industry's

good in this industry's production, with the first entry showing the use of the last good in the production of the first, and no entry will be zero. Consider in turn each of the principal submatrices of order $n-1$ in C, M_{ii}. Each sub-matrix consists of $n-1$ industries and $n-1$ corresponding columns of consumption. A principal submatrix of this rearranged input matrix necessarily omits one diagonal entry. Since total production for each industry is set at unity, at least one of the sums of the columns in a principal submatrix must be less than unity and none can be greater (i.e., $s'M < 1$). The price of (e.g.) the first industry's product is the rate at which the net amount not in its own production, $c_1 - c_{11}$, exchanges for the products of other industries which it does need. Since $s'(I-C)=0$, $c_1 - c_{11} = c_{21} + c_{31} + \ldots + c_{n1}$, and for the same reason, the amounts of the various goods needed by the producer of c_1 are exactly the amounts by which production in the submatrix exceeds consumption. Since this is true of the relation of every principal submatrix to the eliminated industry and consumption column, exchange is possible between each industry and the rest, and hence all prices must be positive. Further, since the amounts by which production in the submatrix exceeds consumption are *exactly* the amounts needed by the eliminated industry, only these exchanges are possible; hence the price ratios are unique.

9. In the 15th century towns pushed their advantage a good deal further than this. Siena, for example, conquered the nearby countryside, and set up fortified granaries to ensure its food supply. It built an elaborate and sophisticated aqueduct system to safeguard its water sources. Florence established garrisons in nearby towns and villages to control the local countryside. Coupled (at first) with a citizen's army and control over the marketplace, towns were able to turn the terms of trade to their advantage, and appropriate a good part of the countryside's surplus.
10. Assume that machinery lasts a fixed number of years and allow for a common depreciation rate in both sectors, d. Then the equations would be:

$$(d+g)(a) + (1+g)cAQ = 1 \tag{13.21'}$$

$$(d+g)(b) + (1+g)cBQ = Q \tag{13.22'}$$

$$Q = B/A(1-(d+g)a) + (d+g)b \tag{13.23'}$$

$$dQ/dg = (b - aB/A) < 0 \tag{13.24'}$$

Similar adjustments can be made throughout the study. Nothing much is gained, and I have sought to keep the exposition as simple as possible by sticking to the case of circulating capital.
11. The same mechanism which in equations (13.26) – (13.28) applies between Industry and Agriculture, could also work within Industry, determining rents for business premises or, more likely, licences to practice certain crafts or trades. I am neglecting differential rents here, which can easily be added to the argument.

References

Baumol, W. (1974) 'The Transformation of Values: What Marx "Really" Meant, an Interpretation,' *Journal of Economic Literature* (March) pp. 51–61.
Coulton, G.C. (1945) *The Medieval World* (Oxford: Oxford University Press).
Engels, F. (1967) *Capital*, Vol. II (New York: International Publishers).
Engels, F. (1965) 'The Law of Value and the Rate of Profit,' Appendix, *Capital*, Vol. III (New York: International Publishers).
Marx, K. (1967) *Capital*, Vol. I (New York: International Publishers).
Marx, K. (1965) *Wage, Price and Profit* (New York: International Publishers).
Morishima, M. and Catephores, G. (1978) *Value, Exploitation and Growth* (London: McGraw-Hill).
Nell, E.J. (1967) 'Wicksells Theory of Circulation,' *Journal of Political Economy* (August) Vol. 75 no. 4
Nell, E.J. (1968) 'The Advantages of Money over Barter,' *Australian Economic Papers* (December) pp. 149–176.
Nell, E.J. (1988) 'On Monetary Circulation and the Rate of Exploitation,' in P. Arestis (ed.) *Post Keynesian Monetary Theory* (London: Edward Elgar)
Nell, E.J. (1990) *Keynes After Sraffa* (London: Macmillan).
Ochoa, E. (1984) *Labor Values and Prices of Production: an Interindustry Study of the U.S. Economy, 1947–72*, Ph.D. Thesis (New York: New School For Social Research).
Samuelson, P. (1971) 'Understanding the Marxian Notion of Exploitation: A Summary of the So-called Transformation Problem Between Marxian Values and Competitive Prices,' *Journal of Economic Literature* (June).
Val'tukh, K. (1987) 'Statistical Verification of the Theory of Value: An Analysis of Price Indexes,' in G. Gandolfo and Marzano (eds), *Keynesian Theory, Planning Models and Quantitative Economics* (Milan: Dott. A. Giufre Editore).

14 The Price Revolution and Primitive Accumulation

Immanuel Wallerstein's *The Modern World-System* is a massive and magnificent work of historical scholarship and deserves the highest praise for combining breadth of vision with attention to scholarly detail. Yet like all attempts to synthesize many different kinds of studies, carried out from many different points of view, it runs into the problem that the underlying theoretical ideas may not always be consistent with each other. I shall concentrate on one such problem which emerges largely in the second chapter. This is the question of the initial emergence of capital, the first concentrations of control over the means of production, held in money form, which Marx called 'primitive accumulation.' Wallerstein surveys the debate over the 'price revolution,' which provided one explanation of the emergence of capital, and he goes over the demographic evidence, which provides a different explanation for the same series of price and wage movements. His own view is clearly that what really matters is the emerging world division of labor, including the patterns of labor control, which result from specialization in supplying the world market, but in arguing for this, he overlooks important developments in the re-organization of the guilds, and he appears to accept some arguments, both from the monetarists and from the demographers, that no serious scholar should countenance. The major problem, however, is that he does not see that the emergence of capitalist relationships in the domestic economy is based on institutions which will inhibit its later functioning.

1 THE STALEMATE AT THE END OF THE 15TH CENTURY

The state of affairs during the 15th century can be seen as a kind of stalemate. Towns, and within towns the artisans, had acquired a position of economic dominance in which they could steadily increase their share of the net product. Real wages and craftsmens' real earnings rose all over Europe, from the Battle of Courtrai to the Battle of Bosworth, at which time, in Southern England, they reached a peak higher than any previously recorded, and not reached again until precisely 400 years later. In many towns, especially in Flanders and in Italy, artisans came to play a leading role in town government, sharing power formerly reserved to merchants,

* *Peasant Studies*, 6(1) (January 1977).

and sometimes for short periods dominating the political scene. They never wholly displaced the merchants, however, for the latter were able to work together, whereas the fact that craft guilds frequently competed across the market, e.g., millers and bakers, smiths and armorers, often stood in the way of political cooperation, especially in areas concerned with the regulation of economic activity. (See Appendices to Chapter 12.)

Yet this prosperity and prominence was bought at a heavy price, for neither merchants nor nobles were prepared to accept such an erosion of their position. Alliances of the nobility and the patriciate (e.g. the Leliarts) were often formed with the express design (among others) of subjugating such economic power to political, or if necessary, military restriction. (The wage and price legislation in England during the 14th century and the frequent attempts of nobles to control the town markets are examples.) It has been suggested by Postan that the failures of these moves to halt the downward trend of noble revenue led to more drastic measures, to outright brigandage and preying on trade, which brought them into conflict with the merchants. Thus a system of shifting alliances developed – merchants and nobles were as one in trying to depress wages and artisan earnings, but artisans and merchants shared a common interest in protecting trade and the independence of the towns.

As long as the central government remained weak, the protection of trade could not be assured and economic power could not decisively displace military power as a foundation for the ruling class. For this, the destruction of the power of nobles to resist superior central authority was necessary. The development of gunpowder effectively shifted the balance of military power from the defense to the attack. If the central authority could muster its troops and arm them adequately, the provincial nobility could no longer hold out in impregnable fortresses. The crucial condition for effective central government thus became the ability to raise adequate revenue to support an army and a bureaucracy. The foundation of the power of the central government thus shifted from the military to the economic sphere, and with this shift came an alliance between the state and the towns.

The shift of economic power to the artisans led the merchant class to two courses of action: the purchase of land in both the countryside and in towns (thus allying themselves with the nobility) and entrance into industrial production via the putting-out system. These responses were frequently combined, and during the 15th century a movement of industry from towns to the countryside took place. A further advantage lay in the fact that wages and craft earnings in the countryside tended to lag behind those in the towns; moreover, feudal rights and restrictions could be used to hold them down. Thus new content was poured into the old forms.

But by itself such activity would not have changed the trend of events, or led to the subsequent dramatic fall in real wages and earnings in the 16th century (illustrated by figures 12.1–12.3). The consolidation of state power on a new basis played a large role, since the necessity for adequate finance made the state dependent on the merchants as the financial class which controlled the supply of loanable funds. The resulting close cooperation made it possible for merchants to secure remarkably favorable legislation. But perhaps the crucial, purely economic fact was the separation of the producer from his product, which came about with the growth of capitalistic production transforming guilds into proprietorships, and the development of capitalistic agriculture. Instead of the worker owning his own tools and materials, so that his earnings depended on the price of his product, as was the case with both peasant and artisan, a new class of landless peasants and workers without tools emerged. The earnings of this class depended not upon the price of the product they produced, but on the price they could get for their labor, bargaining in a free market.

These slow but inexorable changes in institutional practice fundamentally altered the conditions of labor and set the stage for the entrance of capital. But a very different case has been argued: It has been claimed that the two centuries long decline in real wages, following the discovery of the New World, by creating exceptional profits, begat and began the modern era. This decline in turn resulted from the influx of New World treasure, driving up prices relatively to money wages, which were held down by a substantial population expansion.

2 CHANGES IN THE RELATIONSHIP OF PRODUCERS TO THE MEANS OF PRODUCTION

At the end of the 15th century direct producers – those who did the work – in both agriculture and industry had substantial control over the means of production, the nature and pace of work, the conditions of employment, the choices of method of production, and the design of products. Democracy and egalitarianism in the guilds should not be exaggerated but must be acknowledged. No one can deny, however, the detailed control exercised by the guilds over all phases of production, marketing, and the training of labor. Feudal landlords, by commuting labor services to money rents and granting leases, changed the land holding system from one of service based on hierarchy and status to one based on contract, and in doing so created a class of independent farmers, i.e. farmers who could decide *what* to produce, how to rotate crops, how to mix arable and pasture, what animals to keep, as the largely or partly dependent serf, working demesne land, could not.

By the end of the 17th century substantial numbers of direct producers in both sectors had lost control over both the means and conditions of production. A large class of propertyless workers with nothing to sell but their labor had been created. Small farms had been consolidated into large estates, the yeomen of England had become a sometimes nomadic rural labor force, and guilds had been converted into mercantile trading companies.

3 CHANGES IN THE PATTERN OF COMPETITIVE PRESSURES

Capitalism is a system in which earnings are figured on the value of total advances. So natural does this procedure seem today that we forget it was not always so. Under the arrangements of the feudal economy, earnings were computed not on capital advanced but on labor time expended. Prices were set to cover direct and indirect labor costs. No one 'advanced capital' because no one controlled the entire process of production. Feudal lords extracted work from serfs and the value of a manor, as a security for a loan, say, depended on the amount of labor services owed, together with the average productivity of that labor. (For a description of an idealized feudal economy and its pattern of trade with an idealized urban economy, cf. Chapters 11 and 12 below.)

To see how this works consider an establishment, a bakery or smithy, operating according to guild rules. From its revenue from sales, funds are set aside for replacement of equipment, purchase of materials and the like. Guild dues and city taxes are paid on a per capita basis for all the members of the establishment. The remainder is then divided among masters, journeymen, and apprentices in proportion to time worked, weighted by seniority. Establishments where earnings are above average will attract apprentices and journeymen; those where earnings are below average will experience difficulty recruiting. The principle operates between guilds as well as between establishments within a guild. Thus labor will tend to move towards high earnings and shun low, pressuring the former to expand and the latter to shrink. However, this works differently between guilds and within a guild. In the latter case, the high earning establishments tend to drive the others out of the market or reduce them to serving small local markets of tied customers, since competition in the product market and the rules of 'just price' require charging a common price, one which just covers the direct and indirect labor costs. In the former case, between guilds producing different products, high earning guilds will tend to expand, low earning ones to contract, leading the price of the former's products to fall, and the latter to rise, assuming normal demand patterns. This will tend to reestablish a common rate of earning for labor-time.

The situation is quite different when the control of the production process is concentrated in the hands of a single authority possessing the right, and having the opportunity (if he so wishes), to liquidate the assets. In an important sense the master craftsman was bound to his journeymen and apprentices as much as they were to him. He could not (easily) dismiss them or sell up the enterprise and go into a new line of business. He could not for two reasons: first there was no capital market, no way of liquidating an enterprise. And second, he was not allowed to, for he was under obligations to provide livelihood for the other members of the establishment. Ideally, though certainly not always in practice, he was *primus inter pares*. He was not an employer in the modern sense.

By contrast, the capitalist employer is both unencumbered by such obligations and is well able to find markets for disposing of entire business enterprises. For him the issue is return on his entire capital, the funds for materials, equipment, depreciation, and wages. He pays such wages as he must, given the state of the labor market, and (if he is rational) he will certainly not employ labor beyond the point where the extra payments needed to attract labor reduce his return below what he could obtain elsewhere.

One issue, then, in accounting for the rise of capitalism, is to explain the institutional change from the master–journeyman–apprentice system to the capitalist employer–employee relationship. Only when this change has taken place can capital accumulated elsewhere, e.g. in overseas trade or in the colonies, enter into domestic industry and proceed to transform handicrafts into modern industry. But the very process of this change may create difficulties for the free mobility of capital, as we shall see later.

4 THE OLD ORTHODOXY

The Hamilton–Keynes thesis holds that the influx of precious metals from the New World, aided by renewed output from Southern European mines and by gold brought from Africa by the Portuguese, and abetted by manipulations of royal mints, caused prices to run ahead of money wages. Exactly why price increases outstripped money wages is not clear; and it was not universal. In Spain after the early 16th century they did not. Part of the explanation may have been population growth. Certainly in Spain emigration to the colonies and the expulsion of the Moriscos contributed to a labor shortage, which helped money wages to rise. Another part of the story may be that prices rose first among those goods which figured in international trade, so that money wages would tend to lag. But in any event the effect was a rise in revenues above costs, creating a Profit Inflation, the benefits of which accrued, in this view, primarily to the more active, mercantile section of the community at the expense of rentiers and, most heavily, the laboring population.

Orthodox it may be, acceptable it is not. A number of by now standard observations simply cannot be squared with this account. France experienced a greater price inflation and a greater profit inflation than England but appears to have invested much less in industry. Spain experienced a much greater price inflation, but little or no profit inflation. England seems to have experienced a considerable price inflation on the basis of a very much smaller influx of specie than the others. Though it is difficult to trace the movements of specie, it does seem clear that price increases occurred in many places throughout Europe during the 16th and 17th centuries without the stimulus of a prior influx of treasure.

There are theoretical objections too. According to much modern economic theory, liquidity, not the quantity of money is the relevant factor in raising effective demand. The inflow of specie could have ended up in hoards; hence, in addition to the quantity of treasure one must consider the institutional and economic variables which determine the desired level of liquidity. Further, one must also consider the available varieties of means of payment – 'near monies.' A given influx of specie may have a greater or lesser effect depending both on the extent to which bills of exchange, bank notes and the like are used and on the way these are tied to the precious metals. In any case, as we saw above, the quantity theory by itself cannot explain a profit inflation.

Even if these difficulties could be overcome, one central fact still could not be fitted in. The period was one in which the terms of trade between town and countryside moved steadily in favor of agriculture. Indeed the major part of the decline in real wages was due to the rise in the price of grain and other foodstuffs. This movement of the terms of trade requires explanation, and the Hamilton–Keynes thesis, as usually stated, can throw no light on the matter.

5 THE OLD ORTHODOXY REVISED

All the same, American treasure was important, and before turning to the New Orthodoxy we might try to make the best of the position, even if the end result does not look much like Hamilton or Keynes, or Wallerstein, either.

The influx of treasure moved first and foremost in the channels of international trade. As long as treasure was *flowing* a gap tended to open between sellers' prices and buyers' prices, creating opportunities for merchants, who consequently flourished. An increase in profits will lead merchants to bid up the prices of the goods they buy, particularly wheat and wool. The existence of opportunities for favorable arbitrage will lead profit-minded landlords to convert a higher proportion of their capital to a more liquid form, by shifting from arable to pasture, thus reducing their wage bill and also their fixed capital requirements. This shift is not necessarily more profitable, it simply means that less capital is committed to long-term projects and less is tied up in wages and seed. It is a shift to greater liquidity.

One result of sheep and cattle driving people off the land is an exodus to the cities, where the newly dispossessed help to keep down money wages. Another is to accentuate the rise in the price of grain. The low level and slow rise of money wages helps to reduce cost pressures on the urban craft industries, whose products, leather goods, harness, bricks, furniture, stonework, tools and implements, armor and so on, do not enter international trade, and so tend to rise in price more slowly anyway.

Merchants depend on contracts and connections for information and upon information for profit. An individual builds up a set of personal relationships upon which his success depends. These cannot so easily be passed on; each generation must make its own way anew. There is therefore a considerable temptation to move into a less risky, more settled, more permanent way of life. Merchants buying land will bid up land prices, and, when they take over an estate, they will bring a new and more commercial spirit to the management of it. Thus, the famous 'rise of the gentry.'

The movement of capital into foreign trade and the development of colonies, from which the influx of treasure flows, can also be seen as the consequence of exceptionally high levels of wages (a corresponding political ascendancy of artisans) prevailing at the end of the 15th century. Capital fled the towns, investment slowed. Merchants bought agricultural products for shipment abroad, or invested in fleets of privateering ships. With the influx of treasure, these tendencies were exacerbated, and not only investment in the towns but also demand for urban products fell off, owing to competition from colonial and New World goods and luxuries from Africa and the Far East. Thus urban and industrial prices lagged, and the urban demand for labor was not sufficient to absorb the dispossessed from the countryside.

In short, the high wages and artisan power of the late 15th century drove the custom and the capital of merchants and nobles abroad, the first great imperialist expansion. The treasure of the New World, in turn, made it possible to drive down real wages and break the power of the guilds.

This version is better but it still does not work. Cloth and cattle are the two counter-examples. Cloth, as a finished product of urban industry, was a major item in foreign trade, yet its price rose only slightly, very much less than grain. Cattle and beef products, not prominent in foreign trade, nevertheless rose substantially in price, though less than grain. Perhaps more important, the model does not explain how the power of the guilds was broken. Competition of foreign goods might weaken them, but that can hardly have been decisive for bakers, blacksmiths, and masons. And finally the model tends to talk of shifting capital about, as if this were already possible, when the object is to explain not the *growth* of industry but the *development* of capitalist institutions.

6 THE NEW ORTHODOXY

The Hamilton–Keynes thesis relies too much on the mechanics of the Quantity Theory of Money and, in any case, cannot explain the different patterns of development in different sectors. At best, as Wallerstein points out, the influx of treasure made possible or facilitated the emergence of events or movements already present in embryo, but though a contributory factor, it should not be considered among the basic or ultimate causes. The modern explanation of the changes observed in these two centuries returns to Malthus and demographic pressures, and Wallerstein appears to agree, although only if considered in conjunction with effects of the development and partitioning of world markets. Population pressure in the 16th century resulted from the exceptionally high wages of the 15th century; given the available technology and resources and the ability to finance their use, the rise in population created the pressures that produced the observed pattern of price and wage movements, made easier by the influx of New World gold and silver. The pressure of population on the limited supply of arable land led to rising food and grain prices, while the increased supply of labor kept wages low or rising more slowly, thus creating a 'profit inflation.' The differences in these price and wage movements, in turn, helped to define the New World division of labor, for too high a level of real wages, as in Venice, cut into profits and retarded capital formation, whereas too low a level (France, Spain) inhibited the development of the local market. A middling level of wages, as in England and Holland, permitted capital accumulation and the development of the domestic market to proceed together. These faster-growing states then came to form the core of the world economy.

Stated so simply, the argument has the ring of truth; examined more closely, cracks and flaws appear. To begin with, there are no less than *three* different and to some extent incompatible versions of the 'population pressure' thesis. Worse still, none of them is really acceptable. And finally, there is a serious methodological flaw in this eclectic approach. Let us consider each of the versions of the population theories in turn.

The first is the textbook doctrine of marginal productivity. This is a *cost*-based explanation and in its simplest forms relies on the assumption of competitive markets. It can be adapted to 'imperfect markets,' but they can only be imperfect in certan ways. Were the markets of the 16th century really that similar in form to the markets of advanced capitalism? We will return to this question later. The basic argument is that unit costs move inversely to productivity. If productivity at the margin falls, while demand price and input purchase prices remain constant, then costs rise and profits fall. A rise in population raises the labor-land ratio, and so reduces the marginal productivity of labor on land; hence, real wages will fall and marginal food costs rise.[1] Industry is supposed to produce under conditions of constant returns to scale, allowing for easier expansion. Thus, either the population pressure will not affect the labor-capital ratio as much as the labor–land ratio, or the changes in the marginal productivities of labor and capital will be offsetting, whereas those of labor and land will not, so that marginal costs will not rise as much in industry as they do in agriculture. (Notice that there are two *different* possible versions of this argument, one turning on investment – capital can be expanded *pari passu* with population, while land cannot – the other on the nature of technology – more labor applied to limited land leads to rising marginal costs, whereas more labor applied to limited supplies of tools and materials leads to working them more intensively, and so to constant or more slowly rising marginal costs. The assumption, in this late case, is that innovation in working routines is easier to implement in towns than in the countryside.) Either version of the argument leads to the conclusion that the terms of trade between agriculture and industry will turn in favor of agriculture.

The entire argument is based on the assumption that *prices* move with *costs*, which in turn move as productivity dictates, where the movement of productivity is accounted for by the behavior of the three-factor aggregate production function exhibiting continous variability and diminishing marginal returns. None of these underlying assumptions should be accepted by serious economic historians for a moment. First, quite obviously, price movements were not dictated by cost movements, which in turn did not simply follow productivity movements; both demand prices and input prices were changing. Secondly, even though *population* rose, it is by no means clear that the labor force employed in agriculture rose by anything like as much, for there was at this time a considerable shift of arable into pasture. Moreover, there was a great deal of polder-making and clearing, so that the labor-to-land ratio may not have altered much. The new land appears to have been, not 'marginal,' but excellent, so that its productivity would in fact lead to lower costs of production. (The costs of clearing land or of polder-making are *capital* costs, not land costs, so are recoverable over a long period and, in accordance with conventional doctrine, should have little influence on the current price of agricultural output.) Thus it is by no means evident that there were diminishing returns to agriculture. Finally, it is not clear that 'capital, (meaning here, industrial means of production) accumulated relative to land, nor is it likely that innovation in this period was in any obvious sense easier in the towns, where extensive guild restrictions were still in force, than in the countryside, where capitalist farming was developing, and indeed, where new industries were moving precisely to escape the guild restrictions of the towns. Thus neither form of the argument seems adequate to explain the relative movement of agricultural and industrial prices.

(In any case, textbook marginal productivity theory has been subjected by modern economists to a devastating critique,[2] and it should be left to die quietly.)

The second version of the population pressure argument avoids the textbook conception of marginal productivity theory and relies on a much simpler and more old-fashioned doctrine. Agricultural price movements are still explained by changes in productivity, but this time it is Ricardo rather than J. B. Clark. Population increase means higher demand, which in turn necessitates the bringing of inferior land into production, so that costs at the 'extensive' margin increase. By contrast industry can be expanded without any such problem, since industrial means of production are themselves produced; hence agricultural prices will rise relative to industrial prices. But the increase in population will produce an excess supply of labor, tending to keep money wages down or rising more slowly.

Most of the same objections apply. The cost-productivity assumptions are not easily reconciled with the historical record; moreover nothing in this argument explains the shift from arable to pasture. Indeed, if the *extensive* margin is being pushed outward, economic theory would suggest that the *intensive* margin should be extended also, which would imply that existing land should have been cultivated by more rather than less labor-intensive techniques. There is another problem. If the industrial means of production can be expanded without seriously increasing costs, why does industry not expand enough to keep the demand for labor up to the supply of it, particularly if wages are lagging? The enormous decline in real wages implies, given the highly imperfect markets of the time, a very considerable labor surplus, very apparent in the historical record. But if industry could be expanded at constant cost, why was this slack not taken up? An *additional* explanation will be required to complete the argument.

The third line of argument is in fact the one most commonly advanced, and is moreover the simplest, though perhaps the least respectable from the point of view of orthodox economics. It explains the movement of prices and wages by reference to changes in *demand*, making only the simplest assumptions about supply. Marginal productivity is simply dropped; no account is given of the supply curve at all. Supply curves are there and have the shape they have, and that is that. There are basically two kinds of markets: agricultural goods have inelastic supply curves and elastic demand curves; labor markets and markets for manufactured goods have elastic supply curves and inelastic demand curves. These can be drawn as follows.

The supply and demand curves in agriculture are pretty standard; for labor and industrial goods a word of explanation is needed. The supply curve reflects the fact that a large supply will be forthcoming at a certain slightly rising price, though there may be an upper limit, and it is possible that at substantially higher prices, *less* would be offered – a 'backward-bending' curve – showing that suppliers can obtain their desired or traditional income by producing less, when price is higher. The demand curve shows that at very high prices demand will fall off sharply and at very low prices will increase substantially but that over a large range, the range of likely variation, it will be roughly constant. The assumption of the population pressure theorists appears at first to be that increases in population shift the demand curves for goods out and up, the supply curve of labor out and down, while the demand curve for labor shifts out due to the increased demand for both kinds of goods. The two shifts in the labor market tend to be more or less offsetting; prices of manufactured goods tend to rise slightly and those of agricultural goods, substantially.

This sounds more plausible, and is not committed to any particular theory of the supply curves, so is not open to the objections to either version of marginal productivity theory, though, of course, it just pushes the problem of explanation back one stage. Buth there are two important difficulties, one theoretical and one empirical. The theoretical difficulty is simply that an increase in population does not by itself increase the demand for either agricultural or manufactured goods. There are more people, it is true, but they cannot buy goods of any sort unless they have incomes. Incomes come from wages profits and rents, and in orthodox theory, these follow from the marginal productivities together with the amounts of the factors employed. But even ignoring orthodox theory, an increase in the supply of labor which lowered the supply curve in the face of an inelastic demand for labor would tend to lower the total wage bill, *reducing* the demand for grain and workers' demand for manufactured goods such as cloth. Thus we would expect agricultural prices to fall, manufacturing prices to stay steady, while the change in real wages would depend upon the proportion of grain, etc. in the worker's budget and the relative elasticities of the supply curve in agriculture and the demand curve for labor (see Figures 14.1 and 14.2). If the former is highly inelastic, the latter comparatively elastic, and the share of the wage spent on grain very high, the real wage could remain substantially the same.)

The way around this is to assume that the wage level is fixed at a traditional point, so that the increase in the labor supply will not lower the money wage rate. This is certainly what must be meant, since in fact money wage rates rose during the great inflation. But then we come up against the empirical difficulty. For the demand curve for agricultural products cannot shift (as a result of population increase) by more than the proportional increase in the wage bill. Moreover, there is evidence that the supply curve for agriculture shifted outward due to improvements in productivity, the opening of new lands, etc. Hence the percentage rise in the price of grain must be less than the percentage increase in population, and will be still less of the supply curve is not perfectly vertical. The real wage in England and elsewhere in Western Europe declined between 1500 and 1575 by about one-half. But by no account can one argue that in that same period population doubled, let alone, as would be required, considerably more

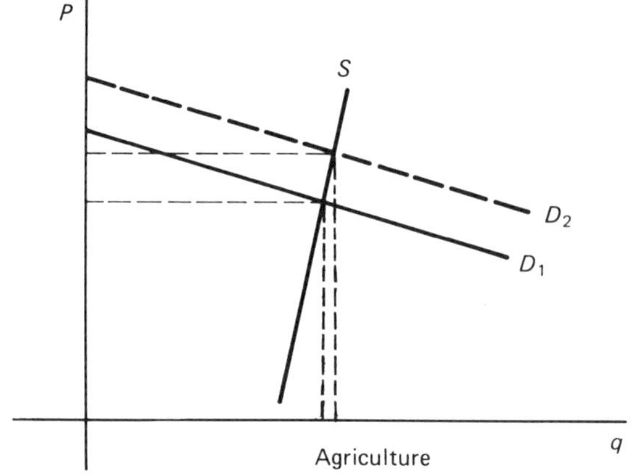

Figure 14.1

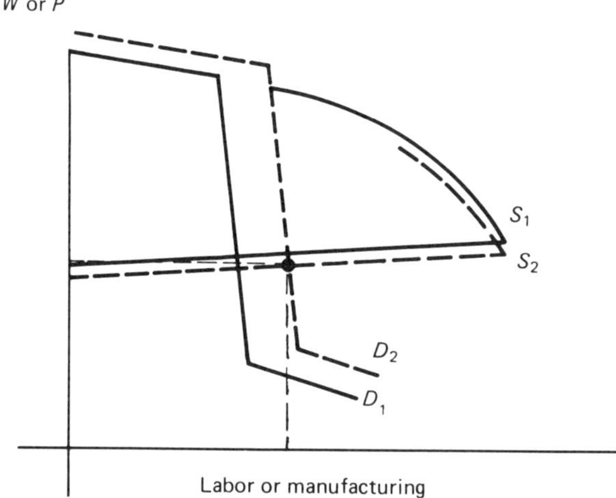

Figure 14.2

than doubled. Moreover, from 1450 to 1500 population was increasing, yet during this period real wages continued to rise, though more slowly than in the previous century. Not only is the new orthodoxy riddled with theoretical ambiguities; there seems to be no way of reconciling its implications with the historical record.

Wallerstein's account of the movement of price and wages, of course, puts great stress on the context of the world market, but his distinctive contribution comes in his argument that the pattern of inflation helped to develop the distinction between the core and the outer rings. The argument he gives, however, fails for reasons quite similar to those just examined. In 'highwage' states we should expect to find the domestic demand for agricultural products to be strong enough to push agriculture to its limits, bidding up the price of grain and other products. Thus the 'high real wages' should turn out to be temporary; as the price of grain rises, the real wage will fall. In 'low wage' states, the demand for agricultural products will be weak, and since such products do not keep without loss, it is likely that grain and other prices will prove weak. So again the 'low real wage' would prove relatively temporary, tending to rise back to a level compatible with the sale at an acceptable supply price of the entire output of the available land. The point can be put this way: given the acreage of arable land and the methods of cultivation, and given the established guilds, their equipment and methods of work, the total wages paid in agriculture and manufacturing must be such as to enable the total output of consumables to be cleared from the market at a price which will provide capitalists and landlords the profits and rent to finance their planned purchases of investible goods. If the money wage bill is too low, the price of consumables will fall; if money wages are too high, the price will rise, lowering real wages. *Provided investment plans are in balance with investment output*, the market will adjust the distribution of income to provide the required finance in the form of profits. This is an important proposition in the neo-Keynesian analysis of capitalism, but it is highly questionable whether it belongs *at all* in an account of the working of very early and only partly capitalist markets in the 16th century. In any case Wallerstein's notion of a 'medium wage level' as 'optimal' in balancing the size of the profit margin against the size of the local market simply cannot be sustained. Supply and demand are always good for a run, but they just do not make it around this track.

7 THE EMERGENCE OF CAPITALISM: THE FORMATION AND FUNCTIONING OF CAPITAL

In addition to the above difficulties the Old and the New Orthodoxies share a common methodological fault. Both treat certain crucial economic categories – wages and labor, profits and capital, rent and land – as applicable more or less independently of the particular economic institutions of different historical periods. To be sure, the writers who use these terms recognize different degrees of development, or 'perfection,' of the markets at different periods, but they regard the phenomena to which they apply categories as essentially the same.

Surprisingly, for he discusses different modes of exploitation of labor in some detail, Wallerstein appears to accede to such usage of these terms. Thus in relation to the cities of Italy and Flanders he quotes Cipolla: 'labor costs seem to have been too high in Italy in relation to wage levels in competing countries' and 'worker's organizations succeeded in imposing wage levels which were disproportionate to the productivity of labour.' Wallerstein himself comments that it is 'precisely as a result of the "strength" of the workers and the progress of capitalist mores that both northern Italian and Flemish cities would decline as industrial centers in the 16th century. Shortly after this (p. 84), he advances the argument, already criticized,, for the 'optimal' wage level 'for a local investing class,' summarizing his conclusions:

> Inflation was thus important both because it was a mechanism of forced savings and hence, capital accumulation, and because it distributed these profits unevenly.

The methodological fault is as simple as its implications are far-reaching. The phrase 'labour costs' implies that labor is on a footing with other purchased inputs; that is, that labor is a *commodity*, bought and sold freely on the market. That, however, is exactly what was *not* the case in the guild-dominated cities of northern Italy and Flanders at this time. Labor was not a commodity, for the guild workers participated in the running of the guilds according to the rights and privileges of their respective ranks, shared in the earnings, and took an active part in defining the rights and privileges of their guild in relation to others. In many countries in the 16th and 17th centuries the guilds fell under the sway of oligarchies of masters and merchants, who were able to establish control over the guild's licensing power and were able to exclude the lower ranks from decision-making and participation, using the licensing power to exclude troublesome members of lower rank who challenged their policies. But in just these cities this process met with substantial and at least partially effective resistance. Hence labor did not become a commodity; once apprenticed a worker was not mobile, nor was he dimissable at the will of an 'employer.' A guild master was not an employer in the modern sense; *how he became one – or was replaced by one – is precisely the question at issue.*

Similar remarks apply to the contention that 'wage levels' were 'disproportionate to the productivity of labour.' Presumably this means 'lay above the marginal productivity of labor;' otherwise the remark is literally nonsense. But if it does mean that, it implies theoretical assumptions which presuppose the existence of both capital and a competitive return to capital. For it does not *matter* whether the wage lies above marginal productivity (all the better for workers – and prices can be kept down by squeezing out profits), except that it drives the return to capital down below its competitive supply price, leading capital to *withdraw* from that sphere of production. But in a guild system there is no way to withdraw capital and invest it elsewhere; businesses cannot be bought and sold. The formation of capital markets, that is, the emergence of institutional arrangements making it possible to buy and sell operating productive activities (activities carried out by employees of the one selling the business) is again part of what has to be explained.

Thus the reference to an investing class is premature, as is the reference to capital accumulation as a result of saving out of profits. The 16th century is part of the period preceding capitalistic accumulation on a regular basis; it is the period of 'primitive accumulation', in which there occurs the formation of hoards of wealth, the concentration of control over the means of production, and the expropriation of direct producers, forming a property-less labor force. This is the principal kind of capital accumulation that takes places in this era; it is the formation of capitalism, rather than its normal functioning, that is happening. Capital accumulation by saving out of profits is certainly a regular and important feature of developed capitalism, but it is not a part of primitive accumulation, where there is still no developed capital market.

To see the importance of appreciating this point, let us look again at the Flemish and Italian cities. It is not because of the strength of the workers and the progress of capitalist mores that those cities declined relatively, but because capitalist mores never became firmly established. The old order did not break down completely; the oligarchs were not able to establish firm control. They were not able effectively to expel the lower ranks from participation in decision-making, and hence members of those ranks could not be summarily dismissed, nor were the masters able to choose the methods, timing and pattern of work. Control over the means of production was not effectively monopolized by any class, nor were the direct producers dispossessed. The explanation is therefore not that wages were too high, but that 'wages' were not paid at all! The decline is not attributable to a return on capital so low that capital either moved elsewhere or was unable to grow at a competitive rate, as is implied by the contention that wages were too high, but rather that capital was not formed at all. The arrangements of production remained substantially those of the preceding system.

This example also suggests some of the dangers of concentrating too heavily on the development of the world market, to the neglect of the domestic, in explaining the rise of capitalism. The older arrangements had to be subverted, the authority of the guilds had to be usurped, and their power concentrated in a few hands, before capitalism could emerge in full dress. The growth of the world market provided both stimulus and, in the inflation, a means of creating dependency through indebtedness, but it was by no means certain that the result would be achieved.

The method by which the authority of the guilds was usurped, the same as that by which feudal prerogatives were transformed into private property, is as interesting as it is important. The power of the newly emerging State was invoked both to redefine the system of rights and privileges and to legitimize the changes. It was through the power of the State that the right of the masters to license, without the participation or agreement of the other ranks, was confirmed. The State, and not as previously the guilds by agreement among themselves, conferred monopolies, determined marketing practices, and defined both the status of apprentices and the qualifications conferring the right to enter a trade. To be sure, the medieval monarchy had claimed the right to define these matters but had never possessed the means for enforcing its will, for that required a bureaucracy, which in turn, as Wallerstein emphasizes, rested on an effective tax system, something that only emerged with the growth of world trade and the corresponding rise in revenues from duties and market taxes. The use of State power to regulate, restrict and reorganize industry and trade was as essential to the formation of capitalist relations in production as it was inimical to the proper functioning of capital, once formed.

Indeed, certain methods of achieving the concentration of control stood in the way of further progress towards full capitalism. For the *formation* of capital must be distinguished from its effective *functioning*. Capitalism requires a free field of movement for both capital and labor; the concentration of control in a few hands, together with the dispossession of the rest is not enough. That control must be expressed in terms of the *market value* of the means of production, and the fund of value must be freely convertible from one form to another, from goods into money into goods again. Moreover, it must be transferrable from one sphere of production to another. But the formation of capital through the usurpation of the authority of the guilds and through the development of merchant control through advances and 'putting-out,' rests on precisely the institutions and restrictions that have to be abolished to provide the field for capital to function in. The new form of control over the means of production arises from the corruption of the old. Thus the old system is the indispensable framework of primitive accumulation. It is the authority of the guilds and, in the countryside, the authority of the feudal landholding system that provides the grounds for the legitimacy of the new private property for it is that authority which is being usurped and transferred to new purposes. Hence, when it first emerges, the new form of control over the means of production, capitalist control, will be hedged in with all sorts of restrictions remaining from the institutions of the old system. These are not swept away by the growth of the world market; indeed they may proliferate during such growth, for many arise not so much from the old system as from the struggles for control induced by the disintegration of the feudal system. Thus capital or capitalist control emerges in the domestic economy, particularly in handicraft industry, in conditions which will inhibit its successful functioning. These conditions will have to be swept away before capital can undertake the job of transforming 'manufacturing properly so-called' into modern industry. Yet this contradiction in the conditions under which capital emerges, crucial to the understanding of the destruction of the State bureaucracy in 1641[3], does not find a place in Wallerstein's analysis.

Notes

1. The production function *could* provide for an offsetting change in the marginal productivity of land, and still have the conventional form, so the rise in the marginal cost of foodstuffs does not actually follow from the textbook theory, though it is *consistent* with one form of that theory.
2. Summarized in Harcourt (1972). See Part II of this volume.
3. 'The destruction of the royal bureaucracy in 1640–41 can be regarded as the most decisive single event in the whole of British history': Hill (1967) p. 76.

References

Harcourt, G.C. (1972) *Controversies in the Theory of Capital* (London: Cambridge University Press).

Hill, C. (1967) *Reformation to Industrial Revolution* (London: Weidenfeld & Nicolson).

Nell, E.J. (1967) 'Economic Relationships in the Decline of Feudalism,' *History and Theory*, 6.

Wallerstein, I. (1974) *The Modern World System* (New York: Academic Press).

15 Cyclical Growth: the Interdependent Dynamics of Industry and Agriculture*

Accumulation is one side of the golden coin of capitalism; the creation of the proletariat is the other. Historically, accumulation has meant the simultaneous dispossession of people and concentration of property, so that the dispossessed face the propertied in the free labor market (see Marx (1967), I, pp. 614, 620, 624).

Yet many economists today, oblivious to economic history, still tend to argue that under competition, given smooth and infinite substitution between factors, the economy will grow at a stable balanced rate, compatible with full employment and technical progress. Even where instability and imbalance are acknowledged, the institutional conditions of capitalism are assumed, rather than shown to develop through the accumulation process itself. Even where development is mentioned, the longest revolution, the ending of settled agricultural life, is not recognized. The capitalization of agriculture, beginning in the early sixteenth century, and reaching its climax at the end of the nineteenth, has torn man's roots from the earth, separated his work from his life, and reduced his family to the nuclear unit. The theory of accumulation should be able to account for this transformation.

The theory of accumulation, then, is part of the theory of history; the mechanics of an economic model are interesting to the extent that they are (or illuminate) the mechanics of history. What such models yield are not the steady-state movements of economic variables, but the pressures that result in the transformation of institutions. What follows begins from Marx's theory of the early stages of this process, in which urban industry and rural life exist separately, linked only by trade, and goes on to consider the impact of mechanization on agriculture, resulting in a cyclical model which I shall then use to criticize some contemporary thinking about

* W. Semmler (ed.), *Competition, Instability and Nonlinear Cycles* (Berlin: Springer-Verlag, 1986). Thanks are owed to Felix Jimenez for working through the equations and saving me from many mistakes.

growth. The historical background is the economy of Northern and Western Europe during the Industrial Revolution.

We begin with an economy divided into towns and countryside. Population grows steadily at a low rate; by far the greater part of the people live on the land. Industry is relatively primitive. Competition, however, has emerged and, within each sector, tends to equalize profit and wage rates. But movement between the sectors is sometimes inhibited by important barriers. Capital can move freely from rural areas to towns now that the power of guilds has been cracked, though of course capital goods are specialized and fixed. Thus capital flows will involve shortages and surpluses of productive capacity, with consequences for market prices and investment plans. Going the other way, capital can move, but not freely, from towns to the countryside. In this direction there is a tariff – the former feudal seigneurs, possessing a monopoly of land, demand the payment of 'absolute rent' (Marx (1967), III, Ch. 45) 'Nulle terre sans seigneur;' there is no no-rent land. (There may also be differential rents.) This is made possible by enforcing a trading position against industry and the working class, whereby grain and country products are sold for their labor value instead of for their (lower) prices of production (Marx (1967), III, pp. 761–3). This will be explained in detail below.

Within limits, then, capital is mobile. Not so labor. Within a town or a district, we might expect enough shifting from job to job to roughly equalize rates of pay subject to skill and risk differentials. But it is quite another matter for labor to move from one sector to another. Communications are poor, education limited, and travel slow; to finance such a move would require savings which laborers do not have. In any case rural labor still possesses residual rights in land, including common lands, and often in cottages, farm buildings, and forests as well. These will not be given up lightly (Marx (1967), I, Ch. 27). Labor does move, of course, but it has to be pushed out; it will not ordinarily leave in response to the attraction of higher wages in another sector.

There are, therefore, two essentially separate labor markets, in each of which population grows slowly, so that investment has a tendency to run up against labor shortage, at which time wages rise as capital competes for workers (Marx (1967), I, p. 619). This, in turn, leads to a fall in profits, which reduces growth. But the two sectors don't react in the same way or at the same time. And they affect one another through prices. Let's see how this works. First we will look at the conditions of long-run equilibrium in profits and growth, and then we will turn to a short-term model in which profit and/or wage rates may differ between the sectors. Finally, we will develop an oscillatory dynamic that will help to explain the pressures causing the migration of labor.

The Conditions for Expanded Reproduction

Under competitive conditions, differential earnings set up pressures which will shift resources between the sectors. To analyze this, we will first examine how the system would work without such pressures, i.e., we examine the position about which the oscillations, which are our primary interest, will move. I shall use a variant of a familiar notation in which Roman letters stand for inputs and variables associated with urban industry, and Greek for those concerned with agriculture. Urban industry is not highly advanced. Capitalists earn and reinvest profits, which they compute on the entire sum of their advances, including their wage bill. Products of urban industry – 'manufacture properly so-called' in Marx's terms – include cloth, tools, equipment, weapons, clocks, early machinery, and so on. I shall assume that urban industry produces a composite input good, 'machines,' whose components are always used in the same proportions, and similarly that agriculture produces a composite consumption good, 'corn,' again always consumed in the same proportions. Thus we can write the input–output matrix

$$\begin{bmatrix} a & b \\ \alpha & \beta \end{bmatrix}$$

Where the top row shows 'machine' and 'corn' (labor support) inputs into machine production, and the bottom row machine and corn inputs into corn; 'b' and 'β' represent corn needed to support the requisite number of laborers at the established subsistence level for one year; 'a' and 'α,' however, represent the required machinery which lasts for more than one year. Hence, we must figure annual depreciation, which need not take place at the same rate in both industries. But it will simplify the model to assume that it does. So, I shall use 'μ' for the depreciation rate in both industry and agriculture, and 'r' and 'g' will be the net rates of profit and growth. The wage rate 'w,' deserves some comment. It represents the gross (subsistence plus net) wage *rate* (a pure number, e.g., 120%); it is the ratio of the total command over consumption, subsistence plus surplus, to that necessary for the socially-defined subsistence. We can treat the wage rate in this way, perfectly analogous to the rate of profit, because we defined the labor coefficients in terms of the consumption goods that are needed to support labor for a period of time. 'π' will be the price of corn expressed in machines (i.e. the machines that will exchange for a unit of corn), and 'λ' will be the output ratio of corn to machines, which will need careful interpretation, since, out of equilibrium, it can refer either to *capacity* or to *expenditure*. Finally, 'ϱ' stands for the level of absolute rent per acre of land, a concept we will explain in a moment.

First we write equations for wages, profits and prices. These are essentially markup equations, where the left hand side is cost, including normal profit, and the right hand side revenue.

$$(\mu + r)\, a + (1 + r)\, wb\pi = 1 \tag{15.1}$$

$$(\mu + r)\, \alpha + (1 + r)\, w\beta\pi = \pi \tag{15.2}$$

$$\pi = (\beta/b)\, [1 - (\mu + r)\, a] + (\mu + r)\, \alpha \tag{15.3}$$

$$(d\pi/dr) = \alpha - a\, (\beta/b) = a[\alpha/a) - (\beta/b)] < 0 \tag{15.3a}$$

$(\beta/b) > (\alpha/a)$, by assumption (Marx (1987), III, Ch. 45)

$$\pi_{max} = e = \mu\alpha + (\beta/b)\, (1 - \mu a) \tag{15.3b}$$

$$w = \frac{[1 - (\mu + r)\, a]}{(1 + r)\, [(\mu + r)\, (\alpha b - a\beta) + \beta]} \tag{15.4}$$

$$(dw/dr) = -\, [(1 + r)\, (\alpha b)/A^2] - [w/\, (1 + r)] \tag{15.5}$$

$$= -\, [(1 + r)^2\, \alpha b + wA^2]\, /\, [(1 + r)A^2]$$

where $A = (1 + r)\, [\beta + (\mu + r)\, (\alpha b - \beta a)]$, so $(dw/dr) < 0$, since the numerator and the denominator are both > 0.

When $r = 0$, $w = w_{max} = (1 - \mu a)\, /\, [\mu\, (\alpha b - a\beta) + \beta]$, and when both sectors have the same composition of capital, $w = w_{max} = (1 - \mu a)/\beta$.

In this case, when $w = 1$, $r = r_{max} = (1 - \beta - \mu a)\, /\, (a + \beta)$.

Consequently, when $(\beta/\alpha) > (b/a)$, w_{max} will be greater than in the pure labor theory case, but no simple rule can be stated for r_{max}.

Let $X = \alpha b - a\beta$. Then, in general, when $w = 1$, $r = r_{max}$ is found from

$$Xr^2 + [X(1 + \mu) + a + \beta]\, r - [1 - \beta - \mu\, (a + X)] = 0$$

then

$$\frac{dr}{dX} = -\, \frac{r^2 + r\, (1 + \mu) + \mu}{2Xr + a + \beta + (1 + \mu)X}\ ;$$

factoring and rearranging

$$\frac{dr}{dX} = -\, \frac{[(1 + r)\, (\mu + r)]\, /\, [(1 + r) + (\mu + r)]}{X + \{(a + \beta)\, /\, [(1 + r) + (\mu + r)]\}}$$

$X > 0$ implies $(dr/dX) < 0$

$X < 0$ implies $(dr/dX) > 0$ if $|X| > (a + \beta) / [(1 + r) + (\mu + r)]$

Next we write equations for growth, consumption and output. Here the left hand side stands for input requirements, respectively in consumption and investment, while the right hand side is output. $(\mu + g)$ is applied to 'a' and 'b', because industry must operate at an intensity sufficient to satisfy replacement demand, just as agriculture must meet per capita consumption demand. The equations are

$$(\mu + g)\, a + (1 + g)\, c\alpha\lambda = 1 \tag{15.6}$$

$$(\mu + g)\, b + (1 + g)\, c\beta\lambda = \lambda \tag{15.7}$$

Equations exactly mirroring (15.4) and (15.5) are easily deduced. More important, however, is:

$$\lambda = (\beta/\alpha)\, [1 - (\mu + g)\, a] + (\mu + g)b \tag{15.8}$$

$$(d\lambda/dg) = [b - (a\beta/\alpha)] < 0 \tag{15.8a}$$

The growth and profit sets of equations can be connected by the simple assumption that all profits are saved, while all wages are consumed. Under these conditions,

$$r = g, \text{ and} \tag{15.9}$$

$$\lambda = (b/\alpha)\pi \tag{15.10}$$

Of course, capitalist consumption is important (although worker saving probably is not), since it provides a large component of effective demand. And if the capitalist propensity to consume varied with profit conditions, cyclical demand fluctuations could be intensified. But capitalist consumption is financed to a large extent by fixed income, which is relatively insensitive to sales fluctuations; moreover, our interest here concerns the shifting pattern of investment as it moves between the sectors. (A more relevant consideration would be the division of investment between 'basic' and 'nonbasic' industries, but to take this into account would distract from our central purpose.)

Absolute Rent

The long-term model relevant in the early stages of capitalist development is a variant of the above, in which 'π' is fixed at 'e,' the value of corn established in the urban-rural exchange, under conditions in which earnings are proportional to labor, rather than to inputs as a whole. (This implies that the maximum wage rate in the two sectors is the same.) In agriculture, feudal land tenure has been transformed into capitalist property rights, permitting the former feudal landlords to charge absolute rent, 'ϱ', per acre of land, which depends on the difference between 'e' and 'π,' the price that would rule for the prevailing wage and profit rates, under competitive exchange. This assumes, of course, that the pre-capitalist urban–rural exchange reflected the direct plus indirect labor costs in the respective sectors, a case argued earlier, in Ch. 13. We therefore rewrite the price/profit equations:

$$(\mu + r)\, a + (1 + r)\, wbe\, (1 - \varrho L) = 1 \tag{15.11}$$

$$(\mu + r)\, \alpha + (1 + r)\, w\beta e\, (1 - \varrho L) = e\, (1 - \varrho L) \tag{15.12}$$

Since 'e' is fixed 'r' and 'ϱ' will vary, so that

$$e(1 - \varrho L) = (\beta/b)\, [1 - (\mu + r)\, a] + (\mu + r)\, \alpha \tag{15.13}$$

and

$$(d\varrho/dr) = (1/eL)\, [(a\beta/b) - \alpha]$$

$$= (a/eL)\, [(\beta/b) - (\alpha/a)] > 0 \tag{15.13a}$$

under Marx's assumptions.

Observe that the price of land is given by capitalizing the rents at the rate of profit: $\varrho L/r$. Under the foregoing system, then, absolute rents, and so the price of land, will vary with distribution quite apart from growth or expansion of cultivation. Further and most important, absolute rents and the rate of profits move together relative to the wage. Landlords and capitalists therefore have a common long-term interest in forcing wages down.

But growth also affects rents and land values. To see this, we must reconsider the growth-consumption-output equations for the case of absolute rents. Here, however, 'λ,' unlike 'e,' will be variable. Drawing on (15.9) and (15.10) we can write,

$$\pi = (\alpha/b)\, \lambda = (\alpha/b)\, \{(\beta/\alpha)\, [1 - (\mu + g)\, a] + (\mu + g) b\}$$

$$(d\pi/dg) = (\alpha/b)\, [b - (\beta/\alpha) a] = [\alpha - (\beta/b) a] = a\, [(\alpha/a) - (\beta/b)] < 0$$

But

$$(d\pi/dg) = d[e\, (1 - \varrho L)]/dg = -eL(d\varrho/dg)$$

so

$$-eL(d\varrho/dg) = a\,[(\alpha/a) - (\beta/b)]$$

and

$$(d\varrho/dg) = -\,(a/eL)\,[(\alpha/a) - (\beta/b)] > 0, \text{ since } (\beta/b) > (\alpha/a)$$

Hence, rents and growth move together as a result of expansion, without any variation in land quality, providing landlords and capitalists a common long-term interest in growth.

The Short-term Model

Before capitalism flowers fully in the garden of history, profits may blossom, but will surely vary in size and hue, between sectors, even if uniform within a region. And the same will hold for the wage. Capital but not labor will possess the means to shift between sectors in response to differentials, which means that the proportions in which investment is divided between sectors will vary, creating excess capacity and shortage. This we shall show sets up an oscillatory dynamic, which creates sufficient pressure, but in one direction only, to cause labor to move. To examine this we rewrite the basic price equations with subscripts for the urban and agricultural sectors, respectively:

$$(\mu + r_u)\,a + (1 + r_u)w_u\,be\,(1 - \varrho L) = 1, \quad e(1 - \varrho L) = e' \tag{15.14}$$

$$(\mu + r_A)\,\alpha + (1 + r_A)w_A\,\beta e\,(1 - \varrho L) = e\,(1 - \varrho L) \tag{15.15}$$

$$\max r_u,\ w_u = 1 \tag{15.16a}$$

$$r_u = \frac{1 - \mu a - be'}{a + be'}$$

$$\max r_A,\ w_A = 1 \tag{15.16b}$$

$$r_A = \frac{e' - \mu\alpha - e'\beta}{\alpha + \beta e'} = \frac{e'\,(1 - \beta) - \mu\alpha}{\alpha + \beta e'}$$

$$\max w_u,\ r_u = 0 \tag{15.16c}$$

$$w_u = \frac{1 - \mu a}{be'}$$

$$\max w_A,\ r_A = 0 \tag{15.16d}$$

$$w_A = \frac{e' - \mu\alpha}{\beta e'} \cdot \text{So } e' = \mu\alpha + (\beta/b)(1 - \mu a)$$

Equations (15.14) and (15.15) are rectangular hyperbolas, and can be put in standard form:

$$\begin{cases} w_u = \dfrac{(-a)r_u + (1 - \mu a)}{(be')r_u + (be')} \\ \text{center: } w_u = -1,\ r_u = a/be' \end{cases} \tag{15.17}$$

$$\begin{cases} w_A = \dfrac{(-\alpha)r_A + (e' - \mu\alpha)}{(\beta e')r_A + (\beta e')} \\ \text{center: } w_A = -1,\ r_A = \alpha/\beta e' \end{cases} \tag{15.18}$$

Since $(\beta/\alpha) > (b/a)$ the agriculture wage curve cuts the industry curve from above at the max w, which is the same in both sectors. This is easily seen:

$$\max w_u = (1 - \mu a)/(be');\ \max w_A = (e' - \mu\alpha)/\beta e'$$

Since $e' = \mu\alpha + (\beta/b)(1 - \mu a)$

$$\max w_A = [(\beta/b)(1 - \mu a)]/\beta e'$$

$$\max w_A = (1 - \mu a)/be'$$

so $\max w_A = \max w_u$

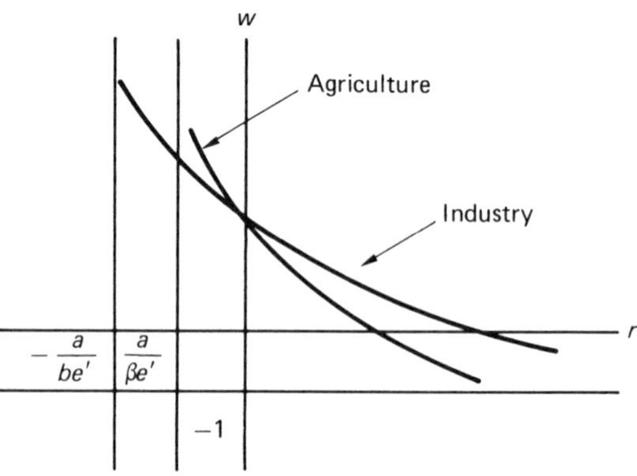

Figure 15.1

(The possibility remains that the curves might intersect again in the positive quadrant. This could happen if the industry curve were relatively flat and the agricultural curve very steep. The conditions for this, however, have no clear economic interpretation.) If profits are above 0, therefore, and if a uniform rate prevails over both sectors, agricultural wages will lie below urban industrial wages. Towns will seem prosperous compared to the countryside.

If profit rates differ, and capital is at least partially mobile, investment will shift, creating capacity shortages and surpluses. This will affect prices, and so profits. Investment in agriculture will also run up against rents, so we must know how rents will affect profits.

Define $\pi'_m = \pi_m (1 - \varrho L)$, to be the market value of corn, where

$$\pi'_m = e' (D/S) \tag{15.19}$$

where D and S are demand and supply. Then

$$(\mu + r_u)\, a + (1 + r_u) w_u\, b\pi'_m = 1, \tag{15.20}$$

and

$$\frac{dr_u}{d\pi'_m} = -\frac{(1 + r_u) w_u b}{a + w_u b\pi'_m} < 0;$$

$$(\mu + r_A)\, \alpha + (1 + r_A) w_A\, \beta\pi'_\mu = \pi'_\mu, \tag{15.21}$$

and

$$\frac{dr_A}{d\pi'_m} = \frac{1 - (1 + r_A) w_A \beta}{\alpha + w_A \beta\pi'_m} > 0.$$

Given the definition of π'_m, it is clear that the short-run effects of a change in rents will be just the opposite: a rise in rent will raise 'r_u' and lower 'r_A.'

$$(dr_u/d\varrho) > 0 \tag{15.20a}$$

$$(dr_A/d\varrho) < 0 \tag{15.21a}$$

Now turn to Growth–Consumption–Output in the Short-Run:

$$(\mu + g_u)\, a + (1 + g_A)\, \bar{c}\alpha\lambda' = 1, \tag{15.22}$$

$$\lambda' = \lambda (1 - \varrho L)$$

$$(\mu + g_u)\, b + (1 + g_A)\, \bar{c}\beta\lambda' = \lambda', \tag{15.23}$$

where

$$\bar{c} = \frac{w_u\, b + r_A\, \beta}{b + \beta},$$

and $\bar{c}$ is total *per capita* consumption.

Industrial input demand for machines, which also depends on the average rate of per capita consumption demand, equals total machine supply. Industrial input demand for grain plus agricultural input demand for grain, which depends on the rate of per capita consumption, equals grain output. The expression for 'λ' depends only on 'g_u'

$$(\mu + g_u)\, b + (\beta/\alpha)\, [1 - (\mu + g_u)\, a] = \lambda' \tag{15.24}$$

$$(d\lambda'/dg_u) = [\mathrm{b} - (a\beta/\alpha)] < 0$$

The effect on 'λ' of an increase in 'g_A' which reduces 'g_u' is exactly the same as if '$\bar{c}$' had increased at the expense of an overall uniform growth rate. Hence, we can see the changes in 'g_u' and 'g_A' which take place in response to profit differentials 'r_u' and 'r_A' reflected in 'λ'. Shifts in investment *ex ante* mean shifts in demand; hence 'λ' shows not only relative *capacity* once the construction of an investment project has been completed, but also relative investment *demand*, which is to say, expenditure. Starting from an initial position then we can analyze the relation between demand and capacity, both in relation to fluctuations of market price around 'e,' and in relation to investment.

For this purpose we shall make two assumptions. First, that in a given period, according as demand exceeds or falls short of capacity, market price exceeds or falls short of 'e,' with the effects on sectoral profit rates noted earlier. Notice that, together with the classical saving assumption, this implies that the market *price mechanism* shifts capital from one sector to another, through the medium of capital gains and losses. We do not have to suppose, implausibly, that established urban enterprises shut up shop, sell out, and buy farms. Second, if in a given period demand falls short of capacity in a sector, so that capital losses are being made, in the succeeding period net investment will drop toward zero. It cannot be assumed that the uninvested funds will shift into the other sector, for there may not be any appropriate investment opportunities. If there are not, then a shortage of effective demand will compound the difficulties of the sector making losses.

Investment in agriculture has certain special features, however. If land is acquired it is reasonable to suppose that it is worse land or more inconvenient, so that 'L' will rise relative to 'α' and 'β.'

$$\frac{dr_A}{dL} = -\frac{e\varrho[1 - (1 + r_A)\, w_A\beta]}{\alpha + w_A\, \beta e\, (1 - \varrho L)} < 0 \tag{15.25}$$

Clearly it would be advantageous for capital to enter agriculture by means other than acquiring land. Consider the possibility of investing by substituting men for equipment on already cultivated land. Suppose first that we simply *convert* existing wage capital into fixed plant, at the going price of machines in terms of grain, '$1/e$.' Then $d\alpha = -\, eyd\beta$, where 'y' is a technical coefficient stating how much machinery will be needed to replace a given reduction of manpower. In the short period, wages and rents will be unaffected by this conversion. Hence,

$$\frac{dr_A}{d\beta} = \frac{A\left[\dfrac{d}{d\beta}\,(e' - \mu\alpha - w_A\, \beta e')\right] - r_A\, A\, \dfrac{dA}{d\beta}}{A^2}, \tag{15.26}$$

where $A = \alpha + w_A\beta e'$

$$= \frac{[-\, \mu\, (d\alpha/d\beta) - w_A\, e' - r_A\, (d\alpha/d\beta) - r_A w_A e']}{A}\,.$$

Then since $(d\alpha/d\beta) = -\, ey$ this simplifies to:

$$= -\frac{w_A e'(1 + r_A) - ey\, (\mu + r_A)}{\alpha + w_A\beta e'}$$

and this will be negative if w_A is substantially > 1, if y is near 1, and if μ is not too large.

It therefore pays to convert wage capital into machines. Intuitively this is obvious; profit is earned on both kinds of capital, but wages must be paid on subsistence capital. So long as 'y' is low, agricultural manpower will be replaced. But there are two circumstances where it would pay even if 'y' were high. It would pay if rents or lease money 'ϱ,' were high and available land of poor quality. It would be better to earn low profit than go into poor land. Secondly, it would make a difference if the actual market price of machinery lay below 'e',' as for example when investment shifted to agriculture and there were excess capacity in industry. The consequences of converting existing or incoming wage capital into machinery are not confined to agriculture. Labor displaced by machinery means people uprooted from land and villages 'cleared.' The homeless and propertyless must find work. They will drift to the towns where the markets and labor exchanges are, where they will drive wages down:

$$w(t) = w(t - 1)\ (D/S), \tag{15.27}$$

where 't' indicates the time period.

Cyclical Accumulation

First I will describe the process informally, then more precisely using a diagram, and finally, I will compare the results to modern neo-Classical theory. Let us start with the formation of a rate of profit out of the surplus value in each sector. Initially we can expect the industrial profit rate to exceed the agricultural (15.17, 15.18). If it did not, investment in agriculture, expanding cultivation, will lower 'r_A' relative to 'r_u' (15.20, 15.21), so that eventually $g_u > g_A$. The consequence is to bring down 'λ'' (15.24), which implies that corn demand falls relative to corn capacity, while industrial demand rises relative to capacity; so there will develop a shortage of urban goods, and an excess of corn. Market price changes (15.19) will thus cause a further widening of the spread between the profit rates (15.20, 15.21), with a further shift of investment to industry; 'g_u' will now lie well above the growth rate of the skilled population of laborers, and by next period wages will rise in rough proportion (15.27). This has two effects: it reduces the overall growth rate (15.6, 15.7) especially that of industry (15.20, 15.21) and it increases consumption. Thus the new 'λ' rises, swinging towards corn production (15.24). This yields a price effect at once, as corn rises and machines fall, bringing 'r_A' up towards, perhaps above, 'r_u.' But the principal effect, as far as investment is concerned, is to create excess capacity in the now expanded urban sector. This excess capacity will cause net investment next period to fall dramatically, as capital shifts to agriculture. The shift in turn brings a further relative price rice in corn, exacerbating the demand shortage in industry, where prices fall further.

But to flow into agriculture, capital must pay the tariff of absolute rent (15.14, 15.15) and any substantial influx would bid up wages. Yet at this phase, machines are at their cheapest. It is therefore peculiarly advantageous to mechanize (15.25, 15.26), for it takes advantage of cheap prices, avoids the tariff of absolute rent, and moderates or avoids the rise in wages. (By contrast, when wages rises in industry, machine prices are at their highest). The agricultural demand for machines will therefore absorb some or all of industry's excess capacity and strengthen its prices. (By providing employment this also prevents urban wages from falling.)

But the cycle will not swing back until the displaced agricultural labor hits the urban market. *Then* wages will fall, and industrial profits soar. Urban growth rises and 'λ' swings towards machinery. Agricultural prices weaken, mechanization ceases and the short-term effects of rents eat into rural profits, driving off potential investment. With the shift of new capital to industry the cycle begins again.

This mechanism can be illustrated with a diagram. Note that the heavily shaded vertical axis is a line of division, measuring profit rates on the left and farm output on the right. Initially suppose wages are at subsistence in both sectors, the price ratio is e' and output 'λ',' equal to capacity in both sectors. But '$r_u > r_A$' which implies that both outputs and prices must swing towards industry. (See dotted arrows) This will shift the 'r_u' curve up and the 'r_A' curve down, increasing the discrepancy between 'r_u' and 'r_A,' and causing a further change in 'λ'.' (Such changes, however, initially mean a rise in the demand for industrial goods, and so there emerges a shortage of industrial capacity, thus raising the urban market price.) The attempt to expand industrial output eventually leads to a bidding up of the urban wage, as shown in the lower right hand quadrant. (Below subsistence, the wage moves slowly with output, above, it moves rapidly.) This lowers urban profits and raises the demand for farm products, raising the profit rate in agriculture. As a consequence 'λ'' moves back towards agriculture (perhaps shortening in the process), causing the emergence of excess capacity in the now-expanded urban industry. Excess capacity in towns, together with increased demand for farm products leads prices to shift also, so the profit curves shift back towards their original levels. The consequence will be investment in agriculture, eventually producing an outflow of labor that will shift the urban wage curve, reducing the urban wage again to subsistence, as shown in Figure 15.2.

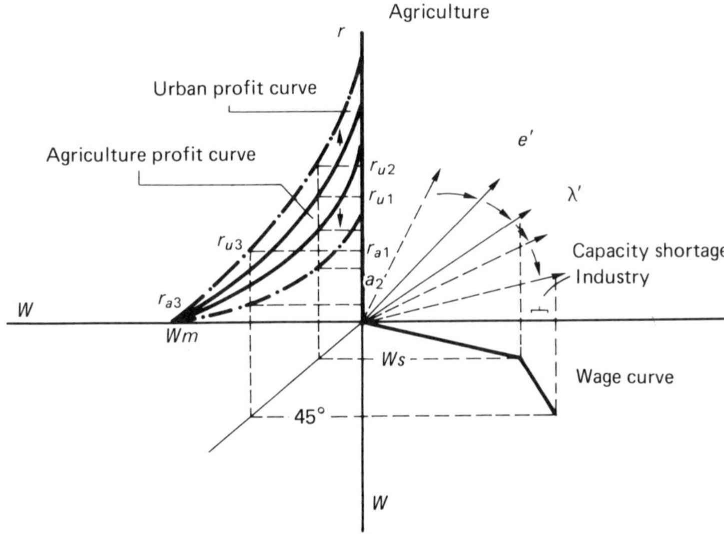

Figure 15.2

The process can be simplified by considering it in two stages.

Stage 1 $r_{u1} > r_{a1}$ to a shift towards industry in demand and prices, creating capacity shortage in industry, shifting the urban profit curve up and the agriculture profit curve down, putting further pressure on industrial capacity and bidding up the wage, thus lowering both rates of profit (see Figure 15.3).

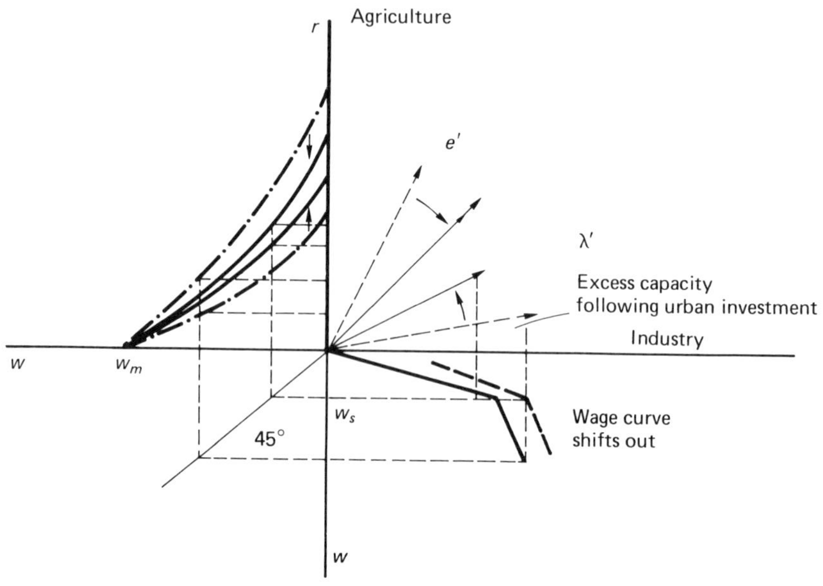

Figure 15.3

Stage II The higher wage leads to a shift of demand and output back towards agriculture, bringing excess capacity in the expanded urban sector, causing industrial prices to fall, encouraging mechanization of agriculture, which shifts the urban wage curve out, bringing wages back to the initial subsistence level.

This model is not in Marx so many words but it is kin in spirit, 'Marx after Goodwin,' one would say. Its central feature is the cyclical and asymmetrical pattern of pressure leading to mechanization of agriculture, creating homeless laborers who drift to towns in search of work. Technical change is the source of the labor supply, but comes about only as a result of the effects of intersectoral trade upon income distribution. When it does, it changes not only economic variables, but also, over time, the pattern of daily life throughout much of society. The accumulation of capital is also the develoment of capitalism.

References

Goodwin, R.M. (1972) 'A Growth Cycle,' in E.K. Hunt and J.G. Schwartz (eds), *A Critique of Economic Theory* (Harmondsworth: Penguin).
Goodwin, R.M. (1948) 'Secular and Cyclical Aspects of the Multiplier and Accelerator,' in *Income, Employment and Public Policy: Essays in Honor of A.H. Hansen* (New York: Norton).
Hicks, J.R. (1950) *A Contribution to the Theory of the Trade Cycle* (Oxford, Oxford University Press).
Kaldor, N. (1940) 'A Model of the Trade Cycle,' *Economic Journal*, 50.
Marx, K. (1967) *Capital*, Vols I, II and III (New York: International Publishers).
Nell, E. (1985) 'Finance, Risk and Investment Spending,' in A. Barriere (ed.), *Keynes Today: Theories and Policies* (London: Macmillan).
Nell, E. (1967) 'Economic Relationship, in the Decline of Feudalism,' *History and Theory*, V.
Nell, E. (1976) 'Population, The Price Revolution, and Primitive Accumulation,' *Peasant Studies*, 6 (1)
Nell, E. (1984) *Historia y Teoria Economica* (Editorial Critica, Barcelona).
Schumpeter, J.A. (1939) *Business Cycles* (New York: McGraw Hill).

16 Transformational Growth: From Say's Law to the Multiplier*

There's a famous Sherlock Holmes story in which the clue is the dog that didn't bark. The history of economic thought presents us with a similar clue – in the multiplier that wasn't there, in the work of Ricardo and Marx and, indeed, other 19th century economists. Why, when they developed many analytically more difficult ideas, did they fail to develop the multiplier? In the case of Ricardo and Marx, the problem is particularly striking, since the direct and indirect labor embodied in a good *is* the employment multiplier for that good, and the set of labor values for the economy as a whole is the matrix employment multiplier for the economy. Why, when they developed the theory of labor values, did Ricardo and Marx not take the further step of defining the employment multiplier?

The dog didn't bark because nothing unusual occurred; perhaps Ricardo and Marx didn't define a multiplier because no such processes took place in their time when investment or exports varied. This may be an important clue to the nature of early capitalism – and even more significantly, to the way capitalism has developed.

Early capitalism consisted largely of family firms and family farms operating production technologies that depended on the presence and cooperation of skilled workers, working together. Such an economy tended to run at full employment, unless seriously disrupted by business failures; markets tended to clear through price adjustments. Employment remained fixed in the face of fluctuations in sales; when output varied it was through changes in the productivity of labor. But this system created strong incentives to change the methods of production – in particular, to make current costs variable, especially labor. By the end of the 19th century the methods of Mass Production were developed and came into prominence, but their successful adoption depended on the simultaneous emergence of a mass market. This process can be called 'transformational growth' for, once adopted, these innovations in technology change the way the system works, replacing price with multiplier adjustments and full utilization with normal excess capacity. Changes of this kind are continuing and we can perhaps see the beginnings of a new kind of economy, based on information systems.

* Written for this volume.

1 FIXED VS VARIABLE EMPLOYMENT

We begin by examining an aspect of technology that has largely been overlooked, namely the extent to which the process of production permits inputs or costs, and even output itself, to be varied so as to adapt to fluctuations in the state of demand. There are several dimensions of variability and examples may help: if there is no refrigeration or method of storage, the whole current supply of fish and vegetables must be offered for sale – otherwise it will spoil. If demand has fallen, supply on the market cannot be reduced, so price will be forced down. Sometimes output cannot be varied: spring planting (and the weather) determines the fall harvest; if demand has dropped in the meantime, output cannot be changed, although grain can be stored, so supply could be changed – at a cost. In a traditional blacksmith's shop, the forge must be lit, and the apprentices on hand, whether much or little work is to be done. Energy and labor costs will be the same for quite a wide range of levels of daily output. Lighting the forge and in steam-driven factories, building up a head of steam is time-consuming and labor-intensive. Thus, faced with fluctuations in demand, the methods of production may or may not permit:

- supply offered to the market
- output produced
- employment
- energy costs

to be varied *pari passu*. To the extent that all or any of these cannot be varied, excess or shortage of supply will exert pressure on prices. But employment is the key: if it cannot be varied then the largest part of current costs will be fixed, and output can be made variable only by changing productivity.

To see the contrasts sharply, compare 'pure' stylized cases. As an example of a Fixed Employment system we will take an idealized Artisan economy, in which small family firms – and farms – practise traditional crafts. The system is capitalist, in that a (more or less uniform) rate of profit prevails and governs investment, but it is not industrial. Craft methods are practised by teams of workers following long traditions. Craft work requires the presence of the entire work team, full time, for there to be any output at all. Start-up and shut-down costs are typically large, as are storage costs. The little technical progress that takes place is unsystematic and there are few, if any, economies of scale.

In such an economy, in the long run, prices must cover costs (including normal profits), so will reflect distribution, but in the short run, employment will be relatively stable since work teams cannot easily be broken up, with the result that a high proportion of current costs will be fixed.[1]

Needing to cover these costs and lacking technology for storage and preservation, when demand weakens goods will have to be sold for whatever they will bring, so that prices will adjust to the requirements of market-clearing. Employment and output will tend to be stable, prices flexible.

Artisan production may have a well-developed division of labor, and it may also be highly mechanized. (Adam Smith's pin factory has the first, and Marshall's examples of the printing and watch-making trades exhibit the second as well.[2]) Prior to Mass Production the use of machinery replaces the workers' energy; but the machine system drives essentially the same tools, though on a much larger scale.[3] Such use of machinery does not affect the system's characteristic mode of operation. For neither division of labor nor mechanization will have proceeded to the point where the pace and quality of production is controlled by the machinery, as in the assembly line.

In the Artisan economy the work team must be kept together; everyone works or no one works. In the extreme case, layoffs are simply not possible. If machinery is used it must likewise all be used. Work is skilled and workers have to coordinate their efforts; workers themselves largely set the pace of work, so that productivity depends heavily on morale. A work crew that functions well together is highly important. Moreover, (especially with the use of steam power) start-up and shut-down costs are significant, so that the firm cannot go on half time or close down for part of the week.[4] (At a later point, however, we will consider variations in employment through reorganization of work, while continuing to use the same tools and methods.) Finally, products are non-standard: they are made to order, and storage facilities are both poor and expensive; losses in terms of wastage and decay are heavy.

The system of mass production differs in every one of these respects; products are standardized, and storage facilities climate and pest-controlled. The pace of work is governed by the speed of the assembly line, or other machinery; jobs are broken down into their simplest components, reducing the need for skill. Skills remain important but, ideally, no worker need have more than one basic skill, to be exercised repetitively, in conditions where precision equipment eliminates much of the need for judgement or timing. Tasks are regularly simplified through time and motion studies. Work is continually reorganized, resulting in a persistent, though variable, tendency for output per worker to rise. The labor force has no need to interact, so morale counts for nothing, and workers are dispensible and interchangeable. Finally, start-up and shut-down costs are minimal; power is provided by petroleum-based fuels and electricity. These differences in technology and labor requirements make possible a very 'different form of market organization – the corporate industrial system of mass production.

Here, production is carried out by corporations, organized as large bureaucracies, the ownership of which is decided in the financial markets. Technical progress is regular, economies of scale are widespread. New products and new processes are frequent and innovation is one aspect of competition. The size of an operating unit in the Artisan economy will be limited by difficulties of coordination, cost of transport for distant markets, storage costs and increasing risks; in many cases, craft technologies will dictate a 'natural' size for the plant, and family firms will tend to operate a single plant. In the case of Mass Production, however, a larger plant confers economies of scale which must be balanced against increasing risks and distribution costs. But plant size does not determine firm size. Growth is inherent in the system, and investment is carried out as far as possible by existing firms – who will not leave it to newcomers. For new entrants would threaten the arrangements in existing markets since new equipment will normally be superior to old, providing newcomers with a competitive edge. Hence firms will do their own saving, in the form of retained earnings. Price guidelines will be set so as to earn just enough on normal operations to finance the expected required investment, given the anticipated growth of the market at such prices. Actual prices will be held close to the guidelines; fluctuations in demand will be met by adjusting production and employment.

The Artisan economy fundamentally has only two levels of operation: all out or zero. To cut back output, work must be done more slowly – but the entire crew will still be working. Given time, work can be reorganized, so some variation in employment is possible, but given an organization of work the only way to adjust output is to vary productivity at the margin. By contrast the Mass Production system is able to maintain productivity while varying output. The Artisan system thus has fixed capacity utilization and variable productivity, while Mass Production has variable capacity utilization and fixed productivity at the margin. Hence an Artisan process will have low variable and high fixed costs, but the fixed costs will in large part be current costs, set in real terms, rather than capital costs fixed in monetary terms. The industrial economy, on the other hand, will have much higher variable costs, and its fixed costs will be capital costs set in monetary terms.[5] In the Artisan economy, therefore, changes in demand may lead to changes in the intensity with which workers work, but not to changes in employment. If demand increases, then output *per capita* may be increased, although output per unit of effort may actually decline – indeed, normally will decline after a point. Conversely, when demand declines, output *per capita* will decline, although output per unit of effort could remain constant, or increase.

Since employment is largely fixed, worker consumption will be governed by real wages. Money wages will be set at the time of employment, and since employment tends to be relatively constant, money wages will not vary much either. Prices, on the other hand, will reflect the need to earn as much over current costs as demand and the competition permit; hence when demand is below normal, competitive price cutting will take place, and when it is above normal prices will rise. Prices will therefore be quite flexible. Hence real wages will move inversely to variations in demand. If the chief cause of variations in overall demand is investment, reflecting 'the general state of business confidence' then, since consumption will tend to change in the opposite direction, the system has a built-in stabilizing mechanism.[6]

Real world economies will always be a mixture; very likely no economy was ever purely Fixed Employment or purely Mass Production. But the two systems differ profoundly in their mode of operation, a point which shows up most clearly in the way markets adjust to variations in demand. In the Mass Production economy adjustment takes place through the multiplier, but in the Craft economy the adjustment process concerns prices and distribution (and therefore, also, costs) and it affects different sectors and markets differently. It turns out, in fact, to be a complete system of market relationships of very traditional form, revolving around the system's long-period position.

2 NORMAL PRICES: THE LONG-RUN SETTING FOR BOTH SYSTEMS

Both systems are capitalist and are therefore described by the basic equations of prices, wages and profits, showing how production generates a surplus, provides for reproduction, and divides the surplus between labor and capital. But these equations are too abstract to capture the difference between Craft and Mass Production technologies. Nor, therefore, can these equations provide an understanding of the adjustment processes, though they do provide the setting (i.e., the 'normal' values). Present capacity was built because it was believed that with the sizes and techniques chosen, at the given locations, operations could be run at wage and price combinations that would provide profits at a normal rate. These various anticipated valuations, entering into formal and informal contracts, thus reflect the generally prevalent beliefs and expectations about prices and wages, sales and profits, and form the basis for all long-term decisions about the construction of capacity.[7]

Grouping all the various industries into two major sectors, capital goods and consumer goods respectively, we can refer to the equations for normal prices, as developed in earlier chapters.[8] The capital goods sector produces a composite output which is used both in its own production and in the production of consumer goods. This composite good lasts for more than one period of production and depreciates at a given rate each period.

The consumption goods sector produces a composite output, one unit of which supports workers and their families at the socially normal standard of living for one period. The wage rate will then be a percentage of this, say 110% or 95%. (Making the real wage here a pure number ensures compatibility with the monetary real wage, which is 'money wages/time period' divided by 'money value of consumer goods/time period' – a pure number.) These are *average* rather than best-practice coefficients because we are setting out the long-period relationships underlying the actual economy, as it is operating now.[9] The normal coefficients contain very minimal information; they are incapable of distinguishing between Craft and Mass Production technologies.

In the Craft economy businesses will be set up largely with borrowed capital, mobilized by banks from the savings of capitalist families; hence the rate of interest on money capital will govern the organization of new businesses, which will have to earn at least that, plus the normal compensation for management and the normal premium for risk, to be viable. Thus competition will have established, if not a uniform rate of profit, then a system of profits such that the non-uniformities stand in fixed and clearly defined relationships. In the Mass Production economy, the financial system is more complicated, but arbitrage between growth stocks, blue chips and bonds tends to bring interest, dividend earnings and financial growth together. Financial growth, however, reflects the market's judgement of firm's investment policies; in the long run, and barring major speculative disturbances, it should therefore mirror real growth. So growth, profits and the rate of interest will be brought into line with one another. (Ch. 21, below). Looked at another way, prices in the corporate industrial economy have to be set to provide the profits that will be adequate to underwrite normal growth (Eichner, 1976; Sylos-Labini, 1985; Ch. 17, below).

For simplicity, let us approximate this by a uniform rate. (Non-uniform profit rates provide no problems so long as the profit differentials are stable, see Semmler, 1984) It can be assumed that, sharing a common class position, all workers consume at the same rate, and that both sectors will grow in tandem, each being necessary for the successful functioning of the other. Capital goods will be used up and newly invested in proportion to the scale of each sector in which they are employed; consumption goods will be consumed in proportion to the employment in each sector. Then the equations will be those we have already seen for the price and quantity systems. The wage-profit and consumption-growth tradeoffs can be derived, and we can explore the behavior of relative prices and quantities.

Next we need a relationship between wages and consumption and/or between profits and investment. To allow for full generality, there must be room for both worker saving and capitalist consumption; therefore let consumption be a function of both wages and profits: $c = f(w, r)$. Then from the quantity equation knowing q, we have g, from which we obtain c by means of the c, g equation. Hence we have $c = f(w, r)$ and the w, r tradeoff, two equations to determine the two unknowns, w and r. Provided the consumption equation is of simple form this will always be solvable. Then, once r is known, the price equation yields p, and the solution is complete. Given the capacity sizes of the sectors the long-run valuations inherent in the system can always be computed on the assumption that the capacity is utilized as expected.[10] (Cf. Ch. 17.)

But the capacities of the sectors do not represent 'endowments' in the neo-Classical sense. They have been constructed in the expectation of a certain pattern of demand, which in turn reflected the anticipated distribution of income. Thus the relative capacities do not 'close' the system: they are determined rather than determining. Moreover, there is no sense in which these productive capacities could be 'scarce'; they are the results of past investment and they will change with current investment. Long-run prices accordingly are governed by distribution and the requirements of reproduction, not by the relation between endowments and preferences, mediated by technology.

Precisely because these are the 'inherent' prices, no one expects them to be actually realized at any particular time. They will appear as averages and function as guidelines; current prices will be established by considering the deviation of current market demand and supply from the normal position.

3 PRICES, SUPPLY AND DEMAND UNDER FIXED EMPLOYMENT

Given the normal prices and the normal rate of profit, variations in demand will lead to price and output adjustments in the Fixed Employment system. These, in turn, give rise to pressures for innovations that will reduce the costs and risks of such adjustments.

The Optimal Size of the Firm

In a Fixed Employment economy firms will seek their optimal size, and continue to operate at that size indefinitely (Robinson, 1931). When technical progress is irregular and economies of scale rare, existing firms will normally not risk overextending themselves by making new investments, especially when markets are local and transport and storage costs are high. By contrast under conditions of Mass Production, firms will invest and grow, keeping pace with the growth of the market. Growth under conditions of Fixed Employment therefore implies investment in the formation of new firms, rather than investment in the expansion and renovation of existing firms – 'extensive' rather than 'intensive' expansion.

The reasons can be seen quite easily. Plot plant size on the horizontal axis against costs and gains on the vertical. The larger the size the larger the earnings, but economies of scale are relatively few; assume for the sake of the argument that there are also relatively few diseconomies. (This is to avoid the traditional argument that there are first economies of scale then diseconomies, yielding a U-shaped average cost curve, the optimal size of the firm being that at which average costs are a minimum. Sraffa (1926) has argued that the ideas of increasing and diminishing returns cannot be combined in this way.) The relation between size and earning can therefore be approximated by a straight line, implying constant marginal returns to size. At low sizes the costs and risk due to size will be nil; at some point, however, a larger size will begin to imply significant transport and storage costs – the plant will be larger than the immediately accessible market. As the area served increases, these will rise rapidly, under conditions of Craft technology.

Further, while a small and localized operation may be relatively immune to variations in the state of demand, a larger operation will not be. The amplitude of fluctuations and the degree to which they affect all localities may be assumed to be more or less normally distributed. A small localized firm will therefore be affected only by relatively rare (or large or universal) depressions. But a larger operation extending into a number of regions will be vulnerable to smaller and more frequent fluctuations in the state of trade, and will, therefore, face a greater risk of losses due to overproduction. More precisely, assume that in general the smallest firms are only affected by the largest and most widespread downswings in demand, and larger firms by correspondingly smaller downturns. Then as firm size increases, the number of recessions which will affect a firm (and therefore the risk it faces) will be given by the cumulative frequency of the distribution of fluctuations, calculated as fluctuations decrease in size from largest to smallest. Hence starting from a normal small size of firm, risk will increase rapidly with size until firms become quite large (at which point it will increase more slowly, following the shape of the cumulative frequency curve). In addition, a larger firm can be expected to require a higher proportion of external finance. Since employment is fixed, and variable costs low, the burden of adjustment falls on profits, so the larger the share of external finance the greater the risk of bankruptcy.

Turning to the graph in Figure 16.1, the cost–size relationship will begin from a positive point on the horizontal axis, rise slowly at first, and then turn up steeply, eventually cutting the size–earning line. The optimal size of the plant will be found at the point where the marginal cost just equals the marginal gain due to extra plant size.

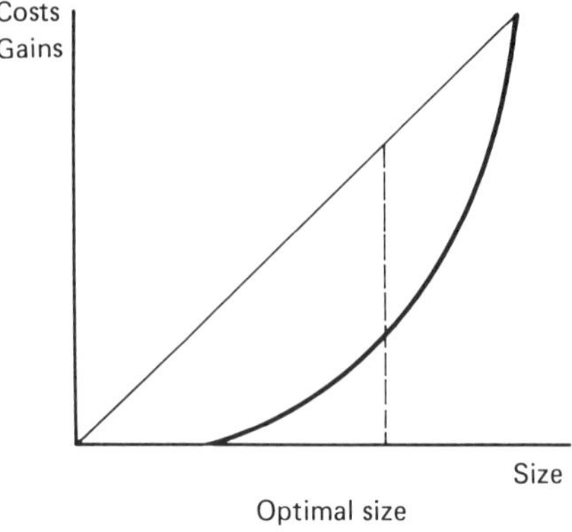

Figure 16.1

The optimal number of plants which a given management coordinates depends on the organizational arrangements and on the effectiveness of communication. It may be wiser for a family to diversify its portfolio, rather than invest it all in one line of business.

Given that growth takes place by founding new firms of optimal size, the savings–investment nexus must now be explored.

Finance and Savings in the Craft Economy

The financial market mobilizes savings, which will come chiefly from capitalist families, and channels them into new investments, normally made by new firms. So firms will pay out all their profits, since they have no need of retained earnings. The market therefore collects household savings and makes them available to entrepreneurs founding new enterprises.[11]

Savings out of profit income, and therefore loanable funds, will obviously be higher, the higher the rate of return.[12] Two observations are relevant at this point. First, the cross-sectional pattern of saving is easily explained by this approach; high income households normally have a large component of property income, most of which they save. Low income and most middle income households have only wage income, and save little.[13] Second, in early capitalism, operating Artisan technology, we would not expect saving to be tightly related to current income – since consumption and investment are inversely related.[14]

The Marginal Efficiency of Capital Schedule

Using the prices determined in the analysis of the long-run setting the various possible investment projects can be evaluated and ranked.[15] In an Artisan economy the number of possible projects can be considered given at any time; innovation is irregular and infrequent. Each project creates a new firm, and each such firm will be of 'normal' size – an optimum given by the number of employees a family firm can effectively manage, balancing the limited economies of scale against the increasing risks of size.[16] Each project will have a cost – the price of plant and equipment – and each will generate a stream of returns – gross revenue minus wage and other current costs – over the expected lifetime of the project. The marginal efficiency is the discount rate that equates the discounted sum of this stream to the project's cost. Projects can be ranked by their marginal efficiencies and the amount of investment in successive projects can be measured on one axis with the progressively lower marginal efficiency on the other. If investment projects now are as numerous and as profitable as expected when the capacity in the capital goods sector was installed, the amount of investment demanded at the marginal efficiency just equal to the current rate of interest will equal the normal capacity of that sector, and this will also just equal the saving out of normal profits (and wages). This is the normal position.

Under normal conditions new investment projects will produce the same goods by the same methods as existing firms. The new projects will differ in location and in the experience and skill of the workers and entrepreneurs. But in a period of innovation many investment projects may be designed to produce new products or to employ new techniques.

Now consider the effects of changes in the state of confidence, due to anything which affects a business's estimate of future sales. If the future looks bleak, prices will be expected to fall, if it looks rosy, they will rise, relative to normal prices. Consider the evaluation of an n-period project:

$$p_1q_1 = (p_2q_2-wn) \,/\, (1+\varrho) + (p_2q_2-wn) \,/\, (1+\varrho)^2 + \\ \ldots (p_2q^2-wn) \,/\, (1+\varrho)^n$$

If p_1, p_2 and w all rose or fell in the same proportion, the marginal efficiency, ϱ, would be unaffected; but if p_1 and p_2 change in the same proportion, but w remains fixed or changes by less, then the earnings stream changes relative to the cost, and ϱ will change. Changes in prices relative to money wages will therefore shift the marginal efficiency curve; a rise will shift it outwards, a decline inwards.

Such changes will also affect the rankings of projects; when prices rise relative to their normal levels, the real wage declines, and the more labor-intensive a project is, the more profitable it becomes. Thus the largest increases in profitability will take place in projects requiring the least investment; projects previously far down the line may be moved up to the forefront. Hence the shift will be irregular and the shape of the curve may change. The intercept on the horizontal axis shifts out because the cost

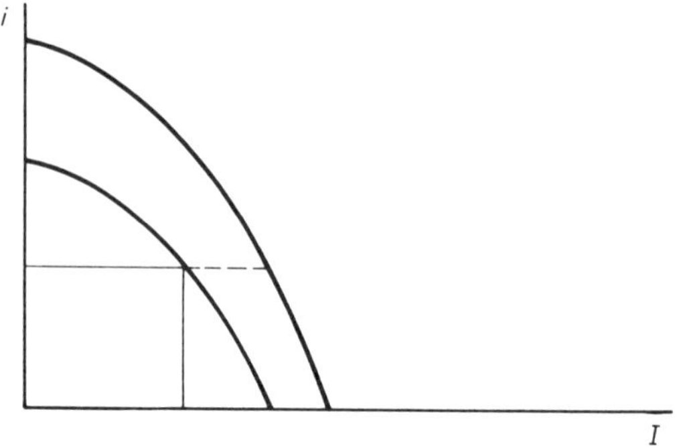

Figure 16.2

of each project increases as the prices of capital goods rise. In the new ranking the most profitable projects will be grouped near the origin on the horizontal axis; thus at these levels the curve will shift up the most (Figure 16.2).

Shifting the Marginal Efficiency Curve in the Short Run

Start from the marginal efficiency curve in its normal position, and consider an improvement in the state of confidence; the curve will alter position and shift up and out, as shown in Figure 16.2. (Employment in existing firms is taken as fixed during the period under analysis; variations in employment due to reorganization will be examined later.) At the initial level of the interest and profit rates, saving – loanable funds – equalled investment. Investment demand is now higher, but the anticipated profit rate on existing operations will also be higher, since the real wage is lower. (The increase in profits on current operations will be more pronounced in labor-intensive industries.[17]) Hence, funds will not be loaned at the old rate of interest new loans will be made at a higher rate, reflecting the higher rate of profit. In turn, the demand for loans will be higher, but at the higher interest rate investment demand will, of course, be less than at the initial rate. Hence both the interest rate and the level of savings rise, the first reflecting the increase in the realized rate of profit, the second relecting the level of profit generated by the larger investment demand, resulting in the higher level of prices. Neglecting savings out of wages, the relationship will be

$$i = s_p P/K,$$

where s_p is the saving propensity out of profits, P, and K is the capital stock evaluated at the long-period prices.

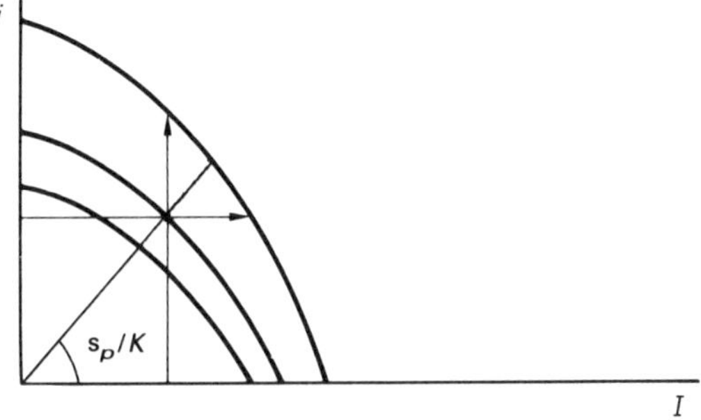

Figure 16.3

An exactly parallel analysis holds for a decline in the state of confidence, leading to lower prices relative to money wages, resulting in a downward shift of the MEC schedule, bringing lower profit and interest rates. These in turn bring lower levels of saving and investment, but because of the lower interest rate, the decline in investment will be less than indicated by considering the initial shift in the marginal efficiency curve at the normal level of interest. The relationship between interest and savings is thus a line from the origin with a slope of s_p/K. The diagram of the two schedules (Figure 16.3) thus presents a falling marginal efficiency curve coupled with a rising interest-rate/savings curve, which looks for all the world exactly like the traditional picture.

An implication of this analysis is that when the marginal efficiency schedule shifts, prices and interest rates will move together; as prices rise and fall relative to the money wage, they generate movements in the same direction in realized profits, which in turn (no doubt with some lag) bring a corresponding movement in the rate of interest. Since these are movements around the 'normal' level, we should see deviations in both directions, corresponding to periods of boom and slump. This corresponds to the pattern discussed by Keynes under the heading 'Gibson's Paradox' (cf. Keynes, 1973, *Treatise on Money*. Vol II, pp. 198–208).

Construction of Demand and Supply Curves

An increase in investment demand will not only bid up the price of capital goods; it will also increase their output, as workers in the capital goods sector intensify their efforts. In the same way a decline in investment demand, due to a collapse of confidence, shifting the marginal efficiency curve in, will lead to a fall in both price and output. Let us explore this in a diagram (Figure 16.4).

Plot price on the vertical axis and the output of capital goods on the horizontal. Then since the marginal efficiency–saving–interest market fixes

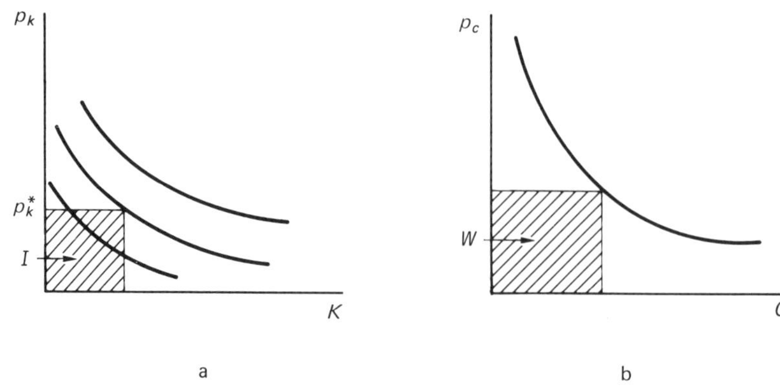

Figure 16.4

investment demand in nominal terms as an amount, I, the demand curve for capital goods will be a curve of unit elasticity, the area under which will be I. An increase in I means a shift outwards of the curve.

When p_k is at the normal level, $p_k{}^*$, I will purchase the number of capital goods needed for expansion to supply the expected growth in the market. So when $p_k > p_k{}^*$ too few goods will be purchased, resulting in a growing shortage of output in consumer goods, leading prices there eventually to rise. Similarly when $p_k < p_k{}^*$ capital goods will be bought in excess, leading to overbuilding and downward pressure on prices. (Initially firms may buy the correct amount of capital goods more cheaply; but competition will force prices down, leading to expansion of consumer demand, and hence to increased derived demand for capital goods, so the full amount of I will be spent.)

A version of marginal utility analysis can help to explain the way wage-earning consumers adjust their spending when conditions change. A normal pattern of consumption must be taken as given at the outset – explained by household technology and social conventions. Income will be divided into categories of expenditure between which fixed ratios will hold in normal circumstances. Then two kinds of variation can take place: money incomes can change, with prices fixed, or prices can change, with money incomes fixed. On the assumption that marginal utilities are in equilibrium in normal conditions, changes in expenditure patterns can be explained by the *relative* changes in marginal utilities. With prices given, when money income changes, expenditures on goods A and B will change according to the relationship between MUa_1/MUa_2 and MUb_1/MUb_2, where '1' indicates the initial position and '2' the position after the change. Similarly when prices change, incomes given, spending will depend on a comparison of the changed marginal utility of A with the changed marginal utility of B. It will never be necessary to compare the marginal utility of A directly to that of B – the utility from additional furniture per unit money

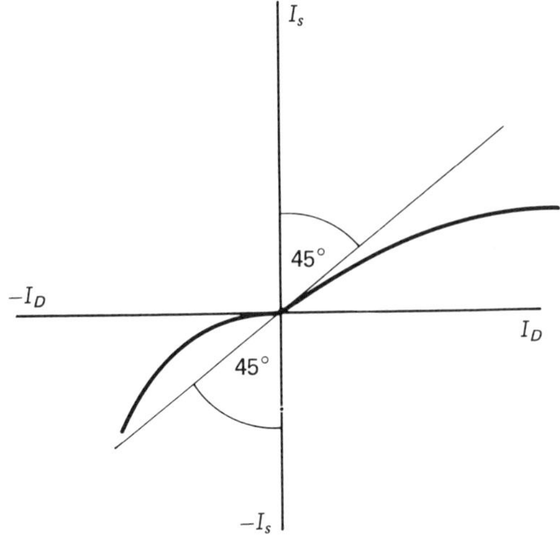

Figure 16.5

need not be measured against that from additional heating or entertainment per unit money. Only the rates of change have to be compared. So long as marginal utility is always positive but diminishing, the changes in expenditure on the different categories of consumption will be determinate. But what is explained is not the normal pattern of consumption – that is assumed given – but the changes in consumption due to changes in income or prices.

Next consider the ability of production to respond to an increase in demand to a point above the long-term normal level. For small increases in demand the intensification of effort will yield the required output; but as the increases become larger, the proportion which can be supplied falls off (Figure 16.5).

The positive vertical axis measures output supplied, while the negative section shows output diminished; the horizontal shows demand above and below normal. The 45° line indicates that demand and supply are equal. In the positive quadrant the curve falls away from this fully adjusted line, indicating that higher levels of demand are progressively harder to supply through intensification of work effort. When demand falls below normal capacity there will be a tendency to maintain production – not adjust at all – and only when the shortfall is large will supply adjust. This is shown by a curve which runs along the horizontal axis to the left, then turning in towards the 45° line.

Now consider an outward shift of the unit-elasticity curve, representing a horizontal shift in investment demand. The production-response function determines the proportion of this increase in demand which can be supplied. Mark this off, and then read upward to the new unit-elasticity curve

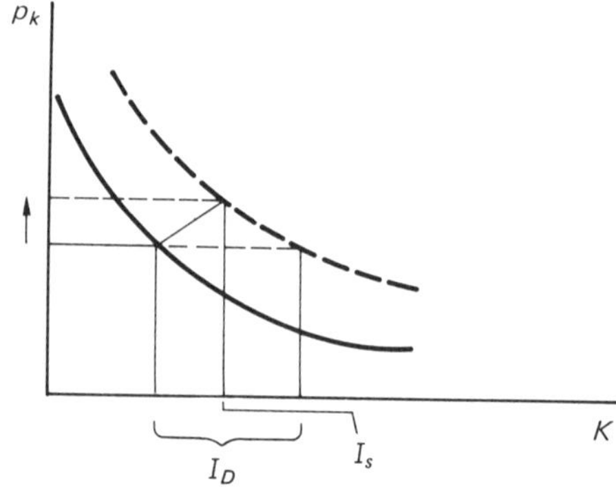

Figure 16.6

to find the new price. Consider a different (larger or smaller) shift in demand, and repeat the process. Joining the resulting points traces out a 'rising supply curve.' The same procedure, using the negative section of the production-response function, can be followed to trace out declining prices and output (Figure 16.6).

The curve traced out in this way looks exactly like a traditional supply curve, but it does not reflect scarcity of endowments in relation to preferences, and in particular it does not reflect marginal costs. It does, however, reflect the difficulty of adjusting output through intensification of work using given produced means of production – something like Marshall's 'real costs.'

A Shift in Production at the Margin

The higher price of capital goods signifies higher costs of production in consumer goods, where prices will now have to be raised. Since money wages and (initially) employment are fixed, the higher price of consumer goods means a decline in real wages and so a proportional decline in demand. Pressure will therefore develop for work to be done less intensively in consumer goods, more intensively in capital goods. It is plausible, therefore, to consider a shift of some marginal workers from the consumer goods sector to the capital goods sector.

In equilibrium, $w\Delta N_c = \Delta Cp_c$ and $w\Delta N_k = \Delta Ip_k$ will both hold; if the additional wage cost in either sector were less than the value of additional output, it would pay to hire more workers; if it were greater it would pay to dismiss some. However, there is no need to suppose that adjustment will take place through the contribution to output of additional workers diminishing; instead here the additional output will lead to a decline in price. What look like marginal productivity conditions both hold and govern adjustments, but the pattern of causation is different.

The above conditions also imply

$$[\Delta N_c/\Delta C] \,/\, \{\Delta N_k/\Delta I\} = p_c/p_k$$

So when p_c and/or p_k change there will have to be changes in the ratio of the productivities. This can be accomplished through changes in the intensity of work, as indicated earlier. Thus when p_c rises – for example, due to greater demand – work intensity for the given labor force will increase, and (analogously with Figure 16.5) labor effort required per unit of output will rise. This is acceptable provided variations in 'work intensity' or 'labor effort' mean *longer hours*, which are therefore equivalent to additional labor time. But in an Artisan economy work intensity may not always be expressible in terms of additional work time; craft workers may adjust their work pace, working harder at some times to meet exceptional demand, taking it easy at other times when demand is slack. In such a case, it would not be possible to adjust the ratio of the productivities to the new price ratio.

Even where it is possible, working at greater intensity than normal can be presumed to be harder, more dangerous, or less healthy. Surely there were good reasons for establishing the normal level in the first place? Hence such work can be only temporary; in traditional terms, it involves an increase in the disutility of labor, at the same time that the real wage is diminished. Working harder for less pay requires that the conditions of work will have to be changed. This means investment, the construction of additional capacity, so that the pace of work can be returned to its normal level. The role, then, of the 'marginal disutility of labor' is to require that the adjustment be merely temporary, and that the additional output brought about by more intensive use of existing facilities be replaced with additional output from new capacity. The converse case will also have to be short run; when output is reduced through working at less than the normally intensive pace and this is coupled with higher wages, employers will eventually want to dispose of workers that are both expensive and underutilized.

Thus, rather than (or in addition to) changing work intensity in response to changes in the price ratio, workers will shift from the contracting sector to the expanding one. Such a shift will make sense if

$$w\Delta N_k < \text{ or } = \Delta I p_k, \text{ and } w\Delta N_c > \text{ or } = \Delta C p_c$$

that is, if starting from equilibrium, p_k has risen and p_c has fallen. To restore equilibrium enough labor must shift to change the relative sizes of sectoral outputs sufficiently in relation to the new pattern of demand to lower p_k and raise p_c. Of course, this may require small and/or temporary variations in the money wages rates as between the two sectors. (The

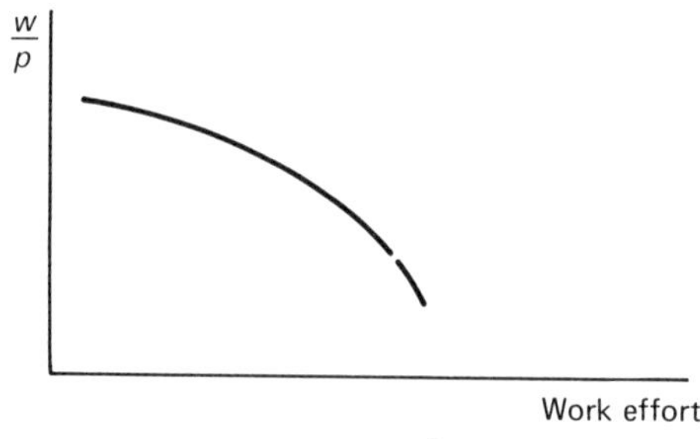

Figure 16.7

traditional formulation of Say's Law stressed that an expansion in one area would be matched by contraction in another, and vice versa.)

The adjustment process works so that a rise in investment demand leads to an increased output of capital goods, together with a diminished output of consumer goods: investment, profits and savings rise, consumption and real wages decline. Bearing in mind that all the changes are fluctuations around a normal position, these adjustments are stabilizing.

Some very traditional relationships can be seen here in several different forms. The increase in demand drives up prices relative to money wages; therefore the real wage declines, but at the same time, work effort and output increases. Hence we have a declining real wage accompanied by increased work, measured in units of effort. Also, as the real wage declines, marginal workers will be transferred to the sector where output is increasing, and price has risen. As output increases, with a given labor force, work effort becomes progressively less effective; when output increases with a rising labor force, and a given demand, price falls; in either case, the 'marginal value product' declines. In all of these we have an echo of the traditional theory, but nowhere have we assumed scarcity conditions in regard to employment, nor does the relationship say anything about opportunity costs (Figure 16.7).

Changes in Costs in Relation to Supply

Variations in demand may require the use or release of 'marginal' factors – 'marginal' in the sense not only that they are dispensible, but also that they are not of the same quality as the regular labor force or equipment. Expansion will thus be accompanied by diminished productivity at the margin, so by rising costs. Less well-trained or educated workers, less fertile land, older or previously retired equipment, may be brought into service, at higher costs, which can be met out of the increased prices. These increased costs are *permitted* by the higher prices: they do not *explain* them. In the traditional theory the higher costs, resulting from intensive and extensive diminishing returns, are the cause of the higher supply prices

– the supply curve of the individual firm is the rising section of its marginal cost curve and the supply curve for the industry is the horizontal sum of the individual supply curves of the firms. Because these rising costs both governed prices and reflected diminishing returns to the employment of scarce factors, a price could be said to measure opportunity costs, and an equilibrium to imply efficient allocation. In spite of the apparent similarities in the shapes of the functions, however, nothing of the sort can be inferred here. Supply price increases because of changes in demand, and costs change because distribution – the real wage – changes.

4 AGGREGATE ADJUSTMENTS

The price adjustments just considered have important macroeconomic implications for the relationship between investment and consumption, and for employment and productivity.

The Elasticity of Consumption With Respect to Investment

Even though employment will not vary with changes in investment, output will, although less and with a greater lag than price. But consider the 'pure' or extreme case, where the entire effect of a change in investment initially falls on price (i.e., investment demand falls by a certain percentage, and price drops by the same percentage). This means that the costs of capital inputs into consumer goods have declined by this percentage, so competition should lower the price of consumer goods in proportion, while keeping the rate of profit uniform. As a consequence, the real wage will rise in proportion, and on the assumption that the whole of real wage income is spent on consumer goods, consumption demand will increase in the same proportion.

Spelling this out formally, with I as investment demand, Y_k as current capital goods output, Y_c the output of consumer goods, p_k the price of capital goods, p_c the price of consumer goods, w/p_c the real wage, and C the demand for consumer goods, we have the following.

Since $I = p_k Y_k$ in equilibrium, $dI = Y_k dp_k$, when output remains fixed; dividing both sides of the second equation by the first,

$$dI/I = dp_k/p_k$$

The effect of a change in p_k on p_c is the result of two sets of pressures. First, a decline in p_k lowers costs in the consumer goods sector; competition then forces p_c down. Secondly, the possibility of entry and exit, of moving productive resources between the sectors (See above), ensures that the rate of profit will move in the same way in both sectors. Thus a fall in profitability in the capital goods sector will be transmitted to consumer goods. In per capita form we have the price equations:

$$p_k = Rk_k p_k + wn_k$$

$$p_c = Rk_c p_k + wn_c$$

which, solving each for R, and equating, differentiating and rearranging, will give:

$$dp_k/(p_k - wn_k) = dp_c/(p_c - wn_c).$$

When capital–labor ratios are equal in the two sectors, however, following the same procedure yields:

$$dp_k/p_k = dp_c/p_c.$$

$$dp_c/p_c = dp_k/p_k$$

When the capital–labor ratios of the two sectors differ, this equality will not hold. Suppose capital goods is capital-intensive and I falls; then the matching fall in the rate of profit in consumer goods will not be enough to release the funds needed for the labor-intensive wage bill, which means that the consumer goods price will not fall as much as the capital goods price (i.e., $dp_c/p_c < dp_k/p_k$). Just the reverse holds when the capital goods sector is labor-intensive.

When the consumer goods price changes, the real wage changes in the opposite direction. Since dw = 0,

$$d[w/p_c] \ / \ (w/p_c = -wdp_c/p_c^2/(w/p_c) = -dp_c/p_c$$

Ex hypothesi, all real wage income is spent on consumer goods; since employment is fixed, consumer demand must rise at the same rate that the real wage increases. Yet there seems to be a paradox here – the demand for and output of consumer goods are to rise while the price falls! And this in conditions in which prices are relatively flexible, compared to output and employment. But the paradox dissolves on closer inspection: capital goods demand is falling, which brings down capital goods prices and profits; this is the initiating cause. Consumer goods prices fall only because costs have fallen and competition forces them down. Consumer goods profits are reduced by the threatened or actual movement of capital out of the capital goods sector. But the resulting reduction of consumer goods prices raises real wages and therefore consumer demand. Firms and workers able to move

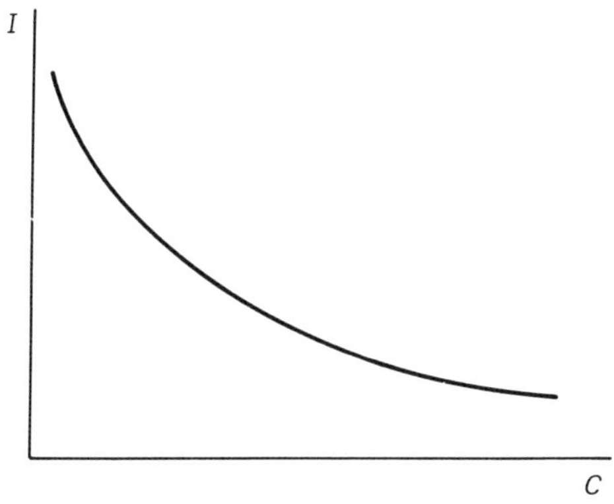

Figure 16.8

will therefore shift from the capital goods sector, where demand is falling to consumer goods where demand is rising. Hence, in ideal conditions,

$$d[w/p_c] \,/\, (w/p_c) = dC/C = dY_c/Y_c$$

Putting all this together, we see that

$$dI/I = -dC/C, \text{ or } [CdI/dCI] = -1$$

The elasticity of consumption with respect to investment is − 1 (assuming equal capital–labor ratios). A proportional rise or fall in investment is exactly offset by the corresponding proportional fall or rise in consumption, brought about by the working of competition and the price system. This can be expressed in a simple diagram of negative unitary elasticity (Figure 16.8). (Note that the price mechanism does not produce a perfect Say's Law offset; that would require the constancy of $I + C$, rather than the product $I \times C$.[18] However, the adjustment mechanism is significantly stabilizing: since $C > I$, and $dC/C = -dI/I$, $|dC| > |dI|$. So when I falls, adjusted total income, $Y+dY = C+dC+I+dI > Y$, and when I rises, $Y+dY < Y$. In the first case, the increase will tend to stimulate investment, in the second, the decline to diminish it, thus providing a corrective in the right direction.)

(A *caveat* must be entered here. Not all producers will be equally efficient. A fall in price may put some high-cost producers out of business, leaving their labor force unemployed, and thus reduce consumption spending. This reduction in consumer demand may create additional bankruptcies – a bankruptcy multiplier. If the number of high cost producers is large enough and the fall in price severe enough, the effect of bankruptcy in reducing consumption could rise to the point where it offsets the stimulating effect of the rise in real wages. The result will be a 'general glut.')

Aggregate Employment and Marginal Productivity

Yet a Craft system is not so inflexible that no changes whatever take place in employment. Given a sufficient period of time – a Month, compared to the Week we have been considering – existing firms can vary the pattern of work, extra hands can be taken on, extra work stations can be set up, using spare parts or reserve equipment, or fallow fields can be brought into cultivation. Work crews can be augmented or cut back, and all such changes will see corresponding changes in output. The different ways of organizing work can be ranked, and if tradition is to be believed the ranking will exhibit diminishing returns in output to additional employment. This employment–output function is not a conventional production function; the technical coefficients are given and relative prices are fixed. Only the labor coefficients vary, and the ranking associates increased (but progressively smaller) output with increased labor employed.

The outputs of the two sectors can be aggregated in terms of the prices embedded in the system. Normal output and normal employment are also known; but there will be a range of possible variation above and below normal levels, provided a longer period of time is considered, during which work can be reorganized. Even below (and certainly above) the normal level, additional employment and/or increased work intensity will yield diminishing increments of output. The normal level of activity is what has been planned and expected. Plot aggregate output on the vertical axis, and total employment on the horizontal. The origin indicates the lower limit of the range of variation. This function shows the variation in output with changes in employment and/or intensity of work *with given equipment and technique* (Figure 16.9).

Next, a straight line rising from the origin with the slope w/p will indicate the wage bill corresponding to each level of employment, which by assumption, will also equal worker consumption. (State transfer payments are negligible in early capitalism.) If we neglect capitalist consumption, this will also be total consumption. (The argument is unaffected by a constant level of capitalist consumption.) Then normal Investment can be designated by a point on the vertical axis, and total demand, $C+I$, will be given, for each level of employment by a line starting from the Investment point, rising parallel to the Wage–Consumption line. Suppose this line lies wholly above the output curve; demand would exceed supply at every level of employment. Prices would be bid up, so the real wage would fall, until the demand line swung down so as to just touch the output curve at the level of normal employment (since we began from normal Investment). If the demand curve intersected the output line below normal employment,

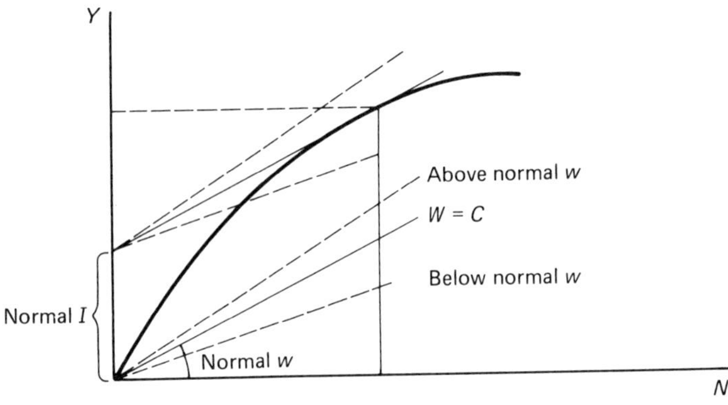

Figure 16.9

profit could be increased by cutting prices, raising real wages and employment, and so increasing output to the point at which the demand line is tangent to the output curve. Hence at the level of normal activity, the real wage will equal the short-run marginal product of employment, in the given technical conditions.

Now consider fluctuations in the level of Investment. If Investment falls below its normal level, total demand will intersect the output curve below the level of normal employment; it will then be possible to raise profits by cutting prices and raising real wages and employment. Output will rise until the demand line is tangent, which will be at a point near to but below the normal level. When Investment is above its normal level, total demand will be excessive, and prices will be bid up, until the real wage falls, bringing the demand line down, until it is tangent again, at a point near to but above the normal position. Changes in prices adjust the real wage, and employment as well as output, so that movements in consumption offset variations in investment.

Another possible adjustment must be considered. When the aggregate demand line lies wholly above the normal output–employment curve, pressures will build to increase the intensity of work at every level of employment, so that the normal output curve will tend to shift up – and conversely when aggregate demand lies below the normal output curve at the normal level of employment. These shifts due to changing work intensity may not be very large, but they will increase the stability of normal employment, and reduce the size of the price fluctuations required to restore equilibrium. With variable prices, then, the real wage will adjust to equal the marginal product of employment, and aggregate profit will be maximized, at a rather stable level of employment (Figure 16.10).

When money prices change relative to the money wage, changing the real wage, the most labor-intensive industries will be affected the most. For

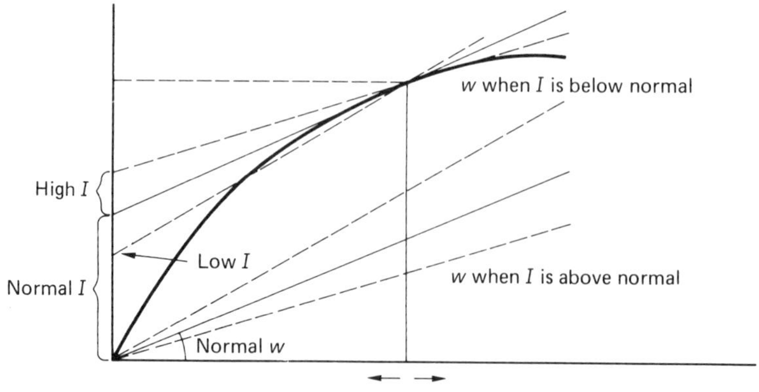

Figure 16.10

example, when the real wage falls, money prices have been bid up, and output increases, but labor productivity falls when reorganization takes place and production rises above the normal level. Similarly, when the real wage rises, output will fall below the previous norm and productivity will increase when employment is cut back. The more labor-intensive the industry the greater the proportional change. This would seem to call for appropriate changes in relative prices.

But relative prices depend on the normal position and the normal rate of profit is not supposed to be realized at any particular moment of time. It is an average over good times and bad; investment fluctuates and so therefore do profits. If the fluctuations in investment average out to the normal level, then gains from above normal earnings and losses from below normal earnings in the various sectors will average out also, regardless of differences in labor intensities. Relative prices will therefore remain fixed, while employment and the real wage will adjust in such a way as to maximize profit. The real wage will equal the marginal product of aggregate employment. But this is not an equilibrium relationship. It is the condition determining the pattern of adjustment around the normal long-term position of the system. So investment in the Craft economy can be expected to fluctuate around a normal level.

The Neo-Classical Production Function

A well-behaved neo-Classical production function has the following property: if factors are paid their marginal products, and output is 'exhausted,' where $Y = Y(K, N) = y(k, 1)$ in *per capita* terms, then $dr/d(w/p) = -n$, where $n = 1/k = N/K$.[19]

Now suppose that techniques are given and do not change, so that there are, in fact, no marginal products in the theoretical sense. But demand varies, and output adjusts with only negligible changes in employment, while prices vary substantially relative to money wages. When demand falls, employment and money wages will be only slightly affected, but prices will decline significantly, so that the real wage will rise. In a similar fashion, with expansion the real wage will decline. To those looking at the world through neo-Classically tinted glasses, this will appear to trace out a downward sloping demand curve for labor. To see the way this works, write:

$$pY = wN + rKp$$

(which is implicitly a 'one-good' economy). Then, taking the total differential,

$$Ydp = Ndw + K(pdr + rdp)$$

and manipulating this, we find the following expression for the change in the average profit rate:

$$dr = (wN/Kp)\ [dp/p - dw/w]$$

The profit rate changes in proportion to the difference between the proportional changes in the price level and the money wage. This is as we would expect. But it is also exactly the result obtained by expanding the above condition implied by marginal productivity theory. For

$$dr = -nd(w/p) = -N/K\ [(pdw - wdp)/p^2],$$

which becomes

$$dr = (wN/Kp)\ [dp/p - dw/w]$$

Hence, fluctuating demand and the consequent variation of prices relative to money wages create a pattern of changes that appear to confirm marginal productivity theory and imply the existence of a well-behaved production function, but which actually arise from the working of the system of effective demand in conditions in which no changes in output and employment take place. (See Ch. 9, esp. footnote 2; also Ch. 24.)

Growth Paths and Adjustment

Aggregate demand will tend to balance aggregate capacity. Let $g = I/K$ be the path along which the economy should tend to move, if the adjustment processes just examined can be extended to the long run. But the growth of the labor force, g_n, may be greater or less than this. Suppose $g_n > g$; a labor surplus will tend to emerge, and money wages will be driven down. This lowers both costs and demand in consumer goods, in the same proportion. Output should therefore be unaffected. The lower money wages, however, will mean that costs of investment projects are down. This suggests that the MEC curve should shift outwards, increasing investment. If investment were to increase, profits would rise, and the growth rate would rise towards the natural.

The shift in the MEC schedule, however, depends on the nature of the investment projects. If normal conditions obtain – new projects are the same as old – lower money (though unchanged real) wages will mean reduced consumer spending in money terms and proportionately lower expected net earnings per period. So the lower costs of investment projects will be offset by lower returns and there will be no outward shift of the MEC schedule. In these circumstances the system will sink into a deflation, as falling prices chase falling wages while the growing labor surplus keeps downward pressure on money wages. In these conditions, the system will not adjust.

But if new investment projects concern new or improved products for which demand could be expected to be strong if the project is successful (since these new goods would tend to replace existing ones), then a decline in money wages would reduce costs but leave expected demand unchanged – so the MEC schedule would shift, and the warranted rate rise towards the natural. (The new goods would, at least initially, carry the price of the goods they replace.)

Just the reverse process will take place when $g_n < g$. Money wages will rise, reducing profits, tending to bring down the rate of accumulation, (on the assumption that the negative effect of higher money wages on profits is not offset by higher consumer spending) while speeding up family formation and attracting immigrants. Again the nature of the projects making up the MEC schedule will be crucial: investment projects which simply duplicate existing facilities will be demand sensitive, while projects involving new and/or improved products will respond chiefly to cost changes. If the projects are chiefly duplications then a rise in money wages will set off an inflation; but if the projects chiefly involve new designs or new technologies, then a rise in money wages will lead to a downward shift in the MEC schedule. However, in this case there will be an important – and largely irreversible – further effect: when wages are bid up by rapid growth, mechanization will take place, displacing labor and raising productivity – thus adding to the pool of available labor (Ch. 24).

In the long run, there will be a pattern of adjustment, but no pressure for 'market-clearing.' An excess supply of labor will simply keep wages from exceeding the 'normal' cost of living. A too-rapid growth of labor will lower money wages; in normal conditions, this will lead to a deflationary spiral, but in periods of innovation this will tend to raise investment, and so the growth rate, which, in turn, will keep prices up. So real wages will decline, which will tend to slow the growth of the labor force. Too slow a growth of labor will, in a similar manner, tend to raise money wages, which will either lead to inflation, under normal conditions or, in innovative periods, tend both to reduce accumulation and increase labor force growth. The system adjusts only in periods of innovation.

Workers are produced by families: children must be fed, socialized, and trained in a trade, all of which depends on family income. The labor force is not a given; it is itself determined by the productive powers of the system. But it certainly need not be established at a full employment level; the adjustment process can be expected to generate an appropriate labor reserve. It may also generate cycles; periods of rapid and slow growth may chase one another in oscillating fashion, more Marx and Goodwin than Harrod or Solow.

Say's Law, Traditional Theory and Effective Demand

What has sometimes been called the 'Cambridge theory of distribution' turns out on closer examination to be a pattern of adjustment around 'normal' prices of production – the long-period position – in a system with a certain inflexibility in its technology, characteristic of the early stages of capitalism. This adjustment mechanism, by which an Artisan economy responds to fluctuations in aggregate demand, approximates the traditional idea known as Say's Law, that any decrease in demand will be offset by an increase in some other sector. Further, this comes about through the working of the interest rate and prices in a set of very traditional-seeming supply and demand functions, and an examination of the impact on labor yields what look like marginal productivity relationships.[20] But none of the traditional assumptions have been made, and these functions do not in any sense measure opportunity costs or scarcities. Nor is there any reason to suppose that full employment will be established. Morever, normal prices of production, likewise unrelated to scarcity, are determined by the embedded system of normal price–profit–capacity relationships; the supply and demand functions concern deviations from the normal positions. They represent adjustments to changes in effective demand in an economy in which competition has not extended to the sphere of technological innovation, and in which Mass Production has not yet made its appearance.

5 VARIABLE EMPLOYMENT SYSTEMS

Transformational growth arises from the fact that the normal working of the economy sets up pressures for innovation. These pressures explain the changes in the Craft economy which have brought about the system of Mass Production.

The Pressures for Change

A Craft economy has a pattern of stabilizing adjustments, which depend on market-clearing prices. From the point of view of the system this may be good, but from the point of view of individual producers these adjustments have some undesirable properties. For example, when demand falls off, production will be run more slowly but, exceptions aside, the full labor force will still have to be on hand. From the individual owner's point of view, this is an unfortunate expense, which necessitates injurious price competition. The burden of adjustment falls heavily on profits – when the markup is 50% a 5% drop in demand is a 10% fall in profits. If capital were 2/3 external, a 17% falling off of demand could bring bankruptcy. Hence leverage must remain restricted, under these conditions. Conversely, when demand is strong, the rate at which production can take place will depend on the morale of the labor force, and its willingness to put in extra effort. The capitalist does not have full or satisfactory control over the pace of work, or the level of costs.

What the capitalist needs, first, is greater control over the process of production, especially over the productivity of labor and the pace of work. Motion and time studies were developed to provide just this (Barnes, 1956). Secondly, firms need to be able to vary costs when sales are varying, which requires being able to lay off and rehire labor easily which, in turn, depends on being able to schedule and reschedule production. To do this start-up and shut-down costs must be minimal. Thirdly, firms need to be able to store output without spoilage. If when sales fall, output can be cut back, and along with output, costs can also be cut and, at the same time, unsold inventory can be stored without significant loss or other costs, a great deal of pressure for potentially ruinous price-cutting will be lifted. Part of the problem thus reduces to a technical question, which is, how can production be run at less than full blast, without all workers having to be present? Alternatively, how can production be started up and shut down, easily and costlessly, so that a drop in demand can be met by running short time?

The normal working of the system throws these questions up; the answers will help businesses to compete more effectively. Inflexible output and costs, resulting in overproduction and cut-throat price competition, is potentially ruinous. The system itself thus creates the pressures which lead to the technological developments that make labor a cost that varies with output, which in turn varies with demand. The result is an improvement in the flexibility of the firm's response to changing market conditions.

Business will attempt systematically to gain greater control over the production process, substituting mechanical power for labor power, and mechanical or electronic control for human skill, as far as possible. In general, the larger the scale on which operations take place, the better the prospects for doing this – an aspect of economies of scale – 'the division of labor is limited by the extent of the market.'

These pressures also tend to change the nature of competition; previously it centered on prices in a comparatively simple way. But now the chief focus will become technological development, especially in relation to market share – since an increase in share can permit a larger size, which in turn will make it possible to extend the division of labor, reaping economies of scale that in turn will permit the consolidation of a lower price – and so on. Once an advantage is achieved, a 'virtuous' cycle develops, enabling the successful firm to establish a leading or even dominant market position.

With competition centering on a race for improvements in technology, the strategic situation of firms changes. Firms will no longer seek to establish their optimum size and remain there, and it will no longer be possible to permit new firms to supply the growth of the market. For new firms will be able to build plants and buy equipment embodying the latest technology; they will therefore be able to establish a cost advantage and invade the markets of established firms. Hence existing firms must invest regularly, incorporating new technology into their plants, and growing enough so that, taken together, they will supply the expansion of the market. Prices will therefore have to be set with an eye to providing the profits that will finance growth. To facilitate such growth, firms will withhold profits, investing them directly, rather than distributing them to shareholders. Both the pattern of competition and the working of financial markets is altered by the move to Mass Production technology and the shift from extensive to intensive growth (Chandler, 1977).

Consequently, when the new technology becomes widespread the system as a whole will begin to work differently. First, when demand for a particular good falls (say) due to a general decline in investment spending, workers will be laid off, and prices will tend to fall comparatively little. Thus instead of consumption varying inversely with investment, as it did when a decline in demand led to a greater proportional fall in prices than in money wages, consumption will now also decline, since the laid-off workers and their families will now have to curtail their consumption spending. The elasticity of consumption with respect to investment will now be positive.

The Multiplier and the Elasticity of Consumption

In a Mass Production economy employment reflects the degree to which capacity is utilized. Variations in demand are met by varying utilization, keeping prices and productivity constant. When demand falls, workers are laid off; when it increases they are re-employed, up to and even beyond rated capacity. Investment constitutes the demand for capital goods;

neglecting other forms of consumer spending, wages provide the demand for consumer goods. Gross profits are withdrawn at each stage in both sectors. Given a variation in investment spending, the multiplier sequence will be:

$$\Delta C_1 = wn_k\Delta I$$

$$\Delta C_2 = wn_c\Delta C_1 = wn_k wn_c\Delta I$$

$$\Delta C_3 = wn_c\Delta C_2 = wn_k(wn_c)^2\Delta I$$

Hence, the sequence converges to

$$\Delta C = \{(wn_k) / [1 - wn_c]\}\Delta I.$$

This is the multiplier; a change in investment generates an accompanying change in the same direction in consumption. In this form, the multiplier depends on the share of variable costs in revenue, and on the real wage. The psychological propensities of households are not significant.

In a Mass Production economy, money wages and money prices are stable or move together, so that with fixed productivity, output is adjusted to sales. Fluctuations in investment will then lead to changes in employment, as workers are either laid off or rehired or find themselves working short time or overtime, resulting in changes in their pay and so in consumption spending. Rises and falls in investment will be accompanied by changes in the same direction in consumption. This can be illustrated on a diagram that is a simple variant of Figures 16.9 and 16.10. The output–employment function will be a straight line, since productivity is fixed by the nature of the equipment. Consumption, investment and the wage will be the same as before, and the equilibrium will be as shown in Figure 16.11, with a multiplier of $1/(1 - wn)$.

Let the term in brackets be M; it then follows, by integration that $C = MI$. Dividing the former by the latter, it follows that

$$dC/C = dI/I, \text{ and } [IdC/CdI] = 1.$$

If I and C are interpreted as final demand composite commodities – vectors – produced by vertically integrated sectors (each producing all necessary means of production for itself), M will take the form of a matrix multiplier, and the elasticity formula will hold for the general 'inter-industry' case (see Ch. 20, Appendix).

A proportional change in investment generates an equiproportional change in the same direction in consumption. Under Mass Production the market maintains the constancy of the *ratio*, I/C, rather than the product of the two, as in the Fixed Employment Economy.

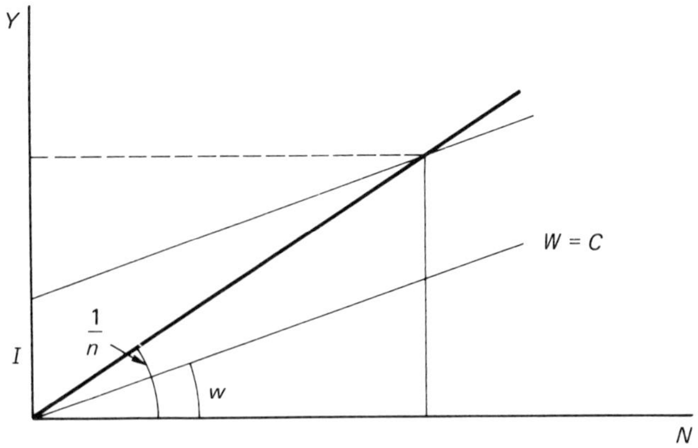

Figure 16.11

Excess Capacity

Mass Production systems have a tendency to generate excess capacity, a feature that explains many paradoxes of modern economics (Nell, 1988, Ch. 10) This tendency arises, initially, as an effect of economies of scale in choosing competitive strategies. Each firm can calculate the pricing and investment plans of the representative, average firm, and can thereby determine the amount of additional capacity it should build to maintain its market share. But this determination is subject to two kinds of uncertainty: the future expansion of the market can be estimated only within a range, and the exact impact of technological improvements on costs and output can be only approximately judged. But it is known that economies of scale exist. Let us suppose that no firm has any definite technological or managerial advantage, so that no one has an incentive to try to improve their market position. Nevertheless, they will have to decide whether to build for the high demand and low technical progress estimates, or for the low demand/high technical progress – i.e., whether to err on the side of overbuilding, or on the side of underbuilding.

Consider the strategic position of a representative firm *vis-à-vis* the rest of the firms:

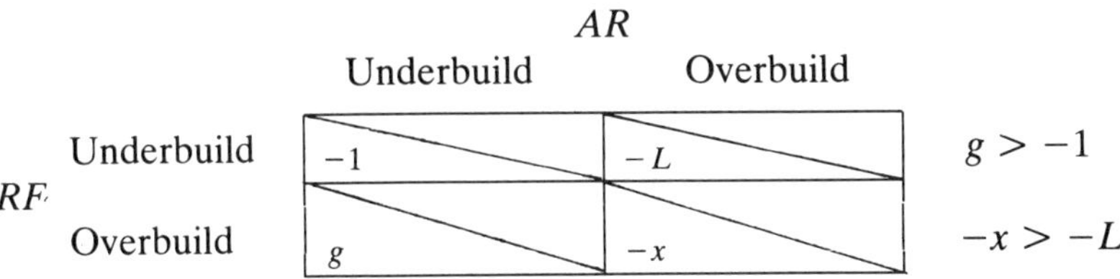

		AR		
		Underbuild	Overbuild	
RF	Underbuild	-1	$-L$	$g > -1$
	Overbuild	g	$-x$	$-x > -L$

If 'all the rest,' *AR*, underbuild, and *RF* also underbuilds, the result will be unsatisfied demand, creating room for entry, so that both *RF* and *AR* will suffer losses, -1, due to new competitors. If *AR* underbuilds and *RF* overbuilds, then *RF* makes a gain, g, since it increases its share. If *AR* overbuilds and *RF* underbuilds, *RF* suffers a substantial loss in market share, $-L$, since the overbuilders will both enjoy economies of scale and be under pressure to press their competitive advantage. If *AR* overbuilds and *RF* also overbuilds, *RF* suffers only a small and uncertain loss, $-x$, due to carrying excess capacity, which will be partly offset by economies of scale.

The best strategy for *RF*, therefore, is to overbuild, or build ahead of demand. This applies to every firm taken successively in isolation, and considered against all the rest. Hence there will be a tendency to excess capacity. (By contrast, in a Craft economy, with little technical progress and few economies of scale, new competitors would create no necessary problems, while overbuilding will carry a heavy penalty in risk. The safest strategy will be underbuild). This interacts strongly with the multiplier, in ways that we cannot explore here. Very roughly, when there is excess capacity, we find that expenditure times the multiplier is less than the capital stock times its productivity.[21] The effects of competition, we shall see, in these circumstances, will tend to reduce the multiplier and to raise productivity, thereby worsening the pressure – and discouraging investment. New products and new processes will be needed to offset the potential for stagnation. Traditionally, this has involved the appropriation of the activities of the household by industry.

6 TRANSFORMATIONAL GROWTH

Mass Production requires a mass market. The shift from small, localized Craft production to modern industry is possible only if appropriate new markets emerge *pari passu*. Fortunately, the two go hand in hand.

The Impact of Transformational Growth on the Household

In the early stages of capitalism the basic provisioning for social existence – food, clothing, shelter, transport, education – was still carried out within the household or domestic economy, by the methods of the traditional crafts. The family household was the unit that raised and socialized the new generation. The pattern of control over these activities was defined by the kinship system, which determined the inheritance of property and therefore of the power to make decisions about investment, location, production, employment and training. The system of inheritance has traditionally been that of male primogeniture, embedded in a patriarchy, with various local modifications.

Fixed employment systems cannot expand so easily at the expense of the household. First, they employ essentially the same technologies, so that their products are not necessarily either cheaper or better. Second, because of the inflexibility of labor costs, and the consequent risks of size, they are inhibited from building large enough plants to take advantage of what economies of scale do exist. But with advent of variable employment systems it becomes first possible to build on a large scale, and then competitively necessary. At this point, then, the drive to replace household production goes into high gear.

Growth in 19th century America began from a largely rural and small town system of family farms and family firms operating traditional crafts, which expanded by adding new regions. This was gradually transformed into modern corporate industry and corporate farming, operating large-scale scientific industrial methods, marketing on a mass basis, and controlled by a professional career management, largely independent of the kinship system. A kinship-based class and property system has thus been (partially) transformed into an educational-and-career-based income hierarchy. (Class and property, of course, provide a head-start in education and career.) Activities and control were shifted from the kinship-oriented domestic economy to the bureaucratically controlled industrial system, creating new markets in the process. It is this pattern of development that has created the long-term pressure for technological change and investment.

The production system that directly supported everyday life, even as recently as a century ago, was largely organized through the household. More than half the population still worked the land, and another third lived in small towns. These households grew much of their own food, put up preserves every autumn, cooked whatever they ate, made their own bread, cookies, cakes, etc. mended their own clothes (and made many of them), made soaps and candles, grew or collected herbs for medicinal purposes, mended and often made furniture, and repaired and sometimes even built the houses they lived in. Of course, the basic consumer goods and most means of production were produced in factories, managed by capital, even then. Shoes and leather goods, for example, cloth, most basic clothing, patent medicines, building materials, staple foodstuffs, oil and kerosene, lamps, household furniture, stoves, kitchen utensils and all luxury goods, all were produced for profit and marketed on what was already becoming a national basis. But the household was not a 'final consumer'; the household produced. Indeed, members of the household were skilled in many serious crafts – sewing, wood-working, cooking and preserving, carpentry, herbal medicine, and many others. But besides craft work many activities now routinely conducted outside the home went on within it. For example, birth and death and serious illness were largely handled in the family, with the assistance of outside specialists, to be sure, but the basic work was done in the home. Moreover, the family did much of the educating of the children and virtually all of caring for the aged and infirm.

Of course, not every family possessed all the skills or performed all these activities. Some households would specialize and exchange would take place, either barter within the framework of the extended family, or monetary exchange within the local community – perhaps more commonly, both. However, such local specialization and exchange still remained fundamentally within the sphere of the household. Even though money might change hands, the activities were neither industrial in their technology nor capitalist in their organization.

The production activities of the pre-modern, nonurban household were much more extensive than is generally recognized. The everyday circumstances of our grandparents or great grandparents were something they largely created themselves, through the exercise of craft skills in the home. By contrast, we buy the circumstances of our lives in the shopping center and from the real estate developer, together with service contracts, should anything go wrong, as it certainly will. A glance over the very partial list of crafts, skills and activities mentioned above is enough to reveal a central, and often overlooked, feature of our economic develoment over the past century. Every one of these domestic crafts and household skills has been replaced by a major industry, dominated by one or more giant, multinational firms. The household has been depleted, and has lost the power to control or shape its everyday circumstances (a loss actively resisted by the 'do-it-yourself' movement, and by the counter-culture), while the market has expanded. The growth of capital has taken place at the expense of the household.

Of course, it can be immediately protested that this is a distorted and perverse way of describing a well-known phenomenon – the freeing of both men and women from onerous toil. Progress, indeed, should be measured by the replacement of old-fashioned, even primitive, ways of doing things with modern technologically superior mass production. We can buy bread cheaper than we could make it; perhaps homemade bread is better than the supermarkets', but the same could hardly be said about homemade clothes or furniture or soaps or cosmetics or medicines. (*Hand*made clothes or furniture – that is, made by skilled craftsmen – may be better than mass produced ones, but the modern crafts have themselves been transformed by industrial technology, and use its tools and materials.) The reasons for these developments are simple: the new products are frequently better, always cheaper, and moving production out of the household has provided a vast increase in leisure time.

There is no reason to deny this, and the only criticism of this view is that it is seriously incomplete. True, the new products are cheaper, frequently better, and their introduction lightens the burden of daily work. But this is not simply the onward march of progress; along with growth there is destruction. Basic activities have all been moved out of the home and traditional skills have been lost. The market and the state between them have taken over most of the functions previously performed by the family. Small wonder, then, that the extended family has ceased to be a significant feature of modern life, and even the nuclear family shows signs of disintegration. Apart from the conceiving of children and caring for them while they are quite young, the family system is no longer the sole or even the central agency responsible for the reproduction of the material and social circumstances for everyday life. The development of the economy – and of the state – has been a process of taking over these functions, producing the goods and services required on an industrial scale, by new and more powerful processes, and then marketing them commercially, with the state providing the infrastructure to make this possible. With rapid and endogenous technical progress jobs are continually changing; fathers can no longer pass their skills along to their sons. Education and vocational training have fallen largely into the province of the state, partly into the hands of private entrepreneurs. That, for better or worse, has been the process of transformational growth.[22]

The Information Economy

A new pattern has begun to emerge, however: just as crafts gave way to industrial mass production, drawing on massive sources of power and economies of scale, so the latter is giving way to automated and computerized systems of production, drawing on accumulated information. The industrial economy substitutes energy for the skills of the craftsman; the computerized economy substitutes information and control of complex operations for the energy and scale economies of the industrial system. In the first movement factory work expands at the expense of agriculture and the crafts; in the second, office and white collar work expand at the expense of manufacturing. In the first, classes are transformed into hierarchies and the Night Watchman State turns into the Welfare State; in the second, capital is institutionalized and sets out to dominate the state. Schematically, the Craft economy gives way to Modern industry, as capital develops an appropriate technology, and this in turn, yields to the Information economy, as capital develops appropriate controls and institutional forms.

One phase of transformational growth, the development of industrial mass production, is drawing to an end, while what apears to be the next phase, the setting up of the Information economy, has hardly begun. The cost structure of business in the new mold is going to be different, just as it changed with the shift from Crafts to Industry. In the Craft economy variable costs were low in relation to output, because a large part of the labor force was fixed. Hence fixed costs were high, but consisted of current charges, rather than capital, and were set in real rather than monetary terms. By contrast, in Mass Production, variable costs are large, while fixed costs are amortized and are set in monetary form. The chief effect of the change to the Information economy is to reduce – even in some cases, when automation is virtually total, to eliminate – variable costs. In addition, sunk costs (that is, non-recoverable developmental or set-up costs) will be different in the three regimes. In the Craft economy these will largely be current labor or entrepreneurial costs; under Mass Production they will be capital costs, but in both cases they will be low compared to other costs. In the Information economy, however, they will begin to loom large, becoming in some cases the dominant cost for a product. Let's set this out in a table first, and then explain it further.

Table 16.1 The changing cost structure of Business

Costs: / *Type of economy*	*Variable*	*Fixed*	*Sunk*	*Nature*
Craft:	Low	Current	Current (Low)	Real
Industrial:	High	Capital	Capital (Low)	Monetary
Information:	Low	Capital	Capital (High)	Monetary

When variable costs are a high proportion of output, adjusting output to sales minimizes the pressure on profit margins. But when this cannot be done, there is a great temptation to cut prices to gain sales at the expense of competitors – yet if they follow suit everyone is worse off, a classic Prisoner's Dilemma. (Even worse, prices can be driven down very far indeed, as demand for manufactures tends to be inelastic.) Control over the market is therefore strongly desired.

In the Craft economy consumption spending tended to offset changes in investment since, because of the cost structure, prices were more flexible than money wages. With low variable costs, there cannot be much of a multiplier. By contrast, in the Mass Production system, consumption and investment will move together, because of the high variable costs and the multiplier. And because the fixed costs are monetary, prices will be set in money terms with an eye to recovering capital over a certain write-off period. Hence prices will be insensitive to demand changes.

But we have already seen the emergence of new forms.[23] In Europe, employment has long been less flexible than in the USA. With the emergence of the Information economy employment and money wages will tend to be stable, but output will be variable. Low variable and high monetary capital costs suggest that prices will be programmed over the whole of the expected product cycle, and will certainly not be lowered in the face of short-term fluctuations in sales. Since labor costs are likely to be low relative to the other systems, even if they occurred, favorable distributional changes would be a less effective stabilizer. And they are unlikely to occur; on the contrary, giant capital-intensive firms with loyal customers and differentiated products will possess substantial market power. They are likely to try to move prices countercyclically – when demand growth ceases, and current demand falls, such firms will tend to raise prices to maintain cash flow. (They would not do this ordinarily, since raising prices will inhibit market development). As a result, productivity in value terms will tend to be more stable than productivity in physical terms.

(If counter-cyclical price adjusting is widespread, a curious kind of 'price multiplier' could develop. Suppose that a fall in investment demand leads to an offsetting price rise, which then drives up consumer goods prices. Real wages thus decline, so real consumer demand falls; this triggers a further price rise, further reducing real wages and consumer goods sales. And so on. As long as the proportional price increase is less than the proportional sales decline each period, this sequence will converge.)

Automation will substitute energy and equipment use for skilled and expensive labor; with computerization and flexibility in production components can be contracted out, all over the world. It will no longer be necessary to keep large capacity and skilled production teams on hand, so large production systems will be broken down. But high set-up and development costs will keep firm sizes large, even if production units can be smaller. Fluctuating sales in the face of high monetary fixed costs will lead to financial difficulties; borrowing will rise, and reorganizations will become more frequent. With low variable labor costs there will be less of a cushion, hence there will be downward pressure on wages and costs to create a margin of safety in profits. This continues the tendency to stagnation.

But low labor costs need not mean that variable costs are low; capital charges can become variable. Interest rates can be made changeable, and dividends are certainly variable. Raw materials, intermediate products and energy vary with adjustments of output to demand. A new multiplier can be defined, in which expenditures for energy, materials, etc. are related to output, dividends are tied to sales revenues, while retained earnings and depreciation allowances are the chief withdrawals. Dividends will, of course, be partly saved, but part will be assumed to be paid to foundations, universities and other bodies that pass the funds along in further, mostly consumer expenditures. Investment will be the volatile factor, while overhead labor and managerial salaries will be fixed expenditures which underwrite stable patterns of consumption. A balance can thus be struck between withdrawals and injections, through the adjustment of expenditures that vary with sales and/or output.

To take a simple example: let I be net investment, C be consumption of workers and managers $= wL$, where w is an average of wages and salaries and L is total fixed employment, $E = eY$ is energy expenditures per unit output, $M = mY$ is materials per unit output, and $D = dY$ (not to be confused with the calculus operator) is dividends paid out per unit sales revenue, where the receipt of the dividends finances consumer or other spending. Then $Y = [E + M + D] + C + I$, where C is stable and tends to be constant, but I will be volatile. Then,

$$Y = [C + I] / \{1 - (e + m + d)\}, \text{ and } 1 / \{1 - (e + m + d)\}$$

is the multiplier, based partly on variable costs of production, and partly on the passing along of earnings in proportion to sales. Like all multipliers, it depends on prices remaining largely stable. If firms are successful in moving prices countercyclically, the impact of demand fluctuations on profitability will be dampened, but successive rounds of price increase may be triggered.

7 CONCLUSIONS

In the conditions of early capitalism prices and markets will function so that consumer spending will vary to offset fluctuations in investment, keeping total output and employment relatively stable. But this system has serious disadvantages from the point of view of individual firms, setting up incentives to innovate in ways that will change it. These are among the chief incentives that shape and drive technological innovation. The result is a new technology, the system of Mass Production which, in turn, gives rise to a new pattern of inter-connectedness between markets – the multiplier, which amplifies variations in spending, resulting in a tendency to generate excess capacity and unemployment. This dampens the propensity to invest, but innovation that creates industrial methods for performing tasks traditionally carried out in the household sets up competitive pressures to develop new markets. This has supported investment up to the present – but this process appears to be coming to an end. Mass Production appears to be giving way to a new system, with a different characteristic cost structure. It is too early to predict the shape of the new economy, but it is likely that it will contain a multiplier relation, and it may also exhibit a new pattern of price movement.

Notes

1. In practice, of course, there will be dispensible laborers, and opportunities for partial shut-downs, but the aim here is to draw the contrasts sharply, basing them on distinctive features of the respective technologies. When workers are not laid off, demand changes will not be transmitted as changes in income and spending. It is this transmission which characterizes the short-run adjustment process of the multiplier. *Any* linear relationship can be expressed in 'multiplier' form: If $x = a + by$, then $y = (x - a)/b$, and $1/b$ is a 'multiplier'. What makes this significant economics, rather than algebraic trivia, is the existence of normal business practices that establish market processes that converge dynamically to the result expressed by the linear equations. These business practices are the tendency to hold the line on prices, while laying off / rehiring workers in the face of variations in sales – practices which did not exist in the early stages of capitalism, characterized by fixed employment technology.
2. In the pin factory each man specializes in a particular operation, drawing the wire, straightening it, cutting, pointing, grinding, putting the head on, whitening or polishing, etc. amounting to about eighteen distinct operations, which can be divided up in several different ways. Clearly they have to be coordinated, and each worker has to complete his operation in a manner that eases the way for the next. The description makes it clear that the division of labor itself requires practice; the advantages cannot be reaped without effort and skill. Moreover, much of the machinery and improvements 'were originally the inventions of common workmen, who, . . . naturally turned their thoughts towards finding out easier and readier methods' (Smith, 1776, p. 9). Marshall argues that while machinery displaces purely manual skill, it increases the demand for judgement and general intelligence. Again his examples illustrate the need for coordination of the work force and for high morale (cf. 1961, pp. 255–64).
3. With characteristic acumen Marx observed, 'On a closer examination of the working machine proper, we find in it, as a general rule, though often, no doubt, under very altered forms, the apparatus and tools used by the handicraftsman or manufacturing workman; with this difference, that instead of being human implements, they are the implements of a mechanism, or mechanical implements. Either the entire machine is only a more or less altered mechanical edition of the old handicraft tool, as, for instance, the powerloom, or the working parts fitted in the frame of the machine are old acquaintances, as spindles are in a mule, needles in a stocking loom' (Marx, n.d., Vol. I, p. 373).
4. Adam is not the only Smith we can cite:

   Under a spreading chestnut tree
   The village smithy stands
   The smith, a mighty man is he
   . . . .
   His brow is wet with honest sweat
   He earns what e'er he can
   . . . .
   Week in, week out, from morn till night
   You can hear his bellows blow
   You can hear him swing his heavy sledge
   With measured beat and slow.
   Henry Wadsworth Longfellow

'He earns whate'er he can,' that is, he works steadily, 'week in, week out,' although his earnings may vary with demand. That a craftsman works steadily but receives earnings which fluctuate with good times and bad is an idea so natural that it appears almost unconsciously in poetry and novels. Of course, the practice of 'putting out' – a relic of earlier times – enabled employers to pass on the burden of reduced demand to labor, but at the cost of forgoing the greater efficiency and economies of the factory system (Mantoux, 1961).

5. The failure to appreciate this may be due to a common confusion of two distinctions, between fixed and variable costs on the one hand, and capital and current costs on the other. Fixed costs are incurred at a set rate so long as the firm is in business; variable costs are incurred in proportion to the level of output. Current costs are those incurred in the current accounting period; capital costs are spread over many accounting periods. Variable costs are always current; but not all current costs are variable. Labor costs are current; but in the Craft economy (and in part, in Mass Production, too) labor may be fixed. Nor are capital charges necessarily fixed. Depreciation is a capital charge, but it may be varied with output; interest and dividend payments may be varied with earnings. (Cf. Marshall, Book V, Ch. IV.)
6. Marshall clearly understood that prices and money-wages had different degrees of flexibility, though he largely failed to draw out the consequences: 'when prices are rising, the rise in the price of the finished commodity is generally more rapid than that in the price of the raw material, always more rapid than that in the price of labour; and when prices are falling, the fall in the price of the finished commodity is generally more rapid than that in the price of the raw material, always more rapid than that in the price of labour.' Even though he seems to have reversed the actual relationship between the variability of the prices of finished goods and raw materials (Pedersen and Petersen, 1938), he grasped the main point: 'statistics prove that the real income of the country is not very much less in the present time of low prices, than it was in the period of high prices that went before it. The total amount of necessaries, comforts and luxuries which are enjoyed by Englishmen is but little less in 1879 than it was in 1872' (1961, Vol. 2, pp. 714–16). Kaldor, in 1938, clearly understood that if prices were flexible relative to money wages, the resulting distribution effects would bring a Wicksellian 'cumulative process' to an end (Kaldor, 1960, pp. 110–11).
7. The simplest long-run model of prices was presented by Marshall. According to this view, in the long run the stock of appliances for production can be varied in response to demand, so that if they are produced and used under conditions of constant cost, the long-period supply curve will be a horizontal straight line. Price will therefore be determined exclusively by 'costs of production' (including the allowance for normal profit), while a downward-sloping demand curve will determine the quantities of the various goods that will be produced. A striking but little remarked feature of this system is its independence from any condition of scarcity. Prices are determined by input requirements and normal profits; quantities are determined by demand – but demand depends upon income, which in turn depends upon the relation between the marginal utility of goods and the marginal disutility of work. This is a matter of preferences, not of endowments; there need be no binding constraints in this case. We are in a Ricardian, rather than a Walrasian, world. For when there are no binding constraints, prices cannot reflect relative scarcities. Prices will be governed by 'costs of production,' which in turn will reflect distribution. If distribution is determined not by 'supply and demand' but, for example, by a real wage that

reflects convention and the cost of living, then neo-classical theory has no foothold at all. The Marshallian model, however, does not tell us enough. A linear analysis of prices, the rate of profits and production presents the same picture in more detail.

8. Such a framework, of course, does not distinguish between Artisan and Mass Production technological systems; the relationships portrayed are common to both – they comprise the basic structure of capitalism. These technological, class, property and power relationships have been analysed to derive the conditions for the system to maintain and reproduce itself, both in regard to the production system and to the lifestyles of the classes, as expressed in domestic and contractual relationships. (Of course, it will be necessary to simplify and abstract; the point is not to abstract from anything *essential*, cf. Hollis and Nell, 1975, Chs 4, 9.)
9. Best-practice coefficients would overestimate the outputs that the sectors can produce, and would therefore call for higher wage and profit rates, and lower prices, than can in fact be realized. Over time the inefficient techniques will be phased out, mistaken procedures will be corrected, etc. (although new mistakes will be made and new failures will occur) so that production can be said to tend towards best-practice levels. The best-practice model shows the tendencies inherent in the system, but the average-practice model shows the valuations actually embedded in the system.
10. Yet the long-run position has been derived from the actual economy's capacity, which may embody mistakes, and is the result of investments which may turn out to be unrealistic or ill-founded. Actual demand and actual market conditions may differ considerably from what was expected. Why should anyone pay any attention to the embedded values? If current information is better, why base current behavior on valuations that reflect ignorance or mistakes? This confuses two different matters: investment and current production. Newer and better information is certainly relevant, but to planning for new construction, not to the running of plants that already exist. It is of no importance for today's production that the firm could have built a better plant or designed a better product. The product produced today will be priced according to today's costs, not tomorrow's. Current production necessarily uses present technology, which governs current prices even when the better technology is in active competition; the best-practice firm cannot serve more customers than its capacity permits. At any given time, the remaining customers will have to buy the more costly products, even though over time the best-practice firms will expand at the expense of the others.
11. The loan market will be assumed to be fully competitive, in the sense that new firms will be able to borrow all the funds that they can effectively manage at the going rate of interest. The security for the loan is the project in which the proceeds are invested; such projects must therefore be judged risk-worthy in the eyes of the bankers.
12. Utility theorists normally introduce 'time preference' – Irving Fisher called it 'impatience' – to explain the relation between interest and savings. Consumption now is preferred to consumption later; interest is needed to compensate for the delay. The higher the rate of interest the more consumption will be postponed, etc. Of course, some kinds of delays are extremely annoying, but to generalize this to all consumption of all kinds is absurd. Many consumer items, especially consumer durables, stand in natural sequences; Act II cannot be appreciated before Act I, dessert follows dinner, marriage follows graduation, buying the house waits on the promotion, and the furniture and appliances on

the house. When we set out a plan for the household's life-cycle this kind of natural order becomes apparent. There is no role for generalized impatience.

13. The majority of households own no income-yielding property and depend upon the breadwinner's wages to support the family. The normal level of real wages will normally just cover the long-run socially necessary expenses of family life – allowing for normal variation, etc. Normal saving out of wage income, therefore, can be only what is required to provide precautionary funds, or to finance expenditures later in life. But a minority of households receive profit incomes. The profits of business include normal remuneration for management by the capitalist owners; such remuneration will likewise generally just cover the expenses of living in the style appropriate for proprietors. So savings out of these 'wages of superintendence' – as Mill termed them – can cover only precautionary funds and funds set aside for later consumption. When such remuneration is subtracted from general business earnings the result will be the true net earnings. The savings out of these earnings – profit income – will then be available for lending.
14. A family's status in the community will depend on the size of its wealth holding relative to those of others; hence there will be strong pressures to save at the same (or a higher) rate as other families. Competition will thus tend to establish a common or general rate of financial accumulation. Moreover, it will require the rate of interest at which savings are supplied to the market as loans to be the same as the risk-adjusted rate of net earnings on marginal projects.
15. The marginal efficiency schedule has been severely criticized in recent years, and correctly – for an industrial, corporate economy. But the criticisms do not apply in the present context: For example, 'reswitching' objections do not arise, since the 'normal' MEC schedule is defined only for the prices, etc. derived from the long-run setting, and shifts in the MEC schedule are understood to be deviations from the normal position. The problem that changes in interest rates require the readjustment of prices to re-establish equilibrium (and thus the reranking of projects, so one can never 'move along' a schedule) does not arise since the interest rate changes only when the MEC schedule is out of its normal position – the argument only applies to adjustments around equilibrium. It has been claimed that the MEC calculation is wrong because the firm's future investments will have 'external' effects on future earnings from the present investment; to know the returns of future periods correctly these effects must be estimated – but the future investments might not be made unless the present one is successful. This may be a problem for industrial corporations engaged in regular investment, but not when each new project is carried out by a separate new firm.
16. Growth has a different character in the two systems. In the Craft economy it will be extensive, spreading out to new locales, reaching to new populations, but new investments will simply replicate old. There will be little innovation and new capital will not necessarily compete with existing. In the Mass Production economy, however, each firm will grow indefinitely through internal investment, because new capital is technically superior to old; hence new firms would have a competitive advantage over old. Firms are thus compelled to grow by investing, and growth will be intensive, involving increases in capital per head and output per head, as well as innovations in processes and products.
17. The fact that the profit rate has temporarily become nonuniform, because of the unequal capital–labor ratios of the sectors will not necessarily lead to significant movements of capital. Some firms may be positioned to switch from

one market to a related one easily, but to suggest that in general firms should leave a low-profit sector to enter a higher, is misleading when the differentials may be temporary. Firms would be ill-advised to act in response to *current market* prices and profits; major investment decisions should be made only on the basis of long-term judgements about the relative future courses of prices and profits.

18. Say's Law has been formulated in many ways: 'supply creates its own demand,' and 'all savings are automatically invested,' are the two most common. But as the argument between Ricardo and Malthus showed (Sraffa (1951) Vol. 2, Costabile and Rowthorn 1985; Vol. 2), the first is best interpreted as saying that production distributes income equal to the value of output; it is a separate question whether all income is spent. The second is directed to this point; it has to mean that invesment will always rise to the level of *potential* (full capacity) savings, and empirically this is obviously false. Theoretically it has been hard to justify; neither interest rate mechanisms nor real balance effects have proved plausible. It is often argued that the postulate of Say's Law began as a wrong but inspired guess, but has now become a part of the free market ideology (Morishima and Catephores, 1985). The suggestion here is that a 'Say's Law' economy is a Fixed Employment system, in which movements in Consumption and Investment spending are offsetting.

19. Given $Y = Y(K, N) = y(k)$, with p = price level; then from Euler's Theorem,

$$w/p = \text{real wage} = mp \text{ of labor} = y(k) - ky'(k)$$

$$r = mp \text{ of capital} = dy/dk = y'(k)$$

Then

$$d(w/p) = y'dk - ky''dk - y'dk = -ky''dk; \text{ and } dr = y''dk.$$

Hence

$$d(w/p) \;/\; dr = [-ky''dk]/(y''dk) = -k, \text{ i.e.}$$

$$dr/d(w/p) = -n$$

20. In 'cross-dual' dynamics, inequalities of supply and demand lead to prices changing, and differentials in profit rates lead to shifts of capital (and therefore labor), exactly as in the Fixed Employment economy. Flaschel and Semmler, 1986, formulate such a system, introducing a vector showing the direction and rate of change of profits in each sector as a further influence on capital movements. This improves the stability of their model. The rate of change of profits is similar to the ratio of the marginal efficiency of capital to the general rate of profit; cross-dual dynamics appears to demonstrate the general stability of a Fixed Employment system.

21. The Harrod–Domar 'warranted rate of growth,' $g = s/v$, is formed from an equation similar to this inequality. When I/s represents Aggregate Demand and K/v Aggregate Supply, the two will balance along the growth path, $I/K = g = s/v$. Two problems then come to the forefront. First, there is no reason to suppose that this will be compatible with the growth of the labor force; second, if Aggregate Demand > Aggregate Supply, business will experience a shortage of capacity, so will try to invest more; conversely if $I/s < K/v$. The warranted

path appears to be unstable. This is misleading; no actual economy ever moves along the 'warranted' path. Capitalist economies all operate with excess capacity; Eastern bloc economies with excess demand. The warranted path should be thought of as a dividing line between two modes of operation of a system employing Mass Production technology (Nell, 1990).

22. At low levels of income households will chiefly be concerned with meeting basic material needs – food, clothing, shelter, transport. These will be largely private goods in the economist's sense, although some transport may be collective. But as income increases the household will increasingly try to introduce 'higher' – more distinctly human – levels of activity into their consumption pattern. For example, education, entertainment, and communication, all of which are essentially collective, all rise as a percentage of household budgets, as we consider higher income levels. These are necessary to running economy, and progress in them is necessary to expanding productivity – but the public aspects can lead to government regulation and conflicts with private capital.

23. It might seem that these are analogous to different techniques, or, perhaps, to different operating methods, between which firms could choose, according to the criterion of cost minimizing. This would be a serious misunderstanding. These are cost structures which reflect the evolution of technique, under the pressure of economic incentives. The 'choice of technique' framework treats these as given, with input coefficients per unit output knowable in advance. But the speed and efficiency with which a labor force can operate plant and equipment, the flexibility with which plant can be shut down and re-started – the variability of costs, in short – only emerges in practice, as the result of learning by doing, through innumerable sequential improvements, small and large. They develop during the use of the technology, which changes as it is applied; but these features of the system are not given in advance.

References

Barnes, R.M. (1956) *Motion and Time Study* (New York: John Wiley).

Chandler, A. (1977) *The Visible Hand* (Cambridge, Mass.: Harvard University Press).

Costabile, L. and Rowthorn, R. (1985) 'Malthus' Theory of Wages and Growth,' *Economic Journal*, June.

Domar, Evsey (1957) *Essays in the Theory of Growth* (New York: Oxford University Press).

Eichner, Alfred (1976) *The Megacorp and Oligopoly* (Cambridge: Cambridge University Press).

Fisher, Irving (1930) *The Theory of Interest* (New York: Macmillan).

Flaschel, P. and Semmler, W. (1986) 'The Dynamic Equalization of Profit Rates for Input–Output Models with Fixed Capital,' in Semmler, (ed.) *Competition, Instability and Nonlinear Cycles* (New York: Springer-Verlag).

Garegnani, Pierangelo (1983) 'Two Routes to Effective Demand,' in J. Kregel (ed.), *Distribution, Effective Demand and International Economic Relations* (London: Macmillan).

Gershuny, Jonathan (1983) *Social Innovation and the Division of Labour* (Oxford: Oxford University Press).

Goodwin, R.M. (1983) *Essays in Linear Economic Structures* (London: Macmillan).

Harrod R. (1966) *Towards a Dynamic Economics* (London: Macmillan).
Hegeland, H. (1954) *The Multiplier Theory* (New York: Augustus Kelley).
Hirschhorn, Larry (1984) *Beyond Mechanization* (Cambridge, Mass.: MIT Press).
Hodgson, Geoffrey (1988) *Economics and Institutions* (Oxford: Polity Press and Blackwell).
Hollis, M. and Nell, E.J. (1975) *Rational Economic Man* (Cambridge: Cambridge University Press).
Kaldor, N. (1960) *Essays on Economic Stability and Growth* (London: Duckworth).
Kalecki, M. (1939) *Essays in the Theory of Economic Fluctuations* (London: Allen & Unwin).
Keynes, J.M. (1973) *The Collected Works of John Maynard Keynes*, Vols V and VI: *The Treatise on Money*; Vol. VII, *The General Theory* (London: Macmillan).
Mantoux, P. (1961) *The Industrial Revolution in the Eighteenth Century* (London: Methuen).
Marshall, Alfred (1961) *Principles of Economics*, variorum edn (London: Macmillan).
Marx, Karl (n.d.) *Capital* (New York: International Publishers).
Morishima, M. and Catephores, G. (1985) 'Say's Law and Anti-Say's Law,' University College, Department of Political Economy, Discussion Paper.
Nell, E.J. (1982) 'Growth, Distribution and Inflation,' *Journal of Post Keynesian Economics*, vol. 5, pp. 104–13.
Nell, Edward (1988a) *Prosperity and Public Spending: Transformational Growth and the Role of the State* (London: Unwin Hyman).
Nell, Edward (1988b) 'On Monetary Circulation and the Rate of Exploitation,' in P. Arestis (ed.), *Post-Keynesian Monetary Theory* (London: Edward Elgar).
Nell, Edward (1989a) 'Accumulation and Capital Theory,' in G. Feiwel (ed.), *Joan Robinson and Modern Economic Theory* (New York: New York University Press).
Nell, Edward (1989b) 'On Long Run Equilibrium in Class Society,' in G. Feiwel, *Joan Robinson and Modern Economic Theory* (New York: New York University Press).
Nell, Edward (1989c) 'Notes on Finance, Risk and Investment Spending,' in A. Barrère (ed.), *Money Credit and Prices in Keynesian Perspective* (London: Macmillan).
Nell, Edward (1989d) 'The Rate of Profit in Kalecki's Theory,' in M. Sebastiani (ed.), *Kalecki's Relevance Today* (London: Macmillan).
Nell, E.J. (1990) 'Demand Scarcity and Supply Shortage in Capitalism and Socialism,' in E. Nell and W. Semmler (eds), *Nicholas Kaldor and Mainstream Economics: Confrontation or Convergence* (London: Macmillan).
Pasinetti, Luigi (1977) *Lectures on the Theory of Production* (New York: Columbia University Press).
Pasinetti, L. (1980) *Essays on the Theory of Joint Production* (New York: Columbia University Press).
Pedersen, J. and Petersen, O. (1938) *An Analysis of Price Behaviour* (London: Humphrey Milford, Oxford University Press).
Robinson, E.A.G. (1931) *The Structure of Competitive Industry* (Cambridge: Cambridge University Press).
Semmler, W. (1984) *Competition, Monopoly, and Differential Profit Rates* (New York: Columbia University Press).
Smith, Adam (1776) *The Wealth of Nations* (New York: Modern Library).

Sraffa, P. (1926) 'The Laws of Returns in Competitive Conditions,' *Economic Journal*, vol. 36, December.
Sraffa, P. (ed.) (1951) *Works and Correspondence of David Ricardo* (Cambridge: Cambridge University Press).
Sylos-Labini, P. (1985) *The Forces of Economic Growth and Decline* (Cambridge, Mass.: MIT Press).

Part IV Prices, Investment and Effective Demand

Multiplier effects depend on prices remaining steady in the face of variations in demand. This will happen when mass production technology is dominant. The first study (Chapter 17) explains why, and analyzes competition and price-setting in these conditions, showing the relation between pricing and investment under conditions in which firms may or may not be able to influence the growth of their markets. The next two studies (Chapters 18 and 19) develop certain aspects of the theory of effective demand, as it has been presented in the mainstream IS–LM model, analyzing stability questions and the impact of the government. These studies show that certain very common claims – for example about the stabilizing impact of 'wealth effects' – are not true in general, and further suggest that the conceptualization of those effects, and consequently of the government deficit, is not coherent. But the IS–LM model does not even have an equation for the payment of income; income consists of claims to the surplus – so the surplus approach's account of effective demand will have to be built on firmer ground. The fourth study (Chapter 20) develops a better account of the multiplier, which is then extended in the fifth (Chapter 21) to an account of investment spending and finance. This gives rise to a simple and elegant business cycle. It also raises questions about the connections between the rate of interest, the rate of profit, and the rate of growth, which are further examined in the sixth study (Chapter 22). The multiplier as developed here implies that the real wage is positively, rather than negatively, related to the demand for labor; this requires a new look at the labor market, and at inflation, especially in regard to its effect on income distribution and on bearing the burden of changes in costs, Chapter 23. These questions are further explored in Chapter 24 in connection with the Harrod–Domar problem. Part IV concludes with three critical essays (Chapter 25), in each of which the author examined has failed, in one way or another, properly to account for the process of income generation – that is, the payment of claims to the surplus to the various categories of claimants. This failure is traced to an inadequate conception of income – the surplus – which, in turn, reflects a faulty understanding of the relationship between the real and the monetary aspects of the economy.

17 Demand, Pricing and Investment*

Economists dissatisfied with the conventional theory of the firm have recently begun to examine the connections between a corporation's pricing and investment decisions. Prices are seen as linked to potential output, rather than to current output, as in conventional theory. Perfectly competitive firms take prices as given and choose the optimal output, while in imperfect markets firms take the demand curve as given and choose the optimal combination of price and current output. In both cases productive capacity and the cost structure are taken as given. This may be reasonable for a small family firm, which at the outset makes a once-for-all choice of its optimal size, thereafter adjusting its current activity to changing conditions. But modern industrial corporations do not choose an optimal size; they invest regularly and grow. The conventional picture is not so much wrong as out of place – it is as though someone had painted a scene from the Middle West and tried to pass it off as a portrait of the Rockies. There are similarities, to be sure. The sky is blue and the grass is green, in both cases, and the sky lies above the land. Granted, but prairies are not mountains; it is not even 'as if' they were mountains. Corporate firms grow, and their pricing policies must be understood in relation to their growth if we are to accurately picture how the modern economy works.[1]

Three studies of pricing and investment particularly stand out – those of Alfred Eichner, Geoff Harcourt and Peter Kenyon, and Adrian Wood. All three try to determine not only prices and quantity of investment, but also the choice of the optimal method of production and the division between internal and external finance. At the same time, however, these three models also exhibit a basic defect in this approach, as it has developed so far. For all three fail to give adequate attention to the relationship between investment, pricing and the growth of *demand*, and, as result, ignore significant relationships while relying on unacceptable *ad hoc* principles. Eichner employs the Keynesian marginal efficiency schedule, in spite of having assumed market conditions in which it would not be valid, while Harcourt and Kenyon, and in a different way, Wood, treat the growth of demand as exogenous, and rely upon an implicit accelerator, and so wholly fail to connect prices with the growth of demand.

* Written for this volume.

1 INVESTMENT, PRICING AND DEMAND: CRITICAL NOTES

Eichner and the Marginal Efficiency Curve

Eichner sets out to determine, not the markup itself, but the change in the markup from some given initial situation. His strategy is to consider the demand for and supply of funds for investment in relation to a rate of interest. In the case of the demand for investment, the traditional marginal efficiency schedule relates the quantity of investment that will be demanded to the market rate of interest. Individual investment projects can be ranked according to their marginal efficiencies, which are determined by finding the discount rate that equates the net earnings of a project over its lifetime to its supply price or cost of construction. The schedule is then created by aggregating, for each level of the marginal efficiency, all the projects earning that level or above. It will thus be rational to invest in all projects whose marginal efficiency is equal to or greater than the supply price of funds; when the supply price falls, investment will increase, since more projects will become viable. The supply of funds, on the other hand, depends on the markup, which generates profits which can be retained, but a high markup will also lead to entry by competitors and substitution by customers, thus reducing the flow of funds, especially in the longer term. For each markup there will be a stream of internally generated funds, such that higher markups are associated with higher profits, but also with more substitution and entry. The loss due to substitution and entry, appropriately discounted and summed over the lifetime of the project, divided by the lifetime gains (also appropriately discounted), due to the higher markup provides an implicit rate of interest on internally generated funds, which can be compared to the going rate of interest on external funds. This defines a rising supply curve. For each level of the markup an increasing amount of external funds can be raised at a proportionately higher implicit interest rate. Thus with the demand curve for investible funds sloping down and the supply curve rising, the amount of funds, and the markup, will be determined. Then by comparing the implicit interest rate (equal to the marginal efficiency of the investment) to the going rate of interest, the proportion (if any) of external finance can also be settled. If the demand curve for investment cuts the supply curve at an implicit interest rate above the going market rate, then internal funds will be supplied up to the point where the implicit interest rate equals the market rate, and external funds thereafter, until the marginal efficiency of capital has fallen to the level of the market interest rate (see Figure 17.1).

Eichner emphasizes the important connection between pricing and investment, which he treats as expansion, rather than adjustment, in contrast to the mainstream approach.[2] His analysis of pricing is therefore consistent with modern growth theory.[3] Moreover, he develops an

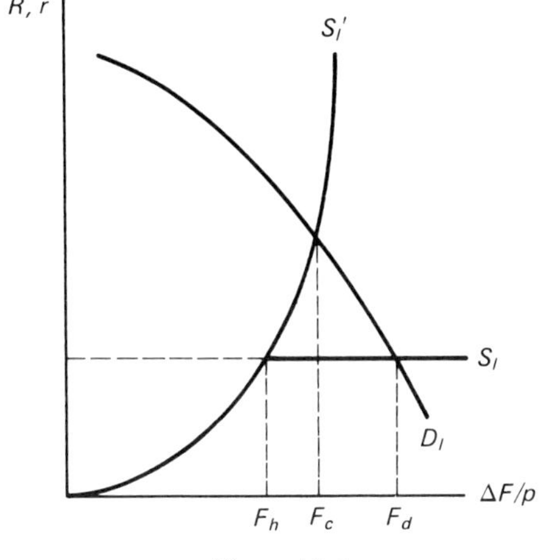

Figure 17.1

interesting discussion of internal and external funds, but the demand side is seriously inadequate. First, the marginal efficiency schedule poses problems under the best of conditions. If it is a disequilibrium construction we need an explanation for the long-term stability of the prices according to which we value output and inputs over the lifetime of the projects. If it is an equilibrium concept, however, when the rate of interest changes, equilibrium will not be re-established until the rate of profit has realigned itself. But changes in the rate of profit imply changes in prices and capital values. As the reswitching controversy showed, the order of projects may change, and the capital values involved may change sharply. For example, a fall in the rate of interest could lead to a decrease in the amount of investment, if the consequent decline in the rate of profit engendered a sufficient drop in the prices and (due to switches of technique) quantities of inputs in the viable projects.

If this were the only problem, Eichner would be in no worse a position than traditional Keynesians. A suitable, if necessarily *ad hoc*, explanation would be required for the disequilibrium stability of the prices of inputs and outputs over the lifetime of projects. The foundations might be weak, but the construction could be defended as useful or illuminating.

Unfortunately, there also appears to be an internal inconsistency in the argument. The implicit cost of funds, *R*, on the supply curve is positively related to the margin above costs. But as this margin is increased, substitution and entry of competitors cut into the expected market, reducing expected revenue. For that very reason, as we move up the supply curve, *required capacity will be less with each successive step*. In other words, the demand curve *also* depends on the margin above costs, by Eichner's own reasoning, which shows that the higher the margin above costs, the lower

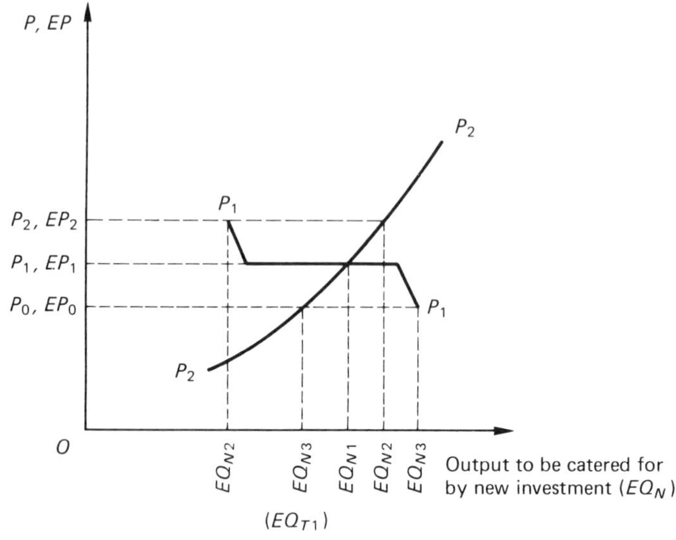

Figure 17.2

must be the demand for investment. This implies that there will be a *family* of investment–interest demand curves, one for each choice of profit margin. Spelling this out: in Eichner's notation, a higher R must imply a higher n, so will imply substitution and entry cutting into the cash flow. But this reduction comes about by *reducing physical volume*, while price increases. Hence less capacity will be needed, since fewer items will be sold. Thus as the markup rises the need for new capacity falls. In short, the supply curve for funds and the demand for investment are not independent. So Eichner's model is overdetermined and is thus not acceptable.

Harcourt and Kenyon and 'Vintages'

Harcourt and Kenyon also have a problem with demand. They draw two curves, plotting expected price or cost against the level of output to be catered for by new investment (see Figure 17.2). The p_1p_1 curve is downward sloping at each end, but has a long horizontal stretch in the middle. It shows the price that will have to be charged to cover costs for providing capacity to cater for different levels of output. The negative slope, surprisingly, is explained from the supply side. The firm is assumed to operate plants of varying vintages, older vintages having higher running costs. The higher the price, therefore, the older the vintages that can be currently operated, so the less new investment will be needed to provide the capacity to meet expected future demand. Conversely, the lower the price the fewer the vintage plants that will be operable, so the more investment will be needed. The horizontal stretch indicates that while a new plant can be run at varying levels of output, the price that will be charged *this period* to generate the internal funds to build up the plant will depend only on the fact that the plant has to be built. Any expected output within that range will require construction of a new plant, and will require the same corresponding price this period. Harcourt and Kenyon then draw their p_2p_2 curve, rising from left to right and intersecting p_1p_1. This second curve shows the output that will be producible by the plants that can be built with the funds generated by a certain price, assuming a given best-practice technique. So we have an intersection of a supply of funds curve from retained earnings and a demand for funds for investment.

This intersection is supposed to show the unique point at which expectations regarding the supply and the demand for funds are consistent. Yet their own interpretation of these curves suggests other possibilities. For example, suppose prices were set higher than the intersection, and in particular, above the horizontal pattern of p_1p_1. Then only a small amount of new capacity will be required, since vintage plants will provide most of the required output, but a large amount could be *afforded*; so, after meeting demand, funds would be left over. Then why not construct a large capacity plant, replacing some of the older vintage equipment, and use any extra funds in a selling or marketing campaign? To be sure, this might be a gamble, but in the world of the large corporation, high markups and heavy marketing often win out over low markups and reliance on normal demand.

On the other hand, suppose little or no older vintage capacity is available (e.g., older vintages can produce only goods of uncompetitive quality, or the market has expanded so much that vintage plants make up only a tiny proportion of total capacity)? What will replace the p_1p_1 curve under these conditions?

But the main problem is that the expected future demand (i.e., the growth of demand from its current or immediately past level) has been taken as independent of the markup chosen. The authors argue, correctly, that the evidence shows that oligopolistic producers adapt output to variations in short-run demand, leaving price unchanged, since price has been set to provide internal finance. But the reason for trying to maintain the flow of finance is that it is needed to build capacity; and they assume that decisions to build capacity will be taken whenever long-period expectations of demand change. Clearly these latter are of prime importance, yet no account whatever is provided of the determinants of long-period demand. It is simply taken as given, exogenous to the representative firm, presumably determined by macroeconomic forces. Yet by their own admission (when discussing Eichner's work) if the markup is above normal, substitution and entry can be expected which, of course, reduces the future level of demand. Surely this must be taken into account in planning the construction of capacity? If so, however, firms must be admitted to have some ability to influence their own future levels of demand. Since the approach deals with oligopolies, this can hardly be distressing, but somehow it never made it into the formal analysis. What of expenditures on selling, or investment in establishing distribution networks? The authors are silent. Perhaps they can be forgiven for overlooking this topic, but not for making their firms schizophrenic: they have them invest in long-lived plant on the basis of *given* expectations of demand, and choose a markup to finance this investment, even though they also hold expectations about the effect of changes in the markup on the physical volume of demand in the periods ahead.

Harcourt and Kenyon basically accept Eichner's theory of the supply of investible funds, but have replaced his use of the marginal efficiency of capital schedule by a demand construct based on given expectations and the notion of vintages of plant and equipment.[4] The main problem has been left untouched: a given markup, by providing the finance for investment, is associated with a certain growth of capacity; but it *affects* demand by encouraging or discouraging substitution and entry – and, unmentioned so far, the ability of the firm to develop new markets. Hence it should also be linked theoretically with the growth of demand.

Wood, Exogenous Demand Growth and the Accelerator

Adrian Wood tries to do this, but he bases his analysis on a problematical relationship of the investment coefficient to the accelerator principle, which creates difficulties not unlike those of Harcourt and Kenyon. The theory is simple and elegant. He defines an 'opportunity frontier,' showing the highest profit margin attainable for each rate of growth of sales, given the capital–output ratio, and a 'finance frontier,' showing the profit margin required to finance each rate of growth, also depending on a capital–output ratio. On the opportunity frontier, the relation between the profit margin and the rate of growth is negative for the given capital coefficient. On the finance frontier, it is positive. For a given profit margin, the relation between the capital coefficient and the growth rate will be positive on the opportunity frontier (more capital per unit output means lower labor and current costs per unit output, so a higher profit margin) and negative on the finance frontier. The object of the corporation is to maximize its growth rate of sales. The model determines the growth rate, the profit margin and capital output ratio together (see Figure 17.3).

Attractive as this theory is, there are nevertheless serious difficulties.[5] To define the finance frontier Wood argues that, given the capital coefficient, the growth rate of demand will determine the amount of investment needed to provide the required capacity. Then given the external finance ratio and the payment rate, the profit margin necessary to generate the

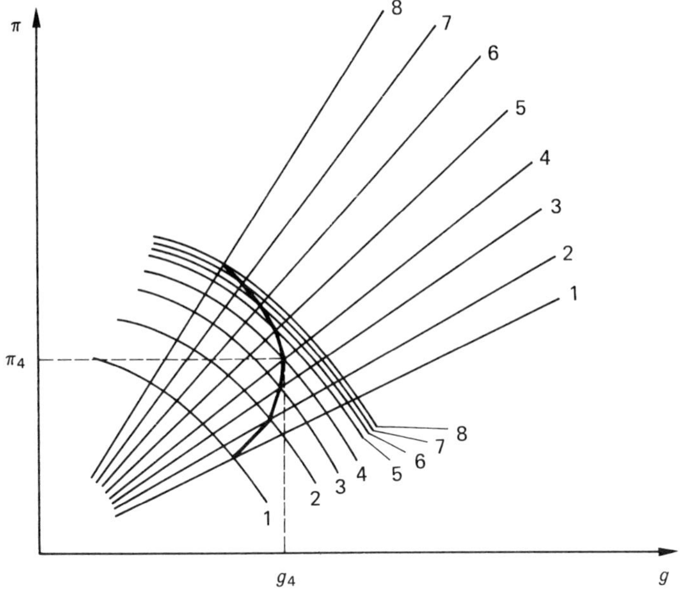

Figure 17.3

required internal finance follows. The capital coefficient thus functions as a one-period accelerator.

However, this creates a considerable difficulty for the interpretation of the opportunity frontier. Wood clearly wants to present a theory in which the corporation can exercise some *control* over the growth of its market, as in fact corporations obviously do. But if capital investment takes place exclusively in *response* to growth of demand, as the accelerator requires, then the only variable left by means of which the corporation could influence the growth of demand is the profit margin. But the relation shown in the opportunity frontier between the profit margin and the growth rate of sales is repeatedly described as 'the maximum profit margin attainable *given any particular growth rate of sales*' (pp. 66, 68, 69, 82, emphasis added). That is, the growth rate of demand is the independent variable, and the profit margin the dependent one. At first glance this may seem a matter of convention, but the economic interpretation is significant. For if the firm takes the growth rate of sales as given and *reacts* by setting the best profit margin it can get in the light of what its competitors are doing, then Wood is not entitled to say, as he does on p. 84, '[when the investment coefficient is given, a firm] . . . can increase the growth of demand for its products only by reducing its best attainable profit margin.' To say this implies that by reducing its profit margin a firm can raise its growth rate of sales, quite a different matter from saying that faced with a rise in the growth rate of its sales, the firm will find that the best profit margin it can get will decline because of the pressure of its competitors.

Nor is that all. Wood's analysis determines three variables – the rate of growth, the profit margin, and the investment coefficient. The latter is supposed to influence both the opportunity frontier and the finance frontier. The effect on finance is obvious: a higher capital coefficient implies a greater need for finance per unit of output. But the alleged effect on the opportunity frontier is easily understood only if the rate of growth of demand is exogenous to the firm: given such a growth rate, a higher capital coefficient, by reducing unit operating costs, will increase the maximum attainable profit margin. This is straightforward. By contrast, it is more difficult to argue that, given a profit margin, a higher capital coefficient will make it possible for the firm to increase the growth rate of its sales. To maintain a given profit margin with lower operating costs, price would have to be cut proportionately; but why will a lower price raise the *rate of growth*, as opposed to the level of demand? Further, if price and the rate of growth of demand are related in the appropriate way, then price should replace the profit margin as the variable to be determined.

The point underlying Wood's approach is certainly reasonable; he claims on the one hand that by reducing prices demand will be stimulated and, on the other, that when unit selling costs have been increased (for good reasons, of course) sales will be stimulated – i.e., the demand curves facing firms will be shifted as a consequence of the increased sales effort. So the growth rate of demand (this period's demand minus last period's, divided by last period's) will be increased – at least this appears to be the argument (pp. 65–6.) Taken literally, however, the implication is that an unchanged profit margin will be associated with a *zero* growth rate of sales; only changes in the profit margin will be associated with changes in demand, and levels with levels, as in traditional theory. Why a lower profit margin will raise the rate of growth of demand, as opposed to its level, is left unexplained.

Another aspect of the argument leads to an additional problem. An increase in selling costs means adding more sales personnel, more office equipment, perhaps more office space. Capital costs, as well as current costs, will be involved. Within limits, selling effort, as measured by unit selling costs, sales personnel, etc. could no doubt be increased temporarily by using existing office equipment and space more intensively. But in the long run changes in the capital invested in office space and equipment will be required. In the light of this, consider the interpretation of the capital coefficient. Some increases in capital – increases in sales capital – will tend to cause changes in demand, while other changes in capital – production capital – will come in response to changes in demand. The simple and valid point that corporations can affect their demand by incurring selling costs sits uneasily in the company of the accelerator principle.

These problems are compounded by the fact that Wood explicitly takes the growth rate of aggregate demand as given exogenously (p. 64) and describes companies as competing 'for a limited total amount of demand' in any period (p. 66). So any given company or sector can deviate from the general growth rate in a given period only if other companies or sectors deviate in exactly offsetting ways. One party's growth boom requires another's growth slump.

In short, either Wood intends the growth of demand to be exogenous, or he assumes that firms can influence it. But if demand growth is exogenous, the value of the analysis is more limited than it appears, and the reason that higher growth rates lead firms to lower their margins is unclear. If firms are supposed to influence the growth of demand, then the relationship intended is clear enough, but the price (rather than the margin) is the appropriate variable, and it still needs to be explained why lowering price or margin raises the growth rate rather than the level of sales.

Conclusions

All three make the point that the markup on the output of normal capacity must be set so as to provide the funds which will finance the construction of the capacity needed to supply the expected future demand. All make the further point that the choice of the markup will influence and be influenced by the division of finance between internal and external funds, and two of the three also relate the markup decision to the choice of the best method of production. But none of them successfully connects the markup to the growth of demand: indeed, all three fail to provide an adequate treatment of the relation of pricing and investment to demand. That is the task to which we must turn now.

2 GROWTH AND DEMAND

Two Patterns of Growth

Prices in a capitalist economy can be expressed by 'normal cost' equations: the price of one unit equals its wage cost plus the input costs plus the profit. Breaking this down shows the coefficients of the various inputs into each process, each multiplied by the amounts employed and by its price, aggregated to get total input cost. This figure will be multiplied by the gross rate of profit – the net rate plus the rate of depreciation – and then combined with the labor inputs times the wage rate. This results in the familiar 'Sraffian' or Classical matrix expression for prices and the rate of profit, given the wage.

This equation shows how prices, once firms fix them, interact with each other and with the rate of profits, but it does not tell us how firms settle on the prices they will charge, nor do the coefficients tell us how the system of production operates. To arrive at an account of how firms set their prices and realize them in the market, it is necessary to know more about the technology. In particular, we will distinguish two idealized systems, based on historical conditions, but defined as pure types – a stylized 'Artisan' economy, in which production is carried out on a small scale by groups of specialized, skilled workers, assisted by animal, water or mechanical (steam) power, and a stylized 'Industrial' economy in which mass production is carried out by workers operating along an assembly line or similar system that sets the pace of work. ('Artisan' conditions thus characterize much primary sector production, and 'Industrial' conditions correspond to manufacturing.) Each can be considered a complete economy, capitalist, described by the Classical equations and capable of growth. But the way investment brings about growth will be different in each, and so will the behavior of costs and prices when demand fluctuates (Leijonhufvud, 1985; Ch. 16, above).

An Artisan economy can either operate in stationary equilibrium or it can grow. If it grows it will characteristically expand through the lending of household savings to new firms, which set up shops that replicate existing ones, but serve new customers. But – at least under certain conditions – it need not grow, and its prices do not depend on growth. By contrast, an Industrial economy cannot settle into stationary conditions; in general it must expand or fall into recession, and its prices do reflect its growth. The reason for this lies in the different relationship of technology to competition in the two cases.

In the Artisan economy success in competition comes through the development of the skills and morale of workers. The successful firm has the better product, has more reliable delivery times, and quicker production times (with unit costs therefore lower), etc. – all of which depend on worker skills and their ability to function together as a team. Such characteristics are personal and intangible; improving them does not depend on rebuilding factories or re-equipping shops. But they are also unreliable: sickness or disaffection of key workers could undermine the whole year's effort.

In the Industrial economy competitive success likewise depends on cost-cutting and improved product design, but the difference is that these are objectively grounded in the production process, rather than based on intangible personal characteristics. They are therefore reliable, but depend on the design and characteristics of the technology. Improvements require retooling or rebuilding when they are 'embodied' technological innovations, and require investment. Plants have to be shut down and renovated or scrapped and rebuilt. Even 'disembodied' technical change, however, requires redesigning the work flow and the organizational chart.

An improvement provides a competitive advantage and must therefore be matched. So there will be need and incentive for the economy to contain a sector that specializes in supplying the means of production, and large enough to meet the demand for rebuilding entire industries. Investment will be more or less continuous, and productivity will regularly rise, though not necessarily in step with demand.[6]

Competitive improvements (cost-cutting, product quality) thus shift from depending on personal characteristics of artisans to being embodied in equipment and job design; as a result, the nature of labor changes. In an Artisan economy a high proportion of labor is fixed. The entire work team must function continuously in order for there to be any production at all. The firm has only two choices: to produce or to shut down. The only way to vary production is to vary the productivity of labor. As a consequence, the ability of firms to respond to fluctuations in demand by adjusting output and costs will be very limited. (This is the clue to understanding the Marshallian short-run production function.)[7] By contrast, in an Industrial economy productivity is built into the equipment, and labor is highly simplified. Tasks are broken down into their components and jobs are deskilled as far as possible. The work crew is less important, and productivity no longer depends on workers. Output can be quickly adapted to the level of sales; labor can be laid off or put on short time; it becomes a variable cost, and its productivity is fixed.

The shift from Fixed Employment to Flexible Employment technology also changes the nature of the saving–investment process. When the Artisan economy expands, household savings will be loaned to set up new firms. The system of small establishments will replicate itself; growth will not normally be undertaken by adding to the capacity of existing firms, for there are few economies of scale in traditional crafts, while adding to the investment under one management increases risk. (There is a problem, however, in the traditional account of a 'perfect capital market'.)[8] Industrial systems, on the other hand, do provide economies of scale, both in the design of equipment and in the organization of work. Even more important, however, technological competition between suppliers of capital goods means that new equipment is likely to be better or cheaper than old.[9] New investors will have an edge; existing firms cannot afford to remain satisfied with their present scale of operations, leaving growth to new entrants, for new firms will be able to undercut them in their own markets.

But existing firms do not necessarily have to scrap and rebuild every time there is a significant innovation. This would be wasteful, both socially and privately. Instead they can adopt the innovation in building new capacity to meet growing demand, carefully building just enough – at an appropriate price – to prevent newcomers from entering. The industry will then consist of a number of firms each having both new and old plants, rather than of older firms with outdated plants and newer ones with superior equipment.

To achieve this, however, growth must proceed differently than in the Artisan economy. To avoid competing for household savings, firms will retain their earnings and invest them directly. So long as their investments are judged to be wise, the value of their equity will rise in proportion – which means that shareholders desiring funds can obtain them by selling off an appropriate part of their holdings at the higher price (Ch. 21, below).

Growth in an Industrial system thus differs fundamentally from growth in an Artisan economy. Competition requires regular investment, financed by retained earnings, with a consequent rising price of equity. Labor becomes a variable cost, and output and employment vary together in line with sales, while productivity, fixed by technology, stays constant. Capacity capable of meeting the maximum likely demand can be installed, thereby ensuring that there will be no room for newcomers, without any risk of having to meet the labor cost of that capacity when it is not in full use.

But perhaps the most relevant differences, for the present discussion, concern costs and prices. In an Artisan economy, or in the primary sector of a modern economy, labor costs are largely fixed; variable costs are therefore confined to materials. Start up and shut down costs are large; variations in demand cannot be matched by variations in running costs. Output can be adjusted only by varying productivity. So when demand falls, for example, profits will be hit the hardest. And, since output cannot be readily contracted, excess inventories will have to be 'dumped' for whatever they will bring, forcing prices down. Prices will therefore reflect the requirements of market-clearing. In an Industrial economy, or in the manufacturing sector, by contrast, labor and other costs will be variable, so that operating costs and output can be adjusted to variations in demand, keeping productivity constant, and shifting part of the burden of adjustment from profits to wages.

In the Artisan world, growth simply replicates existing stationary relationships and market prices reflect the current balance of *spending* and output. We examined the variation of Fixed Employment prices around their normal levels when we analyzed the elasticity of consumption in relation to investment in the preceding chapter.

By contrast, in the Industrial system growth is a major agent of innovation and change and is central to the normal working of markets: for example, it must occur for potential profits to be realized. Of even more relevance here, it is part of the competitive process. If markets currently clear, but there is an imbalance between rates of growth of supply and demand they will fall into disequilibrium in the future. If they do not clear now, but their rates of growth are in balance, they will eventually even out. Prices are obviously both affected and influential – at low prices new customers can adopt a new good, so demand can expand; but low prices mean low profit margins, so little finance for construction of new capacity. This suggests that a price might be found that would just balance the rates of growth of supply and demand. We will need, however, to take a closer look at demand in a modern industrial economy.

Demand and Prices

To plan their market strategies, firms must know how the market will react to changes in prices. This depends on the composition of the prospective customers in terms of social class and income level, on the one hand, and on the way they have planned their household budgets, on the other, bearing in mind that this will take different forms in different classes. To keep matters simple we will distinguish only two classes here – the professional and managerial, and the working class. (A class is a class of families each earning similar incomes by performing jobs of similar status, exercising the same kinds of skills, and producing a new generation capable of occupying the same social positions, while also reproducing themselves.) We will assume that these are the only two classes.[10] But within each class there will be hierarchical relationships also; some groups will tend to set the fashions for the rest, and in some (but not all) fields, the highest level of the professional class will set the standards for the whole society.

We shall assume significant differences in household economic behavior between these classes – not just that they characteristically consume in different patterns. Members of the professional and managerial classes normally seek advancement along a career path; they hope and expect to rise in the social order, to find regular promotion to positions of higher status and pay – and they expect and hope that their children will also advance. They therefore plan their normal household budget with an eye to setting funds aside, after meeting the requirements of the household, to invest in furthering their or their childrens' careers. By contrast, members of the working class do not enter on careers, cannot normally expect much in the way of promotion (as opposed to wage raises) and do not expect to rise in station in life. Their extra time and income will be spent on hobbies, vacations, and leisure-time activities.

Families in each class must therefore spend their incomes in ways designed to meet the expectations of the world. Social life is governed by norms regulating the foods we eat, the clothes we wear, the kind of houses we live in, and so forth. These norms will differ for the two classes, but families in each must maintain the ability on their breadwinners to work adequately and attentively – at a minimum they must be well-fed and rested, dressed properly, with suitable transport to work from homes comfortable enough for them to bring up the next generation. The consumption of each class will be guided by a conception of its appropriate lifestyle, given its place in the social pyramid. (Such styles are displayed and debated in the media of the day, whether radio, TV, and movies – or in earlier times, newspapers, novels and traveling players, or even sumptuary laws and the pulpits of the churches.) A lifestyle will be expressed as a vector of standards, $s_1, \ldots, s_m$, where the elements express the level and style that must be achieved in each area, such as nutrition in diet, elegance in clothing, size of housing, and so on. Observe that a lifestyle is specified by levels of characteristics (Lancaster, 1966, 1979), not by quantities of goods.[11] The consumption of goods contributes in various ways to achieving levels of these characteristics, posing the problem of choosing the right mix of goods.

Given the basic requirements of life and the appropriate designations of style (including normal saving for retirement), each class will face a similar budget problem: to minimize the expenditures needed to cover these basics in adequate style, in order to release resources for investment in advancement, or for hobbies and leisuretime activities, respectively. Thus both classes face a straightforward optimizing problem:

$$\begin{array}{ll} \text{Min:} & C = p_1x_1, \ldots, p_nx_n \\ \text{S.T.} & a_{11}x_1 + \ldots + a_{1n}x_n \geq s_1 \\ & a_{21}x_1 + \ldots + a_{2n}x_n \geq s_2 \\ \hline & a_{m1}x_1 + \ldots + a_{mn}x_n \geq s^{m} \\ & x^1, \ldots, x^n \geq 0 \end{array}$$

Here C is the cost of living, $p_1, \ldots p_n$ are the prices of consumer goods, $x_1, \ldots, x_n$ are the choice variables, namely the quantities of the various goods that will be purchased by the household budget, $s_1, \ldots, s_m$ are the lifestyle parameters, representing the level and quality required of the various characteristics making up the standard of living, and the coefficients a_{ij} indicate the contribution of each of the n goods towards attaining the required levels of each of the m standards.

Once it is determined how to achieve the standard for minimum cost, the second problem emerges. For the working class (and those in the professional class whose careers have peaked), the question is how to spend the discretionary component of their income most agreeably. Hobbies, vacations, sporting events, entertainment, and do-it-yourself, will all figure here. But precisely because these are luxuries, spending on them may be subject to relatively sharp fluctuations resulting from changes either in fashion, or in views of the future.

Professional households, on the other hand, must examine their opportunities for advancement and decide, given the uncertainties, what their best investments will be. Each opportunity may be considered to have a present cost (perhaps in foregone earnings as well as actual payments) and to yield an (uncertain) stream of future benefits, in the form of higher

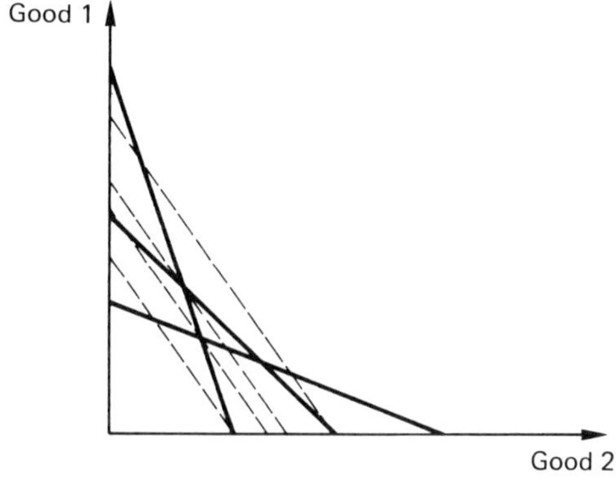

Figure 17.4

status and salary-plus-benefits. When present values are calculated, the projects can be ranked in terms of internal rates of return; investment will be limited by the excess of income over the cost of meeting the expected standard of living. (A more sophisticated treatment would analyze the conditions of possible tradeoffs between investment in career advancement and meeting the normal standard of living. Here, however, we assume the decision ordering to be lexicographic.)

Now consider the equilibrium of a representative family, say of the professional class, assuming two goods and three constraints (Figure 17.4).

So long as the price ratio (the slope of the dotted lines) lies between the slopes of the first two constraints, price variations will not affect the optimal purchasing plan. But if the ratio comes to coincide with the slope of the first constraint, good 2 will drop out of the budget altogether, and there will be a large increase in the purchase of good 1 – which could be the result of a rise only in the price of good 2; the price of good 1 itself could be unchanged. The new corner optimum will be at a higher cost level, leaving less for investment in career advancement, which will therefore have to be cut back or postponed. So a small rise in good 2's price could lead to its complete elimination, together with a large rise in expenditure on good 1, and a cutback in spending on education. (Notice that this could also happen with given prices, as a result of a change in the required standards.)

The moral is that price changes may have little or no effect over a significant range, and then suddenly have large effects, sometimes in unexpected directions. Of course, households will not all be the same, so in the neighborhood of the point at which a representative household would change its consumption pattern, we can expect to find a distribution of actual households, some changing at prices above, some at prices below the representative point. Changes in social standards and expectations may have similar effects. New goods and services can easily be introduced if they can be shown to achieve the same results at lower cost. (As the price of a new goods falls, and it is increasingly adopted, it displaces one or more older goods; the demand curve for the new good has an echo in the displacement curve of the old.) Emulation effects normally follow the social hierarchy; the consumption styles of the rich and famous set standards to which the rest aspire (or, sometimes, against which they react). When prices can be reduced or money incomes raised sufficiently, elements of more prosperous lifestyles will be incorporated into those of lower levels, usually in modified form. (The stereo systems of the rich become the boomboxes of the poor.)

Demand, then, is based on class structure, reflecting money incomes, and on price. There are two kinds of effects, which we may call 'composition' and 'incorporation' effects. Price changes lead, as a rule discontinuously, to changes in the composition of household budgets. Even substantial price changes may have only small effects over some ranges; then small changes may have large effects. In general, however, quantities purchased will move inversely to prices, as a result of household budget planning.

The other effect depends on the cost of a good, or of the meeting of a standard, in relation to income. Substantial changes in prices will alter the ranges of possibility for income groups. (For example, a substantial cut in the price of television sets in the mid-1950s dramatically increased the market.) Lower prices (or cheaper versions) bring goods previously available only to the well-to-do into the purview of lower income groups, allowing them to incorporate those goods into their budgets, creating larger markets. Alternatively, with the same prices, and the same degree of inequality, higher money incomes will increase the size of the market.

The normal growth of demand follows the development of a dominant lifestyle and its extension through each of the main social classes. Since a lifestyle is a way of using goods and services to provide the basic social requisites (food, clothing, shelter, education, transportation, communications, etc.) it distinguishes its components as belonging to a certain class in a certain epoch. Goods and services are fitted together in a way which characterizes them as belonging to one another: modern furniture belongs in a modern house, Victorian furniture in a Victorian. Different lifestyles can to some extent be mixed, it is true, and there can be differences of opinion as to what is 'correct' within a given lifestyle. But a lifestyle nevertheless fits together in a determinate way the methods of filling the basic social functions.

As a result, since the social functions are complementary, the dominant methods of filling them will be also. Of course, even within a given lifestyle a social function can normally be filled in a number of alternative ways, substitutes for one another, so that price changes will lead to changes in consumption. But these substitutes are all goods or services of the same *category*; tea and coffee are both beverages, rice and potatoes are both carbohydrates. Within categories, substitution holds, but between categories complementarity tends to be the rule. Pork and beef are substitutes, but meat and vegetables are not (unless, of course, one becomes a vegetarian – but that is a different lifestyle.) In production, steel and fiberglass are alternative materials, but energy cannot be substituted for materials. The more specific the good, the greater will be the possibilities of substitution, the more general the category, the more fixed the complementarity.[12] At the most general level, there will be the relationship between output of consumer goods and the coefficient of capital goods. The growth of consumer goods will require equiproportional growth in capital goods.

So if we choose a high enough level of generality in the categories of goods it will be reasonable to assume fixed proportions in both consumption and production, bearing in mind that our starting point is a social order in which there is a dominant lifestyle, supported by an already existing capitalist industrial system.[13] The implication of fixed proportions, of course, is that all consumer goods will grow at the same rate, and this will translate into the same rate of growth in all capital goods.

So we have an irregular but inverse relationship between price and the amount demanded of a commodity. This holds for a representative household from either social class, permitting the formation of aggregate demand functions. Likewise, demand depends on income; when the income of a class or subclass rises we can expect the demand–price relationship to shift out, making it possible to analyze the growth of demand. (Somewhat less reliably, it will shift inwards when income falls – though probably not in the short run.) With these two relationships, we can now develop the theory of pricing and investment.

3 BENCHMARK PRICING AND NORMAL GROWTH

The long-term normal 'benchmark' price is the one which will return a normal rate of profit on invested capital, when plant and equipment are used at the planned rate of 'full-capacity' operation. (This will not be the maximum possible rate, for firms will normally carry some reserve capacity for precautionary reasons, just as they carry cash balances in excess of normal transactions needs for such reasons.) Firms may be assumed to use the best technology and face the same wage rate and input prices; hence this benchmark price will be generally known, and will be used by financial analysts in calculating the ability of firms to carry debt.

Consider a market for a well-defined product or class of products. Outside of this market there are no very close substitutes; all the products within are similar and are produced by broadly similar technologies, giving rise to similar cost structures. Since the market is defined by the similarity of the goods other products must be relatively dissimilar. So in the short run there cannot be much in the way of substitution effects. Given more time, of course, consumers could switch in response to price changes, and even in the short run price changes could lead to postponements or stocking up. But under 'normal' conditions short-run demand can be assumed to be relatively inelastic – more precisely, the demand curve will be steep.[14] (Therefore, lowering the market price will not create a level of demand that present capacity will be unable to meet.)

Now consider a representative firm, operating plant and equipment embodying the best-practice technique, as defined by the consensus of the industry. It has built a plant of the optimal size in the light of its competitive position in the industry, given the capital that its owners could put up or raise and provide security for.[15] It expects to operate this plant at the 'full capacity' level, allowing for normal variations. It therefore expects a certain share of the market, based on past performance, location, relations with established customers, etc. Its demand, on the assumption that all firms charge the same price (or move their prices together), will therefore always be the same percentage of the market demand that its capacity is of total capacity – assuming, of course, that all other firms have built capacity in response to similar incentives and expectations (Cf. Ch. 16).

Wages, salaries and fixed costs – debt servicing and normal dividends plus rents and other contractual obligations – are given in money terms. Over the normal range of utilization the firm will use a 'standard cost' system, reflecting the technologically determined level of productivity and implying constant marginal costs. The position of the firm can be shown by plotting costs on the vertical axis and output on the horizontal (Figure 17.5). Here Q_0 is the initial level of normal capacity output and *AFC*, a rectangular hyperbola, is the curve of average fixed costs. The shaded area in Figure 17.5a represents fixed costs; any other rectangle under *AFC* will be the same in area. MC is the level of marginal costs. In Figure 17.5b required investment funds are added on top of marginal and fixed costs; these are the funds needed to expand by the same percentage that demand is expected to increase – shown here as Q_1, so that $(Q_1 - Q_0)/Q_0$ is the expected rate of growth of demand, g. The problem now is to find a price, p, such that initial capacity just balances demand at that price and the profits at that price will, when invested, create just the additional capacity needed to supply the growth of demand expected at that price. Such a price is shown in Figure 17.5c, where the initial and the later demand curves are D_0 and D_1, respectively. At every price, revenue is assumed to grow by the same percentage, $1 + g$, where this growth rate is exogenous – the representative firm cannot affect or control it. Consider the firm's calculation now.

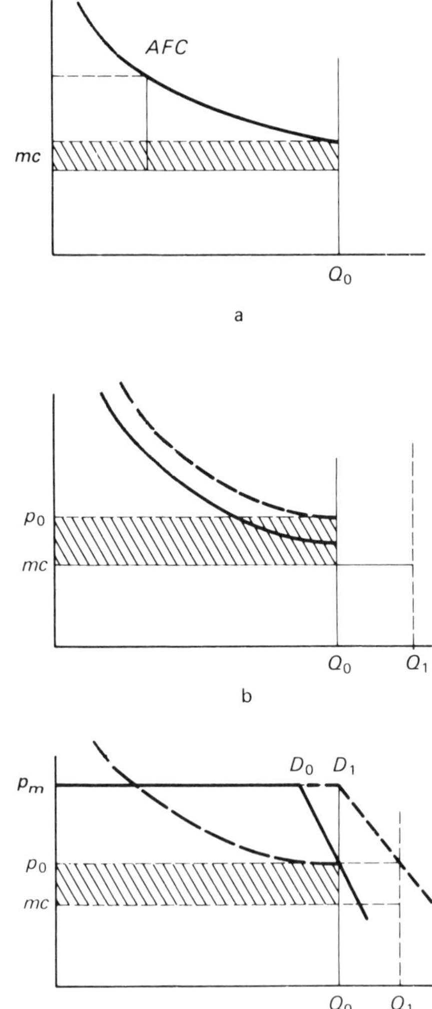

Figure 17.5

Balancing Net Revenue and Required Revenue

The firm has to choose a price that will provide the funds to expand capacity in the same proportion that demand is expected to grow.[16] This price will have to maintained over a certain period of time; it is not a momentary price. It is the benchmark that guides the day-to-day pricing policies of the firm's sales staff. The relevant period is obviously the time

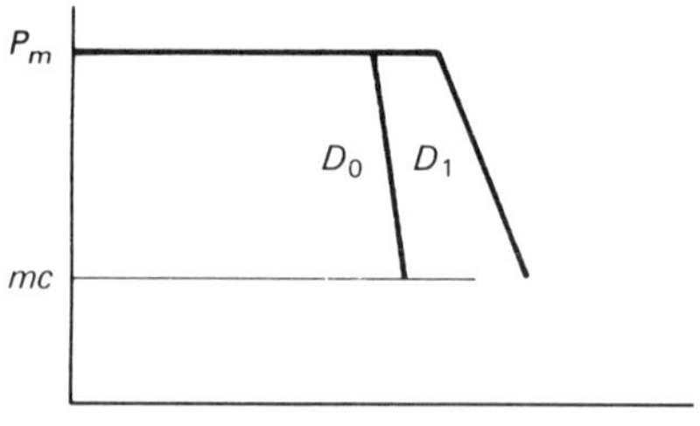

Figure 17.6

required to construct and install new capacity; the profits from normal operations over this period must be enough to finance new plant sufficient to satisfy the new customers added during this same time. But a longer period must be considered also: over the lifetime of a plant, the profit generated by its operation, plus the recovery of its initial cost, both compounded at a rate of interest equal to the normal growth rate, must finance the construction of new capacity equal to the initial demand times normal (compound) growth over that same period.

The capital–output ratio of the representative firm is given by history. The normal growth of the market follows partly from its own conditions and partly from the situation of the economy as a whole. The inelastic demand curve shows alternative prices and corresponding levels of purchase by fully adjusted consumers. However, we also need to think in terms of changing prices. There will be a maximum price such that, if price rose to it from another level, the good would be unaffordable within the short period, and demand would fall to zero. Below that, however, there will be a normal range, in which the good will figure in the budgets and planning of potential users. In this range a lower price will lead to some but not much increased consumption. However, over time, as incomes grow, the market will expand.[17] This is shown here as an outward shift of the inelastic (steep) market demand curve (Figure 17.6).

If the initial demand function is D_0, then the new one is $D_1 = (1 + g)D_0$; if D_0 is $q = a - bp$, D_1 is $(1 + g)\ (a - bp)$. This seems to say that the demand curve progressively flattens out from period to period, eventually becoming quite elastic. This would be a misinterpretation. D_1 is the expected demand, at various prices, as judged by the firm, on the assumption that income is growing. D_1 thus states that if the firm charges the same price from period to period sales will grow at every price in the same proportion that income increases. So it does not show the various quantities that would be bought at various prices; only D_0 can be so interpreted.[18]

It must now be shown that a unique price always exists balancing the revenue earned from normal operations and the revenue required to finance the additional capacity corresponding to the expected shift in demand. Intuitively when the price is higher, the required profits will be smaller; since the demand curve has a negative slope, the higher price

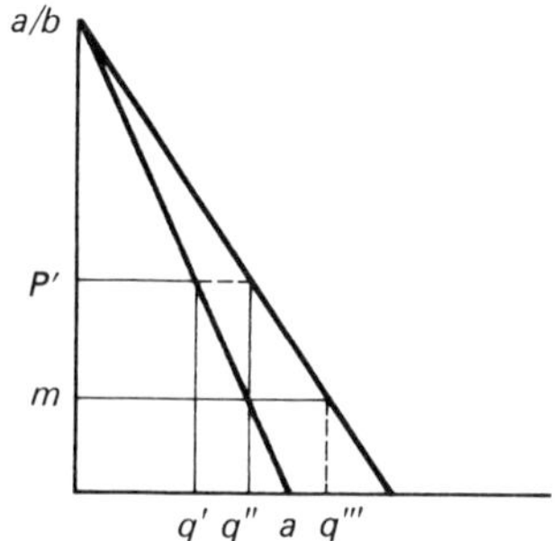

Figure 17.7

implies a lower denominator of the (given) growth rate. Hence the numerator must also be lower, so less investment will be needed. This implies a functional relation between price and investible funds, with a positive intercept on the price axis and a negative slope. On the other hand, it is clear that the higher the price the larger will be the investible funds generated, at least over a range, since the demand curve being steeply sloped, is inelastic over most of the relevant range.[19] There is therefore a second relationship between price and investible funds, this time with a positive slope. The price at which these two functions intersect will equate growth of capacity to growth of demand, and the quantity corresponding to that price on the demand curve will be the required initial capacity level output.

In symbols, let Q_1 be capacity output in a given period, where $q = a - bp$ is the demand equation. The Maximum price will be p' and the minimum price, m, equal to marginal cost. Hence the slope of the curve will be: $-b = (p' - m)/q'' - q'$ (Figure 17.7). The growth of demand changes the slope to $(1 + g)b$. The theoretically maximal price, the intercept on the vertical axis, will be a/b, which will be unchanged by growth.

Now consider the required increase in capacity at different levels of price. At price p', initial capacity equal to demand would have to be q' and next period's would be $(1 + g)q'$, where $g = (q'' - q')/q'$. At price m an exactly similar calculation can be made, showing a larger difference, divided by a larger initial capacity. Hence we can show the change in capacity, ΔQ, as a function of the price. For $p = p'$,

$$\Delta Q_p' = Q_1 - Q_0 = (1 + g)(a - bp') - (a - bp') = g(a - bp')$$

$$\Delta Q_m = Q_1 - Q_0 = (1 + g)(a - bm) - (a - bm) = g(a - bm)$$

The difference between $\Delta Q_p'$ and ΔQ_m is

$$\begin{aligned}\Delta\Delta Q = \Delta Q_m - \Delta Q_{p'm} &= g[(a - bm) - (a - bp')] \\ &= gb(p' - m) \\ &= gb\Delta p\end{aligned}$$

Assuming continuity and integrating, then

$$\Delta Q = -gbp + \text{constant} = ga - gbp,\ p' > p > m$$

The additional required capacity is an inverse linear function of the price. The constant will be the size of ΔQ when $p = 0$, so when p is out of the picture, $Q_1 - Q_0 = (1 + g)a - a = ga$.

To find the required investment funds ΔQ has to be multiplied by the appropriate marginal capital–output ratio (that of the least-cost method). On the assumption that the best-practice technique is given, this creates no difficulties, but unanticipated capital-saving technical progress would imply that a constant price would generate more funds than required. Another adjustment follows from the fact that the capital–output ratios in different sectors reflect the different capital–labor ratios. So the movement of relative prices when the normal expected growth rate of the economy changes will depend on these differences. A sector with a high capital–output ratio, facing an increase in normal growth, will have to raise its price more than a sector with a low capital–output ratio.

Next consider profits, or investible funds, as a function of price. This will be total revenue minus marginal and fixed costs, hence net revenue (remembering actual vintages – if best-practice costs are used net revenue will be overestimated):

$$\begin{aligned} R &= p(a - bp) - m\,(a - bp) - F = (p - m)(a - bp) - F \\ &= ap - bp^2 - am + bpm - F \end{aligned}$$

$$dR/dp = a - 2bp + bm,$$

where $d^2R/dp^2 = -2b$

$$dR/dp = 0,$$

when $p = (a + bm)/2\text{b}$.

Clearly the net revenue or profit function is a parabola which cuts the price axis twice, at $p = m$, where the curve is rising, and again at $p = a/b$, where it is falling.[20] In between, it reaches its maximum at $p = (a + bm)/2b$. So when price rises above m, initially, and over most of the relevant range, profits or investible funds increase (Figure 17.8).

The phrase 'investible funds' should not obscure the fact that profits need not only be invested directly, but may be used to service borrowed funds. This latter, of course, provides leverage; the profit justifies a larger investment, but the borrowing dilutes equity. The firm must decide on its borrowing policy: the more it borrows the greater the risk and the greater

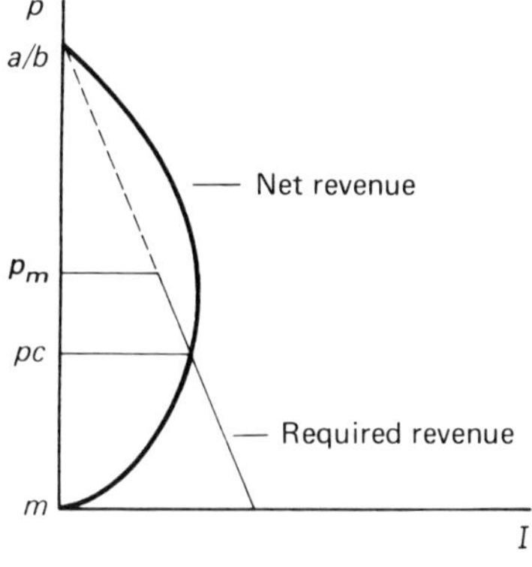

Figure 17.8

the dilution of equity, but the more it can expand and/or the more capital-intensive it can become. Firms must calculate an optimal policy by balancing these as best they can. Since all firms are similar, by assumption, all will adopt similar policies.

These two functions can now be put together to determine the benchmark price. The required revenue function shows the change in needed capacity due to demand growth; to get the required funds it must be multiplied by the capital–output ratio. The generated revenue function shows the net earnings; to find the available funds it must be multiplied by the leverage factor. For simplicity, assume initially that these two cancel each other. For the moment, also neglect fixed costs. Now consider the two functions. From the intercept *a*/*b* the net revenue function curves downwards to intersect the vertical axis again at *m*. The required revenue function also starts from *a*/*b*; then as price drops towards *m*, the revenue required to finance expansion of capacity rises. The two functions will intersect once, determining the benchmark price and the initial capacity output which will enable that price to remain constant while capacity grows in step with demand.

Setting the two functions equal to each other and regrouping yields a simple quadratic:

$$-bp^2 + [b(g + m) + a]p - a(g + m) = 0$$

(where 'm' is still marginal cost).

has the standard form $Ap^2 + Bp + C = 0$. The discriminant is

$$D \;=\; [b(g + m) + a]^2 - 4ab(g + m),$$

which simplified

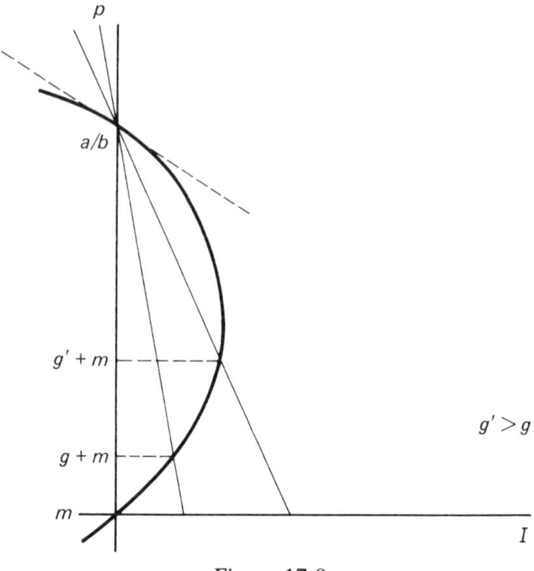

Figure 17.9

$$= b^2 (g + m)^2 - 2ab(g + m) + a^2,$$

a perfect square, whose root

$$= a - b (g + m).$$

When the demand curve is steep, a will be large compared to b, but the assumptions require that $a/b > m$ and $g > 0$. Hence,

$$a \geqq b (g + m),$$

so that $D \geqq 0$ and there will be either two roots or one. When the discriminant is positive, the roots will be

$$p = a/b \text{ and } p = g + m,$$

and when $D = 0$, $a/b = g + m$, and the single root is $p = a/b$. But the upper root, a/b, has to be considered irrelevant, since it represents a price set so high that growth, demand and profits are all eliminated. Only the lower root is economically significant, and given m, it depends only on g (Figure 17.9).

Allowing for fixed costs reduces the available generated revenue, effectively shifting the curve to the left. Allowing for a difference between the capital–output ratio, v, and the financial leverage ratio, f, requires a recalculation. Required revenue must be multiplied by v, generated revenue by f; the resulting equation is

$$-bfp^2 + [b(gv + mf) + af]p - a\,(gv + mf) = 0,$$

where

$$D = [b\,(gv + mf) + af]^2 - 4afb\,(gv + mf),$$
$$= (af)^2 - 2afb\,(gv + mf)^2 + b\,(gv + mf)^2,$$

with root $= af - b\,(gv + mf)$.

When $D > 0$, the two roots will be

$$p = a/b, \text{ and } p = gv/f + m;$$

and when $D = 0$, $af/b = gv + mf$, and the single root is a/b. Again the upper root is irrelevant, and the calculation will always yield a unique price.

The general conclusion has to be that under normal and plausible circumstances, in a steadily growing market with relatively price-inelastic demand, these two relationships will uniquely determine a benchmark price that will hold over a substantial period of time.

Further Analysis

Demand has been assumed to be linear and steeply inelastic as, in fact, is characteristic of manufactured products. Suppose the demand curve were of unitary elasticity; then the generated revenue function would be vertical, the required revenue a hyperbola, and the solution simple. Other forms can be imagined, but with substitution limited the functions will have to be similar to those examined.

Alternatively, suppose that g was high and a/b low, so that the required revenue function intersected generated revenue in the upper region, where demand is elastic. Consider a price above the equilibrium; at that price, generated revenue would exceed required revenue, exactly as it would in the lower region, in which revenue is rising with price. Excess revenue will tend to be translated into additional capacity, leading to a lower price: the movement is stabilizing.

Given the position of the initial demand curve, suppose the initial capacity level of the representative firm were too low, which is equivalent to saying that at some previous time, demand expanded more than expected. With actual capacity less than 'benchmark' capacity, price will tend

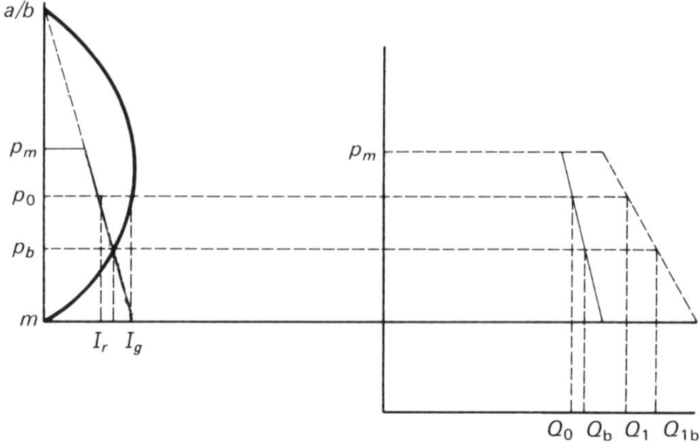

Figure 17.10

to be bid up above the benchmark level. At a higher price sales will expand less from period to period, but the profits generated will be larger (Figure 17.10).

When price is above the benchmark level the net revenue generated is above that required; hence extra capacity can be built to offset the initial shortfall. When price is below the benchmark, required revenue exceeds that generated; if the initial capacity level were too high, the profit margin would be squeezed and requirements expanded. So the relative movements of demand and capacity will be in the right direction for successful adjustment.

Such a process of adjustment raises the possibility of overshooting and cyclical behavior.[21] A purely mechanical analysis would seem to confirm this. But on reflection this is not plausible. For the benchmark price is a fictitious calculation which anyone familiar with the industry can make; it is the price that will prevent entry and ensure stability among the presently existing firms. If the initial capacity level is wrong, then the required funds function will have to be adjusted accordingly. The point is to calculate the price that will properly balance the growth of demand with the growth of capacity; if the starting point is wrong, then it will be corrected as soon as firms realize the error.

Next suppose that money wages rise or that materials become more expensive. What are the effects on the calculation? There are two cases. If the rise is local there will be no effects on the required revenue function, but generated net revenue will be reduced for every level of price except the upper intercept (Figure 17.11).

When m increases the generated revenue curve shifts inward and up, only the intercept, a/b, remaining fixed. Hence the new benchmark prices

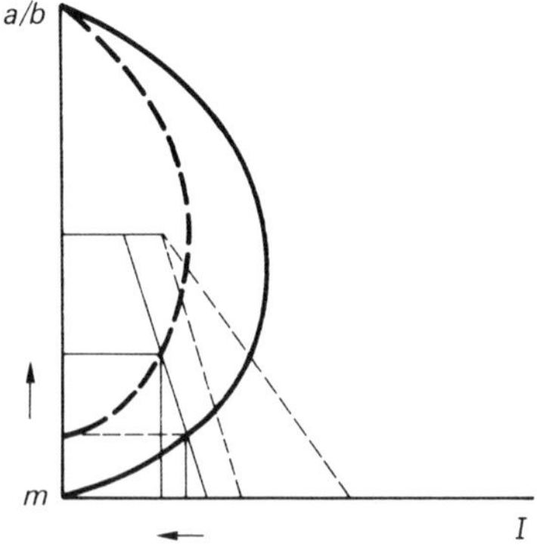

Figure 17.11

will be greater then the old, and the new level of investment funds will be less than the original.

But if the rise is *general*, an economy-wide increase in the wage, it is likely to affect either the level or the growth of demand. The numbers of customers currently in the market and those planning to enter could remain unchanged; if both groups spent more in the same proportion then the growth rate would be unchanged, but the market would undergo a once-for-all increase. So the initial capacity size would have to be adjusted, which implies a temporary outward shift of the required revenue function. Alternatively the rise in wages could bring the budgets of a new group of potential customers to the point where they could accommodate the good. Each period these new customers would join the market in larger numbers than at the old wage. Thus the growth rate of demand would rise, flattening the slope of the required revenue function.

Normal Growth and the Uniform Profit Rate

Under certain assumptions, the prices established here – by marking up marginal costs just enough to provide the profits required to finance the capacity needed to supply normal market growth – will result in a uniform profit rate. The benchmark prices so determined would be the money-price counterparts of 'prices of production.' But the assumptions necessary are quite significant and must be interpreted carefully.

Normal growth may be accompanied by innovations that will make some consumer or capital goods obsolete. However, a new good will often simply replace an old in the same category – the power mower displaces the hand mower and the boy next door – without changing the amount of expenditure on the category. If we assume that innovations are generally of this sort, the monetary flows between the categories will remain stable, while the average coefficients necessarily change slowly, reflecting investment and scrapping.

In addition to innovations, technical progress in the form of reorganizing work and improving productivity will normally take place. But if such progress is general, taking place, under competitive pressure, at the same rate in all sectors, then it will leave the relations between the coefficients unchanged, except for labor.[22] Such technical progress is consistent with balanced growth.

But there are other obstacles to balanced growth. Innovations lead to destruction of industries and productive capacity; the development and spread of a new lifestyle leads to the phasing out of the suppliers of the goods that figured in the older patterns of consumption. Technical progress in the design of goods and working of systems implies that new plant and equipment will be superior to the old. The new coefficients will reflect the competitively dominant costs, to which all prices will eventually have to adapt; but they will overstate the productivity of the system, and thus imply a faster rate of growth than would actually be feasible.

But the analysis started from the *actual* social order, in which households live according to the dominant lifestyle, using goods produced by the currently installed plant and equipment. To study pricing we considered the situation of a 'representative firm' setting a price that would preserve its market share, by permitting it to grow at the same rate as demand. Then we considered a more abstract system, in which demand grows at a uniform rate in all categories. But this would not be sufficient to ensure balanced growth, since innovations and technical progress might lead to rapid expansion in some areas, coupled with slower growth and even decline in other sectors. Innovations can be assumed strictly to displace earlier forms of the good, and technical progress to save labor in a uniform proportion. Finally, we must decide how to treat the coefficients; in practice, they will be the average of the various vintages of investment. But an interesting hypothetical system can be constructed on the assumption that all installed capacity operates with the coefficients of the best practice and most advanced design. The capacity of older factories is considered displaced by the newer; older products are substituted by newer ones in both production and consumption. An artificial system is created with the same scale of operations as the actual, and with the same dominant lifestyles and technology, but in which all equipment is best practice, all products best design and all technical progress uniform. This can be called the *abstract, normal system*.

This is a purely theoretical construction, showing the relationships between prices, wages and the rate of profit, on the one hand, and investment, consumption and industry sizes, on the other. It abstracts from the actual historical mix of mistakes, earlier products and technologies and from the irregularities inherent in technical progress. It assumes 'normal' growth, based on the dominant lifestyles, and determines normal prices and profits, based on the dominant technologies. But, although abstract and theoretical, it is not imaginary; it is constructed from the actual system and has the same scale. Its purpose is to show the relationships that competition would tend to enforce, except for the debris of history and the disorder of ordinary life.

Accordingly, refer back to the simplified model of an abstract normal system with two sectors, consumer goods and capital goods. The price equations, in money terms, were:

$$p = R\,(ap + wb),\ p = P_1/P_2$$

$$1 = R\,(Ap + wB)$$

And the quantity equations:

$$q = G\,(aq + wA),\ q = wX_1/X_2$$

$$1 = G\,(bq + wB)$$

Now multiply each of the q equations by the corresponding prices, and each of the p equations by the corresponding qs, representing capacity output. Then add the resulting pairs. The LHS of both sets of equations will be the value of gross output, price × quantity. Then simplifying, and putting the expression in relative terms, we obtain a relationship we will meet again in Chapter 20:

$$RAp = Gbq;\ \text{or, alternatively,}\ Rbq = GAp.$$

Clearly when prices are set to cover the costs of expansion at the normal growth rate, the result will be an equivalent rate of profit. Under these assumptions, then, normal growth gives rise to a uniform rate of profit and to prices of production.

Of course, the current pattern of normal growth may well not be balanced – technology may have been more or less productive than expected, markets may not have developed as foreseen. An unbalanced pattern of growth can be expected to give rise to a non-uniform pattern of profit rates. But the relations may be somewhat irregular; we cannot always expect to find higher market growth rates (or increases in market growth rates) associated with higher prices. Prices also reflect the costs of inputs, which will be influenced by the growth rates in the markets for those inputs, and if growth rates are varied, input prices may fall enough for a good whose market is growing faster for the price to decline.

When a new long-term pattern of growth emerges, requiring a new configuration of prices, we can assume there will be a first round of price setting, based on the initial costs and the new anticipations of growth. But as the new prices become known it will emerge that the initial costs are incorrect; a second round of price setting will then take place, based on the first round's prices. These, in turn, will have to be modified, based on the second round's prices, and so on. Provided certain conditions are met, the largest price changes in each round will be smaller than the largest ones of the previous round, and the sequence will converge (Nell, 1991). Unfortunately, the issue is too complex to be considered further here.

When the growth of the economy in general rises, on a permanent basis, however, money prices in general will rise, and (unless there is an 'inflation barrier', in Joan Robinson's phrase) real wages will fall, so that the profit rate rises. In this case, then money prices in general will move with the real growth rate; but relative prices will move in both directions! For when real wages fall and the profit rate rises, some prices will rise and some will fall, reflecting the different degrees of labor intensity in different industries (Sraffa, 1960; Part II, above).

4 BENCHMARK PRICES AND MARKET CONDITIONS

Actual conditions are seldom 'normal,' which means that firms will not be selling their 'normal' output. Benchmark prices are guidelines; they can be calculated by anyone familiar with the conditions of the industry; they will be used by bankers to assess creditworthiness and by courts to value assets. Once a benchmark price has become established firms will be reluctant to change it unless the underlying long-run data have changed. But short-term and cyclical fluctuations have to be dealt with. In the face of shortages, surcharges could be added; when there is excess capacity, cuts can be made. Benchmark prices, in short, could well remain stable, while market prices showed considerable flexibility.

Of course, market prices do fluctuate quite a lot. Sales drives, special discounts, 'loss leaders,' dumping, etc. all lead to variation. But price flexibility has a special meaning: prices will systematically fall when actual demand falls below normal, and rise systematically when actual demand reaches or exceeds normal. Demand fluctuates quite markedly, but the expected systematic price behavior does not seem to take place. Why not?

Competitive Strategy

Consider a firm whose demand has fallen substantially below capacity. To attract more trade it could cut price – a delicate operation at best; in the ideal case, it would offer bargains throughout the market while keeping its rivals in the dark, but more often it will act without knowing what rivals will do. In any case a preliminary strategy calculation shows that the representative firms must be prepared to act regardless of the behavior of rivals.

Let *RF* be the representative firm, and *AR* be all its rivals, meaning all 'nearby' firms from whom *RF* could expect to attract customers or to whom it could lose its market. There are two broad strategies, then, cutting price or sticking fast. The initial price will be p, and the change Δp. The size of a typical firm will be q, and *AR* is made up of n firms, so will have an output of nq. When *RF* cuts and *AR* sticks, a fraction x of *AR*'s demand will potentially switch to *RF* Analytically, as a first approximation,

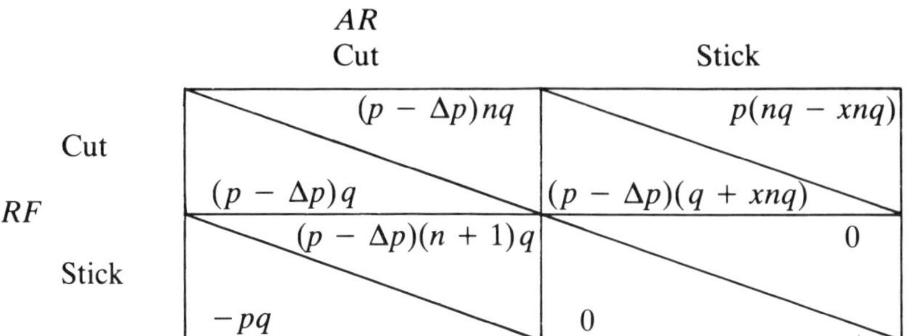

From this it would appear that *RF*'s best strategy is to cut, no matter what *AR* does, since both $(p - \Delta p)q > -pq$, and $(p - \Delta p)(q + xnq) > 0$. If *AR* cuts and *RF* sticks, *RF* stands to lose everything, since *AR*, being much larger, will be able to supply *RF*'s whole market. If *RF* cuts and *AR* sticks, *RF* will attract a large clientèle – but this potential gain may not be realizable. For *RF* cannot (except temporarily) supply more than its capacity permits. Moreover, as we shall see, if a large price cut is necessary to attract demand, and the amount of excess capacity is small, it may not be worth it. What is the use of attracting demand that cannot be supplied? We will examine this point in a moment. First, note that *AR*'s calculation is not relevant, although it would appear that cutting would be best for it, too, if Δp were small and x large (i.e., when lots of customers would move for small price cuts). But such a calculation implies that the firms that make up *AR* can act in concert. If the market is competitive, however, they will act individually, so the calculation for *RF* holds for each of the firms in *AR*, taken separately.

A further reason for firms to favor the strategy of cutting when demand falls short of capacity lies in the fact that a single firm inflicts only a small loss on its competitors, which when spread among them may be hardly noticeable. No one may notice, or bother to retaliate. Thus each firm may be tempted to cut first: which implies that all will cut.

So, at first glance, competitive strategy seems to imply that a representa-

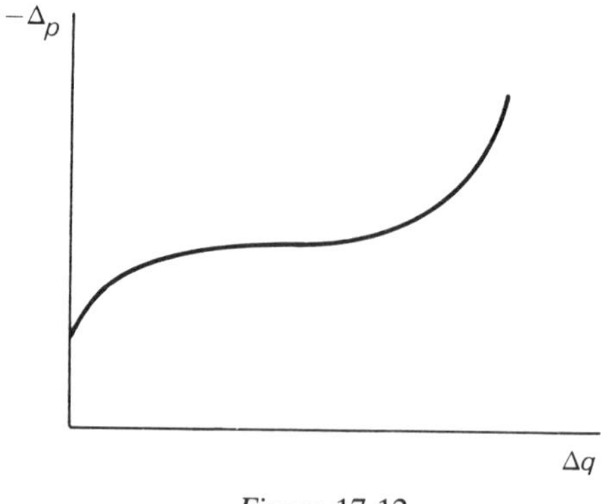

Figure 17.12

tive firm will cut its prices when demand falls below capacity and, by analogy, raise them when it runs over. But it makes sense for a firm to try to attract only demand it can service, and this raises the question: how large a price cut to attract how many customers?

The Customer Attraction Function

Firms each occupy a certain space in the market – a geographical location, and also a position in social space, which together give them a set of habitual customers, who, however, are aware of competitors. Changing suppliers takes time and may disrupt working arrangements between officials of manufacturing and distributing firms or between customers and shopkeepers. Yet if it is worthwhile customers will certainly switch. Firms will try to estimate how much extra trade they could attract by dropping their prices below the benchmark, and also how much they stand to loss if they don't and others do (Figure 17.12). The customer attraction function for the representative firm will show the change in sales and the customers attracted, for price cuts of various sizes. In general, it will have a positive intercept; a small price cut would hardly be noticed, nor would it be worthwhile to disrupt established practices for small gains. But as the cut increases more and more customers will be attracted, until at a certain level a very large number will shift. Beyond this point, however, it will take very large cuts to attract even a small additional number. All the mobile 'nearby' customers have already shifted; those now being attracted are distant, unfamiliar or have significant links with their normal sources of supply. So the general shape will be, starting from a positive intercept, to climb steeply, flatten out, and then climb steeply again. The more 'competitive' the market, the smaller will be the required price cuts and the greater the number of mobile customers, so the lower the intercept and the longer the flat portion. In the extreme case, corresponding presumably to the ideal of 'perfect' competition, the curve would reduce to the horizontal axis, indicating that an infinitesimal price cut would attract an infinite

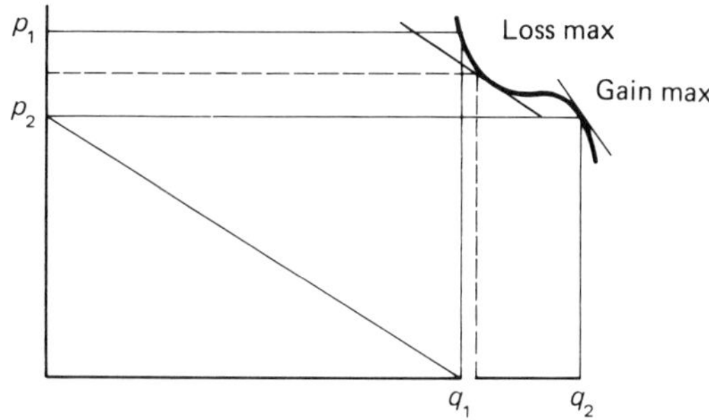

Figure 17.13

demand.[23] But in the normal case changing suppliers, or even seeking out the best bargain, has a cost, which will vary for different customers, giving rise to the functional shape examined above.

Competing for Customers

Suppose demand is less than capacity and the representative firm has decided to cut to try to attract customers. It faces a 'normal' customer attraction function. How much should it cut its price?

For the price cut to be worthwhile, the gain, the new price × the additional quantity, must outweigh the loss, the change in price × the initial quantity. So the new price must be chosen to make this difference as large as possible. Hence,

$$\text{max: } p_2\Delta q - \Delta p q_1, \text{ i.e.}$$

$$d/dp\,[p_2\Delta q - \Delta p q_1] = 0, \text{ or}$$

$$\Delta q\,(dp_2/dp) + p_2(d\Delta q/dp) = q_1(d\Delta q/dp) + \Delta p(dq_1/dp)$$

Assuming continuity and manipulating, noting the zero terms,

$$p_2/q_1 = d\Delta p/d\Delta q$$

and this will be a maximum when the second derivative is negative. In words, when p_2 is chosen so that the tangent to the customer attraction function at the point (p_2, q_2) is parallel to the line from p_2 to q_1, the additional revenue reaches an extreme point, which will be a maximum gain at the place marked in Figure 17.13. It seems that the price p_2 should therefore be selected by the representative firm.

But if $q_2 - q_1$ is greater than the difference between the original level of sales and normal capacity it would be a mistake to drop the price to p_2, for part of the demand attracted could not be supplied. The gap between normal capacity and current sales in proportion to the level of sales must be greater than the price cut in relation to the new price to make it worthwhile to cut at all.[24]

Even if this condition is fulfilled for the representative firm it does not follow that there will be a general spate of price cutting. Actual firms differ from the representative firm and from each other, both in relation to costs and in the loyalty of their customers. When effective demand falls off some firms may bear the brunt and begin cutting; but then the rest have to calculate how much they stand to lose if they stick. For instance, a firm with relatively little excess capacity and whose nearby customers are quite loyal to their normal suppliers would not find it worthwhile to cut, unless it stood to lose heavily. But if its customers are reasonably loyal, so that the proportionate loss in sales is less than the proportionate price cut necessary to prevent such losses, the firm should stick to its price and take the loss. By the same token, price cutters will not gain very many customers, so it may not be worthwhile for them. But if firms are fairly similar and the fall in demand substantial, all may calculate that it would be advantageous to cut.

However, if all cut, no one gains. Worse all lose, since the market demand curve is inelastic. The problem has to be reformulated – cutting below the benchmark price is a strategy that will work only if one's rivals do not follow suit. Since such cuts are dangerous it is unlikely that small deviations will be followed; on the other hand large ones, which may attract sizeable numbers of customers, are increasingly likely to be matched. The probability of rivals following suit is thus an increasing function of the size of the price cut.

But a small price cut merely brings a loss; if a large price cut carries a high probability of being matched, then it, too, 'spoils the market.' Under these circumstances, the best strategy is to hold the line.

Now suppose demand is above capacity, and steady. The firm is in a strong position and its customers should know that alternative sources of supply will be hard to find. This is the time for surcharges. To determine how much to add to the normal price, the firm maximizes the additional revenue (Figure 17.14).

$$\max: \Delta p q_2 - p_1 \Delta q,$$

$$d/dp\,[\Delta p q_2 - \mathrm{p}_1 \Delta q] = 0$$

which becomes

$$q_2(d\Delta p/dp + \Delta p(dq_2/dp) = p_1\,(d\Delta q/dp) + \Delta q(dp_1/dp)$$

Assuming continuity and rearranging,

$$q_2/p_1 = d\Delta q/d\Delta p$$

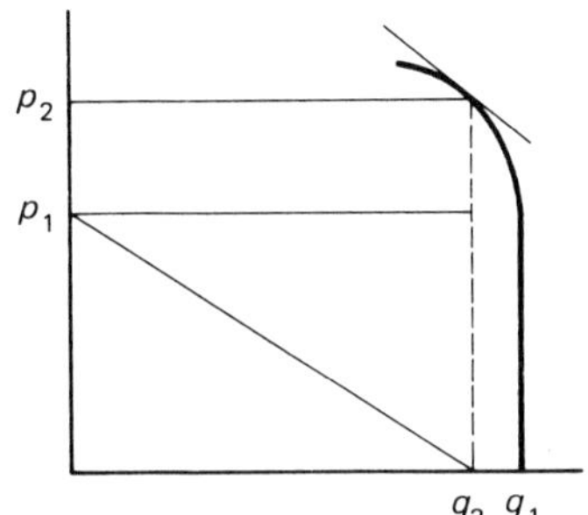

Figure 17.14

price will be raised until the tangent to the customer loss function at (p_2, q_2) is parallel to the line from p_1 to q_2. Hence at or above capacity there will be a tendency for prices to drift upwards, even though firms may believe that their rivals will not follow suit, so long as they believe their customers will be reluctant to shift, at least for small surcharges: prices rise more easily than they fall.

The Customer Attraction Matrix

Consider a market consisting of n firms, all producing a product of identical design, using the same technology, but with the possibility of differences in efficiency and the organization of work – and hence in costs, and also in services related to product delivery and the reliability of quality checking. In the event of a price war, firms will differ in their ability to attract customers from each other. Let a_{ij} indicate the customers attracted by the ith firm from the jth, as the result of a price cut. Rows will therefore show all the customers the ith firm can attract from each of its j competitors, and the row sums will show the total customers attracted by a unit price cut. Columns will show the customers lost by the jth firm to each of its i competitors, and column sums will show the total lost. Hence if a firm's (row sum)/(column sum) > 1, it gains in a price war; if less, it loses. We can number the firms according to their (row sum)/(column sum) ratios, putting the highest first (and noting that diagonal elements are zero):

$$\begin{array}{cccccc}
a_{11} & + \; a_{12} & + \; \ldots + a_{1n} & = & S_{1j} \\
+ & + & + & & \\
a_{21} & + \; a_{22} & \ldots + a_{2n} & = & S_{2j} \\
+ & + & + & & \\
\hline
+ & + & + & & \\
\underline{a_{n1}} & \underline{a_{n2}} & \ldots + \underline{a_{nn}} & = & S_{nj} \\
S_{i1} & S_{i2} & \ldots \; S_{in} & &
\end{array}$$

Clearly if this matrix is symmetric, $a_{ij} = a_{ji}$, with row sums = column sums, price wars will benefit no one. The nearer it is to symmetric, and especially the nearer the majority of row/column ratios to unity, the fewer the gainers and the smaller the gains. But the presence of even a few firms with row/column ratios significantly greater than one will indicate beneficiaries in a price war. The nearer the matrix to a triangular form the clearer is the hierarchy of market strength and weakness. Over time, we can expect competition to eliminate the weaker firms, moving the matrix towards symmetry – in which case we can reasonably speak of the customer attraction function of a representative firm.

Cutting Money Wages

When demand falls workers will be laid off. It might be argued that such unemployment would bid down money wages, with competition then pushing down prices in proportion, so that prices would fall with demand, after all.[25] (It would be harder to argue, however, that a recovery leading to re-employment would bid up money wages, leading prices to rise with demand.)

Wage-cutting is dangerous, however; it upsets relationships between the firm and its employees, endangering technical progress. Worse, it can provoke slowdowns and sabotage – direct retaliation. Moreover, if rivals do not follow suit, the best workers will leave for greener pastures, and the firm will face turnover and training costs. Consider the strategic position of a firm contemplating a cut in the money wages it pays its workers:

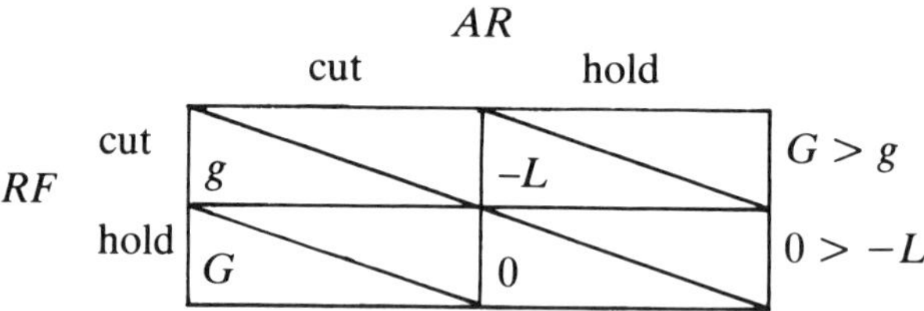

Suppose all the rest are cutting; if *RF* also cuts it will make a small gain, g, due to the lower wages, but it will have to deal with disgruntled employees and low morale. If it holds the line, however, it will attract the best workers from everywhere else, and will reap the rewards of higher morale, which it can cash in the form of worker willingness to accept speed-ups and cost-cutting job redefinitions. These productivity gains, G, could easily outweigh the gains from lowering wages.

Suppose the other firms are holding wages steady. Then to cut would be to become a pariah in the eyes of workers. The best would leave, the rest would turn sullen and obstinate, and the result would be a loss, $-L$, in productivity, outweighing the gain from the cut. To hold the line will leave the situation unchanged. So if workers can speed up or hold back technical progress, so that G and L are large, it will pay the representative firm, and therefore every firm considered in succession, to hold the line on wages, rather than cut, in the face of unemployment and deficient demand.

The Instability of Perfect Competition

The limiting case occurs where an infinitesimal price cut would lead to infinite demand – the entire market would shift to the price cutting firm. In such circumstances, it seems, the representative firm will always produce at capacity. When demand fluctuates, however, the response is unstable. Demand above capacity should lead to price increases – but given the inelasticity of demand, these increases may have to become very large before the excess demand is eliminated. When demand falls substantially below capacity, however, price will immediately be driven down to marginal cost. Any one firm cutting will force the others to follow suit; when all cut, however, demand increases only slightly, so the cutting will continue, down to marginal cost. Firms will therefore not be able to meet their fixed obligations, and so will have to go out of business or be reorganized. Supply will thus be drastically curtailed, leading to a very large price increase. With constant marginal and falling average costs, and inelastic demand (the normal situation of firms in modern industries), the limiting case of perfect competition will be unstable, with price swinging about wildly and firms facing bankruptcy and reorganization.

The result of pushing price down to marginal cost is that profits will fall below the level needed to finance the capacity to prevent entry. New firms will therefore enter, with the latest technology and product design. They will be able to dominate the market and will set about to establish customer loyalty, raising the intercept of the customer attraction function.

Investment in Customer Loyalty

Loyal customers mean that a firm will not have to follow cuts down and will be able to add surcharges in boom times (so long as this does not undermine the loyalty!). Customers are loyal, not as a matter of sentiment, however, but because the firm has made it worthwhile for them to stick by it. To develop a loyal market a firm has to invest in providing customer services – effective sales displays, prompt delivery service, repairs, maintenance and warranties, efficient quality checking, reasonable payment terms and so on. These are costly and also take up management's time and attention. To invest in them requires building offices and training staff – at the expense of investing such funds in additional productive capacity. The return on the investment is the stream of earnings over and above what they would have been with more mobile customers (minus the current costs

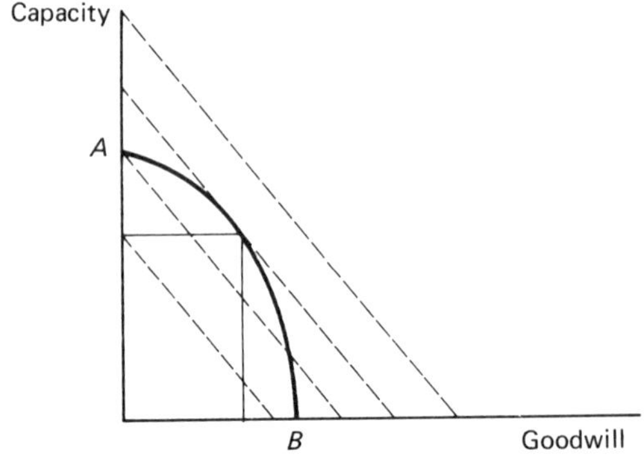

Figure 17.15

of providing the various customer services). These higher earnings reflect higher capacity utilization, steadier prices, and lower risk of default. The rate of return, then, is the rate which discounts the stream of expected earnings, until it just equals the cost of the investment.

This rate must be compared to the rate of return (in terms of earnings growth) anticipated from the construction of new capacity. For given an amount of investible funds, the firm must decide how much to put into new capacity and how much into the development of 'goodwill' or market loyalty. Should the firm sacrifice the construction of some new capacity in order to reduce the downward variance of sales, thereby raising the average rate of capacity utilization and reducing the risk of default? If so, how much?

A very traditional type of calculation can be made. There is a given amount of investible funds. Capacity will be measured on the vertical axis and 'goodwill' on the horizontal, both in units of additional revenue. If all the funds are put into capacity, *A* will be built; if all go into creating goodwill, *B* (Figure 17.15). The production-possibility frontier *AB* then shows the various combinations which could be obtained. This will be concave to the origin, for in developing customer loyalty, the relatively amenable and easy-to-reach will be attracted first, and it will take progressively more effort to reach the others. So in units of additional revenue, there will be diminishing returns to investment in 'goodwill.'

Revenue will be at a maximum when the revenue from additional expenditure on goodwill falls to the same level as that from additional expenditure on capacity. Draw iso-revenue lines with a slope of 45°; the point where the production possibility frontier is tangent to the highest iso-revenue line will give the optimal division of investment.

This calculation looks very orthodox, but it carries an unsettling implication: firms have a normal incentive *to invest in undoing competitive condi-*

tions. Reducing the mobility of customers – improving the shape of customer loyalty functions – increases average utilization, reduces risk of insolvency and improves competitive position; over time, we can therefore expect markets to change character.[26]

A Classification of Markets

The limiting case is *pure atomistic competition*, in which the customer loyalty function takes on its extreme form: there is zero loyalty, and so an infinitesimal price change brings an infinite reaction – the entire market moves. But in this case, industrial markets (in which variable costs are constant and average fixed costs fall, while demand curves are steep) will be markedly unstable. Moreover, it is contrary to both common sense and common observation to hold that mobility is costless. But if there are costs to switching suppliers, customers will not move unless the price differential is large enough to compensate them.

The normal competitive case can be called *practical atomistic competition*. There are large numbers of similar firms and large numbers of customers are willing to move for relatively small price differentials. But firms calculate their strategies and small amounts of excess capacity will not lead to any price cutting, nor will small amounts of excess demand bid prices up. Firms do not wish to spoil their markets, nor do they propose to erode their goodwill. Prices will therefore normally be more stable than outputs.

But firms will regularly invest in creating goodwill, and as customers develop loyalty the market will tend towards *imperfect competition*. Even large shortfalls in demand will not lead to price cutting; on the other hand firms may be able rather easily to add surcharges when demand is strong. Once customers have become attached, small surcharges will not drive them away. Hence in imperfect markets there will be a tendency for prices to drift upwards over time (Figure 17.16).

The three degrees of competition are readily illustrated. Q represents full capacity production, mc is marginal cost, and p_b is the benchmark price. The curve shows the average price charged as demand varies in relation to capacity, and the shading gives an indication of the variance of prices. In pure competition very slight variations in demand will bring very wide swings in price, with almost no variance among firms. In practical competition there will be a significant range over which price will not change or will change very little, extending both below and above normal capacity. But there will be considerable variance among firms. In imperfect competition prices will rise relatively readily, but it will take a very large shortfall in demand to bring about price cutting, although the variance among firms will be much larger.

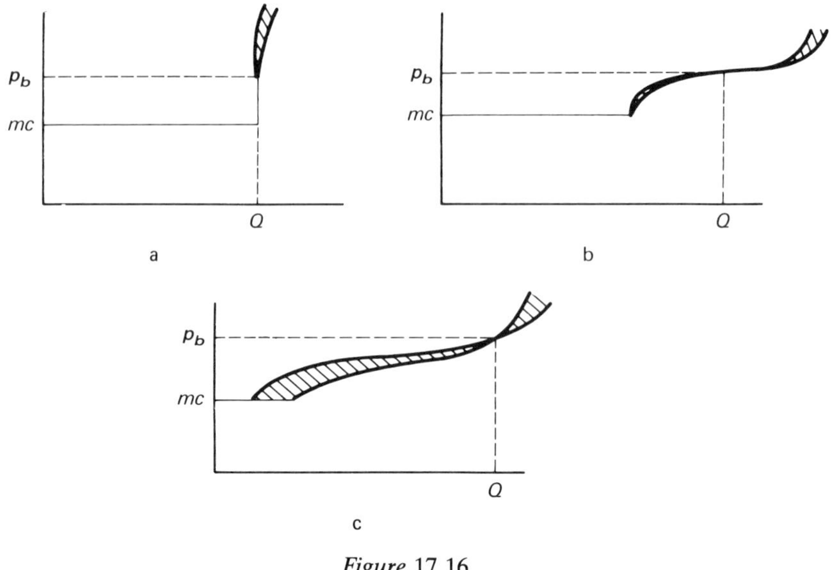

Figure 17.16

Financial Competition and Product Differentiation

Imperfect competition can develop in another way, in which firms develop a differentiated product, each variant being designed to appeal to specific submarkets. This is the result of pressure arising from stagnation after a period of growth. As lifestyles change with affluence, the growth of expenditure may be concentrated in new fields, so that while established markets may remain large, they will cease to grow. But the capital invested in them will still be under pressure either to grow or to pay dividends equal to growth. A company that fails to grow or to pay an equivalent yield will find that its stock is likely to collapse, making it a target for a takeover. To protect itself, management must therefore try to keep up its earnings.

Competitive pricing belongs to the 'Ford' phase of industrial capitalism, along with rapid growth, technical progress, and mass production. When growth slows down and stagnation sets in, however, we come to the 'Sloan' period of product differentiation, advertising and marketing.

Traditional capitalism had just two classes, capitalists and workers. Modern capitalism first created a middle class, and then brought about fragmentation and subdivision in all three classes, ultimately merging capitalists with professionals, and forming distinct styles and patterns of consumption in the various subgroups. In the Ford phase, industry turns out an efficient product which is the same for everyone; in the Sloan phase the product is varied and adapted to the conscious (and the unconscious) needs and desires of each class or subgroup.

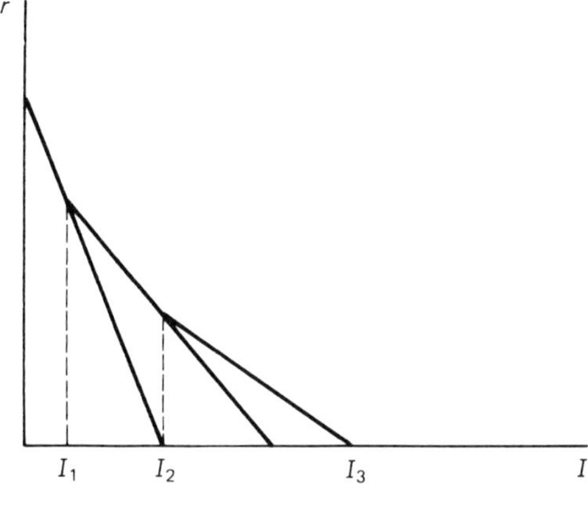

Figure 17.17

The Sloan phase begins when it is clear that the market is stagnant, but the capital is being recovered. Instead of renewing existing plant, the market will be fragmented, and a different product will be designed for each distinct subgroup. The basic production process will remain the same, and the basic underlying product will also. But new plant and equipment will be needed to undertake the modifications necessary to adapt the product to each group – Chevvies for the workers, Pontiacs and Buicks for different strata of the middle and upper-middle classes, Cadillacs for the rich. Each of the new products is sold to a specialized fraction of the original market, willing to pay a higher price in order to obtain a distinctive version of the basic product. So the new prices will be set by marking up the benchmark price of the original product. Higher prices will mean smaller markets, lower larger. Larger markets will be associated with lower rates of return, unless there are sufficient economies of scale to outweigh the price effect. Normally, then, for each potential product there will be a downward-sloping curve showing the size of the investment (needed to serve the market) in inverse relation to the rate of return (Figure 17.17).

Arrange the investments in the different products in order of their highest potential rates of return. The first investment will be in the highest-return project, and the amount invested will be the amount that just brings the rate of return in this project down to the highest level obtainable in the next best project. The amount invested in that project will be the amount that brings its rate down to the highest level obtainable in the third project, and so on, until all the funds are invested. Any residual funds, of course, can be invested in the original product, since the new specialized markets, operating at higher prices, will not absorb the whole of the original demand. The ending of a period of growth will thus bring on product differentiation and imperfect competition.

Investment and Entry

In traditional theory the entry and exit of firms supposedly correct excessive or inadequate profits, establishing the uniform rate through such movements. By contrast, benchmark pricing is designed to keep new firms out by enabling existing firms to expand enough to supply the (exogenous) growth of demand at a stable price, and the uniformity of the rate of profits is established (if at all) on the basis of normal growth; in general, there will be differentials in profit rates, reflecting different expectations of market growth, and of the evolution of costs. The traditional account is part of the conception of pure atomistic competition, and its account of entry is flawed.[27]

In practical competition, however, firms do enter and exit, though not as often as the textbooks suggest. Oligopoly theorists have argued that firms will adjust their pricing strategies to keep prices low enough to discourage potential entrants. But if prices are kept down, profits will be lower, and less investment can be afforded. Will enough capacity be constructed to supply the growing market, particularly given that the lower prices may stimulate or permit faster expansion of the market? If too little capacity is built, then entry will be virtually impossible to prevent. On the other hand if enough capacity – or more than enough – is built entry will be discouraged even if prices are high, since the firms already in place have a natural advantage (assuming that they are normally efficient and well run).

Entry moves are investment decisions and must be considered on the same footing as the investment decisions of the firms already in an established industry. Leaving aside entry of *capital* through mergers, acquisitions and lending, firms enter by constructing new plant and equipment. They will do this only if they believe that existing firms are not planning to build enough (or good enough) capacity. Hence, paradoxically, a firm may enter because it believes the present benchmark price too low! Such a price will encourage the growth of more demand than it will generate the profits to build the capacity to supply. So an outsider will enter anticipating a growth of demand in excess of what the industry has expected and prepared for. Outsiders will thus enter when current profits are too low – just the reverse of the traditional doctrine.[28] Similarly, a relatively weak firm would be well-advised to exit in a period of high current profits, if it believes that demand growth is likely to be weaker at this high price than originally anticipated.

There are two cases where the traditional story holds, however. In a new market, the growth of demand is often likely to be both substantial and erratic, so that the firms already producing cannot expect to satisfy demand when it expands, but may find sales drying up unexpectedly from time to time. In these circumstances high prices may indeed be an appropriate signal to enter, and low prices to leave. But when the market settles down and growth becomes predictable, though still not controllable, then the question of entry will depend on outsiders' assessments of the investment plans of the firms already producing.

The second case concerns a stagnant or declining market. When the market is no longer growing, price cannot be governed by the requirements of investment; with inelastic demand, however, firms could milk the market by raising prices. If entry barriers were weak this could conceivably attract the attention of outsiders. The threat to reduce prices in the event of entry may be a sufficient deterrent; alternatively prices may have to be kept below some temptation level. Much more important, however, is why the market has stagnated; if it is because no potential new customers have been identified, then milking the market by the existing firms may encourage 'oblique' entry by outsiders – modifying the product to make it attractive to a new class of customers whom the outsiders proceed to proselytize and supply. On the other hand, if stagnation has occurred because a new and significantly more attractive product is taking over the functions of the old, then no one is likely to want to enter – but raising the price will tend to speed up the process of decline.

Even though the growth of the industry cannot govern price, firms will try to earn at least normal profits, so as to have the funds available to invest in other projects. Once a market turns stagnant, the firms in it must diversify; otherwise the capital they represent will cease to expand at the normal rate. Their investors will be disappointed and will tend to pull out, or seek to dislodge the managements. The decision whether or not to try to milk a stagnant market will thus depend on the possibilities of diversification, the speed of the market's potential decline and the likelihood of provoking entry.[29]

Rising Supply Price

When demand is above capacity prices tend to be bid up, when demand is below, prices tend to fall. Such price movements were held to serve the important economic function of allocating scarce resources to where they were needed most. This traditional view cannot be accepted, but it is true that the market performs an important function. Prices generate profits where they are needed to finance new capacity to service the expected growth of demand. In a sense prices do allocate investible funds, with the important proviso that there is a significant range of variation of demand within which prices do not respond – and for good reason.

But prices do not reflect scarcities. Traditional theory tried to explain changes in prices, as demand changed, by the movement of costs, requiring the postulate of diminishing returns. In modern industry variable costs are constant and average fixed costs fall with increasing output. Costs, therefore, cannot explain the behavior of prices.

The level of capacity utilization reflects an industry's current demand, which in turn is governed by investment. So when capacity utilization is persistently high, pushing prices up, this indicates that investment in general is high, responding to growing demand in many markets. A high price is therefore appropriate, since profits will be needed to finance the capacity needed to meet the growth of demand. Similarly for low capacity utilization and low prices. Market forces thus tend to push prices in the direction they should move, in the light of their function in providing profits to finance new capacity.

Market forces also weed out inefficient – high-cost, low-quality – producers, since they will earn less than normal profits, and with weaker sales and fewer loyal customers, carry more than normal excess capacity. So they will grow more slowly; high-quality, low-cost producers will earn higher than normal profits, and will grow faster. If all firms start out at approximately the same size, and if 'cost efficiency' and 'quality production' are normally distributed, then growth will result in a *log normal* size distribution of firms, with the larger firms being the more efficient, better quality producers.

But a great deal of the fluctuation in demand is not long-term, nor reflective of underlying trends. It may be cyclical in nature, or it may reflect temporary aberrations, policy decisions, or speculative excesses. From the point of view of the firm, it would be unwise continually to adapt prices and pricing policies to such changing conditions. Since they operate a Flexible Employment technology, they can adjust output and costs when demand fluctuates. It thus makes sense to define a normal operating range, and both strategy and customer loyalty will insulate this range from market pressures. Industrial prices are steadier than outputs.

5 PRICING IN ADMINISTERED MARKETS

Corporate Pricing and Investment Decisions

When firms are small and the market is new, no one firm will have any control over the growth of demand, nor will any one have a body of established and closely attached customers. But with maturity a few large firms producing somewhat differentiated products will acquire a sufficiently dominant position that they will possess a well-defined and identifiable body of established customers and be able to influence, at a price, the growth of their sales. The analysis which follows concerns a representative firm of such a kind.[30]

Established and New Markets

A firm's established market is where it is well-recognized and can count on a loyal and reliable set of customers, either households or businesses, who have incorporated its products into their lifestyles or production processes, so that to switch to an alternative product would entail at least some costs. Switching products thus becomes an investment decision – the stream of gains from the new product, properly discounted, must more than cover the cost of making the switch. Substituting products will therefore not be lightly done, so sales will be predictable and, within some reasonable range of prices, customers will continue to prefer the firm's products. An established market thus carries itself; the current selling effort is negligible and for all practical purposes capital selling costs are sunk.

Established markets can exist for intangibles – services – as well as for tangible goods, and, in both cases, we can distinguish between durable and nondurable purchases. Durable goods last, removing the customer from the market; nondurables require continuous re-entry into the market. Durable services produce results that last – the surgeon as opposed to the pharmacist, the architect as opposed to the gardener. An established market for a nondurable (an operating input into a household or business) means that there is a regular clientèle that repeatedly purchases the good or service for use in its established operating procedures. So it plans for the use of the good, budgets for it, and would have to change its routine to substitute another good or service. In the case of durables, new purchasers similar to those of the past, coming from the same neighborhood, social class or industry, regularly enter along with replacement purchasers, drawn by the product's reputation and suitability, including the ready availability of ancillary services.

Consider a representative firm, or a representative division of a conglomerate corporation, producing a well-defined product with an established clientèle. The firm or division has to earn the profits necessary to finance its own growth, either directly by spending internally generated funds, or by showing earnings that will justify the required level of borrowing. In a moment we will see that, given the various costs, the level at which the firm sets the price will determine the growth rate that it can finance. First, however, we must explore the relationships between the level at which price is set and the rate at which the market can be expected to grow. Over a wide range the large established market will be comparatively insensitive to price, but, by contrast, the smaller new markets which the firm wishes to develop or penetrate will react quite strongly to prices. This can be shown in a pair of diagrams (Figure 17.18a and 17.18b). Figure 17.18a represents the established market, the broken line indicating that it is much larger. The steepness of the demand line indicates that the good is

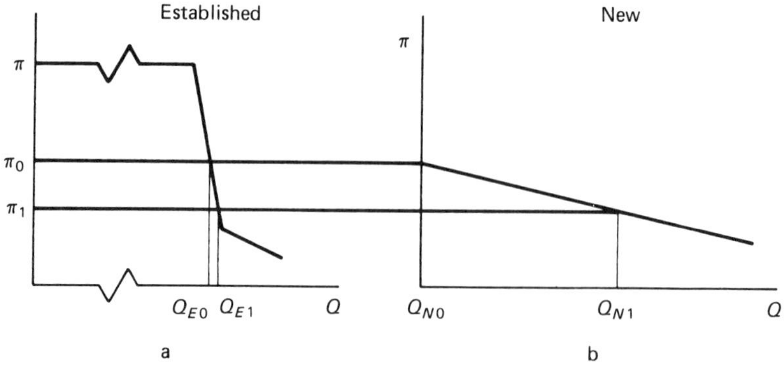

Figure 17.18

strongly complementary with other goods in the household's normal life style, or in business's production systems. The high and low breaks mark the points where substitution will take place, and customers leave and enter. In the smaller new market, shown in Figure 17.18b demand is quite sensitive to changes in price. (The price does not actually have to be the same in the two markets, but if they are different, they must be strictly related and move together.) The current sales drive can be assumed to be concentrated in the new market, and the level of investment in sales and distribution will determine the position and slope of the demand curve,[31] confronting the firm in this market. Other things being equal, the higher this level of investment the higher the intercept and the flatter the slope of this demand curve. (Similarly, the position of the demand curve in the established market depends, among other things, on past investments in sales and distribution.) The implication, then, is that a change in price, say from high to lower, will not affect the established market much, but will have a strong impact on the new. At the lower price, the ratio of the new market to the old will be higher. But this ratio represents the growth of sales.

In the notation of Figure 17.18 at the price π_0, the rate of growth of sales will be

$$\frac{Q_{n0}}{Q_{E0}}$$

at $\pi_1 < \pi_0$, it will be

$$\frac{Q_{n1}}{Q_{E1}} > \frac{Q_{n0}}{Q_{E0}}$$

So as the price falls, the rate of growth of sales increases, for a given investment in sales and distribution. The maximum price for the price –

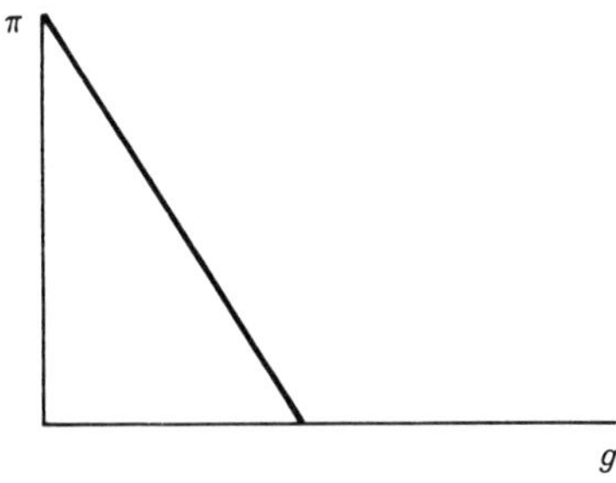

Figure 17.19

rate of growth function will be the price at which the new market vanishes. The maximum rate of growth, corresponding to the minimum price, will be given by the horizontal intercept of the new market's demand curve (see Figure 17.19).

The slope of the growth of demand function, then, will be

$$\frac{\pi_0 - \pi_1}{\dfrac{Q_{n0}}{Q_{E0}} - \dfrac{Q_{n1}}{Q_{E1}}}$$

which can be rewritten

$$\frac{Q_{E0}\, Q_{E1}\, (\pi_0 - \pi_1)}{Q_{E1}\, Q_{n0} - Q_{E0}\, Q_{n1}}$$

In the special case where $Q_E0 = Q_E1 = Q_E$ we have

$$\frac{Q_E(\pi_0 - \pi_1)}{Q_{n0} - Q_{n1}} = -Q_E \frac{\Delta\pi}{\Delta Q_n}$$

If the demand curve in the established market is quite steep this will be a good approximation to the slope of the price–growth of demand function.

To fix the position of the new market demand function, it is necessary to know the investment in sales effort. This should be explained. There are current costs, both fixed and variable, involved in selling, but the larger part of selling costs constitute an investment. The aim is to capture the loyalty of set of customers. The time, effort and expense in selling are to be applied not only to the immediate sale, which may only be a trial order, but to all future sales in that market. A sales[32] campaign requires training and equipping a sales force, providing warehouses, showrooms, office space, personnel, dealers, distributors, delivery systems, servicing arrangements, warranties, and insurance. Independent distributors may be used, but then contracts must be drawn up covering all of the above, and franchises issued. This will involve commitments over various lengths of time. The firm's object is not merely to expand its market, but to develop one that reliable. It is committing resources to building plant and equipment; it must develop a market corresponding to this new productive capacity that will last as long as the new factories, or at least as long as it take to write them off. So the expenses in developing the market should be considered investment; they entail the commitment of capital in construction, training and the assumption of contractual obligations. These are long-term arrangements and they are expected to yield long-term benefits.

Investment in market development will shift the growth of demand frontier, but successive investments will not necessarily shift it the same amount. There are good reasons for believing that there will be diminishing returns to investment in sales and marketing. The 'pool' of potential customers can be defined geographically and socially. Near the center of the pool it will be comparatively easy and inexpensive to convert potential customers into actual ones, but the further from this center the more expensive and problematical the process will become. Transport and transactions costs will rise, and the 'fit' between the potential customer and the product will be poorer. This will be important later on.

To summarize the assumed circumstances: the product is well-defined and the established market is given. The productive capacity supplying it has been built, the sales investment has been made and customer loyalties established. The new market has been targeted and projections drawn. It is expected that sales will follow a certain course, depending on the prices charged and the sales investment made. Other things being equal firms will pursue the most rapid possible course of expansion. Their long-term expectations will be assumed to be correct, though allowance will be made at times for unexpected short-term fluctuations in demand. The analysis, then, will hold for the time it takes to carry the project through – that is, to develop the market and build the capacity to service it. After that, the new market becomes part of the established market and attention can be turned to the next investment project. The length of this planning and execution period will be longer than the conventional short run, because the new capacity has not only to be built, it has to be operated and the new market consolidated. But the time this takes will itself depend on market conditions and may vary from sector to sector, and even from firm to firm.

The Supply of Finance for Growth

Given the foregoing relationships between the corporation's projected growth in sales, its prices, and sales investment, the company's next problem must be to ensure adequate financing to underwrite the investment in sales and to build and equip the new plant to supply the expected new markets. The calculation it must make is relatively straightforward. The company will have a policy, to be explored in a moment, with respect to the burden of debt it wishes to assume relative to its equity. This will depend on the balance between the advantages of leverage and the costs and risk of default. Given this policy the total funds available over the development period will consist of profits plus borrowing, while these funds will be used to cover expenditure on construction of new plant, building up sales and distribution networks, and, of course, meeting existing fixed costs. Thus,

$$P + B = I_F + I_S + F$$

where the symbols stand, respectively, for profit, borrowing, investment in factories, investment in sales development and fixed expenses. So, remembering the earlier symbol for price, and introducing Y for capacity output, W for the capacity wage bill plus materials costs, and g for the growth rate of capacity output, we have,

$$\pi Y - W = I_F + I_S + F - B$$

and rearranging,

$$\frac{\pi Y}{K} = g + \frac{(I_S + F + W - B)}{K}$$

or

$$\pi = gv + \frac{(I_S + F + W - B)}{Y}$$

where

$$v = \frac{I_F}{Y}$$

The rate of growth, g is defined as

$$\frac{I_F}{K} = \frac{Q_n}{Q_E}$$

so that productive investment is proportional to the expected size of the new market. The ratio of productive investment to capacity output, v, is the fraction of normal capacity income or output devoted to increasing productive capacity, and it appears as the slope of the finance relation between price and the rate of growth. This ratio is based on the firm's judgement of its competitive situation, its need for investment spending to keep up with advances in technology, and on its expectations of the long-term development of its markets. The intercept will normally be positive, since we can reasonably expect that

$$(I_S + F + W) > B$$

An increase (decrease) in sales investment will cause the finance relation to shift up (down), just as sales investment causes the price-growth of demand function to shift out or in. In addition, the function will shift up with rises in the wage rate, increases in fixed costs, or restrictive monetary policies which reduce borrowing. Figure 17.19 illustrates these relationships.

Underlying the definition of g, the rate of growth, is the assumption that the firm's marginal capital–output ratio equals its average. That is g can be defined as above because $I_F = \alpha Q_n$ and $K = \alpha Q_E$.

Dividing the second equation into the first, the αs cancel, and the result is g. If the marginal C is not equal to the average, but is constant, Little is changed. The growth of capacity will simply be proportionate to the growth of demand rather than equal to it. But if there are economies of scale in investment – as there often are – then the relationship between the two rates of growth will vary. As the size of the new market increases, the investment required to service a unit of it declines; hence the finance required per unit of the new market also declines. This can be illustrated readily in a modified version of the preceding diagram, as in Figures 17.20 and 17.21. Instead of lines of constant slope, we have curves, starting from the same intercepts and rising, but falling in slope as g rises.

The finance function is defined for capacity output, since the planning period comprises a number of short periods and the relevant concept is the expected norm for the whole period. Nevertheless the model must be capable of analyzing short-period fluctuations, since these are real problems which businesses face. When actual income falls short of the normal operating rate, the finance intercept is increased – the firm will need a higher price to generate the required finance. But the slope of the finance function will remain unaffected, for the firm will not change its judgement of the fraction of its capacity output that it should invest with every shift in the short-run winds.

External Finance

The level of the firm's demand for B will be set by increasing risk. Higher levels of B imply higher levels of F in the future; but F/K is set by a balance

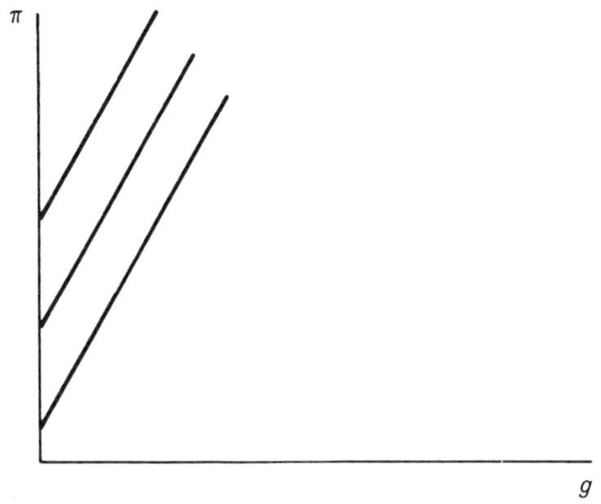

Figure 17.20

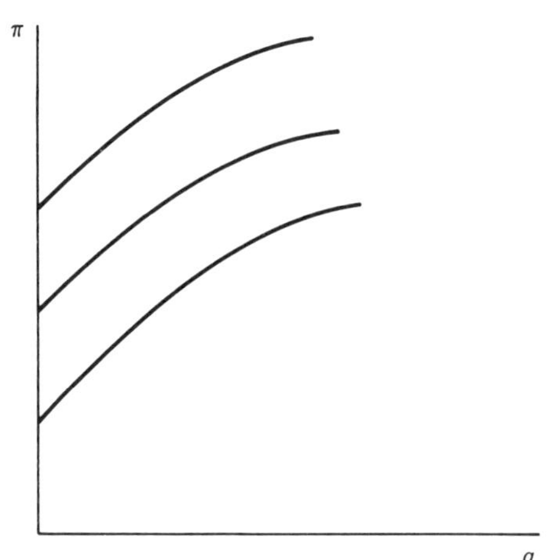

Figure 17.21

between the advantages of additional leverage, and the costs of insuring against default, where the risk and the cost of default increase as *F*/*K* rises. The risk arises from the probability that a downswing will cut into revenue deeply enough to make it impossible to meet *F*; clearly the larger *F*/*K*, for a given normal rate of profit, the smaller the downswing needed to cause trouble. Given a normal size distribution of fluctuations in sales, risk will increase at a rising rate as *F*/*K* rises. The costs of default are the resulting penalties, legal fees, loss of credit rating, and/or reorganization and these clearly increases additively with the severity of the default. But after a point they also interact; when the default is serious, for example, legal fees will be incurred not only to defend the initial default, but also to postpone the penalties, hold off the loss of other credit, defend against reorganiza-

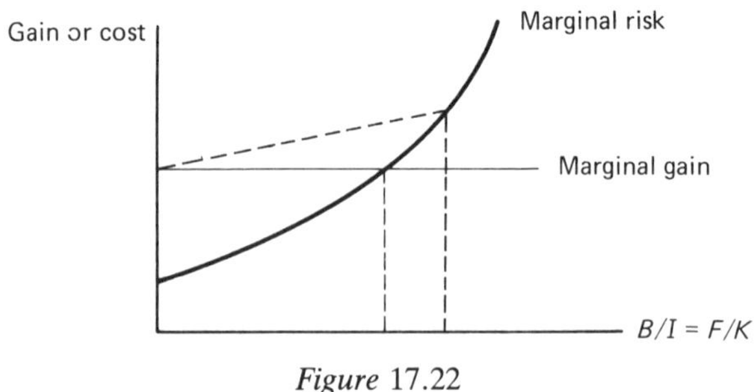

Figure 17.22

tion, etc.; in other words, the interaction will be multiplicative. So the costs will tend to rise exponentially, once they begin to interact.[33]

For a given capital–output ratio, a given rate of interest, and a given normal rate of profit, then, the firm's desired level of $B/I = F/K$ will be set at the point where the gain from additional borrowing (a constant) is just offset by the (increasing) cost of the insurance premium to offset the (rising) risk and cost of default (Figure 17.22). If there were economies of scale the marginal gain from borrowing would increase, as indicated by the dotted line, and a larger ratio B/I would be justified.

Growth and Sales Investment

The growth-of-demand frontier and the finance function can now be put together on the same diagram, remembering that each relationship is also a function of the amount invested in sales[34] and marketing. Increases in sales investment require the finance function to shift up in a constant proportion, but they shift the growth of demand frontier outward in a diminishing proportion. These shifts can be graphed as in Figure 17.23; the intersections trace out the curve indicated. The solution will therefore be to choose the unique price and level of investment in sales that will maximize the rate of growth, g.

Nothing much is changed by the presence of economies of scale in productive investment. As shown earlier, the finance lines will then rise in a progressively shallower curve, but the intersections with the demand lines will still trace out a curve of the same shape, so that there will still be a unique maximizing solution, as in Figure 17.24.

These solutions are predicated on given levels of F, W, B and Y. If either F or W rise, or if B or Y decrease, then the set of finance lines must shift up, and the equilibrium planned price will be higher. The effects on g, however, require a closer[35] look in at least one case. A rise in F or a decline in B, *ceteris paribus*, will simply shift the set of finance lines, having no effect on the growth of sales frontier;[36] hence g will fall. But changes in W are more complicated. A rise in W, if it is general and known to be general,

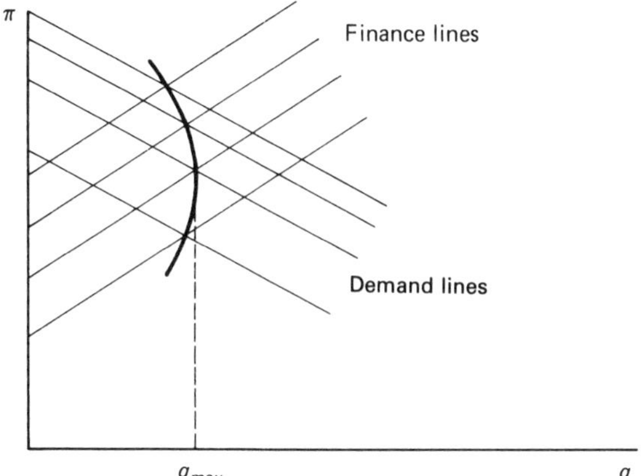

Figure 17.23

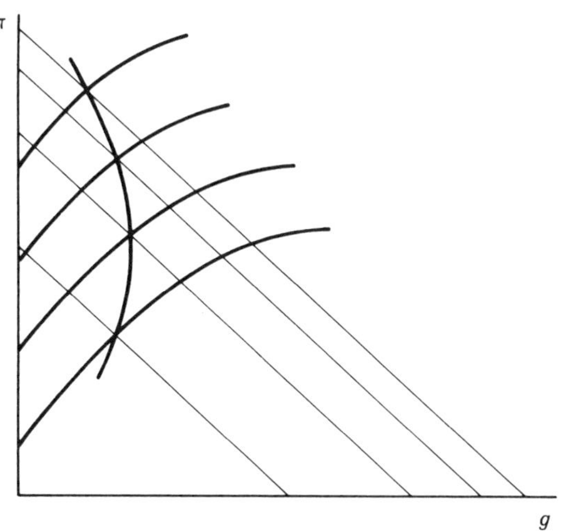

Figure 17.24

implies a general increase in household incomes and so new growth in consumer spending. If the firm's products are consumer goods, the growth of sales lines will shift up, too. Price will increase, but *g* will be unaffected. In Figure 17.25, the rise in *W* raises the finance line, and it also shifts up the growth of sales line. If the two are affected in the same proportion, the growth rate will be unchanged, and the entire effect of the rise in wages will be to increase prices. But there is another possibility. The increase in wages could increase spending (at every price) in the established markets in the same proportion that spending is increased in the new markets. If at every price spending in the old and new markets has increased in the same

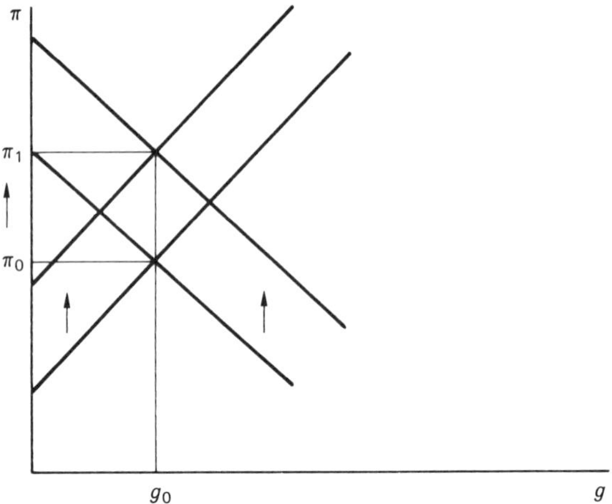

Figure 17.25

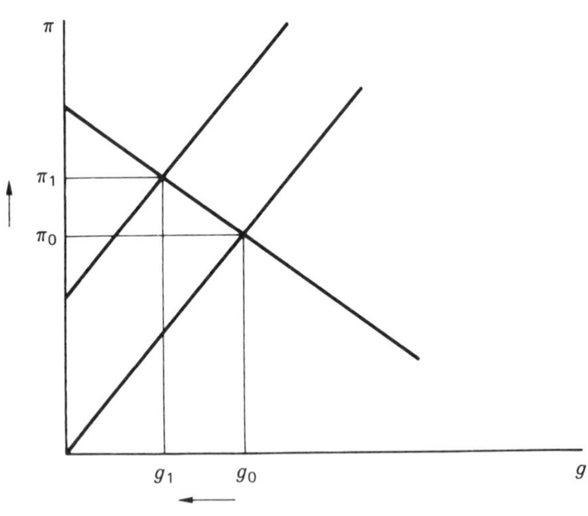

Figure 17.26

proportion, spending in the old and new markets will stand in the same ratio as before the wage increase, so there will be no effect at all on the growth of sales. The rise in *W* will have shifted up the finance line but will have left the growth of sales line unaffected, resulting in an equilibrium with a higher price and a lower rate of growth (Figures 17.25 and 17.26).

Choice of Technique

Modern industrial processes can frequently be computerized and automated, substantially reducing the labor costs, raising fixed costs, and

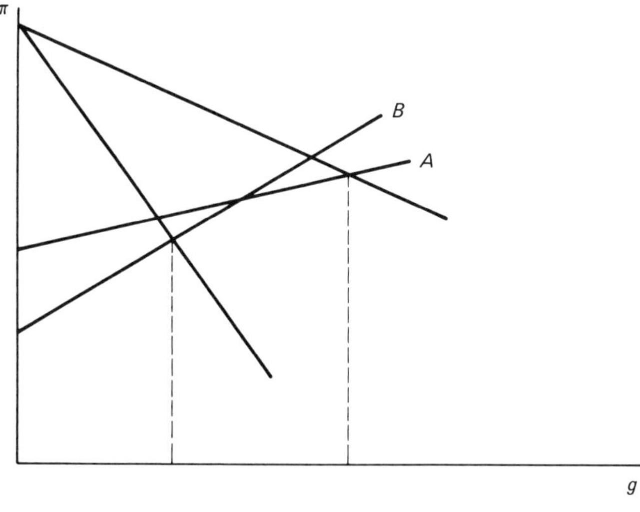

Choice of technique

Figure 17.27

increasing the capital–output ratio. We will assume,[37] however, that fixed costs will be set by the calculation of risk above, and that no technique will be considered which implies a rise in *F*. Alternative techniques therefore change the finance frontier: they cause it to differ in slope and intercept; the technique with the lower intercept – lower *W* – has the higher capital–output ratio, so is steeper, rising from left to right. Consider two techniques as drawn in Figure 17.27: at some point they will cross. If the demand–growth line is steep, cutting the techniques below their intersection, the relatively capital-intensive technique, since it has the lower intercept, will yield the higher rate of growth. But if the demand–growth line is relatively flat and cuts the finance lines above their intersection, then the less capital-intensive technique will give rise to the higher growth rate.

The choice of technique is normally treated entirely in terms of supply-side considerations. By contrast, the analysis here implies that the possibilities for growth of demand play a significant role in determining technique.

Impact of Exchange Rate Changes

Foreign goods may be imported and sold for domestic currency, either with or without further processing; or foreign capital equipment, energy or intermediate goods may be used in production. In either case a change in the exchange rate changes the costs which must be covered by the supply of finance; but in the first case, the change increases the cost of sales inventory, in the second it affects the cost of productive capacity. Hence a

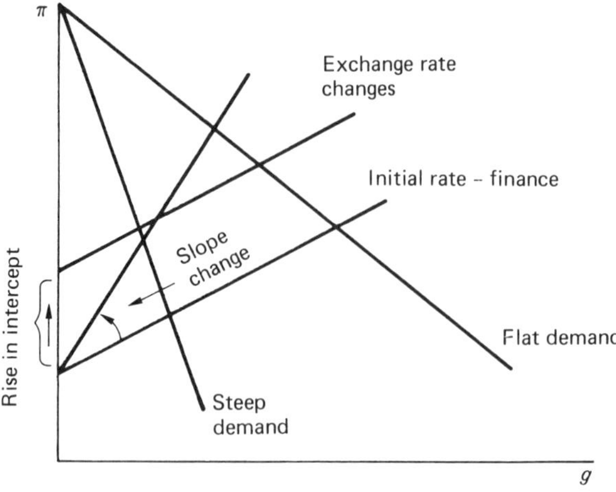

Figure 17.28

change in the exchange rate alters the intercept of the finance frontier of a firm importing foreign goods for sale, while it alters the slope in the case of a firm importing foreign capital equipment.

Consider a firm making candy that imports its chocolate and syrup from Europe, processing it with domestic equipment, and compare it to another firm, making scientific instruments, that imports high-grade equipment from Europe, but uses domestic materials. For the sake of the argument, suppose that the finance frontiers of both initially have the same intercepts and the same slopes, and further suppose that imported materials are the same percentage of the 'intercept' costs that imported equipment is of total capital. The exchange rate change will therefore have the same percentage impact in both cases (Figure 17.28).

In Figure 17.28 both the intercept and the slope are shown to double (a very large change, representing a 50% decline in the value of the domestic currency, if all the relevant costs are incurred in foreign currency). The two new finance frontiers will intersect at a certain point. If the price–demand lines are similar and both steep enough to lie below the intersection we can see that the capital-importing industry will raise its price less and suffer less growth slowdown than the materials-importing industry. If the price–demand lines are similar and both flat enough to lie beyond the intersection, just the reverse will be true. In general, the flatter the price–demand lines, the less the impact on price, and the greater the impact on growth. But in neither case will the full impact of the exchange rate change be passed along as a price increase.

The usual explanations for variations in exchange-rate[38] pass-along, bottleneck and beachhead effects, are based exclusively on supply-side concerns; by contrast, once again, the account here depends crucially on demand, but not on the level of demand – it is the relationship between price and the rate of growth of demand that matters.

Temporary or Cyclical Variations in Demand

The argument so far has been concerned exclusively with expected long-term normal costs and sales, and the variables determined have been planned or 'benchmark' prices and the target rate of growth of sales. But this same framework can be used to determine the appropriate responses to short-run or cyclical variations in aggregate demand, affecting the firm's current and immediately future rate of sales. To make the adaptation, we assume that the underlying parameters remain unchanged, and that the firm wishes to maintain its long-run position as well as possible.

Notice, however, that there is an asymmetry between short-term increases and declines in demand. When demand falls, the firm will not necessarily want to cut investment spending, since the long-term pattern of growth is unchanged. But the recession will probably mean that new markets will temporarily dry up. Hence it will be able to exploit its established market by increasing prices enough to maintain the flow of funds required for growth. When demand rises, however, the new rate of growth indicated by the new intersection could not be sustained (since the increase is temporary). So there is no point in moving to it by cutting price and setting up a sales campaign – which could be rudely upset if demand fell back to normal and prices had to be raised. So a rise in demand will not lead to a fall in price; indeed, if the rise is large enough (and regarded as temporary enough) firms might well react by adding surcharges or service fees to ration the demand.

On the diagram in Figure 17.28, the price–demand growth line is unaffected, since the demand change is only temporary. A fall in demand raises the finance line, a rise lowers it. To maintain normal growth when demand falls firms will have to raise price to the point on the new finance line. When demand rises, since cutting price will not be a desirable strategy,[39] maintaining price permits a buildup of reserves sufficient, if invested at a later date (to make up for a recession), to raise the growth rate by the amount indicated.

Cyclical downturns, however, can become depressions, and last long enough to affect plans. The effects of such a decline can be analyzed in the same way. Consider first the case of a recession, in which (only) new markets will tend to dry up; the sales growth lines will shift down, offsetting the rise in finance requirements. If the shifts are equi-proportional, price would remain unchanged, while the growth rate would fall. If the shifts are not perfect offsets, the major effect will still be on g, while the change in price would be relatively minor. Recessions do not tend to lower corporate prices (Figure 17.29).

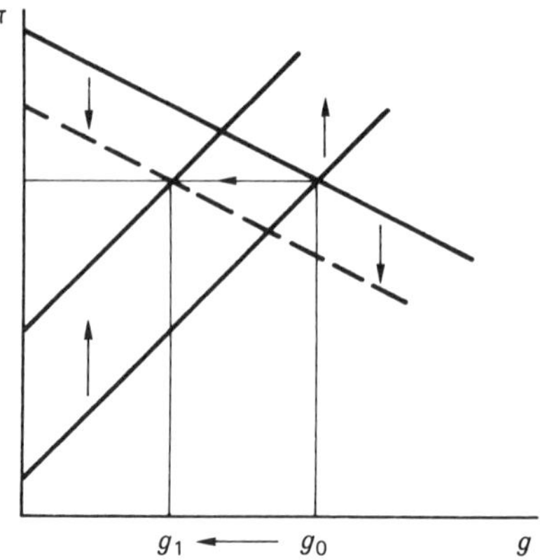

Figure 17.29

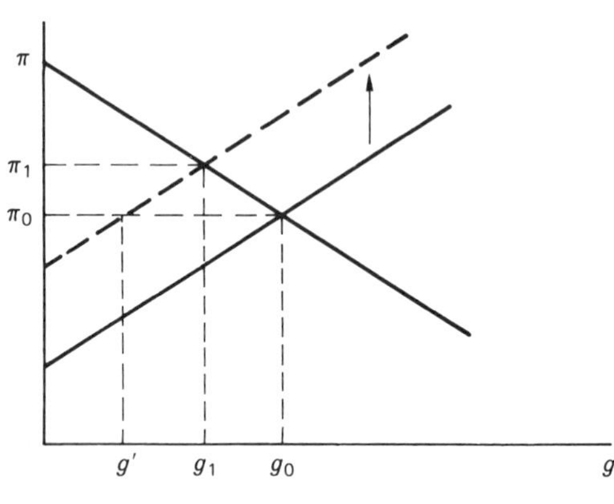

Figure 17.30

There is another possibility. A decline in incomes, perhaps due to layoffs, may reduce demand in the established markets as well as in the new markets. If demand is reduced in both in the same proportion then, as in the case of a rise in W, the ratio of spending in new markets to spending in old, for each level of price, will be the same after the change as before. Hence the sales–growth line will not shift, and the entire impact of the decline is brought about by the upward shift of the finance line, resulting in a higher price and a lower rate of growth (Figure 17.30).

6 CONCLUSIONS

The failure to develop a theory of demand based on class and sociooccupational divisions has prevented the full elaboration of the connections between pricing and investment. As long as demand is thought of in individual terms (or simply neglected) the marketing plans of firms, and their investment in their marketing divisions, will not be properly appreciated. Consider the usual approach: rational individuals need only to be provided with technical information about products and market information concerning price and availability. They then make decisions which hold until the parameters change. On the other side of the market, firms produce goods to given specifications, choosing the cheapest methods from a pre-existing set of techniques. Both consumers and producers are peculiarly passive in this picture – their choices are fully determined by an algorithm over whose terms they have no control. In pure competition firms control only the quantity variables; under various forms of imperfect competition they can, in addition, indirectly influence price, through their control over quantity. But their strategic moves are basically limited to adjustments of output. There is no scope here for imagination, insight, inventiveness or strategic competitive warfare. By treating a household as a member of a social class, however, subject to the rules of conformity and pressures to 'keep up' or advance, that are inherent in its lifestyle, we are able to understand and analyze the way firms try to build customer loyalty, seek out new markets, and develop improved – more marketable – products. Besides price cutting, there is competition to develop products, services and technology.

Two cases can be clearly distinguished. In the first, the firm has no control over the growth of its market. It must estimate this growth on the basis of what it knows about its customers – their incomes, the social pressures under which they live, the hopes and expectations they have for themselves and their children, and the way all of these are changing. Firms make their plans on the basis of this data, given their present position on the market and their estimate of their competitive strength *vis-à-vis* their rivals. To improve their competitive position, however, they will try to bind their customers more closely to them. This, together with the gradual elimination of weaker firms, will lead to a new situation, in which firms (by investing in market development and choosing appropriate pricing policies) are able to exercise some control over the growth of their markets. To understand the differences between the two cases, and the way they are linked by market development, requires a theory of the social influences affecting household decisions to consume and invest. Many different dynamics are imaginable, but all will draw on an understanding of the way new products enter household budgets and the way new markets can be opened.

This perspective also makes it clear that new products and new processes are being developed and introduced continuously. A new product may be a slight modification of a standard product, designed to make it more attractive to a particular group of potential consumers – witness cigarette marketing campaigns in the late 1980s; or it may be a new method of performing the same function – compact discs for tapes for records. Whichever applies, the innovations are part of an ongoing process of adaptation, as are the innovations in production, with which they frequently interact: both result from, and serve to intensify, the pressures of competition.

Actual growth fluctuates quite strongly around the norm of expected growth, and as a result, realized profits also deviate sharply from normal levels. But under conditions of advanced technology, actual relative prices (and sometimes even money prices) show considerable insensitivity to these fluctuations, although output and employment adjust rapidly. Traditional theory suggests that prices rather than outputs should adjust rapidly, and in the earlier conditions of fixed employment, they did. Their failure to do so now has been taken as evidence of market imperfection and the growth of oligopoloy. But traditional theory analyzes markets in terms of a conception of the firm as an artisan plying a craft; its approach to competition will not transfer to an environment of industrial corporations. Limited liability companies operating industrial technology competitively will set price guidelines on the basis of expected market growth, and have good strategic reasons to keep actual prices steady while adjusting output to variations in sales. Competition will play itself out in ways that leave prices largely stable in the face of changes in demand. The prices set in this way can be related to the theoretical ideal of the prices associated with a uniform rate of profit. But competition also has a way of undermining itself over the long run; the strategies pursued will change the nature of the market, leading to closer ties between firms and customers. When this has become widespread, pricing policies will affect market growth, and prices will respond differently to variations in the market.

Notes

1. The relation between pricing and growth has received official recognition. During the late 1960s and the 1970s the British National Board for Prices and Incomes used 'the effect which a particular level of profit has on the firm's ability to finance future investment' as one of the criteria for approving a higher price (Pickering, 1971, p. 232).
2. In the traditional theory, growth is understood to mean movement toward the optimal size. For example, in his classic *Structure of Competitive Industry* E.A.G. Robinson devotes chapters to discussing optimal technical size and

managerial size, the optimum financial unit and the optimal marketing unit, thus necessitating a separate chapter on the 'Reconciliation of Differing Optima'.

3. Eichner (1987) presents a simple algebraic model, starting from the expression for the required investment in an industry.

$$z_t = g_t b_t (p_t q_t) = p_t q_t - c_t q_t$$

where p is price, q quantity, b the capital–output ratio, and g the growth rate of demand, all for the ith product. Then,

$$(p_t - c_t) \,/\, p_t = m_t = g_t b_t$$

or

$$g_t = \frac{m_t}{b_t}$$

which Eichner contends is the Harrod–Domar relationship, since m is the profit margin, or corporate saving ratio. Further, we have

$$p_t = \frac{c_t}{(1 - g_t b_t)}$$

a positive relationship between the growth rate of demand for the ith product and its price. Eichner argues that this enables us to connect pricing and growth in an input–output formulation since costs can be broken down. But what stands out here is that *the rate of growth of demand is taken as given*. The ith industry's price has no influence on the rate of growth of its demand, nor does its investment, which implies either that it does not invest in sales and distribution, or that such investment has no impact.

4. Harcourt and Kenyon accept Eichner's idea that the division of finance between internal and external is a matter of cost. When the implicit interest rate on internal funds lies below the market rate, retained earnings will be used; when investment requirements rise to where the implicit rate exceeds the market rate, the firm will turn to external sources. The firm can raise money by raising prices, or by borrowing, and it will do whatever is cheaper. This implies that in times of low real interest rates firms will turn extensively, even exclusively, to external financing; the historical record does not support this. Nor does this approach mention the problem of increasing risk – the larger the proportion of borrowing, the greater the risk of default in the event of a cyclical downturn. Yet such risk is surely a major factor limiting the use of external funds.

5. Wood and Harcourt and Kenyon both analyse the firm's problems in choosing methods of production. Whatever the other merits of their discussions, both contend that the choice of technique will influence, and be influenced by, the optimal price policy; since both analyses run into difficulties over the price–demand relationships, both solutions to the problem of selecting the best technique must be set aside.

6. An earlier chapter argued that a corporate industrial economy is normally constrained by its level of demand, rather than by resources, capacity or labor.

Further, since demand is scarce in every field, competition sets up pressures for cutting costs and raising productivity, with the result that capacity output is increased and the multiplier reduced, so that the gap between aggregate demand and potential supply is always tending to widen (cf. Ch. 23).

7. The modern textbook short-run production function is a comparative-static construction which shows the different outputs resulting from various amounts of labor combined with a fixed amount of *capital* – not a fixed set of capital goods. In the modern version the given amount of capital, or funds, will be embodied in the most appropriate form at each point, and will always be fully utilized. But, speaking of what he called the 'fixed stock of appliances for production' 'when the supply is excessive' [in relation to current demand], Marshall remarks 'some of them must remain imperfectly employed,' and when the 'supply is deficient, . . . producers have to adjust . . . as best they can with the appliances . . at their disposal. Clearly the idea is that the labor force varies the intensity with which it operates the fixed set of appliances, and as the intensity of utilization varies, so will productivity. By contrast, in an industrial economy, when utilization varies, *employment* changes.
8. In a perfect capital market, any borrower should be able to raise any amount at the prevailing rate of interest. A corollary is that the roles of worker and employer are adopted by choice; labor can hire capital just as easily as capital can hire labor. Here, as elsewhere, the ideas sketched by Marshall in the context of an artisan economy come to grief when applied to industrial conditions. A 'perfect capital market' cannot account for the financial structure of a modern corporation. Consider a bank or a group of investors being offered a bond by an entrepreneur. The security will be the project itself and the return the prevailing rate of interest. Both sides must consider the advantages and disadvantages of owning the actual project. For the entrepreneur, the choice is between borrowing capital and owning the project and so working for himself, or working as a manager for another owner. So the expected profit from the project must exceed the required interest plus the competitive salary for managers. The bank/investor group faces the analogous choice. They can lend to the entrepreneur or hire a manager and own the project directly. If the expected profit from the project exceeds the going interest plus the competitive manager's salary, they should set up the project themselves and hire a manager. If the expected profit falls short of interest plus salary, they would not want to own it – but by the same token, they should not accept the assets of the project as security either, since the income it generates is not sufficient to meet its costs. So when a project is potentially profitable both investors and entrepreneurs will wish to hold the equity, and when it is not, investors should not consider it adequate security. The assumptions have precluded any explanation of financial structure – and this is what lies behind the Modigliani–Miller theorem. (It could be argued that entrepreneurs and investors have different knowledge and skills, and therefore different expectations of profitability. This is sensible enough, but in a 'perfect' market there has to be perfect information. Moreover, if there is imperfect knowledge, there is a good motive for requiring independent security for loans; in which case borrowing power will be limited by net worth.)
9. These improvements may change the nature of the goods or the techniques. It is therefore not possible, in the case of an industrial economy, to start with the assumption that the list of products and the set of techniques is given at the outset. On the contrary, firms will compete to produce new and improved products and cheaper techniques. To assume a fixed list, however large,

implies ruling out the form of industrial competition that determines the nature of both labor and the investment process. Or to put it another way, the assumption of a fixed list is an essential underpinning of the idea that prices and quantities are determined simultaneously by market-clearing.

10. In early or Fixed Employment capitalism an appropriate simplification would be to consider the two classes of capitalist families, the owners of firms, and worker families. But in advanced or Flexible Employment capitalism, capital is no longer lodged with families ; it is held in professionally managed portfolios and/or by financial institutions. The former owners are now beneficiaries or largely passive recipients of interest and dividends; their interests in life center around their careers (cf. Section 2 below).
11. A fuller and more sophisticated treatment would consider the possibilities of tradeoffs between the characteristics composing the lifestyles. This must be done carefully: nutrition and taste may trade off in diet, elegance and comfort may trade off in clothing, or shelter. The possibilities of substitution are much less, however, when it comes to the broader categories of diet, clothing and shelter. A smaller house for better clothing? Eat cheaply to dress smartly? On occasion, no doubt; but as a general rule a certain standard will have to be achieved in each category, while the significant tradeoffs will be in the way it can be reached. For our purposes, however, these questions can be set aside.
12. The neo-Classical tradition emphasizes general substitution in both consumption and production. By contrast, the view here is that substitution cannot possibly be so general. Household consumption produces a lifestyle, in which the present adults are supported in a manner which permits them to work, earning an income, and to bring up their children, educated to an appropraite degree. The concept of a lifestyle lays down specific criteria for behavior, status symbols, education, social and technical skills, etc. which only certain goods and certain patterns of consumption can provide. A similar case be made with regard to production (cf. Hollis and Nell, *Rational Economic Man*, 1975, Chs 5, 8 and 9).
13. If our analysis is based on wide and therefore complementary categories in consumption, it will tend to rule out substitution on the demand side. But by the same token, such wide definitions will surely make it easier to define substitution possibilities on the supply side – not substitution of different inputs to produce the same output, but alternative ways to fulfill the same function. We must learn to draw the line between complements and substitutes in a different way. We must also think more carefully about the nature of commodities. A group of complementary commodities which together serve a function or meet a need may be considered, for some purposes, a single unit, even though supplied separately (especially if the revenue devoted to the need or function is determinate.) Similarly a group of outputs generated jointly by a common process can be considered a unit, even though demanded separately (especially if competition limits or determines the total profit obtainable from running the process.) Whether we have joint or single production, joint or single consumption, therefore, is often a matter of classification, in the light of our theoretical objectives.
14. At any given time the market for a commodity consists of those who are prepared to buy, which means those who have planned their budget to include the good, setting aside a certain portion of their income for the purpose. Households will have fitted the good into their lifestyle; businesses will have judged that it improves productivity, reduces costs or enhances sales. But in any case, being prepared to buy implies having made a commitment, and

therefore having adjusted other plans accordingly. To change the purchase will mean changing plans, and this will take time. This does not mean that demand will be wholly insensitive to price changes; it means only that the response will be slow and uncertain and in many cases not very large. In other words, at this stage the expansion of the market depends mainly on growth in consumer incomes and on changing tastes rather than on cheapening of the product.

15. Why didn't one firm build a huge plant and, drawing on economies of scale, put everyone else out of business, or by doing it first, prevent anyone else from entering? More generally, what determines the optimal initial size of firms? The larger the plant, the greater the economies of scale, but the greater the loss if it should become obsolescent. The earlier the entry, the better the chance to build up a market position, but the greater the chance that one's investment will become obsolescent. So an early entry must balance the likelihood and costs of becoming outdated against the advantages of using economies of scale to build up a strong market position. Plant size will be determined where additional economies of scale are just outweighed by the probability of additional losses from premature scrapping. Since, by assumption, all initial firms face similar situations, all will build plants of similar size.
16. Firms assume that entry will be blocked as the result of their investment strategies, not their pricing policies. A considerable literature has developed around the idea that oligopolists would fix on a price lying above average costs, but still below the level that would induce (or permit) entry – or would threaten to cut to such a price on perceiving preparations to enter (Sylos–Labini, 1969; Modigliani, 1958; Bhagwati, 1970; Wenders 1967). Much of this literature is still wedded to the idea that prices are determined in conjunction with output, thereby missing the connection with investment. In any case, the idea depends crucially on the existence of barriers that permit a gap between average costs and the entry-inducing price. In the present analysis no such barriers are assumed; markets are competitive and entry is always possible – but those already in the market do have the advantages of experience and established connections. Entry is blocked because the existing firms both have the capacity and are already in position to supply the entire potential market.
17. The normal growth of the market (due to income growth) has to be greater than its potential expansion due to any feasible price cut. If a price cut could expand the market by more than normal growth then firms would concentrate on recovering capital and cutting costs, rather than investing in new capacity, for whoever develops a less costly technique will not only capture a huge market, but will have to bring in new capital to service it.
18. To consider further periods requires redrawing the shifted demand curve as an 'initial' one – that is, as one showing the various quantities the market would buy at various alternative prices.
19. As we shall see, so long as the demand curve is linear (or approximately linear), neither slope nor elasticity matter. The investible revenue curve will always intersect the required funds curve in a stable fashion. In the case of unitary elasticity the investible funds curve will be a vertical straight line.
20. The quadratic $R = -bp^2 + (a + bm)p - am$ has two positive roots: $p = \{-(a + bm) \pm [(a + bm)^2 - 4abm]^{1/2}\}/-2b$
21. In Figure 17. , if the initial capacity is $Q_0 < Q_b$, then price will be bid up to $p_0 > p_b$. As a result the investment funds generated, I_g, will be greater than those required, I_r, to move capacity to Q_1, which represents the expected growth of sales at p_0. If v is the capital–output ratio, then $v(I_g - I_r)$ will be the additional capacity that can be built to offset the initial shortfall. Let Q_{1b} be the

level of capacity at which price would return to p_b; the shortfall would be just exactly made up. If $v(I_g - I_r) = Q_{1b} - Q_1$, this will be achieved, but if $v(I_g - I_r) > Q_{1b} - Q_1$ there will be overshooting, and the system will go from shortage of capacity to an excess, leading price to fall below p_b. Further, this could lead, in 'cobweb' fashion, to cyclical swings converging on the benchmark values of progressively diverging.

22. A uniform reduction of labor-time per unit of output in every sector leaves capital-goods requirements per unit of output unaffected, and generates a surplus consisting of the wage goods that support labor. The proof is given in Ch. 4; also cf. Section 3 and Nell (1982).
23. Textbook definitions of perfect competition are misleading. Samuelson, for example, writes, 'The demand curve for the whole industry . . . will look . . . perfectly horizontal [to the firm], with an elasticity of demand . . . of infinity.' He adds, 'The draftsman will have to train a microscope on the relevant point of the industry curve to show how this sloped curve will reappear as . . . horizontal . . . to the Lilliputian eye of the firm.' But a slope is a slope, whatever the units. The point, however, has to be that the demand of the industry is an order of magnitude greater than the demand facing the firm. A quantity is an order of magnitude greater than another if when the first is $f(n)$ and the second $g(n)$, the absolute value of $f(n)/g(n)$ tends to 0 as n tends to 0. Let q be the output of the representitive firms and n be the number of firms. The market will then be nq. As the number of firms increases, suppose that the industry reaps advantages, economies of scale, which are of benefit to firms, so that q increases. For example, $q = an$, where a is some positive number. Then the absolute value $(AV)\ nq/an = (AV)\ nan/an = (AV)\ n$, and the definition is trivially fulfilled. But the fact that the industry's demand is an order of magnitude greater than the firm's tells us nothing about the relation of the industry's demand to its capacity, nor does it say anything about how firms will adjust prices in relation to demand. For this we turn to, for example, Stonier and Hague (1961), who write, 'A limiting case will occur when there are so many competitors producing such close substitutes that the demand for the product of each individual firm is infinitely elastic and its average revenue curve is a horizontal straight line . . . the firm can sell as much of its product as it wishes at the ruling market price. If the firm raises its price . . . it will lose all its customers. If the firm were to lower its price, it would be swamped by orders' (p. 105). The line is infinitely elastic because an infinitesimal price cut will attract the entire market, an order of magnitude greater than the firm, therefore infinite in relation to it. As defined, it is a customer attraction function, positioned at the level of the initial market price. But it is not an average or a marginal revenue function; if the industry's demand curve is continuous, then if more is to be sold, even a very small amount, price will have to drop. Nor does the limiting case of the customer attraction function justify price-taking behavior; quite the contrary. If demand is below capacity, the representative firm will cut price since an infinitesimally small cut will attract all the additional demand it needs. In general, the firm will push production to capacity so long as price covers marginal costs. Thus price will tend to fall to marginal cost whenever demand is below capacity.
24. 'Normal capacity' is not a precise quantity; there is usually a degree of flexibility such that incurring once-for-all costs will allow the firm to produce for a time, or even permanently, at a higher level. But this would require a higher price, to cover these additional costs, and such flexibility is therefore of no relevance to the obstacle imposed by capacity limitations on price-cutting.

25. A considerable Keynesian literature has grown up around the idea that 'implicit contracts' between workers and employers would keep wage rates steady in the face of falling demand (Okun, 1981; Tobin, 1983; Grossman and Hart, 1983). But there is little direct evidence of such contracts. Nor do they represent what workers want, which is a steady income, not a steady wage rate. And why should firms hold to an implicit contract, for which there is no enforcement, during a long period – the slump – when its observance is not in their interest? Since there is no enforcement, how can they be sure that workers will refrain from making demands during the boom? By contrast, the argument here is that refraining from wage cuts will be in the interest of firms, provided the conditions in the text are met.
26. It will be difficult to develop strong *general* conclusions about this, however. The approach easily leads to complicated dynamic processes, where the results tend to depend strongly on the assumptions, which will be different in different particular circumstances. An illustration: start with equal-size firms, and a normal distribution of customer loyalty. This will lead to a corresponding normal distribution of investment in capacity (i.e., of growth rates). Hence, since the growth rate $(1 + g)i$ will be normally distributed, we have a version of Gibrat's 'l'effet proportionnel,' and over time a log-normal size distribution of firms will evolve (Gibrat, 1931; Aitchison and Brown, 1957). But a different distribution of initial sizes, or of customer loyalty, or the addition of other influences on investment, can all affect the outcome – perhaps we can say that the general tendency appears to be to skew the distribution, but it is doubtful that we can go much further. Yet this is no flaw; the search for generality is misplaced and leads to triviality. What is useful is to develop categories of models, showing the different kinds of processes and outcomes that arise in different circumstances.
27. On the analogy of a price cut under perfect competition, when the competitive condition of 'free entry' holds, an infinitesimal superprofit will attract an infinite entry and an infinitesimal subprofit will lead to a total exit. An infinite entry – all the firms from all other industries – means oversupply and a collapse in prices; a total exit of all the firms in the industry means radical shortage and a bidding up of prices. Perfect conditions of free entry and exit thus imply severe instability. To try to limit this instability by placing restrictions on the ability to move implies acknowledging that 'entry' and 'exit' are investment decisions, which brings the discussion back to the relationship of growth in demand to growth of capacity.
28. Asimakopulos (1978, p. 344) cites the case of the Canada Cement Company in the early 1950s, which kept cement prices low and did not expand fast enough, and thus provoked entry to meet the unsatisfied demand, thereby losing heavily, dropping from holding 4/5 of the market in 1946 to one-half in 1957.
29. If the possibilities of diversification are good, firms will wish to exit rapidly, and thus will be likely to raise prices even if the higher prices attract entry and speed up the market's decline. Entering firms may buy out the facilities and brand names of existing firms. However, a speed-up of the market's decline will deter entry, or confine it to 'oblique entry' – those who believe the old market can be used as a base for developing innovations. Nor can a single firm raise price unless it is certain that its lead will be followed.
30. The traditional approach has focussed on the possibility of the firm using price to exercise some control over its current level of demand. In a growing economy with technical progress, prices will have to be related to investment; moreover, macroeconomics suggests that firms cannot reliably control current

demand. But in the long run, there is an important distinction between conditions in which they can and those in which they cannot reasonably expect to influence the growth of their markets. Earlier, we set out an analytical treatment of the case where firms adopt prices that will finance the capacity to serve a growing market over which they have no control. This will normally be a kind of competitive market; certainly it need not be an oligopoly. But prices will tend to be inflexible in the face of short-run variations in demand.

31. Inelastic – steep – demand curves are characteristic of markets for manufactures, both consumer and capital goods, because there tend to be strong complementarities in their use. Consumer goods have to fit together into a coherent lifestyle; capital goods into a manufacturing process. Only rarely can a single element be changed, the others remaining the same. However, at very high prices purchases will be cut back and other less appropriate goods substituted, or perhaps that part of the lifestyle or process will be adjusted, so that many goods will be affected.
32. New markets may be markets of the same social class or group, but located in a different geographical region; or they may be in the same region, but involve an appeal to a new social grouping. In the former case new distributional outlets will be needed; in the latter, a new advertising and promotional campaign will have to be devised. So the implications for sales investment will be different in the two cases, but in each sales investment will be called for.
33. The calculation here concerns borrower's risk. Lender's risk may also exist, in which case the costs of borrowing would rise, rather than being flat as shown in the diagram (cf. Minsky, 1975, Kalecki, 1970, Harcourt and Kenyon, 1976).
34. In the theory of monopolistic competition selling costs are considered, but they are treated exclusively as current costs; the capital costs incurred by developing new markets are never examined (Chamberlin, 1933; Taylor and Weiser, 1972; Eichner, 1976; Kaldor, 1950–1). As early as 1931 E.A.G. Robinson referred to '[the] whole expenditure on wages, buildings, equipment and organization necessary to bring the goods to market' (p. 65) and later noting the long-term effects of a selling effort, he points out that, 'once the market has been won, it can be retained at a lower selling cost than necessary to secure it initially' (p. 68). Clearly long-term costs are incurred for long-term gains.
35. A restrictive monetary policy causing i to rise, will after a time raise F; by the same token, as credit is both more expensive and more difficult to obtain, it will reduce B. Thus restrictive monetary policy both tends to raise prices and lower the growth of sales – it exacerbates inflation and tends to bring recession.
36. The rise in W is due to a rise in the wage rate; hence the new spending will come out of the additional wage income, which might require some adjustment lag, unless some form of consumer finance is available to bridge the gap.
37. The pre-existing 'book of blueprints' is a neo-Classical fiction, and has no role in a realistic theory. There may be – and often is – more than one way to produce a particular item; there are seldom many ways, and in general different methods of production will result in products with different characteristics. (Hollis and Nell, 1975, pp. 235–8) These differences may appear unimportant at first, but later turn out to have considerable significance in marketing. Process innovations tend to arise from learning by doing, and learning by using (Rosenberg, 1980) and product innovation from learning by selling (Thomson, 1989).
38. 'Beachhead' and 'bottleneck' models undoubtedly contain a certain amount of good sense (Baldwin, 1988; Dornbusch, 1987; Dixit, 1987). Entry and exit conditions are asymmetrical; if an exchange rate change induces entry, an

equivalent change back will not cause all entrants to exit; this is the beachhead effect. Bottlenecks occur at full capacity; an exchange rate change is assumed to increase capacity; when it changes back, however, capacity does not decrease. The result will be a discontinuity in marginal costs, and therefore in the movement of prices. But all such models rely on the framework of monopolistic competition, in which current output and prices are adjusted together. Exchange rate changes, however, take place in the context of a growing economy, and their effects have to be examined in the context of corporate planning for the financing of growth.

39. Marshall referred to the danger of 'spoiling the market' by reckless price-cutting; many business leaders have bemoaned cut-throat competition (Brown, 1924).

References

Aitcheson, J. and Brown, J. (1957) *The Log normal Distribution* (Cambridge: Cambridge University Press).

Andrews, P.W.S. (1949) *Manufacturing Business* (London: Macmillan).

Andrews, P.W.S. (1964) *On Competition in Economic Theory* (London: Macmillan).

Asimakopulos, A. (1978) *Microeconomics: An Introduction to Economic Theory* (Oxford: Oxford Univesity Press).

Bain, Joe S. (1956) *Barriers to New Competition* (Cambridge, Mass.: Harvard University Press).

Baldwin, R. (1988) 'Hysteresis in Import Prices: the Beachhead Effect,' *American Economic Review* (September).

Baran, P. and Sweezy, P. (1976) *Monopoly Capital* (New York: Monthly Review Press).

Baron, D. (1973) 'Limit Pricing, Potential Entry and Barriers to Entry,' *American Economic Review*, 63 (4) pp. 666–74.

Baumol, W. (1967) *Business Behavior, Value and Growth* (New York: Harcourt, Brace & World) revised edn.

Berle, A. and Means, G. (1933) *The Modern Corporation and Private Property* (New York: Macmillan).

Bhagwati, J. (1970) 'Oligopoly Theory, Entry-prevention and Growth,' *Oxford Economic Papers*, 22, pp. 297–310.

Blair, J. (1972) *Economic Concentration: Structure, Behavior and Policy* (New York: Harcourt, Brace Jovanovich).

Brown, Donaldson (1924) 'Pricing Policy in Relation to Financial Control. Articles 2–4,' *Management and Administration*, 7, 195–8, 283–6, 417–22.

Cagan, P. (1975) 'Changes in the Recession Behavior of Wholesale Prices in the 1920's and Post World War II,' *Explorations of Economic Research*, (Winter) pp. 54–104.

Chamberlin, E. (1933) *The Theory of Monopolistic Competition* (Cambridge, Mass.: Harvard University Press).

Chandler, A.D. (1977) *The Visible Hand* (Cambridge, Mass.: Harvard University Press).

Clifton, J. (1977) 'Competition and the Evolution of the Capitalist Mode of Production,' *Cambridge Journal of Economics*, 1 (June) pp. 137–51.

Clifton, J. (1983) 'Administered Prices in the Context of Capitalist Develoment,' *Contributions to Political Economy*, 2, pp. 23–38.
Comanor, W. and Wilson, T. (1967) 'Advertising Market Structure and Performance,' *Review of Economics and Statistics*, 49 (November) pp. 423–40.
Cornwall, J. (1977) *Modern Capitalism* (New York, M.E. Sharpe).
Coutts, K., Godley, W. and Nordhaus, W. (1978) *Industrial Prices in the United Kingdom* (Cambridge: Cambridge University Press).
Dalton, J.A. (1973) 'Administered Inflation and Business Pricing: Another Look,' *Review of Economics and Statistics*, 55 (November) pp. 516–19.
Dixit, A. (1980) 'The Rate of Investment in Entry Deterrence,' *Economic Journal*, 90, March pp. 95–106.
Dornbusch, R. (1987) 'Exchange Rates and Prices,' *American Economic Review*, 77 (1) (March).
Eatwell, J. (1971) 'Growth, Profitability and Size – The Empirical Evidence,' Marris and Wood (eds) (1971) pp. 379–422.
Eatwell, J. (1981) 'Competition,' in Bradley, I. and M. Howard (eds), *Classical and Marxian Political Economy: Essays in Memory of Ronald Meek* (London: Macmillan) pp. 23–46.
Eckstein, O. and Fromm, G. (1968) 'The Price Equation,' *American Economic Review*, (December) pp. 1159–1183.
Eichner, A. (1976) *The Megacorp and Oligopoly* (Cambridge: Cambridge University Press).
Eichner, A. (1980) 'A General Model of Investment and Pricing,' in Nell (ed.) pp. 118–33.
Eichner, A. (1987) *The Macrodynamics of Advanced Market Economies* (New York: M.E. Sharpe).
Gibrat, R. Sr. (1931) *Les Inegalites Economiques* (Paris: Libraire de Receuil Sirey).
Godley, W. (1959) 'Cost Prices and Demand in the Short Run. Surrey,' in W. Godley (ed.), *Macroeconomic Themes* (Oxford: Oxford University Press).
Grossman, S. and Hart, O. (1983) 'Implicit Contracts Under Asymmetrical Information,' *Quarterly Journal of Economics*, 98 pp. 123–56.
Hall, R. and Hitch, C. (1936) 'Price Theory and Business Behavior,' *Oxford Economic Papers*, 2.
Harcourt, G. and Kenyon, P. (1976) 'Pricing and the Investment Decision,' *Kyklos*, 29, pp. 449–77.
Hazledine, T. (1974) 'Determination of the Mark-up Under Oligopoly: A Comment,' *Economic Journal*, 84 (December) pp. 967–9.
Herman, E. (1981) *Corporate Control, Corporate Power* (Cambridge: Cambridge University, Press).
Hodgson, G. (1988) *Economics and Institutions* (Oxford: Polity Press).
Hollis, M. and Nell, E. (1975) *Rational Economic Man* (Cambridge: Cambridge University Press).
Hymer, S. (1979) *The Multinational Corporation: A Radical Approach* (Cambridge: Cambridge University Press).
Kaldor, N. (1950–1) 'The Economic Aspects of Advertising,' *Review of Economic Studies*, 18 pp. 1–27.
Kalecki, M. (1971) 'Costs and Prices,' *Selected Essays on the Dynamics of the Capitalist Economy, 1933–1970* (Cambridge: Cambridge University Press) pp. 43–62.
Kaplan, A., Dirlam, J. and Lanzilotti, R. (1958) *Pricing in Big Business* (Washington D.C.: The Brookings Institution).

Lancaster, K. (1966) 'A New Approach to Consumer Theory,' *Journal of Political Economy*, 74, pp. 132–57.
Lancaster, K. (1979) *Variety, Equity and Efficiency* (New York: Columbia University Press).
Lanzilotti, R. (1958) 'Pricing Objectives in Larger Companies,' *American Economic Review*, 48 (December) pp. 921–40.
Lee, F. (1984) 'The Marginalist Controversy and the Demise of Full Cost Pricing,' *Journal of Economic Issues*, 18 (December).
Leijonhufvud, A. (1985) 'Capitalism and the Factory System', in Richard Langlois (ed.) *Economics as a Process: Essays in the New Institutional Economics* (Cambridge: Cambridge University Press).
Levine, D. (1980) 'Aspects of the Classical Theory of Markets,' *Australian Economic Papers* (June) pp. 1–15.
Marris, R. (1964) *The Economic Theory of Managerial Capitalism* (New York: Macmillan).
Marris, R. and Wood, A. (1971) *The Corporate Economy* (Cambridge, Mass.: Harvard University Press).
Marshall, A. (1920) *Principles of Economics* (London: Macmillan) 8th edn.
Means, G. (1935) *Industrial Prices and Their Relative Inflexibility*, 74th Cong., 1st. Sess., Doc. 13.
Means, G. (1959) *Hearings on Administered Prices*, Part 9, Senate Subcommittee on Antitrust and Monopoly, 86th Cong., 2nd Sess., pp. 4745–60.
Means, G. (1972) 'The Administered Price Thesis Recomfirmed,' *American Economic Review*, 61 (June) pp. 292–306.
Milberg, W. (1988) 'Exchange Rate Pass-Through Under Full Cost Pricing' (University of Michigan-Dearborn) (mimeo).
Minsky, H. (1975) *John Maynard Keynes* (New York: Columbia University Press).
Modigliani, F. (1958) 'New Developments on the Oligopoly Front,' *Journal of Political Economy*, 64, pp. 215–33.
Morris, D., Sinclair, P. Slater, M., and Vickers, S. (1986) *Strategic Behavior and Industrial Competition* (Oxford: Clarendon Press).
Mueller, D. (1977) 'The Persistence of Profits Above the Norm,' *Economica*, 44, pp. 371–80.
Munkirs, J. (1985) *The Transformation of American Capitalism* (New York: M.E. Sharpe).
Nell, E. (1980) 'Competition and Price-Taking Behavior,' in E. Nell (ed), *Growth, Profits and Property* (Cambridge: Cambridge University Press) pp. 99–117.
Nell, E. (1982) 'Understanding the Marxian Theory of Exploitation,' in G. Ferwer (ed.), *Samuelson and Neo-Classical Economics* (Boston: Kluwer-Nijhoff).
Nell, E. (1986) 'On Monetary Circulation and the Rate of Exploitation,' *Themes Papers in Political Economy* (Summer).
Nell, E. (1988) *Prosperity and Public Spending* (London, Boston: Unwin Hyman).
Neild, R. (1963) *Pricing and Employment in the Trade Cycle* (Cambridge: Cambridge University Press).
Nordhaus, W. and Godley, W. (1972) 'Pricing in the Trade Cycle,' *Economic Journal*, 82 (September) pp. 853–82.
Okun, A. (1981) *Prices and Quantities* (Oxford: Basil Blackwell).
Penrose, E. (1959) *The Theory of the Growth of the Firm* (New York: John Wiley).

Pickering, J.F. (1971)'The Prices and Incomes Board and Private Sector Prices: A Survey,' *Economic Journal*, 8, (June) pp. 225–41.
Robinson, E.A.G. (1931) *The Structure of Competitive Industry* (Cambridge: Economic Handbooks).
Robinson, J. (1962) 'The Basic Theory of Normal Prices,' *Quarterly Journal of Economics*, 76, pp. 1–19.
Roncaglia, A. (1978) *Sraffa and the Theory of Price* (New York: John Wiley).
Rosenberg, N. (1982) *Inside the Black Box and Technology and Economics* (Cambridge: Cambridge University, Press).
Samuelson, P.A. (1976) *Economics*, 10th edn (New York: McGraw-Hill).
Semmler, W. (1984) *Competition, Monopoly and Differential Profit Rates* (New York: Columbia University Press).
Solow, R. (1980) 'On Theories of Unemployment,' *American Economic Review*, 70.
Steindl, J. (1976) *Maturity and Stagnation in American Capitalism* (New York: Monthly Review Press).
Stiglitz, J. and Shapiro, C. (1984) 'Equilibrium Unemployment as a Worker Discipline Device,' *American Economic Review*, 74.
Stonier, A. and Hague, D. (1961) *A Textbook of Economic Theory* (New York: John Wiley).
Sylos-Labini, P. (1969) *Oligopoly and Technical Progress* (Cambridge, Mass.: Harvard University Press).
Sylos-Labini, P. (1984) *The Forces of Economic Growth and Decline* (Cambridge, Mass.: MIT Press).
Taylor, L. and Weiser, D. (1972) 'Advertising and the Aggregate Consumption Function,' *American Economic Review*, 62, pp. 642–55.
Thomson, R. (1987) 'Learning by Selling and Invention: The Case of the Sewing Machine,' *Journal of Economic History*, 44, June, pp. 433–445.
Tobin, J. (1983) *Macroeconomics, Prices and Quantities* (Oxford: Basil Blackwell).
Wenders, J. (1967) 'Entry and Monopolistic Pricing,' *Journal of Political Economy*, 75, pp. 755–62.
Weston, J. (1973) 'Pricing Behavior of Large Firms,' in J. Weston and Ornstein (eds), *The Impact of Large Firms* (Lexington, Mass.: Lexington Books).
Wood, A. (1976) *A Theory of Profits* (Cambridge: Cambridge University Press).

18 Stability in Simple Keynesian Models*

There are many meanings of 'stability' but simple models need simple concepts. It would be inappropriate to burden an IS–LM model with a complicated theory of adjustment, but it is surprising that the simpler processes have not been more fully investigated. For policy measures initially disturb markets, and if the system is not at least imperfectly stable, in Hicks's sense, it may make a difference to the effectiveness of policy which markets are initially disturbed.

First I shall show that for a standard model simple dynamic and Hicksian static analysis give the same results. In the course of this I shall suggest a reinterpretation of the standard model which strongly supports the possibility that it is not imperfectly stable. Finally I shall consider the alleged effects of wage and price flexilibity on spending and show that this does not improve the system's stability. Indeed when the fiction that wages and prices move together is abandoned, we can develop a model related to the *Treatise on Money*, capable of being analysed by many of the same methods, but giving significantly different results. Allowing wages and prices to vary in a Flexible Employment system does not change the conclusion that involuntary unemployment can exist in an equilibrium that balances 'injections and withdrawals,' but it does open the door on a significant connection between inflation and distribution.

PART 1

I

Much of what follows can be understood by analogy with a single market. 'Walrasian behavior' supposes that the initial disequlibrium is one of quantity, and that demanders and suppliers adjust demand and supply prices, so calling forth altered quantities. 'Marshallian behavior' is equally possible. The initial disequlibrium consists of a divergence between demand and supply prices, and demander and supplier accordingly adjust quantities; so bringing about price changes.

* Spanish version (trans. by L. Argemi), *Cuardenos de Economìa*, 11 (3) (April 1974) pp. 66–90. I wish to thank Professor C.R. Ross and Mr. David Bailey of the University of East Anglia for help and encouragement on an earlier version of this paper.

For Walrasian equilibrium we require that excess quantity demand be zero,

$$E_D = D(p) - S(p) = 0$$

and the corresponding stability condition is that price increases should reduce excess demand,

$$D'(p) - S'(p) < 0$$

For Marshallian equilibrium we require that 'excess price' shall be zero,

$$E_p = D^{-1}(q) - S^{-1}(q) = 0$$

and the corresponding stability condition in that an increase in quantity should reduce excess price,

$$D^{-1\prime}(q) - S^{-1\prime}(q) < 0$$

Given that the demand curve slopes downward, Marshallian and Walrasian stability conditions (conditions for rectifying price and quantity disequilibria) can both be met if the supply curve has a positive slope. But should the two curves slope the same way, the two criteria cannot both be filled. The standard Keynesian model can be analysed in a closely analogous way.

II

In the case of a simple Keynesian model the Mashallian analogue is adjustment to a discrepancy between the investment or real rate of interest and the money rate of interest, while the Walrasian analogue is adjustment to a divergence between income and expenditure. This requires a more careful interpretation of the model than is often given. Let us first examine stability on dynamic assumptions. The model, assuming linear functions for simplicity is:

$$S = a + bY + cr; \qquad b > 0, c > 0 \tag{18.1}$$

$$I = d + eY + fr; \qquad e > 0, f < 0 \tag{18.2}$$

$$L = \alpha + \beta E + \gamma i; \qquad \beta > 0, \gamma > 0 \tag{18.3}$$

$$M = L \qquad M = \text{constant} \tag{18.4}$$

$$S = I \tag{18.5}$$

$$r = i \qquad i \geq i' \text{ (Liquidity Trap)} \tag{18.6}$$

$$Y = E \tag{18.7}$$

Where S is total saving, I is total investment, L is the demand for money, Y is total income, E is total spending, r is the investment rate of interest, and i, the money rate.

Equations (18.1)–(18.3) are behavioral functions, (18.4)–(18.5) are the quantity equilibrium conditions in the money and goods markets respectively, while (18.6)–(18.7) are the corresponding price and quantity equilibrium conditions for the system as a whole. This formulation makes it clear that the decision to save depends on income, the decision to invest on output (where income ≡ output) and the rate of return on capital at the margin, while the transactions and speculative demand for money depend on spending and interest on money.[1] It requires a careful specification of the investment function, and the saving-investment market. An increase in the expected rate of return is required to call forth more saving, but additional investment causes the rate of return at the margin to decline. Investment projects can be ranked unambiguously, and the more profitable projects will be done first. Investment will be pushed to the point where no further savings are forthcoming, i.e., the point at which, for a given level of income (output), the saving and investment curves cross. We will hear more of this later.

Solving for the IS curve,

$$r = \frac{d - a}{c - f} + \left(\frac{e - b}{c - f}\right) Y, \tag{18.8}$$

and substituting $Y = E$, for the LM curve,

$$i = \frac{M - \alpha}{\gamma} - \frac{\beta}{\gamma} Y, \qquad i \geq i' \tag{18.9}$$

The IS curve slopes up if $e > \beta$; the LM curve has a positive slope at all points.

Next we define

$$\Delta Y_t = Y_t - \bar{Y}_t \tag{18.10}$$

where Y_t is income at time t, a time within the short period, and $\bar{Y}_t$ is equilibrium income at that time, and postulate 'Marshallian' disequilibrium behavior:

$$\frac{dY}{dt} = j(r - i), \qquad j>0 \tag{18.11}$$

That is, the speed of adjustment of income will be proportional to the disequilibrium in the prices of asset services.

For stability, $\Delta Y \to 0$. Hence,

$$\frac{d\Delta Y_t}{dt} = \frac{dY_t}{dt} - \frac{d\bar{Y}_t}{dt}, \tag{18.12}$$

and substituting (18.8), (18.9) and (18.11) into (18.12)

$$\frac{d\Delta Y_t}{dt} = j\left(\frac{e-b}{c-f} + \frac{\beta}{\gamma}\right)\Delta Y + j\left(\frac{d-a}{c-f} - \frac{M-\alpha}{\gamma}\right)$$

$$+ j\left(\frac{e-b}{c-f} + \frac{\beta}{\gamma}\right)\bar{Y}_t - \frac{d\bar{Y}_t}{dt}. \tag{18.13}$$

By definition, however, since $\bar{Y}_t$ is equilibrium income,

$$\frac{d\bar{Y}_t}{dt} = j(r-i) = j\left(\frac{d-a}{c-f} - \frac{M-\alpha}{\gamma}\right) + j\left(\frac{e-b}{c-f} + \frac{\beta}{\gamma}\right)\bar{Y}_t = 0 \tag{18.14}$$

Hence from (18.14),

$$\frac{d\Delta Y_t}{dt} = j\left(\frac{e-b}{c-f} + \frac{\beta}{\gamma}\right)\Delta Y_t \tag{18.15}$$

Rearranging

$$\frac{d\Delta Y_t}{\Delta Y_t} = j\left(\frac{e-b}{c-f} + \frac{\beta}{\gamma}\right)dt \tag{18.16}$$

Integrating, then

$$\Delta Y_t = Ae^{jmt}, \quad \text{where } m = \frac{e-b}{c-f} + \frac{\beta}{\gamma} \tag{18.17}$$

At time $t = 0$, $jmt = 0$, so

$$\Delta Y_0 = A \tag{18.18}$$

representing the initial disequilibrium in income due to the divergence of investment and money rates of return. Consider (18.17) as $t \to \infty$. If $m < 0$, as $t \to \infty$, $jmt \to -\infty$; hence $\Delta Y_t \to 0$. If $m = 0$, $\Delta Y_t = A$, and if $m > 0$, $\Delta Y_t \to \infty$ as $t \to \infty$. The stability conditions thus are

$$m < 0; \quad \frac{e-b}{c-f} < -\frac{\beta}{\gamma}\text{ ; tends to equilibrium}$$

$$m = 0, \quad \frac{e-b}{c-f} = -\frac{\beta}{\gamma}\text{ ; constant disequilibrium} \tag{18.19}$$

$$m > 0, \quad \frac{e-b}{c-f} > -\frac{\beta}{\gamma}\text{ ; progressive divergence from equilibrium}$$

Given the sign constraints on the coefficient, if $b > e$ the IS curve slopes down, and the system will be stable. But if $b < e$, as many trade cycle theorists have assumed,[2] the slope of the IS curve must be flatter than that of the LM curve for 'Marshallian' stability.

III

Now consider the 'Walrasian' approach, in section 2 we examined adjustment to a disequilibrium in the asset market on the hypothesis that income and spending moved together. Now we suppose that money and real rates of return move together, and consider adjustment to a divergence between income and expenditure, as the latter affects demand for money.

Solve for Y and E in terms of i

$$Y = \frac{a-d}{e-b} + \left(\frac{c-f}{e-b}\right) i \tag{18.20}$$

$$E = \frac{M-\alpha}{\beta} - \left(\frac{\gamma}{\beta}\right) i \tag{18.21}$$

The adjustment function will be

$$\frac{di}{dt} = g(Y-E),\ g > 0 \tag{18.22}$$

and we define

$$\Delta i_t = i_t - \bar{i}_t \tag{18.23}$$

where i_t is the rate of return at time t, and $\bar{i}_t$ is the equilibrium rate at that time.

Then,

$$\frac{d\Delta i_t}{dt} = \frac{di_t}{dt} - \frac{d\bar{i}_t}{dt} \tag{18.24}$$

By definition the second term on the RHS is zero. Substituting

$$\frac{d\Delta i_t}{dt} = g(Y - E) = g\left(\frac{a-d}{e-b} - \frac{M-\alpha}{\beta}\right) + g\left(\frac{c-f}{e-b} + \frac{\gamma}{\beta}\right) i_t$$

and from (18.23)

$$= g\left(\frac{c-f}{e-b} + \frac{\gamma}{\beta}\right) \Delta i_t + g\left(\frac{a-d}{e-b} - \frac{M-\alpha}{\beta}\right) + g\left(\frac{c-f}{e-b} + \frac{\gamma}{\beta}\right) i_t \tag{18.25}$$

Since the second two terms are $\dfrac{d\bar{i}_t}{dt} = 0$

$$\frac{d\Delta i_t}{dt} = g\left(\frac{c-f}{e-b} + \frac{\gamma}{\beta}\right)\Delta i_t. \text{ Hence,} \tag{18.26}$$

$$\frac{d\Delta i_t}{\Delta i_t} = g\left(\frac{c-f}{e-b} + \frac{\gamma}{\beta}\right) dt. \tag{18.27}$$

Integrating,

$$\Delta i_t = Be^{gnt}, \text{ where } n = \frac{c-f}{e-b} - \frac{\gamma}{\beta} \tag{18.28}$$

At time $t = 0$,

$$\Delta i_0 = B \tag{18.29}$$

which given the size of the initial disequilibrium in the asset market due to the divergence of income and spending. As $t \to \infty$, $gnt \to -\infty$, if $n < 0$; $gnt \to \infty$, if $n > 0$. Hence we have[3]

$$n < 0; \quad \frac{c-f}{e-b} < -\frac{\gamma}{\beta} \text{ ; tends to equilibrium}$$

$$n = 0; \quad \frac{c-f}{e-b} = -\frac{\gamma}{\beta}\text{; constant disequilibrium} \tag{18.30}$$

$$n > 0; \quad \frac{c-f}{e-b} > -\frac{\gamma}{\beta}\text{; progressive divergence from equilibrium}$$

If the IS curve has a negative slope, $b > e$, then $m < 0$, $n < 0$, both Marshallian and Walrasian condition will be filled. But if IS has a positive slope, $b < e$, then $m < 0$ entails $n > 0$, and vice-versa. Only one of the conditions can be met; moreover, one of them must be met. Hence, when the marginal propensity to invest out of income exceeds the marginal propensity to save out of income, if a disequilibrium originating in the prices of assets tends to stabilize itself, a disequilibrium originating in output and expenditure will not, and vice-versa. The initial impact of monetary policy (in a Keynesian model) causes a divergence between i and r; the initial impact of fiscal policy causes a divergence between Y and E. During the upswing of the cycle, therefore, it is likely that either monetary or fiscal policy will be destabilizing.

IV

These results are not changed if we substitute static for dynamic analysis. Rewrite the model in excess demand form:

$$E_i = I - S = (d - a) + (e - b)Y + (f - c)r = 0 \tag{18.31}$$

$$E_L = L - M = (\alpha - M) + \beta E + \gamma i = 0 \tag{18.32}$$

Assuming initial equilibrium, substitute Y for E and i for r. Then consider a small disturbance causing the system to move out of equilibrium. To find the resulting changes in the variables, differentiate totally:

$$dE_i = (e - b)dY + (f - c)di \tag{18.33}$$

$$dE_L = \beta\, dY + \gamma di \tag{18.34}$$

For imperfect stability, all prices are assumed flexible and changes in each market's excess demand are examined on the assumption that other markets adjust. Taking the market for output, and assuming that the interest rate adjusts, we have:

$$dE_i = (e - b)dy + (f - c)di \tag{18.35}$$

$$0 = \beta\, dY + \gamma\, di$$

Using Cramer's Rule:

$$dY = \frac{\begin{vmatrix} dE_i & f-c \\ 0 & \gamma \end{vmatrix}}{\begin{vmatrix} e-b & f-c \\ \beta & \gamma \end{vmatrix}} = dE_i \frac{\gamma}{(e-b) - \beta(f-c)} \tag{18.36}$$

So, for stability,

$$\frac{dE_i}{dY} = (e-b) - \frac{\beta}{\gamma}(f-c) < 0, \text{ implying}^4 \tag{18.37}$$

$$\frac{e-b}{f-c} > \frac{\beta}{\gamma}, \text{ or } \frac{e-b}{c-f} < -\frac{\beta}{\gamma} \tag{18.38}$$

If the IS curve slopes down this will automatically be met but if it slopes up, it must cut the LM curve from above.

Now suppose income adjusts, eliminating excess demand for investment goods, and consider the stability of the asset market.

$$0 = (e-b)dY + (f-c)di \tag{18.39}$$

$$dE_i = \beta\, dY + \gamma\, di$$

Using Cramer's Rule,

$$di = \frac{\begin{vmatrix} e-b & 0 \\ \beta & dE_i \end{vmatrix}}{\begin{vmatrix} e-b & f-c \\ \beta & \gamma \end{vmatrix}} = dE_L \frac{e-b}{\gamma(e-b) - \beta(f-c)} \tag{18.40}$$

So that, stability

$$\frac{dE_L}{di} = \gamma - \beta\frac{f-c}{e-b} < 0, \text{ implying} \tag{18.41}$$

$$\frac{f-c}{e-b} > \frac{\gamma}{\beta}, \text{ or } \frac{c-f}{e-b} < -\frac{\gamma}{\beta} \tag{18.42}$$

Conditions (18.38) and (18.42) are, of course, the same as (18.19) and

(18.30). For imperfect stability in Hicks's sense, both (18.38) and (18.42) must be met. This will happen only if the IS curve slopes down; if the IS curve has a positive slope, as is likely in the upswing, then the system cannot be imperfectly stable. Either the output or the asset market will be unstable, and hence either fiscal or monetary policy will be destabilizing, exactly the conclusion we reached in the dynamic case.

But the Hicksian method brings an important assumption into the open. To examine the stability of a market we assume that the others have successfully adjusted, a proposition more clearly evident in the static approach than in the dynamic. When the *IS* has a positive slope, however, the investment-saving-income adjustment process will itself be unstable, so that it is not easy to see how the goods market could clear. Hence, when $b > e$ it is likely that fiscal policy will always be destabilizing, and if, in addition, the slope of the *IS* is less than that of the *LM* (the most plausible case) monetary policy will be also. The standard Keynesian policies may have difficulty controlling a boom.

V

Keynes appears to have held both that 'underemployment equilibrium,' in some sense of that much-abused term, was possible, and that an unregulated capitalist system was inherently unstable. Critics have claimed that Wealth Effects, in particular, the Real Balance Effect, in addition to guaranteeing the existence of full employment equilibrium, contribute to the stability of the system, supporting the claim that an unregulated private enterprise system 'tends to equilibrium at full employment.'

Adopting standard assumptions, and writing Π for the general price level, the new behavioral relations will be:

$$S = a + bY + cr + x\Pi, \qquad b > 0, c > 0, x > 0 \tag{18.43}$$

$$I = d + eY + fr + y\Pi, \qquad e > 0, f < 0, y < 0 \tag{18.44}$$

$$L = \alpha + \beta E + \gamma i + z\Pi, \qquad B > 0, \gamma < 0, z > 0 \tag{18.45}$$

Liquid assets are assumed to influence both consumption and investment. When the price level rises, the real value of cash holdings falls, so households will reduce consumption in order to rebuild their cash holdings in real terms. Firms will adjust their current rate of investment spending in order to maintain their desired level of cash holding in real terms. The demand for money in nominal terms varies directly with the price level, reflecting absence of a 'money illusion.'

To these equations we must add a mechanism showing how the price level will fall in the face of excess capacity, and rise in times of capacity shortage. In a competitive neo-Classical world this is brought about in the labor market. Excess capacity means the demand for labor is less than full employment supply, so the money wage falls, and competition forces down the price level. Capacity shortage means a bidding up of prices and wages. Any disparity between the movement of money wages and the price level, of course, changes the real wage, thereby creating positive or negative excess demand for labor, changing the money wage so as to restore the equilibrium real wage, equal to the marginal product of labor at full employment, according to the standard view.

We therefore add,

$$\Delta E = E - Y_F = md\pi, \; m > 0 \tag{18.46}$$

which can be illustrated very simply in a diagram. Clearly, when $E = Y_F$, $d\pi = 0$; when $E > Y_{F'}$, $d\pi > 0$; when $E < Y_{F'}$, $d\pi < 0$. (Integrating will be assumed to imply that when $E \rightarrow Y_{F'}$, $\Delta\pi \rightarrow 0$, at a level of π, π^*, compatible with full employment.)

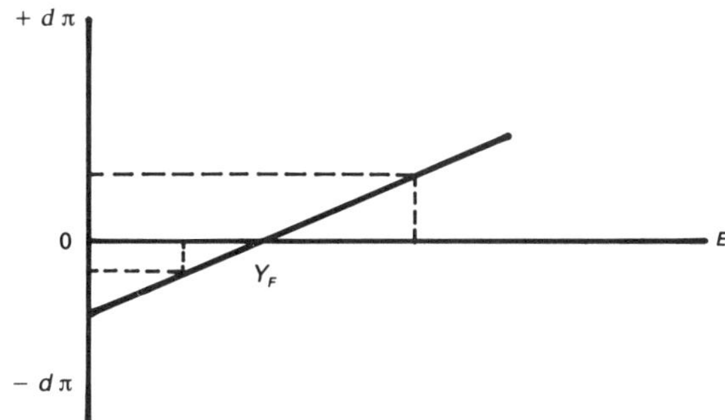

Figure 18.1

The four equations, 18.43–18.46, when combined with the four equilibrium conditions, 18.4–18.7, make up a system of eight equations in the unknowns: S, I, L, Y, E, r, i. If we now substitute the integrated form,

$$Y_F = m\pi^* \tag{18.46$'$}$$

for 18.46, the system will have a unique full employment solution in the positive quadrant, if, but only if, the *IS* and *LM* loci intersect uniquely in that quadrant.[5] (Suppose $b > e$, so the *IS* locus sloped upwards, but remained shallower than the *LM*. Wealth effects could then ensure a full employment equilibrium, but there could also easily be a second equilibrium in the Liquidity Trap region, provided the *IS* locus associated with π^* had a vertical intercept below the interest rate, i'.)

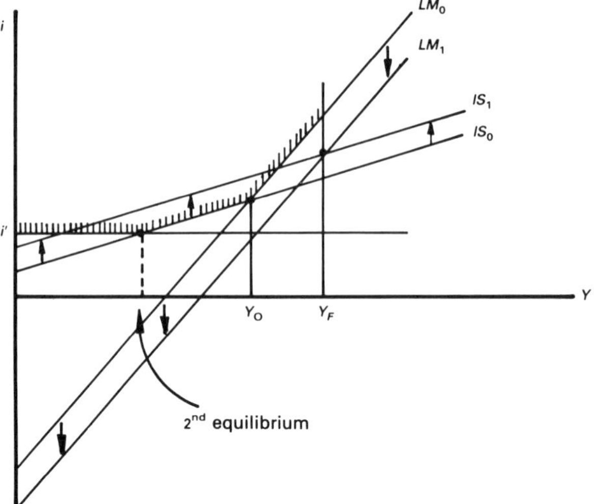

Figure 18.2

Turning to stability, and solving for the *IS* and *LM* equations,

$$i_{IS} = \frac{d-a}{c-f} + \left(\frac{e-b}{c-f}\right)Y + \left(\frac{y-x}{c-f}\right)\pi, \quad \text{where } \frac{\delta i_{IS}}{\delta\pi} = \frac{y-x}{c-f} < 0 \quad (18.47)$$

$$i_{LM} = \frac{m-\alpha}{\gamma} - \frac{\beta}{\gamma}Y - \frac{z}{\gamma}\pi, \quad \text{where } \frac{\delta i_{LM}}{\delta\pi} = -\frac{z}{\gamma} > 0 \quad (18.48)$$

when $d\pi < 0$, $di_{IS} = \dfrac{y-x}{c-f}\, d\pi > 0$, and $di_{LM} = -\, z/\gamma\; d\pi < 0$;

so the *IS* curve shifts up and the *Lm* curve shifts down. A fall in the price level raises the real value of cash balances, stimulating spending but lowering the demand for money.

As before we define,

$\Delta Y = Y_t - Y_F$, and

$$\frac{dY}{dt} = j(i_{IS} - i_{LM}),\ j > 0. \quad (18.49)$$

For stability we require $\Delta Y_t \to 0$. Following the same procedure, substituting and regrouping:

$$\frac{d\Delta Y}{dt} = j\left[\left(\frac{e-b}{c-f} + \frac{\beta}{j}\right)\Delta Y + \left(\frac{y-x}{c-f} = \frac{z}{\gamma}\right)\Delta\pi\right] \quad (18.50)$$

Dividing by ΔY, and multiplying by dt,

$$\frac{d\Delta Y}{\Delta Y} = j \left[\left(\frac{e-b}{c-f} + \frac{ß}{\gamma} \right) dt + \left(\frac{y-x}{c-f} + \frac{z}{\gamma} \right) \frac{\Delta \pi}{\Delta Y} dt \right] \quad (18.51)$$

But $\frac{\Delta \pi}{\Delta Y} = 1/m$, from 18.46:

$$\frac{d\Delta Y}{\Delta Y} = j \left[\left(\frac{e-b}{c-f} + \frac{ß}{\gamma} \right) + \left(\frac{y-x}{c-f} + \frac{z}{\gamma} \right) \frac{1}{m} \right] dt \quad (18.52)$$

Integrating,

$$\Delta Y_t = Ae^{jXt} \quad (18.53)$$

where

$$X = \frac{e-b}{c-f} + \frac{ß}{\gamma} + \frac{1}{m} \left(\frac{y-x}{c-f} + \frac{z}{\gamma} \right) \quad (18.54)$$

which can be rewritten,

$$X = \frac{e - b + 1/m\,(y-x)}{c-f} + \frac{ß + z/m}{\gamma} \quad (18.55)$$

As before, when $X < 0$; as $t \to \infty$, $jXt \to \infty$ and $Y_t \to 0$; when $X = 0$, $Y_t = A$, and when $X > 0$, as $t \to \infty$, $Y_t \to \infty$. Since $(c - f)$ and $(ß + z/m) > 0$, while γ and $(y - x) < 0$, the key relationship is once again $(e - b)$. If $b > e$, i.e. $(e - b) < 0$, then

$$\frac{e - b + 1/m\,(y-x)}{c-f} + \frac{ß + z/m}{\gamma} < 0, \quad (18.56)$$

and the system is stable. But when $e > b$ this may not hold.

To see the relationship more clearly write the expression:

$$\frac{e - b + 1/m\,(y-x)}{c-f} \gtrless - \frac{ß + z/m}{\gamma} \quad (18.57)$$

The *LHS* is the slope of the locus of combinations of i, Y and for which savings equals investment; the *RHS* is the slope of the locus of combinations of i, Y and for which the demand and supply of money are equal. When this augmented *IS* has a negative slope, stability is assured. If it has a positive slope, the system will still be stable, if the slope is less than that of the augmented *LM* locus (subject to the qualification above, concerning the instability of the investment-saving relationship itself.) If the two slopes are equal, there will be no movement, but if the slope of the augmented *IS* is greater than that of the *LM*, the system will be unstable. The addition of wealth effects has not changed the essential character of the system. A 'full employment' price level, π^*, must be assumed to exist, and the wealth effects have contributed nothing to stability.

Clearly the claim that wage and price-flexibility in conjunction with a real-balance effect substantially stabilizes the system is false. But there is a point to introducing the capacity-price level market. For in addition to fiscal and monetary policy, the government has another set of measures at its disposal: direct controls. Through manipulation of nationalized industries and through legislation it may direct that a certain percentage of capacity be used (volume of employment be offered), or it may influence the price level, either directly through legislation, or indirectly through wage and price guidelines, encouragement, and penalties. Direct price controls in effect set $\Delta\pi/\Delta Y = 0$; this reduces the system to the *IS* – *LM* equations of the preceding sections.

PART II

VI

One could agree that one sector short-run aggregative models have their uses particularly if capacity utilization, employment, wages and prices are explicitly considered, and yet still object strongly to the model of Part I. Three features of this model have received well-merited criticism: the real balance effect, the assumption that investment projects can be uniquely ranked by degree of profitability, independently of other short-run economic variables, and the simultaneous use of marginal productivity theory and the neglect of short-run distributional effects. Taking each in turn: there is little or no evidence to support the claim that changes in the real value of liquid assets will affect consumption.[6] Hicks argues that the effect is asymmetrical, a *fall* in the real value of cash balances might necessitate curtailing current spending, but a rise would result in portfolio adjustments, without additions to current spending.[7] In so far as liquid assets are 'inside money,' the effects of price level changes on creditors and debtors will tend to be offsetting.[8] But even 'outside money' and government paper

$$S = a + bY + cr \qquad b > 0, c > 0 \tag{18.72}$$

$$I = d + eY + fr \qquad e > 0, f > 0 \tag{18.73}$$

$$L/\Pi = \alpha + \beta E + \gamma i \qquad \beta > 0, \gamma < 0 \tag{18.74}$$

$$N/N_F = Y/Y_F \qquad N \leqslant N_F \tag{18.75}$$

$$W/W_o = N/N_F \qquad Y \leqslant Y_F \tag{18.76}$$

$$r = \frac{\Pi Y - WN}{K} \qquad \begin{matrix} W \leqslant W_o \\ i \geqslant \bar{\imath} \end{matrix} \tag{18.77}$$

$$M = L \tag{18.78}$$

$$S = I \tag{18.79}$$

$$Y = E \tag{18.80}$$

$$r = i \tag{18.81}$$

The value of capital is taken as given in the short run. Nothing essential would be changed by introducing a proportionality constant into equations (18.75) and/or (18.76). To solve the model, first find the IS curve:

$$r = \frac{d-a}{c-f} + \frac{e-b}{c-f}\, Y, \text{ i.e.} \tag{18.82a}$$

$$r = H + JY \tag{18.82b}$$

Then find the LM curve

$$i = \frac{M/\Pi - \alpha}{\gamma} - \frac{\beta}{\gamma}\, Y, \text{ i.e.} \tag{18.83a}$$

$$= \frac{M/\Pi - \alpha}{\gamma} - QY \tag{18.83b}$$

Then find the profit–employment curve

$$r = \frac{\Pi Y}{K} - Y^2 \frac{W_o N_F}{K Y_F^2} \tag{18.84a}$$

$$= \frac{\Pi Y}{K} - \lambda Y^2 \tag{18.84b}$$

This gives three equations in the three unknowns, r, Π, and Y. To solve we combine (18.82b) and (18.83b) and (18.82b) and (18.84b) to get:

$$\Pi = \frac{T}{Y+U} \tag{18.85}$$

$$\Pi = K\lambda Y + KJ + \frac{KH}{Y}, \tag{18.86}$$

where $T = \dfrac{M-\alpha}{\gamma(Q+J)}$ and $U = \dfrac{H}{Q+J}$

Equation (18.85) is the locus of all combinations of price and income levels consistent both with investment–saving equilibrium and with money market equilibrium. Equation (18.86) is the locus of all price and income levels consistent both with investment–saving and distributional equilibrium. Equation (18.85) is a rectangular hyperbola with asymptotes $\Pi = 0$ and $Y = -U$. Equation (18.86) is not so obvious. Differentiating,

$$\frac{d\Pi}{dY} = K(\lambda - H/Y^2) \tag{18.87}$$

$$\frac{d^2\Pi}{dY^2} = 2KHY^{-3} > 0 \quad \text{if H} > 0.$$

The first derivative will be zero when

$$Y = \pm \sqrt{H/\lambda} \text{ and the second will always be positive;} \tag{18.88}$$

hence there will be minimum points. By inspection, it is easy to see that as $Y \to 0$ through positive or negative fractions, $\Pi \to \infty$. The two curves can be diagrammed together. In the case illustrated, in Figure 18.3, it is assumed that $U < 0$, $H > 0$, $T > 0$, and $H/\lambda > -U$. The condition that $H > 0$ is the Kaldorian stability condition; while $U \gtrless 0$ depends on the familiar relationship $\dfrac{\beta}{\gamma} \gtrless \dfrac{e-b}{c-f}$, if $U > 0$, assuming $H > 0$, then the line $Y = -U$ will shift to the other side of the vertical axis. But $U > 0$ implies

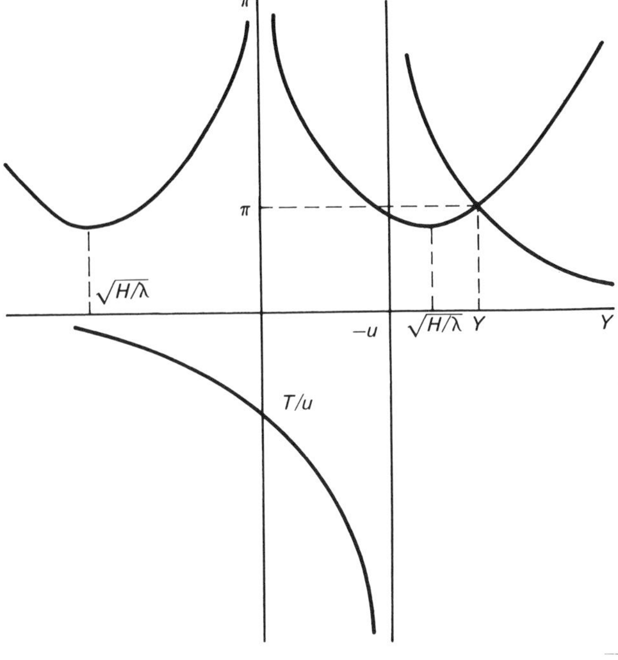

Figure 18.3

$T < 0$; no positive price levels will be associated with positive levels of income. Hence there will be no positive equilibrium. In other words, on the assumption that $H > 0$, $T > 0$ must hold for equilibrium; either the IS curve slopes down, $J < 0$, or if $J > 0$, $|Q| > |J|$; an upward-sloping IS curve must be less steep than the LM curve, in order for equilibrium to exist. If $H < 0$, $T < 0$ is possible, for a positive price level will be associated with positive levels of income so long as $0 < Y < |U|$, where $U < 0$, i.e., $Q + J > 0$, which implies $T < 0$. If $H < 0$, then

$$\frac{d^2\Pi}{d^2} < 0, \text{ so the stationary points } \pm \sqrt{H/\lambda}$$

will be maximum points.

A general stability analysis of this model would require methods more advanced than any we have used. One case can be examined quite easily, however; namely, the response of income to a divergence between demand price and supply price. As before, we postulate

$$\frac{dY}{dt} = j(\Pi_E - \Pi_Y), \quad j > 0 \tag{18.89}$$

$$= j \frac{T}{Y+U} - K\left(\lambda Y + J + \frac{H}{Y}\right) \tag{18.90}$$

Since $\Delta Y_t = Y_t - \bar{Y}_t$,

$$\frac{d\Delta Y_t}{dt} = j(\Pi_E - \Pi_Y) - \frac{d\bar{Y}_t}{dt} \tag{18.91}$$

and for stability $\Delta Y_t \rightarrow 0$. So, substituting and simplifying

$$\frac{d\Delta Y_t}{dt} = j \frac{T}{(\Delta Y_t + \bar{Y}_t) + u} - K\left(\lambda(\Delta Y_t + \bar{Y}_t) + J + \frac{H}{\Delta Y_t + \bar{Y}_t}\right)$$

$$- j\frac{T}{\bar{Y}_t + u} - K\left(\lambda Y_t + J + \frac{H}{\bar{Y}_t}\right) \tag{18.92}$$

$$= j\left(\frac{T}{(\bar{Y}_t + u)\,(Y + u)} + \frac{KH}{\bar{Y}_t\,Y} - K\lambda\right)\Delta Y_t. \tag{18.93}$$

Hence,

$$\frac{d\Delta Y_t}{\Delta Y_t} = j\left(\frac{T}{(\bar{Y}_t + u)\,(Y + u)} + \frac{KH}{\bar{Y}_t\,Y} - K\lambda\right) dt \tag{18.94}$$

Integrating and taking out antilogs,

$$\Delta Y_t = Ae^{j\theta t} \tag{18.95}$$

Where

$$\theta = \frac{T}{(\bar{Y}_t + u)\,(Y + u)} + \frac{KH}{\bar{Y}_t\,Y} - K\lambda$$

Stability requires $\theta < 0$; hence, will be the more likely the larger are actual and equilibrium income. Normally $H > 0$; hence, $T < 0$ if $J < 0$ or if $IQI > IJI$. However $T < 0$ does not permit a positive equilibrium, as our inspection of equation (18.85) showed, unless $H < 0$. In that event stability would be assured – if there existed an equilibrium.

The models of Part II represent in two respects a return to a tradition of thought developed in the *Treatise*, but submerged in the Keynesian Revolution following the *General Theory*. First, the capital stock represents fixed money obligations in the short run, and secondly, short-run movements of wages and prices mean variations in short-run profits – Profit Inflation or Profit Deflation. To examine this in the context of a one-sector 'Keynesian' model requires making the distribution of income explicit, considerably complicating the structure of the model, and adding an equation specifying the extent to which employers can force money wages down in the presence of unemployment. By doing this we acknowledge the existence of economic power and class conflict, taking macroeconomics a step closer to Political Economy.

We have left the model incomplete, in one respect. We have specified a behavioral function only for money wages; not for prices. Yet to do so would certainly be in the tradition of Kalecki and Kaldor.[16]

Such an augmentation would over-determine the model. This should not necessarily be seen as a drawback; an entire tradition of political and economic thought is built around the conception of 'internal contradictions' and their resolution. It has become standard practice to explain inflation as, in part, an attempt to reconcile incompatible wage demands and profit requirements through businesses' ability to set prices. Part and parcel of this ability is the power to generate the finance needed to support a given price level.[17] This means that the 'money supply' becomes, at least in part, endogenous. Such a development of the model, however, takes us into the theory of inflation, a different ballgame altogether.

Notes

1. It is a condition of these models making economic sense that, whatever the theory of distribution assumed, the purchasing power paid out as income should equal the aggregate value of output produced. This is not an equilibrium condition in the usual sense. Parts of this paper take the money supply as given exogenously. This is not plausible for reasons explained briefly at the end of Chapter 19, where the money supply equation

$$M = M^* + \mu Y + \nu i,$$

is introduced. M^* is determined by the central bank; μ shows the creation of money in response to demand pressures, e.g. by activating lines of credit; ν shows the creation of money in response to changes in interest rates, e.g. by expanding new media of circulation, such as credit cards. The LM locus will be

$$i_{LM} = \frac{M-\alpha}{\gamma-\nu} + \left(\frac{\mu-\beta}{\gamma-\nu}\right) Y$$

The greater the responsiveness of the money supply, the flatter the curve.

2. A common model used by Duesenberry (1958) and in 1972 by Cornwall, and criticized by Pasinetti (1974), runs:

$K_t = K_{t-1} + I_t$ (N1.1) Define:

$Y_t = C_t + I_t$ (N1.2) $\qquad G_y = \dfrac{Y_t - Y_{t-1}}{Y_{t-1}}$

$C_t = cY_{t-1}$ (N1.3)

$I_t = \alpha Y_{t-1} - \beta K_{t-1}$ (N1.4) $\qquad G_k = \dfrac{K_t - K_{t-1}}{K_{t-1}}$

$$v = \frac{K_{t-1}}{Y_{t-1}}$$

Then from N1.3, N1.4, and N1.2

$$G_y = (\alpha + c-1) - \beta v \qquad \text{(N1.5)}$$

and from N1.1 and N1.4

$$G_k = -\beta + \alpha/v \qquad \text{(N1.6)}$$

These can be put on a simple diagram (Figure 18N.1). G_k is a rectangular hyperbola, and G_y a line. The diagram and model make economic sense only if $\alpha + c - 1 > 0$, if the marginal-propensity to invest exceeds the marginal propensity to save, both lagged one period.

3. This is not the whole story, of course. Time can only run to the end of the period. If the adjustment process is slow, and the average gestation period for investment projects short, neither movement towards nor away from equilibrium may be able to get very far. Short-period movements may be swamped by long periods.
4. Since $f-c < 0$.
5. We are assuming that a definite equilibrium exists, i.e., that the IS and LM curves, and the investment-saving-price level and capacity-price level curves do not have identical slopes.
6. Evans (1967) pp. 335–51; Haldi and Whitcomb (1967) pp. 373–85.
7. Hicks (1967) pp. 55–6.
8. Gurley and Shaw (1960); Patinkin (1965).
9. Nell (1984) pp. 60–76.
10. Nell (1984) pp. 60–76.
11. Fisher (1969) pp. 553–77.
12. Robinson and Naqvi (1966); Sraffa (1960), Chapter 12; Pasinetti (1969) pp. 508–30.
13. It will not be the existence of excess capacity that will push prices down, so much as the fact that a higher price level will mean greater profits, which will increase saving more than it will stimulate investment, thus weakening effective demand.
14. How nonsensical this would be can be seen from the diagram in Figure 18N.2. Here, an increased willingness to save at any rate of profit leads to a higher rate of profit *and* a higher level of investment. Where do these profits come from? How are they caused by a greater willingness to save? Taken as a determining mechanism this doesn't make sense. But it is perfectly sensible to say that the condition $I=S$ requires, now *ceteris paribus*, that the rate of profit be set at r_2,

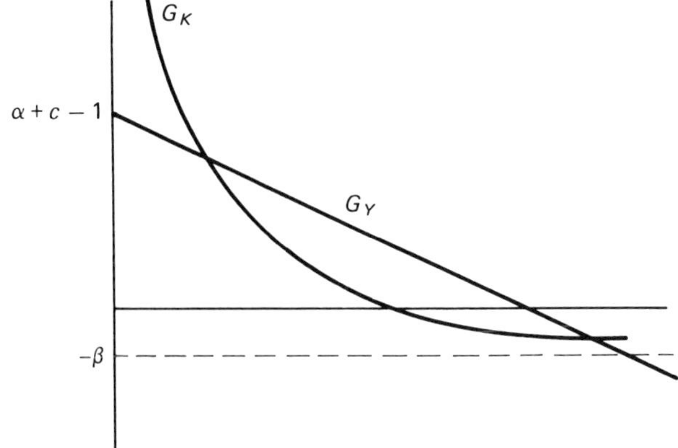

Figure 18N.1

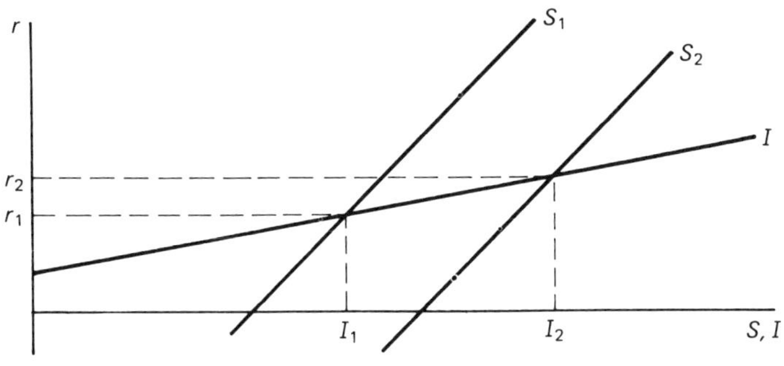

Figure 18N.2

rather than r_1, where it is understood that Figure 18N.2 will be embedded in a more complete model, including a price-setting mechanism for the profit rate.

15. Kaldor (1987) pp. 591–624.
16. Harcourt (1972) Ch. V presents a short-run Kaldorian model, clearly a first cousin to those of our Part II, in which money-wages are fixed and the price level is a function of planned investment, on the grounds that the major investment decision-makers are also the principal price-leaders, and will decide investment and prices at the same time.
17. Kaldor (1970).

References

Cornwall, J. (1972) *Growth and Stability in a Mature Economy* (New York: John Wiley).

Duesenberry, J. (1958) *Business Cycles and Economic Growth* (New York: McGraw-Hill).
Evans, M.K. (1967) 'The Importance of Wealth in the Consumption Function,' *Journal of Political Economy*, 75 (August).
Fisher, F.M. (1969) 'The Existence of Aggregate Production Functions,' *Econometrica* (October).
Gurley, J. and Shaw, E. (1960) *Money in a Theory of Finance* (Washington, D.C.: Brookings Institution).
Haldi, J. and Whitcomb, D. (1967) 'Economies of Scale in Industrial Plants,' *Journal of Political Economy*, 75 (August).
Harcourt, G.C. (1972) *Cambridge Controversies in the Theory of Capital* (Cambridge: Cambridge University Press).
Hicks, J. (1967) *Critical Essays in Monetary Theory* (Oxford: Clarendon Press).
Kaldor, N. (1957) 'A Model of Economic Growth,' *Economic Journal*, 67, pp. 591–624.
Kaldor, N. (1970) 'The New Monetarists,' *Lloyds Bank Review*, July, pp. 1–18.
Nell, E. (1984) *Free Market Conservatism* (London: Allen & Unwin).
Pasinetti, L. (1969) 'Switches of Technique and the "Rate of Return" in Capital Theory,' *Economic Journal*, 74 (September) pp. 508–31.
Pasinetti, L. (1974) *Growth and Income Distribution* (Cambridge: Cambridge University Press).
Patinkin, D. (1965) *Money, Interest and Prices*, Chs 13 and 14, 2nd edn (New York: Harper & Row).
Robinson, J. and Naqvi, K. (1966) 'The Badly Behaved Production Function,' *Quarterly Journal of Economics* (November).
Sraffa, P. (1960) *Production of Commodities by Means of Commodities* (Cambridge: Cambridge University Press).

19 Wealth Effects and the Government Budget Constraint*

In recent years it has been widely argued that a stimulative fiscal policy is inherently ineffective unless accompanied by an expansion of the money supply. The reason is that the government deficit must be financed by borrowing, that is, by open market sales of new government bonds to the private sector, thus raising the private sector's wealth. Since the demand for money is widely held to be an increasing function of wealth, this will raise demand with a fixed money supply, and so will bid up interest rates for all levels of income, counteracting the stimulus to spending provided by the deficit. The new equilibrium is likely to be at about the same level of income, but with a higher level of interest rates. This argument is unacceptable.

1 A STANDARD APPROACH

Figure 19.1, adapted from Blinder and Solow (1973), illustrates the argument. Let S = saving, I = investment, M = stock of money, L = demand for money, and E = equilibrium. Y will be aggregate income, and i the indicator of the complex of interest rates. Starting from less than full employment income, deficit spending shifts the IS curve from IS_0 to IS_1. This requires financing by a new bond issue, which shifts the LM curve up from LM_0 to LM_1, which would lead to a small *decline* in income. But the new bonds, representing new wealth, cause a further shift of the IS curve to IS_2, with the resulting equilibrium, E_3, slightly above the original level of income. (These shifts will be the subject of the following analysis.) Perhaps not everyone would agree that a new issue of government bonds to the private sector (new borrowing from it) represents 'new wealth' of such a sort as to stimulate additional spending in the current short period. But there is general acceptance of the view that deficit spending financed by bonds entails a parallel outward shift of the IS curve, partly or wholly offset by a parallel upward and inward shift of the LM curve. By contrast, when the deficit is financed by money creation, the LM curve shifts out, and continues to shift so long as the deficit lasts.

* Free Market Conservatism (1984) Ch. 3.

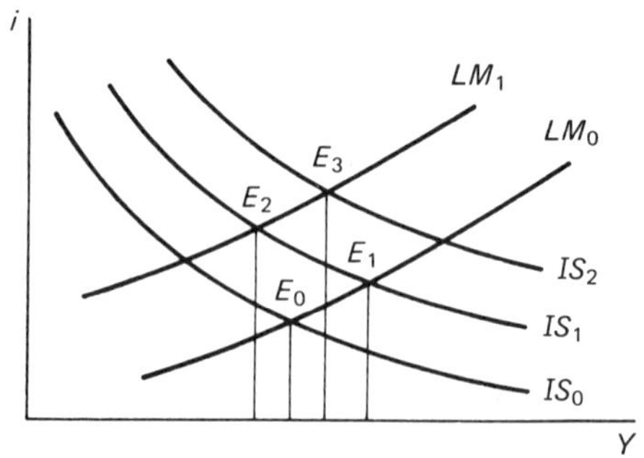

Figure 19.1

One conclusion frequently drawn is that fiscal policy is not independent of monetary policy; another is that fiscal policy, on its own, is ineffectual. It is monetary policy that rules the roost. I shall argue that these conclusions are wholly unjustified because the original argument and most of the subsequent discussion have misunderstood the relationship between the public and private sectors implied in the 'goods market equilibrium' of the simple Keynesian model, and have drawn uncritically on an incoherent concept of wealth.

2 A SIMPLE MODEL

Consider a simple Keynesian *IS–LM* model in linear form (a model we will criticize later):

$$
\begin{aligned}
S &= a + bY + ci \qquad a < 0, b, c > 0 \\
I &= d + eY + fi \qquad d, e > 0, f < 0 \\
L &= \alpha + \beta Y + \gamma i \qquad \alpha, \beta > 0, \gamma < 0 \\
i_T &= \text{minimum, or 'liquidity trap', level of the interest rate} \\
i_e &= \text{equilibrium level of the interest rate} \\
Y_F &= \text{full employment level of income} \\
Y_e &= \text{equilibrium level of income.}
\end{aligned}
$$

Here, the equilibrium conditions are: $I = S$ and $L = M$, where M is fixed by the central bank. Briefly, a is dissaving at zero income; d is autonomous investment; b and e are the marginal propensities to save and invest, respectively; c and f show the influence of interest rates on saving and investment (presumably c is relatively weak, while f, bearing on the marginal efficiency of capital, is significant); α is autonomous demand for money; β is transactions demand for money; and γ is the speculative demand for money.

Solving,

$$i_{IS} = \frac{d - a}{c - f} + \left(\frac{e - b}{c - f}\right) Y \text{ goods market flow equilibrium}$$

$$i_{LM} = \frac{M - \alpha}{\gamma} - \frac{\beta}{\gamma} Y \text{ equilibrium in holding the money stock}$$

$$Y_e = \frac{(c - f)(M - \alpha) - \gamma\,(d - a)}{\gamma(e - b) + \beta(c - f)} \leqslant Y_F$$

$$i_e = \frac{(b - e)(M - \alpha) - \beta\,(d - a)}{\beta(f - c) + \gamma(b - e)} \geqslant i_T$$

Provided $b > e$, and given the usual assumptions, the model can be drawn as in Figure 19.2. Now let us introduce the government. To the investment equation we add G, the government's spending, and to the savings or withdrawals equation we add taxes, in the form tY, where t is the fixed rate of income tax. This yields a new 'injection-withdrawal' (JW) equation,

$$i_{JW} = \frac{G + d - a}{c - f} + \left(\frac{e - b - t}{c - f}\right) Y,$$

or, rearranging;

$$i_{JW} = \frac{G - tY}{c - f} + \frac{d - a}{c - f} + \left(\frac{e - b}{c - f}\right) Y.$$

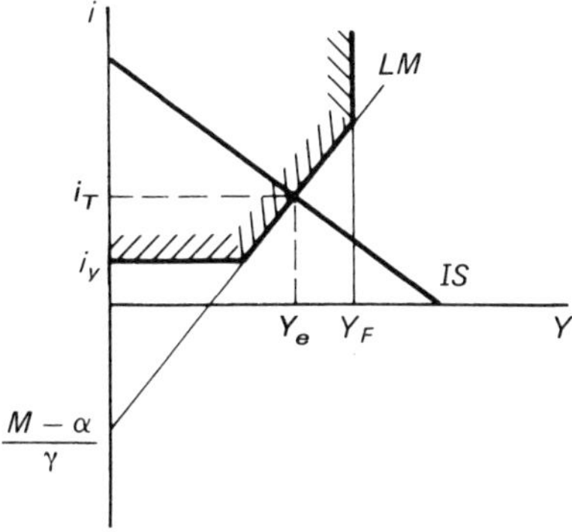

Figure 19.2

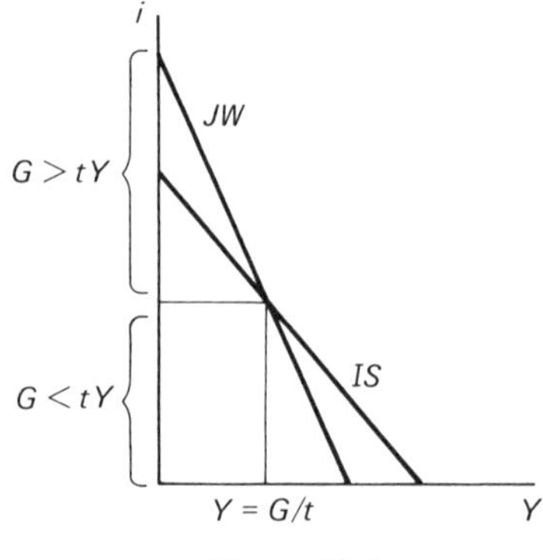

Figure 19.3

(These equations could be written so that saving or both saving and investment depend on disposable income, $Y - tY$, rather than on income. In the first case, then,

$$i_{JW} = \frac{G + d - a}{c - f} + \left[\frac{e - (b)(1 - t) - t}{c - f}\right] Y$$

and, in the second,

$$i_{JW} = \frac{G + d - a}{c - f} + \left[\frac{(e - b)(1 - t) - t}{c - f}\right] Y$$

The intercept remains the same, but the slope is steeper than when saving and investment depend on income.) Call this the *JW* locus. Clearly when $G = tY$, $i_{JW} = i_{IS}$, $Y_{JW} = Y_{IS}$. When $G > tY$, $i_{JW} > i_{IS}$, and when $G < tY$, $i_{JW} < i_{IS}$. The two lines can be graphed. They will cross when $Y = G/t$; for lower levels of Y, the government budget will be in deficit, and for higher it will be in surplus. The further Y from G/t the larger the deficit – or surplus. Adding the government raises the intercept and steepens the slope. When government is in deficit, of course, the private sector will have an equivalent surplus; while a government surplus implies a private sector shortage of savings (see Figure 19.3).

3 BORROWING AND LENDING

The argument from which we began is that a government deficit must be financed either by money creation or by borrowing, i.e., issuing new government bonds. Let us ignore money creation. Hence, writing ΔB for new bonds, with subscripts '*g*' and '*p*' to denote 'government' or 'private,' and using a subscript '*F*' to indicate 'finance required' for *G* and *I*, respectively, we can write that government spending is financed by taxes and borrowing from (lending to) the private sector:

$$G_F = tY + \Delta B_g$$

(If $\Delta B < 0$, the government is lending its surplus.) If the government borrows, the private sector must lend. Hence we have the corresponding condition, which states that finance for private investment equals private saving plus borrowing from (lending to) the government:

$$I_F = a + bY + ci + \Delta B_p.$$

Whatever is borrowed must be loaned:

$$\Delta B_g = - \Delta Bp$$

hence, adding and assuming that the 'required finance' is actually spent:

$$G + I = tY + a + bY + ci = T + S$$

where *T* is total taxes.

This is the condition that defines the *JW* locus; derived here from the assumption that withdrawals will be loaned to finance injections.[1] So we see that the government's deficit or surplus is financed *at every point by the equivalent private sector surplus or deficit*. The multiplier re-spending process generates the required *flow* of funds; there is no need to disturb the *stock* equilibrium represented by the *LM* locus. Changes in *Y* of course, mean the system will move along the *LM* to maintain monetary equilibrium.

4 WEALTH EFFECTS AND THE *LM* LOCUS

Surely the issuing of new government bonds to the private sector counts as raising wealth and hence the demand for money, thus shifting the *LM* locus in and upwards? Let us accept this for a moment and explore the implications of this doctrine. First consider an *LM* line cutting *JW* at the point at which *JW* intersects *IS* (see Figure 19.4). (This is purely arbitrary; however it makes it easy to consider both deficits and surpluses on the government's account.) At this point $Y = G/t$ – the government budget is in balance and private savings exactly cover investment. There is no outstanding government debt. Suppose some exogenous and temporary disturbance in the

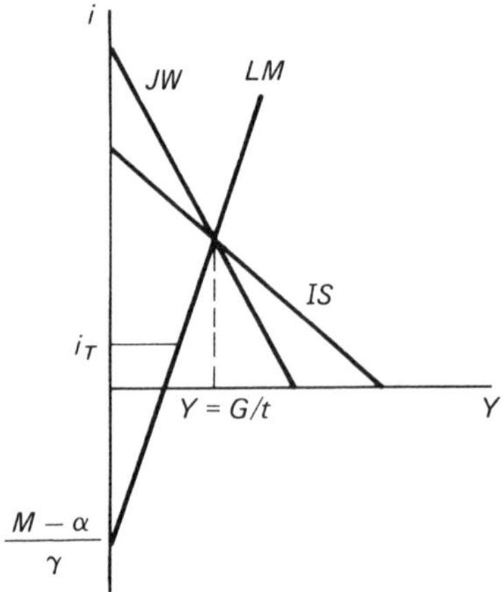

Figure 19.4

supply of money causes *LM* to shift in and up; a deficit will emerge. This deficit will have to be funded and, accordingly, private sector wealth will be permanently increased by the new bonds issued to cover the government deficit. Hence the initial temporary disturbance of the *LM* locus will be compounded by a further shift in the same direction. But this shift in turn will further increase the deficit, leading to still further open market operations, and so on. The economy will contract without limit.

Suppose, now, that the exogenous disturbance causes *LM* to shift out and down; a surplus will emerge. Instead of borrowing, the government now will be lending in the open market. By symmetry, such lending – buying bonds from the private sector – must *reduce* private sector wealth, and so will also reduce the private sector's demand for money. Hence the *LM* curve must shift down and out. But each such shift of the *LM* locus will further increase the surplus, leading to yet another shift, so the economy will expand to full employment, or until i has fallen to i_T, whichever is reached first. Hence there is only one possible equilibrium point, namely, $Y = G/t$, and any slight deviation from this level of income will set up forces driving the economy either to zero employment or to full employment.

If there is initially an outstanding government debt (a quantity of bonds, B), then a change in the level of the interest rate as the *LM* locus shifts will cause them to be revalued. To determine the *net* change in wealth (say as the *LM* shifts in and up from an initial zero deficit equilibrium), the increase in the deficit leading to an issue of bonds will have to be reduced by the effect of the higher interest rate on the value of the existing bonds. If the outstanding debt is small enough and/or the *JW* locus flat enough, the change in the value of the existing bonds will be less than the issue of new bonds, and the previous conclusions will hold. But if B is large and JW steep, then the revaluation effect will outweigh the new issue effect, so that an inward and upward shift of the LM will *reduce* total wealth. Hence the initial shift will be followed by a downward and outward shift, taking the system to the other side of the point from which it began. At this new level of income the two effects will assert themselves once again, but working in opposite ways now. The interest rate has fallen, so revaluation will now raise wealth, but instead of a deficit there is a surplus, so bonds will be retired, reducing wealth. Since the revaluation effect outweighs the issuing effect, the net result will be a new inward and upward shift of the LM locus. Clearly this process can either converge back towards or progressively diverge from the initial equilibrium, depending on how strongly the revaluation effect outweighs the issuing effect.

5 FURTHER WEALTH EFFECTS

Now let us return to the case considered at the outset, where there is no outstanding government debt, and the government budget balances, but where wealth effects shift the IS and JW loci, as well as the LM. Rewrite the equations, adding a wealth term, ω:

$$S = a + bY + ci + x\omega \quad x < 0$$

$$I = d + eY + fi + y\omega \quad y > 0$$

$$L = \alpha + \beta Y + \gamma i + z\omega \quad z > 0.$$

Then, solving, introducing G and t as before:

$$i_{IS} = \frac{d-a}{c-f} + \left(\frac{y-x}{c-f}\right)\omega + \left(\frac{e-b}{c-f}\right)Y$$

$$i_{JW} = \frac{G+d-a+(y-x)\omega}{c-f} + \left(\frac{e-b-t}{c-f}\right)Y =$$

$$\frac{G-tY}{c-f} + \frac{d-a}{c-f} + \left(\frac{y-x}{c-f}\right)\omega + \left(\frac{e-b}{c-f}\right)Y$$

$$i_{LM} = \frac{M+\alpha}{\gamma} - \frac{z}{\gamma}\omega - \frac{\beta}{\gamma}Y.$$

Here $(y - x) / (c - f) > 0$, and $- z/\gamma > 0$, so the *IS*, the *JW* and the *LM* loci all shift upwards with an increase in wealth.

Wealth is defined in the literature as money plus bonds plus real capital, a definition with serious problems, as we shall see shortly. Accepting it for the moment, however, we take both the money stock and the stock of capital as fixed. Hence

$$dW = dB = G - T = t(Y_B - Y_E).$$

The change in wealth is equal to the budget deficit, which in turn equals t times the difference between the balanced budget level of income, Y_B, and the equilibrium level, Y_E (where *LM* cuts *JW*).

Now compare the *IS* and the *JW* equations: $i_{IS} = i_{JW}$ if and only if $G = tY$, i.e., iff $Y = G/t$, regardless of the level of wealth! Hence if wealth increases it will shift both the *IS* and the *JW* loci by the same vertical amount (leaving Y unchanged), since both contain the identical wealth term, which raises the balanced budget rate of interest by that same vertical distance – equal to $(y - x)/(c - f)\ \omega$ (see Figure 19.5).

Start from a balanced budget equilibrium, as illustrated in Figure 19.6. The *LM* locus cuts the *JW* locus where it intersects *IS*; hence $Y = G/t$ and the interest rate is the balanced budget rate. Suppose now some initial disturbance in the money supply shifts *LM* upwards. A budget deficit will emerge and wealth will rise as bonds are issued to finance the deficit. So both the *LM* and the *IS* and *JW* loci will shift upwards. If the vertical shifts are exactly equal (i.e., if $- z / \gamma = (y - x) / (c - f)$), then after the initial disturbance is corrected a balanced budget equilibrium will be established at the same level of income but with a higher interest rate, reflecting the influence of the higher level of wealth. But if the *LM* locus shifts upward *more* than the *JW* and *IS* do, (i.e., if $- z/\gamma > (y - x)/(c - f)$), then the new equilibrium will be established at a level of income, Y_1, *below* $Y_B = G/t$; thus a new deficit will emerge, which will persist even after the initial disturbance has been corrected. This new deficit requires a new issue of bonds, hence further increases wealth. This brings another set of shifts, in which again *LM* will shift upward more than *IS* and *JW*; the new intersection will be at a level of income $Y_2 < Y_1 < Y_B = G/t$. The deficit will again be increased, and the process will repeat itself until income has fallen to zero.

An exactly similar story can be told starting from an initial expansion of the money supply, shifting *LM* down. In this case a surplus will emerge if the *LM* shift is greater than that of *JW*. Each time, therefore, wealth will be reduced, but, since the reduction shifts *LM* further, income will progressively expand and the interest rate fall until either the full employment level of income or the liquidity trap level of interest is reached.

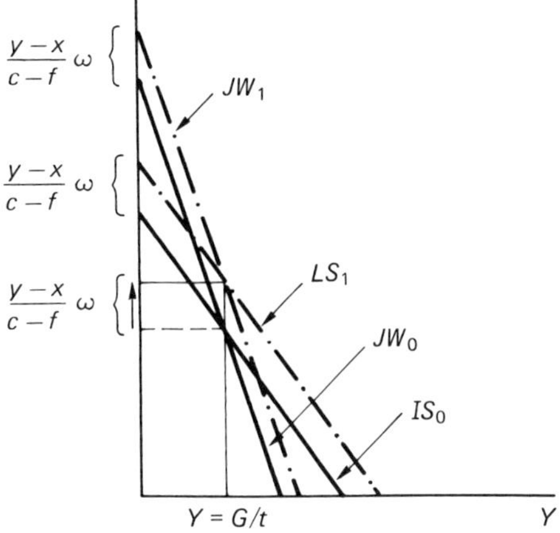

Figure 19.5

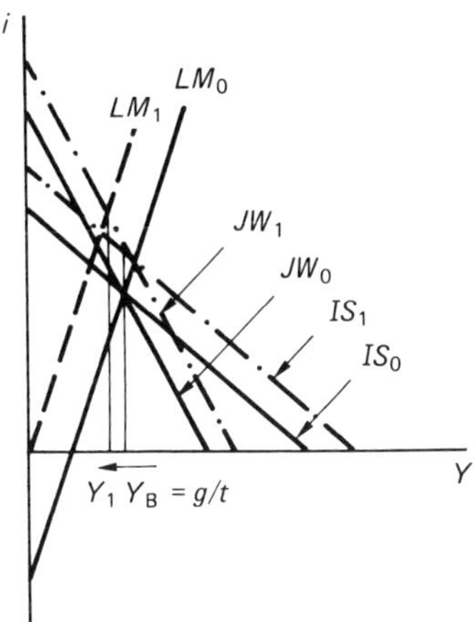

Figure 19.6

Next suppose there is some disruption that causes actual income, Y, to fall below the initial balanced budget equilibrium (i.e., from Y_B to Y_0), thus creating a deficit, but that the wealth effects are such that the subsequent upward shift of the *LM* locus is *less* than that of *JW* and *IS*, i.e., $-z/\gamma < (y-x)/(c-f)$. The new equilibrium will now be to the right of the new intersection of the *JW* and *IS* loci, that is, the new level of income $Y_1 > Y_B = G/t > Y_0$. The government will thus be running a *surplus*, and so will retire bonds, which will reduce wealth. Both the *LM* and the *IS* and *JW* loci will now shift down, but the shift of the *JW* and *IS* will be relatively larger. There are now three cases, depending on whether the surplus equals, is less than or is greater than the initial deficit, $t(Y_B - Y_0)$. If the surplus equals the initial deficit, $|t(Y_B - Y_1)| = |t(Y_B - Y_0)|$, then the downward shifts of both *JW* and *LM* will exactly reflect the initial upward shifts and the original balanced budget equilibrium will be restored in one stroke. If $|t(Y_B - Y_1)| < |t(Y_B - Y_0)|$, then the downward shifts of both will be less than required to restore the initial equilibrium, and at the new intersection there will still be a surplus, but it will be smaller. Hence there will be further shifting (possibly including overshooting) until equilibrium is reached. If $|tY_B - Y_1)| > |t(Y_B - Y_0)|$, then the downward shift will overshoot the balanced budget equilibrium, creating a deficit, but a smaller one than initially existed. Hence there will follow an upward shift of both loci, but smaller than previously, resulting in a smaller surplus, which, in turn, will produce downward shifts to an equilibrium that will yield a deficit, but a smaller one than before. The oscillations will continue back and forth, eventually converging upon the balanced budget equilibrium.[2]

Two points stand out. First, the borrowing or lending consequent upon a deficit or surplus takes time; thus the movement towards or away from balanced budget equilibrium will take place over a substantial stretch of time – certainly not within one 'short period.' This virtually eliminates the possibility of 'short-run equilibrium' or of determinate short-run adjustment processes, since wealth effects will be causing income–expenditure changes all the time. Second, the model is completely arbitrary. If wealth effects on consumption and investment are relatively weak or non-existent the model is radically unstable. If wealth effects on consumption and investment are strong relative to such effects on the demand for money, the model is stable, though it will not adjust within a short period. But there are no intuitive or institutional reasons by which to explain such a conclusion. It rests on nothing but mechanics.

6 THE BASIC ERROR

In fact, no such instability exists; it is a sign that something has gone wrong in the analysis. The error comes in thinking that government borrowing or lending necessarily affects the *stock* equilibrium in the holding of assets. What we actually have is a flow equilibrium between injections and withdrawals. The total finance required will have to cover investment plus the government deficit, if any; the total finance currently available will consist of savings plus the government surplus, if any. For any feasible level of income, in equilibrium, the total finance currently demanded will exactly equal that currently available. Hence moving from one point to another on the *JW* locus (*or*, 'considering the difference,' to stay within the bounds of comparative statics) does *not* require a shift of the *LM* locus.

8 WEALTH AND MONEY

Even if wealth did increase as a result of the sale of bonds to the private sector, it is not clear why this should raise the demand for money. Why should the private sector demand more money just because it has more government bonds? Is it for transactions reasons? Look at it another way: just before the private sector bought the bonds it had the savings on hand with which to buy them; why did portfolio managers not make the optimal division of these savings between money and bonds at the moment of purchase? (Why do they not also demand more money as a result of, or in connection with, their purchases of private bonds?) But why should this optimal division lead to higher cash balances? Surely if the ordinary transactions, precautionary and speculative motives are satisfied, there is no further reason to add to non-yielding balances.

Finally, if the money supply is itself partly endogenous, the *LM* locus will be relatively flat. Let the money supply function be

$$M = M^* + \mu Y + \nu i, \quad \mu, \nu > 0$$

Here M^* is determined by the central bank, μ is the coefficient showing the creation of money in response to aggregate demand (e.g., by shifting funds from time deposits or short-term securities to demand deposits, or by activating previously negotiated lines of credit), and ν is the coefficient showing the creation of money in response to the level of interest rates (e.g., the introduction of new media of circulation). Then

$$i_{LM} = \frac{\bar{m} - \alpha}{\gamma - \nu} + \left(\frac{\mu - \beta}{\gamma - \nu}\right) Y$$

which will have a positive slope if $\beta > \mu$, but will be flatter than the previous *LM* locus (horizontal if $\beta = \mu$). Hence a given government deficit will have a larger effect. If a wealth term is now added to the demand for money, we could argue symmetrically that the endogenous supply of money could also respond to wealth – just as it does to income. As wealth increases, the banking system creates money to fund it. Thus, even if the wealth effects discussed above made sense, and even if they caused a rise in the demand for money, this could be partially or wholly offset by endogenous money creation.

9 CONCLUSIONS

The wealth effects that supposedly result from the government's financing of its deficit make the *IS–LM* equilibrium implausibly unstable. On closer inspection these 'wealth effects' turn out to be based on an arbitrary and invalid conception of wealth. Moreover, it is not clear that a rise in wealth necessarily raises the demand for money, or that, if it did, such an increase could not be offset by an endogenous increase in the money supply. Wealth effects have been the basis of argument that the *IS* cannot shift independently of the *LM*, so that fiscal policy rests on monetary. This is not true. Every link in the anti-fiscalist chain of reasoning is suspect.

Chapters 18 and 19 suggest that the very common Aggregate Demand and Aggregate Supply constructions, featured in much recent research, may be invalid. If, in fact, positions of aggregate demand equilibrium can be unstable, and if wealth effects do not reliably correct such instability, a locus of combinations of aggregate demand and the price level, for which investment equals savings and demand for money equals supply, will not be a viable tool of analysis. If any points on this locus are unstable the economy could not 'move along' such a curve, since the unstable points could not be approached. Nor for the same reason could policy interventions move the system towards desired points on such a curve. This issue will come up again in Chapter 25.

Appendix

The *JW–IS–LM* diagram can be used to examine other policy questions, dropping all reference to wealth effects. Consider a 'supply-side' tax cut, lowering t from t_0 to t_1, first with G constant. According to received supply-side doctrine, this should lead to an increase in savings, lowering interest rates, so raising investment, and expanding income, perhaps enough to generate sufficient new tax revenue to offset the cut in rates and balance the budget. Now, look at Figure 19A.1.

Start from a balanced budget equilibrium. The lower tax rate t_1 swings the *JW* locus out from JW_0 to JW_1. The new intersection with the unchanged *LM* locus therefore occurs at a higher level of income but also at a higher rate of interest. Since JW_1 intersects *IS* at a much lower i and higher Y (compared to JW_0's intersection with *IS*), the new equilibrium involves a substantial government deficit, with a corresponding excess of private saving over investment. Investment is higher, but savings have risen even more. So the supply-side analysis is wrong on three counts; the new interest rate is higher, the government is in deficit, and savings have increased more than investment.

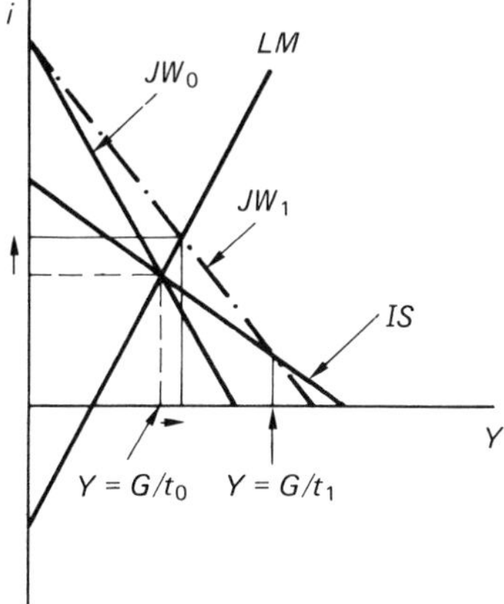

Figure 19A.1

Next, if G were reduced in proportion to the tax cut, the *JW* locus would rotate around the initial (balanced budget) equilibrium point, saying within the angle made by JW_0 and *IS*, and there would be *no* effect on either interest or income.

Notes

1. The government need not lend its surplus by buying new private sector bonds. Instead it could retire old government bonds held in private hands. Either way the funds required by the private sector to finance its investment spending are made available to it.
2. To complete the analysis, the new issuing effects just discussed should be compared with the revaluation of existing government bonds, due to changes in the rate of interest. But this will not change the central point. The outcome will depend on the relative strength of the two effects, which is altogether arbitrary. If the outstanding government debt is small and other conditions are appropriate, the conclusions above hold; otherwise the result may be a convergence back to the initial equilibrium, or a divergent oscillation about it. But whether the system is stable or not does not seem to depend on any plausible economic rationale. In any case it makes little sense to introduce a stable quantity of 'existing government bonds' into a model in which the issuance of those bonds would have provoked violent instability.
3. Perhaps this point about finance can best be seen by separating the multiplier completely from the monetary system. Assume a simplified Kalecki–Robinson system, where I is wholly independent of i; all I is financed by retained earnings, all profits are saved, and all wages consumed. Here the injection-withdrawal condition will be: $G + I = T + P$, where $T = tY$ and $P = Y - wN$. Further, let $I = d + eY$, as in the text. It then follows that $Y = (G + d) / |1 + t - wn - e|$, where $n = N/Y$, and is assumed constant as the level of utilization varies. Under these circumstances, a government deficit will always be exactly matched by the excess of private sector profits over private sector investment (deficits are good for profits), and this will be brought about by the multiplier. Such a *JW* locus would be vertical in (i, Y) space, and would therefore affect the interest rate without being affected by it.

Reference

Blinder, A.S.J. and Solow, R.M. (1973) 'Analytical Foundations of Fiscal Policy' in A.S Blinder *et al.* *Economics of Public Finance* (Washington, DC: Brookings Institution).

20 The Simple Theory of Effective Demand*

Keynes set out to show that orthodox economic theory was flawed. To that end he accepted its postulates and general approach as the starting point for his argument. In particular he accepted marginal productivity theory as an account of the demand for labor, even though his own work in the *Treatise* had already suggested a different theory of distribution. Accepting marginal productivity theory committed Keynes to more than is generally realized, and marks a decisive difference between this model and Kalecki's. It opened the way to the IS–LM interpretation and to the 'neo-Classical synthesis.' Kalecki's approach, by contrast, fits well with mark-up pricing and a realistic notion of market behavior, in both small and large scale industries.

The crucial commitment in the Keynesian approach comes at the very outset. The economic system is pictured as a circular flow of transactions between households and firms. Productive services are sold by households to firms and, with the proceeds, households in their turn purchase goods and services from the firms. Income is paid in exchange for productive services, which are combined to produce goods and services of equivalent value, which are sold back to the households as the income is spent. Obviously, as the flow is circular and continuous, it need be measured only at one point to establish its level for the entire circuit. Thus income is normally expressed as a sum of expenditures, necessarily equal to business receipts, which in turn exactly cover equilibrium factor payments.

But according to an older tradition of economics, and one that Kalecki explicitly drew on in his formulation of the theory of effective demand, income is not paid to factors for productive services. Instead, it is the distribution to social classes of claims to the surplus generated by production, where such claims are expressed in exchange value. The payment of income is not a market process of the same kind as the expenditure of income and its causes and consequences require a separate analysis. The significance of this change comes out very clearly in quite simple models, and at the risk of losing readers who are accustomed to more sophisticated fare, I would like to explore some very elementary problems in macroeconomics from the general standpoint developed by Kalecki and Joan Robinson.[1]

* *Political Economy at the New School* (New York: New School for Social Research, 1977). Warm thanks to Rosemary Rinder for detailed and constructive suggestions which saved me from many mistakes and greatly improved the presentation of the argument.

1 INCOME

One of the striking features of the orthodox 'income–expenditure model' is that it contains no expression at all for income. Output and expenditure are clearly indicated. Output is the product generated by employed labor working with the given stock of fixed plant and equipment, assumed constant in the short run. Output is the sum total of value added. Expenditure is the total for consumer spending, government spending, net exports, and new capital formation, minus transfers and inventory adjustments. Both these notions are represented in orthodox models, usually by the same symbol, Y, which is often called 'income,' but which it is not.

Aggregate income is the sum of payments received for productive services and, in the case of 'unearned income,' as a consequence of property rights. So it will be found by aggregating wages and salaries and the income of unincorporated business, on the one hand, and rents, interest, dividends and undistributed corporate profits, on the other hand. Making suitable adjustments for transfers and for defects in statistics, the result should be two broad categories: income from employment and income from property, each paid out regularly though not at the same rate per unit time as each other. Wages will normally be paid daily or weekly, salaries monthly, and profits quarterly or even yearly. Thus, we should be able to define two variables, W for employment income and P for property income; for simplicity we think of them as "wages" and 'profits.' The total income, Y, will equal $W + P$, and the income so paid out should be equal to the value of output. In general, the types of income aggregated into W will be paid out more frequently and will be adjusted quickly to the rate of sales, as these forms of income represent variable costs to firms. Property income, on the other hand, consists partly of fixed costs, such as debt servicing, and partly of residual income. Fixed costs must be paid at the contractually stated time, anywhere from quarterly to annually, while residual income can only be known for certain upon completion of an audit. So the incomes aggregated into P will not vary so readily with sales, and none of them will be actually paid out in full during the short period.

In short, wage income is available to finance money expenditures and is varied by business with the level of sales. But property income – profits – does not vary so readily, and is not paid out and may very well not even be known during the short run; hence for the purposes of short-run analysis, property income is withheld from the flow of responding. This is not the same as calling it 'retained earnings' or 'business saving,' as these terms are normally understood. For in their usual sense, these terms refer to the final disposition of income. But regardless of that disposition, property income is not available to underwrite or influence spending in the short run.

The point is that wage income and other variable cost spending (purchases by the consumer goods sector of materials and replacements) is directly and immediately connected to spending for consumption goods (and by the consumption goods industries for materials, etc.). So when wage income varies, consumer spending varies *pari passu*. Working class families are assumed to have no other means of financing consumer spending, and are sufficiently needy that they will spend the whole of their income at once. By contrast, capitalist families with income from shares and lands are able, in the short run, to maintain their consumption spending since they possess assets which they can put up as security for loans. Short-run variations in property income will not affect capitalist consumption spending; because of this, and to keep the argument simple, I shall largely ignore capitalist consumption spending in what follows.[2]

These points on consumption and wages are worth summarizing, together with plausible qualifications:

> Consumption is strongly and stably related to wage income. It includes the consumption of wage earners, which amounts on average to the whole of their wages, though this will normally be arranged over the short run to minimize downward adjustments in consumption. It includes also the consumption of capitalists and quasi-capitalists, which probably has some constant rate of growth, not influenced by short-term changes in anything. It can, therefore, practically be disregarded in an analysis of short-run changes in employment, output, and income, although it should be remembered that capitalist consumption has a stabilizing influence on aggregate C, which in general provides a slight cushioning effect against changes in demand for consumption goods caused by a change in W.

The important point is that workers' consumption expenditures – the bulk of total consumption demand – are cut (in practice, of course, as little as possible), when choices of capitalists create cutbacks in employment and income. Thus, consumption responds passively; it is dependent on the spending decisions of capitalists.

Three clear and distinct ideas: income, output and expenditure are often and confusingly represented by a single symbol in orthodox models. The relationships between the three are close but complex, and it will take some care to disentangle them. Most orthodox models clearly separate output from expenditure, even when both are indicated by the same symbol. But they do not represent income at all, which leads to problems in two directions. First, the costs and profits generated by producing output cannot be known until the correct income payments are determined. Second, the pattern of expenditure cannot be settled until the income of the various spending units is determined. So determining income and its distribution is essential in determining economically significant aspects of both output and expenditure. Let us explore these relations more closely.

In the aggregate, real income must equal the value of real output. This is a consequence of the property system. Everything produced must be owned, and the owner of the product – including all positive or negative liabilities incurred during production – is the firm. Hence, the residual earnings of the firm ensure that total income generated will equal the value of the total output produced. This does *not*, of course, ensure that money payments made during the period of production will exactly add up to the value of the product, let alone to the revenue generated by sales during that period. So there are several relationships here to keep clear:

(1) money claims = value of output
(2) money payments = value of output
(3) money payments = revenue from sales
(4) money claims = revenue from sales
(5) value of output = revenue from sales.

Only (1) is necessarily an equality. The total money value of claims against the product necessarily adds up to the value of the product. That is, the costs incurred by the firm for materials, labor, energy, depreciation, etc. are subtracted from the value of the output to give the firms net expected operating profit, and this residual, together with the costs, then constitutes the total of money claims issued, necessarily equal to the value of the product. There is a moral here for price theory, too. The *price* of the product will normally be set so as to generate a net operating profit of a certain size, so that it will stand to the invested capital of the firm in the normal ratio.

Now consider (2). The total money payments issued by the firm will include operating expenses, plus dividends distributed, plus debt servicing; and to make the case as strong as possible, add also the actual corporate retained earnings from the period. But this need not equal the value of the product for the simple reason that everything produced during the period may not have been sold. (According to neo-Classical theory, this should lead to a fall in price, which would increase sales and reduce the value of output. But this would also lead to a revaluation of the entire output, requiring recalculation of the money payments.) Of course, in equilibrium the money payments, including corporate retained earnings, will equal the value of output; but even out of equilibrium when an audit has taken place and inventory value adjustments made, the money value of *claims* must equal the value of output. But money payments actually made during the period, including the banking of retained earnings, need not exactly equal the value of output.

On the other hand, money payments including retained earnings will tend to equal current revenue from sales, (3). For retained earnings, positive or negative, will make up the difference between costs paid out and current revenue. But this is not necessary in the same sense as (1), for costs and dividends could be pegged to the level of current production, determined by expected sales. So if current sales revenue were unexpectedly low, money payments could exceed revenue. Of course, this would require borrowing or running down cash balances, an important qualification. For money payments plus capital adjustments necessarily equal current revenue from sales; adding capital adjustments turns (3) into an accounting identity.

Finally, money claims will equal revenue from sales if and only if all production is sold for the planned price. (Since money claims necessarily equal the value of output, this covers: (5), value of output = revenue from sales.)

So we can say: in equilibrium, these will all hold. Out of equilibrium, however, only (1) and the modified version of (3) hold as accounting identities. Both (1) and (3) are consequences of the property system: (1) depends on the fact that everything produced is owned; (3) depends on the fact that all funds used must have a source. Payments cannot be made unless they can be financed; funds must come from somewhere and if not from sales revenue, then from capital or from borrowing. Thus (1) and (3) illustrate fundamental truths about the economic system.

These truths, however, sit awkwardly with the neo-Classical doctrine that income arises as payment for a productive service. If that were true, all income payments would be costs of production and there would be no room for residual income. But it is precisely the claims to residual income that ensure the truth of (1). In the case of (3), on the one hand, revenue not equal to money payments requires an adjustment of assets, building up or running down capital holdings, to provide a source for the money payments; and on the other hand, revenue arises from spending which in turn must come from a source, either money payments of wages or profits, borrowing, or running down assets. Either way, revenue not equal to money payments requires a change in assets and liabilities, an adjustment of financial holdings, quite apart from any question of productive services or marginal products. The point is that the relation of income payments to the value of output and to the level of expenditure reflects the nature of the property system, the crucial characteristic of which is that capitalist firms own the means of production, giving them title to the entire results of production, while a non-propertied class must work on a contractual basis for wages. The *net* residual claims of the property-owning institutions consist, therefore, of the entire product Y, minus the contractual payments to employees, minus payments for materials and other inputs.

2 OUTPUT AND EMPLOYMENT

Now let us examine a simplified model of production in such a class-based, or exploitative system, where output is constrained in the short run by industrial capacity. The obvious questions then, are: first, how much of the industrial capacity will be used, and secondly, what will be the pattern of income distribution and employment? The questions are easy, but the answers may be harder to understand. In neo-Classical theory we expect to find equilibrium, the resting place of the system or the conclusion of a dynamic process, at the point where the market clears. And if the market does not clear, it will be because imperfections in it have prevented prices from adjusting sufficiently.

But we have just seen that the payment of income is not analogous to the buying and selling of final commodities. Both the payments to labor and those to capital have special features, intrinsic to the capitalist system, which differentiate them from each other and from market transactions for other goods. These features largely center on the employer-employee contract and entail that the system may settle into a stable position, as the result of a dynamic adjustment process, in which there is unemployment and excess capacity yet no prices have a tendency to move, nor need there be any 'market imperfections' of the usual sort.

To understand this, the institutional setting must be clear. To see what is implied, assume a drastically simplified capitalist industrial society. There are two sectors: industry which produces capital goods both for itself and for agriculture, where factory-farms produce consumer goods. Capitalist institutions own all the enterprises in both sectors and loyal managers run them. Capitalist firms own the results of production, which they sell. In order to produce, they hire workers to operate their plant and equipment, paying them wages, which constitute the workers' only source of income, and which workers spend in total on consumer goods.

The wage is at least sufficient to support workers and their families for a given period of time. (If it were insufficient, in the long run the working class would die off or emigrate.) In return, workers do the jobs their employers set for them during the time for which they have contracted. The faster they work, the more raw materials they process into finished goods, and the greater will be the employer's potential profits. But the faster they work the harder the job. Workers will, therefore, resist speed-ups and job reorganization. To maintain work discipline and keep productivity high, employers design equipment to run at the highest speed consistent with safety and accuracy in work, paying workers the minimum premium above subsistence necessary to induce them to accept the resulting working conditions. When sales fall off in the short run the plant cannot be redesigned, so parts will be shut down or run part-time, and workers on various shifts will be laid off until business picks up.

In a capacity constrained system, employment reflects the degree to which capacity is utilized. Demand in excess of capacity cannot be met, nor will it lead to the employment of more labor. Employment as well as output is constrained by capacity. No more men can be employed than there are places on the assembly line; jobs reflect the equipment installed in factories. Jobs will be offered as demand increases up to capacity; workers will be laid off as demand falls below capacity. Output will increase or decrease to meet demand as employment is varied. So there will be a definite functional relationship between employment and output, assuming that the level of output is uniquely correlated with the level of employment, that is, with the degree of capacity utilization, regardless for example of whether utilization reached that level by increasing or decreasing.[3] When employment increases output will increase.

But how fast? Will output always increase in the same proportion when employment increases? Or will output increase more or less than in proportion? There are three possibilities: constant, increasing, and diminishing returns to the utilization of capacity.

Remember, there is no substitution here. Techniques of production, job definitions, organizational structures, plant and equipment, and business location are all fixed. What varies is the degree to which the given production system is *utilized*. The correspondence between the utilization of plant and equipment and the amount of employment depends on the rigidity of job definitions. The precise tasks are specified, together with the sequencing and the pace of work on the assembly line, as well as use of the labor force to clean up the shop, make repairs, and so on.

Utilization functions can be defined for each plant and aggregated to show the correspondence between output and employment for the whole society.[4] What is the shape of the resulting function? Tradition would have it that successive doses of additional labor applied to fixed equipment will bring declining increments of output. But this belief is based on a misunderstanding. The argument for diminishing marginal returns depends on successive doses of employment being applied to *efficiently utilized* equipment. Each time labor was added, the use and perhaps also the nature of the equipment changed; only its amount as capital remained constant. Different levels of employment might be engaged in very different types of labor. Each level of employment, therefore, represented the 'best practice' technique for that amount of labor applied to the *given amount of capital*, which, however, will generally be embodied in very different concrete forms at different points in the function. That such a function cannot be constructed has been demonstrated in the recent 'capital theory' controversies; but this in no way affects the very different concept of a utilization function. However, for the same reason, the traditional arguments for diminishing returns have no weight either. Why should returns diminish when the plant is being run more nearly at the rate for which it was

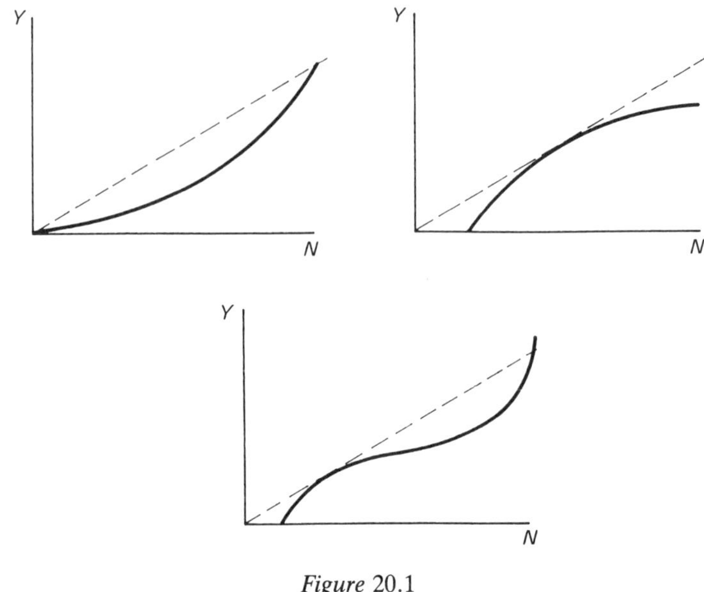

Figure 20.1

designed? Surely one might expect returns to be higher, user cost per unit lower, at the rate of output for which the engineers planned. And this is what some evidence seems to suggest.

But the evidence is not conclusive. The appearance of diminishing or increasing returns could result from different patterns of labor hoarding, by an industrial system which was actually characterized by constant returns. Suppose that near the full employment point industry tended to hoard labor, while at lower levels of employment it became progressively more willing to vary the labor force in proportion to demand. The result would be a curve apparently exhibiting 'increasing returns,' but in fact lying along its whole length below the true constant returns line. (Figure 20.1) In the same way a ready willingness to dismiss workers, at high levels of employment coupled with labor-hoarding as employment falls towards the core of long-term experienced employees, will give rise to an impression of diminishing returns, the curve lying below and to the right of the true constant returns line. The two cases could be combined: labor hoarding could exist near full employment and again at low levels, where experienced long-term workers were threatened. This would yield a plausible function showing first diminishing and then increasing returns, just the reverse of the relationship assumed by conventional theory.

A conventional short-term production function shows alternative positions of fully adjusted equilibrium. Capital is embodied in the best choice technique, labor is organized efficiently, and so on. Hence, the system cannot move from one level of employment to another, for to do so would require reorganizing and perhaps rebuilding the capital stock. By contrast, a utilization function shows alternative levels of employment when a *given* industrial system is run more or less intensively, according to capitalist principles. So there is no difficulty describing movement from one level of activity to another. It is precisely the appropriate concept for analyzing short-run changes in activity.

The argument so far can be summed up concisely as follows:

1. $Y=f(N)$, output varies with the level of employment of labor and capacity. Returns to capacity utilization are probably increasing, perhaps constant, unlikely to be decreasing.

2. $Y=E$, employers adjust output and employment to the point where all output is sold at current prices.

3. $Y=C+I$, definition of sectoral output.

4. $E=W+P$, definition of class-based income streams.

5. $W=C$, a theory of consumption.
6. $\therefore P=I$, deducted from 3, 4, and 5.

It is the capitalist firms who initiate spending, who set investment and so determine the level of output and employment which generates the expenditures which assure that the output will be sold at prices the capitalists set. Observed profits will only roughly equal investment spending over rather long periods of time, especially if the consumption function is modified in the direction of greater realism, and because of the volatility of observed profits, which is greater than that of investment spending. But, the fact that the tautological result, $P = I$, is only approximate, and only holds on average, does not weaken the theoretical point, which is that profits are passive, a result of the active investment decisions which essentially drive the whole economy.

Finally, output consists of sectoral outputs, just as incomes are the incomes of separate classes. We will return to this point later.

3 EFFECTIVE DEMAND

The basic principles of effective demand can be illustrated most easily by concentrating on the constant returns case. First, the functional correspondence between employment and output needs to be explored further. Below a certain level, one would expect output to turn negative, indicating

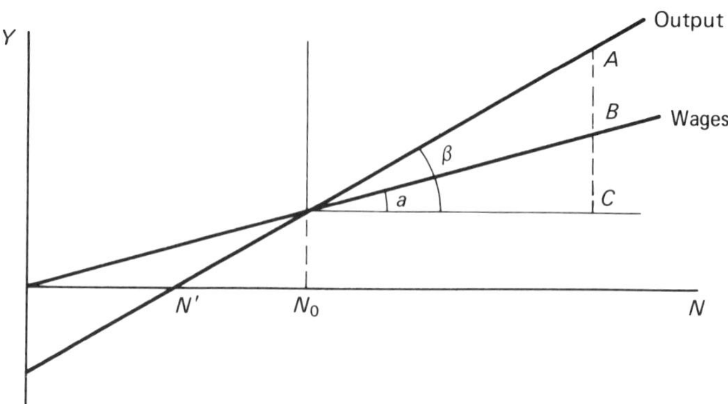

Figure 20.2

that workers use up more in the value of materials, energy, and user cost than they produce. However, this section of the utilization function can be ignored so long as the wage is always positive. For workers will not take employment in a capitalist system unless they are paid wages, which, having no assets to speak of, they must spend at once to support their families. Hence employment generates positive spending on consumption goods which in turn generates further employment. So long as the wage line lies above the output line, employment at such levels would generate demand in excess of output. (Figure 20.2) Conversely, the costs of such employment would exceed the returns from it. Either way, the range of values below N_0 is infeasible. So N_0 becomes the effective origin.

The slope of the wage line is shallower than that of the output line, reflecting the fact that the working force in the factory system as a whole produces more than is needed to sustain and reproduce itself, given the life style of the working class. Thus the ratio between the angles β and *a*, β/*a* or, between the corresponding line segments, *AC*/*BC*, gives the short-run rate of exploitation, or more accurately, the ratio of total output to wage cost, or the markup over wages.

The real wage bill here, as a function of employment, is represented by a straight line, indicating that the real wage rate is constant in the short run for different possible levels of employment. A change in the real wage would thus be shown as a change in the angle ß. Yet surely, according to traditional thinking, if employment is below capacity, the unemployed workers will drive the wage down? But this argument is defective. There is first a practical point. In the competitive areas of the economy business tends to be small scale, with less division of labor and lower mechanization. So the production process tends to depend on skilled and experienced workers and their crews, making it difficult to break into the cycle and fire presently employed workers to replace them by the unemployed at lower money wages. The loss in production and delay during training makes it inefficient. Unemployment will have an effect but not within the short period. In large scale industry, workers are more easily replaced since the division of labor, mechanization and automation have gone further, but so has unionization. In the short run such workers are protected by their union contract. Only in advanced industries with a highly developed division of labor and no unions, the least likely situation to be found in practice, would the emergence of short-run unemployment have a direct and immediate effect on money wages.

There is also a theoretical reason why the emergence of unemployment does not drive money wages down in the short run even when conditions are broadly competitive in a realistic sense. Workers do not set wage rates – employers do. Firms define jobs and announce openings at publicly stated rates of pay, which workers can accept or reject. If a firm cuts its money wage scales below the current market rate it will lose all or part of its labor force, unless all others cut by the same amount or more. But in the absence of collusion, no firm can know that others will also cut. A firm knows only that *its* sales have fallen off; it does not know, reliably, and certainly not at once, how its rivals are doing. And in the case of labor, it has to know not only what its rivals are doing, it has to know how all other markets are doing since workers can take employment in other industries as well. Thus, any given firm will be inhibited in offering lower money wages by uncertainty – the fear that others will not follow suit.[5] (Ch. 17.)

In any case, it is very easy to show changes in the real wage: the slope (angle) of the wage line changes. It is important to remember that this may happen as a result either of changes in money wages or changes in consumption goods prices. In either case the change is likely to be the result of interaction between a number of factors, and so should be derived precisely, rather than assumed. Hence, for the basic analysis, it is best to begin on the assumption of a given real wage, reflecting current prices and the established money wage.

Since capacity, output, and capacity employment are fixed, each can be taken as 100 per cent, and the axes of the diagram (Figure 20.3) showing the functional correlation between employment and output can be measured in percentages. The constant returns diagram will then be a 45° line, and the wage, equal to worker consumption spending, will be given by a ray from the origin lying beneath the 45° line.

Investment *spending* can now be shown. Investment *decisions* are taken by firms in the light of their long-run prospects – for new markets, developing new products, in the anticipation of growth of demand in existing markets, moving their present products into new regions or classes of the population, or in the case of capital goods, persuading new categories of business to adopt improved or new capital equipment. But current investment spending depends upon how rapidly businesses feel they should implement, carry through or complete the projects they have decided

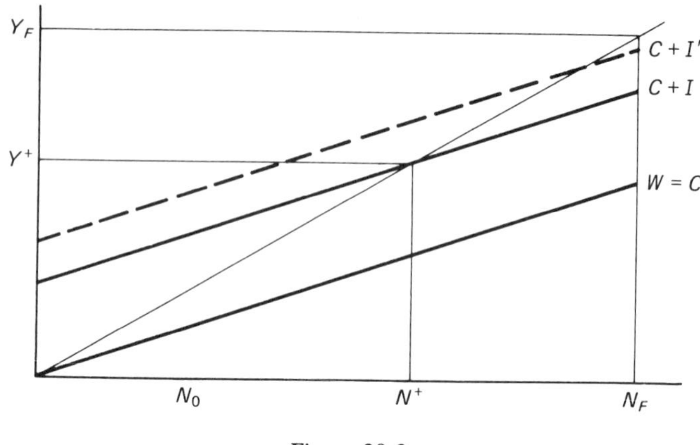

Figure 20.3

upon. It is a matter of timing; they have decided what to do, now the question is how fast to complete it. This will depend partly upon their ability to finance investment spending, and partly upon their confidence that the time is now ripe to bring these projects into operation. For our purposes, however, it will be best to leave the determinants of investment spending to one side, so as to concentrate attention on its effects. Assume for simplicity then, that investment spending is determined independently of the current level of employment and output. Aggregate demand will then be the sum of investment spending plus consumption spending (neglecting government spending and consumption by the capitalist class at this time). The intersection of aggregate demand and the employment utilization function then gives the short-run equilibrium output and employment as percentages of capacity output and employment. Equilibrium output is Y^+, and W^+ is the corresponding total wage bill. The difference, $Y^+ - W^+$, then, is profit, P; so the division of the vertical line rising from N^+ to the 45° line gives the distribution of income between wages and profits, and also between consumption and investment. Notice that this diagram cannot deal with changes in productivity. Henceforth, output and employment will be measured in natural units. Other things being equal, then, the lower is the productivity of labor, the higher will be the level of employment, for a given real wage and level of investment.

Consider an upward shift in investment (the dotted line $C+I'$). Employment and output both increase, by a multiple of the increase in investment. Profits increase by the exact amount of the additional investment. This follows tautologically from the definitions $Y=W+P$, $E=C+I$; the equilibrium condition $Y=E$; and the assumption $W=C$. But there is more than mere tautology behind this. 'Workers spend what they get; capitalists get what they spend.' The point of this aphorism is that the direction of causality is different in the wage-consumption and profit-investment relationships. Wages are the source of consumption spending; workers have no income-yielding assets, so cannot sustain a spending stream unless they receive wage income. By contrast, capitalists, owning the means of production, are in a position to initiate spending, which then generates the profits to underwrite it. The multiplier depends exclusively on the slope of the real wage line; it is the reciprocal of the complement of the wage rate, $\frac{1}{1-w}$. The aggregate 'propensity to consume,' based on psychology, has nothing to do with it. Profits are retained in the short run, and used for finance. Wages on the whole, are spent. The multiplier reflects the real wage and the characteristics of the property system in this simplified model.

Suppose, for some reason, business offered a level of employment different from the equilibrium. Can we say, on the basis of this analysis, what would happen? In orthodox theory, dynamics is notoriously tricky, requiring special assumptions, which often prove difficult to justify, about the pattern of market adjustment to disequilibrium. But here no special assumptions are necessary. All that is necessary for a rudimentary dynamic analysis has already been incorporated into the concept of the utilization function. Employers adjust their current production to their current sales, keeping inventory stocks constant.[6] If the employment offered is below equilibrium, say at N_1, then the aggregate demand, $C_1 + I$, will be greater than Y_1, the output corresponding to N_1. Inventory will be run down, and additional plant and equipment, idle initially, will be brought into operation, leading to the employment of more workers. Employment will rise to N_2, but at this level of employment the wage bill, and so consumption spending, is now greater. Hence, aggregate demand now equals $C_2 + I > Y_2$. Again, inventory will be run down and more idle plant and equipment will be brought into operation, with employment rising to N_3 and aggregate demand to $C_3 + I > Y_3$, and so on until the equilibrium point is reached. Starting from an increment of investment, the resulting change in output is given by summing the series of the rounds of respending. The first term is given by the wage times the amount of additional employment, caused by the increase in investment; the second term by the wage times the first term, and so on. Hence, the additional consumption each time is the fraction of investment spending that goes to wages, which will be the wage rate times the amount of employment generated by the investment spending. Employment per unit output, $n=\frac{\Delta N}{\Delta Y}$, is reciprocal of the productivity of labor, the slope of $Y=f(N)$. So, the multiplier series is,[7]

$$\frac{\Delta Y}{\Delta I} = 1 + wn + (wn)^2 + \ldots = \frac{1}{1-wn}$$

$$\frac{\Delta N}{\Delta I} = n(1 + wn + (wn)^2 + \ldots) = \frac{n}{1-wn}$$

In the case where $n=1$, because employment and output are both measured as percentages of capacity levels, this becomes $\frac{1}{1 - w}$.

Notice that the effects of the multiplier are concentrated in the consumer goods sector after the initial round of spending. It is there that employment and output increase.

At this point it is evident that it will not do to treat the economy as if it consisted of 'one sector' only. Investment demand and consumption demand are directed to different parts of the economy and need to be treated separately. Accordingly, the preceding account of the multiplier needs to be restated. Define:

n_I as the labor coefficient in investment goods

n_c as the labor coefficient in consumption goods

w as the real wage, assumed to be wholly spent

u as the ratio $\frac{w - z}{w} > 0$, where z is the level of spending which can be sustained by an unemployed worker, financed by borrowing and the Welfare State

a as the coefficient of replacement demand by the consumer goods sector for investment goods.

Let $x = uwn_c$
$y = uwn_I$

Then when effective demand varies due to a change in investment, ΔI:

$$\Delta C_1 = y\Delta I$$

$$\Delta C_2 = xy\Delta I + ay^2\Delta I = (x + ay)y\Delta I$$

$$\vdots$$

$$\Delta C_n = (x + ay)^{n-1}y\Delta I.$$

So the series will be:

$$y\Delta I\,[1 + (x + ay) + (x + ay)^2 + \ldots]$$

which gives,

$$\text{multiplier} = \frac{\Delta C}{\Delta I} = \frac{y}{1 - (x + ay)} = \frac{uwn_I}{1 - uw(n_c + an_I)}.$$

This formula shows sectoral coefficients explicitly together with the intersectoral relationship. The principal impact will take place in the consumer goods sector; the effect on employment in investment goods will be secondary. It also shows the effect of welfare and unemployment compensation. The higher z is, the lower will be u and so the lower the multiplier. This is intuitively obvious; the change in spending as a result of moving from employed to unemployed, or vice versa is not so great.[8]

Now suppose $z = 0$. Rewrite the formula and cross-multiply. We have:

$$wn_I\Delta I = [(1 - w(n_C + an_I)]\Delta C.$$

The left hand side is the additional consumption goods demand resulting from additional employment in the investment goods sector; the right hand side is the additional sales of consumer goods, *minus* the additional sales of consumer goods to workers in the consumer goods sector itself, *minus* the additional sales of consumer goods to workers newly employed in investment goods to produce additional replacements for consumer goods. In short, the equation reads:

> the extra demand for consumer goods by investment goods workers = the extra supply of consumer goods (over and above the costs in consumer goods of producing this supply).

This is, therefore, a dynamic and more complex form of the famous Marxian 'balancing condition' for expanded reproduction (Marx, 1967).

In this formulation (as in the simpler version above) the multiplier no longer depends on anyone's 'psychological propensity' to consume.[9] The multiplier here is based upon structural and institutional features of capitalism. It depends first and foremost on the level of real wages, which reflects the division of income between pay and profits, or, more generally, between *variable costs* and the *mark up*. It further depends on the labor coefficients in the sectors and on the degree of technical dependence between them, and finally, upon the welfare policy of the State. Of course, if workers save a portion of their income this can easily be taken into account; workers will simply spend a fraction of their wage, rather than the whole of it. A more serious modification may be required to take into account the fact that it takes households time to adjust their spending habits when real wages change. But this would take the argument out of the realm of simple models.

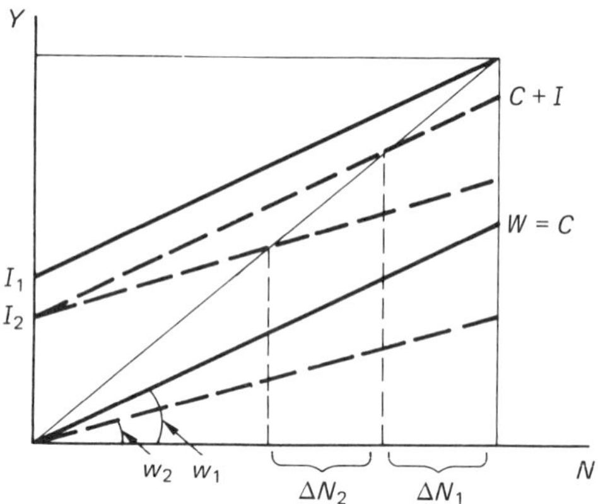

Figure 20.4

It has already been argued that there are good reasons for supposing both money wages and prices to be unresponsive in many circumstances to short-run changes in the degree of utilization. However, there certainly are plausible conditions in which changes in utilization would be accompanied by either price or money wage changes or both. Such changes can easily be incorporated in the analysis. Consider a decline in investment spending, causing unemployment. Suppose that producers have a tacit agreement not to 'spoil the market,' so that prices fall very little, but the labor market is highly competitive and the division of labor has proceeded far enough that workers are easily interchangeable appendages to the assembly line. So wages will fall while prices stay steady, or decline more slowly. To keep the argument simple, look at the 45° diagram in Figure 20.4. Initially investment was sufficient at I_1 to provide full capacity employment. It then shifts down to I_2 generating unemployment ΔN_1. This leads to a fall in the wage rate, a change in the slope of the wage line, from w_1 to w_2, lowering the wage bill, and creating additional unemployment ΔN_2, entirely concentrated in the consumer goods sector.

These two processes will take place together. The decline in investment spending will create initial unemployment, which will then lower the money wage (and so the real wage) a certain amount; these two effects will together lower spending on consumer goods, creating more unemployment which will then further lower the money wage; the two effects then causing a further reduction in consumer spending, and so on.

Formally (using the simpler version of the multiplier), $\Delta Y_1 = w_1\Delta N + N_1\Delta w + \Delta w\Delta N$ (ignoring the last term) $= w_1 n\Delta I + N_1 xn\Delta I = (w_1 + xN_1)n\Delta I$, where w_1, N_1 is the initial wage-employment position, n is the (aggregate 'one-sector') labor coefficient, and x is the fraction by which the wage changes when employment changes, assumed to be constant through the process and to be the same for increases and decreases. So $\Delta w = x\Delta N = xn\Delta I$,

$$\Delta Y_2 = [w_1 - \Delta w) + x(N_1 - \Delta N)]\ (w_1 + xN_1)n^2\Delta I$$

$$\Delta Y_3 = [(w_1 - 2\Delta w) + x(N_1 - 2\Delta N)]\ [(w_1 - \Delta w) + x(N_1 - \Delta N)]\ (w_1 + xN_1)n^2\Delta I;$$

and

$$\begin{aligned} \Delta Y_k &= [(w_1 - (k-1)\ \Delta w) + x(N_1 - (k-1)\Delta N)]n\Delta Y_k - 1 \\ &= [w_1 - (k-1)xn\Delta I + x(N_1 - (k-1)n\Delta I]n\Delta Y_k - 1 \\ &= [(w_1 - xN_1) - (k-1)(1+x)n\Delta I]n\Delta Y_k - 1. \end{aligned}$$

By taking k sufficiently large, the last term in brackets can be made zero; hence $\Delta Y_k = 0$. The series is therefore a finite sum of $(k - 1)$ positive terms.

If cut-throat competition caused prices to fall, while money wages remained sticky in the short run, then the real wage would *rise* when investment demand fell. Such a rise would dampen, or, in the extreme case, reverse the effects of the decline in investment spending on employment and output. (See Ch. 16.)

And this brings out a very important proposition: a rise or fall in the real wage brings about a corresponding rise or fall in the level of employment in the consumer goods sector, together with a secondary effect (through the coefficient, a) on employment in investment goods. In the theory of effective demand, employment and the real wage vary together.[10]

This means that existing unemployment (at least in consumer goods) can always be eliminated by a large enough increase in the real wage. Suppose present investment is too low to generate full capacity employment, yielding instead employment, N_0. (Figure 20.5) Draw a line, *IF*, from the investment intercept on the Y axis to the full employment point F. Then the real wage required for full capacity employment is the wage line parallel to the dotted line *IF*.

Another way to put the same point: the level of investment necessary to produce full capacity employment is a unique and inverse function of the real wage. Given a factory system with a fixed capacity, the higher the real wage, the lower the level of investment and government spending needed for full capacity performance.

A qualification is necessary, however. The increased employment $N_F - N_0$, will chiefly take place in the consumer goods sector, with a secondary effect in investment goods due to increased demand for

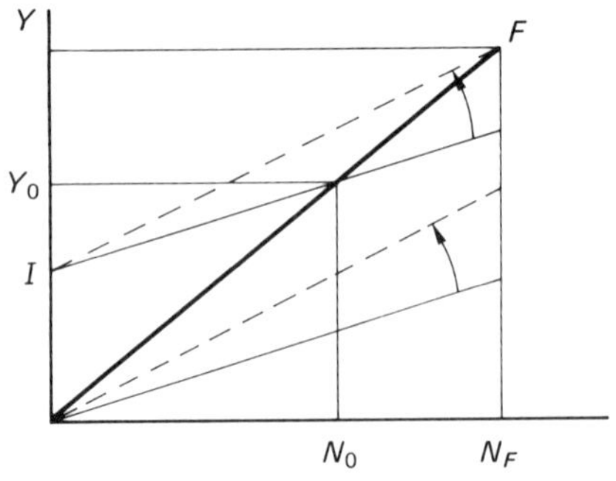

Figure 20.5

replacements of worn out consumer goods equipment. This secondary effect may not be very large, so the higher real wage can assure full capacity employment only in the consumer goods sector.

Notice, however, that the profits of capitalists are the same absolute amount at both levels of employment, N_0 and N_F. Since the capital stock is given, whether used or not, both yield the same average rate on invested capital. Profit is determined by investment spending (plus exports, government deficit spending, and capitalist consumption, all neglected here) not by the level of the real wage. In the short term, changes in the real wage have no effect at all on realized profits.[11]

The argument can be developed a step further by dropping the convention of measuring output and employment as percentages of capacity. Measure them instead in money value and manhours. Then for given levels of investment and real wages, the lower the productivity of labor, the higher will be the level of employment. On the diagram, (Figure 20.6), the dotted line shows a lower level of productivity, with the corresponding high level of employment, *ceteris paribus*. Employers will not employ more workers than they need to produce the output they can sell. So the interests of workers and employers are clearly opposed, since employers will not wish to pay high wages on long run and on competitive grounds. (What is true for the aggregate need not hold for the individual taken separately.) The interests of the workers and employers are clearly opposed in the short run.

Assume that technical progress increases the effective capacity of existing plan and equipment. Suppose that such 'disembodied' improvements raise the output-employment function from $Y_1(N)$ to $Y_2(N)$, (Figure 20.7), and that the wage rate rises in the same proportion, so the wage line swings up from W_1 to W_2. Suppose further that there is no lag in the spending of the additional wage income, and that investment spending remains constant at the level planned for the period. Then total expenditure will rise from E_1 to E_2. The new aggregate demand line, IE_2, will therefore be

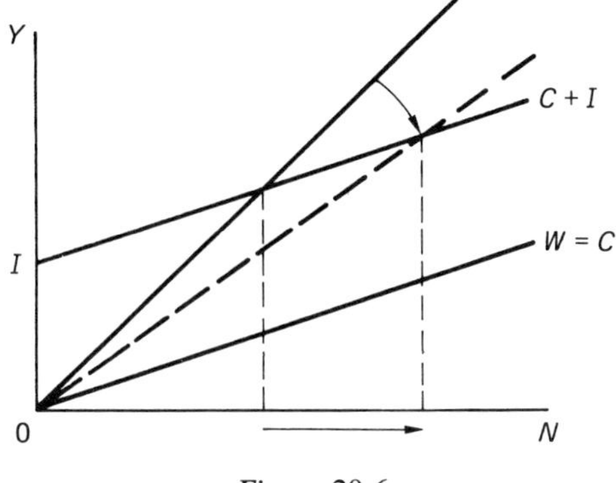

Figure 20.6

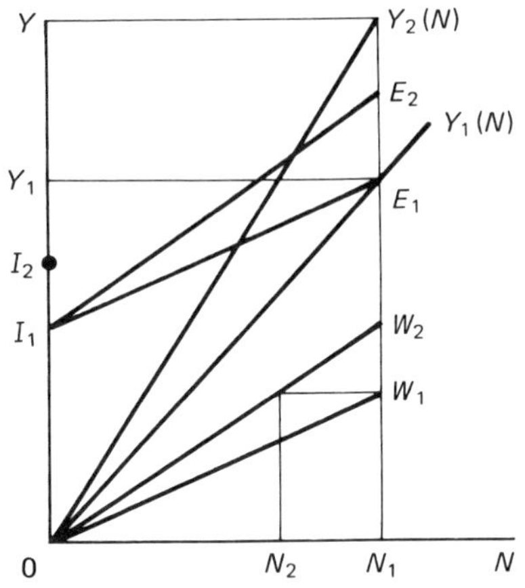

Figure 20.7

parallel to the new wage line OW_2. But for employment to remain constant at N_1, the aggregate demand line would have to intersect $Y_2(N)$ at the point where that line cuts a vertical line rising from N_1. Such an IE line starting at I_1 would not be parallel to OW_2. If investment rose to I_2, increasing in the same proportion as both wages and productivity, then I_2E_2 would be parallel, and employment would remain at N_1. But if investment remains as planned, employment, N_2, must lie below N_1. Now consider equilibrium output, originally at Y_1. With I constant at I_1, aggregate demand equals $I_1 + C_2$, where $C_2 = W_2N_2$. But the wage rate (and so consumption per head) rises in the same proportion that labor required per unit of output falls. Hence $W_2N_2 = W_1N_1$, and $C_2 = C_1$. Consequently total output is unchanged.[12]

Thus technical progress with the wage rising at the same rate as total productivity reduces employment, but leaves total output unaffected,

$N_2 < N_1$, $Y_2 = Y_1$. The idea that raising wages *pari passu* with productivity is somehow 'neutral' or 'fair' will not stand inspection.

It is important to remember two caveats: first, that the propositions demonstrated here, with the exception of those concerning the multiplier, are all *comparative static*. Secondly, I am neglecting the important relationships between finance and investment spending, and between aggregate spending and finance. So, investment spending is taken as exogenous; and when the text speaks, e.g., of 'the increase in productivity' or of a 'rise in real wages,' this should be understood not as an actual change in historical time, but as a comparison between two equilibrium positions, in one of which productivity or wages is higher, with everything else the same.)

4 MARGINAL PRODUCTIVITY

In short, the theory of effective demand is a theory of employment in the short run. But neo-Classical theory is committed to the theory of marginal productivity, according to which an increase in employment can come about only if the real wage *declines*. And Keynes explicitly adopted this position in *The General Theory*:

> in general, an increase in employment can only occur to the accompaniment of a decline in the rate of real wages. Thus I am not disputing the vital fact which the classical economists have (rightly) asserted as indefeasible. In a given state of organisation, equipment and technique, the real wage earned by a unit of labor has a unique (inverse) correlation with the volume of employment. Thus, *if* employment increases, then, in the short period, the reward per unit of labour in terms of wage-goods must, in general, decline and profits increase. This is simply the obverse of the familiar proposition that industry is normally working subject to decreasing returns in the short period during which equipment etc. is assumed to be constant (1936, p. 17).

Keynes could hardly have been clearer. He accepts the whole of marginal productivity theory – short period decreasing returns, the real wage equal to the marginal product, and any increase in employment implies a decline in the real wage. However, he does say that, 'equipment etc. is assumed to be constant.' But if factories and their equipment are given, then we are considering the question of utilization, and there is no reason to suppose that returns diminish. So long as labor's marginal product is *greater* than the real wage, it will pay business to employ labor in *proportion to the demand for goods*, up to capacity. The question then arises, are there no forces acting to equate the real wage and the marginal product?

In the true neo-Classical case, the short period is defined by the amount

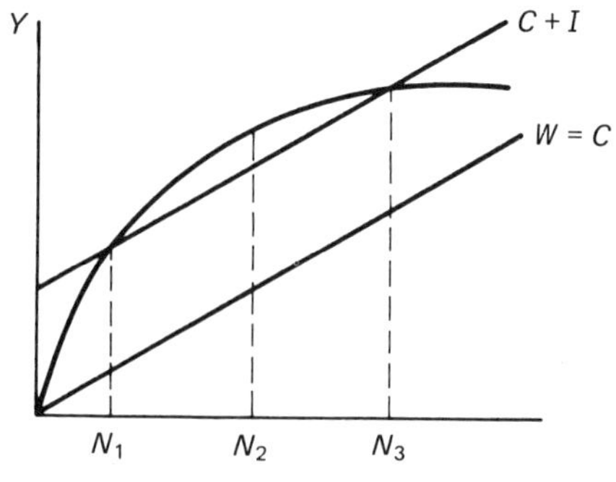

Figure 20.8

of capital, which remains constant. Every point on the production function is efficient; labor and capital are combined in the technically optimal manner. Hence each point represents a complete adaptation of the capital equipment; each point has its own unique history. In this case the neo-Classical supply and demand curves for labor can be used to define 'full employment,' and 'involuntary unemployment' will then exist only when labor is 'off' its supply curve. But such a conception is wholly unsuitable for analyzing short-run changes in employment. Moreover this is precisely the conception of the production function which the capital theory controversy has shown to be in general untenable.[13] Short-run changes in employment must be analyzed in terms of changes in capacity utilization.

First there is the question of the shape of the utilization function. If returns are constant or increasing then it is impossible for the real wage to equal the marginal product of labor. Employers will hire labor so long as the real wage is less than or equal to the marginal product, but if additional employment increases the marginal product or leaves it unaffected, there will be no tendency for the two to be equated. Diminishing returns to factory utilization is therefore the only case consistent with orthodoxy; though perhaps the least plausible empirically.

Even this implausible case gives unacceptable results. Suppose the real wage is given, as above, and that a certain amount of investment spending is scheduled. Suppose that this gives an effective demand that cuts the employment function in two places as drawn, (Figure 20.8). At the lower point, N_1, the real wage is less than the marginal product, at N_2 they are equal, and at N_3, the real wage is greater than the marginal product. N_2 should therefore be the profit maximizing point, and it is indeed the point at which potential profits, output minus wage costs, are the greatest. But realized profit is equal to investment, and so will be the same at all these levels of employment, at N_2, however, or anywhere between N_1 and N_3, there will be unsold output; only at N_1 and N_3 are output and expenditure just balanced. But there is a significant difference between the two points:

just below N_1 demand is greater than output, while just above it output exceeds demand. So if employment is near N_1, business will be motivated to raise or lower it in the direction of N_1. By contrast, if employment is just below N_3 output is greater than demand, leading business to lay workers off; just above N_3 demand exceeds output, leading to further expansion, and a still wider discrepancy. In short, N_1 is a stable equilibrium point, and N_3 is unstable. N_2 maximizes unsold output.

This is the true – and only – significance of the marginal productivity doctrine in this case. At a level of employment where the real wage is less than the marginal product, the corresponding aggregate effective demand function will intersect the output curve in a stable point, when the real wage is greater than the marginal product, the point of intersection will be unstable. This follows very simply from the fact that as long as investment spending is autonomous, the slope of the effective demand function is given by the real wage. Hence when the real wage is less than the marginal product, the demand function cuts the output curve from above – and the point is stable.

In its microeconomic form, marginal productivity is a theory of employment; employers face a given wage and hire workers until their marginal product declines to the level of the wage. But here, given the level of investment, and given that employment will be adjusted until output equals demand, for the theorem to hold the real wage would have to adjust to the profit maximizing marginal product. When there are diminishing returns to utilization, given any level of investment there is always a real wage such that the effective demand line will just be tangent to the output curve. (For each level of investment, e.g., I_1, measured on the vertical axis, Figure 20.10, one and only one line can be drawn tangent to the curve, given the latter's convexity and continuity. The required real wage, w_1, will then be the ray from the origin parallel to the tangent line.) Given any real wage, e.g., w_2, there is always a level of investment, I_2, such that the effective demand line will be just tangent to the output curve. But there do not seem to be any economically plausible pressures that would tend reliably to move either the real wage or investment to the level corresponding to the tangency position.[14] If the wage were less than the marginal product it would have to rise, even though unemployment existed. Alternatively, investment would have to rise, even though there existed unused capacity. Nevertheless, suppose that investment spending were increased just enough so that the effective demand line became tangent to the output curve at N_2, on Figure 20.8. The real wage would then exactly equal the short-run marginal (utilization) product. Now consider some simple dynamics. At levels of employment just below N_2, demand > output, so employment will move towards N_2; but at levels of employment just above N_2, demand will also be greater than output, leading inventories to run down, inducing business to hire more to meet

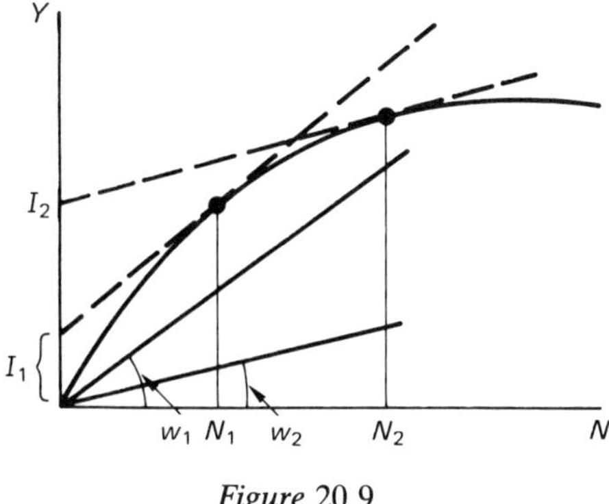

Figure 20.9

the demand. The fact that output in the aggregate does not keep pace does not reduce profits, which remain equal to investment. Inventories, however, are run down increasingly, until output hits capacity. At that point, output can no longer be increased further, and demand (plus the demand by business to restore inventory) pushes up prices. This reduces the real wage, until the effective demand line has swung down until it just meets the output curve at full capacity (Figure 20.9).

At this point, the factory system is fully utilized and no more labor can be hired; there are no places on the assembly line. So, given investment spending, demand cannot increase further. But if for any reason, employment should temporarily fall below the capacity level, output will then be greater than aggregate demand, leading to overstocking and inducing business to lay workers off. The consequent reduction in worker spending will reduce demand more than the layoffs will reduce output, and the recessionary gap will first grow, and then diminish as employment is progressively reduced, finally reaching stable equilibrium at the comparatively low level N_0, below the level at which the wage equals the short-run marginal product. (Figure 20.10).

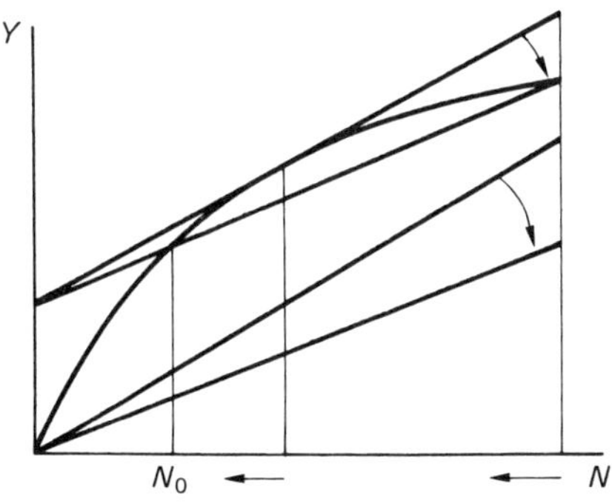

Figure 20.10

The theory of effective demand, then, is a theory of employment of labor in the short period, where labor is employed to operate equipment of fixed capacity, and to produce an output adjusted (with allowance of maintaining inventory) to the current level of demand.

But although this is a theory of employment and of aggregate output, in Keynes' sense, far from being opposed to the theory of distribution (as Keynes thought it had to be) it is at the same time a theory of distribution. Investment (and related kinds of spending) determines profits, while wages determine consumption. At capacity, excess effective demand will cause prices to rise relative to money wage rates until profits generate the appropriate savings to offset investment. It is a short-run, and over-simplified theory, but it establishes the connections between effective demand and the distribution of realized income at a very general level. It allows us to see the error in the orthodox theory quite plainly: orthodoxy assumes that employment will settle at the point where the difference between output and wage cost is at a maximum, regardless of whether the resulting product can be sold. The assumption is plain: whatever is produced will be sold because supply creates its own sufficient demand. By contrast the theory of effective demand determines employment at the level where output will be exactly matched by demand.

In this light the argument seems simple and obvious, yet it runs counter to almost all the conventional wisdom of both monetarists and Keynesians. The theory of effective demand really supports neither side of the current dispute between the two branches of orthodoxy although it is unquestionably closer to the Keynesians. But, it does show quite clearly why neither can present an adequate account of their relationships between inflation and unemployment: both sides start their analysis by assuming marginal productivity theory.

5 WEALTH EFFECTS

The orthodox reply will be that everything presented so far depends on 'sticky' money wages and prices, i.e., on market imperfections. With fully flexible money wages and prices, the emergence of a shortage of effective demand would lead to an equi-proportional fall in both, resulting in a higher real value of cash balances. This improvement in household and business wealth positions would entail higher spending, overcoming the demand shortfall. Strictly speaking, the argument is a comparative static one; it states that there always exists a low enough level of prices and money wages to raise the value of cash balances enough to provide a full employment level of spending. (It is generally agreed that even if money wages and prices were flexible downward, no dynamic argument could be made, since declining wages and prices are likely to set up adverse expectations.)

Consider an economy with given plant and equipment, financed by some given pattern of borrowing. (Orthodox theorists often assume for simplicity that all capital is raised by selling bonds.) Given expected money outlays and revenues and the requirements of debt servicing, businesses and households will hold certain nominal cash balances. Now suppose that the level of consumption and investment is insufficient to employ the economy's full capacity at the initial level of money wages and prices. Suppose money wages and prices were lower, but that everything else – the real wage, plant and equipment, debt structure, and nominal cash holdings – remained the same. Could we expect a higher level of spending?

(It cannot be argued that because the nominal value of plant and equipment is lower, the nominal amount of debt will also be lower; because, then, by the same token, nominal cash balances would also be less. Holding cash is an alternative to paying off debt; if the one is fully adjusted, the other must be also.)

The orthodox answer is that the higher real value of cash balances, making households and businesses wealthier, will cause the psychological propensities to consume and invest to shift upwards. The increased wealth does not yield an increased flow of purchasing power; it merely stimulates economic agents to spend more out of their existing and unchanged flows of income.

Two problems spring to mind at once. Since the present model assumes that all wage income is spent and that only wage earners consume, there is no room for the 'wealth effect' in consumption. Room could be made by allowing worker saving or introducing a salaried and parsimonious middle class, but this just pushes the problem back a step. What happens when the 'wealth effect' has done its work, stimulating consumption until saving disappears, and still $C + I <$ full capacity output?

The second obvious point concerns installment buying and resale value. Plant and equipment, houses, automobiles, and many consumer durables are commonly financed by vendor's mortgages. An important component in the decision to buy is the expected resale or second-hand value, at the end of a certain period, with which the tail end of the mortgage will be retired. Lower money prices will affect this calculation, and would require a curtailment of current spending.

But the chief defect in the doctrine of the 'wealth effect' is that it ignores the increase in the real burden of debt. When money wages and prices both decline, so does the absolute size of gross profits. This can create problems in debt servicing, and lead to insolvency; if it goes far enough, it will reduce gross profit below the level of interest plus principal. Instead of deflation leading to expansion, deflation leads to bankruptcy, which, in practice, of course, it always has. (If cash balances are run down to meet the demands of debt servicing, bankruptcy may be avoided – *this* period! – but all possibility of expansionary stimulus is gone.)

So the orthodox position *has* to be that the burden of indebtedness can be reduced by rolling over the original bonds at a new, *lower* rate of interest. The rate of interest will be lower because the transactions demand for money is lower, owing to the lower level of wages and prices. In rolling over the debt, the volume of new bonds demanded will be exactly the same as the old bonds being retired, hence the operation, skillfully managed, finances itself and should have no effect on interest rates.

The trouble is obvious as soon as one looks at the deal with the eyes of a banker. A firm has machinery and plant initially worth $\$x$ and mortgaged for that amount. Prices have fallen, however, and the new value is $\$x/y$; where $y > 1$. It wishes to pay this mortgage off now, by issuing bonds or borrowing $\$x$ at a lower rate. But the security it has to offer for this new loan is now worth only $\$x/y$. Why should a bank or any sensible financier lend against such inadequate security? The only possible justfication for lending against inadequate security is that the rate of interest offered is high enough to warrant the risk. But the orthodox position requires that the new rate of interest be *lower*, even though the risk is manifestly greater!

Flexible money wages and prices provide no escape from the conclusions of the theory of effective demand.

6 SECTORS

Enough has been said already to show the importance of separating the economy into sectors, and it is time to develop this explicitly. First we will exhibit a position of long-run equilibrium, in which the wage rate and the rate of profit are equal in both sectors at full capacity. Employment in each sector, N_1 and N_c (Figure 20.11) is measured in manpower along the horizontal axis from the origin to the right; capital invested for each sector, K_1 and K_c is measured in money value from the origin to the left along the same axis. The vertical axis reading upward in each case measures output in money value, Y_1 and Y_c, and reading down from the origin it measures capital again.

The sectors are drawn with consumer goods assumed labor intensive and capital goods capital intensive. The slopes of the lines $K_I - Y_I$ and $K_c - Y_c$ give the respective output–capital ratios, those of the lines $K_I - N_I$ and $K_c - N_c$ the capital-labor ratios, and those of $O_I - F_I$ and $O_c - F_c$ are the labor productivities. Angles $W_IO_IN_I$ and $W_cO_cN_c$ represent the wage rates, equal in both sectors, and angles $P_IK_IO_I$ and $P_cK_cO_c$ are the profit rates, also equal. Lines F_IP_I and W_IO_I are parallel, as are F_cP_c and W_cO_c. Hence, O_IP_I and O_cP_c are the respective amounts of profit in the sectors. If all, and only, this profit is invested then the two sectors will grow uniformly.

The balance between the sectors is shown by line W_IP_c, which expresses

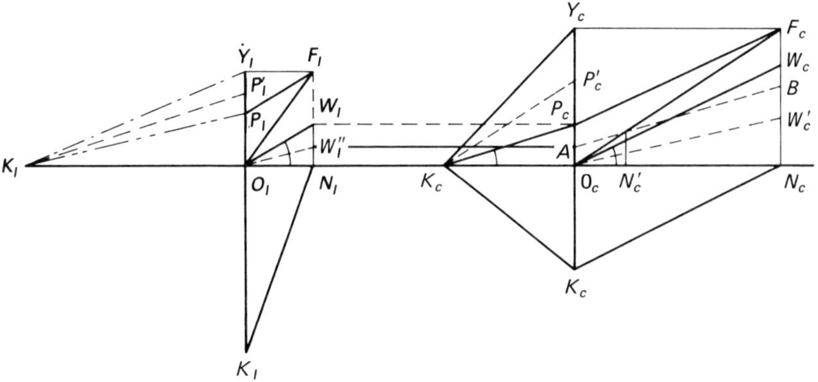

Figure 20.11

the fact that profit in the consumer goods sector equals the wage bill in investment goods.

To see the connection of this with long-run pricing, consider what happens if the real wage were to settle at a level equal to half the value shown. The new *potential* rates of profit at full capacity operation in both sectors are shown by the slopes of the dotted lines $K_IP'_I$ and $K_cP'_c$; clearly the fall in the real wage raises the potential rate of profit in the labor-intensive sector above that in the capital-intensive one. What is required, as is well known from Ricardo, Marx, and Sraffa (1960) is a higher relative price of capital to consumer goods, lowering the potential rate of profit in consumer goods and raising it in capital goods. But if we look at this in terms of monetary magnitudes in the short run, it is not at all clear how this might come about. If the investment goods sector operates at full capacity, its wage bill will now be W'_I; hence, profits in consumer goods will be O_cA, and the line AB will give the total demand for consumer goods. This intersects the output–employment line, O_cF_c, at a level of employment, $N'_c<N_c$. There will, therefore, be unemployment and excess capacity in consumer goods and the *realized* rate of profit will be shown by line K_cA, less in slope than K_cP_c, and far less than $K_cP'_c$. The price of consumer goods and/or money wage rates may fall, liquid capital may shift, investment spending may fall off, and investment plans may alter. These questions are beyond the scope of this paper. The point is that with given plant and equipment and differing sectorial capital–labor ratios, a change in the real wage both renders the potential profit rates at full capacity unequal and also undoes the short-run sectoral balance. The restoration of full equilibrium requires that both conditions be corrected.

(We could show the relative price ratio explicitly. Measure real output on both vertical axes, and leave out the capital stocks. Include the price vector, rising to the left from the consumer sector origin, with the horizon-

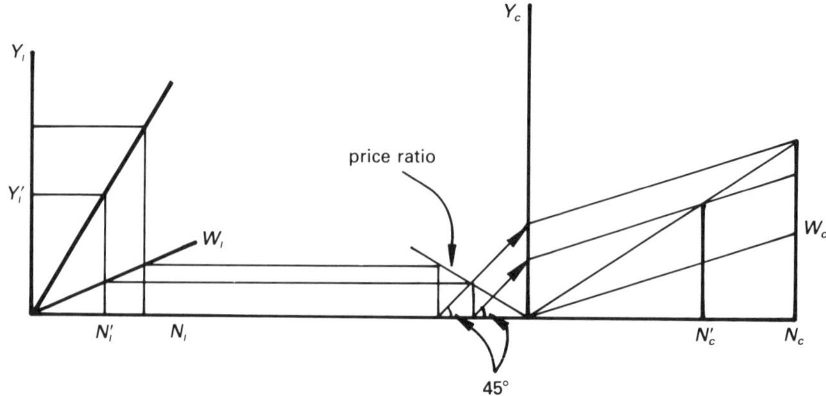

Figure 20.12

tal axis showing consumer good output to the left (and employment to the right, as before.) The investment sector wage bill is a quantity of capital goods; mapping this on to the price vector gives us the equivalent quantity of consumer goods, which a 45-degree line transfers to the vertical axis of the consumer sector diagram. Fig. 20.12.)

Here, however, our concern is with the short run. Putting aside the problems of prices, unequal rates of profit, etc., consider the relations between the sectors in terms of effective demand, using the core of the same diagram (Figure 20.12).

The discussion which follows concerns comparisons of equilibrium positions before and after changes in the value of some variable or variables, in spite of the fact that the language may appear to refer to movements in variables. To study movements – dynamics – we would have to take into account the effects of movements upon expectations, etc., and derive the explicit time paths of the variables, an enterprise beyond the scope of this study.

Initially gross investment demand is at capacity and with the given real wage, employment in consumer goods is N_c and output Y_c, both also at capacity. Now let investment demand shift down to Y_1', so that equilibrium employment falls from N_1 to N_1'. This reduces the wage bill in investment goods from W_1 to W_1', and consequently lowers profit, output, and employment in consumer goods. But the decline in employment in investment goods depends only on the labor coefficient there, whereas the decline in employment in consumer goods depends both on the productivity of labor in consumer goods and on the real wage. The higher the productivity of labor, given the real wage, the smaller will be the decline in consumer goods employment for a given fall in investment demand. Given the productivity of labor, the higher the real wage, the larger the decline in employment. If investment goods is capital intensive and has, therefore, the higher productivity of labor, then, especially in high wage economies,

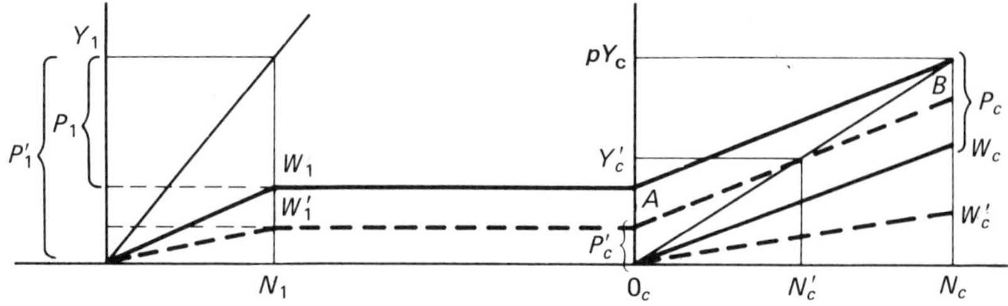

Figure 20.13

fluctuations in investment demand may cause greater changes in employment in consumer goods than in the investment sector itself.

Now consider a change in the real wage, for a given level of investment spending, using the same diagrammatic apparatus, (but ignoring the price relations) (Figure 20.13). We have already seen this above, but it is worth a closer look.

Gross investment demand stays steady at Y_I. At the initial level of the real wage both sectors are fully employed. (This is for simplicity only; there could be unemployment in both, which might cause money wages to fall further than prices, bringing about the lower real wage.) Now consider a lower real wage. In investment goods, profits are now $P'_I > P_I$, while employment and output remain the same. In consumer goods, however, equilibrium profits decline from P_c *to* P'_c, output falls to Y'_c and unemployment $N_c - N'_c$ emerges. But the *total* profit remains the same, for the increase in investment goods profit, W_1–W'_1, exactly equals the decline in consumer goods profit, $P_c - P'_c$. Just the reverse would happen with a rise in the real wage. Thus in investment goods, profit varies *inversely* with the real wage, while in consumer goods, it varies *directly* – a proposition which should lead the capitalists of the two sectors to take different approaches to economic policy.

The decline in employment and output in consumer goods is brought about by two causes, represented respectively by the changes in the intercept and the slope of the consumer goods total demand line, AB. The new intercept shows the decline in the demand for consumer goods by capital goods workers due to their lower wages; the new slope shows the lower wages (and no consumption) of workers in the consumer goods industry itself. It is clear that high real wages benefit all parties in the consumer goods sector in the short run.

Now let us turn back to the question of productivity increases. Let investment spending be given. Suppose first, implausibly, that productivity rises at the same rate in both sectors, and that the real wage is raised by the same percentage, a supposedly desirable and non-inflationary increase. In the investment goods sector, the rise in productivity will reduce employment, leaving output unchanged, but the rise in the wage will exactly offset the reduction in employment, leaving the wage bill unchanged. Profits are

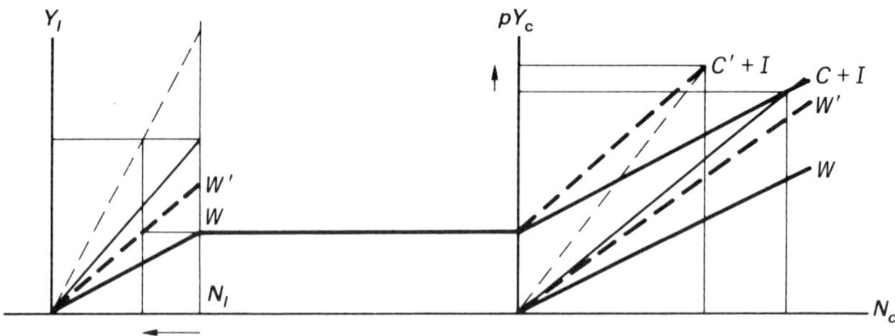

Figure 20.14

therefore also unchanged. Since the investment sector's wage bill is unchanged, profits in the consumer goods sector will be the same. But output in consumer goods will be up and employment down, as can be seen by inspecting the diagram, which is the same as that considered for the economy as a whole (Figure 20.14).

Again assume that investment spending is fixed. Suppose now that productivity increases faster in investment goods than in consumer goods, but that wages are raised by the average of the increases in the sectors, weighted by their sizes. Profit will increase in the investment goods sector, because the decrease in employment will be proportionally greater than the rise in wages. Hence the wage bill will diminish. So, by the same token, profits in the consumer goods sector will be down. The total profit will be the same, of course. If productivity increased faster in consumer goods than in investment goods, profit would be squeezed in investment, and the increased wage bill there would raise profits in consumer goods.

Now consider what happens when, with capacity fixed and no technical progress, total demand for investment exceeds capacity. According to the 'Cambridge' theory of distribution, when aggregate demand is greater than capacity, prices will be higher relative to money wages (excess demand for goods does *not* imply excess demand for labor, since the demand for labor is limited by the number of places on the assembly line), so profit will be larger, providing the saving to balance the investment, i.e., reducing consumption demand. The problem is that while the price of investment goods will be bid up, which will increase profits in that sector, additional profits do not mean additional capacity. The demand still cannot be met. So long as the money wage and the price of the consumer goods are unchanged, no real adjustment is possible. However, the higher price of investment goods raises the cost of materials and replacements in consumer goods. Hence, the price of consumer goods must go up. With given money wages, this means a decline in the real wage. Hence, output and employment decline in consumer goods. So the demand by the consumer goods sector for materials and replacements from investment goods will be lower, and it is this which provides the free capacity to meet the initial excess demand. The adjustment takes place by creating inflation in investment goods, which is passed on to consumer goods, where it is transmuted into recession, which in turn frees capacity in investment goods. A higher price of investment goods is sufficient to balance saving and investment in *value* terms; but higher profit by itself does not mean more serviceable capacity. Nor does a lower level of consumption, for that creates excess capacity in consumer goods, the wrong sector. It is the decline in the consumer goods sector's demand for the products of the investment goods sector which finally frees usable capacity.

The purpose of this paper has been to present the basic elements of the theory of effective demand in a manner making it possible to compare and contrast these ideas with those of orthodox theory. The detailed argument could be carried much further, but the basics should be clear by now.[15] The post-Keynesian approach takes a realistic view of the economy and society. It starts from the reality of social classes and industrial sectors. There are rigidities and they have important consequences. Property and property incomes are hedged about by rules which make the pattern of payment different from that of wage income. When these matters are taken into account, a theory of employment in the short run emerges which stands in flat contradiction to the neo-Classical theory of marginal productivity. It also suggests promising new ways to account for 'stagflation' and other contemporary problems. The next step is to look at investment and the financial sector.

Appendix: The Matrix Multiplier

The simplest matrix multiplier follows from the linear production equation: $x = Ax + y$, which implies

$$x = [I - A]^{-1}.$$

Here x will be the column vector of gross output, y of net, and A the square, non-negative, irreducible input coefficient matrix. Several variations are possible on this theme, but all center on the idea that, behind any net output, there lies a 'vertically integrated' sector of inputs – the direct plus indirect labor required, for example, or, calculated in the same way, the direct plus indirect quantities of each of the various means of production. Then on the assumption of constant returns, an increase or decrease in an output will imply a corresponding increase or decrease in the vertically integrated inputs, and the ratio between these will be the multiplier.

But this is not the multiplier of Keynesian economics, which gives the magnitude of the secondary changes brought about by the short-run adjustments to a given initial change. Vertically integrated inputs can be calculated for *any* interdependent industrial system exhibiting fixed coefficients or constant returns in some sense. For example, in a Fixed Employment system, the labor and inputs required for a unit of the consumer good can be calculated, and then the labor and inputs required for each of those inputs, and so on. This will sum to a definite magnitude, provided the A matrix is productive, etc. – but no short-run variation is possible, as we have seen. In the long run, however, an expansion of production of the consumer good will require the calculated secondary expansion of labor and inputs, and labor and inputs for labor and inputs, etc. This simply reflects the logic of interdependent production, and is important in that context; but it tells us nothing about the pattern of short-term adjustment. This depends on the passing along of expenditures, therefore upon variable costs (and household withdrawals, if any.)

As a first approximation, assume that all labor costs are variable; assume also that the means of production of consumer goods must vary with consumer goods output, and when they do, their labor inputs vary. Wages will be paid in units of command over the composite consumer good; all wages will be spent on consumption. Then we have,

$y = c + i$, where c and i are the vectors of consumption and

investment. Then $c = wNx$, where w is the real wage, N is the vector of direct labor inputs, and x the vector of gross output. Hence,

$c = wN[\mathrm{I} - A]^{-1}y = wL^*y$, where $L^* = N[\mathrm{I} - A]^{-1}$, that is, L^* is

the total direct and indirect labor employed per unit output. So we have,

$y = wL^*y + i$, and, rearranging,

$y = [\mathrm{I} - wL^*]^{-1}i$, a matrix reformulation of the multiplier of

Section 3. It depends on the real wage and on productivity; prices do not enter explicitly (as they would have to, if for example, there were savings out of income, or if we had to aggregate different patterns of consumption for different classes.) It also depends on the assumptions about variability; if only part of the labor costs are variable, the vector N will have to be adjusted accordingly for the analysis of changes in y corresponding to changes in investment.

Notes

1. No one else should be implicated in the specifics which follow, especially the diagrams, for which I (and many years of New School students) must take the responsibility. But the general approach is that of the post-Keynesian tradition. See Nell and Hollis (1975), Introduction and Chapter 1. But the purposes of this paper are strictly limited. The determinants of investment, and particularly the role of finance, are not considered. In orthodox terms, this paper examines the 'IS' side of macroeconomics (See Ch. 21).
2. To deal with it properly would require separating salaries from wages, on the one hand, and a closer look at consumer finance on the other. Both are beyond the scope of this study.

   The large and growing category of salaries in modern capitalism creates an empirical problem for this highly simplified theory of consumption. Some salaries (bank tellers, etc.) clearly fit into the theoretical concept of wages – they are variable and directly influence consumption spending: others (bank president, etc.) clearly contain large elements of profits, are quite stable, and do not influence spending. The empirical problems in separating categories, however, need not detract from the theoretical validity of the categories.
3. One can easily think of reasons why the direction of movement might have an effect. For example, when employment is diminishing, worker 'morale' is likely to be low: that is, workers are likely to resist layoffs by slowdowns and work-to-rule. When employment is increasing, on the other hand, morale and productivity may rise together.
4. Aggregation, as always, causes problems. If the sectors have different capital–labor ratios, different levels of employment may be associated with a given level of aggregate demand, according to how it is made up of consumption and investment. This is a good reason for keeping the sectors separate, as set forth in the last section of the paper.
5. This also acts to inhibit price cutting when sales fall off in the short run. If a firm is the first to cut price, it will attract sales, but by the same token it will then need its full labor force, which it will risk losing by announcing a wage below the prevailing rate. To cut price it must, therefore, be prepared to cut its markup, which *ex hypothesi* has been set to earn some target rate of return over the expected economic lifetime of the capital equipment (Ch. 17).
6. More complicated dynamics are easily developed following well-known models. Time lags could be introduced, movements could be assumed to generate expectations of further movement in the same direction, and so on, producing familiar patterns of inventory fluctuation. See Allen (1959), Kalecki (1971), Gandolfo (1983).
7. These two series are derived from the following sequences:

$$\Delta Y_1 = \Delta I$$
$$\Delta Y_2 = \Delta C_1 = wn\Delta I$$
$$\Delta Y_3 = \Delta C_2 = wn\Delta C_1 = (wn)^2\, \Delta I, \text{ etc.}$$

$$\Delta N_1 = n\Delta I$$
$$\Delta N_2 = n\Delta C_1 = n(wn\Delta I)$$
$$\Delta N_3 = n\Delta C_2 = n(wn)^2\Delta I, \text{ etc.}$$

8. Let m be the multiplier, and let A stand for wn_I and B stand for $w(n_C + \alpha n_I)$. Then,

$$\frac{dm}{du} = \frac{A}{(1 - uB)^2} > 0.$$

9. Keynes, in a letter to Beveridge (28 July 1936) presents the multiplier in this light, rather than, as in *The General Theory*, depending on a psychological propensity. 'Take the case of an increase in investment say, the building of additional houses. The men who are directly employed in building the houses will have a higher income than before. They will spend this income on consumption . . . except when there is full employment, there is an elasticity of supply in the consumption-goods industries, and . . ., if more men are employed in building houses, more men will also be employed in making things for the house-builders to consume . . . The additional men employed in the consumption industries will themselves consume more, so that we have a whole series of repercussions,' (1940, pp. 57–8). Joan Robinson's account of the multiplier runs along these lines (Robinson, 1971, pp. 15–22). R.F. Kahn in his famous original article takes account of both inputs and the 'dole' (welfare support of unemployed), but mistakenly believes, first, that an increase in employment will yield an increase in realized profits in the short run, and, secondly, that there will be current spending out of these profits. See Kahn (1972, pp. 11–12). This erroneous perception of the role of profits in the short run pervades the entire Keynesian literature. By contrast, Kalecki was always clear that investment expenditure (and capitalist consumption) determined realized profits, which, therefore, exercised no influence on current spending.
10. The contrast is worth spelling out: in marginal productivity theory a lower real wage implies more employment – employers are stimulated by cheap labor. In the theory of effective demand a rise in the real wage implies a rise in consumption sales – employers are stimulated by inventories running down.
11. Might not a rise in the real wage induce a decline in investment spending, and in this way bring about a decline in profits? This is certainly possible, but the relationships involved go beyond the simple model of this study. Investment *spending*, taken as exogenous here, depends on prior investment *decisions*, which the firm takes in pursuit of growth. The firm will be eyeing potential markets, net products, new technical processes, and balancing this against further expansion in its existing markets. Investment decisions are decisions to build a certain plant, embodying a certain technical process, to produce a certain product, designed (literally) to sell in a certain market. The level of real wages expected both during construction and later in operation, will obviously be relevant to such decisions, as costs; and the general level of real wages will be relevant in terms of the expected size of the market. Once investment decisions are taken, there is the further question of how rapidly to implement them. Investment *spending* can be speeded up or slowed down, depending on

the phase of the trade cycle, the availability and cost of finance and the political and social climate. Here again, the level of real wages will be important, but the effects will probably be different in the different sectors.

12. More compactly, in equilibrium. $Y = E = I + C$. Hence, since $dI = 0$, $dY = dE = dC$. But $C = wN$, according to our over simplified theory of consumption. Hence

$$dY = d\,(wN) = Ndw - wdN \text{ where } dN < 0$$

$$= wN\left(\frac{dw}{w} + \frac{dN}{N}\right)$$

$$= 0.$$

On the other hand, suppose consumption (Fig. 21.1) contains a welfare component, so that $C = C_c + wN \div Z\left(1 - \frac{N}{N_F}\right)$, where Z is welfare spending. Then, $dC = wN\left(\frac{dw}{w} + \frac{dN}{N}\right) - \frac{Z}{N_F}\, dN$ and when the first term is 0, $dC > 0$. Hence consumption rises, and $dY > 0$. In these circumstances, paying a real wage increase equiproportional to the increase in productivity, will still reduce employment, but will increase output.

13. For a recent account of the controversy, see Laibman and Nell (1977). Also for a full history, Harcourt (1972); cf. Part II.
14. What if prices were allowed to change? If excess capacity implies lower prices, unemployment should imply lower money wages. If the effects are the same, the real wage remains unchanged. But why should one effect systematically outweigh the other? There seems to be no clear answer. If prices were more flexible than money wages, then excess capacity would lower the real wage and so capacity utilization: if money wages were the more flexible, the real wage would rise, reducing excess capacity. Both effects were discussed earlier along with the multiplier, but neither tend to move the real wage towards the marginal product. To keep things simple, however, it has seemed best to assume that neither prices nor money wages change (or are different) when demand varies at levels below full capacity (See Ch. 16).
15. Too much should not be claimed. This study has abstracted from the determinants of investment. To complete the short-run analysis it will be necessary to provide a theory of finance which will explain the willingness and ability of business to carry through its spending. Both willingness, and ability may well be affected, for example, by the shifts in profits just described. But short-run analysis cannot stand alone. It must fit into a framework which explains (as much as possible!) the long-run expansion and structural change of capitalism. Thus, the present argument must be complemented first by a theory of investment finance, and secondly by an account of investment decisions which fits into the theory of growth and development (See Ch. 21).

References

R.G.D. Allen (1959) *Mathematical Economics* (New York, London).
G. Gandolfo (1983) *Economic Dynamics: Methods and Models* (New York: North-Holland).
G.C. Harcourt (1972) *Some Cambridge Controversies in the Theory of Capital* (Cambridge).
R. Kahn (1972) *Selected Essays on Employment and Growth* (Cambridge).
M. Kalecki (1969) *Studies in the Theories of Business Cycles 1933–1939*, (Oxford).
M. Kalecki (1971) *Selected Essays on the Dynamics of the Capitalist Economy 1930–1970* (Cambridge).
J.M. Keynes (1930) *A Treatise on Money* (New York).
J.M. Keynes (1936) *The General Theory of Employment, Interest, and Money* (London).
J.M. Keynes (1971) *The Collected Writings of John Maynard Keynes*, for The Royal Economic Society, Vol.14 (New York).
D. Laibman and E. Nell (1977) 'Reswitching, Wicksell Effects, and the Neo-Classical Production Function,' *American Economic Review*, 67 (Dec) pp. 878–88.
A. Lowe (1976) *The Path of Economic Growth* (New York, Cambridge).
K. Marx (1967) *Capital*, Vol. II (New York).
E. Nell and M. Hollis (1975) *Rational Economic Man* (London, New York).
J. Robinson (1940) *Introduction to The Theory of Employment* (London).
P. Sraffa (1960) *Production of Commodities By Means of Commodities* (Cambridge).

21 Notes on Finance, Risk and Investment Spending*

1 INTRODUCTION

Ordinary macroeconomics presents three essentially incompatible theories of investment spending, each corresponding to a separate branch of the subject. When dealing with short-run questions, investment is held to depend on the level of income and the rate of interest, in accordance with the marginal efficiency calculation. It is this function which enters into the construction of the celebrated *IS* curve. But when the matter of the cycle is broached, investment is suddenly seen to depend not on the level, but on the *rate of change* of income, appropriately lagged, while the influence of the interest rate quietly evaporates. The crucial parameters are the saving ratio, the capital–output ratio, and the time lags. However, the cycle cannot really be studied without consideration of the trend, which, of course, depends on investment. So to explain the trend we have a third theory of investment. The form of the function is the same, with the same parameters – the saving and capital–output ratios, and time lags – but now the parameters must assume *different values*. For one range of values will produce cycles, while another is required for exponential growth. So the textbook explanations of growth and the cycle are inconsistent with one another. They both draw on the accelerator mechanism, but they assume different ranges of values for the parameters. And both are inconsistent with the theory used in short-run analysis.

The object of this study is to present a theory of investment consistent with the simple theory of effective demand, which accounts for the business cycle and which can be integrated into a theory of growth and development capable of explaining the significant changes over time in the working of the system – a theory of transformational growth.

2 INVESTMENT DECISIONS AND INVESTMENT SPENDING

To develop a theory of business spending on investment it is first necessary to disentangle long-run and short-run aspects of the question.[1] Building a factory is a complex project which involves making a series of expensive,

* A. Barrère (ed.), *Money, Credit and Prices in Keynesian Perspective* (London: Macmillan 1989). Revised for this volume.

risky, interconnected, and often irreversible long-term commitments. The type of product (and its technical specifications) must be decided, in the light of the market for which it is intended, and the competition it must meet. The scale of the plant must be determined, usually in conjunction with the choice of technology to be employed, which may also influence the quality and specifications of the product. A plan of marketing and distribution must be developed and its cost and effectiveness estimated. What can be expected from the competition? Will the product appeal to the market? Will the technology work? Will construction proceed without mistakes or cost overruns? Will new products or processes be developed before the project has paid off? All these questions involve long-run calculations; they are part of the firm's plan for its own growth and development. The interaction of the decisions of all the firms, taken together, will lead to cumulative pressures bringing about institutional changes over the long run.

In a mass production economy, moreover, the investment decision must go hand in hand with pricing. In Ch. 17, we saw that prices were determined by long-run considerations, remaining fairly steady in the face of short-run fluctuations. The goods currently produced in existing capacity must be priced high enough to generate the profits needed to cover fixed costs and finance the new investment, but the price must be low enough to permit the development of the market on a scale sufficient to employ the new capacity. In addition, it must be foreseen that the price for the product produced by this new capacity will be high enough both to cover fixed costs and finance further investments, but low enough to continue to encourage market growth. The pricing decisions, then, are the long-run complements of the decisions as to the nature and scale of investment.

Until and unless these issues are resolved, at least provisionally, a plan of investment spending cannot be drawn up. But once they are resolved, a further question still remains – how fast to implement the plan. For the decision to build a plant of a certain size to produce a certain product using a certain process does not by itself answer the question when it is to be done. Of course the plan will establish some limits. The choice of technology and scale will determine some minimal construction period. It cannot come on line any sooner than some future date. And estimates of what new developments by potential competitors are in the pipeline will very likely establish a future date beyond which it would be too risky to go ahead with the plan, at least in its present form. But between these two dates, which themselves may not be very firm, there will normally be a good deal of latitude. Construction can begin at once, orders for equipment can be placed immediately, and arrangements for distribution can be set up, or the firm can take things more slowly, spending at a lower rate, doing one thing at a time. The *investment decision* defines the plan which sets the total amount of investment, and establishes a general time frame, but within these limits the *rate of investment spending* can vary, in accordance with the firm's perception of its short-run position.

3 THE SHORT RUN

In the short run, the productive capacity of the economy is taken as given (although it is being regularly augmented), and the question is, to what extent will it be actually utilised? This, of course, depends on effective demand – that is, demand backed by income or finance. We do not have to assume that productive capacity actually remains constant. Instead we can assume that the expansion rates of various 'long-run' features of the economy – productive capacity, the labour force, fixed long-term debt, the size of the government sector, the size of the managerial class – are all equal, so that the proportions between key variables of the economy are not changing. Of course some of these may change as a result of changes during the short period, but then the effects of such changes will be shown as shifts in the functions in the short period under consideration.

4 ENTREPRENEURIAL BUSINESS

The theory of investment spending outlined here concerns business firms which are, in a broad and realistic sense, competitive. This is the early stage of mass production, before the impact of the forces making for concentration has been felt. In each market I shall assume there are a large number of relatively similar small firms, none dominant, managed by or for a definite group of owner-shareholders. All are joint stock limited liability companies, but in each case there is an identifiable controlling interest group for whom the management works. The controlling groups will normally consist of members of a *family*. None has any special access to sources of finance; all have similar costs and marketing positions. Customers are assumed to be mobile. The methods of mass production are employed, implying that workers are subject to the discipline of the machinery, which sets the pace of work. Economies of scale are important, and businesses invest competitively, jockeying for the best places in growing markets.

By contrast to such business, the modern giant corporation operates under quite different conditions. It normally has (or shares with one or two other giants) a dominant position in one or more markets, in which a large body of customers are closely to tied to it. It has access to special sources of finance, and can frequently obtain privileged treatment by governments. Like small business the giant corporation will be a limited liability company, but unlike them the typical corporation will no longer have a readily identifiable and permanent locus of shareholder control. Not that large shareholders are unimportant; far from it. But management is in the saddle, and shareholder interests are only one – though important – among its concerns. Both giant oligopolies and small competitive corporations can generate internal finance, but the giants can vary the amounts they generate to match their needs through their control over market prices – or, more precisely, through their ability to influence the growth of their markets. The large corporation therefore adjusts its supply of finance to its investment plans. For the small competitive firm the direction of adjustment runs the opposite way: investment spending must be adapted to the constraints of finance.

A word about prices. Competitive industrial firms and oligopolies both set prices; there are no 'price-takers' in conditions of mass production. The difference is that in competitive conditions market prices will tend to be kept near the benchmark level, but if they move at all will vary directly with demand changes, whereas oligopolies may tend to vary market prices *inversely* with sales, in order to try to dampen fluctuations in revenue (Nell, 1988; Okun, 1982; Eichner, 1976; Ch. 17).

5 CRITERIA FOR INVESTMENT SPENDING

At any given moment the small entrepreneurial firm will have a certain level of fixed costs – management salaries, debt servicing and special contracts of various sorts (e.g., for accounting or legal services). So its earnings must lie high enough above its variable costs to at least cover these; if this is all, however, there will be nothing left to cover the additional costs of finance charges on funds borrowed for investment. And, of course, the higher the proposed investment spending, the more will be borrowed, and the higher the total additional finance charges. Thus for every level of proposed investment spending the firm can compute the rate of return required to cover its given fixed costs plus the finance charges newly incurred. But there is another consideration. Firms at any time have expectations about their likely sales in the coming period. The higher the level of investment, the higher the required rate of return, so the higher – and, broadly speaking, less likely – must be the firm's level of sales. In other words, in addition to the requirements of finance, the firm must add an 'insurance premium' to cover the possibility that sales revenue will prove inadequate to cover the old and the new financial obligations. This risk premium can be expected to increase at an increasing rate as higher and higher investment levels are considered.

The calculation described above is one which can be made by an individual firm. If the firm is 'representative,' then such calculations can be summed over all levels of investment, and the result will be an Investment–

Finance function showing the rates of return required for each level of investment. The intercept will be given by the level of fixed costs divided by the value of the capital stock, as determined by whatever system of accounting firms commonly employ. From the theory of effective demand we know that any given level of investment will determine a corresponding level of profits, which divided by the same value of the capital stock gives the rate of return generated by that level of investment. Clearly a level of I cannot be sustained if the generated rate of return lies below the associated required rate for that level, and equally it can be argued on dynamic grounds, a level of I will be established if the generated rate of return lies above the required. The incentive to invest is already there; the firms have made, and are making, investment decisions, based on their judgements of their respective long-term situations. They will therefore spend in order to carry out such decisions, as much as they prudently can, in the light of short-term conditions and the financial obligations such investment spending creates.

But comparing the required current rate of return with that generated by the system is not the end of the story. Long-run considerations have been taken into account already, in the investment decisions. In between, however, lies a kind of middle ground, in which we see the effects of current-period investment spending upon later-period values of variables entering into short-run decisions. Next period's long-term rate of interest, for example, will reflect the level of investment spending in this period. The rate of growth of share values and expectations of sales also depend in part on previous levels of investment.

The long-term rate of interest and the rate of growth of share prices, however, are also relevant to current decisions to spend on investment. If share prices are growing at a rate higher than the rate of interest, this is a sign that the market puts a higher value on the firm's investments than on the bank's money. Investment is clearly called for. But if the rate of interest lies above the rate of share price appreciation, the market values the additions to capital less than it values an equivalent amount of money. In such circumstances, spending on investment makes sense only if the firm thinks it can outguess the market, so that eventually its increased share prices will come to outweigh its additional debt.

Much of the volatility of investment spending arises from the fact that these two market criteria frequently give mutually destabilising signals. To see how this works we must take a closer look at the firm's short-run position. The next two sections will present the basic ideas.

6 THE GENERATED RATE OF RETURN

In the short period any given firm will consider the rate of return it would have to make to finance each possible level of investment spending, and

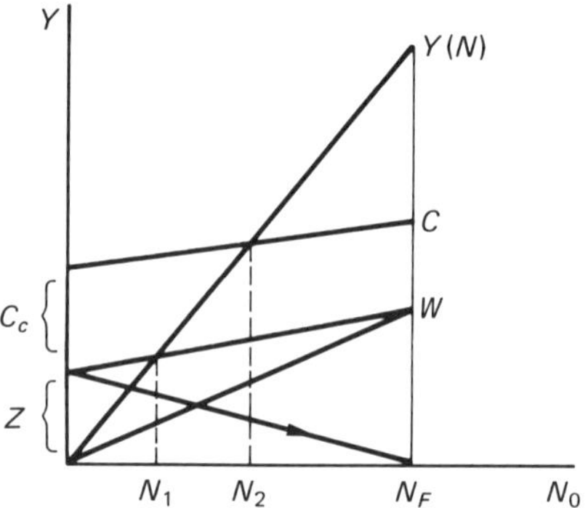

Figure 21.1 Investment spending and the realized rate of return

will compare that to the return they foresee on the basis of their position in the current market. (Notice that this is *not* a comparison of construction costs with the lifetime discounted returns from a project. It is a comparison of current expected earnings with current planned expenditure.) But for firms taken as a whole, the aggregate level of investment spending actually undertaken determines the realized rate of return through the multiplier. This can easily be seen on a simple diagram (Figure 21.1). Assume constant returns to utilisation and plot Y as a function of N. Then the wage rate will be the slope of the line OW, where N_F is the full capacity level of employment. But when workers are unemployed the state, through unemployment compensation, their family and friends and their wits, combine to enable them to sustain an average level of consumption spending z. Then $Z = \Sigma_i^n z$ is the level of consumption when all workers are unemployed. As employment rises, spending by the unemployed falls, as indicated by the downward-sloping line ZN_F. Employed workers will spend all and only their wages; all, because they are paid approximately what is needed for support and reproduction; only, because in general they have nothing else. (Any assets must be set aside against the day some family members become unemployed.) So the total consumption demand, by employed and unemployed workers taken together will be given by the line ZW. This intersects $Y(N)$ at a level of employment, N_1, below which employment cannot fall, so long as the unemployed are able to maintain a level of spending of z per head. But there is still a further aspect of consumption. The well-to-do managers and owners also consume. Their spending reflects their established life style, backed by property, wealth and power. Profits and employment both vary, but neither will affect the consumption spending of the managerial class. Worker employment is irrelevant; managerial employment depends on different issues. Nor does profit income matter. Capitalist consumption depends on taste and style, not on current income; the salaried and the well-to-do have short-term

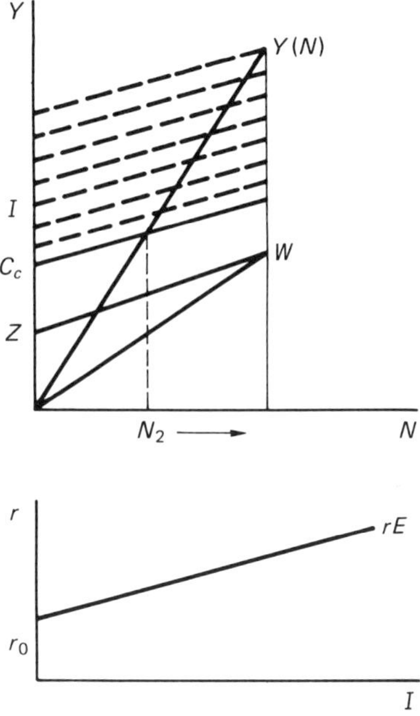

Figure 21.2 Levels of investment

borrowing power, which will enable them to sustain their consumption when profit income drops off.[2] Nor will a rise in profits necessarily stimulate consumption, beyond that impetus that boom psychology always has. Hence the consumption of owners and managers can be treated as a constant in the short-run, and is shown in Figure 21.1 as C_c. (In a slump, of course, management salaries and even managerial employment will fall off. Legal and accounting services will be cut back. The professional and managerial classes will therefore borrow (i.e., sell bonds) to maintain C_c. Hence they will help to maintain a high level of interest rates. During the upswing, salaries and employment for professionals and managers will be booming, making it possible to retire debt. Hence these classes will be buying bonds, repaying loans, thus helping to hold interest rates down.) So the line C_cC shows the total level of consumption, by workers, capitalists and unemployed, for each level of employment. This line cuts $Y(N)$ at N_2, which is the minimum level of employment given both Z and C_c.

Now consider different levels of investment (Figure 21.2). Each successive level of investment will be uniquely associated with a correspondingly higher level of employment, rising from N_2 when $I = 0$ to N_F when I equals its full capacity level. At each level of employment, profit is equal to investment plus capitalist consumption. Hence given the value of the capital stock, as investment spending is higher, the realised rate of return will be higher. The resulting function can be graphed. The intercept is the rate of return when $I = 0$ and $N = N_z$; the slope is $1/K$. The equation, neglecting Z, is

$$r = r_0 + \frac{I}{K}, \quad \text{where} \quad r_0 = \frac{C_c}{K}$$

It is important to interpret Figure 21.2 with care, for it will play a role in a dynamic argument, in spite of being itself the offspring of comparative statics. Figure 21.2 states that a level of aggregate investment *generates* a certain corresponding level of the average rate of return. A direction of causality is definitely implied: investment spending causes business profits, not the other way around. Figure 21.2 is a straight line because short-run constant returns has been assumed. Of course, not every firm will realise the average rate of profit; how well a firm does depends on its competitive position in sales. But we can take the structure of markets as given during the short run. Hence the generated rate of return, adjusted by a factor indicating the firm's competitive position, will represent the realised earnings of firms.

7 THE REQUIRED RATE OF RETURN

To undertake a constant level of investment spending in the current period, a firm must be reasonably sure of making at least a level of earnings that will cover both its fixed costs and the finance charges associated with that level of investment. This last depends on how much the firm normally borrows – its debt–equity ratio – and of course on the long-term rate of interest. Suppose the firm borrowed nothing and invested only out of retained earnings. Then its profit, after deductions for fixed costs, would have to equal the desired level of investment. Hence the required rate of return would equal the rate of growth. Suppose, on the other hand that the firm planned to finance the entire investment through bonds. Then the profit, after deductions for fixed costs, would equal only the interest on the investment, plus one period's repayment of principal. (This last would depend on the term of the loan. But assume the length of loans to be constant, though it could vary consistently with the interest rate – shorter loans at higher rates, longer at lower – without affecting the argument.) On the first supposition, the required rate of return would differ from the generated rate only by virtue of taking 'fixed costs' rather than 'capitalist consumption' into account. If fixed costs – e.g., salaries and interest income – all go to underwrite capitalist consumption, then the two equations will be the same. But fixed costs and capitalist consumption would be related in other ways; in particular, changes in fixed costs may not be reflected in changes in C_c. On the second supposition, the required rate will lie beneath the generated rate by a large margin. More generally, a portion of investment will be financed by borrowing, the rest by retained earnings. The larger the share of borrowing, the lower the required rate compared to the maximum possible such rate, which would equal the generated rate, if fixed costs were equal to capitalist consumption. This can be expressed very simply in an equation. Let F stand for fixed costs: salaries, debt servicing, contracts for business services, and so on. Then i will be the long-term rate of interest, and b will be the ratio of debt to investment spending, D/I while K is the given value of the capital stock. The required rate of return is:

$$r_r = \frac{F}{K} + [\,(1 - b) + ib]\,\frac{I}{K},\ 0 \leqslant b \leqslant 1$$

This can be called the 'investment finance', or *IF* curve. When

$$b = 0, \quad r_r = \frac{F + I}{K}$$

when

$$b = 1, \quad r_r = \frac{F + iI}{K}$$

The debt–investment ratio, b, will reflect the same forces that shape the overall debt–capital ratio for the firm. Too high a ratio, though profitable to shareholders, is risky: too low a ratio dilutes ownership. For any given short run, b will be taken as fixed, but it is a parameter which can vary over the curve of the cycle as a whole, and will change as the long-run rate of interest changes in relation to the rate of profit and the rate of growth.

Putting the required and generated rates of return together, we have the diagram in Figure 21.3.

Most likely $F > C_c$ – that is, either there will be some saving out of fixed cost incomes, or there will be some fixed costs which do not correspond to incomes underwriting capitalist consumption. But should $F \leqslant C_c$ the situation will appear as in the case of the dotted line, IF'. Since the slopes of IF and IF' are the same, and $1 - b + ib < 1$, IF is the shallower line. The generated rate of return will lie above the required at all levels of investment; hence as this situation comes to be reflected in expectations of sales, actual I will rise to capacity output, or to the level of demand corresponding to long-term investment decisions, whichever is lower. (If capacity is reached first, a bidding up of capital goods prices may follow.) When $F > C_c$ the required rate will lie above the generated rate for levels of $I < I^*$. Levels of investment spending in that region cannot be

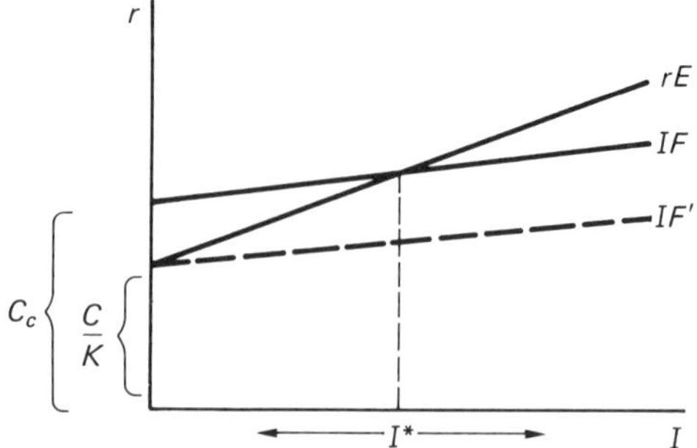

Figure 21.3 Required and generated rates of return

sustained, and would have to be cut back. The intersection point I^* is therefore *unstable*; levels of investment spending just below it will be cut back, but levels just above it will be expanded.

If either i or b rises, the slope of IF increases; over time the intercept F will also rise, and vice-versa if i or b fall. These movements will be examined shortly.

8 INCREASING RISK

Another factor applying chiefly to the consumer goods sector has to be considered in determining the required rate of return – namely, the risk that by undertaking investment spending, the firm will find itself with too little revenue to meet its (now larger) fixed obligations. Clearly the higher the level of sales and the lower the level of initial fixed costs, and of the rate of interest, the less risk there will be. Also, given the levels of sales, of fixed costs and interest rate, it is intuitively evident that the larger the amount of investment spending, the greater the risk that something might go wrong. In order to clarify this, we will study the case of realistically competitive markets composed of small, very similar industrial firms, with a highly mobile clientele.

For any given firm the risk depends on the probability that, when aggregate spending in the market is expected at a certain level, their sales will fail to cover their fixed obligations. And this depends on the *distribution* of sales among the firms making up the sector. To get an idea of this we can draw a frequency graph (see Figure 21.4). On the vertical axis measure the number of firms achieving a certain level of revenue from sales; on the horizontal axis plot the level of revenue from sales as a percentage of capacity. Each point then represents an amount of revenue as a per cent of capacity revenue for a firm. (We assume all firms are of equal size and growing at equal rates.) It is reasonable to expect very low levels of sales revenue in relation to capacity to be rare; similarly, compar-

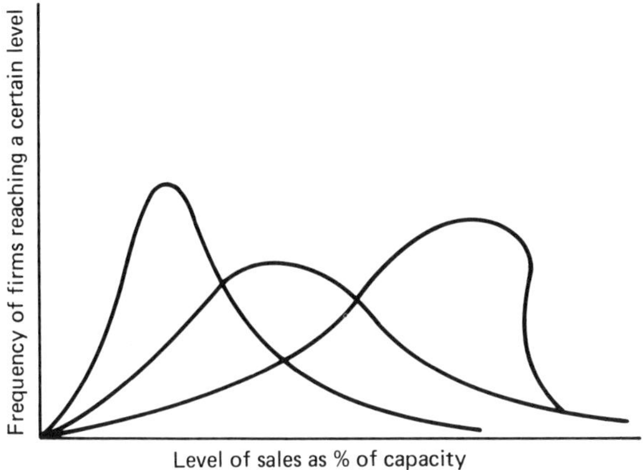

Figure 21.4 A frequency graph

atively few firms will achieve very high ratios of sales to capacity. Most will fall in the middle somewhere – but the precise shape of the distribution can vary for many reasons. Firms will sell different amounts as customers move about looking for the best deals, and firms will sell earlier or later, thus bearing different carrying costs for inventory. Revenue will therefore be lower on later sales and this difference will be variously distributed. If sales are systematically postponed, then revenue will be down, because of higher carrying costs. The distributions – all having the same total area (i.e., the same total revenue) – can take many different shapes, being skewed toward the lower end or the upper end, having large or small variance, and so on. These different shapes will reflect, on the one hand, relatively permanent or long-run characteristics of the market – its degree of competitiveness, the relative sizes of firms and customers, and so on – and, on the other, the effects of changes in the short-run situation. Among these the most important will be changes in the expected level and composition of spending. Changes in the level of spending will shift the distribution in or out, but won't necessarily alter its shape. Changes in the overall composition of spending, however, brought about either by changes in the distribution of income, or because the ratio C_c/C has changed, may change the shape.

We have assumed a large number of family firms, all of about the same size and skill, all facing markets of highly mobile customers. The distribution of sales among firms should therefore be random, with most firms selling at the same level during the period. But not all customers make expenditures of the same size. Capitalist consumption purchases will typically be larger; either they will buy more, or they will pay extra for higher quality. So the ratio C_c/C shows the proportion of large purchases in the total. The higher that ratio the more skewed to the right the distribution will be, since there will be a higher proportion of large purchases. Thus in the short run, for a given degree of competitiveness, and so forth, the *position* of the expected distribution of sales among firms in a market will depend on the expected state of effective aggregate demand – in other words, on employment – but the skewness of the distribution will depend on the ratio of C_c/C which (since C_c is fixed) will move inversely with employment. In other words, C_c by providing a stable number of large individual spenders ensures a higher probability of firms making large sales in poor times, while this effect will be less noticeable in good times.

The distribution of sales, *ex post* shows how many firms did well and how many did badly. But customers are not tied to firms; they are mobile and shop around. Thus the fact that a firm did well in the recent past is no assurance that it will do well this coming period, except as other firms also did well. If a firm did well and most others did badly, it could not expect to do as well again.

If a firm could rationally expect to do well relatively to the rest next period because it had done so this, it could then afford to invest at a higher rate than the rest, and so to grow faster than the rest. But if over time, the relative growth rates of firms were proportional to their respective earlier successes, a *normal* distribution of sales among firms of *equal size* would grow over time into a *log-normal* distribution of *capacity sizes* and market shares, assuming that the market grows in proportion of the appropriately weighted average rate of growth of capacity – or that the rate of growth of the market is given exogenously, and determines the average rate of growth of capacity. In many cases, this could be considered realistic. But I wish to avoid this complication and develop a theory of the cycle in markets that remain characterised by competition among firms of equal size and ability.[3] Hence I assume that there are no grounds for a firm to expect its immediate future to resemble its recent past. Rather it will think of its prospects in terms of the market it belongs to as a whole. It has the same chances as its rivals do; hence it sees the coming period in terms of the size distribution for the market. Roughly, taking last period as the guide to the coming one (and allowing for any modifications on the basis of surveys and newspapers or other information) a firm will assume that its chances to obtain any given amount of revenue will be in proportion to the number of firms who earned that much or more last period. The distribution, then, defines the probability of earning various amounts of revenue.

Now draw in the level of financial obligations corresponding to the initial level of fixed costs plus the interest and other charges entailed by some given level of proposed investment spending (Figure 21.5). Clearly as I varies this vertical line will shift in and out over the range $0 \leqslant I \leqslant I_m$ where I_m is the maximum called for by the present investment decisions. The cumulative frequency up to the point on the vertical axis corresponding to this line shows how many firms can be expected to earn less than the

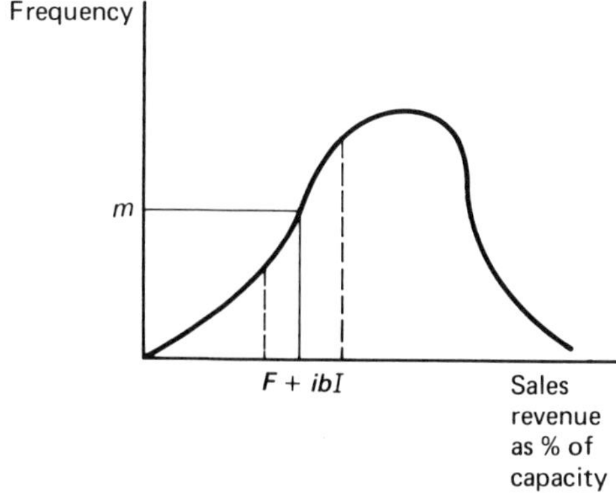

Figure 21.5 Financial obligations and proposed investment spending

amount needed to cover the financial obligations required by that level of investment. The ratio of that cumulative frequency to the total number of firms then gives the probability for any firm of being unable to meet the financial obligations of that level of investment. The costs of failing to meet such obligations – penalty payments, legal fees, court costs, and audit, and so on, plus the inconvenience and loss of competitive position, and independence – will be taken as measured by some fixed sum. Then the cost of raising that sum multiplied by the probability of having to do it measures the risk associated with any level of investment. The rate of risk, then, is that sum in proportion to the total capital, and this must be added to the formula for the required rate of return:

$$r_r = \frac{F}{K} + [1 - b + ib]\frac{I}{K} + \varrho$$

where $$\varrho = \frac{\sum_{i=1}^{m} f_i X}{mK}$$

X = cost of bankruptcy
f = frequency at each point
m = number of firms corresponding to point $F = ibI$
n = total number of firms

Clearly prudence will dictate a maximum acceptable level the probability of failure will be an increasing function of the level of investment and, given the likely shape of the distribution, one which increases at an increasing rate.

Figure 21.5 presents the situation of a representative firm. In a market in which growth is uneven, so that concentration is rising, the probabilities of

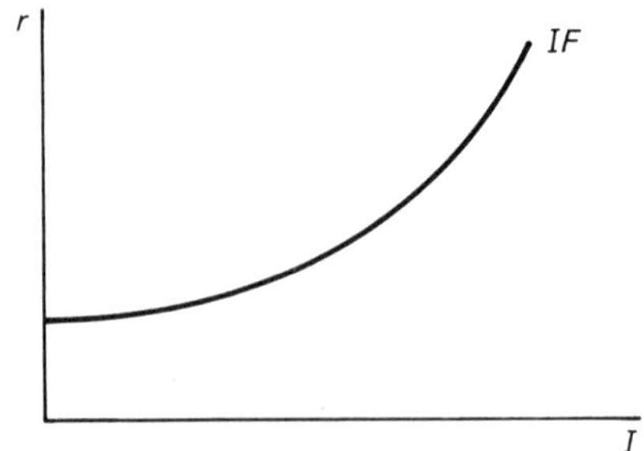

Figure 21.6 The effect of increasing risk

failing to achieve the required levels of sales will be different for different categories of firms, and each category will therefore be described by a separate version of Figure 21.5. Otherwise the analysis remains the same.

The *IF* curve can now be redrawn (Figure 21.6), showing the effect of increasing risk. For low levels of investment spending, the addition to financial commitments adds negligibly to risk, but after a certain point risk turns the curve upward sharply, at an increasing rate, until further investment would require an unimaginable increase in the required rate.

9 THE *rE* AND *IF* CURVES – STABILITY AND DYNAMICS

The generated and required rate of return curves can now be interpreted together (Figure 21.7). Suppose for the sake of argument that $F > C_c$. There will then be two intersections I_1 and I_2, of which the lower will be unstable, while the upper will be stable. Taking I_1 as an example, if $I \leqslant I_2$, $r_g > r_r$ and investment spending can be safely increased in accordance with investment plans, while if $I > I_2$, investment spending must be cut back. Of course, the *rE* line shows the rate of return that *will* be generated; whereas firms will plan their investment spending according to what they *expect*. (Notoriously, their expectations may be wrong. Nevertheless, that plays no systematic role in what happens here. I shall assume that firms have good and correct information about what is going to happen in their markets. When they believe that some level of spending will take place, resulting in a certain level and pattern of sales revenue, they do so because they have good reason: that level and pattern of spending is about to take place. If it does not ultimately happen, that will be because a parameter has shifted in a manner which could not reasonably be foreseen. So their expectations are, in a sense, rational expectations, but they are also limited. As we shall show, financial markets are unstable at certain points in the cycle, and F depends on financial costs. (Hence reliable expectations can only be formed for sales and receipts in the near-term future.)

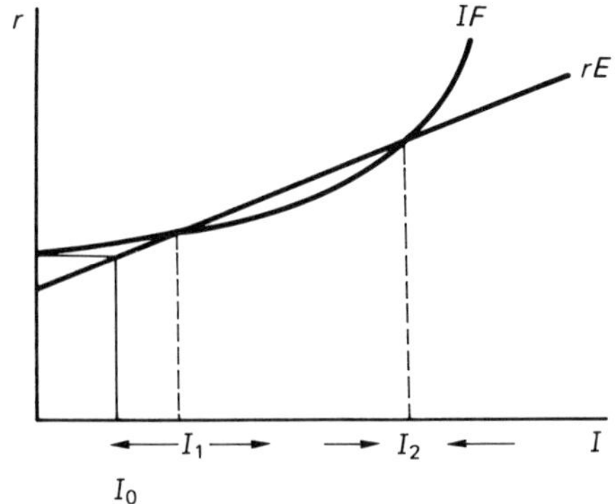

Figure 21.7 Interpreting the generated and required rate of return curves

Below I_1 any level of I must fall back to zero; since $r_r > r_g$, the level of I is too high to be safe. A horizontal line from F across to the rE line shows the level of the rate of return required simply to cover F. That is, a level of spending equal to I_0 will have to be established somehow; no investment spending equal to or below I_0 could possibly be chosen because the revenue generated would not cover the initial level of fixed costs.

Above I_2, any level of I must fall back to I_2; again $r_r > r_g$ and the level of spending engenders commitments which are too high for safety. The rate of return generated will be substantially higher than the ratio of financial commitments to capital; but in addition to such direct commitments the firm must consider the risks of failing to meet its obligations, and it is the 'insurance premium' for this which pushes the required rate above the generated in the range above I_2.

In the open interval $I_2 - I$ (Figure 21.8a and 21.8b), any level of investment spending will rise to I_2, since $r_g > r_r$, so long, of course, as $I_2 > I_m$. Firms will correctly expect to earn r_g and will calculate that $r_g > r_r$, and will therefore expand their planned spending, since they would like, if it were safe, to expand to the full level called for by investment decisions, I_m. Of course F may not be greater than C_c. In that case there would only be one intersection, which would depend entirely on how *rapidly risk rose*. If risk rises slowly, $F < C_c$ will be a sufficient condition for $I = I_m$. On the other hand, risk may rise very rapidly. Then, even though $F > C_c$ and $(1 - b + ib) < 1$, as risk shifts up, the two intersections converge to a point of tangency, so that $r_r > r_g$ at all other points, while the point of tangency itself is unstable downwards.

Thus the relation between the two curves determines both the *direction of movement* of I, and the places of rest. But by itself this tells us nothing about the speed with which levels of I will be adjusted. To move to a dynamic theory, this will have to be specified. On the basis of the argument

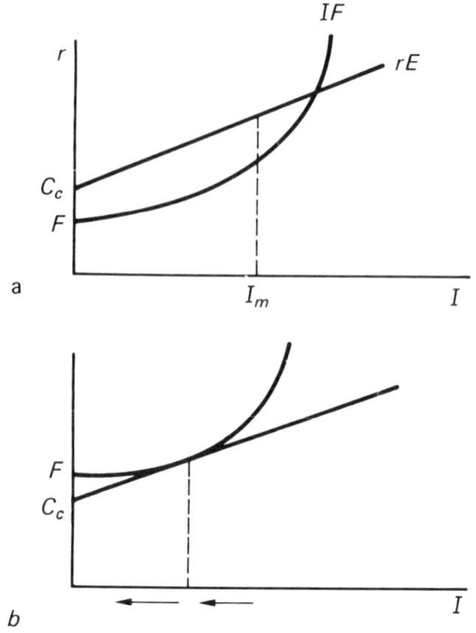

Figure 21.8 Level of investment spending

so far, it is reasonable and convenient to assume that the movement in *I* indicated by the relationship of *rE* and *IF* will be carried out within one short period.

This raises a problem, however. If *I* changes, then surely the demand for loans changes. How then can the long-term interest rate remain unchanged – as it must if the slope and shape of the *IF* curve is to remain unaltered? But just as *I*-spending creates a demand for loans, so does it create a corresponding supply. For a given level of investment spending creates a corresponding amount of profit. Hence *both* demand and supply of loanable funds will rise or fall as *I* rises or falls. The same applies to the demand and supply of money; the banking system will accommodate the needs of business, through the device of lines of credit. The 'transactions demand,' therefore, has no effect on the rate of interest, which, however, will vary over the cycle, and plays an important role in what follows (Nell, 1988; Moore in Arestis, 1988).

A simple sketch can now be given of an investment cycle.[4] Initially, the rate of interest falls in the slump. This lowers the *IF* curve until *I* rises. But the long-term rate stays low since profits rise with *I*. (Also, the managerial classes will be ceasing their indebtedness, increasing supplies of loanable funds.) In the boom, however, the rate of interest eventually rises (to keep pace with the rate of growth, as we shall see in a moment). This shifts *IF* up, and raises risk. When *IF* rises to the point of tangency, *I* will collapse entirely, but the rate of interest will not fall during the downswing. On the contrary, its relative stickiness will contribute to the development of panic in the capital markets. Once the bottom has been reached, however, F will be reduced through reorganisation and bankruptcies, and the rate of interest will fall, beginning the upswing again. To develop this picture we must now examine the determinants of the long-term interest rate, to show how it moves over the cycle and contributes to the changes in F. Notice that the fluctuations in investment spending, and therefore in output and employment, are determined by the movements of the IF and rE curves, which reflect 'required' and 'realised' profits, respectively. Physical or capacity constraints play no role in this – the boom is not cut short by any form of factor or supply limitation. Scarcities are not in evidence – the entire cycle is defined by the changing relationships between conditions encouraging and those discouraging expenditure. The cycle is demand-determined.

10 THE LONG-TERM RATE OF INTEREST AND THE RATE OF PROFIT

It has long been taken for granted both in orthodox and in Marxist theory that arbitrage will bring the money rate of interest into equality with some variant of the rate of profit. Wicksell, quoted favourably by Mandel, saw the relationship between the money rate of interest and the natural rate of return (on real capital) as the central mechanism governing the price level. Keynes, of course, saw the rate of interest as being equated to the marginal efficiency of capital (the expected rate of return on the marginal investment project) by changes in the level of investment. Sraffa suggests that the rate of profit might be determined by the rate of interest in money, while Marx seems to argue just the opposite, that the money rate of interest will be determined by the general rate of profit, though the relative availability of money capital will from time to time exercise an independent, temporary, influence.

The view that the rate of interest on money and the ratio of profit on capital will be equalised by market forces is nearly universal. Yet for the modern world, it is surely wrong. In the Stationary State, where all profits are consumed, it would certainly be true. There is no saving and no investment in such a state; hence only *already existing capital* can be borrowed. There are plenty of reasons to borrow even though there is no new investment. (For example, a firm may wish to diplace labour by a machine – convert variable circulating capital to constant, fixed capital. Or it may wish to replace buildings or equipment, or carry inventory). But such capital already earns the rate of profit. To induce a capitalist to lend it, at least as much must be offered in interest, allowing for risk, as the capital already makes.

A craft economy behaves as if it were in stationary conditions. Households save, but these savings are borrowed by entrepreneurs interested in establishing new firms, and who will pay interest equal to the going rate of profit. Existing firms do not invest; they set up at their optimum size and function unchanged thereafter. But in conditions of mass production firms will be competing in regard to technological innovation, in both products and methods, and will therefore be continually re-investing in their own operations, in search of improvements and economies of scale (Ch. 17).

A growing mass production economy works differently from a stationary-like craft system. New savings are withdrawals from the stream of earnings, and have to be placed before they can bring a return. They can be placed according to a contact of loan, which guarantees the payment of interest at a fixed rate, and repayment according to some agreed upon schedule. Or such funds can be used to acquire an ownership interest in a business. Or finally, and perhaps most important, savings can be taken directly out of profits by companies and used to finance their own investment spending. This is obvious, but there is a hidden implication: in the stationary economy earning the rate of profit is the alternative to earning the rate of interest, because at any time all capital has to get one or the other. All capital has an institutional form. But in a growing economy new capital has yet to assume that form. To *become* earning capital, private savings must be invested, and this can be done either by buying *shares* or by buying *bonds*. So the alternative to the rate of interest will be the rate of growth of *shares*; not the rate of profit on capital. The rate of return on shares, of course, is the rate of share price appreciation plus the rate of dividends. But household savings is only part of the story. Companies also save, by retaining part of their earnings. Retained earnings can either be invested – or they could be loaned out at interest. They will be invested if the market is expected to grow; indeed the expectation of growth is the reason for the saving in the first place. But this means that the disposition of retained earnings will be governed by the relation between the rate of growth and the rate of interest. If the expected rate of growth exceeds the rate of interest, the invested retained earnings will increase the value of shares by an amount that would exceed the earnings of that sum loaned at interest.

In a growing economy, in other words, new savings have to *become* capital, which means they have to be invested in (and/or by) a firm. This act of investment will cause the value of the shares of the firm to appreciate, and it is this rate of share appreciation, rather than the rate of profit, which is the alternative in a growing economy to the rate of interest. Only *existing* capital, institutionalised in firms, earns the rate of profit. The only way to participate in such earnings is to buy the bonds or the shares issued by firms. But then the question becomes, which is the more attractive deal, shares or bonds?

But surely, it will be argued, in the case of investment it is the *prospective* profit that matters. Of course, only existing capital earns the current rate of profits, but each investment project must be examined in the light of its prospective earning power. So the expected rate of return on each project, over its lifetime, will be compared to the rate of interest.

There is a curious imbalance of terms in this very common argument. The rate of return on an investment *project* is to be compared with the rate of interest on bonds. How does a project 'earn returns'? The returns are the returns of the *firm*; it is the firm that will build and operate the project, and negotiate the finance for it. So it is the *firm's* returns that matter and it is the firm that will have to pay interest. So, of course, the firm's rate of return must be, on average, sufficient to pay interest. But a new project, in itself, might be unprofitable, if, for example, undertaken for essentially defensive reasons, to protect markets or forestall competition. In other words, the rate of return on the project is not the same thing as the rate of return to the firm, and the latter is the relevant concept.

Calculating the rate of return on a project presents formidable difficulties. The lifetime of the project must be known, the prices of inputs, wages, and the product must be known for every future period; and the degree of utilisation must be known for every period. The likelihood of breakdowns and the costs of repairs must be accurately foreseen. All these have to be known for the future stream of net returns to be written down. None of these can be known in advance with any degree of reliability – not even the lifetime of the project. Not only might the engineers be wrong; but new inventions or new products might render it obsolete or uncompetitive. But this is not all; besides the direct costs of the project, it must be assigned its share of the company's overhead, particularly of those overhead costs (such as selling costs) which vary in proportion to output. Notoriously, allocating overheads presents problems, especially looking ahead to the future. And the future poses a dilemma: in the relatively near term market conditions can be estimated more or less reliably, but the technology may well be crawling with 'bugs;' in the more distant future, the technology will have been made reliable, but it will no longer be possible to estimate the market. Finally, there are the purely technical problems; the stream of net returns may have such a form that the calculated 'internal rate of return' is not unique.[5] Different investment criteria (e.g., present value, internal rate of return, payoff period) can yield different orderings of alternative projects. And relatively small and plausible variations in the expected future stream of returns can produce quite dramatic changes in the orderings of projects, using a given criterion.

At this point it could be argued that the computation of the 'marginal efficiency of investment' is a *reductio ad absurdum* of rational economic calculation in the Marshallian tradition. It is as though Keynes were saying: this impossible list of future specifics would have to be known to make the calculation. They cannot conceivably be accurately foreseen; therefore investment is governed not by rational planning but by animal spirits.

That animal spirits are involved in investment *decisions* cannot be denied, for such decisions require planning to start building capacity now to meet the expected growth in demand some time hence, when the construction is complete and the plant can be brought into operation. A gamble on the future is inescapable. But it does not follow that rational calculation can only take the form outlined in the theory of marginal efficiency. In particular, once the investment decision is made (the long-run gamble), investment spending may be governed by quite reasonable calculations, which take a very different form.

The crucial step in reformulating the calculation is seeing that the rate of return on the *project* is not the appropriate concept. As argued above, it is the effect of the new project on the *firm*'s rate of return that has to be considered. But the firm may be undertaking several different investment projects at any one time. Separating out the effects attributable to each may be virtually impossible, in view of their respective 'external' effects on other activities of the firm, and in view of the difficulties in allocating overheads. Moreover, if the contribution to profits were to be compared to the interest cost of capital, it would have to be considered not for one year, but over the entire period of the loan. But next year and later there will be further investments, including investments in overhead, which will modify, develop and otherwise affect the plant and equipment installed now. So the contribution of today's new investment, even if it could be calculated now, will become progressively more difficult to identify as time passes. Nor is this a minor problem. Characteristically, firms will plan a *series* of investment projects, each feeding into the next. For example, this year a new factory designed for a new process but still operating the old, next year modifications which will enable the product to be improved, the year after a sales campaign to open new markets, upon which the old process will be scrapped and a new one installed in the factory: four distinct stages, financed by four separate fund-raisings, but all interconnected parts of a general plan. Yet because each stage is contingent upon successful completion of the previous one, the plan cannot be evaluated in separate parts. The profit earned in each stage cannot be attributed solely to that stage. But to take the plan as a whole and compute its present value makes no sense either. For the funds are not going to be expended all at once, so do not have to be raised now, and in most such plans some of the funds for later stages will be generated by the earlier ones. The simple fact is that the firm will plan its various investment projects – now and in the future – not only with an eye to the returns on each project which are clearly attributable to that project during its expected lifetime, but also (and sometimes more importantly) with regard to those effects which are *external* to the separate projects but *internal* to the firm as a whole. So the criterion for the firm has to be: will its investment plans enable it to continue, over the foreseeable future, to make its target rate of return on its total capital?

Why a target rate? Why does it not *maximise* its profit rate? Because it must consider the long-run *development* of its market position. It must choose a rate of return that enables it to grow along with its market, and maintain or improve its market share. Single-minded pursuit of profits may endanger its long-run market position, or make it cash-rich and ripe for a takeover. But for present purposes it doesn't matter *on what grounds* it has chosen a target rate; it may have done so by solving a long-run maximising problem, however implausible that may seem. What counts is that it has a long-run target rate, and that the capital market knows this (Ch. 17).

11 SHARE PRICES AND THE RATE OF GROWTH

Neither the firm, nor the observing economist nor the Stock Market, then, can evaluate the firm's investment projects, one by one. But what the Stock Market can and will do, often on the advice of observing economists, is say whether or not it trusts the management to earn its target rate of return on all its capital, old and new, next period. If it is expected to do so, then next period the new capital in place will be valued the same as the old is, the value of the old remaining unchanged, assuming the target rate is unchanged. Hence, assuming that the capital goods sector sells capital goods for what they are worth (assuming, that is, that they make *their* target rate on the sale), the value of the firm's capital will increase in the ratio: $I/K = g$.

The effect of this on share prices can easily be seen. To keep the argument simple, let us assume that all spending for new capital is financed either by borrowing or from retained earnings. Then let:

N = number of shares
p = price of one share
I = new investment
K = value of existing capital
F = total fixed obligations
D = new indebtedness

Clearly, from the assumptions:

$$Np = K - F.$$

If no new shares are issued,

$$Ndp = dK - dF = I - D.$$

Hence,

$$(pN/K)\ dp/p = I/K - D/K.$$

Define

$$v = Np/K = 1 - F/K.$$

Then

$$dp/p = \frac{g - D/K}{v} = \frac{I - D}{K - F}.$$

But, if the ratio of new indebtedness to investment is the same as fixed obligations to capital (constant debt–equity ratio) $D/F = I/K = g$. In such a case, since

$$v = 1 - F/K, \qquad dv = \frac{E}{K}\left(\frac{dK}{K} - \frac{dF}{F}\right) = 0;$$

the value of shares will stand in the same ratio to the value of capital. Hence

$$\frac{dp}{p} = \frac{I - D}{K - F} = g$$

This assumes that the rate of interest is steady, the same for F and for D. But if it changes, then even though the same proportion of the funds needed for investment is borrowed, the resulting changes will be greater. So for non-steady state conditions the formulae must be amended, letting subscript B indicate borrowed funds and t time periods:

$$\frac{dp}{p} = \frac{I - D}{K - F} = \frac{I - i_t I_B}{K - i_{t-1} K_B} = g \text{ iff } \left\{ \begin{array}{c} i_t = i_{t-1} \\ \frac{I}{K} \quad \frac{I_B}{K_B} \end{array} \right.$$

$$dv = \frac{F}{K}\left(\frac{dK}{F} - \frac{dF}{F}\right) = \frac{iK_B}{K}\left(g - \frac{K_B di + idK_B}{iK_B}\right)$$

$$= \frac{iK_B}{K}\left[g - \left(\frac{di}{i} + \frac{dK_B}{K_B}\right)\right]$$

12 THE RATE OF INTEREST AND THE RATE OF GROWTH

From the point of view of managers, then, a firm's retained earnings will yield to the owners an immediate rate of return (realisable in the Stock Market) of $dp/p = g$. On the other hand, had the managers *loaned* these funds, or bought relatively safe bonds, they could have realised a rate of return equal to the rate of interest. Hence the effective alternatives to management are interest and share appreciation, as far as the immediate return to shareholders is concerned.

This is exactly the situation in which managers of portfolios of finance capital find themselves. Their alternatives are to buy shares, in the hopes of appreciation in value – 'growth stocks' – or to buy bonds for the interest. The alternatives are *not* interest and profits; the rate of interest is not an alternative to the firm's rate of profit, still less to a project's 'internal rate of return.' Instead it is an alternative to the rate of appreciation of the shares of a firm, and this, in turn, reflects the real rate of growth of capacity.

13 DIVIDENDS

Before this can be developed further, however, one obvious matter remains to be cleared up. Companies pay out dividends. Yet this seems hard to justify. For, *ex hypothesi*, they have investment programs planned for several years ahead that need funding. To pay out dividends simply reduces the funds available to support real growth. The investment of such funds, on the other hand, would be reflected in the appreciation of the firm's shares. Why, then, do firms pay out dividends?

The answer is simple enough. Share price appreciation will not be *realisable* unless there is a market for the share. For a market to exist the share must be actively traded and widely held. Moreover – and at least as important – for the original group of shareholders to be able to exercise control leverage (maintain effective control with less than majority holdings), the outstanding shares not in their possession must be widely held in small amounts. For both these reasons management, acting in the interests of the controlling shareholders, will seek a wide dispersal of small holdings actively traded. Paying dividends is an effective way to encourage financial managers to include a share in their portfolios; dividends can be regarded as a kind of premium for foregone liquidity.

Let d be the ratio of dividends to share capital, or (dividing by N) the ratio of earnings to price, for a representative firm. Then, assuming that portfolio managers attach some positive value to liquidity, there will be a minimum level of d, below which no one will hold the shares, except the original owner-operators. This minimum will, of course, be different for

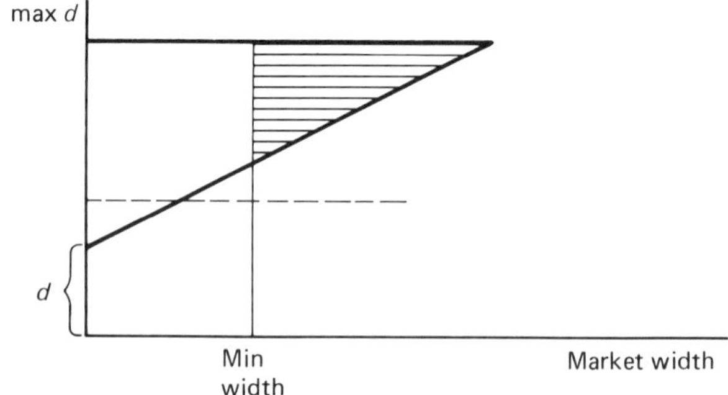

Figure 21.9 Cost of supporting the market in the firm's shares

different kinds of firms, and for different particular firms, also. As d rises, more and more portfolios will be willing to include them. This is not an inducement to the market to absorb more shares; it is an inducement to portfolio managers to include the share among their holdings. It is a *widening* of the market, not a deepening. Management, in turn, will want a market for certain minimum 'width,' even at the price of a high dividend rate, but there will also be a dividend rate above which it will not be prepared to go, at all. Rather than pay more, management would give up any prospect of supporting the market in the firm's shares. This can be shown on a diagram as in Figure 21.9.

Any point within the shaded triangle is feasible, but will drift horizontally to the hypotenuse. (If the max d were the dotted line, it would mean the max d was not feasible, so the firm would continue with its given pattern of shareholding.)

As the dividend rate rises, the firm will be progressively less willing to raise it further, and will require a progressively greater addition to the 'width' of the market, to compensate for the extra payout. The dividend rate will settle at the point where the additional dividend rate which firms are willing to pay to widen the market has fallen to the level of the inducement in extra dividends actually needed to widen it by a unit amount (Figure 21.10).

The needs to be interpreted with care. The maximum d that a firm is willing to pay, and the minimum width of the market that it seeks are functions of its long-term prospects. But the change in d per unit desired widening of its shareholdings should properly be a change in its dividend rate compared to the dividends it believes other firms similar to it are willing to pay. For any given firm seeking to widen the holdings of its shares is competing for customers with other firms. Yet if all firms together try this, the result will be a rise in d with little or no significant change in share-holding patterns. But there is no need to suppose that firms will all

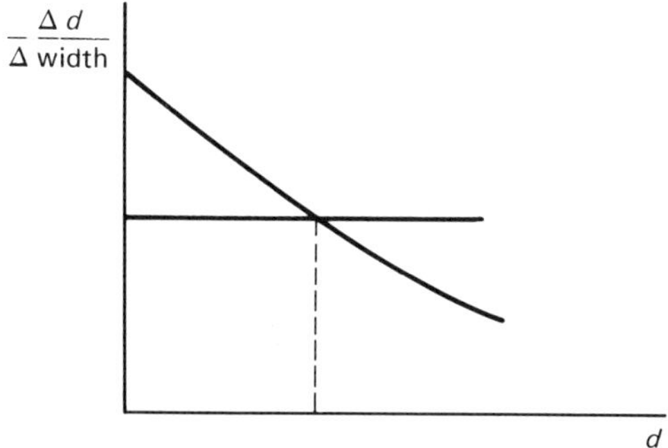

Figure 21.10 The new dividend rate

make this decision at the same time. Establishing a dividend policy is a long-term decision; it will be *revised* from time to time in the light of current rates and the needs of the controlling shareholders. But firms will not all be making such revisions at the same time. Hence, we can assume that each firm will establish its policy taking the position of the others as given.

But will not changes in sales require changes in pay-out rates? Not necessarily; if realised earnings fall, and are expected to stay down, the valuation of the firm's shares will fall, so the rate of pay-out per unit share value can stay the same. But a prolonged fall in share values may so inconvenience owners that the firm will have to try to reverse the downtrend by raising its pay-out. And, of course, a very wide swing in sales, which endangered the firm's ability to meet fixed obligations, would have to lead to a cut-off of dividends. By contrast, however, a boom in the firm's shares would *not* lead to a corresponding rise in dividends paid out; instead d would fall, for the very good reason that a boom in share prices implies there is already a fine market which needs no further encouragement.

14 THE RATE OF PROFIT, THE RATE OF GROWTH AND THE RATE OF INTEREST

As a result, then, we can say that the firm will attempt to adjust its investment spending so that the rate of profit it expects to realise just covers its required rate, and that the capital market will adjust its holdings of shares and bonds so that the rate of interest is brought into line with the rate of share appreciation (which reflects the rate of growth) added to firms' established dividend policies. Hence we will normally find: $r > g + d = i$. This must be examined further.[6]

Given a level of d, both i and g are functions of I, the level of investment spending. The rate of growth of capacity simply rises proportionately with

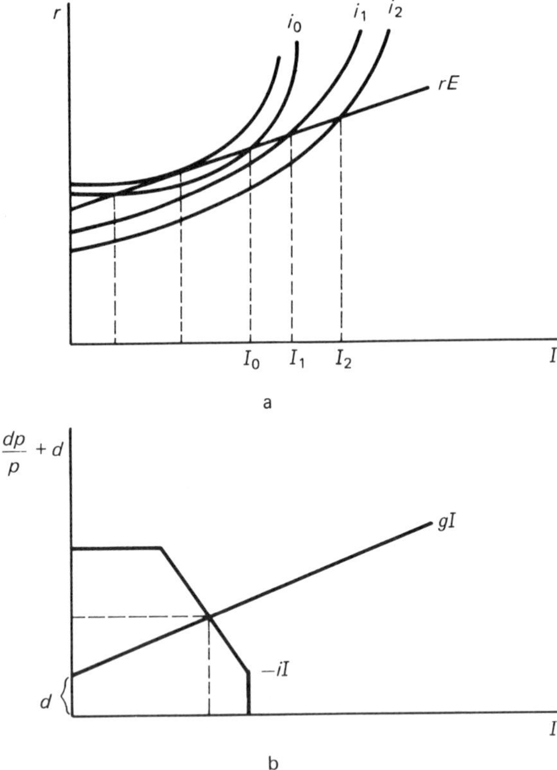

Figure 21.11 Rate of interest and level of *I*

I. The rate of interest increases the level of fixed costs, and so raises risk; hence the higher the rate of interest, the lower the level of *I* which will equate r_r to the expected r_g. But this has to be interpreted carefully, since the *IF* curve may cut the *rE* more than once (Figure 21.11a and 21.11b).

Consider an *rE* line and a set of *IF* curves, and look at the upper intersections. Higher rates of interest, $i_0 > i_1 > i_2$, are associated with lower levels of *I*, $I_0 < I_1 < I_2$. When the rate of interest reaches a certain level, then all *I*-spending will cease. When *i* is sufficiently low, *I* will reach the maximum level called for by investment decisions. Hence the $i - I$ relation for the *upper equilibrium* can be put together with the rate of share appreciation plus dividends.[7] This shows that under plausible assumptions there exists a unique level of investment spending at which the rate of interest equals the rate of growth, and the generated rate of return equals the required rate. A unique upper equilibrium always exists.

But, of course, things are quite different as regards the lower intersection points (Figure 21.12). There, $i_0 > i_1$ and $I_0' > I_1'$. A succession of *IF*

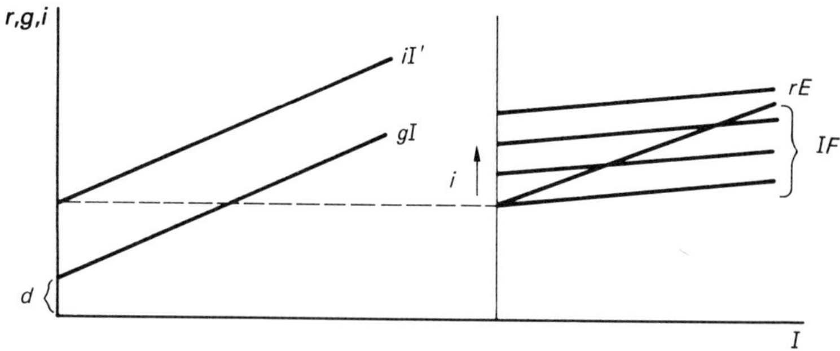

Figure 21.12 When I has fallen to 0

curves, starting from one whose vertical intercept coincides with that of rE, trace out a series of intersections with rE. The resulting iI relation simply reproduces rE. Since $r_0 > d$ (C_c is financed not only by dividends but also by salaries and fixed interest), and since the slope of both rE and gI is $1/K$, these two lines will never intersect. There is no lower equilibrium; the system will come to rest only when I has fallen to zero, that is, to its practical minimum.

The i, g relationship differs from $IFrE$ significantly. In the latter case, firms holding expectations as to their sales adjust I until $r_r = r_g$. But adjusting I has no immediate effect on iI. That curve is the locus of combinations of i, I for which $r_r = r_g$. But different levels of I do show up as different levels of g, as the spending is translated into usable capacity, whereupon they appear in the capital market as various levels of dp/p. So movements in the level of investment spending tend to originate in the considerations modelled in the $IFrE$ diagram (Figure 21.12). But the i, g diagram (Figure 21.13) represents an important set of relationships, too: the capital market. For it is here that pressures causing the rate of interest to vary will be found. Let us see how this works.

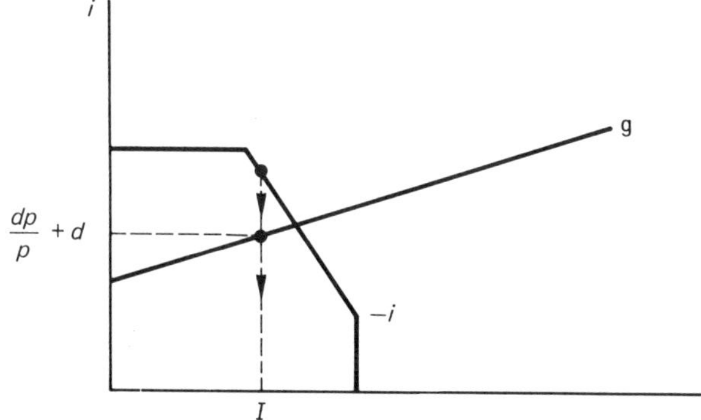

Figure 21.13 I at a level where $r_r - r_g$

Suppose that I settles at the level where $r_r = r_g$ and the initial rate of interest, defining F and D, is such that $i > dp/p + d = g$. Once this level of spending and revenues has become established, there will be incentives to portfolio managers to switch out of shares into bonds, since the return on bonds is greater. Hence bond prices will be bid up; not all at once, of course, for it will take some time for the market to judge the prospects of firms and the effectiveness of their investments. But once information is available and opinion congeals, the movement of funds can be quite rapid. The effect of funds switching from shares to bonds, however, is not only to raise bond prices, lowering i; it also lowers the rate of appreciation of share prices. So dp/p falls. Hence the discrepancy between i and dp/p is maintained, and the incentive to switch funds remains. (However, the fall in i does not lower F, for such costs were established in the past, at the earlier level of the interest rate. Over time, loans can be rolled over, but in general it will not be easy for a firm to renegotiate its long-term debt at a lower interest rate when its share prices are collapsing. The behaviour of the firm's shares appears to indicate that the market does not think highly of its prospects – what, then, is the worth of the security the firm is to put up for a new loan at a lower interest rate?)

But this situation becomes progressively more uncomfortable for the owners. The addition to capacity is valued by the market at less than its opportunity cost – i.e., more would have been earned by lending the funds and distributing the resulting interest as additional dividends. Of course, this would mean postponing or abandoning the firm's long-range investment plans, and possibly endangering its market position by letting its competitors get a jump ahead. So there are good reasons why a business firm will not put its capital funds into the bond market. But owners still may wish – or need – cash; management has a certain responsibility to them and so must try to prevent the collapse of share prices. Hence as the fall in dp/p becomes more pronounced the firm will raise its dividend payment. In order to do this, of course, they will have to cut back on investment spending, which will lower dp/p still further.

Now suppose that the level of investment spending which equates r_r and r_g is quite high and the initial interest rate low, so that $dp/p + d > i$ (Figure 21.14). Then there will be an incentive for portfolio managers to sell bonds and buy shares. Bond prices will fall and the interest rate rise; but share prices will be bid up faster will than ever. Since the market in shares proves so active, firms will feel less pressure to pay dividends. There is no need, after all, to support or widen the market for shares; it is active enough anyway. Hence the funds normally used to pay dividends can be directed to investment. In addition, if share values reach exceptional heights, the firm might be tempted into an issue of new equity, on the grounds that a great deal of money would be raised for a negligible dilution of ownership. In short, when $dp/p + d > i$, the movement of funds in the capital market is

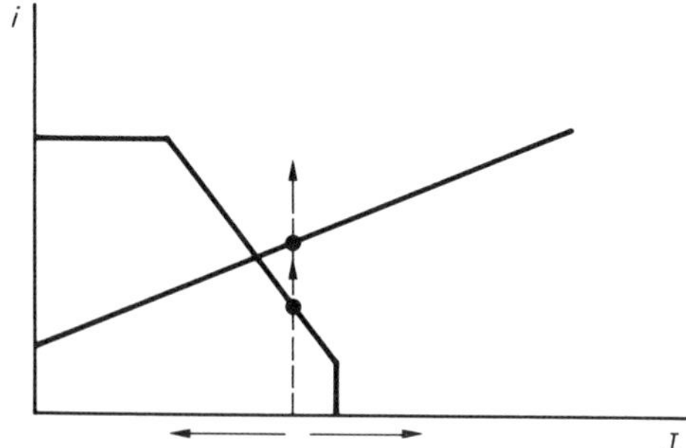

Figure 21.14 Level of investment spending when $dp/p + d > i$

such as to encourage and facilitate further investment spending – which, of course, will tend to raise dp/p even more.

In other words, although an upper equilibrium exists, and is stable with respect to firm's earnings and costs, the capital market is unstable.

The consequences of this for the dynamics of investment spending are important. Let's return to the brief sketch of the investment cycle already proposed. The upswing starts the boom in the capital market, which tends to increase interest rates and, eventually generates a rise of F. But the speculation continues after the IF curve has moved above rE and has brought about a decline of investment. Share prices will be pushed upwards by the speculative fever, and as bonds are sold to buy shares, this will engender a further rise in interest rates. But with the slowing-down of investment the real basis for the rise of share prices disappears. Furthermore – and more important – the multiplier effects of the decrease in the investment spending reduce receipts, and make the payment of dividends more difficult. As these effects become more apparent, share prices stop increasing. But interest rates remain at a high level, so there is a rush to reswitch from shares to bonds, and the resulting collapse of share prices is likely to give birth to a panic, generating bankruptcies and a reorganisation, as well as a decrease in interest rates. Both these cumulative effects lower the IF curve. Investment can thus start again, but interest rates do not increase immediately. As the activity increases, so does the rating of bonds, whereas financial investors remain suspicious toward shares. They will not buy unless payouts rise, or they see other clear evidence of the success of firms' investment strategies. Then, although the rate of return on most shares will still be low, while that on most bonds will still be high, the yield on some shares will rise to equal or exceed that of lower-return bonds. This will start the switching of funds to shares, bidding up their prices, while simultaneously raising the yields on bonds. As the prices of shares rise, more and more funds will switch, pursuing speculative gains, and by doing so, further accelerating price increases. At the same time rising share prices will drag up interest rates, leading eventually to higher fixed costs, which shift *IF* up. Speculative movements in the capital market, aggravated by instability, thus ultimately shift the *IF* curve, intensifying the cycle.

The ties between financial markets and production and investment are thus tenuous but real. Interest rate changes ultimately affect fixed costs, which in turn influence investment spending; investment determines growth of capacity, which will eventually be reflected in share values. But, notoriously, share prices are also influenced by speculative fever, the news of the day, rumors and random events. So they may move independently of capacity growth. The instability of financial markets thus plays a part in the variations of financial costs, which result in cyclical shifts in the *IF* curve. In short, a mixture of productive and monetary forces combines to dance a reel in the shadow of the casino.

Notes

1. By 'investment' I mean construction of fixed plant and equipment, for the purpose of production. I do not consider investment in inventory, or investment in housing. Important though they are, both are left to one side here.
2. A high rate of profits relative to interest might lead consumers to purchase durables now rather than later, on the grounds that interest rates could rise in the future. By the same token, a low rate of profits would lead to postponing consumer durable purchases whenever consumer financing was important. So purchases of consumer durables will move with the cycle, exacerbating its swings.
3. One simple assumption would be sufficient in the present context, but others could be given. Firms who earn high revenue one period are in a stronger position the next. But, by the same token, the firms who earned little are now at a greater risk. They will therefore work harder to recover than their counterparts will to preserve and exploit their advantage. The marginal utility of a sum lost is greater than the marginal utility that sum gained. The assumption then is that the greater effort of the losers just offsets the stronger position of the ones who did relatively better.
4. Notice that if we identify the rate of profit and the rate of interest, we have a two-variable dynamical system in I and r, in which the change in I is proportional to the negative level of r and the change in r is directly proportional to the level of I. This suggests that some variant of the Lotka–Volterra equations might describe the interactions of these variables. However, we cannot identify the rate of profit with the rate of interest here; under certain circumstances, they do not even move together. The financial system contains its own dynamic which interacts with and influences the dynamics of productions and sales.
5. The internal rate of return can be shown to be unique if the process can be suitably 'truncated' – cut off. But that means scrapping and replacing the process, which may not be desirable in view of its complementary relation to other activities of the firm.

6. Notice further that the rate of profit as calculated from input-output and capital stock data will appear high because no risk or insurance premiums have been taken out. These would both reduce the general rate and affect prices, since they will normally differ from sector to sector, but, being in part subjective, are hard to estimate.
7. When $I = 0, g = 0$; hence $dp/p = 0$. But if dividends are treated as a fixed charge by the firm (albeit fixed by themselves and so variable in a crisis), then $d > 0$.

References

Arestis, Philip (ed.) (1988) *Post-Keynesian Monetary Economics* (London: Edward Elgar).

Eichner, R. (1976) *The Megacorp. and Oligopoly* (New York: Cambridge University Press).

Minsky, H. (1986) *Stabilizing an Unstable Economy* (New Haven: Yale University Press).

Nell, Edward (1988) *Prosperity and Public Spending* (London and Boston: Unwin Hyman).

Nell, Edward (1992) *Keynes after Sraffa* (London and Boston: Urwin Hyman).

Okun, Arthur (1982) *Price and Quantities: A Macroeconomic Analysis* (Oxford: Basil Blackwell).

22 Does the Rate of Interest Determine the Rate of Profit?*

Does the rate of interest on money, as fixed by the Central Banking Authorities, determine the rate of profit? There is a suggestion to this effect in Sraffa (1960, p. 33) and Pivetti (1985) has interpreted this to mean that the 'normal' rate of profit, as opposed to the actual rate, will be governed by the effects of the rate of interest on the ratio of money prices to money wages: a fall (rise) in the rate of interest will lower (raise) costs, so will lead to lower (higher) prices, but there will be no similar effect on money wages. So a fall (rise) in the rate of interest will bring a rise (fall) in the real wage; thus the rate of profit will move in the same direction as, and by a magnitude proportional to the change in the rate of interest. In short, 'lasting changes in interest rates must be followed by corresponding changes in normal profit rates' (Pivetti, 1985, p. 81). Similar arguments have been advanced by Panico (1985) who finds the root of the idea in Keynes' Chapter 17, by Vianello, (1985) and by Schefold, (1985), who limits the claim by arguing that the mechanism works only under historical conditions of slow accumulation.

The proposition is admitted to be subject to a number of qualifications: the monetary authorities may be institutionally limited in their power to adjust the rate of interest; strong unions may set an inflation barrier, which in a open economy may prevent the raising of prices; the historical or international position of the country may set limits on the acceptable level or movement of the real wage, etc. The double-edged central point, however, is that the real wage is set by the ratio of prices to money wages – no labor market jointly determines real wages and employment – and this ratio is governed, not by aggregate demand, but by long-term monetary policy. The first part is Keynes, the second Sraffa.

What is a 'lasting change in the rate of interest'? What could this mean, when such a change is a matter of policy? Monetary policy can be changed at any time, and will very likely change with changes in the political climate. The 'normal' rate of profit is the rate obtainable by firms using the dominant technique and producing at the expected capacity levels for normal market conditions; it is not observable, but it is that rate towards which actual profits are always tending as the result of competitive press-

* *Political Economy*, 4 (2) (1988).

ures. Such a rate will not vary with evanescent circumstances. How then can it be affected by policies which necessarily change with the political winds? Surely a more appropriate procedure would be to first examine the way a purely private, profit-driven monetary system would establish interest rates and the provision of finance, defining a long-period position in which private banking and private industry interact (Nell, 1986). (Would not the provision of financial services be a non-basic industry? So the rate of profit would determine the rate of return on such services.) Then it would be possible to consider the effect of introducing a Central Bank as a lender of last resort with regulatory powers and not subject to the profit motive. But following the line suggested by Pivetti and others, surely the best that can be argued is that the current *actual* rate of profit will be set by the temporary ratio of prices to money wages, where the current rate of interest will be one of the influences determining the deviation of the actual ratio of prices to money wages from the normal ratio.

Even this runs into difficulties, however. A chief way in which the monetary authorities set interest rates is by manipulating the money supply; to raise interest rates, the money supply will be constricted, and vice-versa to lower them. But if prices move directly with interest rates, where these latter are governed by policy, then prices must move inversely to the supply of money! This flatly contradicts virtually all thinking on the role of the Quantity of Money; we need not accept the Quantity Theory to view an *inverse* relation between the price level and the money supply with suspicion. As a matter of theory it might be possible to accept a decline in interest rates, brought about by an increase in the quantity of money, leading to a fall in prices, since the additional money could be absorbed by idle balances – provided interest rates fall far enough for the rise in liquidity preference to become large enough. But the reverse movement is much more difficult to swallow: the idea that interest rates and prices can both rise, concurrently with the money stock falling, runs into the problem that there need be no idle balances to discharge the required money. Velocity could rise, and new forms of money could be created – but then what is the justification for supposing that the monetary authorities can set the long-term real rate of interest? Why do changes in velocity or in money creation, which support increased profits, have to wait on action by the authorities?

A merit of the view under discussion is that it makes sense of the great body of evidence, discussed by Keynes under the heading of 'Gibson's Paradox,' which shows that interest rates and the price level are positively rather than inversely correlated (Keynes, 1930 Vol. II, pp. 198–210). But an equally large body of evidence shows that the price level and the quantity of money are also positively correlated – whichever way the causation may run. It will be hard to reconcile this second body of evidence with the view that a policy-determined rate of interest sets the rate of profits. But these two bodies of evidence are both consistent with the view that the money supply adjusts to demand and that the anticipated growth of demand significantly influences the rate of profit, to which the 'normal' long-term rate of interest, in turn, adapts (Nell, 1988). (On this view, monetary policy would find its major field of operations in controlling short-term rates and the volume of certain kinds of lending, but would have little effect on long-term rates.)

The 'normal' rate of profit is defined in terms of normal capacity output, which implies producing for a normal level of demand. Output is divided at least between consumption goods and capital goods; hence there must be a normal level of investment demand, so a normal rate of growth. Both mainstream and 'Cambridge' theories hold that aggregate demand will tend to move inversely to interest rates; Pivetti, following Garegnani (1983) argues that there will be conflicting tendencies and that no general rule can be asserted.

Consider first the case where a decline in the interest rate stimulates both investment demand, and consumer durable demand. Both capital goods and consumer goods industries find their expected demand has increased and feel the need to increase their capacity (beyond the normal growth they have already planned for). Their interest costs, however, are down and borrowing terms are easier. If they lower their prices their demand can be expected to increase still further. The question they must ask is, at what prices will their profits be at least sufficient to finance the maintenance and construction of the capacity required to service the expected demand they will face at those prices? If demand is initially at capacity, a rise in demand will require additional plant and equipment; the decline in interest certainly need not add enough to profits to finance this, let alone to leave enough over for a price cut which will further increase demand. (The cost savings from the decline in interest will depend on the debt–equity ratio on existing capital; the amount needed to finance new capital will depend on the size of the increase in demand, and the capital–output and debt–equity ratios for new capital.) So a decline in interest rates that brought a sufficiently large increase in demand, or occurred with techniques having a sufficiently high capital–output ratio, could lead to no change or to a rise in prices.

Next suppose that there is no effect of interest on investment or on worker consumption, but that interest payments provide income to a rentier class, while profits net of interest finance investment. Let subscript 'k' indicate the capital goods sector, and 'c' the consumption goods sector. Let 'I' be investment, 'D' $= D_k + D_c$, debt, 'K' and 'C' the output of capital goods and consumer goods, respectively, where $K = K_k + K_c$, the capital goods used in each sector, and $C = C_r + C_w$, the consumption of rentiers and workers respectively. 'P_k' and 'P_c' will be the two prices. 'N' $= N_k + N_c$, employment, and 'w' will be the fixed money wage.

If competition were to establish

$$r^* = [IP_k - wN_k]/K_kP_k = [CP_c - wN_c]/K_cP_k$$

there would be no reason why changes in interest costs would affect money prices. Only if interest charges are subtracted as a cost on a par with wages will prices be changed; hence

$$r = [IP_k - iD_k - wN_k]/K_kP_k = [CP_c - iD_c - wN_c]/K_cP_k$$

and $rK = I$, indicating that r is adequate to finance g. Also,

$$iD = C_rP_c \text{ and } wN = C_wP_c, \text{ so that } CP_c = iD + wN.$$

Profits underwrite investment, interest payments finance rentier consumption and wages support worker consumption.

Now consider a fall in the rate of interest. Any producer can now earn the same rate of profit as before while charging a lower price; each will be tempted to try to expand their market share by undercutting the others. All will therefore cut, and no one will gain. But the price changes will offset the change in the rate of interest:

$$dP_k/P_k = [iD_k/(iD_k + wN_k)]di/i, \text{ and}$$

$$dP_c/P_c = [iD_c/(iD_c + wN_c)]di/i.$$

The competitive price-cutting will be carried only to the point where the lower prices have re-established the original rate of profit. There will be no change in the rate of profit, but the relative price $p = P_k/P_c$, will change, since the price change will be greater in the sector with the higher ratio of interest to wage costs. But the most important effect will be to reduce the income and therefore the consumption of rentiers, while raising the real income of workers. Thus C_r will fall and C_w will rise.

However this result does depend on assuming a very simple kind of capital market, in which there is only one kind of income-bearing security. If there were common stock which appreciated at the same rate as real capital accumulated, then stock prices would continue to rise at rate $g = I/K$ (Nell, 1985). Hence when the interest rate fell, rentiers would tend to switch from bonds to stocks, depressing bond prices and raising the rate of interest. Such arbitrage in the securities market would make it difficult for the authorities to depress the long-term rate of interest. The rentier class would be able to defend its level of consumption, and the scope of monetary policy would be limited.

This can be argued in another way: for the authorities to try to move the interest rate against the growth rate endangers the stability of the Stock Market. Suppose the growth rate is high and the authorities try to drive interest down. They will have to increase the money supply, which will flood the market and lead to a boom in share prices. Suppose the growth rate is low, and the authorities try to raise interest rates; they will restrict money and credit, which will tend to collapse share prices. If orderly financial markets are to be maintained, the Central Bank's effective control is limited to moving interest rates in the same direction as growth rates.

These examples show that once the level and rate of growth of demand are taken into account changes in the rate of interest cannot easily affect the ratio of prices to money wages in the manner supposed. It is much more plausible to argue that the normal rate of profit determines the long-term normal rate of interest. The real question concerns the way the normal rate of profit is related to the long-term normal growth of demand.

References

Garegnani, P. (1983) 'Notes on Consumption, Investment and Effective Demand,' in J. Eatwell and M. Milgate (eds), *Keynes' Economics and the Theory of Value and Distribution* (London).

Keynes, J.M. (1930) *Treatise on Money*, Vol. II (London).

Nell, E.J. (1985) 'Notes Sur le Financement, le Riscue et la Depense d'Investissement,' in Alain Barrère (ed.), *Keynes Aujourd'hui* (Paris: Economica).

Nell, E.J. (1986) 'On Monetary Circulation and The Rate of Exploitation,' *Thames Papers in Political Economy* (Summer).

Nell, E.J. (1988) *Prosperity and Public Spending* (Boston, London: Allen and Unwin).

Panico, C. (1985) 'Market Forces and the relation between the Rates of Interest and Profit,' *Contributions to Political Economy*, 4.

Pivetti, M. (1985) 'On the Monetary Explanation of Distribution,' *Political Economy*.

Schefold, B. (1985) 'Cambridge Price Theory: Special Model or General Theory of Value?,' *AEA Papers and Proceedings* pp. 144–5.

Sraffa, Piero, (1960) *Production of Commodities by Means of Commodities* (Cambridge: Cambridge University Press).

Vianello, F. (1985) 'The Pace of Accumulation,' *Political Economy* 1 (1).

23 Wages, Inflation and the Labor Market*

The revival of the approach of the Classics has resulted in a multiplier which implies that an increase in the real wage will increase employment. This requires a close examination of the labor market. But the real wage is a composite construct – it is the money wage divided by the money price of consumer goods. These money variables can move independently of one another, and they do in inflationary processes. We must therefore explore inflation as a wage—price spiral, in which money wages and prices, moving at different rates, change distribution.

1 THE EMPLOYMENT MARKET

To make matters as simple as possible we will provisionally adopt the assumption, taken over from Marx, that the capital–labor ratios of the two sectors are the same. This makes it possible to simplify the multiplier expression, using 'n' for both n_I and n_c. The formula can then be rewritten to show the relationship between aggregate employment and real wages, for a given investment spending:

From Chapter 20 in this volume, and having in mind that $\omega N = C = W$ we obtain

$$N = \frac{n}{1 - \omega n} I, \tag{23.1}$$

where n takes the place of n_c and n_I, and ω is the real wage.

This tells us the total employment, N, generated directly and indirectly by investment spending, I. Suppose we now take both n and I as fixed, and consider the effects of changing ω on N. Clearly

$$\frac{dN}{d\omega} = \frac{In^2}{(1 - \omega n)^2} > 0 \tag{23.2}$$

* Written for this volume based on materials previously published in *Prosperity and Public Spending* (1988).

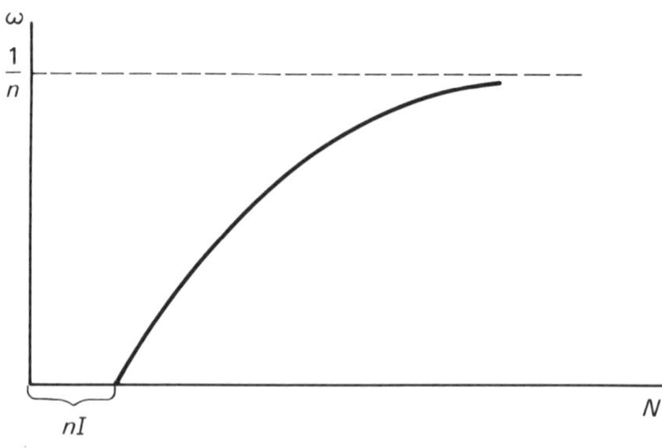

Figure 23.1

Increases in ω will *increase* employment, by stimulating activity in the consumer goods sector, and vice-versa for decreases in ω. Moreover,

$$\frac{d^2N}{d\omega^2} = \frac{2In^3}{(1 - \omega n)^3} > 0. \tag{23.3}$$

That is, the higher ω is, the greater will be the impact on N of a given change in ω. The real wage-employment relation can therefore be represented on a simple diagram (Figure 23.1). There will be a positive intercept, nI, when $\omega = 0$; as ω increases to its maximum, $1/n$, N tends to infinity. (Of course, this is not practically possible; N is constrained by the feasible capacity of existing plant and equipment.)

Next consider a simple labor supply function, showing the number of workers seeking jobs for each perceived level of the real wage. There is some evidence that this number will rise with the real wage, possibly just reflecting the fact that in boom times, when real wages are high, there are more opportunities; so that it is the rise in job openings, more than the rise in wages, that calls forth labor supply. For the sake of argument, however, let us accept the conventional positively sloped labor supply function, and add it to Figure 23.1 (see Figure 23.2).

Clearly, for a given level of I, a unique equilibrium exists, (ω_e, N_e), which clears the labor market. (If the S curve were shallower, and had an intercept lying between the origin and nI, then two equilibria would exist.) The position of the demand for labor curve will shift in and out according to whether I is smaller or larger. Somewhat paradoxically, at first glance, a smaller I implies a higher ω_e and a higher N_e; a larger I, a lower ω_e and N_e. But, in fact, there is no paradox. If investment spending is, for example, higher, there will be more employment in the investment goods sector, and therefore a larger wage bill. But the labor force varies only slightly; when

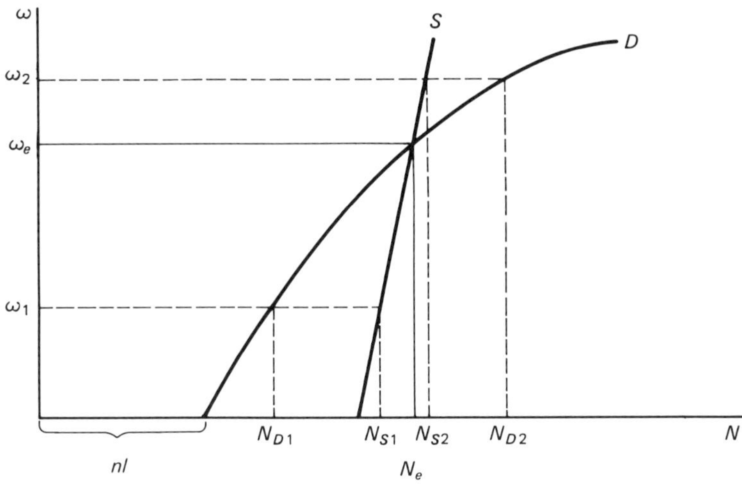

Figure 23.2

employment is larger in investment goods, less employment will be needed in the consumption goods sector to make up the total. Consequently less additional consumer spending is needed to generate the demand for employment; hence a lower real wage will be necessary in order to ensure that only the required amount of consumer demand will be forthcoming. Hence, a higher demand for labor at every level of the real wage – an outward shift in the labor demand function – implies a *lower* equilibrium real wage, and, if the labor force supply function has a positive slope, a lower equilibrium level of employment. The labor market works just the reverse of the way neo-Classical theory assumes that most markets work.

Next, looking again at Figure 23.2, consider a level, $\omega_1 < \omega_e$; demand for labor will be $N_{DI} < N_{SI}$. There will therefore be excess supply of labor, putting downward pressure on money wages. What happens to the real wage then depends on how prices move, assuming flexibility, for the sake of argument. But the likelihood is that prices would fall at the same rate or more slowly; excess supply in the labor market does not necessarily mean unwanted excess capacity. As argued earlier, businesses plan to carry some excess capacity and prefer to locate where there will be some excess labor. So there is no reason to suppose that the circumstances represented by ω_1 will put strong downward pressure on prices. The situation is likely either to be stable, prices falling at the same rate as money wages, or one in which the real wage drifts downwards, as money wages fall faster than prices. In the first case the excess supply of labor will remain constant; in the second, it will increase. Flexible wages and prices are not going to eliminate unemployment.

Now consider $\omega_2 > \omega_e$. This will require looking at another diagram

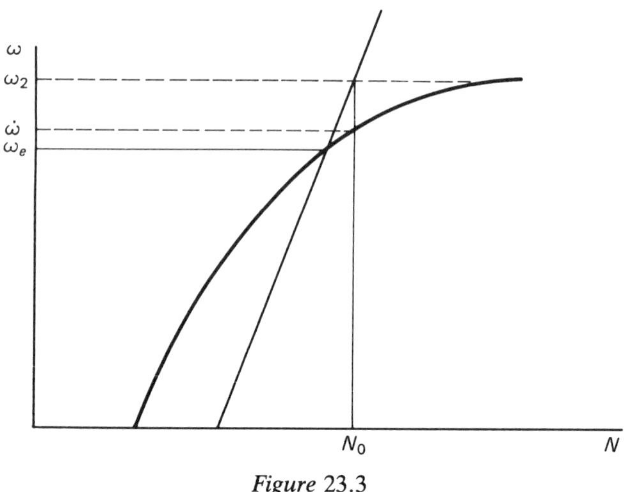

Figure 23.3

(Figure 23.3). The labor supply at ω_2 is only N_0; hence the *respending of wages*, creating additional employment, cannot take place. Thus the section of the labor demand curve lying beyond N_0 is inoperative. But there is nevertheless excess demand for labor. The wage required to generate employment equal to N_0 is $\bar{\omega}$; the actual wage is ω_2. There is therefore excess demand for labor equal to:

$$(\omega_2 - \bar{\omega})N_0 n_c = \Delta C_0 n_c; \tag{23.4}$$

and of course the corresponding excess demand for consumption goods is:

$$(\omega_2 - \bar{\omega})N_0 = \Delta C_0. \tag{23.5}$$

The *proportional* excess demand for labor is therefore

$$\frac{\Delta C_0 \mathrm{n_c}}{C_0 \mathrm{n_c}} = \frac{\Delta C_0}{C_0},$$

which, of course, is equal to the proportional excess demand for consumption goods. Hence the *pressure* in the labor market is the same as the *pressure* in the consumer goods market. If the two markets respond to pressure in the same way, wages and prices will rise in the same proportion. So the real wage will remain unchanged, while money wages and prices rise in a general inflation. Too high a level of the real wage has no tendency to correct itself any more than too low a level. Upward flexibility of money wages and prices no more eliminates a labor shortage than downward flexibility cures unemployment.

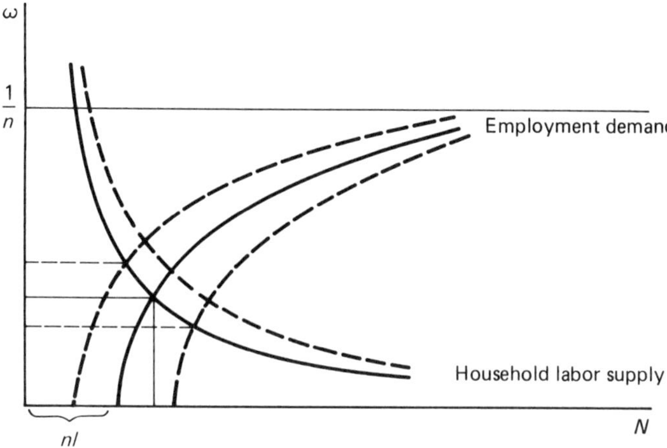

Note: The dotted lines represent shifts: the employment function shifts when investment spending changes, and the household labor supply shifts with changes in the normal standard of living. The labor demand curves differ in their intercepts along the horizontal axis, but they asymptotically approach the *same* limit on the vertical axis – that is, when $\omega = 1/n$, N tends to infinity, and this is true for all the curves, regardless of the level of I. The labor supply curves are asymptotic to both axes.

Figure 23.4

An even more extreme contrast can be obtained by reconsidering the labor force participation function. In place of the preceding conventional idea, imagine a household determined to maintain a certain standard of living. At high wages, only the chief breadwinner will work, putting in a normal work week. At lower wages, the breadwinner will put in for overtime, then will add a part-time job. At still lower wages, other members of the family will enter the market, first for part-time, then for full-time work, and so on. In the extreme case the curve will be a rectangular hyperbola where proportional cuts in the real wages will just be matched by proportional increases in the hours of work offered. Put this together with the wage–employment function and we have the exact opposite of the conventional picture (Figure 23.4): a rising demand for labor, and a falling supply curve. Here a shift in the demand for employment implies perverse movements only in the wage. A shift outward, for example, would require the wage to fall, in order to force enough workers into the labor market. But, of course, an outward shift would, if anything, tend to drive wages up. As before, above the 'equilibrium' real wage the excess demand is not operative, since with no workers available to be employed, there will be no respending. But below the equilibrium the excess labor force surely exerts some downward pressure. Hence there will be tendencies for the market to move into disequilibrium.

So, there are two differences between the labor market and the normal neo-Classical conception of a market. First, shifts in the demand function, *ceteris paribus*, cause the equilibrium wage and, in some cases employment levels to move *inversely*, and secondly, deviations from equilibrium, in either direction, have no tendency to self-correction. In the short run, therefore, there will be a tendency for deviations from equilibrium to persist or grow worse.

2 REAL WAGES AND PRODUCTIVITY

Our project so far has been to examine the short-run effective demand relationships between real wages, employment, productivity and investment. These are summarized in the formula with which we have been working, written in simplified form:

$$N = \frac{n}{1 - \omega n} I. \tag{23.1}$$

First we took n and ω as fixed and examined the effect of changes in I on N, the traditional multiplier relationship in a new format. Then we took I and n as fixed and examined the effects of changes in ω on N. Now we shall treat I as given and look briefly at the effects of the joint variation of ω and n on N. For the foundation of modern anti-inflation policy is that wage increases must be kept equiproportional to rise in productivity. Such a wage increase, according to the conventional wisdom, will be the only possible 'neutral' change, the only change that will not affect prices, employment, profit or other key variables.

But, in fact, in the short run increasing real wages in step with productivity will *reduce employment*. Take the total differential of the multiplier equation, with I fixed:

$$dN = d\omega \frac{\delta N}{\delta \omega} + dn \frac{\delta N}{\delta n'} \tag{23.6}$$

where

$$\frac{\delta N}{\delta \omega} = \frac{In^2}{(1 - \omega n)^2} \quad \text{and} \quad \frac{\delta N}{\delta n'} = \frac{I}{(1 - \omega n)^2}$$

Substituting and rearranging gives:

$$\frac{dN}{N} = \frac{1}{1 - \omega n} \left[\omega n \ \frac{d\omega}{\omega} + \frac{dn}{n} \right], \tag{23.7}$$

since, *ex hypothesi*,

$$\omega n < 1, \text{ and } \frac{d\omega}{\omega} = - \frac{dn}{n} \text{ ; clearly } \frac{dN}{N} < 0.$$

In words, when the real wage is such that the value productivity of labor is positive (rate of exploitation positive) and real wages rise in step with increases in productivity, then the level of employment will steadily fall.

To be sure, this is over-simplified. At the very least the productivity changes in the different sectors should be distinguished. But the point should be clear: the productivity rule is not neutral in terms of its short-run effects on employment. Of course, these could be offset by an investment policy or by planned government spending. But most discussions of income policies have not recognized their short-run impact on employment, or the need to offset this through demand management policies.

3 THE IDEA OF A DEMAND-CONSTRAINED SYSTEM

So demand is the key. But we will have to think about it carefully, for the point has proved so difficult and strange that even those who, like Keynes, first proposed it, have backed away from its full implications. To say that the system is 'demand-constrained', that is, that there is normally a shortage of demand, is to say that output is not constrained by the available resources, which clearly implies that they are not being fully utilized. So they are not 'scarce' in relation to effective demand. Not being scarce means they are not costly to use; they would just be the idle otherwise. In economists' terms, being demand-constrained means that Say's Law – 'supply creates its own demand' – does not hold. No one can assume that whatever they produce will automatically be sold. Producers must compete with each other for the available customers; hence, incentives to efficiency will be strong, but markets, and particularly labor markets will not necessarily clear. In other words (and this is one of the points traditionally trained economists have found hard to accept), the very factor that creates the pressure for efficiency on the part of each agent entails that the overall system will be inefficient, because some available resources are not fully used.

To see the force of this point, consider an opposite kind of system, one that is supply-constrained, or, rather, resource-constrained. In such a system (procurement for the Defense Department, or a centrally planned economy) everything produced can easily be sold. Individual producers will therefore have incentives to overrun costs in order to turn out as much as possible. Since there is excess demand, as long as the output is passable it doesn't have to be good. The shortage of demand is what creates the competition for markets, thereby setting up powerful incentives for cost-cutting and the efficient use of resources. When demand is plentiful, then, quality will tend to deteriorate and costs will tend to rise, so that shortages will become chronic, for every individual producer. In the aggregate, however, the system will be efficient: no resources will be underutilized.

Notice the paradoxical contrast between whole and part: what is true for each and every individual unit is the *opposite* of what is true for the whole. In the first case, each unit is constrained by demand scarcity to cut costs and be efficient – but the system as a whole wastes resources and tends to generate surplus output or capacity. In the second case, each unit tends to overproduce wastefully – but the system as a whole uses resources efficiently and suffers from shortages.

In a demand-constrained system, costs must be cut, the product must be attractive and effective, and service must be prompt in order to compete for sales. Hence both products and processes of production will be designed to be maximally efficient, which means that functions will be separated and tasks will be divided, just as Adam Smith prescribed. But while division of labor and separation of function cut costs, they do not conserve scarce resources. 'The division of labor is limited by the extent of the market,' said Smith; the implication is that there is enough labor to perform the separate jobs. If labor had to be conserved, then division of labor would not be called for; workers would each have to perform a number of functions. Exactly that happens in resource-constrained systems where the pressure of chronic shortages leads to product and process designs that systematically combine functions and multiply rather than subdivide tasks. A shortage economy develops the aerospace plane, the David gun, the space shuttle – systems, rather than products, which are designed to perform several functions simultaneously, and which have to be run by operatives who have mastered a number of distinct skills. Adam Smith's separation of function and division of labor are impossible. In a demand-constrained system, product and process design will tend towards simplicity, while jobs will tend to become repetitive and monotonous. In a shortage economy, product and process design will tend towards the baroque, while jobs will become excessively demanding.

Bureaucracies are inherently resource-constrained systems in at least one respect: time and attention at the top are limited, hence projects will be tailored to conserve top management time, which means combining and coordinating different ventures. Bureaucracies also normally face political constraints; coordinating ventures and combining previously separate functions can help in forming coalitions in order to obtain support for projects. Thus there will normally be pressures for combining functions and multiplying tasks in project design.

When functions are combined and tasks multiplied, so that a project's complexity increases, scarce resources are conserved, but the impact of a breakdown is increased dramatically. For now a breakdown in any one function will mean a breakdown for all the rest; the combination has increased the costs and the output of the project arithmetically, but has raised the costs of a breakdown *geometrically*. If such breakdowns are a major cause of shortages and bottlenecks, then, as output rises, shortages can be expected to rise faster.

The characteristic operation of corporate capitalism can be expressed as $I/z < K/v$ (a shortage of aggregate demand), where $\frac{1}{z}$ is the multiplier and $\frac{1}{v}$ the productivity of capital, so that the pressure cut costs and operate efficiently would lead to a tendency for z to rise, and v to fall, maintaining the tendency of effective demand to lie below capacity. The objective will be to minimize costs. Analogously, the characteristic operation of a planned economy can be expressed as $I/z > K/v$, which signifies excess demand in the aggregate, which will set up incentives that will lead z to fall, and v to rise, intensifying the condition of demand pressure. The objective will be to maximize output. (If anything, I will tend to fall in the first case, since there is already excess capacity, and to rise in the second, since there is a capacity shortage. But investment plans are too complicated and depend on too many other factors for us to draw conclusions about them from such simple premisses. By contrast, cost-minimizing and output-maximizing behavior depend precisely on the factors under examination.)

(It may be worth noting that the relationships here are not so apparent when the multiplier is based on *saving* rather than profit. When there is scarcity of demand, there is pressure to cut costs, which raises the profit margin and reduces the multiplier, but there is no pressure to cut savings. The present formulation reveals things the conventional one conceals.)

So the US economy normally functions as demand-constrained, although from 1941 to 1945, and perhaps again for a shorter time during the Korean and Vietnam wars, it operated as a 'supply-constrained' system so that output was limited not by demand (i.e., what the market will absorb), but by capacity constraints, bottlenecks and shortages of raw materials. In World War II, whatever could be produced at once found a market, without difficulty, and efficiency considerations were not significant. There was no need to compete for sales, the war effort absorbed everything, and there were plenty of complaints about quality.

Finally, let's relate this point to our earlier distinction between two forms of capitalism. An industrial economy is demand constrained, but what about a craft economy? Is it supply-constrained? As we saw, in such a system output and employment do not vary much with changes in demand, in the short and medium term, since a high proportion of labor costs in family firms are fixed in real terms, whereas, for the same reasons, prices and productivity are variable. Moreover, these latter changes imply that variations in investment spending tend to be offset by variations in consumption spending, helping to keep aggregate demand stable. So the system will tend both to lie near and to move towards the point where aggregate demand and supply just balance. However, because of the volatility of both investment and the discretionary consumption of the well-to-do, there will always be the danger of demand shortage, and therefore competition and pressure for efficiency will be strong. In a sense, the craft economy has the best of both worlds – demand shortage plus an in-built tendency to move to full employment. (Nothing like this can be said about the emerging information economy, where the cost structure is different, and prices are likely to be inflexible relative to money wages.) But the ability to reap economies of scale is limited in a craft system. Now let's go on to examine the way prices work in a demand-based system.

4 PRICES IN A DEMAND-CONSTRAINED SYSTEM

Fixed Prices, Variable Sales

In a modern industrial economy, prices are set by firms, not by customers, (although there are occasional auctions, which, as in the case of oil, sometimes assume importance). The first concern of a business firm is to ensure that it covers its costs, the second that its price will permit its market to develop. But if the market expands, then the firm must increase its productive capacity – otherwise its market share will fall. So the firm's prices must be such that the sale of its normal capacity output will generate the profit necessary to finance the investment required to keep up with the growth of the market.

But wait a minute, what has happened to supply and demand? Why won't competition force the prices down to the level of marginal costs, as the textbooks tell us? Remember, we are not in the world of agriculture and handicrafts; we are talking about a modern industrial capitalist system, in which agriculture and primary production serve the needs of urban industry – and the pricing system works accordingly. This does not mean that competition is unimportant or that it has been superseded. Far from it, but it takes on a different form. In particular, firms compete by improving and modifying their products, their production processes, and their selling techniques. They also compete in terms of price – but what is the use of capturing a market you cannot afford to supply? Prices have to remain high enough to generate the profits that will enable firms to finance the construction of the new factories and offices that will be needed to service the new markets. To put the difference between this approach and that of the textbooks in a nutshell: in a capitalist industrial economy, prices are set to equate the *growth* of supply with the *growth* of demand, rather than equating the levels, as in the pre-industrial, pre-capitalist world. This means that prices are planned and administered over the lifetime of the investment.

The Law of Demand

From this perspective one of the oldest 'laws' of economics – that a rise in price will reduce demand, and a fall increase it – takes on a different meaning. According to the standard view, demand varies inversely with price because 'individuals' (either persons or households) will change their purchasing habits, and consume more of the cheaper goods and less of more expensive ones. The aggregate response is just the sum of these individual choices. From the present point of view, by contrast, the crucial factor in the reaction of demand to a change in price will be the distribution of household incomes. High-income households can afford high-priced goods. If sales of a good are to increase, the price must come down to put the product within reach of moderate- and low-income households. Thus larger sales are associated with lower price, because the income distribution is such that the high-income groups are small and the lower the level of income the larger the set of households, until very low levels are reached. (Note that larger sales also justify lower prices because they make it possible to take advantage of economies of scale in production.) Moreover, demand will normally be price-elastic, since the income distribution is pyramidal in shape, so that a successive lowering of prices will bring increasingly larger populations into the market. On this view, then, the 'law of demand' is not a matter of individuals making rational choices – though that could be involved – but is rather a reflection of the inequality in the distribution of income.

This way of thinking about demand ties it closely to investment, because each price level is implicitly associated with not one, but two distinct markets. There is first the established market, consisting of all those families and spending units who can afford the good at that price or higher, and then there is the new market, those who can just afford the good at that price. If these two markets are combined we have a conventional-looking demand curve, showing lower prices associated with larger total sales. But this would be a mistake, on two counts. First, we are not talking about an abstract 'reversible' functional relationship. The idea is that, as prices are successively lowered, new groups of consumers can be brought into the market; a later rise in price would not necessarily lose the same amount of trade. (The relationship between these two will depend on the *microeconomic* problem: how, why and with what consequences do consumers introduce new goods into their household budgets?) Second, the established market and the new market at each price should be kept separate; their ratio shows the growth of demand for that level of price, which will have to be matched by a corresponding growth in supply. If such an expansion of supply cannot be financed at that price, then price cannot be cut to that level. So we are not talking about a 'demand curve' at all; in fact, demand curves for manufactured goods in modern economies tend to be price-inelastic. What we have instead is a set of relationships between prices, investment, finance and income distribution.

Price Competition

There is an important qualification, however. The preceding discussion really refers to *planned* prices, the benchmark prices that firms set as guides for their sales staff. What actually happens depends, of course, on people's tastes and information and prejudices – on the pattern of current demand, in short. So perhaps the textbooks have a point after all?

Not really. Consider what happens when current demand, at the benchmark price, is either below or above current capacity output. Suppose demand is above capacity. If this is because the market is now growing faster, demand will always be high, in which case a higher benchmark price is justified, but, if it is due merely to current special conditions, raising price might cut back the market's growth rate. Suppose demand is below capacity. Cutting price may attract more customers, but it also cuts into profits and hence into the ability to supply a larger market on a permanent basis. In either case it may very well not pay to change price.

All of this makes sense, but a textbook economist would object that it makes sense only for oligopolies or monopolies, or at any rate for markets with some kind of 'price leadership', because it doesn't concern the prices that are the outcome of competitive behavior. If firms are really in competition, they will try to take customers away from each other by cutting prices, especially when demand falls below capacity. And when demand is above capacity, competitive customers will bid up prices in their attempts to attract the available supply away from each other. This sounds plausible enough, but, for example, how much of a differential would be required to attract how many customers away from their normal suppliers? If the differential in proportion to the initial price is greater than the number of new customers in proportion to the initial sales, the price cut isn't worth making. But to attract *any* new customers a price cut will have to be of a certain size – or it won't even be noticed. Changing suppliers takes time and may cause trouble; a price differential may have to be fairly large to make it worth while, particularly in industries where firms go to some lengths to differentiate their products and to provide auxiliary services. This makes it easy to see why a small drop in demand below capacity might have no effect on price at all: if the demand shortfall in relation to capacity output is less than the ratio of the price cut required to attract demand to the initial price, then the price cut cannot possibly be worth while. Even a large collapse of demand may have little or no effect on price, becauses the price cut then required to reliably attract a large amount of demand away from competitors might push the price down dangerously near to, or below, the level of variables costs[1] (Ch. 17).

Primary Products vs Industrial Goods

Broadly speaking, there are two cases. In manufacturing (including both capital goods and consumer goods), variable costs – materials, labor, energy – are a relatively large production of total costs, and the price cuts required to attract demand away from competitors are both sizeable and likely to invite retaliation. Hence price-cutting could quickly push prices down to the break-even point. It is not in general a desirable strategy; as a result prices can be expected to be relatively sticky downwards in the face of changes in demand. By contrast, in primary industries – mining, agriculture, petroleum – variable costs are a small proportion of total costs, the bulk of which consist of overheads and capital charges (or, in the case of family farming, the family subsistence for the year), while the price cut required to attract demand will be negligible, since product differentiation will be minimal. Price-cutting will therefore be an attractive, even a necessary, strategy when demand declines, and consequently in these areas prices will be responsive to changes in demand.

Next, consider price increases when demand outruns capacity. Producers of manufactured goods are generally trying to expand their markets over time, breaking into new geographical or social areas, and will be reluctant to snatch temporary profits at the risk of jeopardizing their long-term market growth. Again this contrasts with the situation of the primary producer. Primary products are generic: they may vary in quality, but, given quality, they are the same regardless of the particular producer. Hence a relatively small price differential between firms may bring about a sizeable shift in custom. Further, they are used as the basis of manufacturing, so the growth of demand for them depends on the growth of manufacturing as a whole. Since they are the most basic inputs of the system, the overall demand for them will be highly price-inelastic, that is, will depend very little on price. Thus, when current demand outruns current capacity no potential new markets are thrown in jeopardy by price increases – and it will take very big price increases to reduce demand. Moreover, unlike manufacturing where capacity can be increased by building new factories, or in many cases simply by installing additional equipment in existing ones, primary productive capacity is limited by natural barriers that cannot normally be pushed back without technological innovation, in addition to investment. To increase the full capacity rate of production from farms and mines either new methods of working or new supplies must be found. Hence excess demand may, at times, tend to push up primary prices very dramatically.

Notice also that this configuration provides an excellent basis for a cartel: the primary good is absolutely necessary; substitutes will be difficult and expensive; and overall demand is price-inelastic, being basically growth-determined. But any *particular* firm's demand will be quite elastic with respect to a difference between its price and that of a competitor, while supply requires heavy investment in overhead costs. Under these conditions price wars will be both tempting and disastrous; a cartel will be extremely useful.

In short, prices of primary products will tend to respond to changes in current demand, while those of manufactured goods will tend to be insensitive to such changes, particularly in the downward direction. This difference in the way these two large groups of goods react to changes in demand is the key to understanding the inflation-stagnation problems of the 1970s.

5 COST-SHIFTING INFLATION

Traditional theory recognizes two basic types of inflation – 'cost-push' and 'demand-pull.' The first results from a push by unionized workers, or by a cartel or a monopoly or oligopoly, raising money wages or some group of prices, thereby setting off a wage–price spiral. 'Demand-pull,' by contrast, starts from excess demand, either in the aggregate or in some major sector, which bids up prices, leading to catch-up wage demands by workers and so to a wage-price spiral. Note how closely these two types of inflation are connected: the initiating wage increase of the 'cost-push' variety creates demand inflation in the second round, while the 'demand-pull' inflation that initially bids up prices causes a cost-push in the second round.

In the mainstream view there is an even deeper connection, however, which shows demand-pull to be the more basic. In the absence of generalized demand pressure, a cost-push would be a temporary disequilibrium, leading to substitution and a new equilibrium. The reason a cost-push becomes inflation is that there is generalized excess demand, so nothing is available to serve as substitute. Nor is this surprising, for the traditional theory assumes that the system is resource-constrained.

It is a peculiar characteristic of virtually all orthodox discussions of inflation that they treat it as merely a costly reflection of excess demand, serving no function or purpose. It is treated as a disequilibrium pure and simple; once started, a wage–price spiral is assumed to go on forever, unless brought to a halt by policy or by some other exogenous force. Yet this is not how things are: inflations begin, accelerate, reach a peak and decline, gradually petering out. They have a natural shape, so to speak, or perhaps several. Social phenomena so ubiquitous and complex, appearing in so many varied guises, seldom turn out to be simply pointless.

Precisely because it is so varied, inflation may sometimes be what the orthodox theory says it is. But this is not likely. The reason for claiming that the orthodox view is implausible lies in the fact that it is grounded on the neo-Classical assumption that markets tend to reach an equilibrium that can be described in *real*, that is, barter, terms. However, relative prices are the only relevant ones; hence if one or another money price changes, equilibrium will be disturbed unless all the others change in the same proportion. Since the usual, though not the sophisticated, presentations of neo-Classical micro theory assume that markets are stable, that is, tend to return to equilibrium if 'disturbed', it is natural to assume that the disturbance caused by the rise of some money price or other will be corrected by all others rising in the same proportion. Otherwise the market system would not be 'stable' in the normal sense.

Such inflations can be called 'neutral': they do not affect income distribution or the proportions in which goods are produced and labor employed. Most inflations, and certainly those of the post-Vietnam era, are not neutral. They bring about significant changes in distribution, and sometimes in demand as well. Moreover, these changes can be seen as their *raison d'être*. Non-neutral inflations have been discussed in several quarters. Post-Keynesian critics of the mainstream hold that inflation arises from excessive wage demands imposed under imperfect market conditions, and will continue indefinitely, unless checked by policy. A related school contends that it is not excessive wages, but excessive claims overall – wages, salaries, profits, rents – that set off inflation. A neo-Keynesian view, however, sees inflation as a price rise, relative to money wages, due to excess demand, bringing about a rise in profits that will increase saving enough to offset the excess demand. This is a good example of a non-neutral inflation, but it is a variation on the theme of a demand inflation. The 1970s suffered from a decade of demand shortage. Let's instead consider a non-neutral cost inflation.

Suppose that the system is faced with a major cost increase, such as a huge jump in the price of a necessary import, like oil. How is this cost to be shared? Who will pay how much, and how will this be decided, on what grounds, and how long will it take to make the decision? (Notice that essentially the same questions arise when the cost increase is internal, such as a rise in the money wages of unionized labor or, a few years ago, in the price of steel.) In some economic systems such questions are decided by administrative fiat – sometimes reflecting a popular consensus, and sometimes not. In modern capitalist economies, however, it is the function of the market to provide the answers. The market is the arena in which economic power can be exercised: those with power can pass along the increased costs; those without must bear them. More precisely, costs increases can be passed along in proportion to the ability to raise prices by a certain amount in a given time. Let's examine this more closely, using a simple numerical example.

Suppose initially that the import bill and the wage bill are the same size, but are composed differently. Let's say that the price of imports (oil, no doubt) is $5 and the quantity 20; money wages (*w*) are $4, and the number of workers 25 (millions, perhaps – but the quantities are arbitrary). The markup factor is 2, and the output will be taken as fixed at 100 units. So we have, at the outset: 2 [$5(20) + $4(25)] = $*p* (100); hence the price of output (*p*) will be $4, and the real wage (*w*/*p*) will be $4/$4, or 1; and the price of oil in terms of both output and labor will be 5/4.

Now the price of oil doubles; corporations are well-placed in their markets and are able to defend their markup, but labor's position is weak – a large majority of the labor force is nonunionized, the government is conservative and hostile, and too aggressive a posture will lead to extensive automation and/or factory flight overseas. Hence labor can push up its money wages by only 50 per cent of the rise in the cost of living in any given period:

$$(\text{change in } w)/w = 1/2\ (\text{change in } p)/p.$$

These are the assumptions; now let's see what happens.

The easiest way is to write it out period by period, starting with period zero:

0: 2[$5(20) + $4(25)] = $4(100)
1: 2[$10(20) + $4(25)] = $6(100); *p* goes from $4 to $6.
2: 2[$10(20) + $5(25)] = $6.50(100); *w* goes from $4 to $5, half the previous period's increase in *p*, and, since the markup is held fixed, *p* now rises from $6 to $6.50.
3: 2[$10(20) + $5.21(25)] = $6.61(100); here 0.21/5 = one-half of 0.5/6 and then, to maintain the markup, *p* rises to $6.61. But now the increases will be very small; *p* has risen from $6.50 to only $6.61, and *w* will rise in proportion by only half as much.
4: 2[$10(20) + $5.254(25)] = $6.627(100). Here *p* has only risen by about 2 cents; the inflationary impulse has petered out.

The effects are plain, however: the real wage (*w*/*p*.) has fallen from $1 to $5.25/$6.63 = $0.792, a drop of a little over one-fifth. Oil in terms of labor is now $10/$5.25, almost 2 to 1 instead of 5/4, and oil in terms of output is $10/$6.63. The burden falls more heavily on labor, but note that both ratios are better than the initial 10/4 ratio that prevailed before the inflation. This, however, may merely lead the oil producers to raise their price again, setting off another round to inflation. This process would then be repeated until oil producers achieved their desired price ratio of oil to output – assuming that they have the market power to keep raising prices, which they may very well not. As we saw, primary products are highly demand-sensitive and, for reasons we shall explain in a moment, a rise in import prices will tend to cause a recession, cutting demand. Now consider a different case.

Suppose that labor were stronger, strong enough to raise money wages each period in the same proportion that prices rose. Then we would have, starting from the same initial position:

1: 2[$10(20) + $4(25)] = $6(100)
2: 2[$10(20) + $6(25)] = $7(100)
3: 2[$10(20) + $7(25)] = $7.50(100)
4: 2[$10(20) + $7.50(25)] = $7.75(100), and so on.

Notice that the inflation progressively slows down as the money wage and price level approach $8. When the ratio 10:8:8 = 5:4:4 is established, the real initial relations between oil, labor and output will be restored, and the inflation will cease unless there is another increase in the oil price.

Inflation, then, serves a definite economic function: it determines who will bear the burden of a cost increase, and it does so by testing the market power of the various groups in the economy. Corporations will try to maintain their markup, workers will try to maintain their real wage (standard of living). If both are equally successful, no one will accept the burden, and the inflation will tend to restore the initial real price ratios, eliminating the problem if the cost increase were a once-for-all accident, but leading to perpetual motion if the initial cost increase is one that has to be accepted in real terms. On the other hand, if some parties are successful in passing along cost increases, while others are not or are less able to do so, then the burden will tend to be shifted to the weaker groups, and the inflation will gradually peter out, unless or until there is another cost shock.

Of course, we've looked at a very over-simplified picture, with only two groups, labor and corporations. Even here we've only considered two cases, where the parties are equal and where corporations are in the stronger position. But in some countries, at some points in time (Scandinavia in the 1960s, perhaps), labor might be in a stronger position, in which case the markup would drift down and the real wage rise, since money wages would rise faster than prices. The inflation would be relatively slow and there would be less likelihood of it leading to a further increase in import costs, since the price of oil (or other imports) in terms of output would not be so much affected by the inflation, and the price of oil in terms of domestic labor is not of any interest to oil producers.

A more realistic approach, however, must take into account the distinctions between different groups of workers – union vs non-union, salaried white-collar and office workers, state employees, middle management, and so on. Also, the power of small business over its markups is likely to be much less than that of the major corporations. Finally, the earnings of the financial system and the other recipients of interest income will be frozen during an inflation – at least during the early stages. In general, non-union workers, white-collar and state employees, and fixed-interest recipients (e.g. savings and loan institutions and other financial bodies) are unable to raise their money incomes, and tend to lose out in the race. Union workers and big business set the pace, some parts of small business can keep up, while others get squeezed. The distribution of earned incomes tends to widen, and the concentration of capital tends to increase.

Now think back to section 4. There we said that the different reactions of primary and manufactured products to changes in demand would provide the key to understanding the inflations of the post-war era. Demand for primary products is highly inelastic – unresponsive – to price changes, either up or down (but very responsive to changes in income or activity levels); hence when demand is strong (because of high activity), a cartel can enforce very great price increases. But demand changes don't affect the prices of manufactured products very much; if costs are increasing they will be passed along, as far as possible, even in the face of weak demand. Strong demand, on the other hand will not set off an inflation by raising manufacturing prices, although it might lead to increases in primary prices, which will then be passed along. But such an inflation will tend to peter out, eventually, particularly since rises in primary import prices tend to create slumps. Demand for primary goods is price-inelastic; hence a run-up of prices raises the import bill – a withdrawal. The inflation raises export prices, reducing sales, and so employment. These slumps bring inflation to a halt not by weakening the ability of corporations or unions to raise prices and wages – the orthodox explanation – but by preventing further increases in primary products, so that when the inflationary spiral runs down it will not be kicked off again. Of course, the danger recurs when recovery comes, but if in the meantime stockpiling of the relevant primary products has taken place, the expansion could proceed without creating the kind of demand pressure that would trigger primary price hikes.

6 MODELLING INFLATION

Inflation has different but symmetrical causes in the two systems. In a demand-constrained economy, inflation originates in changes in costs; in a resource-constrained economy inflation arises from the effects of demand or changes in demand. To put it another way: a demand-constrained system has cost inflation, a resource-constrained system has demand inflation.

In a demand-constrained economy inflation is the market process by which it is determined which groups shall bear the burden of increased costs. In a resource-constrained economy inflation is the market process by which it is determined which groups shall bear the burden of the shortages. This needs to be spelled out, taking the capitalist economy first.

The process can be illustrated with a single-equation model. Let k stand for means of production per unit (aggregate) output, and n labor per unit output, with m as the aggregate markup. \$ will be the price of capital goods, w the money wage rate and p the money price index of output. Initially,

$$mk\$_{t-1} + mnw_{t-1} = p_{t-1}$$

\$ then increases and p increased accordingly, w remains fixed.

$$mk[\$_t - \$_{t-1}] = p_t - p_{t-1}$$

However, once prices go up, households respond by demanding wage increases to compensate:

$$[w_t - w_{t-1}]/w_{t-1} = x[p_{t-1} - p_{t-2}]/p_{t-2}, \text{ where}$$

$0 \leqslant x \leqslant 1$. The parameter x indicates wage-earner's market power; if $x = 0$ they are not able to raise the money wage at all, and the full burden of the cost increase will fall on them; if $x = 1$ they are able to keep pace fully with price increases, and the wage–price spiral will continue until the original ratio $\$/w/p$ is re-established. Any value in between means that workers can keep up partially, but will end up bearing the larger share of the burden. (In a labor-dominated system workers might be able to keep up fully with any cost increases, but business would be able to raise prices only a fraction: interchange the ws and ps in the equation.) In any event the wage–price spiral comes to an end when the burden, reduced by inflation, is distributed.

In a resource-constrained context inflation will result from the impact of an increase in excess demand, e.g., a rise in investment; prices will be bid up by the competition for the scarce goods as consumers and enterprises try to shift the burden of the shortage to those who cannot afford higher prices. But as prices rise workers will demand pay increases, and enterprises in turn will increase output prices as their costs rise. Some groups of workers and some enterprises will be relatively successful; but those in weaker market positions will do poorly, and will end up bearing the burden of the shortages, reduced by the effects of the general price increases. Here, however, the Kaleckian dictum, 'workers spend what they get, capitalists get what they spend,' must be adapted and considered. Workers can only spend more if they receive raises; enterprises, however, will collectively get back whatever they collectively spend – from each other for capital and intermediate goods, and from consumers spending their wages on consumer goods. In the nature of things, then, enterprises will keep up with demand pressure.

Let us suppose that some input in short supply is bid up in price, to ration supplies to those who can afford them. Enterprises using the input then try to pass the costs along; enterprise spending in the aggregate returns to them. Households respond to the higher prices by demanding wage increases. If they get them, their wages return to enterprises in the form of receipts from consumer goods sales. To the extent they fail to keep up, real wages are reduced, and workers bear the burden of the shortages. A corollary is that real supply and effort will tend to shift away from the consumer goods sector to production for inter-enterprise transactions. (Trying to reduce demand pressure by cutting back money wages could backfire if, in anticipation, enterprises intensified this shift.) Such processes may be open or suppressed.

In both economic systems inflation is a market response to an external shock, whose function is to determine who will bear the burden – of the cost increase in capitalism, of the increase in shortages in socialism. In each case the rise in prices and wages reduces the burden to be distributed, while shifting it to the weakest, those least able to pass along or keep up with the increases. The more evenly matched the market positions of the various players, the longer the process will continue, and the lower the final burden to be distributed. (Austerity policies, of course, by creating unemployment generally weaken labor more than business, and therefore tend to bring inflationary processes to a conclusion, even though, paradoxically, a rise in interest rates, by raising costs to business, often initially leads to additional price increases.)

7 CORPORATE PRICING AND AGGREGATE DEMAND

In the modern economy the largest part of output is produced by giant firms with substantial market power, operating large-scale industrial processes with significant indivisibilities. Let us assume that we can neglect the behavior of small businesses, so that the aggregate relations between prices and investment are dominated by what corporations do.

To examine this, the economy can be subdivided into two sectors, producing capital goods and consumer goods respectively. In each case the output will be a composite commodity, and the sector will consist of the capital and labor required, directly and indirectly, to produce the normal capacity output.[2] Each capital coefficient thus consists not only of the various capital goods directly required, but also of those required to make

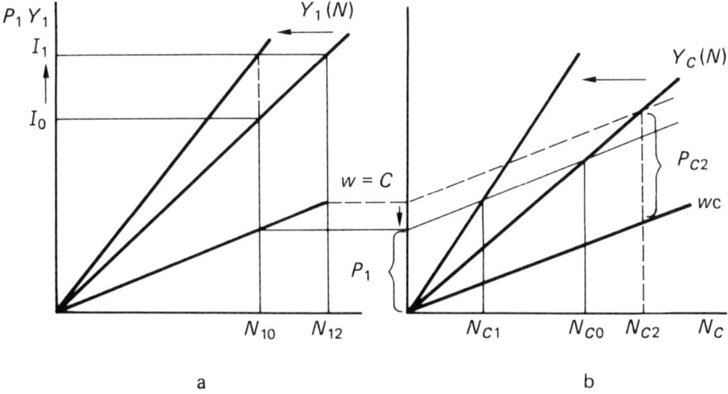

Figure 23.5

the direct inputs, and those further required to manufacture the inputs of the inputs, and so on. Similarly, the labor inputs are those directly required, plus those required for the indirect inputs, etc. An increase in demand for investment will thus require an increase not only in the direct inputs of labor and capital goods, but also in the inputs of suppliers of these direct inputs, and of suppliers of these suppliers. This impact runs through all the input–output relationships of the economy, and is summed up in the sectoral coefficients; but it consists purely of inter-industry relationships: the spending by households of the additional wages paid when investment output rises, is not included. That effect, showing up in additional demand for consumer goods, is a relationship between the sectors. It is the subject of what follows.

Each sector's coefficients can be reinterpreted as a utilization function, showing, for given capacity, output as depending on the level of employment in that sector. (Nell, 1988, Ch. 5, Appendix). The real wage can be taken initially as given, so the wage bill in each sector will also be a direct function of employment. Wages will be assumed to be wholly consumed, investment will be taken as exogenous. For simplicity, and because it is reasonable, all the functions will be assumed to be linear in the relevant ranges. All quantities are shown in money values – that is, 'output' is the money price of output × the amount, the wage bill is the money wage × the amount of labor. The wage rate is shown in each sector by the angle of the wage line, indicating the fraction of the money value of that sector's output that the money wage commands. The price ratio of the two composite outputs must be such that the real wage per unit of labor is the same in the two sectors (Figure 23.5).

Now consider Figure 23.5, showing the demand relationship between the two sectors. The spending of the wage bill in the capital goods sector generates the realized profit in the consumer goods sector. When businesses keep prices steady and adjust output an increase in investment demand will therefore raise employment and output in both sectors. But now consider a rise in investment demand in conditions of corporate markets. Faced with increased demand which they may fear to be temporary, while training and start-up costs may be large, such firms could reasonably choose to raise prices to ration demand. (Faced with a decline in sales, and the drying up of new markets, they might also raise prices, to try to maintain their cash flow, in view of their financial commitments.) Suppose that prices are raised in the capital goods sector just enough to absorb the increased demand.[3] Employment, output and the wage bill will be unchanged, but profit will be higher.

But since the relative price of capital goods has increased, to restore the terms of trade between the sectors, firms in consumer goods industries must raise their prices also – not, however, in exactly the same proportion, but more or less than in propertion, according to the ratio of their capital–labor ratio to that in the capital goods sector. For example, if the consumer sector is relatively labor-intensive, as drawn here, their price will rise less than in proportion. But the equality between the full capacity profit rates of the two sectors must be restored: if it is not, credit ratings in the less profitable sector will decline, and borrowing there will become more expensive – bringing an upward shift of the finance frontiers of consumer firms. In anticipation of this, to protect their credit rating, consumer sector firms must raise prices. But such price increases will have unfortunate short-term consequences for the sector as a whole: both employment and output must fall, although the level of profit will remain unchanged.

The strategy of raising prices rather than output in the face of increased demand works in the short run to the benefit of firms in the capital goods sector at the expense of consumer goods firms and workers. This applies even when the new demand is directed at the consumer goods sector itself, so long as both sectors raise prices in order to maintain the relation between their profit rates. For the price rise in the capital goods sector lowers its wage bill and thus correspondingly reduces the profits of the consumer sector, transferring to the former a portion of the profit arising from the additional demand for consumer goods. If consumer goods firms had increased output, they would have captured the entire additional profit from the increased demand. But, of course, no individual firm could know this. To a price leader, for example, it might seem that the increased demand could turn out to be temporary, so that raising prices would be more sensible than going to the trouble of hiring more workers. Nor can any individual firm know for certain that firms in another sector will follow suit (Figures 23.6 and 23.7).

As we saw earlier, a decline in demand will normally shift the finance function up, but in some cases may leave the sales–growth frontier unaf-

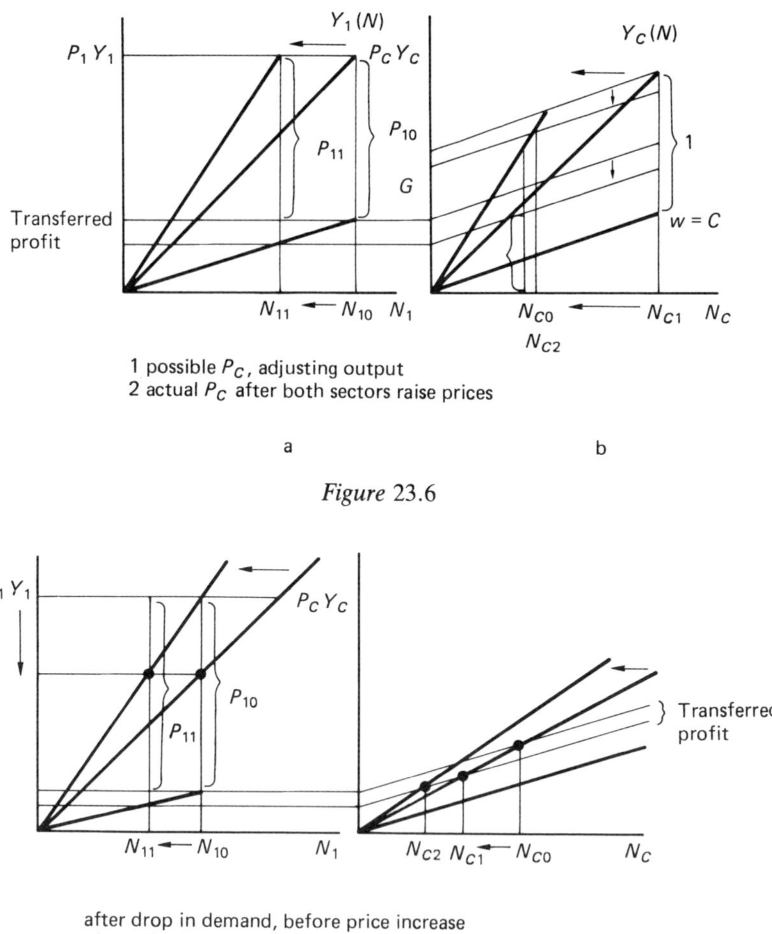

Figure 23.6

Figure 23.7

fected, resulting in a rise in price. If this behavior becomes dominant in the capital goods sector, the new lower level of money demand will be accompanied by a still lower level of output and employment – lowered in proportion to the price rise. Consequently, with a lower wage bill, consumer profits, output and employment will be reduced, and the need to raise prices in consumer industries to maintain credit ratings will reduce output and employment still further. But although total profits remain the same, the realization of profits is shifted from the consumer goods sector to capital goods.

So, in the short run, with a given money wage, a policy of raising prices in response to demand changes tend to benefit the capital goods sector at the expense of workers and the firm in the consumer goods sector, regardless of the direction of the initial change in demand. Not surprisingly, a symmetrical result can be established for price declines. If demand falls and prices are lowered, say, in the capital goods sector, more items will be sold, so if the drop is equiproportional to the decline in demand, employment will be maintained unchanged, and consequently the wage bill will be the same, though profits will be less. Competitive pressures may tend to lower prices in the consumer goods sector. If they do, then output and employment will be higher than otherwise there, too. Since the wage bill of the capital goods sector generates the profit of the consumer goods sector, the effect will be to raise the proportion of profit realized in the consumer goods sector.

A policy of raising prices in response to variations in effective demand tends to lead not only to inflation, but to sluggishness or even recession in output and employment, while a policy of price cutting in response to demand declines can tend to help to prevent slumps from worsening. This corresponds to empirical findings: in the era of pre-corporate capitalism, before the rise of the great oligopolies and conglomerates, downturns showed up primarily in falling prices, with relatively minor fluctuations in output. Since the 1920s, however, prices have fallen very little or not at all during downswings, in recent years even rising, while the fluctuations in output and employment have been considerable (Nell, 1988, Ch. 4; Sylos-Labini, 1984, Part III; Semmler, 1984, Ch. 3).

Conventional economics treats inflation as a disorder, a disequilibrium, pure and simple, whether arising from monetary causes or demand/supply imbalance. It has no economic function itself; it is a part of the problem, not of the solution. By contrast, the view proposed here sees inflation as *the way the price mechanism works today*. Inflation is the process of market adjustment; it may arise from either the labor or the product market, and in either case, the working of the system may produce 'stagflation' – a joint increase in prices and unemployment. Labor market adjustments, in particular, may not converge to a new equilibrium. But the most notable examples of recent inflation are responses to a change in the aggregate costs or pressures impinging on the system as a whole. This form of inflation reduces the burden, on the one hand, and shifts it to the weakest members of the economy, on the other. It is not, therefore, fair or wholly desirable, but it is certainly not pointless, or a mere symptom of disorder. Nor can it, or any of the other dynamic forms considered, be described, let alone explained, by the kind of formulae known as 'Phillips Curves'.

Notes

1. Mainstream attempts to explain the comparative stickiness of prices in the face of demand fluctuations have centered on the role of money wages, assuming that if wages hold steady prices will also. But if prices are not governed by marginal costs, this assumption may well be unjustified. Their explanations of money wage rigidity are likewise unconvincing. Rigidity has been attributed to 'implicit contracts,' to 'efficiency wage' considerations, and to 'imperfections' such as inadequate flows of information and the absence of an auctioneer. But the important implicit contract for labor, one US unions long tried to make explicit, would concern 'incomes' – a Guaranteed Annual Income – not wage rates. It is simply not clear why and how an implicit contract on wage rates would benefit both sides sufficiently to ensure voluntary compliance over the cycle. Why should either side continue to comply during a long period of boom/slump in which the maintenance of the contract is to their disadvantage? As for efficiency wage explanations, they rely on 'ad hoc' assumptions about asymmetry of information, set in the context of a wholly implausible account of labor supply. Inperfectionist arguments can be used to justify 'rationed' supply and demand functions, but the foundations are therefore once again 'ad hoc.' A further strain on credibility comes with the requirement that the current spending of 'firms' is to be constrained by their current income. If this were so, we would not have the kind of credit markets that we do have.
2. The output of each sector consists of heterogeneous goods that must be aggregated, and Figure 23.5 cannot be drawn unless we know the amount of consumer goods that a unit of capital goods commands. These value relationships are derived from the long-term 'normal' prices in the established markets, for these are the prices on the basis of which contracts have been drawn, fixed capital constructed, and employment relationships established. These prices, of course, are not strictly fixed, but they will tend to move slowly. Such prices correspond to Classical 'natural' prices or prices of production; they are associated in each industry with a normal rate of profit. The rates vary between industries according to special conditions. The chief of these, we have argued, are variations in the growth possibilities of new markets, in conjunction with technological requirements expressed in the capital output ratio. Together with the conditions for external finance, these explain the deviations from the norm in the profits of particular firms.
3. Such a price increase cannot be distinguished from a productivity increase on the diagrams here. Both are represented by an upward swing of the productivity line, since every level of employment will produce a higher money value of output. If the diagrams were in real terms, then the distinction is easily made; but we are taking investment demand to be set in monetary terms.

References

Nell, E. (1988) *Prosperity and Public Spending* (London: Unwin Hyman).

Semmler, W. (1984) *Competition, Monopoly and Differential Profit Rates* (New York: Columbia University Press).

Sylos-Labini, R. (1984) *The Faces of Economic Growth and Decline* (Cambridge, Mass.: MIT Press).

24 Growth, Distribution, and Inflation*

As is well known, the warranted rate of capital accumulation is unstable. This rate is defined by the equality of aggregate demand, I/s (where $1/s$ is the multiplier), to aggregate supply, K/v (where $1/v$ is the productivity of the capital stock), and v is assumed constant, so that fixed coefficients prevail. Also there is either no, or Harrod-neutral, technical progress. Relative prices are assumed practically fixed, changing only slowly, with changes in the rate of profit. There is a given, initial money wage.

Hence $I/K = \Delta K/K = s/v = G_w$, the warranted rate of growth. If the actual rate, $G \gtreqless s/v$, then aggregate demand would be greater or less than aggregate supply, $I/s \gtreqless K/v$; hence I would be raised or lowered by the attempts of firms to adjust capacity appropriately. But the effect would be to worsen excess or shortage of demand. Thus a disequilibrium will be exacerbated.

Not only is the warranted rate unstable, there is the further question of its relation to the 'natural rate' G – the growth rate of the labor force, adjusted for skill and technical training. For example, if $G_w > G_n$, it cannot be sustained, and the system will finally plunge into recession. But if $G_w > G_n$, then growing at G_w will lead to long-term unemployment. Since it is unlikely that $G_w = G_n$, except occasionally, by accident, full employment seems unattainable.

Economists of all persuasions have found this conclusion over-simplified and extreme. Capitalism is unstable, but not *that* unstable. Periods of steady growth do occur; something is missing from the model. Neo-Classicists argued that the problem arose because of the lack of substitution between labor and capital. By postulating an aggregate production function, they made v variable and were able to show that G would adjust to G_n. But this procedure did not address the question of the instability of G_w, since it *assumed* that all saving would automatically be invested. Moreover, the Capital Theory controversy has shown the aggregate production function to be deeply flawed. The neo-Classical answer, therefore, misses half the problem and gives an unacceptable analysis of the rest.

By contrast, Kaldor, and following him most post Keynesians, have argued that the share of profits will adapt to the ratio of investment to income, thereby bringing savings into line with investment.[1] Not only will

* *Journal of Post Keynesian Economics*, 5 (1) (Fall 1982) pp. 104–13. Thanks to Chidem Kurdas for helpful comments.

this bring G_w to equality with G_n, it will also stabilize G_w. From the income and saving identities, plus the equilibrium condition:

$$Y = P + W \tag{24.1}$$

$$S = s_p P + s_w W \tag{24.2}$$

$$I = S, \tag{24.3}$$

we obtain

$$\frac{P}{Y} = \frac{1}{s_p - s_w}\frac{I}{Y} + \frac{s_w}{s_p - s_w}, \tag{24.4}$$

where $s_p > I/Y > s_w$.[2] Letting $r = P/K$ and $v = K/Y$, the rate of profit required for steady growth is

$$r = \frac{G_n - s_w/v}{s_p - s_w}, \tag{24.5}$$

where $s_p/v > G > s_w/\mathrm{v}$.

So, within the stated limits a solution exists. But Kaldor and Pasinetti have suggested more; namely, that 'there is in the system a price mechanism by which the level of prices with respect to the money wages (i.e., profit margins) is determined by demand.' Hence the above 'income distribution and rate of profit will not only exist (in the mathematical sense) but also will be the ones that the system actually tends to produce' (Pasinetti, 1974, p. 106).

This price mechanism works because at or above full capacity utilization, prices are more flexible upward than money wage rates. When there is excess demand for goods (because of high investment spending in relation to income), prices will rise; but money wage rates will be bid up less because at full capacity there are no more jobs. All equipment is already being operated; there are no more places on the assembly line. (Of course, overtime will raise labor costs; not all industries will reach capacity simultaneously; there will be wage bidding for special skills, etc., the normal qualifications.[3]) Hence profits, and so savings, rise. On the down side, below full capacity, however, the system works differently. Assuming constant returns to utilization, employment and output decrease proportionately. Hence both profits and wages decrease in the same ratio. So savings decrease in proportion to income; the weighted average of s_w and s_p remains constant.

But this argument does not yet meet the problem. For the above statement and the models it summarizes (Harcourt, 1972, pp. 210–15, 232–40) take investment as exogenous. But the Harrod–Domar model rests on an accelerator principle. To provide an answer to the Harrod–Domar problem, we have to base the argument on that postulate. Let us see if it works out.

From the preceding assumptions it follows that money wages will not rise as fast as prices at or above normal capacity, and this will determine the change in profits for that case. For assuming output, capital, and labor constant, differentiating

$$\pi Y = wN + rK\pi \tag{24.6}$$

where π is the price level and w the money wage, we get

$$dr = \frac{wN}{K\pi}\left(\frac{d\pi}{\pi} - \frac{dw}{w}\right) \tag{24.7}$$

Shares will move, in real and money terms, in favor of profits if the proportional rate of price inflation exceeds the proportional rate of wage inflation, which is to say, if the elasticity of money prices with respect to money wages exceeds unity.

This can provide a basis for a simple but precise account of price and wage inflation in terms of elementary growth theory. It draws on the accelerator and the class-based savings function, both. Investment varies directly with the ratio of aggregate demand to aggregate supply. It also assumes, realistically, that business's propensity to save out of profits is greater than household's propensity to save out of wages. The demand for labor at any given time depends on the actual capital stock (indirect labor) and the current degree of utilization (direct labor). The supply of labor in efficiency units for given family structure and social habits is given by the growth of population. Changes in money wage rates will be determined by growth in demand and supply. Hence when the actual of growth, G, exceeds or falls below the natural rate,G_n, positive or negative money wage inflation will develop[4] (though from experience we would expect money wage rates to be slower to move downward). Hence

$$\text{sign }(G - G_n) = \text{sign }\frac{dw}{w} \tag{24.8}$$

But how can the actual rate of growth lie above the natural? Clearly a long-term steady state G cannot lie above G_n. Year in and year out the growth rate of capital cannot lie above the growth rate of the labor force consistently with a given, technically fixed capital–labor ratio. But for a few periods, especially during processes of adjustment, G can certainly lie above G_n. If G previously lay below G_n, there will be pools of unemployed to soak up; temporary entrants to the labor force may provide an assist; the existing labor force can put in overtime; equipment and processes can be run short-handed. But these are expedients. If G lies strongly above G_n, the combination of available job opportunities and rising money wages will tend to pull G_n up. On the other hand, businesses finding the labor market tight will tend to delay construction, not wishing to be saddled with plant they cannot staff. Hence G will tend to fall, i.e.,

$$G > G_n: \quad \frac{dG}{dt} < 0, \frac{dG_N}{dt} > 0 \tag{24.9}$$

Next consider the relationships between G and G_w. When the actual rate of growth is above the warranted, there will be capacity shortage and a tendency for it to increase farther; when the actual rate lies below the warranted, there will be excess capacity and a tendency for actual growth to fall. In the first instance there will be inflation; in the second there will be, not price reduction, but revenue reduction. Lower revenues will lead to attempts to reduce variable costs, so to layoffs and short hours. But the effect will be more on earnings than on wage rates.[5] Hence:

$$G > G_w: \quad \frac{d\pi}{\pi} < 0$$

$$G < G_w: \quad \frac{dG}{dt} > 0 \tag{24.10}$$

When $G > G_w$, price inflation will take place, and the question is whether it will be more or less rapid than wage inflation. At this point we need a further assumption in order to compare the pressures in the two markets. If there are no special 'imperfections' in a market, it is both reasonable and traditional (Samuelson, 1947, pp. 257–76) to postulate that the rate of change of price will be proportional to the discrepancy between the quantities. In the case of prices the adaptation of this doctrine is straightforward, since a discrepancy between G and G_w *is* a divergence between Aggregate Demand and Aggregate Supply. But prices don't fall when $G < G_w$; instead output and employment adjust, while the price line is held firm. In the case of wages, however, suppose that $G > G_n$, but there is a large pool of long-term unemployed workers. Why should money wages rise just because capital is *growing* faster than the pool of unemployed?

The question is reasonable, but there is a solid answer. When capital grows faster than the labor force, the pool of unemployed is reduced; but in general, firms will have hired the 'best-quality' labor first. The unemployed being absorbed will be the least-skilled, poorest-trained, blackest, most female, etc., of the workers. Hence they will be eligible only for the lowest-paid jobs. But the new capital, embodying the latest innovations, will demand workers of higher 'quality'. Consequently, new capital will have to *bid* for workers in existing jobs; those employers will have to bid for slightly lower-grade workers, and so on down the line, until jobs of suitably low status open up to absorb a portion of the long-term unemployed. Hence the process of absorbing the unemployed workers involves bidding up the money wage all along the line; the faster this process, the higher the bidding.

We can put these two points together in one formula:[6]

$$\frac{w}{\pi}\frac{d\pi}{dw} = f\left(\frac{G - G_w}{G_n - G}\right), \; 0 < f \leqslant 1, \; G > G_w. \qquad (24.11)$$

When $w/\pi \; d\pi/dw > 1$ there is a shift to profits and savings rise, and vice versa for $w/\pi \; d\pi/dw < 1$. To complete this framework for analysis, we need to consider the consequences of the actual rate lying below the warranted.

When $G < G_w$, excess capacity emerges and business revenue declines. Layoffs and reduced workweeks cushion this by shifting the burden to labor; but in the initial downswing, the effect on profits will usually be greater due to labor-hoarding. Hence $G < G_w$ implies a temporary shift in shares in favor of wage-earners, so a fall in savings, though this may be wholly or partially offset by the effect of $G_n > G$ on the rate of wage inflation.

The six cases of wage and price inflation corresponding to the permutations of the three growth rates are informally analyzed in the following table:

I $\quad G_n > G > G_w$: $\dfrac{dw}{w} < 0, \; \dfrac{d\pi}{\pi} > 0$

II $\quad G_w > G > G_n$: $\dfrac{dw}{w} > 0, \; \dfrac{d\pi}{\pi} \leqslant 0$ (short-run shift to wages)

III $\quad G_n > G_w > G$: $\dfrac{dw}{w} < 0, \; \dfrac{d\pi}{\pi} \leqslant 0$ (short-run shift to wages)

IV $\quad G > G_w > G_n$: $\dfrac{dw}{w} > 0, \; \dfrac{d\pi}{\pi} > 0$

$$\text{V} \quad G > G_n > G_w\text{:} \quad \frac{dw}{w} > 0, \; \frac{d\pi}{\pi} > 0$$

$$\text{VI} \quad G_w > G_n > G\text{:} \quad \frac{dw}{w} < 0 < \frac{d\pi}{\pi} > 0 \text{ (short-run shift to wages)}$$

In case I the profit rate rises, so G_w rises toward G, which in turn rises toward G_n (which might tend to fall in the long run as birth rates and marriage ages are generally sensitive to real wages).[7] In case II real wages will tend to rise and profits to fall, on the basis of both (24.10) and (24.11), so that G_w will fall toward G which will drift down toward G_n, which could tend to rise to meet it if marriage ages fell and births rose because of $G > G_n$. But this long-term effect would be offset in the short run by the slump indicated by $dG/dt < 0$. However, the effect on G_w will be reinforced by the short-run shift to labor. In these two cases, then, differential inflation tends to adjust shares to bring actual and warranted growth rates into line with the natural, although it is not possible to say on the basis of this analysis how long this might take. In case IV, $w/\pi \; dk/dw < 1$, and both rising, so there will be a fall in profits and savings. This means that G_w and G will both fall toward G_n, the latter at a lower rate; but the movement will be toward the steady-state path. In case V, $w/\pi \; d\pi/dw > 1$, and both are rising; hence there is a shift to profits. G_w will rise toward G_n, but in the short or medium term G will move progressively further above G_n, preventing the attainment of a steady state. However, in the long term it must eventually adjust to G_n. In any event, at the point $G_w = G_n$, the system switches to case IV and tends to move toward the steady state.

In these four cases, then, there is a clear-cut tendency for the system to move toward a steady state, although this can only be stated definitely in cases IV and V on the basis of a postulate of the sort embodied in (24.11). The simple 'Cambridge' argument unambiguously applies only to I and II. And even so, nothing can be said about the rapidity of the adjustment.

The analysis takes on a different form in cases III and VI. Here the fact that $G_w > G$ in both cases leads, by (24.10), to a slump. (Note that (24.11) does not apply.) Prices, however, in line with Keynesian thinking, do not fall, while money wages, in line with (24.8), do, since $G_n > G$ in both cases. This leads to a rise in *potential* profits. But because of the slump, *actual* profits fall, since investment spending is down (Kalecki, 1971; Nell, 1979). Moreover, the fall in the real wage will further exacerbate the slump (Kalecki, 1971; Nell, 1979). The result is a pronounced decline in G, while full employment, or potential, G_w rises. In both cases, since $G < G_n$ to start with, the pool of unemployed workers tends to grow, further pressuring the wage down, deepening the slump. Here the growth rates show no tendency to come together. Within the framework of this analysis, the prognosis for these two cases must be for an ever-deepening slump.

The fact that when $G_w > G$ (for instance, when $G_n < _w$) there is excess capacity, leading firms to cut back on investment, so that G tends to fall, can be regarded as a generalization of the 'Keynesian paradox' that a high saving ratio is dangerous for an advanced capitalist society. When the full capacity savings ratio is high, in the short run it will be harder for government policy to ensure full employment, and in the long run G_w will be high. If it lies above G_n there will be a tendency to long-run stagnation. These are points of which current policy discussions have lost sight.

There is no basis here for the claim sometimes made (Kaldor, 1961) that the 'Cambridge theory of distribution' provides a mechanism guaranteeing the long-term stability of full employment. This conclusion is very much strengthened when we abandon the "one-sector" framework within which we have worked so far and distinguish the production of investment goods from that of consumer goods. Indeed, the 'Cambridge' argument suggests an explanation of 'stagflation.' For, according to that theory, when aggregate demand is greater than capacity, prices will be higher relative to money wages (remembering that excess demand for goods does *not* imply excess demand for labor, since the demand for labor is limited by the number of places on the assembly line), so profit will be larger, providing the saving to balance the investment, i.e., reducing consumption demand. The problem is that the price of *investment goods* will be bid up, which will increase profits in that sector, but additional profits do not mean additional capacity. The demand still cannot be met. So long as the money wage and prices of the *consumer* goods are unchanged, no real adjustment is possible. However, the higher price of investment goods raises the cost of materials and replacements in consumer goods. Hence the price of consumer goods must go up. With given money wages, this means a decline in the real wage. Hence output and employment decline in consumer goods. So the demand by the consumer goods sector for materials and replacements from investment goods will be lower, and it is this which provides the free capacity to meet the initial excess demand. The adjustment takes place by creating inflation in investment goods, which is passed on to consumer goods, where it is transmuted into recession, which in turn frees capacity in investment goods. A higher price of investment goods is sufficient to balance saving and investment in *value* terms; but higher profits by themselves do not mean more serviceable capacity. Nor does a lower level of consumption, for that creates excess capacity in consumer goods, the wrong sector. It is the decline in the consumer goods sector's demand for the products of the investment goods sector which finally frees usable capacity where it is needed.

In short, the Cambridge price mechanism works, but only sometimes and not very well. Just like the real world.[8]

Notes

1. When the share of profits changes, however, sectoral rates of profit, equal for the initial (equilibrium) share, will diverge if sectoral capital-labor ratios differ, at the initial prices. To restore uniformity in the rate of profit, relative prices must change. If the system is not in Standard proportions – growing on a von Neuman ray – relative shares will change when prices change (Sraffa, 1960).
2. Since $I = s_p Y + (s_w - s_p) W = s_w Y + (s_p - s_w) P$, we can write:

$$\frac{I}{Y} - s_p = (s_w - s_p) \frac{W}{Y}$$

and

$$\frac{I}{Y} - s_w = (s_p - s_w) \frac{P}{Y}$$

The RHS of the first will be negative, that of the second positive. Hence $s_p > I/Y > s_w$.

3. These qualifications are important because a permanent change from one growth path to another requires a change in the relative sizes of industries – it is a movement to a different von Neuman ray. As Lowe has shown (1976), when industries operate with strict capacity limits, such 'traverses' are not generally possible without a period of unemployment and excess capacity, since before any other sectors can grow faster, the capacity of the most 'basic' sector must be expanded, and this can only be done by reducing the demands of other sectors on its output, allowing it to rechannel that output into expanding its own size. Then, larger, the Basic sector can supply the additional investment goods for the other sectors, enabling them to grow at a higher rate. But the temporary reduction of demand required implies that before the system can grow faster, it must first go through a depression in order to change the relative sizes of sectors. Under such circumstances the accelerator cannot work; moreover, the assumption of rigidly fixed capacity is extreme. Clearly, shift working provides flexibility; when demand exceeds *normal* capacity, the second and third shifts are beefed up to provide (at a higher cost) temporarily higher output. In order to examine the working of the Harrod–Domar mechanism, we will assume that shift working enables us to evade the 'traverse' problems Lowe studied. It should be clear that this assumption can only be provisional.
4. Note that it is the actual growth rate in excess of the natural, not planned investment in excess of planned saving, which leads to a bidding up of wages. Only *when* realized will investment add to the demand for labor. Planned investment in excess of planned full capacity saving puts pressure on prices.
5. In the Keynesian spirit we assume that quantities are more flexible than prices, up to full capacity.
6. Notice that this formula determines the *rate of change* of money wages. In good Keynesian fashion we began from an initially given, exogenous money wage. Moreover, we can expect that from time to time the level of money wages will be adjusted through bargaining and social/political pressures. This is perfectly consistent with growth-determined rates of change of money wages.
7. One could also argue that labor force participation, absenteeism, and sick leave vary with real wages (or perhaps with earnings), the first directly, at least up to a

point, the next two inversely in the short run. But the evidence is conflicting, since these variables reflect the struggle over conditions of work.

8. A capitalist economy cannot easily generate excess demand for long; 'automatic' pressures will tend to expand capacity and cut back expenditures. Indeed, it can be shown that, under reasonable assumptions, investment and excess capacity will grow cyclically together, in a fashion reminiscent of the Lotka–Volterra system (Nell, 1991). The price mechanism studied here must therefore be considered a short-run adjustment process. Moreover, the normal pattern of adjustments will be more likely to reflect excess capacity than excess demand.

References

Domar, E. (1987) *Essays in the Theory of Economic Growth* (New York: Oxford University Press).

Harcourt, G.C. (1972) *Some Cambridge Controversies in the Theory of Capital* (Cambridge: Cambridge University Press).

Harrod, R.F. (1939) 'An Essay in Dynamic Theory,' *Economic Journal*, xlix (March) pp. 14–33.

Kaldor, N. (1961) 'Capital Accumulation and Economic Growth,' in F.A. Lutz and D.C. Hague (eds), *The Theory of Capital* (London: Macmillan).

Kalecki, M. (1971) *Selected Essays on the Dynamics of the Capitalist Economy* (Cambridge: Cambridge University Press).

Lowe, A. (1976) *The Path of Economic Growth* (Cambridge: Cambridge University Press).

Nell, E.J. (1979) 'The Simple Theory of Effective Demand,' Chapter 20 in this volume.

Nell, E.J. (1980) 'Employment and Effective Demand: Keynes After Marx,' New School for Social Research (New York).

Nell, E.J. (1991) 'Demand and Capacity in Capitalism and Socialism', *New School Working Papers in Political Economy*, no. 22; forthcoming in the *Economic Record*.

Pasinetti, L. (1974) 'The Economics of Effective Demand,' in *Growth and Income Distribution* (Cambridge: Cambridge University Press).

Samuelson, P. (1947) *Foundations of Economic Analysis* (Cambridge, Mass.: Harvard University Press).

Sraffa, P. (1960) *Production of Commodities by Means of Commodities* (Cambridge: Cambridge University Press).

25 Controversies in Macroeconomics: Patinkin, Friedman and Marglin*

The challenge posed to modern economics by the revival of 'political economy,' the redevelopment of the approach of the Classical authors and Marx, cuts across contemporary ideological lines. The central issue is the relation between production and the payment of income through the market. This requires an understanding, on the one hand, of the institutions of production, which may involve taking account of some subtle forms of social coercion and, on the other, of the way the market works, and this depends among other things on the way the technology has developed through transformational growth. Each of the major schools of modern economics, 'the grand neo-Classical synthesis,' led by Patinkin, free-market conservatism, championed by Milton Friedman, and modern Marxism, represented by S. Marglin, has failed to connect the generation of monetary income payments with the productive process in accordance with the technology in use. The following three essays explore the resulting problems.

1 THE REAL BALANCE EFFECT IN NEO-CLASSICAL THEORY: MICRO AND MACRO

Surprisingly, neo-Classical theory has no generally agreed-upon theory of the relationship between monetary and real variables. In the modern literature, this issue appears in the guise of arguments over the nature of the 'transmission mechanism.' In a somewhat earlier, but still post-war, literature, it took the form of arguments over 'valid' and 'invalid' dichotomies', between real and monetary aspects of the economy, to which we shall now turn. Our argument will be first that monetarists have never

* Edited for this volume from E.J. Nell, *Free Market Conservatism* (1980) and 'Jean-Baptiste Marglin: A comment on "Growth, Distribution and Inflation,"' *Cambridge Journal of Economics*, 9 (2) (June 1985).
Thanks to Alex Azarchs, who co-authored parts of the Chapter in FREE MARKET CONSERVATISM, from which these excerpts have been taken.

successfully addressed the question posed in that dispute, and hence have *no* account whatever of the causal connections between monetary changes and the real economy. Secondly, we shall contend that, for related reasons, both mainstream and Keynesian approaches are also inadequate.

The Dichotomy

The problem is both simple and deeply rooted. Neo-Classical theory determines the equilibrium of supply and demand for commodities, in one, a few or all markets together, as a function of *relative prices*. So the general price level is indeterminate on the basis of supply and demand for goods. This seems to leave room for another market, one for money, in which supply and demand will then determine the general price level. The equation of exchange, $MV = PY$ (where M is the money stock, V is velocity of circulation, P the general or average price level, and Y real output), has often been interpreted as such a market balancing, or 'excess demand' equation. (Excess demand functions show demand minus supply at various prices, with the equilibrium price being the one at which excess demand is zero.) Given an exogenously fixed M, with Y determined by the supplies and demands for goods, which also determine V (since V simply reflects the simplification by money of a predetermined pattern of barter), the price level follows straightforwardly.

But there is a hitch – indeed, worse, a contradiction. The quantities – not the relative quantities, but the absolute amounts exchanged in equilibrium – are functions of relative prices, which means that if *all* prices were, say, doubled or halved the equilibrium quantities would be unaffected, since no *relative* prices would be changed. (Technically, this is expressed by saying that the excess demand functions are homogeneous of degree zero.) But the equation of exchange will be thrown out of balance if, from an initial equilibrium, all prices are doubled or halved. The equation of exchange, in fact, is homogeneous of degree one. Yet, according to Walras' Law for multi-market equilibrium, if $n-1$ markets of an $n-$commodity system are in equilibrium, the nth market must also be.

This had better be explained: it follows from the fact that, in the aggregate, total demand must equal total supplies, since the demand for any good is always an equivalent supply of another and saving is supplying capital funds. To put it another way, in a neo-Classical market system, every purchase by a given agent implies an equivalent sale by that same agent, since goods are purchased with goods (for these purposes, money is just another commodity that has to be purchased with, for example, labor services). Hence excess demand anywhere implies equivalent and offsetting excess supply somewhere; alternatively, in the aggregate excess demands/supplies always sum to zero.

Returning to the argument: if the equation of exchange is an excess demand function of the same character as the others, then, if all markets for goods are in equilibrium, so must the money market. But we have just seen that this is not so; if all prices were doubled, equilibrium in the goods markets would be preserved (since no *relative* prices would be changed), but the money market would be upset. Is the equation of exchange different, then? Or perhaps Walras' Law does not hold for monetary economies? Or perhaps the supply and demand equations for goods are mis-specified?

The first two possibilities have to be dismissed if the analysis is to stay within the traditional framework. When the equation of exchange is written in the Cambridge form, $M = kPY$ (where $k = 1/V$ is the proportion of the real volume of planned transactions to be held as cash balances), it can be seen to be a supply and demand equation. It should therefore enter the system on the same footing as any other. Hence Walras' Law should continue to hold when the money market is taken into consideration, just as it would if any other market were added to the system. The difficulty comes about because the general price level is really a weighted average of individual money prices, and money prices have no influence on supply and demand.

Consider an imaginary experiment, in which there is a doubling of the price level – regardless of how it comes about. If there were equilibrium in holdings of real balances before such a change, there cannot be afterwards. It might be argued that such a change could not come about except by a doubling of the money stock or of the velocity or some combination of the two, and that therefore the whole question is moot. In other words, given equilibrium in outputs and relative prices, the price level can change only if M or V or both change, and then only in the same proportion. In that case the preceding difficulties disappear, but only because we have ceased to interpret the equation of exchange as an equilibrium condition for the money market. Instead it would be interpreted as an identity defining the general price level. But the general price level is the inverse of the value of money and, in neo-Classical theory, 'value' is determined by the interaction between preferences and scarcity, taking place in competitive markets. Thus the value of money should be determined by its quantity, given the demand for it, which will depend on the level of economic activity, on the one hand, and the average institutional practices of payment on the other. The first of these will be given by Y, the second by V, although a more sophisticated analysis would have to include the interest rate, and perhaps the yields of other assets, too. Then the equation of exchange would express the *equilibrium condition* determining the price level at which excess demand for money becomes zero. This is clearly the only interpretation consistent with the neo-Classical approach. Since an equilibrium condition cannot be an identity, we cannot accept the above objection that our imaginary experiment could only come about through a doubling of M or V or both. The problem stands: according to Walras' Law, if all goods markets are in equilibrium, the money market necessarily should be also, if the value of money is determined by scarcity and preferences. But our thought experiment shows that money market equilibrium does not follow.

Blind Alleys

There have been attempts to escape from this bind. Petri (1982), for example, argues that the relative money balances of agents cannot be among the given endowments with which the analysis begins. Long period equilibrium requires that the agents have the right money balances to sustain their equilibrium activity levels; hence these balances will have to be established in the process of moving towards equilibrium. By contrast, Patinkin and others treat initial money endowments for each agent as among the data of the system. Even so, once an equilibrium is established, a uniform change of money prices upsets the money market, but not the goods markets. Nor does Petri tell us how supply and demand lead each agent to obtain the correct money balance for equilibrium. The agents must start with *some* balances, even if they are not the final ones, but he nowhere explains the path that will be followed. So the difficulties remain.

Jurg Niehans (1978) proposes a complicated revision of Walras' auctioning system. A 'compensation fund' must be established that will lend to those short of cash, and to which those with cash surplus must contribute. Then, starting with some price fixed arbitrarily in money equilibrium, relative prices are determined. These relative prices are then frozen, and in the second stage, returning everyone to their original cash balances, the arbitrary price level is varied until monetary equilibrium is reached. First, this procedure is impossibly cumbersome, and runs counter to economic incentives. Why should those with surplus cash pay it into a 'compensation fund'? Secondly, Niehans nowhere addresses the issue of how the correct distribution of cash balances is to be brought about – the issue, that is, of the correct relative size of cash holdings, the point that Petri considers central. Otherwise the compensation fund will have to be permanent. Finally, once the equilibrium price level is disturbed, the contradiction reemerges, even in Niehans' world.

The Real Balance Effect

The favored way out of this impasse has been to re-specify the supply and demand equations for goods so that, besides relative prices, supply and demand functions contain *real cash balances*. Real balances yield utility to consumers because they permit the bridging of gaps between sales receipts and purchases, and enable individuals to take advantage of unexpected opportunities (Patinkin, 1965, pp. 14, 78, 80). For exactly the same reasons, they yield productive services to firms. Individuals are enabled to consume more easily, firms to produce more easily, the larger are their real balances. In other words, higher real balances lead to greater spending. As a result, a change in the general price level, or in the supply of nominal money, will have effects that show up in the adjustments of supplies and demands for goods, as well as in the money market. A doubling of prices will therefore *not* leave goods markets undisturbed; since it will halve real balances, supplies and demands for goods will have to adjust. Both goods and money markets will be disturbed, and both will have to readjust, a process in which they will interact. So the contradiction disappears.

At first glance the argument seems to work out very nicely. At the macro level the real balance effect provides the grounds for contending that a perfectly, or even a reasonably, competitive economy, one with sufficient wage and price flexibility, would always tend towards full employment equilibrium. This, of course, while true in theory, would be modified in practice, since market imperfections would prevent downward wage and price flexibility in many areas, and even where such flexibility existed the adjustment processes might prove too slow or too painful. There would therefore exist good *practical* grounds for Keynesian policies, while at the same time the theoretical optimality of the competitive market system could continue to be upheld, ideological implications intact. The causes of unemployment and inflation are in the system's imperfections, not in the system itself.

At the micro level the argument looks equally attractive. For the long run, the 'neutrality' of money could, it seemed, be affirmed: a rise in the money supply would raise the real value of money balances, increasing spending. If the levels of output and employment were initially in equilibrium, the effect of extra spending would not affect outputs but would increase the price level in proportion to the increased money supply. This, of course, is crucial to neo-Classical theory's claim for both the efficiency and the optimality of market equilibrium: relative prices and quantities must reflect only resource scarcities, technological possibilities and relative preferences. Individual choice is constrained by niggardliness of nature; money is a mere veil – monetary changes have no real long-term effects on equilibrium. Hence *government policy* has no such effects. If money *did* affect long-term equilibrium, then it would be impossible to argue that such an equilibrium represented the highest achievement of preferences subject to constraints imposed by nature, or that prices reflected relative scarcities – for both relative prices and quantities would vary with government monetary policy, which normally has nothing to do with consumer preferences or with natural scarcities.

So, according to proponents of this line of argument, the real balance effect does not upset the long-run 'neutrality' of money. To put it another way, the static comparison of two equilibria would not reveal the real balance effect at all, for 'in [full equilibrium] comparative statics the real balance term may immediately be removed from the functions without making any difference whatever to the solution of the system' (Patinkin, (1965) p. 17), 'but the dynamic adjustment process would depend fundamentally on it' (Patinkin, 1965, p. 57). This means that when equilibrium has changed, or indeed whenever the system is out of equilibrium, the real balance effect will propel the system toward the equilibrium. Suppose there is unemployment: prices and money wages will fall, raising real balances and stimulating spending. Suppose there is excess aggregate demand: prices and money wages will rise, real balances will fall and spending will be curtailed. Thus the real balance effect helps to guarantee the stability of markets although it leaves the traditional conclusions of the quantity theory largely intact – resting them on somewhat more stringent assumptions (e.g. starting from equilibrium), but providing them with a precise grounding in individual maximizing behavior.

A Problem: Money and Debt

A closer look reveals some flies in the ointment. First, the real balance effect requires money holdings to consist of 'outside' money, that is, money that is a medium of exchange and store of value but is not at the same time some other agent's debt. However, most 'money' is in fact precisely that: obligations of banks, the government, financial intermediaries, and so on. Only gold and silver are truly outside monies. When money is entirely or largely 'inside money' – debt – a change in the real value of an agent's money balances implies an equal and opposite change in the value of some other agent's obligations. Each effect may be supposed to provide an opposite stimulus; it is difficult if not impossible to state on *a priori* grounds which will be the stronger. Nor are these easy to measure empirically.[1]

The problem might be avoided by assuming that inside money consisted of obligations of the financial sector (and the government), and that these will change their spending very little in response to a change in the value of their obligations. Thus, although a change in the price level will alter the value of the obligations of financial intermediaries (a fall in P will raise the real value of what they must repay) and will lead them to change their portfolios (a matter the analysis already accounts for), it will have a negligible effect on their spending since such institutions do not spend much. (Most of their expenses are fixed costs.) The only effects will be on households and businesses, and the system will behave *as if* all money were outside money.

This leads to a second general point: no account has been taken of the fact that both households and firms have financial obligations and claims holding over time that are denominated in money. Generally, businesses are net borrowers, households net lenders. Deflation increases the burden of debt to business. When, with output constant, both prices and variable costs fall in a certain proportion, profits will fall in the same proportion; so they decline in relation to *fixed* costs denominated in money, which, of course, increases the risk of bankruptcy. Given the higher burden of fixed costs and increased risk of bankruptcy, prudent firms should clearly cut back on new projects, and prudent banks should refuse them credit if they do not. On the other hand, for exactly the same reasons, households, being net creditors, will find themselves receiving a higher real value of debt servicing payments, and thus will be stimulated to increase their consumption expenditures.

The usual observation at this point is that, while the debtors' losses equal the creditors' gains, there is no way of saying, in general, whether or not the negative stimulus of loss will outweigh the positive stimulus of gain (although that would probably be the implication of diminishing marginal utility in a Marshallian approach!). Since we cannot really say what the net financial effect will be, we cannot rule out the possibility that it will outweigh the positive stimulus of pure cash balances, particularly if the holders of large cash balances have a low marginal propensity to consume and/or tend to switch from cash into non-produced stores of value.

So everything is up in the air. This unsatisfactory state of affairs, however, results from an inadequate picture of the financial system of corporate business. Firms are not 'family firms', run by an owner-operator who borrows the savings of other families – owners or workers – through the mediation of a bank. Instead corporations are *legal persons*, with limited liability, who own their buildings and equipment and other assets outright. Holders of the corporation's equity are not the 'owners' of the corporation, in the way the family head owns the family firm. Owners of a public company's stock are entitled to a share in its earnings and to vote for its directors. That is all. So when a company's burden of debt rises because of deflation, we can expect to find its stock collapsing.

Households, besides holding bonds (having lent to business) also hold equity in business. Indeed, any well-managed portfolio should contain a balanced mixture of bonds and stocks and cash. In a deflation, bonds and cash will rise in real value, but stocks will fall and, as businesses near the bankruptcy point, will fall precipitously. Thus a deflation will have a negative effect on business, while its effect on households will depend on the composition of their portfolios, which may well be different for different classes of households. But if the deflation goes far enough so that businesses approach or reach the bankruptcy point, then not only will the value of equity fall precipitously, but also bond prices of endangered firms will collapse. Thus the effect of a sufficiently pronounced deflation on households must also be negative. Failure to see this is simply the result of failing to distinguish between stocks and bonds, equity holdings and contractual lending.

Given inside money and/or money-denominated contracts, therefore, there are problems in the short-run adjustment that the real balance effect is supposed to provide. It is simply not possible to argue that in general, if unemployment emerges in a competitive market economy, real balance effects will correct it. If there is inside money this will not necessarily be so, and if investment loans are denominated in money – as, of course, they are – the net effects of wage and price flexibility are likely actually to exacerbate the slump.[2] Since all modern capitalist industrial economies operate in large part with inside money and denominate contracts in money, there is very little left of the vaunted claim that real balance effects will, in theory stabilize the system and keep it at full employment[3] (Chs 18, 19 and 20).

A Further Problem: Demand Theory

What of the claim that in long-run analysis the real balance effect enables neo-Classical theory to overcome the contradiction between the monetary excess demand functions and the demand functions for goods and services, while preserving the 'neutrality of money,' the essential conclusion of the traditional quantity theory?

Here we can only summarize the results of a complex argument. Since the price level is a weighted average of all prices, *any* price change must have a real balance effect when utility is a function of real balances. But it has been shown by Cliff Lloyd (1964), and admitted by Patinkin (1965), that, apart from the case of *all prices changing equiproportionally*, the real balance effects associated with ordinary price changes are of indeterminate sign and size. Theoretically, such effects could even swamp substitution effects for normal goods.

Consider a good, x, the consumers of which are highly sensitive to the value of their real balances, and another good, y, where consumers are insensitive to real balances. Then let a non-proportional price rise take place, with x rising very little or not at all, while y and other goods rise substantially. The relative value of x will therefore have fallen, and we should expect the demand for it to increase. But because the consumers of x are highly sensitive to their real balances, which have fallen, they will cut back their spending, whereas the consumers of y, being insensitive, will not. Thus sales of x may fall, in spite of the substitution effect in its favor. If real balance effects are strong enough to ensure full employment, they are strong enough to influence the relative demands for various individual goods in ways that undermine the conclusions of conventional demand theory. Patinkin's 'integration of real and monetary theory' results in an indeterminate theory of demand at the micro level.

Thus the real balance effect overcomes one set of problems only to introduce others. This is especially true in macroeconomics, the arena in which the most intensive fighting between monetarists and Keynesians has occurred. Since both sides agree that the *IS–LM* system provides a useful general model – though they disagree on exactly how it works – we had better examine the role of the real balance effect in such a system.

Macroeconomics

Beginning with Patinkin, real balances were treated as entering into household or consumer preference functions, just like commodities. An increase in real balances increases 'utility', but at a diminishing rate. However, if real balances provide convenience in purchasing for consumers, they surely do likewise for business firms, so they should enter into production functions. This seems straightforward enough, but the consequences are unsettling. In orthodox theory, real balance effects have been confined to product markets in which businesses supply and households demand. There is no justification for this; if real balances enter into utility and production functions, then they affect household *supply* and business *demand* as well. However, these effects upset the usual results. Let us examine this.

Let us start with the most widely accepted model of modern macroeconomics. It can be represented by a three-quadrant diagram (see Figure 25.1). In the lower left are the labor supply and demand curves, derived respectively from the households' work/leisure choice and from the firms' profit-maximizing, subject to the production function, which itself is drawn in the right-hand quadrant. In this, the most usual representation, there are no real balance effects in the labor market. No reason is given for this arbitrary exclusion. In the upper right quadrant, then, are the sets of *IS* and *LM* curves, respectively defined for each possible price level. Real balance effects appear here, but only here. Because of real balance effects, lower price levels are associated with *IS* curves positioned higher and to the right; for each level of the interest rate, investment and savings balance at higher levels of income because the greater monetary wealth associated with lower prices stimulates both consumption and investment spending. Lower price levels are also associated with a rightward positioning of the *LM* curve, since demand and supply of money will balance at higher levels of income for each interest rate, owing to the lower transactions requirements when the price level is lower.

Solutions

There are several ways of illustrating the solution to this system graphically. We will adopt the one that best exhibits the Keynesian–neo-Classical disagreement. First, we derive the relationships between the price level and real output for the *IS* and *LM* functions above, holding interest constant. That is, for a given interest rate we construct the locus of combinations of *P* and *Y* that equate investment and savings, and the

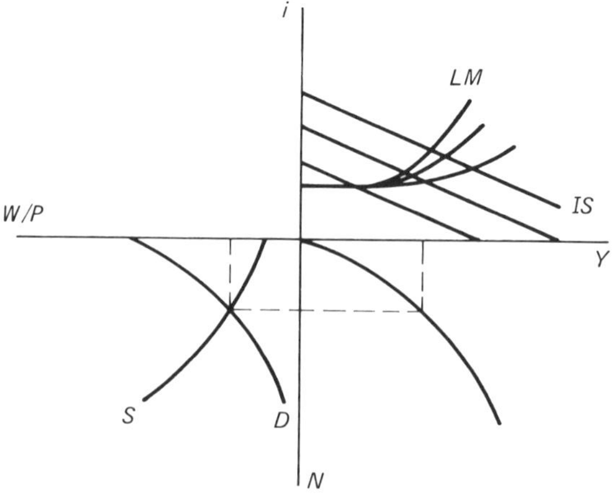

Figure 25.1

demand for and supply of money, respectively. For a given interest rate, a lower price level implies higher real balances, hence more of both real consumption and investment; thus a higher level of real income will be required to generate the greater offsetting savings required. Thus the price level and real income will be inversely related along such a locus. For a given interest rate, a higher price level implies a higher demand for money; with a given supply, determined by the central bank, this requires a lower real income to equate demand to supply. Moreover, it is reasonable to assume that the lower real income must be equiproportional to the higher price level, since both reflect the same nominal transactions demand. Thus the relationship – LM_p – will be a rectangular hyperbola, with *PY* a constant. It can, however, be cut either from above or from below by the *IS* price-level (IS_p) locus. Figure 25.2a and 25.2b illustrates the two cases.

Alternatively, we could derive the relationships between *P* and *i*, respectively, from the *IS* and *LM* curves (see Figure 25.3). For a given *Y*, a lower *P* means higher monetary wealth, so greater consumption and investment spending. Hence a higher *i* will be needed to encourage saving and discourage investment, in order to equate them. So *P* and *i* are inversely related in the *IS* market. In the money market, the *i, P* relationship for given *Y* will be the same as the *i, Y* relationship for given *P*. We have a replica of the usual *LM* curve. Putting the two together, we can determine *i* and *P* for given *Y*. Higher levels of *Y* shift the *IS* curve inward and the *LM* curve outward.

Now look back to the original three-quadrant diagram (Figure 25.1). In the labor market, equilibrium employment, *N*, and the equilibrium real wage, *W*/*P*, are determined. From the production function and *N*, we obtain full employment output, *Y*. Then with a given *Y* we can select the

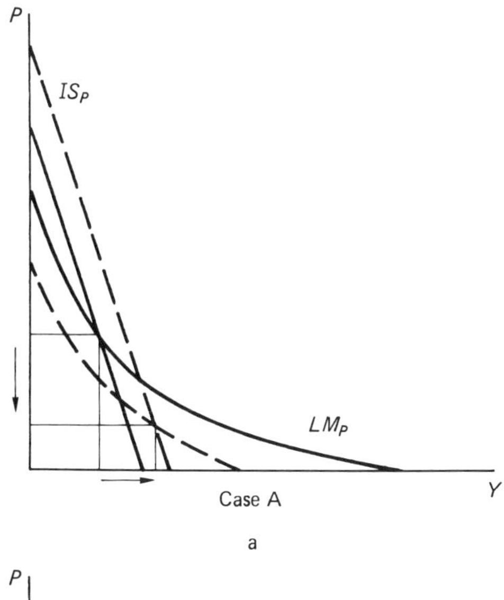

a

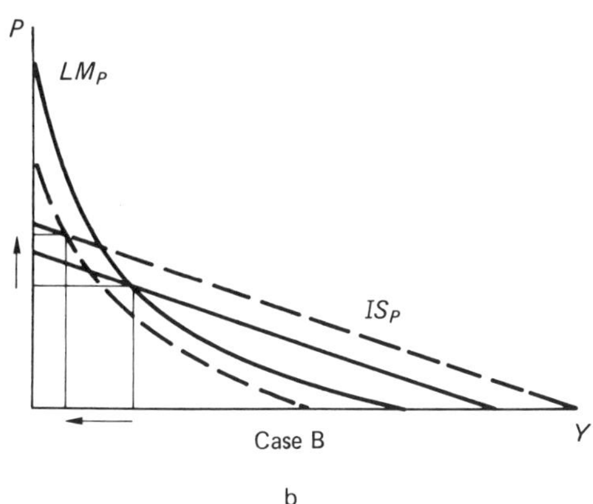

b

Figure 25.2

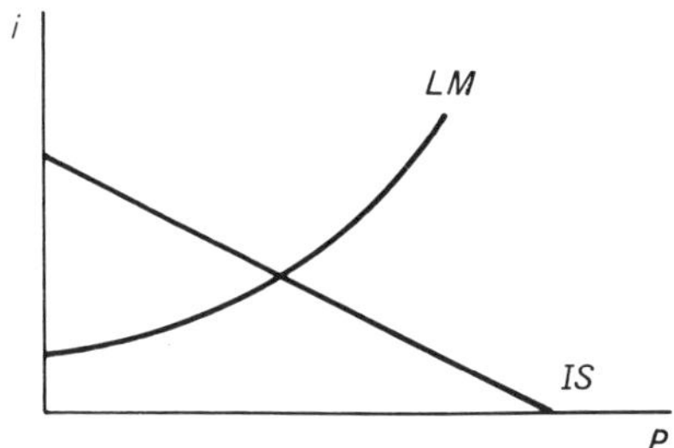

Figure 25.3

appropriate *IS* and *LM* loci in (*i*, *P*) space, and their intersection will determine the full employment rate of interest and price level. Finally, we substitute the price level into the real wage to find the money wage rate, and using the interest rate and income level we can calculate savings investment, consumption and the demand for money. The solution is complete, and given the usual assumptions – in particular that the *IS* curve has a negative slope – it will be unique.[4] Note that an increase in the supply of money will not affect the labor market or the full employment level of output, but it will lower the interest rate and raise the price level, for it will shift the *LM* curve in (*i*, *P*) space to the right. Thus the 'neutrality of money' is confirmed – with respect to employment and output. The case with regard to stability is not so clear, however.

Stability

There are two versions of the *IS* and *LM* diagram in (*P*, *Y*) space, as seen above.[5] This leads directly to a question about the system's stability. Look at Figure 25.2 again. In Case A a large rise in *P*, lowering real balances, has an effect on consumption and investment that can be offset by a small fall in *Y*. In Case B just the opposite holds.

Now suppose that, at the initial rate of interest, the level of real output at which these lines intersect is below the full employment level. By implication, the rate of interest is too high. The excess output will imply excess savings, and the rate of interest will fall.[6] A lower rate of interest will shift the LM_p line inward, since a lower rate of interest implies a higher speculative demand, there being less to be divided between the two influences on the transactions demand. Similarly a lower rate of interest increases both consumption and investment, thus shifting the IS_p upward and to the right, since a higher level of income will be required at each price level to generate the required savings; or, alternatively, at each level of income, a higher price level will be necessary to lower real balances enough to offset the effects of lower interest on consumption and investment. In Case A the results are unambiguous: both movements lower the price level and increase income. The outcome will therefore be a tendency towards full employment income at a lower price level. In Case B things are not so agreeable: both movements lower the balancing level of income; but both movements also *raise* the price level. So the overall movement is *away* from full employment income, while the effects on the price level are inflationary. In this case the real balance effect tends to create 'stagflation'.

Case B makes it clear that the real balance effect, by itself, is not enough to ensure stability. Contrary to what is widely believed. However, even in Case A, Keynesian arguments can be made, even after accepting the contention that, when income is below the full employment level, interest rates will fall. For when interest falls, the speculative demand for money increases. When bond prices rise high enough, the speculative demand will absorb all available cash, so that interest rates will decline no further. So for large discrepancies between actual and full employment income, the movement to full employment will depend on the IS_p locus shifting when interest rates decline. If this response is weak and the speculative demand strong, then full employment may not be reachable in Case A. This is possible even though prices are flexible and the real balance effect is alive and well. Hence, it must be assumed, in addition, that the speculative demand for money is weak or non-existent and that the investment–saving locus is strongly interest-elastic. In short, the claims for the stability of full employment equilibrium simply have no basis.

Real Balances Again

Now let us go back to the basic model. We noted that real balance effects appeared only in the goods markets, although real balances were assumed to enter into household utility and business firm production functions. Logically, they should also affect households' labor supply and business' labor demand decisions. In neo-Classical theory, especially in general equilibrium theory, decisions are interdependent. The decisions to demand goods and to supply labor are not separate decisions; they are part and parcel of the same utility-maximizing problem. The same holds for business decisions to supply goods and demand factors; again, they are two aspects of the same maximizing process. If real balances enter into one part of the problem, they must enter into the other. A rise in real balances, for example, should reduce the supply of labor for every level of real wages. Since households are wealthier, they can consume more, hence, will opt for more leisure and less work. Furthermore, a rise in real balances should increase the demand for labor at every level of the real wage, since it enhances productivity.[7] So, holding the real wage constant, we can define a direct functional relationship between the price level and labor demand. On normal assumptions these two curves will intersect in a unique point, determining the equilibrium price level and employment. A change in the real wage, on the other hand, will shift each curve – higher real wages being associated with an inward shift of D and an outward shift of S (See Figure 25.4). Each shift lowers P, but the effect on N is indeterminate. It could go either way, or, in the extreme case, remain unchanged if two influences were to offset each other exactly.

Leaving this special case to one side, there will no longer be a unique 'full employment' level of N; nor will there be a uniquely corresponding Y, since to every level of N there will correspond many Ys depending on the level of real balances. But the preceding line of argument depended on comparing the full employment income with the actual or initial level of income. If $Y<Y_F$, then interest (or, in most textbook accounts, the price level) would fall, setting off the equilibrating movements. When real balances enter into utility and production functions and influence labor

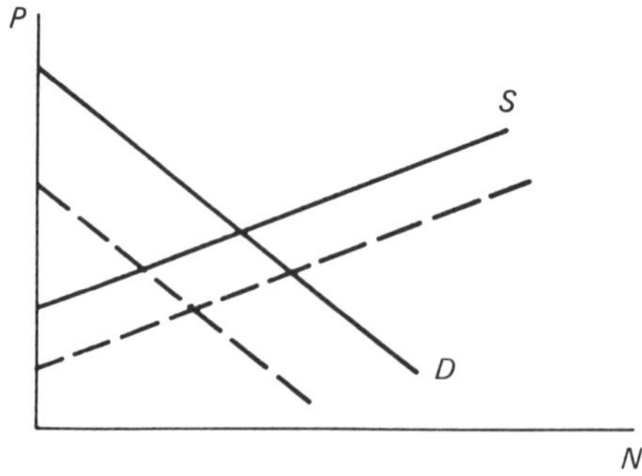

Figure 25.4

demand and supply, the equilibrating process will itself cause the 'full employment' level of income to change. The process can no longer work.

More technically, as we have already seen, without real balance effects (that is, with fixed labor supply and demand curves), the system could always be solved and the solution would normally be unique. But when we add two new functional relationships, between employment and the price level, derived from real balance effects in the labor market without any new variables, we have an over-determined system, which will normally end up generating contradictions. For example, starting from a given labor market situation – which implies a given level of real balances, and so a given price level – we can calculate as before; whereupon we determine P and i together, for full employment Y. But the initial labor market situation *already implied a price level*, since without it the level of employment would not be determined. It would, however, be a remarkable accident if this were the same price level that cleared the product market. In general they will be different. Hence the system is self-contradictory.

In other words, when we take the real balance effect *fully* and *properly* into account, far from 'integrating real and monetary theory,' it engenders an overdetermined, self-contradictory system, even apart from the issues of inside money and the burden of debt.

Income

Finally, what about the empty quadrant? Doesn't something belong there? It almost cries out to be filled. And there is, in fact, an important relationship between i and W/P, which derives from

$$PY = W/N + iKP,$$

which is the expression for the distribution of total money income between the money wage bill and the money returns to capital. Here i represents interest on money capital, and it is assumed that capital values will be adjusted in the stock market, so that the rate of dividends plus capital gains on shares will be equalized to the prevailing rate of interest on bonds. (Alternatively it may be assumed, as Patinkin does explicitly, that all capital is borrowed. Hence the only form of security traded will be bonds.) It may be objected that the condition that the rate of interest be adjusted so that $PY = WN + iKP$ is 'long run', whereas only 'short-run' questions are at issue. It is hard to see what this means. Money income *has* to equal money wages plus money returns to capital; those are the only two possibilities the model allows. Money income has to be paid out in the 'short run', because it finances expenditure. It should be added that the rate of interest determined by the income equation will equal the marginal product of the capital stock, if the production function is first degree homogeneous. From the above we derive,

$$i = \sigma - \frac{W}{P} n, \qquad \text{where } \sigma = Y/K,\ n = N/K.$$

This is a straight line with intercepts $W/P_{\max} = Y/N$, $i_{\max} = Y/K$; and slope equal to N/K. It states that, given the stock of capital, the full employment labor force and full employment output, the equilibrium real wage implies a corresponding full employment rate of interest. This rate of interest is necessary in order for total earnings plus total wages to add up to the total money value of output. If this condition is *not* met, then the spending of full employment income *cannot* purchase all and only full employment output at the going price level. This equation is a precondition for short-run equilibrium and is frequently taken for granted. But once it is written down explicitly, it is easily shown that the system is overdetermined and therefore, except by accident, inconsistent, as can be seen from Figure 25.5.

Rewrite the *IS* and *LM* loci in terms of *i* and *P*, for the full employment level of income, Y_F. This results in the loci of (i, P) that equate full employment saving and investment, IS_{Y_I}, and full employment demand for money to the given supply, LM_Y. The intersection will determine the full employment rate of interest and price level. The full employment money wage follows from this price level and the real wage. But the equation for the payment of income in conjunction with the real wage fixed in the labor market determines the interest rate that will ensure the capital income and money wages jointly exhaust the total value of output. There is no reason why this interest rate should equal the one determined by the *IS–LM* functions. Except for accidental cases, then, the system will be contradictory; it will determine two inconsistent levels of the interest rate (see Figure 25.6). Yet this is the basic model that has been employed by both

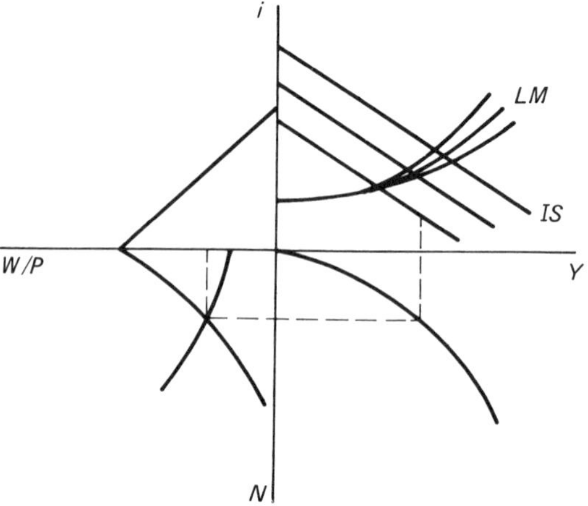

Figure 25.5

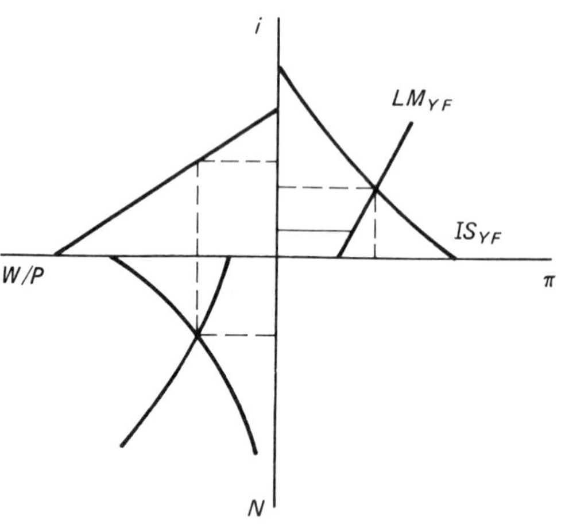

Figure 25.6

sides in the debate between monetarists and Keynesians, and, as we shall now see, it is the model that Friedman himself uses.

2 MILTON FRIEDMAN'S MONETARY THEORY

The preceding section has made it clear that neo-Classical theory as a whole, not only monetarism, still faces substantial unresolved problems in relating its monetary theory to its basic supply and demand analysis of prices and outputs. If it simply proceeds by way of determining relative prices and quantities from the data of preferences, production possibilities and initial endowments, and then introduces a quantity equation, it engenders a contradiction. This is the procedure dubbed by noeclassicists themselves the 'invalid dichotomy.' But if it introduces a 'real balance effect' in order to overcome this, it can generate the desired conclusions for aggregate analysis (full employment, neutrality of money) only if it confines its analysis to pre-modern and implausible monetary systems – *no inside money and no money contracts*. Furthermore, when we consider the disaggregated system in detail, the neutrality of money is lost except in the unusual and implausible case of all prices changing in exactly the same proportion. Nor does the argument support the often-repeated claim that full employment equilibrium is stable. But much worse, most writers, following Patinkin, consider real balance effects only in the product markets. When they are introduced, as they should be, into the labor markets, the resulting model is over-determined and contradictory.

The Monetarist Strategy

Faced with these, from their point of view, depressing conclusions from two decades of rigorous work, monetarists have proceeded in the most straightforward and effective way imaginable. They have simply ignored all the modern work. By and large, they have not changed the basic questions and neither have they challenged or replaced the modern answers. They have simply shouted the old ones louder.

Of course, it will be argued, this is not really quite fair. Serious and important work has been done and new approaches have been developed. Perhaps, but a very great deal of what has been taken to be new is nothing but the old flock of sheep herded forward in fine new wolf-garb. Lest we be thought to be criticizing scarecrows rather than shepherds, we shall take as our illustration the work of the chief shepherd himself, Friedman.[8] We will begin by showing that his arguments repeatedly – in various forms and contexts – embody the 'invalid dichotomy,' to which he has never given an adequate response. In particular, it is because he implicitly assumes the invalid dichotomy that he finds it unnecessary (or impossible?) to give an explicit account of the 'transmission mechanism' by which an increase in the stock of money principally affects prices rather than, as Keynesians have always argued, outputs and employment when the economy is below full capacity. Outputs and employment are 'ground out by the Walrasian system of equations' (Friedman, 1956, p. 15), that is, by the Walrasian equations, *not including real balances and/or wealth in the form of obligations denominated in money*, because if these are included, the results (long run as well as short) will not be those of the traditional quantity theory. But if the Walrasian equations depend only on relative prices, then the quantity equation determines the price level, and the 'transmission mechanism' is trivial. However, as seen, the model is then inconsistent as a whole.

Although Friedman is attracted by the simple quantity theory, he proposes an alternative version, which he calls the 'monetary theory of nominal income,' in which the supply and demand for money determine nominal income, that is, *PY*. Real output is determined through the labor market and the production function, thus fixing employment and so 'the natural rate of unemployment.' However, as we saw earlier, false expectations may at times be generated in the labor market, leading to temporary deviations from equilibrium employment and output levels. As workers and employers learn to form their expectations more adequately, this will happen less frequently and be corrected more rapidly. Thus in equilibrium the monetary theory of nominal income can be put together with the natural rate of employment/unemployment, and the equilibrium price level simply follows. However, Friedman has simply bypassed the determinants of aggregate demand: there is no reason to suppose that this price level is the one that would generate the full employment level of aggregate demand through the real balance effect.

The Phillips Curve and Irving Fisher

It is convenient to start an examination of Friedman's position by looking at his interpretation of the Phillips curve, which he claims to base on Irving Fisher's work. Phillips viewed the relationship between output and employment as a problem in Marshallian equilibrium analysis in a Keynesian world. Output and/or employment are the independent variables, with prices tending to adjust any resulting shortages or surpluses. Prices, or money wages, are clearly the dependent variables. Wages (or the rate of change in wages) are determined by conditions in the labor market as measured by the rate of unemployment. Fisher (1930), on the other hand, writing in a pre-Keynesian framework, drew on a Walrasian approach. Price is the independent variable, of which the offer and demand curves for labor are functions. Thus, he poses the question of what is likely to happen to output and employment in the face of a general increase in wages and prices. Fisher argues that though wages (variable costs) and business receipts may rise proportionally, since a substantial fraction of costs are fixed in money contracts, total costs will rise less than proportionally. Resulting windfall profits ought to increase employment. Higher inflation, in other words, reduces unemployment.[9]

It is important to note that, though these windfalls may be temporary because the contracts will eventually be renegotiated, they are not *illusory*. Friedman's version of the Phillips curve, on the other hand, presents a very different picture, one that is actually inconsistent with Fisher's approach. For while he takes from Fisher the concept of price as the independent variable, he totally ignores the question of lags in the process of adjustment, and substitutes the stimulative effects of various illusions for the stimulative effects of real and permanent transfers of wealth. He argues that the equilibrium level of employment, or the 'natural rate of unemployment,' or 'the level that would be ground out by the Walrasian system of general equilibrium equations' (Friedman, 1968), is determined by the offer and demand schedules for labor for a real wage:

$$N = N\frac{(W)}{P}$$

$$\frac{1}{P} \cdot \frac{dP}{dt} = \frac{1}{W} \cdot \frac{dW}{dt}$$

From this equation we see that a change in money wages (W) and prices (P) does not result in any change in real wages, (W/P); moreover, if there is no change in real wages, the equation shows there should be no change in employment (N). Thus, a change in absolute price that is not a change in relative price will not result in any changes in the equilibrium quantities, i.e. these will depend only on the given supply and demand equations. Any shifts in the curves can be due only to traders misinterpreting the data, i.e. capitalists mistakenly believing that $1/P \cdot dP/dt > 1/W \cdot dW/dt$, and workers mistakenly believing the reverse. Since he tacitly assumes that changes in the rates of fixed costs to revenue have no consequences for employment, Friedman is quite correct in arguing that any change in the equilibrium level of employment from such errors in calculation can only be temporary. 'You can fool some of the people some of the time, but you can't fool all the people all the time', says Friedman in his most statesman-like mood (Friedman, 1973, p. 27). Traders will base their behavior either on experience or on 'rational expectations' of price changes 'on the basis of a correct economic theory.' Once they have corrected any misperceptions, there will be no effect on employment from price inflation; in other words, the Phillips curve will be vertical. There is, therefore, a unique natural rate of unemployment and the government can push the system away from this level only by 'fooling people' – and they will soon catch on. But note that this approach determines output *entirely* from the 'supply side.' Nothing has been said about whether or not there is sufficient real aggregate demand to ensure that this output – no more, no less – can be *sold*. This was the original question for the Keynesians, and Friedman simply ignores it.

Nor is he even true to Fisher. There is a difference between employment changes due to windfall profits, as in Fisher, and employment changes due to miscalculation of costs and revenue. In Fisher's model there is no reason for employment to revert to its original position, for it was not due to a disequilibrium. Employers and workers were not fooled, and the increases in their offers were based on real factors. Friedman changed the nature of Fisher's argument by totally ignoring the whole question of fixed costs. His approach resembles Fisher's only in the choice of the price level as the independent variable. For the rest, his argument assumes a simple old-fashioned labor market in which supplies and demands depend on the real wage. There are no real balance effects, although in the *text* he repeatedly suggests that prices begin to rise because of an increase in the supply of money. This is what sets off the inflationary process during which the various agents misperceive or miscalculate. He assumes the validity of his 'monetary theory of nominal income', but, as we shall see, it does not deal with demand.

Moreover, if there are no real balance effects, how does Friedman propose to avoid the inconsistency? He refers to a 'Walrasian general equilibrium,' so Walras' Law must hold; if it does, the quantity equation cannot be tacked on to the rest. As already mentioned, the point holds equally for micro and for macro models, as we shall shortly show. But Friedman is silent on the subject.

The Transmission Mechanism

Let us approach the subject from another point of view. Friedman supposes that an increase in the supply of money will raise prices. These price increases will then be misperceived, etc. by various agents who will adjust their supplies and demands. Keynesians, by contrast, would expect an increase in the supply of money to lower interest rates rather than raise prices, and then, as a result of lower interest, investment spending might increase, which if the increase were large enough might push up prices. The Keynesian account of the 'transmission' of effects through the economy is quite detailed. Friedman rejects the Keynesian account and holds that changes in the money supply *directly and immediately* affect prices. How? What is his alternative account of the transmission process?

In 'The Quantity Theory of Money – A Restatement' (1956), Friedman attempts to integrate monetary theory into the general framework of neo-Classical value theory. To a utility-maximizing individual, the demand for money is determined in the same way as the demand for any other commodity or asset – a combination of income and substitution effects. The demand for money is part of a portfolio equilibrium decision: 'To the ultimate wealth-owning units in the economy, money is one kind of asset, one way of holding wealth' (Friedman, 1956, p. 4). As such, its demand will be determined by the level of wealth and the return on alternative assets and their expected rate of change. Friedman defines the following symbols (in addition to the ones we have used before):

Let r_b = rate of return from bonds (fixed in nominal terms)
r_e = rate of return from equities (fixed in real terms)
w = ratio of 'non-human' to 'human' wealth
u = variables that affect taste and preference
P = price level or the implicit return from goods.

Then, first writing a demand for money in nominal terms and dividing through by P, we get a demand for real cash balances:

$$L = f\left(r_b, r_e, \frac{1}{P}\frac{dP}{dt}, w, Y, u\right).$$

This equation describes an individual wealth holder. The aggregate function is derived by aggregating over all relevant individuals. The questions as to who these are, and what should be the aggregation weights, will come up in a moment.

According to Friedman, the quantity theorist is distinguished from other economists in holding that:

1. This demand for real cash balances is highly stable.
2. The supply of and demand for money are independent, i.e. there are important factors affecting the supply of money that do not affect the demand.
3. The liquidity trap is not important; quantity theorists reject the doctrine that the demand for money becomes perfectly elastic at very low rates of interest.
4. Quantity theorists interpret wealth and the spectrum of assets more broadly than conventional economists.

All this may be interesting but it does not add up to an account of the transmission process. Friedman was satisfied to end his restatement with 'the proof of the pudding is in the eating' (1956, p. 17) But puddings, no matter how tasty, should be eaten only for dessert. For an entrée it would be reasonable to ask to be shown why a stable demand for money function when linked to an increase in the supply of money would lead to *price* rather than *output* change. In other words, we need a theory of the determinants of spending in the process of short-run adjustment. Finally, in his 'A Theoretical Framework for Monetary Analysis' (1970), Friedman attempted to come to grips with this problem, as well as to try to specify the difference between his monetary framework and the Keynesian system.

Asset Choices

Friedman couches his explanation of the transmission mechanism in an asset choice framework so as better to contrast it with what he believes to be the Keynesian challenge and, surprisingly, the argument is essentially the same as the approach of Patinkin. (The reason for surprise is that if he accepts the real balance effect, he must accept the results that go with it – and these do not square with the conservative position. Specifically, Patinkin's approach provides an important role to aggregate demand, and so to government.) Let us see what he says.

Money is regarded as one of a spectrum of assets, yielding a service similar to other assets and having similar properties of diminishing marginal utility. An increase in the quantity of money in an economy initially in asset equilibrium induces a disequilibrium in the structure of asset holding; that is, there is excess supply relative to a stable demand for real cash balances. This induces a generalized substitution from money to other assets, driving down their rates. The fall in rates on assets raises the implicit, non-observable rates of return on consumer durables. At the same time, the price of current consumption in terms of foregone future consumption (Marshall's 'reward for waiting') has fallen, which, in principle, ought to increase the demand for non-durables as well (Friedman, 1970; in Gordon, 1974, p. 28).[10] We therefore have an increase in money expenditures generated by the increased money supply due to the constant demand for real cash balances. But the excess supply of money is not eliminated by simply being passed around like a hot potato. Friedman and the Keynesians both agree that one person's expenditure is another person's receipt. To restore equilibrium it is necessary for the real value of cash balances to be restored to what the public desires to hold.

It is here that monetarists and Keynesians part company. Friedman argues that the equilibrium will be restored by inflation, which will reduce the value of money until real cash balances are returned to their equilibrium level, while Keynesians would argue that increased expenditures would stimulate employment, which will increase the number of individuals holding cash balances. Taking his cue from Leijonhufvud (1968), Friedman reduces this difference to one of adjustment velocities. Which adjusts faster, prices or quantities? It is important to emphasize this point. While Keynes has been accused (many would argue falsely) of achieving his results by assuming fixed prices, for Friedman to derive *his* transmission mechanism from money to prices, he must assume fixed employment. Though he admits 'there is nothing in the logic of the quantity theory that specifies the dynamic path of adjustment, nothing requires the whole adjustment to take place through P rather than through [real variables]' (Friedman, 1970; in Gordon, 1974, p. 17), he does not offer a satisfactory solution as to which it will be. It is not sufficient to claim, as he does, that this is an empirical question; the empirical results are contradictory, as is well known. (See Ch. 18 for flexible prices in Keynesian models.)

Even more seriously, his empirical work raises questions for his theory.

In *A Monetary History of the United States* (Friedman and Schwartz, 1963), the claim is that the *long-run* changes in the quantity of money have a negligible effect on real income, so that nonmonetary forces are all that matter for changes in real income. For shorter periods, changes in the supply of money will be reflected in all three variables, velocity, price level and real income. But if in the short run a change in the money supply will change real income, presumably it will also change employment and therefore the aggregate amount of money the public wishes to hold, since the total demand for money function is specified in terms of individual demands, which must then be aggregated. If the disequilibrium condition initiated by monetary expansion is solved by employment changes, the aggregate demand for real money (the foundation of the transmission mechanism for long-run price changes) must shift since the number of individuals overs which aggregation takes place and the weights accorded them will have to change with changes in employment.

Friedman's attempt to deal with the problem of the missing mechanism through analysis of asset adjustment is wholly unsatisfactory. The details of such a transmission mechanism are hard to pin down. Variations in money income are made up of fluctuations in both real income and prices, and Friedman has given us no grounds on which to explain their relative magnitude. Furthermore, as Laidler points out,

> Although the practice of treating the determination of variation in money income as a problem prior to and separate from that of breaking such variations down between real income and prices would, as Friedman (1971) argued, greatly simplify macroeconomics, the premises [for doing so] are factually wrong. How much money income will change in response to a given change in the quantity of money depends upon how much of that change comes in real income and how much in the price level (Laidler, 1978, p. 162).

This approach will not provide Friedman with his transmission mechanism. First, the basic model, being Keynesian, strongly suggests that changes in money will affect interest rates and output initially and prices only later. Worse, if real balance effects are excluded, the model is inconsistent; but if they are included, Friedman's simple labor market analysis of the Phillips curve must be rejected, for the reasons advanced earlier.

The Monetary Theory of Nominal Income

These and related objections were advanced from many quarters and Friedman finally took up the challenge to present his complete theory, showing exactly how the monetary theory of nominal income differs both from standard Keynesian theory and from earlier, presumably inferior, versions of the quantity theory. He begins by presenting 'A Simple Common Model' that 'would be accepted alike by adherents of the quantity theory and of the income–expenditure theory' (Friedman, 1970). Let us look at this carefully.

Using our previous notation, but now designating the interest rate by r, to indicate that it is defined in Friedman's sense, the model is:

$C = f(Y, r)$ where C is consumption
$I = g\ (r)$
$Y = C = I$ or $S = Y - C = I$
$M^d = P{\cdot}1(Y, r)$, or, if elasticity of the demand for money with respect to Y equals unity: $M^d = PY{\cdot}1\ (r)$
$M^s = h\ (r)$, or later $M^s = H{\cdot}m\ (r)$ where H is high-powered money and $m\ (r)$ is the money multiplier
$M^d = M^s$

This is a system of six equations with seven unknowns: C, I, r, P, M^d, M^s, Y.

Two comments immediately come to mind:

1. Friedman's investment function is a great simplification of Keynes' investment function, but the idea of separating expenditures into induced (C) and autonomous (I) is correct in spirit.
2. Most *IS–LM* models treat M^s as an exogenous policy-determined variable. To do so, however, requires an assumption that policy is unaffected by changes in the other variables, i.e., the central bank ignores P and r when deciding on changes in M. To Friedman such a state would be desirable (the Fed on automatic pilot), but he recognizes that as an assumption of actual M^s it is unwarranted.

Friedman then states (in Gordon, 1974, p. 31), 'There is a missing equation. Some one of these variables must be determined by relationships outside the system.'[11] He proceeds to consider:

1. The simple quantity theory: hold Y constant. Friedman admits that to do so 'is the essence of what has been called the classical dichotomy' (p. 32).
2. The simple income–expenditure model: hold P constant.

Friedman admits (p. 44) that both of these assumptions lack grounding in theory and are not well supported by evidence. He rejects both of these therefore and puts forth his own, third alternative, which he describes as a combination of Keynes and Fisher.

Yet, amazingly, since his account of the Phillips curve is based on it,

Friedman has simply ignored the labor market! That market, of course, consists of three substantive equations (ignoring the equilibrium condition) – labor demand, labor supply and the production function – while introducing only two new variables, the money wage and employment. The complete model therefore has nine equations and nine unknowns. Indeed, the model is, in all essentials, precisely the one we analyzed in the preceding section. There is no 'missing equation.' How could Friedman have overlooked this?[12]

Moreover, and crucially, when we add the labor market to his 'Simple Common Model,' determining full employment output, the invalid dichotomy is present and the contradiction discussed earlier is implicit. Further, it can easily be explained in macroeconomic terms. Assume inside money and no real balance effects. Start from full employment and then assume an increased money supply. This must involve the banking system buying bonds, i.e. lending more, so lowering interest rates. Hence aggregate demand will rise above the full employment level, creating an inflationary gap, so that the price level begins to rise. With a higher price level, bank deposits will rise, making available a larger supply of loanable funds. But with a higher price level, the funds needed to finance investment will have to be larger. Both demand for and supply of bonds therefore rise in the same proportion. The same thing happens in the commodity markets: earnings are up in the same proportion as costs. Hence in these markets no check exists to the rise in the price level. In the money market, by contrast, the implication is that the increase in income due to the fall in the rate of interest shifts the demand for money schedule by a definite amount so that it intersects with the new supply at a definite price level (see Figure 25.7). But as Walras' Law implies, the money and bond markets are simply *alternative* ways of expressing the same relationships. They cannot give different answers. Hence this formulation of macro theory is inconsistent.[13]

By contrast, when a real balance effect exists, it acts to check the rise in the price level in both the commodity and the bond markets. As prices rise, real balances fall; hence demand will be cut back in the commodity markets. Falling real balances will similarly require portfolio adjustments, cutting back the demand for bonds. The real balance effect therefore eliminates the inconsistency noted above.

Friedman does not explain why he believes such a contradiction can be avoided, however; he simply presents the model and claims that the real balance effect 'is not significant empirically' for short-run analysis. He does not explain how the *theoretical* problems can be overcome. Is the 'invalid dichotomy' acceptable in the short run? Why? As far as we can tell, he never discusses these problems. Does he or does he not accept the Walrasian analysis of markets? If he does not, why does he continually appeal to the equations of general equilibrium? If he does, what happens to Walras' Law in short-run equilibrium?

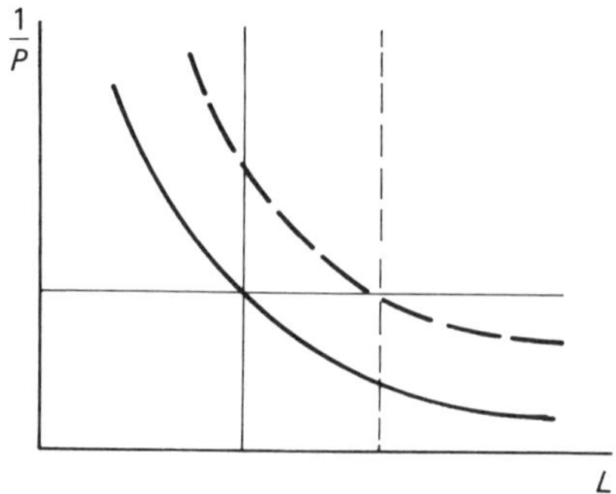

Figure 25.7

He claims at one point that wealth effects ensure that the long-run equilibrium position will always be a full employment one: 'There is no fundamental "flaw in the price system" that makes unemployment the natural outcome of a fully operative market-mechanism' (in Gordon, 1974, p. 16). So evidently he accepts the real balance effect for the long run. But notice that he is talking about the 'price system' here, not about steady growth. In replying to critics of his approach, he states, 'for the most part I was concerned with the short run . . . and I have never believed that the real balance effect is of much empirical significance for the short run' (Friedman, 1974, p. 175). This would seem to imply that he accepts the 'invalid dichotomy' for the short run, which means that Walras' Law would not hold for a short-run equilibrium in which the monetary theory of nominal income was combined with the product market side of the economy. Why this should be acceptable is never discussed. Nor is it clear that this is what he actually intends, since his discussion of the 'transmission mechanism', which is clearly a Keynesian-type short-run linkage, is indistinguishable from a real balance analysis. Why is the real balance effect sometimes treated as 'long-run' and other times as 'short-run'?

Friedman's Theory of Interest

Finally, let us look at Friedman's own approach (1970; in Gordon, 1974), which he describes as a combination of Keynes' interest rate (determined by expected future rates) and Fisher's distinction between the nominal rate (r) and the real rate (ϱ):[14]

$$r = \varrho + \left(\frac{1}{P} \frac{dP}{dt} \right).$$

This equation must be viewed as an identity rather than a theoretical statement. Though one could say that the true 'burden of debt'

$$\varrho = r - \left(\frac{1}{P}\frac{dP}{dt}\right),$$

this is an *ex post* concept. When the debt is contracted, only r is known. The rate of change of prices over the life of the debt is not known, and therefore cannot be calculated until the debt has been repaid. As Keynes pointed out, however, decisions must be made even in the face of uncertainty. Using * to denote expected values, Friedman's equation reads

$$r = \varrho^* + \left(\frac{1}{P}\frac{dP}{dt}\right)^*.$$

The nominal rate equals the real rate plus the rate of change of the price level. Or the true 'burden of debt' equals the nominal rate minus the rate of inflation.[15] This has a Fisherian flavor, but, to repeat, it is well defined only as an *ex post* concept. Since $Y = PY/P$, this can be written:

$$r = \varrho^* + \frac{1}{PY}\frac{d(PY)^*}{dt} - \frac{1\,dY^*}{Y\,dt},$$

or

$$r = \varrho^* - g^* + \frac{1}{PY}\frac{d(PY)^*}{dt}$$

where g^* is the expected rate of growth of real output, and

$$\frac{1}{YP}\left[\frac{d(YP)}{dt}\right]^*$$

is the rate of growth of money income.

Next Friedman argues that the difference, $\varrho^* - g^*$, designated by k_0, is both constant and small, so that

$$k_0 = \varrho^* - g^*,$$

and even if k_0 changes,

$$k_0 < \frac{1}{P}\frac{dP}{dt}.$$

Hence, he concludes:

$$r = k_0 + \left[\frac{1}{YP} \frac{d(YP)}{dt} \right]^*.$$

He then writes:

$$M^d = PY1(r)$$
$$M^s = h(r)$$
$$M^d = M^s.$$

Since he claims (Gordon, 1974, p. 38), 'At any point in time $(1/YP\ [d(YP)^*/dt])$, the "permanent" or "anticipated" rate of growth of nominal income is a predetermined variable . . . based partly on past considerations outside our model.' With r determined this way, the supply and demand for money determine nominal income, PY.

Now we can see quite plainly what Friedman has done. The level of nominal income so determined is nothing more than the level of nominal income that equates the supply of money to the demand for it, at the fixed interest rate. There is no reason to suppose that this is the level of income that will actually prevail in the economy, since nothing has yet been said about *spending*. It is through spending that goods are sold and prices and outputs actually realized, and Friedman has not yet told us about consumption and investment. He has done nothing more than determine which level of nominal income will establish equilibrium in the holding of money for the given rate of interest, as determined by expectations of future rates and of price changes. If these expectations are not realized in the present period, they will very likely change. Friedman's determination of r^* depends upon expectations being realized, that is, upon goods being sold in the anticipated quantities at the anticipated prices. But there is no reason for this to happen, since there is no way to reconcile the consumption and investment side of the 'Common Model' with the rest of his analysis. This can be seen in Figure 25.8. Friedman's monetary theory of nominal income determines r^* and the LM_{P_1} locus, which together with the labor market and the production function determine equilibrium in the following way: the labor market determines W/P and N; from the production function we obtain Y_F; then from the LM locus, given Y_F and r^*, we obtain the price level, P, which substituted in the equilibrium real wage determines the money wage, W. Since we know r^* and Y_F, we can substitute these values in the consumption and investment functions to determine C and I. *But there is no reason to suppose that the C and I so determined will add up to* Y_F! If the IS locus – the set of points for which $C + I = Y$ – is in the position shown, they will add up to less than full employment Y_F. There is plainly a contradiction here; it seems that unemployment could perfectly

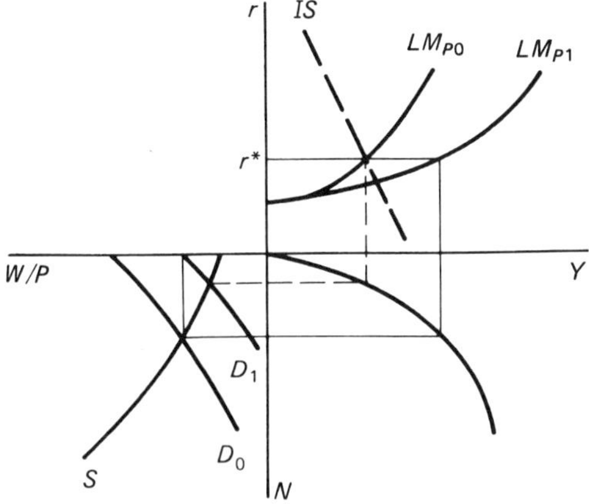

Figure 25.8

well be a natural outcome of the market system, conceived this way.

One way of analyzing this result proceeds by arguing that the *effective* demand for labor must be shifted down, reflecting the inability to sell the product. Thus employment is adjusted to sales. The new effective labor demand curve, D_1, reflecting under-utilized capacity, cuts the supply curve at a lower real wage and level of employment, corresponding to the output that can be sold. (Whether this is an adequate theory of labor market adjustment is another question. But if no adjustment takes place we simply have a contradiction.) Now we see a remarkable and wholly counter-intuitive implication of Friedman's theory. To re-establish equilibrium in the supply and demand for money at the given interest rate, the price level must *rise*, to take up the slack created by a lower real output. Correspondingly, given a higher price level, the money wage must fall substantially, both because the real wage must be lower and because the price level must be higher. Thus excess supply (or potential excess supply) causes money prices of goods to rise but the money price of labor to fall and, indeed, to fall sharply. This makes no sense at all. Of course, defenders of Friedman might reply that they do not believe the labor market adjusts its current demand for labor to current sales or sales expectations – but then they have to explain what happens when the *IS* curve fails to intersect the *LM* curve at the full employment level of real output.

To put the argument briefly: Friedman's monetary theory of nominal income can be combined either with the *IS* curve to determine output and the price level, or with the supply-side equations. But it cannot be combined with both without an explanation of what happens when the two levels of output are not the same.

Of course, the standard neo-Classical way out of this impasse – a failure of aggregate demand to equal full employment output – has been to rely on the real balance effect. But the real balance effect will only work if the *rate of interest is flexible*. For, as we saw earlier, the real balance equation will determine the price level and the rate of interest together, for the full employment level of income. Hence this approach would require jettisoning Friedman's 'Keynes–Fisher' theory of the rate of interest.

There are good reasons to dismiss Friedman's theory. The crucial step comes in the definition of k_0 (the difference between the real rate of interest and the growth rate of real output) and its separation from the growth rate of nominal income. Friedman contends that the growth of output is a function of the growth of capital, which will only change slowly over time through the accumulation of savings. But for Keynesians and mainstream economists generally, the growth of capital depends on its actual productivity (and its actual profitability), and this in turn depends on its rate of utilization, as determined by aggregate demand. Utilization and demand will also affect the price level. For these reasons the actual nominal rate at any point in time may differ from the expected nominal rate that Friedman's equations depend on. (That is, both the actual rate of growth of real income and the actual rate of growth of nominal income may differ from the 'permanent' or 'anticipated' rates because of fluctuations in aggregate demand.) In other words, Friedman has simply divided off the real forces, productivity and thrift, which in his view determine real growth, from monetary forces, which determine the growth of prices. But this is arbitrary. Once we allow that real growth may be influenced by monetary developments and that the growth of prices may be affected by real forces, then Friedman's equation for the nominal rate no longer holds and his simple quantity theory result – that supply and demand for money determine nominal income – cannot be derived. Once again Friedman's conclusions depend on an illegitimate dichotomizing of real and monetary forces.

Rates of Growth

Finally, another peculiarity of Friedman's approach should be considered. The variables with asterisks are interpreted as 'permanent' or 'anticipated' rates of growth. Presumably, then, they are growth paths along which supply and demand are balanced – 'warranted' rates of growth in Harrod–Domar terminology. If the economy's transmission mechanism involves quantity adjustments and the multiplier, then a deviation of the actual rate of growth of either real or nominal income from its warranted or permanent level will set up a cumulative movement increasing the divergence between the two. This is the familiar Harrod–Domar result.[16] But in his discussion of the adjustment process, Friedman nowhere explains why he neglects this problem.

Let us consider this point a little further. Like Friedman, Harrod (1948) assumes a fixed interest rate, which, he contends, means that the capital–labor ratio will stay fixed. Under these circumstances he argues that the warranted growth path is unstable, and that it will be unlikely to equal the growth rate of the labor force. So, in the long term, there will be a tendency to instability and unemployment. Does Friedman accept these conclusions? Presumably not, but he nowhere discusses them.

The by-now standard neo-Classical answer is given by Solow (1970), who allows the capital–labor ratio to vary. Hence the warranted rate of growth will adjust to the natural, i.e. to the rate of growth of the labor force plus technical progress. According to Friedman (1970), however, the growth rate of nominal output will adjust to the growth rate of the money supply. If the growth of real output were determined by the growth of labor plus technical progress, then the growth of the money supply would determine the rate of inflation, and we would have a long-run version of monetary neutrality (see Gordon, 1974, pp. 56–7). But can the interest rate be unaffected by the rate of growth of the money supply? If interest *is* affected, then will not the rate of interest affect the rate of accumulation? Monetary growth would then have effects on real growth.

The problem becomes even more complicated when we take account of the fact that saving out of profits is usually much greater than saving out of wages. The distribution of income between profits and wages therefore matters, so that the effects of monetary changes on distribution should be considered. Friedman nowhere discusses these questions, nor do most mainstream economists.

The conclusion we reach is in some ways a startling one, in this age of monetarism. It is that neither monetarists nor mainstream neo-Classicals have an adequate theoretical account of money or, consequently, of the role and impact of the state. Monetarists, exemplified by Friedman but by implication including all who accept the NRH, are committed to what mainstream discussion agreed upon years ago as the 'invalid dichotomy,' and they have so far failed to show why their models should not be rejected on these eminently Walrasian grounds. But mainstream economics itself is also in trouble, for its integration of monetary and value theory has inherent defects, first in its adoption of an incoherent concept of wealth and 'wealth effects.' Indeed, except in the unlikely case of uniformly proportional money price changes, real balance effects in the product market results in indeterminate demand changes, upsetting traditional results. Secondly, difficulties arise from the inadequate way it considers the effects of changes of the price level on money contracts. Finally, its generally inadequate aggregate model fails to include real balance effects in labor supply and demand decisions, and fails to include an expression for income, i.e., wages plus profits. The conclusion must be that the basic framework is defective. The theory that relates monetary and real economic phenomena will not rise on these foundations.

The consequence is therefore that conservative economists have no grounds for holding that government interference with the free market will result in damage to the economy. The claim that the free market system will tend towards full employment cannot be sustained, since the 'real balance' models, on which it rests, prove to be contradictory. Nor does the real balance effect work for modern monetary systems with contracts and inside money. Indeed, since neo-Classical economics has no adequate theory of money, it cannot have an adequate theory of economic policy. The most basic tools of neo-Classical theory actually prevent modern economists from understanding the role of the state in managing the economy.

3 JEAN-BAPTISTE MARGLIN: A COMMENT ON 'GROWTH, DISTRIBUTION AND INFLATION'[17]

It is not mere politeness to describe this article by Stephen Marglin as an extraordinary work, a synthesis, both clear and profound, of the central elements of two great traditions of economic thinking. It brings together and contrasts, then synthesises, basic ideas from the Marxist and the neo-Keynesian traditions. It does so in an exceptionally clear and simple analytical framework admirable suited for the purpose.

Yet, its very clarity makes it possible to see its shortcomings all the more plainly. The first question that springs to mind is whether the project is, in fact, possible. Can it be done at all, at least in the way Marglin proposes? This is not an idle question. Of course, in one sense, it can be done, and very well, too. Marglin has done it. But the question is whether what he has done is legitimate. To compare neo-Marxist and neo-Keynesian theory, they have to be made comparable. The Marxist tradition pays little attention to problems of aggregate demand, which are central to the Keynesian. Marglin adopts the Marxist position, and re-interprets the neo-Keynesian approach, setting it in a framework in which problems of effective demand are eliminated by assumption. Whatever is produced will be sold, and the neo-Keynesian principles come into play in determining the relative shares of workers and capitalists. But for Keynes, the point of *The General Theory* was to change the question from one of distribution to the determination of the level of output as a whole. Keynes without effective demand is Hamlet without the Prince.

Marglin's Approach

Marglin begins by defining a one-sector framework of capitalist production. Corn is produced by workers planting seed-corn, in accordance with fixed coefficients. The output after subtracting the necessary seed-corn is divided between consumption and investment. Growth is defined as the ratio between next year's output and this year's. The price of corn is defined in relation to labour cost, and the profit rate is defined in terms of the current price. Both prices and wages are defined in terms of money, although no account of the monetary system is ever provided. Output equals consumption plus investment and also equals wages plus profits. But output is fixed in size, which is taken as unity in any given period. Next Marglin turns to savings behaviour, which he takes to be fundamentally a matter of class. Workers do not save, capitalists do, but also consume. Hence the growth rate (since all savings are invested) will be given by the product of the capitalist savings propensity and the rate of profit. But this does not close the model; there are two unknowns, g and r, but only one equation connecting them. A second is needed and Marglin canvasses two candidates. Neo-Marxian theory completes the model by determining the real wage through the reserve army, while neo-Keynesian theory closes it by determining the level of investment through the interaction of the rate of interest, the rate of profit and the price level. Each of these ways of closing the model appears to capture a significant insight into the working of modern capitalism, but together they would overdetermine the system. Yet this need not be a defect; it might, on the contrary be an important insight in itself (Nell, 1970), for it could provide the basis for an account of inflation, and the last part of the study is devoted to this.

Fixed Output and the Quantity Theory

But the assumption of fixed output is crucial to the entire argument, and seriously distorts his account of the neo-Keynesian approach, although it echoes a famous stance once adopted by Kaldor – and mocked by Samuelson (Kaldor, 1956; Samuelson, 1964). This shows up very dramatically in the derivation of the basic neo-Keynesian behavioural functions. Both the short-run investment function, for example, and the long-period growth formula are derived by setting aggregate demand equal to aggregate supply, where the latter is assumed to be fixed by technology (Marglin, 1984, Equations 16 and 18, and Figure 6). Fixing supply in this way, however, leads to some difficulties. Consider the short-run analysis. By assumption, workers consume their wages, which are assumed fixed in money terms in the short run, while capitalist investment demand is also fixed in money terms, in the short run, by decisions to borrow taken on the basis of last period's price level and rate of profit. Current real investment demand therefore varies inversely with the current rate of profit and price level. The level of real investment must equal that of real savings, so this is determined together with the price level. That is, given total demand in money terms, with total supply fixed, the money price level follows immediately, and the rate of profit is calculated by finding the real wage.

For once the price level is known, since the money wage is given, the real wage follows, and so the rate of profit is determined. It is simple. It is also precisely the approach of the old Quantity Theory of Money.

According to the Quantity Theory, the money supply determined the level of money spending, given the velocity, so that with total output fixed, the price level followed. Similarly Marglin has fixed both the level of money spending, corresponding to MV, and total output. But he gives no reason why firms cannot adjust their levels of borrowing for investment purposes in the light of the difference between this period's price level and last period's. If they could, then firms could be supposed to make their real investment plans on the basis of the current price level and rate of profit. This would result in the normal neo-Keynesian argument: when (real) investment demand is below/above savings, the price level will fall/rise, so the real wage will rise/fall, on the assumption that money wages are less flexible than money prices. The real wage adjusts to clear the product market, rather than the labour market. But this no longer treats the real wage as a residual; far from it. The level of the real wage sets one component of effective demand, and investment the other. This adds a dimension to wages not present in the Marxian scheme – or in Marglin's version of neo-Keynesian thinking. Moreover, there is no reason to suppose that investment and savings will be equated only at full capacity. At less than full capacity, adjustments will primarily take the form of income changes rather than of movements in the price level. The assumption of fixed output, Equation 16, and the entire subsequent discussion, runs counter to the Keynesian approach. (Cf. Ch. 16 on Fixed Employment systems.)

Credit and the Rate of Interest

There is another respect in which Marglin's argument parallels the Quantity Theory: both neglect the relationships between money, credit and interest. Marglin claims to capture the central neo-Keynesian insight that because of the credit system, capitalists, unlike workers, operate without a budget constraint, at least in the usual sense. That is, given attractive projects a firm's ability to raise money will not be constrained by its current earnings; in general, business's investment spending is not constrained by current earnings in the way household consumption spending is by current income – contrary to the way business decisions are portrayed, for example, in much contemporary 'disequilibrium' literature. This is, indeed, a crucial element in the neo-Keynesian vision. But Marglin tries to present it in a model which includes money borrowed and lent, but has no specification of the money supply and no determination of the rate of interest. Yet he himself points out that investment depends not simply on the (expected future) rate of profit, but on the ratio of this rate to the current (and expected future) rate of interest. Consider the effects of this point on his short-run investment demand function. Suppose the system is in disequilibrium, with the rate of profit too high. Savings will exceed investment, and the price level must fall, so that real investment can increase. But the investible funds will have been borrowed at the current rate of interest, equal to or proportional to the initial rate of profit. If the price level falls, the rate of profit comes down, and it is going to be difficult to service debt contracted at the earlier, higher rate of interest. But if the debt can be rolled over, why are firms supposed to be constrained, in the short period, to a certain level of money expenditure? Of course, if they are not so constrained then Marglin's short-period story collapses, and we are back with the more traditional neo-Keynesian system, in which investment and saving need not balance at full capacity.[18] But, to repeat a point made above, if output and employment vary with effective demand, we are outside the Marxian framework. The two systems cannot be mixed, if one of them assumes that output is fixed, while the other treats it as variable. Of course, the Marxian framework could be used to examine the long-period path of accumulation, while the Keynesian dealt with fluctuations about that path. But that is not Marglin's approach; nor is it adequate, since there are long-period problems of demand.

Say's Law

It might be replied that since the problem being studied is long run, it is reasonable to neglect the (essentially short-run) variations in sales due to the vagaries of effective demand, in order to concentrate on the true problems of accumulation and distribution. From a neo-Keynesian perspective this is nonsense. Effective demand is not a matter of short-run 'vagaries;' it is a matter of investment, i.e., of capital accumulation. The growth of capacity must keep in step with the growth of demand. This is the essense of the multiplier-accelerator process, more generally expressed as the capital stock adjustment principle. There are problems in this approach, and it may well be that some of them have never been adequately dealt with, but the idea that capital accumulation must proceed *pari passu* with the growth of demand is surely not subject to doubt. Indeed, Say's Law is nothing but the statement that this happens automatically because supply always creates adequate demand. By contrast, the *fundamental* proposition of the Keynesian tradition is that neither in the short run nor in the long is there any reason to suppose that this balance will be achieved at full capacity by the unregulated market, except by accident, or as a temporary phase in a cyclical movement.

This point can be illustrated by examining a remark of Marglin's in connection with the pattern of causality in the neo-Marxian model: 'change the conventional wage and both the distribution of income and the growth rate change: change the propensity to save and *only* the rate of growth changes' (1984, p. 119). The second part of this will be true only if Say's Law holds, that is if all and only what is saved is automatically invested. Otherwise, suppose at full employment of capacity, with a given real wage, and a given level of investment, the propensity to save changed. Suppose it fell; at the initial rate of profit, investment would then exceed savings, so prices would be driven up, the real wage would fall, and the rate of profit increase. The process would stop when savings once again equalled investment – unless the higher rate of profit stimulated further investment, in which case the process might repeat itself, perhaps indefinitely. But if the propensity to save rose, the changes would not be symmetrical, for when savings exceed investment, income and employment will be adjusted downwards, rather than prices. Nevertheless, in either case a change in the propensity to save changes the rate of profit; when the propensity to save falls, this follows from a change in distribution, but when it rises, from a change in income and employment.

Real Wages and Growth

There is an even deeper problem. Is it, in fact, the case that a rise in the growth rate at full capacity can only come about through a fall in real wages? This is certainly the neo-Keynesian tradition, and is also in the spirit of Ricardo and Marx, but is it really true? Of course, if we assume no technical progress, no change in labour intensity, rigid coefficients and strict capacity limits, etc., we can *make* it true tautologically – no help to anyone. The serious question is whether this is a good way to theorise about increasing the growth rate when the economy is operating at what is regarded as the normal level of capacity utilisation, let alone during a period of stagnation. One of the largest sustained expansions ever recorded under capitalism took place in the USA in the early 1940s, yet real wages rose faster than productivity throughout this period, so that the share of wages and the rate of growth *both* increased (Nell, 1983). Of course a wartime economy is special; nevertheless, high employment together with high and rising wages led to a burst of productivity increases, due partly to increased effort on the part of labour, and partly to modernisation. High and rising wages, after all, can be expected to stimulate labour-saving innovation. Nor does it make much sense to think of capacity as rigidly fixed. Firms normally carry excess capacity for the same reasons they carry inventories and precautionary money balances. Of course, these are comments, not about Marglin's argument, but rather about his assumptions. But they turn out to be crucially important to his policy conclusions.

Inflation

When we come to his account of inflation, however, some questions about the argument itself arise. The neo-Marxian determination of the real wage gives rise, according to Marglin, to a simple adjustment process, in which the current real wage adapts by moving towards the equilibrium level. But when the price level is determined by the short-run neo-Keynesian mechanism, the neo-Marxian pressures will govern the movements of money wages. Which of these sets of pressures is stronger, and why? Under what circumstances? Marglin does not inquire. Instead he assumes a steady-state condition, that the rate of money-wage inflation exactly equals the rate of price-level inflation. When this holds the real wage is steady, and so therefore are the profit and growth rates. Starting from some initial position, the long-run equilibrium is determined, with a permanent inequality between savings and investment, disequilibrium real wage, and steady inflation.[19]

But why do the pressures of aggregate demand on aggregate supply just exactly balance the pressures that workers can exert over money wages? Marglin's steady state is possible, but why is it a more likely outcome than any other? What economic forces, with what strength and speed of operation, tend to pull the two rates of inflation into line with one another? And which of the two tends to adapt the most to the other? These questions are never raised, much less answered. Further, the answers are likely to depend on the way investment and effective demand are treated. If the accelerator principle were introduced, the story might look quite different (Nell, 1982). And it might be important to provide an account of the monetary and financial system (Ch. 24).

Worse, there are difficulties in each of the adjustment equations. The wage-adjustment equation (Marglin, 1984, Equation 20 or 31) implies that if the initial real wage is above the equilibrium, money wages will fall, even if the economy is at full employment, with prices rising due to an excess of investment demand over savings. This is surely not plausible. Similarly, if savings exceed investment, prices will fall even if money wages are rising (Equation 22). Marglin can reply that he only intends to draw on these adjustment equations in conditions of steady, balanced inflation, but this means that he cannot use his model to analyse the forces that would tend to establish such a state. In other words, he could not, in principle, answer the questions of the previous paragraph.

At this point, too, the one-sector assumption becomes problematical. Suppose two distinct kinds of goods had been assumed, produced in different sectors: investment goods and consumer goods. An excess of investment demand over savings would then imply an increase in the price of investment goods, but the shift in the distribution of income required to increase savings would need a fall in the real wage, i.e. a rise in the price of consumer goods. The price increase, in other words, takes place in the wrong sector, and moreover, changes the relative price ratio as well. Clearly the pattern of adjustment will have to be substantially more complicated, and it cannot be assumed that it will always work out (Nell, 1982).

Policy Implications and Conclusions

As so often, these theoretical questions have policy significance, but the implications are not as exact as well-organised and tidy minds might desire. Most of what Marglin says would be supported by the ideas I have drawn on in criticising him. But there are a few crucial areas where a difference might arise. For example, Marglin accepts the necessity for the Left to 'respect the logic of the economic situation. Productivity does place limits on wages, and not just physical limits. As long as profitability remains the mainspring of investment, there are economic limits that constrain the wage share. Under capitalism, profits are indeed the geese that lay the golden eggs' (p. 47). This rests squarely on his assumption of Say's Law; when output is determined by effective demand, investment governs current profitability, not the other way around.

Marglin wants the Left to demand worker participation in management in return for agreeing to wage restraint. Reasonable enough, but is a generalised policy of wage restraint necessary or even sensible in modern conditions? First, modern economies have clearly not been operating at anything like full capacity during the past decade and a half. Rising wages would increase demand in consumer goods markets. But, secondly, it would also increase the pressures on backward firms to modernise or go out of business, an effect that does not depend on the economy operating at less than capacity. This raises productivity, but it also leads to investment. In short, under suitable conditions raising wages may stimulate growth. Of course, wages could be raised too much, or in the wrong spheres, leading to bankruptcies and collapse. Likewise, an investment strike could be provoked, or a flight of capital abroad. It is easy to imagine scenarios in which high wages could be fatal (although controls on prices and capital movement might prevent or mitigate these effects). But it is hard to avoid the conclusion that the phenomenal growth of US capital had something to do with the high wages imposed by the existence of the frontier, high wages which generated a huge market, on the one hand, and strong pressures to innovate on the other. In any event Marglin's framework, since it assumes Say's Law, cannot deal with these questions, and is forced to accept the position that austerity policies are nothing but simple 'economic logic,' which any rational agent must accept. Conservatives could ask no better defence.

Each of the three authors examined here has come to grief through failing to connect the technology of production properly to the system of money wages and prices. Patinkin's real balance effects fail to take account of the fixed money costs required in Mass Production – and also fail to live up to billing: they don't stabilize the system. Friedman tries to avoid the problem of the invalid dichotomy, but can't excape it; then like Marglin he doesn't understand the system of Flexible Employment and output. Both the systems of Patinkin and Friedman lack explicit equations for the payment of money incomes. Marglin's system has such an equation, but misses the point of effective demand in conditions of flexible employment. Transformational growth has changed the way the capitalist system works, from a condition in which variation in investment spending is offset by changes in consumption to one in which consumption compounds fluctuations in investment, by changing in the same direction.

Notes

1. Patinkin (1965, p. 298) considers the case where inside money moves equiproportionally with outside, and shows that real balance effects still work under these very special conditions.
2. Even in a pure outside money system there is a problem. For the same reasons that firms and households hold transaction balances, they also hold inventories of goods. A price change that increases their real balances alters the value of their inventories in the opposite direction. There are other problems as well. Pigou and Patinkin held that the wealth effect would result chiefly in spending on regularly produced consumer goods; Friedman and Schwartz argue that the effect might take place first or chiefly as a switch from money to *durables*, including, but not confined to, consumer durables. But, of course, if this latter portfolio adjustment effect' involves switching from money to *non-produced assets* – antiques, land, Victorian houses, vintage automobiles – the only extra employment generated, if any, will be among the salesmen and refurbishers of such items. Keynes' essential contention is that, when the value of money rises, there will be no switching to *produced* goods; hence no employment will be generated by a general deflation.
3. Tobin (1980) argues that in the short run, with a given debt structure, the effects of changes in the burden of debt will always dominate real balance or Pigou effects. But in the long run, there is a Pigou Effect, since, he contends, allowing for opportunities to renegotiate debt, an economy with a lower level of prices and wages, but with the same nominal monetary base at every point in time, would have a higher level of activity than an otherwise identical economy with higher prices and money wages (pp. 11–12). This is difficult to understand. If the period is long enough for debts to be renegotiated, it is long enough to adjust the supply of 'near monies' to the needs of trade. If prices and money wages are low then the effective money supply will be contracted; if they are higher it will be expanded. Or does Tobin wish to argue that in the long run, there is a rigid relationship between the effective money supply and the monetary base? Neither evidence nor theory supports this. Of course, an

expansion of 'near monies' on a given monetary base may cause interest rates to be higher, which might constrict investment, but this would not in any sense be a Pigou Effect. Tobin does not believe 'long run Pigou Effects' are of any practical importance, in any case.

4. When the *IS* curve has a positive slope, which it easily might in a boom period, multiple solutions are possible, and either fiscal or monetary policy will be destabilizing. See Nell (1974, pp. 66–90) (Ch 18, 19).
5. The origin here is defined by the minimum level of real income and the minimum price level – the bottom point of the trade cycle. So the rectangular hyperbola that approaches the true zero axes asymptotically will appear here as a curve with an intercept on each axis. In this way we eliminate a second but irrelevant intersection of the IS_p line with the LM_p curve. (Even so, a special case can be imagined in which there are two intersections.)
6. This, of course, is just what pure Keynesians deny, as Patinkin (1965) agrees. The excess output will never be produced, for firms will not hire labor, regardless of the real wage, if the output from that labor cannot be sold. This is the origin of the so-called 'disequilibrium school', now represented by Malinvaud and Clower.
7. More precisely, when real balances have risen, at every level of employment additional labor could produce more additional output, since the higher balances make transactions easier, quicker, etc. Thus the marginal product curve will be shifted up, which implies that for every level of real wage, more labor will be demanded.
8. An important reason for choosing Friedman is that his work provides one of the earliest, and perhaps the canonical, statement of the 'natural rate hypothesis' (NRH), upon which later work builds. The rational expectations school, which takes its cue from Friedman, draws even more extreme free market conclusions. But the analysis of the rational expectations is built upon the foundation of NRH models, which in turn rest upon the invalid dichotomy. For rational expectations simply states that economic agents will *expect and plan their responses to economic stimuli in the light of what the best available theory predicts*. This assumes, first, that economic actions are planned responses, planned by maximizing methods, to accurately or inaccurately perceived economic stimuli, and, secondly, in many applications that the best models are uniformly known to be the neo-Classical models that generate the NRH. The first is a necessary assumption of the method, the second for the free market conclusion.
9. But Fisher does not actually argue the converse case, that lower inflation will increase unemployment. The stimulating effect of transferences of wealth from passive (creditors) to active (debtors) members of society has been discussed in a long tradition from Hume to Keynes. Interpretation of the Phillips Curve held that raising or lowering unemployment, e.g. through fiscal policy, would lower or raise the rate of inflation by changing the level of demand pressure in final goods markets. Phelps (1968) and Friedman reversed the direction of causality in their interpretation: monetary policy was assumed to change the rate of inflation, which, in turn, by affecting the real wage, altered the level of unemployment through adjustments in the labor market.
10. A similar account of the transmission of monetary effects is given by Laidler (1978), who attributes this view to Tobin, Meiselman, Brunner and Meltzer as well. Note, however, Davidson's (1974) contention that a produced good cannot effectively serve as a store of wealth unless there is an organized spot market for it. If no such markets exist, it is not liquid, and so cannot function as a substitute for money.

11. He adds the footnote: 'Of course this is speaking figuratively. It is not necessary that a single variable be so determined. What is required is an independent relation connecting some subset of the seven variables with exogenous variables, and that subset could in principle consist of seven variables' (Friedman, 1970; in Gordon, 1974, p. 31).
12. Both Patinkin (1965, p. 119) and Tobin (1974, pp. 81–3) point out that there is no missing equation when the labor market and the production function are properly taken into consideration. However, only Patinkin points out that this requires Friedman to confront the issue of the invalid dichotomy.
13. Yet this is precisely the form in which Friedman presents his 'Simple Common Model'. His equations 9–13 show:

    real consumption a function of real income and interest,
    real investment a function of nominal interest,
    real demand for money a function of real income and interest,
    real income equals real consumption plus investment,
    demand for money equals supply,
    supply of money exogenous or depends on interest.

14. In his reply to Tobin, Friedman calls attention to the fact that his own feelings towards this third approach are ambivalent. Tobin makes the point that by fixing the real interest rate, Friedman ensures that monetary changes will influence prices by shifting the *LM* locus; but the corollary is that deficit spending both increases output and employment and lowers the price level. Friedman replies that he regards the model's treatment of savings and investment as 'unfinished business' (Friedman, 1970; in Gordon, 1974, p. 40). Nevertheless, more than a third of his paper is devoted to analyzing his 'monetary theory of nominal income' or comparing it to other approaches. Since he presents nothing else, it is a fair inference that, unfinished or not, this is where he takes his stand. However, our criticism, unlike Tobin's, does not primarily concern savings and investment; rather our concern is with the connections between real and monetary variables, where once again we hold that Friedman has introduced the invalid dichotomy.
15. This may not really be adequate, for with higher rates of inflation the degree of certainty attached to the expected value may decline, raising the risk, which would require a larger gap between r and ϱ to compensate.
16. Let s be the average (equals marginal) saving ratio, and v be the capital output ratio. Then aggregate demand is I/s and aggregate supply K/v. Hence $g = I/K = \Delta K/K = s/v$, is the warranted growth rate, along which aggregate demand just equals aggregate supply. Suppose now that $I/s > K/v$; i.e., that $g > s/v$. The demand will be outstripping capacity; with shortages everywhere, businesses will increase their investment, so that $I^* > I$; hence demand will rise still further above capacity. Similarly, if $g < s/v$, business will cut back on investment, and the slump will deepen.
17. *Cambridge Journal of Economics*, 9 (1985) pp. 173–8.
18. Notice that if investment is below the capacity level, then employment, and so with a given money wage, the wage bill, must also be below capacity. But total money expenditure will fall short of the full capacity level by *more* than the shortfall in investment itself. This is the multiplier effect here.
19. In Marglin's inflation the realised real wage is always in disequilibrium; so it is hard to understand how the equilibrium level can be 'conventional' or 'normal.' How can something which never happens be the norm?

References

Blinder, A.S. and Solow, R.M. (1973) 'Analytical Foundations of Fiscal Policy' (Washington DC; Brookings Institution).

Branson, W. (1979) *Macroeconomic Theory and Policy* (New York: Harper & Row) 2nd edn.

Davidson, P. (1974) 'A Keynesian view of Friedman's theoretical framework for monetary analysis,' in Gordon (1974) pp. 90–110, esp. p. 95.

Fisher, I. (1930) *The Theory of Interest* (New York: Macmillan).

Friedman, M. (1956) 'The quantity theory of money – A restatement,' in *Studies in the Quantity Theory of Money* (Chicago: University of Chicago Press).

Friedman, M. (1968) 'The role of monetary policy,' *American Economic Review*, 58 (March) pp. 1–17.

Friedman, M. (1970) 'A theoretical framework for monetary analysis,' *Journal of Political Economy*, 78, pp. 193–238; reprinted in Gordon (1974) pp. 1–63.

Friedman, M. (1971) 'A monetary theory of nominal income,' *Journal of Political Economy*, 79, pp. 323–37.

Friedman, M. (1973) *Unemployment and Inflation*, London: Institute of Economic Analysis, Occasional Paper.

Friedman, M. (1974) 'Comments on the critics,' in Gordon (1974) pp. 132–7.

Friedman, M. and Schwartz, A. (1963) *A Monetary History of the US* (Princeton, NJ: Princeton University Press).

Gordon, Robert (ed.) (1974) *Milton Friedman's Monetary Framework* (Chicago: University of Chicago Press).

Harrod, R.F. (1948) *Towards a Dynamic Economics* (New York: Macmillan).

Kaldor, N. (1955–6) 'Alternative theories of distribution', *Review of Economic Studies*, 1.XXIII.

Keynes, J.M. (1930) *A Treatise on Money* (London: Macmillan).

Keynes, J.M. (1971–) *Collected Writing of John Maynard Keynes* (London: Macmillan for the Royal Economic Society): Vol. XIII (1972), Vol. XIV (1973).

Laidler, D. (1978) 'Money and money income: an essay in the transmission mechanism,' *Journal of Monetary Economics*, 4.

Leijonhufvud, A. (1968) *On Keynesian Economics and the Economics of Keynes* (London: Oxford University Press).

Lloyd, Cliff (1964) 'The real balance effect and the Slutsky equation,' *Journal of Political Economy*, 72 (June).

Marglin, S.A. (1984a) 'Growth, distribution and inflation: a centennial synthesis,' *Cambridge Journal of Economics*, 8 (2)(June).

Marglin, S.A. (1984b) *Growth, Distribution and Prices* (Cambridge, MA: Harvard University Press).

Nell, E. (1970) 'A Note on the Cambridge Controversies,' *Journal of Economic Literature*, VIII, (1) (March).

Nell, E.J. (1974) 'Established en modelos Keynesianos simples,' *Cuadenos de Economica*, 2 (3)(April) pp. 66–90.

Nell, E. (1982) 'Growth, Distribution and Inflation,' *Journal of Post Keynesian Economics*, 5 (1)(Fall).

Nell, E. (1983) 'Beyond austerity: economic growth and economic policy,' unpublished ms, New School For Social Research (New York).

Niehans, J. (1978) *The Theory of Money* (Baltimore, Md.: Johns Hopkins Press).

Patinkin, D. (1965) *Money, Interest and Prices* (New York: Harper & Row) 2nd edn.

Petri, F. (1982) 'The Patinkin controversy revisited,' *Quademi dell Instituto di Economia*, 15 (Siena).

Phelps, E. (1968) 'Money Wage Dynamics and Labor Market Equilibrium,' *Journal of Political Economy*, 76(4), Part II, pp. 678–711.
Robertson, D. (1948) *Money* (London: Pitman) 4th edn.
Samuelson, A. (1964) 'A brief survey of post-Keynesian developments,' in R. Lekachman (ed.), *Keynes' General Theory: Reports of Three Decades* (London:
Macmillan).
Solow, R. (1970) *Growth Theory: An Exposition* (London: Oxford University Press).
Tobin, James (1974) 'Friedman's theoretical framework,' in Gordon (1974) pp. 77–89.
Tobin, James (1980) *Asset Accumulation and Economic Activity* (Oxford: Basil Blackwell).

Part V
Profits and Justice

26. Economizing Love
27. On Deserving Profits
28. Justice Under Socialism (*with Onora O'Neill*)

The purpose of Part V is to criticize the use of marginalist techniques in analyzing questions of economic justice, and to show that the surplus approach provides a more appropriate framework. The first study (Chapter 26) takes up the Chicago analysis of marriage and the family, showing that the use of the analogy of the market obscures issues of coercion. The second (Chapter 27) turns to free-market arguments that entrepreneurs deserve their profits, a conception that cannot be sustained when profits are seen to be claims to a portion of the surplus generated in production. 'Who deserves how much of what' depends on a number of factors excluded by neo-Classical assumptions. The third study (Chapter 28) then moves on to the most general issues of social organization, examining justice as the problem of fairly assigning claims to the surplus, and arguing for the traditional Socialist Principle against both the Laissez-Faire Principle and several compromises.

26 Economizing Love*

Gary Becker is a renowned economist whose claim to fame rests largely on the ingenuity with which he argues that there is a calculating little capitalist concealed in all of us. In *A Treatise on the Family* he applies his technique and point of view to what most people would regard as a highly unlikely area – the field of marriage, where one would expect the heart to dominate the purse. Not so, according to Becker. His conclusions are startling, to say the least, and not all of us will recognize ourselves.

Here is why rational people – and Becker sees us all as more rational than not – marry:

> persons marry each other if and only if they expect to be better off compared to their best alternatives . . .
> rational persons marry even when certain of eventually finding better prospects with additional search, for the cost of additional search exceeds the expected benefits from better prospects (Becker, 1981, p. 39).

As for whom we marry: '[In] efficient marriage markets, . . . high-quality men are matched with high-quality women and low-quality men with low-quality women.' Prospective marriage partners estimate one another's 'quality,' in Becker's world, primarily by earning power, although they also calculate the value of intangibles, like satisfaction. Nevertheless, 'Men with higher earnings or other income . . . can attract several wives or higher quality wives. This explains why they marry at younger ages and remarry faster when widowed or divorced' (p. 25).

As for the place of women:

> comparative advantage [implies] that married men will specialize in the market sector and married women in the household sector. Therefore the market wage rates of married men will exceed those of married women (p. 25).

As for love, Becker says it comes from the interaction between an altruist, who takes other people's happiness into account in making his choices, and the altruist's selfish beneficiary, who characteristically thinks only of the pleasures she will get. (Becker's choice of pronouns is always consistent.) In a family or relationship the recipient concludes that some-

* *Free Market Conservatism* (1984).

one else's altruism is good for her, and so in turn behaves altruistically enough to make sure the altruist is well enough off to continue to perform kindnesses for her. In short, love is disguised efficiency.

Of course, 'love [altruism] and other personal characteristics are less readily ascertainable prior to marriage than are family reputation and position:'

> The average divorced person can be presumed to be more quarrelsome and in other ways less pleasant than the average person remaining married because an unpleasant temperament is one cause of divorce (p. 234).

If such traits emerge after marriage, they are 'unexpected information,' which leads to divorce when it reduces the couple's wealth from remaining married 'below their wealth from a divorce.' Thus, since there will be mistakes in an uncertain world, 'modern societies have what may appear to be a paradoxical combination of many love marriages and high rates of divorce.'

Let us now go through the entire argument and see what it really says, for it will emerge that there is a very strong underlying political message – Reaganomics, in fact.

Becker begins with the gains from specialization and division of labor in the household. These explain why marriage is instituted in the first place: the wealth of the parties after marriage will be greater than before. To the altar men bring 'human capital' that is oriented to the market, such as job skills – plumbing or accounting. Women bring 'human capital' that is oriented to the household, such as cleaning or child-caring. Hence, men take jobs outside the home, while women do the housework. This is efficient, i.e., specialized according to comparative advantage. When the distribution of potential 'quality' – productivity or earning power in their separate worlds – is about the same for both the men and women in the pool of suitable marriage partners, monogamy will prevail; but if, say, there is one group of high-quality men with the rest clearly made of inferior stuff and the women are all more or less equal, then an efficient marriage market will theoretically require more than one woman to balance one man's productivity, and hence will promote or at least condone polygamy. Even when pools of partners are about even in 'quality,' high-quality men will usually be matched with top-drawer women and low-quality men with the leftovers, as dictated by the canons of efficiency. Children result from a complex decision involving a tradeoff between their quantity and their 'quality,' which depends both on their cost and the earning potential of both parents but particularly of the mother, since child-bearing will fall on her. This explains both the low birth rates in modern societies, and the recent decline, as women's earnings outside the home have risen. Divorce results from a recalculation of advantages in the light of new information; so that, when it is clear that the wealth from parting exceeds that from remaining married, a couple will divorce. Combined with an analysis of 'optimal bequests,' and mixed with some assumptions about 'luck,' the foregoing can be pulled together into a theory of income distribution, showing this to be a function of 'investment in human capital,' modified by various circumstances.

Without exception, Becker applies to each of the topics he discusses a bald idea of motivation derived from economics: people try to satisfy their preferences (which may include preferences for being altruistic) as far as possible subject to the constraints of scarcity. Exchange takes place because it permits higher levels of satisfaction, e.g. because of 'comparative advantage,' that is, each party specializes in what he or she can do *relatively* best, even if one party can do everything better. Investment in physical or human capital takes place because the sacrifice made now (by not consuming the goods or income) will be more than compensated by the increased income later. Investment in physical capital – building a factory, buying a machine – is no different in principle from investment in human capital – getting a degree, taking a course – except that machines can be scrapped or sold off but degrees cannot.

A delectable morsel, but not cooked up for science alone; there are implications for social policy. There are two important messages. The first is that the marriage market cannot work efficiently if it is meddled with. Welfare programs, like Aid to Dependent Children, will raise the rate of illegitimacy and increase the divorce rate essentially because they reduce the penalties associated with each. Welfare undermines the family. The second is that the government can have no significant long-run effect on income distribution. Government supplementary programs, like Head Start or school lunches, lead to offsetting reductions in parents' investment spending on their children. Less spending means less attention. The government causes child neglect. Hence these programs are wasteful failures. Similarly, the equalizing effects of government 'transfer programs' from rich to poor and inheritance taxes will be offset, eventually, by changes in private behavior, e.g., by reductions of earning efforts by the poor. Nothing can be done to change the income distribution, except temporarily, because it reflects the rational behavior of private households investing in education, given their tastes, their market information – and their luck.

In fact, government transfer programs are worse than wasteful; they undermine the incentive to private charity which *can* make a difference, precisely because it is voluntary and therefore does not provoke offsetting reactions. But the existence of government programs (even though they will ultimately fail) reduces private charity. There is, however, one way the government could help: by underwriting private bank loans to the poor, making greater investment by them possible. The poor should go into debt, and the government should be the debt-collector.

In short, Becker sees all decisions (including those of many nonhuman species) as explainable by means of the model of maximizing 'utility' subject to the constraints imposed by scarce resources. The same calculus that explains the market for goods and services can be adopted to explain the market for husbands and wives. The marriage market, an 'implicit' market, nevertheless works according to the same principles that govern explicit ones and, indeed, simply reflects the making of rational choices subject to the constraints imposed by natural scarcity.

A common reaction to this book will be that best expressed by Wordsworth:

> Count not the cost: High Heaven rejects the lore of nicely calculated less or more.

The cold-blooded and cold-hearted calculation of gain has no place in the analysis of marriage, the having and caring for children, or in the tragedy of divorce. These are affairs of the heart; the proper function of the head is in the world of business and politics or in matters intellectual. If allowed a place here it will only create confusion; analysis is inappropriate since the decisions are properly made on the basis of emotion rather than reason.

To reject Becker on these grounds is too easy – and concedes him far too much. No doubt his calculations often oscillate between the ridiculous and the disgusting; some nevertheless have a point. There is a marriage market, and has always been, as bride prices in primitive communities and the novels of Jane Austen testify. For, after all, the family does perform economic functions and, moreover, within the family there is an often controversial division of labor. Children are both costly and capable of earning income and, as they get older, helping to support their parents. Divorces are often economic as well as emotional disasters or liberations. To reject Becker on the grounds that family life is an area in which economic calculation has no place is absurd; but, worse, it implicitly concedes the field of economics to him.

For Becker's book is not merely an application of economic analysis to the family; it draws on a very special and strongly ideological version of modern economic theory that is highly suspect in the profession today. Economists respect much of the work done at Chicago, but by and large they do not believe it. And Becker's work, in particular, stands out in its uncompromising purity. His version of economic theory is uncontaminated either by reality or by the arguments of critics outside his own narrow tradition. Both are ignored.

Enough of this. Now let us examine his terms.

Becker's analysis of income distribution and the prospects for redistribution is actually flawed even on his own terms. For example, he suggests that the progressive tax system redistributes incentives in such a way as to increase long-term inequality. Yet, even using Becker's own assumptions and methodology, the opposite conclusion is more plausible. For individuals are supposed to choose their life styles, then adapt rationally to relevant variables, including government policies. To demonstrate the ineffectiveness of government intervention, Becker focuses on government income redistribution programs – the progressive income tax and transfer payments. He postulates that families, including the poor, the unemployed and the illiterate, make life-cycle human capital investment plans that span two generations. These investment plans weight the expected rate of return on investment, and consider the families' preferences for leisure and for present and future consumption. Progressive income taxation aimed at redistribution will lower the expected rate of return to investment in human capital, causing families to cut back their investments. Becker feels that the lack of significant change in the percentage distribution of income in the USA during this century, despite the progressive income tax, is explained by this incentive effect (Becker, 1981).

The reduced incentive to invest in human capital, where income is taxed progressively, will not be equally distributed, however, for clearly the well-off are more severely affected than the poor (assuming no tax loopholes, of course). Thus the wealthy would cut back investment in human capital more than would the poor, resulting in *less* second-generation inequality (assuming differential earnings actually do reflect human capital investments, of course).

Other government programs designed to redistribute income – welfare and other outright transfer payments to the poor – are also counterproductive, in Becker's view. They weaken family ties, discourage labor force participation, and encourage illegitimacy, high fertility and divorce in poor families. Becker presents no empirical evidence to back up these propositions, but from his point of view he need not – rational agents will maximize their net family income, and if they can do so by having more babies or abandoning the family, so be it. Becker *must* take this view, since the decision to marry and to stay married and the demand for children are, in his view, simply governed by the desire to maximize household income. But in fact, of course, poor women had lots of babies and poor men abandoned their wives and families long before there was Aid to Families with Dependent Children (AFDC); and illegitimate birth rates are highest in American states such as Alabama and Mississippi where AFDC payments are lowest.

Even if Becker's methodology did not preclude his recognizing other human emotions besides the lure of the dollar, he could still take a different view of transfer payments. Transfer payment programs change initial endowments. So, even according to neo-Classical theory, these could affect the final equilibrium. Indeed, the possibility of government action to change initial endowments has been a standard consideration of neo-Classical 'welfare economics.' Usually, of course, this is presented as 'lump-sum' taxation, transferring wealth from one set of endowments to another. But entitlement programs, financed by taxes, can be treated as lump-sum transfers of 'human capital,' simply by capitalizing the taxes and the payments stream. Moreover, if the taxes fall on income that would have been spent on luxuries or socially damaging consumption (e.g., cigarettes) and the payments support better health or education, the consequence should be judged a *net* increase in 'human capital,' and not merely a transfer.

Becker, however, feels that income supplement programs do not improve the lot of the poor because, he contends, they reduce their efforts to earn in proportion to the grants they receive. Food stamps do not raise the nutritional standards of the poor; they simply make it easier for them to eat and allow them, for example, to avoid taking the low-paying jobs, which are supposedly commensurate with their skills, in order to survive. But as a practical matter (Becker is seldom practical) the vast proportion of the poor in the USA are frail old ladies and small children and their mothers. The reasons these people fail to take paying jobs have nothing to do with inflated wage expectations. They do not work because, given their circumstances, they cannot.

For these people, redistributive government programs make the difference between having an income and not having one, between eating well and eating poorly. Even in the strict terms of rational expectations and human capital theory, such programs make a difference. If individuals maximize utility subject to constraints and the constraints are changed, the consumption patterns clearly shift. Welfare payments permit the poor to increase their 'human capital investments,' so that when they do enter the labor or the marriage markets they do so as well-fed rather than sickly individuals, promising greater contributions to prospective employers or spouses, thus landing better jobs or catching more eligible mates.

Becker, on the other hand, feels that income-providing government programs actually feed people who would otherwise be cared for by 'private charity' – family, friends, neighbors or even errant husbands. This is hard to understand. The inadequacy – and arbitrariness – of private charity was one of the reasons for starting the government programs. In any case, in order for the distributional effect of government programs to be zero, the private charity discouraged must be equal and similarly distributed to the government largess handed out. No one could seriously argue this. For example, the family and neighbors of the poor are generally also poor. So government programs, by redistributing income from the well-off to the poor, may offset private charity that would have redistributed from poor to poor. Thus, in contrast to private charity, the government program would change the income distribution to improve the ability of the poor to invest in human capital, and thus enhance their position in labor and marriage markets – to put it in Becker's terms.

Following the well-trodden path of Jeremy Bentham, Becker assumes that we choose courses of action because they satisfy our preferences as much as possible given the costs and the alternatives, where the costs arise ultimately from scarcity. Both sides of this paradigm – the benefits, ranked by preferences, and the costs, imposed by scarcity – are faulty.

Take the costs first. Many costs, of course, do arise from scarcity, that is, from production, from our ways of transforming what Nature provides into what is useful for human society. But many do not, as people living in Chicago should know. Many costs are *imposed* by one party on others, as parts of strategies to improve income or social position. Thus Al Capone imposed costs on others as part of his strategy to sell liquor. Businesses regularly impose costs on other businesses, on their employees and on their customers. And, just as regularly, the other parties undertake expenditures for defense and/or for retaliation. Becker would no doubt argue that such activities have no place in perfect competition, but surely that is simply another reason why the model of perfect competition should be ignored. When it comes to family life, to the division of labor in the household, and to the distribution of income either within the family or within society as a whole, surely the process of economic warfare – imposing costs and defending against them – must be considered central. Yet for all Becker's apparent hard-nosed rational calculation he never considers what 'costs,' for example, a husband could impose on a wife, at minimal inconvenience to himself, to compel her to do his bidding, or what her optimal defense would be. For Becker, marriage is an exchange relationship and exchange, in his economics, always leaves both parties better off. So much for realism.

Now let us look at the other side – choice based on preferences. According to Becker, *all* of our actions can be explained as choices based on our preferences and constrained by the costs arising from scarcity. But we know this is nonsense. Many of our actions have nothing to do with our preferences in the ordinary sense of the term, particularly when we come to the economic behavior of the family. They are *imposed* on us, often against our real wishes, by our jobs, family responsibilities or social positions. They are obligations resulting from prior commitments. Our present choices and actions reflect the past. Of course, Becker would argue that institutions are simply contractual relationships between individuals, chosen on the basis of their preferences. Most philosophers and social theorists would disagree, but Becker has never confronted the issues in any of his writings. Yet the point is utterly basic: if jobs or social positions or institutions are not 'reducible' to the voluntary decisions of individuals, then their independent influence must be taken into account. Becker's framework is not sufficient.

Think of the effects of the development of the modern corporation out of the family business, and along with it, the development of modern agriculture. Together these largely determined the shape of the modern city, and there can be no doubt that the urbanization – and suburbanization – of the working class has brought immense changes in the family.

Over the last century a large number of functions formerly performed by the family have been taken from it. Education (more generally, socialization) may be the chief example, but pensions, insurance, welfare and much medical care are now provided by the state, where in the past they were the responsibility of the family. Moreover, private capital now performs for profit many tasks formerly handled in the home. Food processing and preserving, the handling of births and deaths, the making and mending of clothes, and the care of the aged, among many others, are all now major businesses, although they once figured among the provinces ruled by our great-grandmothers.

Becker would explain these developments by reference, on the one hand, to the greater 'efficiency' of the market system and, on the other, to the rise in the market earning power of women, who, as a result, choose to work less in the home. This rise in the relative earning power of women is itself unexplained, however. The theory of transformational growth, by contrast, would explain the changed position of the family by reference to the shift away from family production, the resulting urbanization and changes in occupational structure, particularly the rise of large hierarchical bureaucracies. Furthermore, the pace of change also matters, since each generation must be prepared for an occupational structure that is not only new but will change during its working life. Becker's commitment to individualism requires him to try to explain the changes in the family in terms of changes in the characterictics of its members – in this case the earning power of women. Both as description and as explanation this account of the new position of the family is inadequate.

So both sides of Becker's paradigm are flawed. On the cost side he overlooks imposed costs (coercion and economic warfare) and on the preference side he ignores institutional factors. Yet these intellectual defects do not explain the real aversion – even disgust – that reading this book provokes. This deeper problem lies in the paradigm itself, in the idea that human behavior can – or perhaps should – be represented by a model of rational, mathematical choice – 'internalizing the external mechanization of life,' in Wilhelm Reich's memorable phrase. Rational choice is *reactive*; facing given conditions people calculate and make the best of what is presented to them. They change their calculated optimum packages reactively, as the conditions they face, and accept, change. In such a model nothing is created, nothing happens; people choose commodities, not their destiny. They do not weave the fabric of life.

> Let me not to the marriage of true minds
> Admit impediments; love is not love
> Which alters when it alteration finds
> Or bends with the remover to remove.

Two of the most powerful motivating forces in mankind's nature are love and fear. Becker understands neither; all he can analyze is a form of greed – the individual pursuit of pleasure or gain. But he cannot do even that adequately, because he cannot situate his analysis institutionally, or combine it with accounts of the other forces that motivate people. He sees 'free choices' where there are in reality, and necessarily, social constraints, obligations, pressures and coercion; and he fails altogether to see the truly creative freedom of the human spirit, which refuses to accept the given, and brings forth inventions, imagination and poetry – the freedom inherent in love.

Reference

Becker, G.S. (1981) *A Treatise on the Family* (Cambridge, Mass.: Harvard University Press).

27 On Deserving Profits*

After an admirably clear account of the distinction between 'desert' and 'entitlement,' N. Scott Arnold's paper 'Why Profits Are Deserved' goes on to argue that, in general, entrepreneurs in a market system deserve to get and keep for their own use the 'pure' profits that accrue to them as the result of their market activities.[1] Such a judgment of desert is not the end of the matter, for it is both subject to a number of reasonable qualifications and capable of being overriden, for example, by moral judgments about the nature of the product or activity, or about other market or nonmarket consequences. But it does provide a prima facie case on behalf of the entrepreneurs.

The argument is simple. To deserve something is to deserve it relative to some institution, which, in turn, is defined by an essential goal or purpose. Then the basic reason for a desert claim will be an action by a person, in an appropriate context, furthering the essential goals of the institution, and what is deserved should then be proportioned to the magnitude of the action. Turning to the question of profits, the essential purpose of the market system is said to be to allocate scarce resources as efficiently as possible to the uses most desired by consumers. When the allocation is optimal all factors will receive their marginal value product as reward, which means that capital will earn interest, and 'pure' profits will be zero. But while the system tends toward optimal allocation, it never reaches it in practice for the very good reason that both technology and tastes are always changing. Hence there will be opportunities to reallocate resources, making a profit in the process. Entrepreneurs are by definition the people who spot these chances for gain and take advantage of them, shifting resources about to do so. They thus help the market to work better and so deserve a reward in proportion, according to the definition of 'desert.' Given the way the market works, the profit earned will be in proportion to the malallocation being corrected, so what the entrepreneurs get will be in fact what they deserve.

Notice first that this argument can easily be generalized from entrepreneurs to the owners of the other factors, labor, land, and capital. These are demanded in accordance with their productivity at the margin of use, while they are supplied according to a schedule that shows the compensation necessary to overcome the disutility of offering each successive amount. So the rate at which each factor is rewarded is proportional to its productive contribution at the margin, while being sufficient to just compensate the

* *Ethics*, 97 (January 1987) pp. 403–10.

factor owner for the trouble of supplying it. And such offers and demands are essential to making the market system work properly. So the same logic implies that the rewards each factor obtains, in equilibrium, are what it deserves, with entrepreneurs being special in that they deserve nothing in equilibrium but get their just deserts when the market is out of equilibrium but tending toward it as a result of their activity.

Arnold's argument rests on four fundamental propositions about the way markets work to distribute income. These are:

1. The essential aim of the market as an institution is to allocate scarce resources efficiently in line with consumer demand.
2. Entrepreneurial profit can be clearly distinguished from capital's factor reward.
3. Factor rewards are proportional to the productive contributions of the factors.
4. The basic activity of entrepreneurs is to shift scarce resources to more productive uses.

The study seems to take these for granted, yet they are not empirical, and they are certainly not universally accepted: they rest on a particular version of the orthodox theory of competitive markets, a version which has been subjected to a serious, even devastating, and so far unanswered, critique. The approach in question is the aggregate or Standard version of marginal productivity theory; the activity analysis, or general equilibrium version of orthodox theory, is not subject to the critique in quite the same way,[2] but that is because it generates a weaker set of claims about factor market efficiency.

A detailed discussion of neo-Classical theory is not appropriate here, but some comments are necessary, since the desert argument depends on the nature of the market. Both versions define equilibrium on the basis of supply-and-demand functions for both final products and factors of production, but the Standard version defines factors and the markets for them broadly, whereas the activity analysis version defines factors narrowly. Thus in the Standard version labor of all different kinds will be treated as a common factor, even though there are important differences in skill and experience. Nevertheless, all forms of labor have certain things in common: while they may not compete directly, they may be linked indirectly, through competition with other forms of labor. By contrast, the general equilibrium approach treats the different kinds of labor as different factors and hence has no theory of the wage share as a whole. This is awkward enough, but the really bad news is that it has no theory of the return to capital in general. For the theory determines the return to each and every kind of capital good. Worse, it determines the return each capital good obtains in each kind of employment, without relating these returns to the capital good's cost of production. Capital goods are treated like land and natural resources; the fact that they are produced means of production is ignored. There may at times be good reasons for adopting this approach. But it cannot support the line of argument under discussion (Cf. Chs. 6 and 7).

For example, in a general equilibrium framework, propositions 2 and 3 could not be upheld. In order to distinguish entrepreneurial profit from the normal return to capital, the latter must obtain a uniform rate of return whatever the area of the economy in which it is invested. But neo-Classical 'temporary equilibrium' systems do not determine a general or uniform rate of profit on invested capital; instead, different specific capital goods will earn different ratios of 'quasi-rents' to their cost of production. These rewards will be proportional to the capital good's productive contribution in any given employment, but the same fund, invested in different capital goods, may obtain very different earnings, or rates of return.[3] This creates the difficulty that the system would apparently reward a *disequilibrating* move by an entrepreneur, shifting capital funds from a low-earning use to a high-earning one in circumstances where markets were already clearing. This would contradict proposition 4 and make nonsense of proposition 3. (It is, of course, also an indication of the limited usefulness of this theory in the analysis of capitalism.)

But the standard version is unacceptable for two different sets of reasons. First, marginal productivity theory requires that the total incomes paid out equal the value of the product produced, that is, the incomes paid out are, from another point of view, the costs of production. But if incomes paid out in accordance with the marginal productivity principle are to equal the value of output for a wide range of possible outputs (depending either upon demand or upon factor supplies) then long-run marginal costs must be constant. But this means that prices, which must reflect costs, will be fully determined by costs, which is to say that they will be independent of demand, contrary to basic neo-Classical doctrine. Even worse, it means that the distribution of output among firms will be indeterminate. But if incomes paid according to marginal productivity do not equal the value of output over some ranges (e.g., of increasing and diminishing returns) then entrepreneurs will make gains or losses for purely technical reasons, quite independent of any actions they may take. (So, according to the doctrine under discussion, they would not deserve them.) Neo-Classical thinkers have worried about these questions since the end of the 19th century, but there is still no acceptable solution.[4]

If anything, the second set of problems is even more serious. Neo-Classical doctrine requires that scarce factors should be allocated to their most productive uses by means of the price mechanism. (This is the basis of proposition 1, on which the desert claims are based.) To make a long story short, the doctrine of efficient allocation requires that the value of invested capital, and the quantity of labor also, be inversely related to their respective returns, the rate of profits and wages. It can be shown that, in general, this will not be the case. In other words, the price mechanism just doesn't work the way neo-Classical doctrines require.[5] And, of course, this theoretical result has been confirmed by any number of empirical market studies.[6]

So, a general equilibrium framework cannot support claims of desert for money-making entrepreneurs, since they could improve their earnings by making disequilibrating moves, while the standard version of neo-Classical theory contains internal flaws. Serious economic theory doesn't support the idea that the market allocates scarce resources optimally; Arnold has based his desert claims on a piece of ideology. Let us examine this further by considering an alternative conception of the market.

On this account the function of prices is not to indicate relative scarcities but, rather, to show the exchanges required for reproduction given a certain distribution. Prices are determined once the division of the net product between wages and profits is settled.[7] Hence proposition 1 will not hold, and so no prima facie claims of desert can be made for profit earners. But we had better spell this out carefully, to see just what is implied.

As Arnold suggests, it can be useful to start by considering what the world would be like if there were no profit; this is exactly Sraffa's starting point – the 'no-surplus' economy. A certain list of commodities is produced, and these commodities are consumed either as means of subsistence for the population or as means of production, inputs of tools, materials, or energy into one or another productive process. Given the techniques, production will use up the existing stocks of goods, leaving each producer in possession of his output but needing the products of others as inputs or means of subsistence in order to engage in another round of production. It can be shown that in general there will be a unique set of exchange values that will exactly permit reproduction; that is, for each sector or industry, the value of the output will exactly equal the total value of all the required inputs and means of subsistence for the workers. Relative prices are thus determined wholly by the methods of production, independently of demand. When a surplus exists, it will (in the simplest case) be divided between wages over subsistence and profits above depreciation and replacement needs. Once this division is settled, prices are determined by the reproduction requirements, together with the condition that wages and profits be paid as uniform rates of return to labor, whatever the line of work, and to the value of invested capital, whatever its actual composition in terms of capital goods and material inputs. This condition, of course, simply reflects the idea that markets are competitive, so that labor or capital would move to wherever rewards were highest and consequently would settle down only when rates of remuneration were uniform (making allowances for natural monopolies and various noneconomic barriers to free movement). However, when the surplus can be divided between wages and profits, the price system is underdetermined; once we know either the wage or the rate of profit, prices and the other variable are fixed. But until the distributional question is settled, prices cannot be determined.

If there are alternative methods of production, then the one which yields the highest rate of profit (for a given wage) will be chosen. It can be shown that this will normally be the cost-minimizing technique, but it can also be shown that various anomalies and problems exist, especially in cases of joint production. No simple 'efficiency' conclusions can be drawn. More important, no regular rules can be laid down for the allocation of 'capital;' it simply cannot be treated as a 'scarce factor.' (This provides the basis for the critique of marginal productivity theory.)

Introducing demand makes no difference to these results, for, with demand in the picture, the composition of surplus output becomes a variable; we add as many unknowns as new equations. Moreover, we can expect the wants and preferences of wage earners and profit recipients to be different; hence overall relative demands will depend on the distribution of the surplus between wages and profits.

So we can distinguish between two aspects of markets and the price system. On the one hand, we have the fact that exchange makes possible reproduction on the basis of a given distribution (which also determines the most profitable technology), and on the other, we have the determination of that distribution. The first can reasonably be thought of as a technical problem, but the second is clearly a question of class conflict, with very possibly sectoral, regional, or other ramifications. Wages and the rate of profits are inversely related; what one side gains the other loses, although, of course, things are never so straightforward when we move away from the simplest and most general models. In any case, the point is that the market system has two aspects, one technical, relating to the conditions for reproduction, and the other distributional and therefore conflict related. In this aspect, the market can be seen as an arena in which distributional and other, for example, regional, battles are fought over the division of spoils. These conflicts are governed by certain rules, the law of contract and the laws of property, and disputes over the rules are settled in court. But the outcomes are governed by relative economic power and by skill in using it; they are not directly governed by considerations of efficiency, although, of course, efficiency by reducing costs may confer economic advantage. But so may inefficient, cumbersome, but overwhelming, size.

This puts a different face on the earning of profits. If we think of the function of the market as reproduction consistently with a distribution determined through economic conflict, rather than the socially optimal allocation of scarce resources, then the actions of 'entrepreneurs' will simply be part of the conflict over the division of the surplus rather than a contribution toward a social optimum. They 'deserve' their profits no more and no less than workers deserve the wage increase which they get after a successful strike. (And if we remember the robber barons this surely seems right.) Nor can any distinction of importance be drawn between 'normal' profit and 'entrepreneurial' profit. Let us explore this further.

Let us consider a system of modern industries, organized as business corporations, operating successfully with a given real wage and an established rate of profits, that is, reproducing itself period after period (either in stationary conditions or expanding at the same rate as its population). Now consider an innovation in a method of production with the following plausible characteristics (chosen for the sake of the argument): (a) it makes possible an increase in the surplus because it makes it possible to *speed up* the work process; (b) the speedup will be the faster, the better certain tools are made, requiring redesign and retooling on the part of suppliers; (c) besides the speeding up of work, certain other workers will be made redundant, and the resulting unemployment will strengthen businesses in their bargaining with labor; (d) certain other inputs will no longer be needed, greatly reducing the demand for them; and (e) the new method was invented by employees of the corporation and is therefore the property of the company; the inventor's reward is their regular salary.

The decision to introduce such an innovation will be made by salaried managers, subject to the approval of the board of directors, representing the shareholders (most of which will be other corporations, trusts, banks, pension funds – in any case institutions). Assume that the new method will, after suitable adjustments, bring about an increase in the surplus. Who deserves to obtain or share in that increase and why? Let us provisionally adopt a commonsense notion of 'desert' and examine the question.

First, notice that the 'entrepreneurs' have disappeared. Making decisions of this kind is part of the regular job of management, for which they receive their salaries. And approving or disapproving proposed innovations is part of the job of the board. Particularly good decisions may 'deserve' bonuses, of course, but that depends on an analysis of the way corporations define jobs and determine pay, which in turn depends on the particular circumstances of various industries. But surely, if workers are going to have to work faster, they can claim a share in the extra output. (This is coming very close to the question of exploitation; but that is too large a topic for now.) And what about the workers who are laid off? The elimination of their jobs is an essential part of the increased productivity of the new process. Why should the benefits of this go to shareholders or management, when the burden falls on the workers? By the same token, what about the suppliers of previously needed inputs, who have now lost their market? Their suffering is an unavoidable consequence of the innovation. (If the innovation caused pollution, we could add the burden on the community.) Of course, in both these cases it can be replied that the question is one of compensation rather than desert. But that distinction might seem less compelling if we suppose that either the workers or the suppliers could block the innovation, for example, by striking or obtaining legislation banning it. Then by deciding not to take such action they contribute to the increase in productivity and so can claim to 'deserve' a share. Finally, what about the suppliers of the new equipment, who have had to redesign their own plant? The speedup will be the greater the better this new equipment, so these suppliers surely also 'deserve' to share in proportion to the speedup.

On face value, and without going into detail, it looks as though the weakest claim is that of capital, that is, the shareholders, and the next weakest is that of management, while the strongest claims will be those of labor and the suppliers of the new equipment, with reasonable claims for what amounts to compensation being advanced by the newly redundant workers and suppliers. In practice, however, the market outcome is likely to be almost the reverse, with the bulk of the benefit going to capital, including the suppliers of the new equipment, with employed labor perhaps getting something, but both newly redundant labor and the displaced suppliers getting the cold shoulder. But it is important to stress that such outcomes, being the results of conflict and bargaining, cannot be predicted any more (or less) than the World Series.

Suppose that, instead of the company's introducing the innovation, the inventors had founded their own new company to produce and promote it. We would then have identifiable 'entrepreneurs.' Would the case be any different? Perhaps another example could generate more desirable results, but the present one still does not support privileged claims for the entrepreneurs. For the speedup still depends on the workers' working faster and on the suppliers producing the better equipment. And it still displaces workers and input suppliers. Finally, even though the inventors have formed a company to promote the new technology, managers of existing companies still have to decide whether or not to adopt it.

The purpose of this example has been to demonstrate that, when the market is conceived in the 'Classical' (or neo-Ricardian or post-Keynesian) manner, as providing an arena in which to work out class and other economic conflicts, consistently with the technical requirements of reproduction, no *prima facie* general claims to deserve profits can be advanced for entrepreneurs, even accepting a commonsense notion of desert. To the contrary, plausible cases can be made for many other participants in the process of introducing innovations, and in general these claims are likely to conflict. For innovation does not increase output in any simple way. Production in a modern industrial system is highly interdependent; hence any innovation will involve changes in the activities of many different actors and will also impose costs on many of them. It will never be easy and may frequently be impossible to determine the 'productive contributions' of these various agents, and it may also be hard to determine the burdens or costs they are compelled to bear. As a result no general case can be made that any one set of agents or actors deserves, to the exclusion of others, the profits (or losses) from an innovation. Claims are likely to conflict and to be highly sensitive to the particular circumstances and institutional arrangements.

Indeed, it will no longer be possible to accept a simple notion of desert in regard to market activity. For such a notion must be relative to the proper function of the market, but the market does not have any unique or simple function. It is an arena in which conflicts are worked out according to certain rules which will ensure that the conflict will not endanger reproduction. It would, of course, be reasonable to inquire into the social functions of capital and profits. But then we would not ask narrowly who deserves to win or why in the conflict between capital and labor but, more broadly, who bears the costs of this conflict and what are the consequences of it? Yet if we wanted to deal seriously with questions of distributive justice, we would have to go beyond consequentialism and judge the organizing institutions, which provide the framework in which actions and their consequences take place. And that, which is the core of the matter, is beyond the scope of this study.

Notes

1. N. Scott Arnold, 'Why Profits Are Deserved,' *Ethics*, 97. Thanks to Onora O'Neill for comments.
2. Edward Nell, 'Cracks in the Neo-classical Mirror: On the Breakup of a Vision,' in E.J. Nell (ed.), *Growth, Profits and Property: Essays in the Revival of Political Economy* (Cambridge: Cambridge University Press, 1980).
3. Ibid. Also cf. E.J. Nell, 'Capital and the Firm in Neo-classical Theory,' *Journal of Post-Keynesian Economics*, 3 (1980). For a popular and authoritative *defense* of neo-Classical theory, which, however, concedes the point here – that a general equilibrium framework cannot provide a theory of the rate of profit – and adds that it by and large *disproves* the 'Invisible Hand' doctrine, see Frank Hahn, 'General Equilibrium Theory,' in Daniel Bell and Irving Kristol (eds), *The Crisis in Economic Theory* (New York: Basic Books, 1981).
4. Nell, 'Cracks in the Neo-classical Mirror.'
5. G.C. Harcourt, *Controversies in the Theory of Capital* (Cambridge: Cambridge University Press, 1972); P.A. Samuelson, 'A Summing-Up,' *Quarterly Journal of Economics*, 80 (1966); pp. 568–83. E.J. Nell, 'A Note on the Cambridge Controversies,' *Journal of Economic Literature*, 8 (1970); pp. 41–5; David Laibman and E.J. Nell, 'Reswitching, Wicksell Effects and the Neo-classical Production Function,' *American Economic Review*, 67 (1977). (Cf. Part II).
6. F.M. Scherer, *Industrial Market Structure and Economic Performance* (Chicago: Rand McNally & Co., 1980; 2nd edn; Alfred B. Chandler, *The Visible Hand* (Cambridge, Mass.: Harvard University Press, 1977); Edward S. Her-

man, *Corporate Control, Corporate Power* (Cambridge: Cambridge University Press, 1981).

7. E.J. Nell, 'Theories of Growth and Theories of Value,' *Economic Development and Cultural Change*, 16 (1967); pp. 15–26; Martin Hollis and Edward Nell, *Rational Economic Man* (Cambridge: Cambridge University Press, 1975); Luigi Pasinetti, *Lectures on the Theory of Production* (New York: Columbia University Press, 1977); Robert Paul Wolff, *Understanding Marx: A Reconstruction and Critique of Capital* (Princeton: N.J.: Princeton University Press, 1984). Cf. Part I.

28 Justice Under Socialism*

Edward Nell and Onora O'Neill

'From each according to his ability, to each according to his need.'

I

The stirring slogan that ends *The Critique of the Gotha Program* is generally taken as a capsule summary of the socialist approach to distributing the burdens and benefits of life. It can be seen as the statement of a noble ideal and yet be found wanting on three separate scores. First, there is no guarantee that, even if all contribute according to their abilities, all needs can be met: the principle gives us no guidance for distributing goods when some needs must go unmet. Second, if all contribute according to their abilities, there may be a material surplus after all needs are met: again, the principle gives us no guidance for distributing such a surplus. Third, the principle incorporates no suggestion as to why each man would contribute according to his ability: no incentive structure is evident.

These apparent shortcomings can be compared with those of other principles a society might follow in distributing burdens and benefits. Let us call

1. 'From each according to his ability to each according to his need,' the *Socialist Principle of Justice*. Its Capitalist counterpart would be
2. 'From each according to his choice, given his assets, to each according to his contribution.' We shall call this the *Laissez-Faire Principle*.

These two principles will require a good deal of interpretation, but at the outset we can say that in the Socialist Principle of Justice 'abilities' and 'needs' refer to persons, whereas the 'choices' and 'contributions' in the Laissez-Faire Principle refer also to the management of impersonal property, the given assets. It goes without saying that some of the 'choices,' particularly those of the propertyless, are normally made under considerable duress. As 'choice' is the ideologically favored term, we shall retain it.

In a society where the Socialist Principle of Justice regulates distribution, the requirement is that everyone use such talents as have been developed in him (though this need not entail any allocation of workers to jobs), and the payment of workers is contingent not upon their contributions but

* *Dissent* (Summer 1972).

upon their needs. In a laissez-faire society, where individuals may be endowed with more or less capital or with bare labor power, they choose in the light of these assets how and how much to work (they may be drop-outs or moonlighters), and/or how to invest their capital, and they are paid in proportion.

None of the three objections raised against the Socialist Principle of Justice holds for the Laissez-Faire Principle. Whatever the level of contribution individuals choose, their aggregate product can be distributed in proportion to the contribution – whether of capital or of labor – each individual chooses to make. The Laissez-Faire Principle is applicable under situations both of scarcity and of abundance, and it incorporates a theory of incentives: people choose their level of contribution in order to get a given level of material reward.

Principles 1 and 2 can be cross-fertilized, yielding two further principles:

3. From each according to his ability, to each according to his contribution.
4. From each according to his choice, to each according to his need.

Principle 3 could be called an *Incentive Socialist Principle* of distribution. Like the Socialist Principle of Justice, it pictures a society in which all are required to work in proportion to the talents that have been developed in them. Since unearned income is not available and rewards are hinged to contribution rather than need, all work is easily enforced in an economy based on the Incentive Socialist Principle. This principle, however, covers a considerable range of systems. It holds for a Stalinist economy with an authoritarian job allocation. It also holds for a more liberal, market socialist economy in which there is a more or less free labor market, though without an option to drop out or live on unearned income, or the freedom to choose the level and type of qualification one is prepared to acquire. The Incentive Socialist Principle rewards workers according to their contribution: it is a principle of distribution in which an incentive system – reliance on material rewards – is explicit. Marx believed this principle would have to be followed in the early stages of socialism, in a society 'still stamped with the birthmarks of the old society.'

Under the Incentive Socialist Principle, each worker receives back the value of the amount of work he contributes to society in one form or another. According to Marx, this is a form of bourgeois right that 'tacitly recognizes unequal individual endowments, and thus natural privileges in respect of productive capacity.' So this principle holds for a still deficient society where the needs of particular workers, which depend on many things other than their productive capacity, may not be met. Although it may be less desirable than the Socialist Principle of Justice, the Incentive

Socialist Principle clearly meets certain criteria the Socialist Principle of Justice cannot meet. It provides a principle of allocation that can be applied equally well to the various situations of scarcity, sufficiency, and abundance. Its material incentive structure explains how under market socialism, given a capital structure and a skill structure, workers will choose jobs and work hard at them – and also why under a Stalinist economy workers will work hard at jobs to which they have been allocated.

Under the Incentive Socialist Principle, workers – whether assigned to menial work or to specific jobs – respond to incentives of the same sort as do workers under the Laissez-Faire Principle. The difference is that, while the Laissez-Faire Principle leaves the measurement of the contribution of a worker to be determined by the level of wage he is offered, the Incentive Socialist Principle relies on a bureaucratically determined weighting that takes into account such factors as the difficulty, duration, qualification level, and risk involved in a given job.

There is another difference between societies living under the Laissez-Faire Principle and those following the Incentive Socialist Principle. Under the Laissez-Faire Principle, there is no central coordination of decisions, for assets are managed according to the choices of their owners. This gives rise to the well-known problems of instability and unemployment. Under the Incentive Socialist Principle, assets are managed by the central government; hence one would expect instability to be eliminated and full employment guaranteed. However, we do not regard this difference as a matter of principle on the same level with others we are discussing. Moreover, in practice some recognizable capitalist societies have managed to control fluctuations without undermining the Laissez-Faire Principle as the principle of distribution.

Let us call Principle 4 the *Utopian Principle of Justice*. It postulates a society without any requirement of contribution or material incentives, but with guaranteed minimal consumption. This principle suffers from the same defect as the Socialist Principle of Justice: it does not determine distributions of benefits under conditions either of scarcity or of abundance, and it suggests no incentive structure to explain why enough should be contributed to its economy to make it possible to satisfy needs. Whether labor is contributed according to choice or according to ability, it is conceivable that the aggregate social product should be such that either some needs cannot be met or that, when all needs are met, a surplus remains that cannot be divided on the basis of needs.

On the surface, this Utopian Principle of Justice exudes the aroma of laissez-faire: though needs will not go unmet in utopia, contributions will be made for no more basic reason than individual whim. They are tied neither to the reliable effects of the incentive of material reward for oneself, nor to those of the noble ideal of filling the needs of others, nor to a conception of duty or self-sacrifice. Instead, contributions will come forth, if they do, according to the free and unconstrained choices of individual economic agents, on the basis of their given preferences. Preferences, however, are not 'given;' they develop and change, are learned and unlearned, and follow fashions and fads. Whim, fancy, pleasure, desire, wish are all words suggesting this aspect of consumer choice. By tying the demand for products to needs and the supply of work to choice, the Utopian Principle of Justice ensures stability in the former but does not legislate against fluctuations and unpredictable variability in the latter.

So the Socialist Principle of Justice and the Utopian Principle of Justice suffer from a common defect. There is no reason to suppose these systems will operate at precisely the level at which aggregate output is sufficient to meet all needs without surplus. And since people do not need an income in money terms but rather an actual and quite precisely defined list of food, clothing, housing, etc. (bearing in mind the various alternatives that might be substituted), the *aggregate* measured in value terms could be right, yet the *composition* might still be unable to meet all the people's needs. People might choose or have the ability to do the right amount of work, but on the wrong projects. One could even imagine the economy growing from a situation of scarcity to one of abundance without ever passing through any point at which its aggregate output could be distributed to meet precisely the needs of its population.

So far, we have been considering not the justification or desirability or alternative principles of distribution, but their practicality. It appears that, in this respect, principles hinging reward on contribution rather than on need have a great advantage. They can both provide a general principle of distribution and indicate the pattern of incentives to which workers will respond.

It might be held that these advantages are restricted to the Incentive Socialist Principle in its various versions, since under the Laissez-Faire Principle there is some income – property income – which is not being paid in virtue of any contribution. This problem can be dealt with either, as we indicated above, by intepreting the notion of contribution to cover the contribution of one's assets to the capital market, or by restricting the scope of the Laissez-Faire Principle to cover workers only, or by interpreting the notion of property income so as to regard wages as a return to property, i.e., property in one's labor power. One can say that under capitalism part of the aggregate product is set aside for the owners of capital (and another part, as under market socialism, for government expenditure) and the remainder is distributed according to the Laissez-Faire Principle. Or one may say that property income is paid in virtue of past contributions, whose reward was not consumed at the time it was earned but was stored. Apologists tend to favor interpretations that make the worker a sort of capitalist or the capitalist a sort of slow-consuming worker. Whichever line is taken, it is clear that the Laissez-Faire Principle – however undesirable we may find it – is a principle of distribution that can be of general use in two senses. Appropriately interpreted, it covers the distribution of earned and of unearned income, and it applies in situations both of scarcity and of abundance.

So we seem to have reached the paradoxical conclusion that the principle of distribution requiring that workers' needs be met is of no use in situations of need, since it does not assign priorities among needs, and that the principle demanding that each contribute according to his ability is unable to explain what incentives will lead him to do so. In this view, the Socialist Principle of Justice would have to be regarded as possibly noble but certainly unworkable.

II

But this view should not be accepted. Marx formulated the Socialist Principle of Justice on the basis of a conception of human abilities and needs that will yield some guidance to its interpretation. We shall now try to see whether the difficulties discussed above can be alleviated when we consider this principle in the light of Marxian theory.

Marx clearly thought that the Socialist Principle of Justice was peculiarly relevant to situations of abundance. In the last section we argued that, on the contrary, it was an adequate principle of distribution only when aggregate principle output exactly covered total needs. The source of this discrepancy lies in differing analyses of human needs.

By fulfillment of needs we understood at least a subsistence income. Needs are not met when a person lacks sufficient food, clothing, shelter, medical care, or socially necessary training/education. But beyond this biological and social minimum we can point to another set of needs, which men do not have qua men but acquire qua producers. Workers need not merely a biological and social minimum, but whatever other goods – be they holidays or contacts with others whose work bears on theirs or guaranteed leisure, which they need to perform their jobs as well as possible. So a principle of distribution according to needs will not be of use only to a subsistence-level economy. Very considerable goods over and above those necessary for biological subsistence can be distributed according to a principle of need.

But despite this extension of the concept of need the Socialist Principle of Justice still seems to face the three problems listed in Section I:

(1) What guarantees are there that even under abundance the *composition* of the output, with all contributing according to their abilities, will suffice to fill all needs? (There may still be scarcities of goods needed to fill either biological or job-related needs.)

(2) What principle can serve to distribute goods that are surplus both to biological and to job-related needs?
(3) What system of incentives explains why each will contribute to the full measure of his abilities, though he is not materially rewarded for increments of effort? Whether or not there is authoritative job allocation, job performance cannot be guaranteed.

Marx's solution to these problems does not seem too explicit. But much is suggested by the passage at the end of the *Critique of the Gotha Program* where he describes the higher phase of communist society as one in which 'labor is no longer merely a means of life but has become life's principal need.'

To most people it sounds almost comic to claim that labor could become life's principal need: it suggest a society of compulsive workers. Labor in the common view is intrinsically undesirable, but undertaken as a means to some further, typically material, end. For Marx this popular view would have been confirmation of his own view of the degree to which most labor under capitalism is alienating. He thought that under capitalism laborers experienced a threefold alienation: alienation from the *product* of their labor, which is for them merely a means to material reward; alienation from the *process* of labor, which is experienced as forced labor rather than as desirable activity; and alienation from *others*, since activities undertaken with others are undertaken as a means to achieving further ends, which are normally scarce and allocated competitively. Laborers cooperate in production but, under capitalism, compete for job and income, and the competition overrides the cooperation. Hence Marx claims (in the *Economic and Philosophical Manuscripts*) that 'life itself appears only as a means to life.' Though the horror of that situation is apparent in the very words, many people accept that labor should be only a means to life – whose real ends lie elsewhere; whether in religion, consumption, personal relations, or leisure.

Marx, on the other hand, held that labor could be more than a means; it could also be an end of life, for labor in itself – *the activity* – can, like other activities, be something for whose sake one does other things. We would be loath to think that activity itself should appear only as a means to life – on the contrary, life's worth for most people lies in the activities undertaken. Those we call labor do not differ intrinsically from the rest, only in relation to the system of production. In Marx's view a system was possible in which all activities undertaken would be nonalienating. Nobody would have to compete to engage in an activity he found unpleasant for the sake of a material reward. Instead, workers would cooperate in creative and fulfilling activities that provide occasions for the exercise of talents, for taking responsibilities, and that result in useful or beautiful products. In such a situation one can see why labor would be regarded as life's greatest need, rather than as its scourge. Nonalienated labor is humanly fulfilling activity.

In the course of switching from the conception of alienating labor to that of non-alienating labor, it might seem that we have moved into a realm for which principles of distribution may be irrelevant. What can the Socialist Principle of Justice tell us about the distribution of burdens and benefits in 'the higher phase of communist society'?

In such a society each is to contribute according to his abilities. In the light of the discussion of nonalienated labor, it is clear that there is no problem of incentives. Each man works at what he wants to work at. He works because that is his need. (This is not a situation in which 'moral incentives' have replaced material ones, for both moral and material incentives are based on alienating labor. The situation Marx envisages is one for which incentives of *all* sorts are irrelevant.)

Though this disposes of the problem of incentives under the Socialist Principle of Justice, it is much less clear whether this principle can work for a reasonable range of situations. Can it cope with both the situation of abundance and that of scarcity?

In the case of abundance, a surplus of goods over and above those needed is provided. But if all activities are need-fulfilling, then no work is done that does not fulfill some need. In a sense there is no surplus to be distributed, for nothing needless is being done. Nevertheless, there may be a surplus of material goods that are the by-product of need-fulfilling activity. In a society where everybody fulfills himself by painting pictures, there may be a vast surplus of pictures. If so, the Socialist Principle of Justice gives no indication of the right method for their distribution; they are not the goal for which the task was undertaken. Since they do not fulfill an objective need, the method for their distribution is not important. In this the higher phase of communist society is, as one might expect, the very antithesis of consumerism; rather than fabricate reasons for desiring and so acquiring what is not needed, it disregards anything that is not needed in decisions of distribution.

There, nevertheless, is a problem of distribution the Socialist Principle of Justice does not attempt to solve. Some of the products of need-fulfilling activity may be things other people either desire or detest. When need-fulfilling activity yields works of art or noisy block parties, its distribution cannot be disregarded. Not all planning problems can be solved by the Socialist Principle of Justice. We shall not discuss the merits of various principles that could serve to handle these cases, but shall only try to delimit the scope of the Socialist Principle of Justice.

This brings us to the problem of scarcity. Can the Socialist Principle of Justice explain why, when all contribute to the extent of their abilities, all needs can be met? Isn't it conceivable that everyone should find fulfillment in painting, but nobody find fulfillment in producing either biological necessities or the canvases, brushes, and paints everybody wants to use? Might not incentive payments be needed, even in this higher phase of communist society, to guarantee the production of subsistence goods and job-related necessities? In short, will not any viable system involve some alienating labor?

Marx at any rate guarantees that communism need not involve much alienating labor. He insists that the Socialist Principle of Justice is applicable only in a context of abundance. For only when man's needs can be met is it relevant to insist that they ought to be met. The Socialist Principle of Justice comes into its own only with the development of the forces of production. But, of course, higher productivity does not by itself guarantee the right composition of output. Subsistence goods and job-related services and products might not be provided as the population fulfills itself in painting, poetry, and sculpture. Man cannot live by works of art alone.

This socialist version of the story of Midas should not alarm us too much. The possibility of starvation amidst abundant art works seemed plausible only because we abstracted it from other features of an abundant socialist society. Such a society is a planned society, and part of its planning concerns the ability structure of the population. Such a society would include people able to perform all tasks necessary to maintain a high level of material well-being.

Nevertheless, there may be certain essential tasks in such a society whose performance is not need-fulfilling for anybody. Their allocation presents another planning problem for which the Socialist Principle of Justice, by hypothesis, is not a solution. But the degree of coercion need not be very great. In a highly productive society the amount of labor expended on nonfulfilling tasks is a diminishing proportion of total labor time. Hence, given equitable allocation of this burden (and it is here that the planning decisions are really made), nobody would be prevented from engaging principally in need-fulfilling activities. In the limiting case of abundance, where automation of the production of material needs is complete, nobody would have to do any task he did not find intrinsically worthwhile. To the extent that this abundance is not reached, the Socialist Principle of Justice cannot be fully implemented.

However, the degree of coercion, experienced by those who are allocated to necessary but nonfulfilling chores, may be reducible if the planning procedure is of a certain sort. To the extent that people participate in planning and that they realize the necessity of the nonfulfilling chores in order for everyone to be able to do also what he finds need-fulfilling, they may find the performance of these chores less burdensome. As they want to achieve the ends, so – once they are informed – they cannot rationally resent the means, provided they perceive the distribution of chores as just.

The point can be taken a step further. Under the Socialist Principle of Justice, households do not put forth productive effort to be rewarded with an aliquot portion of time and means for self-fulfillment. It is precisely this market mentality from which we wish to escape. The miserable toil of society should be

> performed gratis for the benefit of society . . . performed not as a definite duty, not for the purpose of obtaining a right to certain products, not according to previously established and legally fixed quotas, but voluntary labor . . . performed because it has become a habit to work for the common good, and because of a conscious realization (that has become a habit) of the necessity of working for the common good. V. I. Lenin, 'From the Destruction of the Old Social System to the Creation of the New' (April 11, 1920). From *Collected Works*, English trans., 40 vols (London: Lawrence & Wishart, 1965) vol. 30, p. 517.

Creative work should be done for its own sake, not for any reward. Drudgery should be done for the common good, not in order to be rewarded with opportunity and means for creative work. Of course, the better and more efficient the performance of drudgery, the more will be the opportunities for creative work. To realize this, however, is to understand the necessity of working for the common good, not to be animated by private material incentives. For the possibilities of creative work are opened by the simultaneous and parallel development of large numbers of people. To take the arts, poets need a public, authors readers, performers audiences, and all need (though few want) critics. One cannot sensibly wish, under the Socialist Principle of Justice, to be rewarded *privately* with opportunities and means for nonalienated work.

There is a question regarding the distribution of educational opportunities. Before men can contribute according to their abilities, their abilities must be developed. But in whom should society develop which abilities? If we regard education as consumption, then according to the Socialist Principle of Justice, each should receive it according to his need.

It is clear that all people require some early training to make them viable social beings; further, all people require certain general skills necessary for performing work. But we could hardly claim that certain individuals need to be doctors or economists or lawyers, or need to receive any other specialized or expensive training. If, on the other hand, we regard education as production of those skills necessary for maintaining society and providing the possibility of fulfillment, then the Socialist Principle of Justice can determine a lower bound to the production of certain skills: so-and-so many farmers/doctors/mechanics must be produced to satisfy future subsistence and job-related needs. But the Socialist Principle of Justice cannot determine who shall get which of these educational opportunities. One traditional answer might be that each person should specialize at whatever he is relatively best suited to do. Yet this only makes sense in terms of tasks done as onerous means to desirable ends. Specialization on the basis of comparative advantage minimizes the effort in achieving given ends; but if work is itself fulfilling, it is not an 'effort' that must be minimized.

In conditions of abundance, it is unlikely that anyone will be denied training they want and can absorb, though they may have to acquire skills they do not particularly want, since some onerous tasks may still have to be done. For even in conditions of abundance, it may be necessary to compel some or all to undertake certain unwanted training in the interests of the whole. But it is not necessary to supplement the Socialist Principle of Justice with an incentive scheme, whether material or moral. The principle already contains the Kantian maxim: develop your talents to the utmost, for only in this way can a person contribute to the limits of his ability. And if a society wills the end of self-fulfillment, it must will sufficient means. If the members of society take part in planning to maintain and expand the opportunities for everyone's nonalienated activity, they must understand the necessity of allocating the onerous tasks, and so the training for them.

III

Perhaps we can make our point clearer by looking briefly at Marx's schematic conception of the stages of modern history – feudalism, capitalism, socialism, communism – where each stage is characterized by a higher productivity of labor than the preceding stage. In feudalism, the principle of distribution would be:

5. From each according to his status, to each according to his status – the *Feudal Principle of Justice*.

There is no connexion between work and reward. There are no market incentives in the 'ideal' feudal system. Peasants grow the stuff for their own subsistence and perform traditional labor services for their lord on domain land. He in turn provides protection and government in traditional fashion. Yet, though labor is not performed as a means to a distant or abstract end, as when it is done for money, it still is done for survival, not for its own sake, and those who do it are powerless to control their conditions of work or their own destinies. Man lives on the edge of famine and is subject to the vagaries of the weather and the dominion of tradition. Only a massive increase in productive powers frees him. But to engender this increase men must come to connect work directly with reward. This provides the incentive to labor, both to take those jobs most needed (moving from the farm to the factory) and to work sufficiently hard once on the job.

But more than work is needed; the surplus of output over that needed to maintain the work force (including managers) and replace and repair the means of production (machines, raw materials) must be put to productive use; it must be reinvested, not consumed. In capitalism, station at birth determines whether one works or owns capital; workers are rewarded for their contribution of work, capitalists for theirs of reinvestment. There is a stick as well as a carrot. Those workers who do not work, starve; those capitalists who fail to reinvest, fail to grow and will eventually be crushed by their larger rivals. Socialism rationalizes this by eliminating the two-class dichotomy and by making reinvestment a function of the institutions of the state, so that the capital structure of the society is the collective property of the citizenry, all of whom must work for reward. In this system the connexion between work and reward reaches its fullest development, and labor in one sense is most fully alienated. The transition to communism then breaks this link altogether.

The link between work and rewards serves a historical purpose, namely to encourage the development of the productive forces. But as the productive forces continue to develop, the demand for additional rewards will tend to decline, while the difficulty of stimulating still further growth in productivity may increase. This, at least, seems to be implied by the principles of conventional economics – diminishing marginal utility and diminishing marginal productivity. Even if one rejects most of the conventional wisdom of economics, a good case can be made for the diminishing efficacy of material incentives as prosperity increases. For as labor productivity rises, private consumption needs will be met, and the most urgent needs remaining will be those requiring *collective* consumption – and, indeed, some of these needs will be generated by the process of growth and technical progress. These last needs, if left unmet, may hinder further attempts to raise the productive power of labor. So the system of material incentives could in principle come to a point where the weakened encouragements to extra productivity offered as private reward for contribution might be offset by the accumulated hindrances generated by the failures to meet collective needs and by the wastes involved in competition. At this point, it becomes appropriate to break the link between work and reward. Breaking the link however, is not enough. Both the Socialist Principle of Justice and the Utopian Principle of Justice break the link between work and reward. But the Utopian Principle of Justice leaves the distinction between them. Work is a means, the products of work are the ends. Given a high productivity of labor, workers would in principle choose their occupations and work-leisure patterns, yet still continue producing enough to satisfy everyone's needs. This would be a society devoted to minimizing effort, a sort of high-technology Polynesia. Since it neither makes consumption dependent upon work nor regards work as other than a regrettable means to consumption, it fails to explain why sufficient work to supply basic needs should ever be done. The alienation of labor cannot be overcome by eliminating labor rather than alienation.

Breaking the link between work and reward, while leaving the distinction itself in tact, may also lead to the loss of the productive powers of labor. For without reward, and when the object is to work as little as possible, why expend the effort to acquire highly complex skills? What is the motive to education, self-improvement, self-development? A high-technology Polynesia contains an inner contradiction.

By contrast, the Socialist Principle of Justice not only does not make reward depend upon work but denies that there is a distinction between the two. Because mankind needs fulfilling activity – work that he chooses and wants – those who get it contribute according to their ability.

Yet there still may remain routine and menial, unfulfilling jobs. But who wills the end wills the means. The society must plan to have such jobs done. No doubt, many will be mechanized or automated, but the remaining ones will form a burden that must be allocated.

The Socialist Principle of Justice cannot solve this problem of allocation. But everyone has some interest in getting uncoveted but essential work done. Hence it should not be difficult to find an acceptable supplementary principle of distribution for allocating these chores. For instance, the Principle of Comparative Advantage might be introduced to assign each the drudgery at which he is relatively best. There can be no quarrel with this so long as such alienating work is only a small fraction of a person's total activity, conferring no special status. It is only when alienating work takes up the bulk of one's waking hours, and determines status, that specialization inevitably entails some form of class structure.

The Socialist Principle of Justice cannot solve all allocation problems. But once one understands that it is based on a denial of a distinction between work, need, and reward, it is clear that it can solve an enormous range of such problems. In a highly productive society the only allocation problems the Socialist Principle of Justice cannot solve are the distribution of unmechanized and uncoveted chores and of the material byproducts of creative endeavor.

Concluding Remark

Our analysis of the way an industrial society produces a surplus, and how this is connected, on the one hand, to the formation of wages and prices, and, on the other, to the spending of distributed income, has provided us a view of the causes of unemployment and inflation rooted in the transformational growth of the system – the way technology has evolved in response to the pressures of economic incentives. In turn this has made it possible to address the larger questions of justice, the distribution of the burdens and benefits of economic activity, from a structural rather than an individualistic perspective.

Index